RED HILLS

The **Nordic Institute of Asian Studies** (NIAS) is a research and service institute located in Copenhagen where it collaborates closely with Copenhagen University and the Copenhagen Business School as well as with Lund University in Sweden and the wider Nordic Asian Studies community. Funded in part by the governments of Denmark, Finland, Iceland, Norway and Sweden via the Nordic Council of Ministers and in part directly by the Nordic scholarly community, NIAS works to encourage and support Asian Studies in the Nordic countries as well as actively participating in the international scholarly community in its own right. In so doing, NIAS has published books since 1969 and in 2002 launched **NIAS Press** as an independent, not-for-profit publisher aiming at a premium reputation among authors and readers for relevant and focused, quality publishing in the field of Asian Studies.

The **Institute of Southeast Asian Studies** (ISEAS) was established as an autonomous organization in 1968. It is a regional centre dedicated to the study of socio-political, security and economic trends and developments in Southeast Asia and its wider geostrategic and economic environment.

The Institute's research programmes are Regional Economic Studies (RES, including ASEAN and APEC), Regional Strategic and Political Studies (RSPS), and Regional Social and Cultural Studies (RSCS).

ISEAS Publications, an established academic press, has issued more than 1,000 books and journals. It is the largest scholarly publisher of research about Southeast Asia from within the region. ISEAS Publications works with many other academic and trade publishers and distributors to disseminate important research and analyses from and about Southeast Asia to the rest of the world.

Red Hills

Migrants and the State
in the Highlands of Vietnam

ANDREW HARDY

INSTITUTE OF SOUTHEAST ASIAN STUDIES
Singapore

First published in hardback in 2003 by NIAS Press
This paperback edition published in 2005 by NIAS Press
Nordic Institute of Asian Studies
Leifsgade 33, DK–2300 Copenhagen S, Denmark
tel: (+45) 3532 9501 • fax: (+45) 3532 9549
E–mail: books@nias.ku.dk • Website: www.niaspress.dk

First published in 2005 in Singapore by
Institute of Southeast Asian Studies (ISEAS)
30 Heng Mui Keng Terrace, Pasir Panjang, Singapore 119614
E-mail: publish@iseas.edu.sg • Website: http://bookshop.iseas.edu.sg
for distribution in the ASEAN countries, Japan, Korea, Taiwan,
Australia and New Zealand.

Original publication of this book was assisted by a grant
from the École française d'Extrême-Orient (EFEO)

British Library Cataloguing in Publication Data
Hardy, Andrew
Red hills : migrants and the state in the highlands of
Vietnam. - (NIAS monograph ; 93)
1.Migration, Internal Political aspects - Vietnam
2.Central Highlans (Vietnam) - Emigration and immigration
I.Title II.Nordic Institute of Asian Studies
304.8'09597

ISBN 87-91114-80-2 (NIAS hbk edition)
ISBN 87-91114-74-8 (NIAS pbk edition)
ISBN 981-230-315-4 (ISEAS edition)

Cover design by NIAS Press (photograph by Natasha Pairaudeau).
'Beautiful Land, Rich Country, Everywhere is Home'. Slogans like these were used up to
the 1990s to persuade people to volunteer to clear the land. The use of the emotionally
charged word 'home' (*quê hương*) was a state attempt to transfer migrant loyalties from
their home village to the nation.

Typesetting by NIAS Press
Printed and bound in Singapore

For John
who left

still missing you

Contents

ILLUSTRATIONS

Maps

Figures

Plates (colour section between pages 88 and 89)

TABLES

Preface

'Green Forest, Red Hills'
(*Rừng Xanh, Núi Đỏ*)

*T*his book is a political economy of internal migration in twentieth-century Vietnam. It describes the resettlement of Việt people from the Red River Delta to highland areas, a movement which transformed Vietnam's demographic and political map. The book aims to show how these changes took place and draw conclusions about the dynamics of migration in Vietnam.

The crucial dynamism was an interplay between the state and migrant families. This hindered highland settlement during the French colonial period, promoting it after 1954. Policies of migration and the realities of its practice came together, first in the hills of the north, and subsequently in the central highlands.

From the point of view of the state, it asks how the post-colonial Vietnamese government mobilized several million lowland farmers to move to upland areas, where the French colonial administration failed. From the point of view of migrant families, it examines the extent to which people went along with state migration programmes, avoided or manipulated them, or simply ignored them. Finally, it shows how state organization (creating population bases in previously unknown or unsettled areas) and family/village networking (creating flows of information, capital and people) combined in the 1980s and 1990s to create a free migration dynamic of remarkable potency.

This dynamic transformed Vietnam's highlands. The sparsely populated hills of forest and swidden agriculture inhabited by Vietnam's ethnic minorities, became a 'promised land', especially in the central highlands. The central highlands are now secure from armed ethnic insurgency and invasion from Cambodia, and the red flag of the Socialist Republic of Vietnam flies in every district centre. Coffee and other market crops grown from these *terres rouges* have replaced the green forest canopy, making the fortunes of large numbers of Việt migrants. The highlanders have become minorities in their own provinces of these now *Red Hills*.

Acknowledgements

I would like to express my sincere thanks to David Marr, whose scholarship and friendship have been an inspiration since I started work on this project. I have also been lucky to enjoy the support of Ben Kerkvliet, whose interest in my research has been a constant source of encouragement.

I could not have written this book without the help of Diệp Đình Hoa. To say more would be too little.

At the beginning, I was fortunate to meet Đặng Phong, who has since proved a close friend and great source of enthusiasm, wisdom and adventure. Daniel Hémery helped in the early years in Paris. Later on I found my preoccupations had drawn greatly from advice he gave me then. In Vietnam, Phạm Đỗ Nhật Tân sat for long hours helping me understand the ways in which Vietnamese people live, work and move. I am grateful to John Kleinen, whose advice on research and comment on chapters were both entertaining and insightful.

Animated conversations with Philippe Papin set me off on new leads throughout my research on this book, and I would like to thank him especially for his hospitality and support at the École française d'Extrême-Orient in Hanoi.

In the evolution of my ideas about migration and many other matters, I enjoyed lengthy conversations with Grant Evans, Christopher Goscha, William Smith, Thaveeporn Vasavakul and Nguyễn Văn Chính.

This project was made possible with support from the Division of Pacific and Asian History, at the Research School of Pacific and Asian Studies (Australian National University). A Post-doctoral Research Fellowship at the Southeast Asian Studies Programme (National University of Singapore) gave me the time and resources to turn thesis into book. I would also like to thank the École française d'Extrême-Orient in Hanoi for funding from the research programme 'Les Marches de l'Empire Đại Việt'. Thanks too to all those at HUG for their timely efforts.

In Vietnam, no research can be undertaken without a sponsoring institute. I was fortunate to be invited to Vietnam by the Institute of Ethnology, in the National Centre for Social Sciences and the Humanities. The Institute's director, Khổng Diễn, and vice director, Phạm Quang Hoan, not only enabled my research but supported me with great good humour as, over the two years of my fieldwork, I learnt how things work in Vietnam. Researchers and staff at the Institute always reserved a warm welcome for me, and helped out in numerous ways. I would like to express my thanks to those at the Center's International Cooperation Department, notably Nguyễn Giang Hải and Nguyễn Chiến Thắng, who efficiently made arrangements for my visa. And, finally, my appreciation to Nguyễn Duy Quý, whose words of encouragement during a visit to Canberra spurred me through the final months of writing.

Much of this research was carried out in archives and libraries. Staff at the Vietnam National Archives Centres 1 and 3 helped me find my way around the documents and, with our morning chats over tea before work, made working in the archives a real pleasure. Thanks in particular to Vũ Thị Minh Hương and Lê Huy Tuấn. Staff of the Vietnam National Library also pointed me in the right direction on numerous occasions. In France, I am grateful to Lucette Vachier for the guidance she has given me over the years at the Centre des Archives d'Outre-Mer, in Aix-en-Provence.

The other major information source was oral. I wish to thank more than 200 people who took the time to help me understand about their experiences. Their hospitality was a source of constant pleasure. Meeting them would not have been possible without my friends, Đào Thế Đức, Nguyễn Tiến Đông and Trần Hà, who came with me to the countryside. Phạm Tường Vân introduced me to her friends, family and acquaintances, and helped in informal ways impossible to enumerate here.

Thanks to Dương Trung Quốc, Đào Hùng and their colleagues at *Xưa & Nay*, for their generous support. I owe a particular debt to Đào Hùng, who set me off on the trail for an obscure village called Bờ Rạ. This journey is related in Chapter 1.

I wish to thank the officials in the provinces of Đak Lak, Hoa Bình, Sơn La, Thái Bình, Thái Nguyên and Thanh Hóa for their cooperation and help.

During my stay in Vietnam, many people helped in individual ways. It would be impossible to list them all here, but I would like in particular to express my gratitude to Hoàng Ngọc La and his colleagues at the university in Thái Nguyên, Natasha Pairaudeau, Đỗ Huy, Philippe Le Failler, Lưu Đình Nhân, Phạm Văn Hùng. I immensely enjoyed living with Mr Thành and Mrs Kim in their house in Hanoi. They offered me daily evidence of the warm hospitality of Vietnamese people.

In Nouméa, Jean Vanmai gave me generously of his time, and helped deepen my understanding of the Vietnamese community there.

Back in Canberra, Dorothy Macintosh, Oanh Collins, Julie Gordon, Jude Shanahan, Marion Weekes and Kris Brown helped with all sorts of practical matters, and above all with their cheerful friendship. In Paris, thanks to Béa Narcy.

I am grateful to Ian Brown, David Chandler and Hy Van Luong, to the editors at the Nordic Institute of Asian Studies, and to two anonymous readers, for their suggestions on improving the original text.

Chapter 1 was first published in the *Journal of Southeast Asian Studies* (vol. 31, no. 2, September 2000, pp. 295–320) and Chapter 10 appeared in *Asia Pacific*

Viewpoint (vol. 41, no. 1, April 2000, pp. 23–34). I would like to express my thanks to the editors of these two journals for their permission to reproduce, in an expanded form, this material.

From beginning to end, Harriet Beazley was there with unfaltering moral support and unerring reminders of Riley.

* * *

This is not a village study in the classical sense, where the researcher goes and spends time in a single community, learning, participating, observing. I travelled widely in Vietnam, and spent no more than a couple of hours with the majority of my informants. I did, however, spend more than two years in a village during the writing of the book, although not in Vietnam. I should like to express my appreciation to the people of Major's Creek, on the Southern Tablelands of New South Wales, for the warmth of their welcome to a strange and slightly obsessive scholar who one day arrived in their midst, and for their patience in the pub as they listened to my various struggles with the writing. Thanks above all to Penny and Lado Ruzicka, for making it home. They were the first to read and comment on my endeavours in their little cottage. To Oscar and Mina, for hours of entertainment. To Brian and Deirdre McDonald, for our long chats over the back fence, and for water. To Robin and Virginia Wallace-Crabbe, for their reminders of life outside the academy. And thanks too to Eilish and Richard Kidd at the Elrington Hotel for their friendly welcome. To Richard, in particular, who may not have been aware of the power of his words of tough encouragement one tired day when I wandered up for a frustrated mid-afternoon schooner: 'you just have to knuckle down'. They kept me going for months.

Abbreviations

(Note items in italics here are published journals)

ASI	*Annuaire Statistique de l'Indochine* [Indochina Statistical Yearbook]
BAVH	*Bulletin des Amis du Vieux Huế* [Bulletin of the Friends of Old Huế]
BEI	*Bulletin Economique de l'Indochine* [Indochina Economic Bulletin]
BLD	Bộ Lao Động [Ministry of Labour, later Ministry of Labour, Invalids and Social Affairs]
BSEI	*Bulletin de la Société des Etudes Indochinoises* [Bulletin of the Society of Indochinese Studies]
CAOM	Centre des Archives d'Outre Mer (Centre for Archives from Overseas), Aix-en-Provence
CCTK	Chi cục thống kê (Statistical Office, at province level)
CNV	công nhân viên (workers and civil servants)
CQLNTQD	Cục Quản Lý Nông Trường Quốc Doanh (Bureau of State Farm Management)
DRV	Democratic Republic of Vietnam (North Vietnam, 1954–76)
DTH	*Tạp Chí Dân Tộc Học* [Ethnology Journal]
GGI	Gouvernement Général de l'Indochine (Government General of Indochina)
HTX	hợp tàc xã (cooperative)
IDEO	Imprimerie d'Extrême-Orient (Far East Press)
JAS	*Journal of Asian Studies*
KTM	kinh tế mới (new economy), generally used in the term *vùng KTM* (new economic zone)
KTVHMN	kinh tế văn hóa miền núi (upland economy and culture)
MAE	Ministère des Affaires Etrangères (Ministry of Foreign Affairs, Paris)

NCLS	*Nghiên Cứu Lịch Sử* [Historical Research]
NXB	Nhà xuất bản (Publishing House)
ONS	Ouvriers Non-Specialisés (Non-specialized Workers)
QD	*quốc doanh*, found in the expression *nông trường quốc doanh* (state farm)
QDND	*Quân Đội Nhân Dân* [People's Army]
QNPM	Quảng Ninh Provincial Museum
RF	Résident de France (French Residént – the ranking French official in the administration of a province)
RIJE	*Revue Indochinoise Juridique et Economique* [Indochinese Juridical and Economic Review]
RND	French Résident (see RF) in the province of Nam Dinh
RSA	Résident Supérieur de l'Annam (Superior Residént of Annam – the ranking official in the French administration of the protectorate of Annam (central Vietnam))
RSL	Résident Supérieur du Laos (Superior Residént of Laos)
RST	Résident Supérieur du Tonkin (Superior Residént of Tonkin)
RVN	Republic of Vietnam (South Vietnam, 1954–75)
SHAT	Service Historique de l'Armée de Terre (Army Historical Service)
SRV	Socialist Republic of Vietnam (1976–)
TCTK	Tổng Cục Thống Kê (General Statistical Office)
UBKHNN	Ủy Ban Kế hoạch nhà nước (State Planning Committee)
UNDP	United Nations Development Program
VNA	Vietnam National Archives
XHH	*Tạp Chí Xã Hội Học* [Sociology Journal]

Glossary

Bố Chành	provincial mandarin
Cục	Bureau or Office
dân công	labour, porters
đình	communal house, social and political centre for the men of Việt villages
đồng	Vietnamese unit of currency (in colonial times the piastre)
hộ khẩu	system of household residence registration, based on the Chinese hukou system
hộ tịch	population register of statistics on births, marriages and deaths, or civil status
inscrit	*đinh*, adult male villager registered on the village tax roll (before 1945)
lý trưởng	head of a commune, officially recognized by the colonial government (the word was used quite loosely in some contexts to signify village head, or organizer of a group of settlers or workers; the key function was mediation between people and higher authorities, notably tax collection)
mẫu	measurement of land, divided into ten *sào*. See *Note on Vietnamese Names and Measurements*
nam tiến	'southward advance', the settlement by Viet people of the plains of central and southern Vietnam
nhà quê	peasant, a pejorative word in Vietnamese which was used, often in a more general sense, by French living in Indochina
non-inscrit	adult male villager not registered on the village tax roll (before 1945)
Résident	Résident de France, French Resident – the ranking official at the province level in the French administration of its protectorates in Indochina
sào	measurement of land. See *Note on Vietnamese Names and Measurements*

Sở	Office
sơ tàn	evacuation
Sûreté	French internal security and criminal investigation service
tàn cư	evacuation
Tết	the lunar new year festival, usually in January or February of the western calendar
Thoát ly	separation, leaving home
Tỷ	service
Vụ	department

Notes on Vietnamese Names and Measurements

Vietnamese names are presented here with their diacritical marks wherever possible, with the exception of words familiar to modern readers in a westernized form (Hanoi, Haiphong, etc). Few French sources, however, included the correct marks on names of people and places. In addition, many DRV documents, particularly those dating from the 1950s and 1960s, were written on French typewriters, similarly without marks or in codes using ordinary letters following the word instead of the correct mark. Some publications in English also omitted the diacritical marks. For all these reasons, there were instances when diacritical marks could not be found. In such cases, the name has simply been left without marks. Despite an inevitable loss of historical authenticity, diacritical marks have been restored in citations, although reference details of published works and titles of archival documents have been reproduced with respect to the original text.

Under colonial rule the name for majority ethnic group in Vietnam, known nowadays as Việt or Kinh people, was Annamite. To avoid confusion, this has been rendered as Việt throughout the book. Except in citations, the term 'Vietnamese' is reserved for the inhabitants of Vietnam without reference to their ethnic group. The same principle of translation is followed for the regions of northern, central and southern Vietnam (known now to the Vietnamese as Bắc Bộ, Trung Bộ and Nam Bộ, and to the French as Tonkin, Annam and Cochinchine), and their Việt inhabitants (who the French tended to call Tonkinese, Cochinchinese, etc.), except where an administrative rather than geographical context is implied.

Changes in the boundaries of administrative units from the commune to the province have been a regular feature of Vietnam's twentieth-century history. Except where confusion was likely, I have respected the names for administrative units current at the time of events related.

Two Vietnamese measurements of land area are used throughout the text, the *mẫu* and the *sào*. In northern Vietnam, the *mẫu* is an area of 3,600 m^2 (about 1/3 of a hectare) while the *sào* covers 360 m^2. The *mẫu* was originally a measurement, used for taxation purposes, of the amount of land deemed necessary for a house-hold's subsistence. As Việt people settled what is now central and southern Vietnam, they found that land there was more abundant. The value of these measurements varied from one region to the next as well as within regions. Nowadays, both the *mẫu* and the *sào* cover larger areas in the centre and south. There are, in fact, three different values for each, corresponding to the country's three regions.

In this book, the *mẫu* referred to is usually the northern measurement. Farmers from the northern delta, even when they moved to the centre or south, continued to measure land with the northern *mẫu*. Note, however, that in the central highlands, a region which has been settled recently by people from north, south and centre, all three measurements are commonly in use.

The Vietnamese currency, the đồng, has changed its value on a number of occasions, notably in 1959 and 1985. I have not attempted to follow its fluctuations, but where necessary have given a paddy equivalent value in footnotes. The piastre, currency in French Indochina during the colonial period, was known to Vietnamese as the đồng. Where appropriate the Vietnamese word has been used here.

Twentieth-Century Itineraries

Figure 1: Mr Thức, of Nhà Thờ village
Thức was 96 years old when I met him in 1996. He had just returned from the fields. He told me how, in 1906, he had left his village in the Red River Delta province of Nam Định, with his mother and two elder brothers. After years of wandering, the family settled in the province of Thái Nguyên.
Photograph by Andrew Hardy, October 1996.

1906

Can we know how she reached that decision? To leave home. To walk away from the village in the delta. To take her three young boys far from their father's grave? Her youngest, Thức, was just 6 at the time. For him, of course, there was no decision, no dilemma. Only the journey, two or three days of it, till they reached the hills, till their legs were stiff. Together with twenty families from the same village, the four of them begged for food, asked for work, slept rough, wandered around. They finally settled at Tân Cương, a highland village now famous for its tea, where they had relatives. I met Thức there in 1996. At that time, he was 96 years old.*

1936

Tân Cương was home to Thân, only 10 years old when he arrived there from the same village as Thức, in the delta province of Nam Định. There was no party when they left, just some goodbyes as they went down to the pier at four o'clock one dark summer morning. Dodging the fare was easy – they ran off when the boat reached the city. But the city was hard. Thân's father lost his bag, stolen by the rickshaw man he hired to pull him to the bus station. Despite this disaster, he paid the bus fare and the same evening the family arrived at a small town in the uplands. This was Thái Nguyên, just a street in those days, Thân said. The family spent the night in a guest house. The following day they walked down to Tân Cương, where people from their village gave them lodging, food and work. I met Thân there in 1996.†

1945

Giang was 18 when the revolution came. He left his village in the delta and headed for the hills, enlisting in the armed forces of the Việt Minh. Demobilized on health grounds in 1950, he joined up again two years later and was proud to say he fought at Điện Biên Phủ. Demobilized again, he stayed at the site of the famous battle, building roads there till 1959. Back in his village, he stayed four years before signing up on a government programme organizing migrants to go and clear land in the uplands. But the land he cleared and cultivated was lost, flooded in the Đà River hydro-electric project in the province of Hòa Bình. He

---

*   Thức was from Quận Cống village (Xuân Thọ commune, Xuân Trường district, Nam Định). I met him at Nhà Thờ village (Tân Cương commune, Thái Nguyên city, Thái Nguyên). He was just back from ploughing the fields, his buffalo following behind him. He is pictured in Figure 1. Interview (Thái Nguyên, October 1996).

†   Thân is Thức's neighbour at Nhà Thờ village. The city here was Nam Định. They changed buses in Hanoi, before arriving at Thái Nguyên on the edge of Vietnam's northern uplands, 80 km from Hanoi. At Tân Cương people from home were expecting them. Thân was 10 at the time: he was 70 when I met him. Interview (Thái Nguyên, October 1996). For details of Thân's experiences, see Chapter 3.

was resettled at the village of Bình Lý, not far from the dam. He was still living there when I visited in 1995.*

1963

A similar programme to clear land took Học from home. I tape-recorded his account. His itinerary is presented here in his own words:

> First, at home there was a canal, so we took boats and sampans along the canal and river to the district town. All our luggage went into two pairs of shoulder-pole baskets – that was all we could take! Some young children were even put into the baskets to be carried. At the district, people grouped together and went across [the Red River] to Nam Định. Then we took a train from Nam Định to Hanoi, and another from Hanoi to Thái Nguyên. From Thái Nguyên as far as the stone road we came by bus. There the minority people met us and helped us carry everything down here. They showed us up to the stilt-houses where they lived, and we stayed with them for a short time, five or six people in each house. Then we went out to start clearing land. Once we'd built our houses we moved from the minorities' place out to the village here. That's how it was then!†

1977

Vietnam was reunified in 1975 and the land clearance programme extended to the whole country. Ngọc, three years after abandoning a migrant cooperative in the hills of the north, reluctantly boarded a bus for the central highlands. The journey took five days. Nights were spent in reception centres along the way, where the travellers could eat, wash and watch films. A lorry was provided for their luggage. Ngọc arrived at the upland valley of Lak, but didn't stay for long. He joined the army in 1979, spending six years in Cambodia and Đà Nẵng. Initially reluctant to return to Lak, he conceded in 1996 that life there was better than at his home village in the Red River Delta.‡

---

*   Giang was born at Nam Bình commune (Kiến Xương district, Thái Bình). A migration programme took him to Hào Tráng commune (Đà Bắc district, Hòa Bình) in 1963. He moved to Bình Lý village (Tu Lý commune, Đà Bắc district, Hòa Bình) in 1979. Interview (Hòa Bình, July 1995). For details of Giang's experiences, see Chapter 6.

†   Học was born in Hưng Hà district (Thái Bình) and moved to Bình Nguyên village (Điềm Mạc commune, Định Hóa district, Thái Nguyên) at the age of 12. This account was transcribed and translated from a recording of our conversation in July 1995. I am grateful to Thắng and Liên for the hours they spent transcribing this and many other interviews. The translation is my own. For details of Học's experiences, see Chapters 6 and 8.

‡   Ngọc was from Đông Xá commune (Đông Hưng district, Thái Bình). His first stay in the hills was in Nghĩa Lộ province in 1974 (see Chapters 6 and 8). On his way south in 1977, he stopped at Vũ Thư (Thái Bình), Diễn Châu (Nghệ An), Nam Ô (Quảng Nam–Đà Nẵng), Cầu Qua Di (Nghĩa Bình) and Ban Mê Thuột (Dak Lak). Ngọc was 38 when I visited his home at Đông Giang village (Buôn Tría commune, Lak district, Dak Lak) in November 1996.

1988

At the age of 27, Bắc had finished his military service in Hanoi. He wasn't married. He hadn't settled down. He decided to take an extended holiday. He went south, to the port of Qui Nhơn and the beach resort of Nha Trang before paying a visit to his brother in the central highlands. He found the land was good. He was introduced to a woman he liked. On his return home, he surprised his mother with two decisions. He was moving to the hills and he was getting married. The marriage took place immediately and the move soon after that. He had been living in the same village as Ngọc for six years when I met him in 1996.[*]

1997

Mẫu was born in the same place as Bắc, the province of Thái Bình in the Red River Delta. In 1977 he moved to the central highlands province of Dak Lak on the government programme. But while Bắc prospered, Mẫu decided in 1991 to return home to the plains. Economically things were harder back home, but his mother was unwell. He made the move with few regrets. For the hills and the plains, he cared little one way or the other. Both places made him, as he put it, 'fed up with life'. But fourteen years in Dak Lak left its mark in one respect – a love for 'Cow-Boy' brand cigarettes. When relatives come north to visit, they bring him cartons of this highland speciality. He was smoking a 'Cow-Boy' when I called at his house in Thái Bình in 1997. The empty packets were displayed in the glass-fronted cupboard under his family altar. He was that attached to his ancestors, he offered them a gift – a nostalgic symbol of dreams unfulfilled – brought back from the frontier.[†]

---

[*]   Bắc was from Phong Châu commune (Đông Hưng district, Thái Bình). Interview (Dak Lak, November 1996). For details of Bắc's experiences, see Chapter 10.

[†]   Mẫu was 42 when I met him at Lê Lợi village (Đông Xá commune, Đông Hưng district, Thái Bình) in January 1997. Cow-Boy cigarettes were manufactured in Sông Bé province, on the southern edge of the central highlands. Mẫu's house, like many others, had a glass-fronted cabinet, displaying photographs, ornaments, whisky cartons and other furniture of sentimental value or conspicuous consumption, under the altar with its images of deceased parents, incense and fruit offerings.

Researching Migration in Vietnam

Figure 2: 'A sea of rice': the Red River Delta province of Thái Bình
The heartland of Vietnamese civilization, the rich alluvial plains of the Red River Delta are home to a dense population. In the twentieth century, population growth in this region was one of the reasons prompting the colonial and communist authorities to promote migration to the hills.
Source: *Thái Bình tự giới thiệu* [This is Thái Bình], Sở Văn Hóa Thông Tin và Thể Thao Thái Bình, 1996, p. 95.

How did Thức's mother reach her decision to leave her home? We may never be able to answer this question in any detail, although French archive sources suggest his village was visited by floods and harvest losses that year.[1] In Thức's case, the explanation of destitution may suffice. But the itineraries of the six other migrants outlined in the Prologue suggest that economics offer only one dimension of the history of migration from the Red River Delta. These itineraries give a more complex picture of the practice of Việt migration over the twentieth century, showing how motivations for migration and stimuli for settlement drew on factors of social, political and military

                                    Red Hills

importance as well as factors of livelihood. In particular, they show how men, women and children variously ignored, negotiated and complied with policies of the state, policies which at different times either inhibited or promoted migration.

In these pages I argue that the interplay of migration practice and policy shaped the formation of a frontier in the hills. In so doing, I aim to reach broader conclusions about the dynamics of migration in Vietnam, in terms of 'red' politics, family networks and individual decisions. By the end of the twentieth century, its flag in every town, its settlers in every village, the communist government in Hanoi succeeded, within certain limits, in bringing the highlands under its control. Decisions of life direction by the people and decisions of policy by the state combined to cause the settlement of people from the Red River Delta on new land in the hills. In response to the communist government's policies of 'rational' population distribution, and to individual and family decisions based on a desire for prosperity – which in Vietnam is coloured red – these lands were transformed.

These processes, which took place in the 'red hills' of Vietnam, have been the single most significant long-term change in the country's twentieth-century demographic history.

BACKGROUND

Before relating some of these journeys and analysing the settlement of the hills, it is worth saying a few words about how I came to be interested in them, about my intellectual itinerary. The aim is not only to situate the author in the subject, but more importantly to illustrate the perspectives chosen in the researching and writing of it.

In 1988, tourism was in its infancy in Vietnam. Visitors were admitted on short state-organized packages. Nights in communist luxury at the US-built Rex Hotel in Ho Chi Minh City and the Cuban-funded Thắng Lợi Hotel in Hanoi were followed by days of programmed sightseeing. This was how I first saw Vietnam. On 30 April 1988, from the roof garden of the Rex, I watched people on bikes and mopeds circling Ho Chi Minh City in celebration of the fall of Saigon, thirteen years before.

That was a visual image, but two conversations caught my imagination. In a moment of free time, I slipped out of the Rex to explore the market. Hailed by a street peddler, I sat down to chat. Speaking with an American accent, he asked me, out of the blue: 'What do you want to know about this country? Any questions about Vietnam's society or economy? I'll try and answer'. I asked a few clumsy questions and have since forgotten his answers. What stayed with me was the curiosity he aroused in me about his country, and his desire to respond to it. A few days later I spoke to the tourist guide about the possibility of returning to Vietnam, on a different sort of programme. 'It's easy', he said, 'you just get in touch with a research institute in Hanoi'.

I did not immediately follow his advice. Suffering not only from an interest in Vietnam but from a more conventional dose of Anglo-Saxon infatuation with that country's former colonial ruler, I allowed my curiosity to take me to Paris. Enrolling on a Master's degree course at a university in the Latin Quarter, I set out to explore French Indochina's socio-economic history. The main sources for this were situated in the colonial archives in Aix-en-Provence, a fortuitous circumstance allowing me to indulge a passion for the South of France, after which I submitted a dissertation on French economic planning in Indochina in the 1940s.[2]

This was a study in the economics of colonialism. My conclusion to it was that in the 1940s, after years of colonial exploitation, the French authorities finally decided to deal with Indochina's local economic problems. The most significant of these was the pressure of population in Vietnam's Red River Delta. This had been the subject of considerable debate in the 1930s, articulated notably by a French businessman by the name of Paul Bernard.[3] By the mid 1940s, the French resolved on a programme of industrialization, which they outlined in an economic development plan written by Bernard and published in 1948.[4] The solution came too late. By the time the French found the political will to implement it, the 1945 revolution ensured they had lost the power.[5] And when, in March 1992, I settled into a modest hotel room in Hanoi's Nguyễn Đình Chiểu street, back this time not on holiday but to look for a subject for PhD study, these issues were at the forefront of my mind: the pressure of population and the challenge of French failure. I wanted to know how the authorities of independent Vietnam responded to them.

I quickly left the industrialization question behind. Vietnam was primarily an agricultural country. While some industrialization had taken place after the French defeat in 1954, problems of war and management limited its effectiveness as a solution to the issue of demographic growth. Nor – and this was important, after my discussion in the market four years earlier – did the issue particularly interest the Vietnamese people to whom I spoke. Eventually I went back to my reading of Bernard and one night I recalled one of his other solutions, a policy of internal migration. Next morning, I started asking questions, and quickly made two discoveries. Large numbers of people moved to the hills in the period after the French left. Many of them were migrants on a government land clearance programme launched by the newly independent state in North Vietnam as part of a policy of highland development. This policy was continued after reunification. While some aspects of this programme were politically quite sensitive, I found – and this was my second discovery – that many Vietnamese people, fascinated by their own migrations, were happy to tell me about its practice. Almost everyone had a story.

THE HILLS AND THE PLAINS

The preceding story of my own migration is significant for two reasons. It is my response to the challenge, raised in 1980s 'reflexive' theorizing in anthropology, that researchers reveal in their writings the relations that produce ethnographic knowledge. The reader will, indeed, observe throughout this account a language very different to the 'rhetoric of objectivity'.[6] It is significant also in the presentation of the premises with which I approached this work of enquiry. That is to say, I started thinking about the history of migration in Vietnam in terms of its ability to resolve the problem of population growth in the Red River Delta, and of this problem's impact on the daily lives of ordinary people. I was interested in historical demography and the quest, by both the people and the state, for solutions to the pressure of population in the plains.

I stayed mainly in the plains in 1992. Only once did I put myself through the cumbersome administrative arrangements at that time necessary for a visit to the highlands. I went on a day trip to the old French hill station at Tam Đảo. From the mountain top, I was not the first foreigner to be impressed by the view of the delta before me, although it was no longer possible to conjure up the textured vocabulary used by French writers to describe the forests behind. Most of the giant trees they saw had gone, but the contrast between the hills and the plains – offered by that fabulous view – remained on that trip the central feature of the landscape. It retains that position in this account. Not only for reasons of landscape, however. Back in Paris, under the ornate ceiling of the Bibliothèque Nationale, I learnt that during recent decades, by contrast with previous centuries, the hills became an important frontier for the Viet ethnic group. I read, in particular, a book by Paul Mus, published in 1952.

Mus described the geo-political expansion of the Việt people in the imagery of a flood. Moving southward from their heartland in the Red River Delta, step by step settling the coastal strip as far as the Mekong, they 'flowed over Indochina, in the manner of an inundation, carrying off the other peoples everywhere they occupied low-lying soil, paddy fields or places where paddy fields could be put'. He elaborated on his perception of Vietnam's pre-colonial human geography in language as complex and ornate as the library's ceiling:

> This ethnic adventure stopped at the foot of the high country's buttresses – with the exception of certain political or military points, like the region of Cao Bằng, to the North, or the enclave of Plei Ku, in the Moï country. Leaving Tonkin to arrive as far away as the Gulf of Siam, about two thousand kilometres from there, Viet-Nam, at the relatively recent epoch when we were associated with her history, had practically never broached the habitat of the Moï tribes. Her installation strangled itself between the latter and the sea, following a band a thousand kilometres long which, at places, is only a few kilometres wide, where spurs detached from the mountain ranges do not interrupt it completely.
>
> Shadowed, in the west, by the edge of these forested slopes with their redoubtable endemicity of malaria, her demographic equilibrium was gradually achieved, on the plains, by means and to the profit of flooded paddy fields. With men, the major factor in this landscape as we were soon to find on our own epic journey in Asia, she associated two other elements, land and water, which she subordinated by the elimination of a third, the marshy forest – which, in this climate, is brute nature, on low-lying land.[7]

Mus used exaggerated images, but he described a reality of population distribution which persisted – in its broad outlines – until the mid twentieth century. On the one hand, large numbers of Việt people lived in the plains and grew rice. On

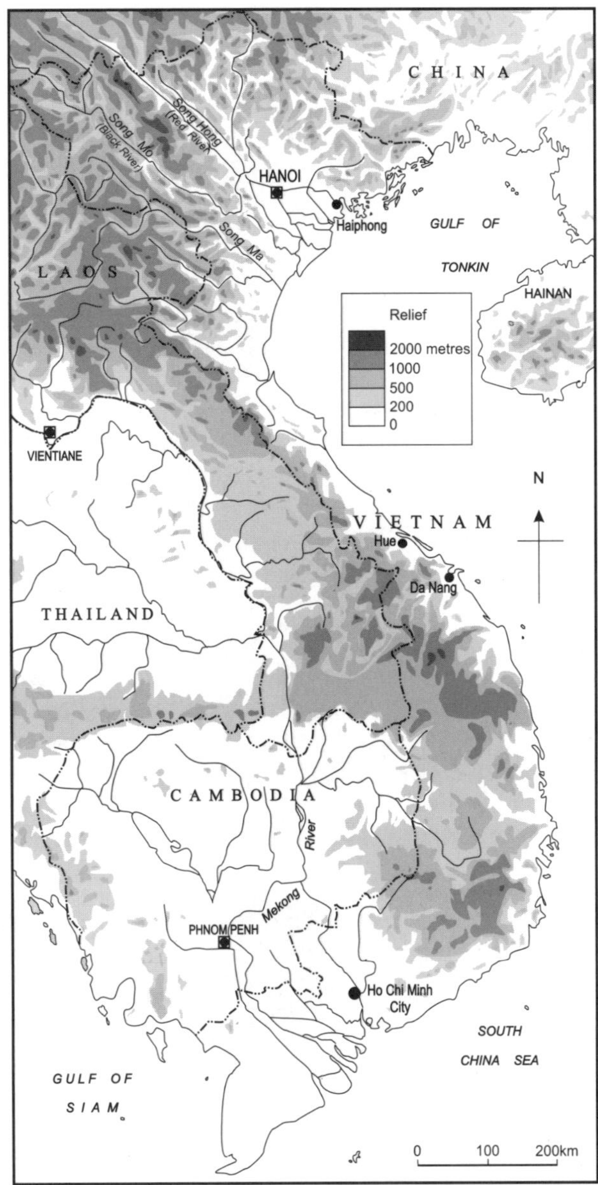

Map 1: The hills and the plains in Vietnam
From the Red River Delta and coastal plains, Việt people moved to the northern high-lands (north and west of Hanoi) and the central highlands (north of Ho Chi Minh City). In the second half of the twentieth century, this became a substantial movement of population from the hills to the plains.
Source: *Địa lý tự nhiên phần đất liên*, Cục Đo Đạc Bản Đồ Nhả Nước, Hanoi, 1989. Redrawn by Lee Li Kheng.

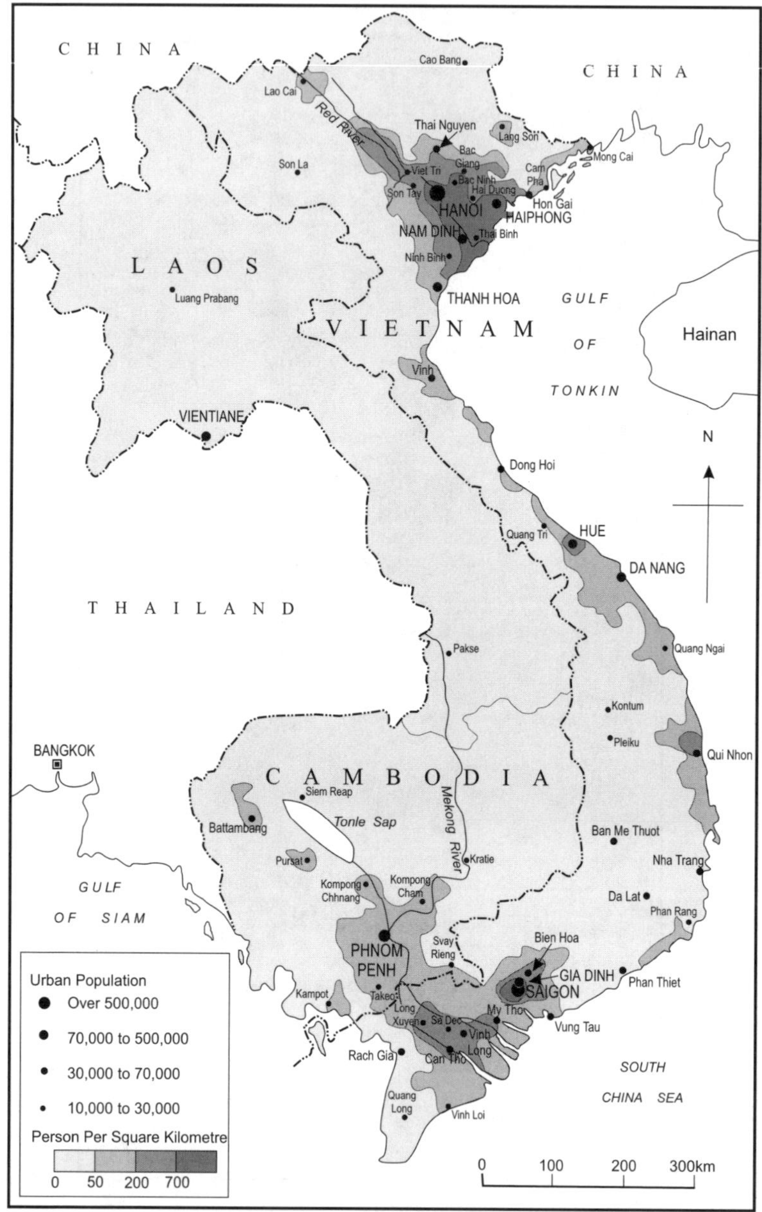

Map 2: Population densities in Indochina, c. 1960
Vietnam's population was heavily concentrated in the Red River Delta in the north, and along the coast as far south as the Mekong Delta. The highlands were, by contrast, sparsely populated.
Source: Unsourced (probably American), map undated (c. 1960). Redrawn by Lee Li Kheng.

the other, Vietnam's two highland regions were sparsely inhabited by a variety of peoples: groups of T'ai, Hmong, Yao and Mon-Khmer speaking people in the northern hills, and the indigenous peoples of Malayo-Polynesian and Austroasiatic origin known to many French writers as 'Moï' in the central highlands.* The contrast between the hills and the plains, a dominant feature of Vietnam's relief, is illustrated in Map 1. In the highlands, most of the inhabitants lived from shifting cultivation and the forest. The plains were crowded with Việt people, and the hills, as was subsequently repeated to me, remained a space of 'wide land and few people'. Maps 2 and 3 show up these patterns of population distribution. Maps 4 and 5 indicate two of the determining factors of Việt settlement: their predilection for wet rice agriculture and their vulnerability to malaria. While French colonization caused some inroads by Việt settlers into the sparsely settled highlands, the demographic balance described by Mus endured well into the twentieth century. As a French geographer noted in 1940, describing Vietnam's major mountain range: 'The Annamitique Chain (…) has played an important role from the human point of view: it served as a refuge for the Indonesian populations and the Việt massed in the coastal plains have not crossed it'.†

At the time Mus wrote his book, major changes were already taking shape. In a short article published in 1951, anthropologist Georges Condominas foreshadowed some of the consequences of French colonization in the central highlands:

> The nuclei of Vietnamese colonization established in the highlands by the French to serve their needs for auxiliaries and manual labourers ultimately provided demographic outlets for the neighbouring Vietnamese areas, even though most Vietnamese continue to dislike the hill country. Accordingly, despite the French restrictions on Vietnamese immigration, the highlands became a colonial area not only for a few European administrators and exploiters but more especially for multitudes of Vietnamese immigrants. Today two peoples at very different stages of technical and cultural development live there in close proximity. On the one hand are the Moï, whose horizon ends at their village boundaries; who are divided among numerous tribes and lack cohesiveness even at the tribal level; who are demographically inert and dependent on rudimentary techniques; and who therefore suffer from a deep-rooted inferiority complex towards their Vietnamese neighbours. On the other hand, the Vietnamese,

---

* The French word *Moï* was a transliteration of the Vietnamese word for the inhabitants of the central highlands (*mọi*, 'savage'), itself drawn from the Chinese tradition of regarding others as 'barbarians' (*man* in Sino-Vietnamese). A more neutral word *montagnard* also existed, which acquired negative connotations by association with the American presence in Vietnam. Here I refer to these peoples collectively as highlanders or ethnic minorities, and specifically by the name for their particular ethnic group. For the sake of clarity, in most other cases I follow the terminology and ethnic classifications of the Vietnamese state. The notable exception to this is that of Vietnam's majority ethnic group, referred to by the ancient term Việt, rather than the more confusing classification Kinh. This usage is discussed in Diệp Đình Hoa, *Người Việt ở đồng bằng Bắc Bộ*, Hanoi: NXB Khoa Học Xã Hội, 2000, pp. 38–42.

† Pierre Gourou, *L'utilisation du sol en Indochine*, Paris: l'Hartmann, 1940, p. 39. The Annamitic Chain is the range of mountains separating the upper reaches of the Mekong River from the seaboard of central Vietnam.

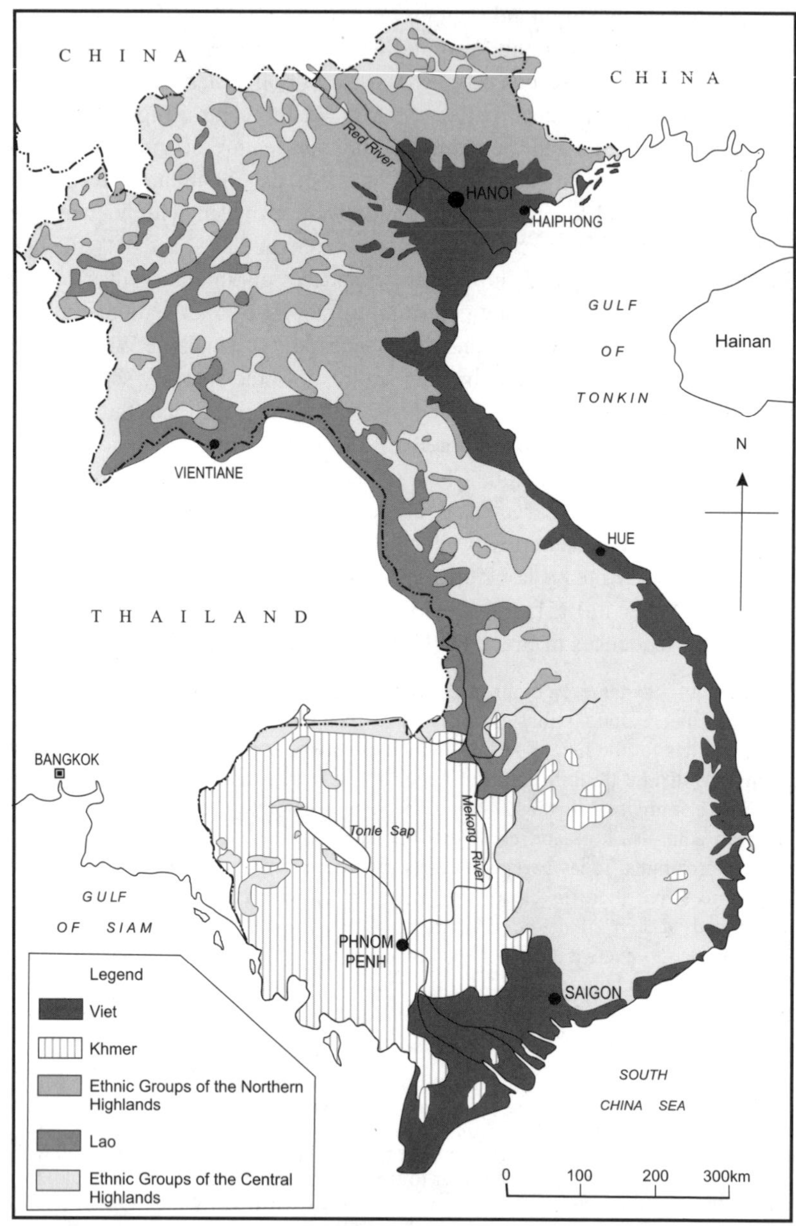

Map 3: Ethnic groups of Indochina, c. 1950
Until the mid twentieth century, Việt people lived mainly in the Vietnamese plains, while other ethnic groups inhabited the highlands. Small settlements of Việt people could be found in provincial centres of the highlands.
Source: 'Carte Ethnolinguistique', Service Géographique National du Việt Nam and École française d'Extrême-Orient, c. 1949. Redrawn by Lee Li Kheng.

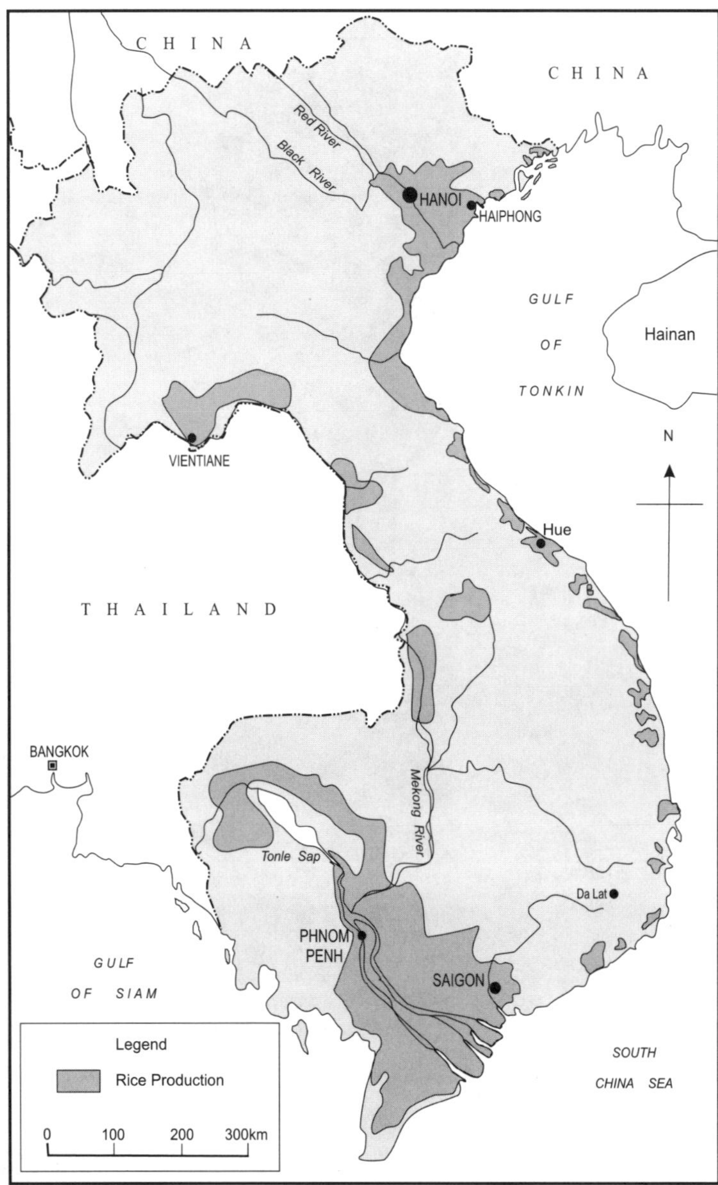

Map 4: Principal areas of rice production in Indochina, 1953
Comparison with Maps 3 and 5 shows that the main areas of wet rice production in Vietnam corresponded to those of Việt settlement and a low incidence of malaria. Wet and dry rice was grown in isolated parts of the highlands.
Source: 'Indochina: Principal Areas of Rice Production', Department of Mines and Technical Surveys, Indo-China, A Geographical Appreciation, Ottawa, 1953, p. 40. Redrawn by Lee Li Kheng.

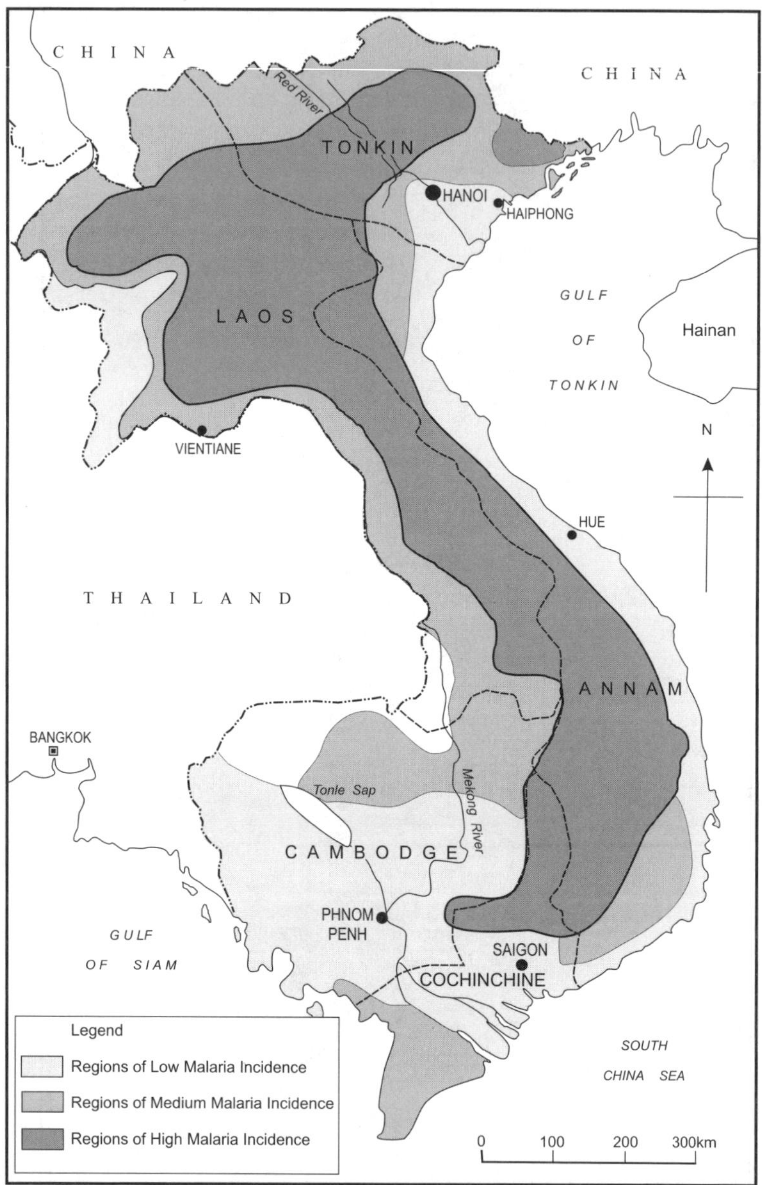

Map 5: Malaria in Indochina, 1907
Areas of low malaria incidence corresponded to those of Việt settlement and intensive rice agriculture. The highlands, by contrast, were the habitat of the Anopheles minimus mosquito, the main vector of malaria in Vietnam.
Source: 'Carte du Paludisme en Indochine, 1907, par Simond', Henry G.-S. Morin, *Entretiens sur le paludisme et sa prévention en Indochine*, Hanoi: Imprimerie d'Extrême-Orient, 1935. Redrawn by Lee Li Kheng.

whose solidly organized communities receive constant reinforcements from the coastal plains, press outward from their established communities. Their overwhelming technical superiority, enhanced by a notable receptivity to Western influences, enables the Vietnamese to best the Moï in all of their dealings with them.[8]

The nuclei of Việt people quickly spread. Forty years on, Việt people made up 40 per cent of the population of the northern highlands and more than half of the population of the central highlands. In a combatively entitled article, 'Internal Colonialism in the Central Highlands of Vietnam', Grant Evans observed dramatic changes in the area's population composition and, in particular, rapid growth of its Việt population. He showed that the major impetus for this change was not French colonization nor even the war, but a migration policy set in place by the government after reunification, presented in Map 6.[9] This was not the first policy of its kind. The central highlands had seen the first government-sponsored Việt settlers arrive under the Republic of Vietnam (RVN) in the late 1950s. In the 1960s and 1970s, meanwhile, the Democratic Republic of Vietnam (DRV) relocated large numbers of Red River Delta peasants to the northern highlands.[10] The extension of this policy to the south after 1975 resulted in a major increase in the proportion of Việt people living in the highlands, illustrated in Map 7. The redrawing of the ethnolinguistic map under the Socialist Republic of Vietnam (SRV) was described in a cheerfully entitled book published in Hanoi in the early 1990s – *The Central Highlands: Potential and Prospects*.[11] While the book does not pinpoint specific locations of Việt settlement in the central highlands, it indicates its general patterns. There were large concentrations around French-period provincial capitals at Dalat, Kontum and Ban Mê Thuột, and smaller pockets elsewhere. Above all, it gives a sense of the scale of the increase.

Much of this increase took place after the mid 1980s. At that time, the practice of spontaneous migration of families started to replace redistributive policy as the main driving force behind the movement of Việt people to the central highlands.[12] Interest in this subject among writers in English remained underdeveloped until the end of the 1990s, obscured by Desbarats' influential but one-dimensional study of migration policy.* Internal migration drew greater attention towards the end of the decade and became the object of a number of valuable monographs.[14] But the international migration of Vietnamese, as boat people to Hong Kong and parts of Southeast Asia, accumulated a much more varied literature.[15] Boat people in the 1970s were mainly southerners leaving for political reasons, but by the late 1980s the majority came from the north, in search of economic opportun-

---

* In 1987, Desbarats published an account of post-1975 migration in Vietnam, often cited until the late 1990s. Her research focused on the rustication of southern urban populations and was couched in language relevant more to the Cold War than to Vietnam's then recent policy of reforms. This perspective detracted from the usefulness of her findings, especially for the peasants of the Red River Delta, where the situation was different to the south. For sources, see note 13.

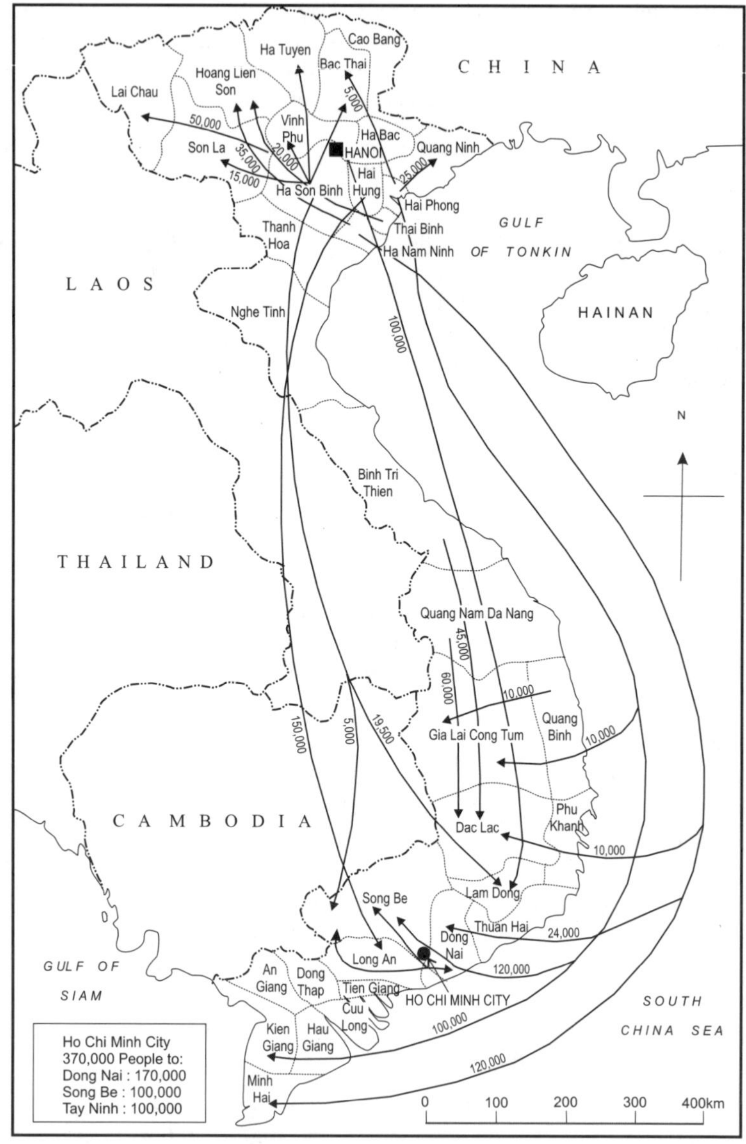

Map 6: The five-year plan for population redistribution in Vietnam, 1976–80
The plan announced at the 4th Party Congress in 1976 aimed to resettle Việt people from the Red River Delta in the northern and central highlands and the Mekong Delta. Despite difficulties in the plan's implementation, large numbers of people did move according to the plan.
Source: Nguyễn Đức Nhuận, 'Contraintes démographiques et politiques de développement au Vietnam, 1975–80', in *Population*, 30 (1984). Figures here are revisions of the original plan to move 4 million people in 1976-80, as reported in *Vietnam Courier*, 58 (1977). Map by Béatrice Narcy, redrawn by Lee Li Kheng.

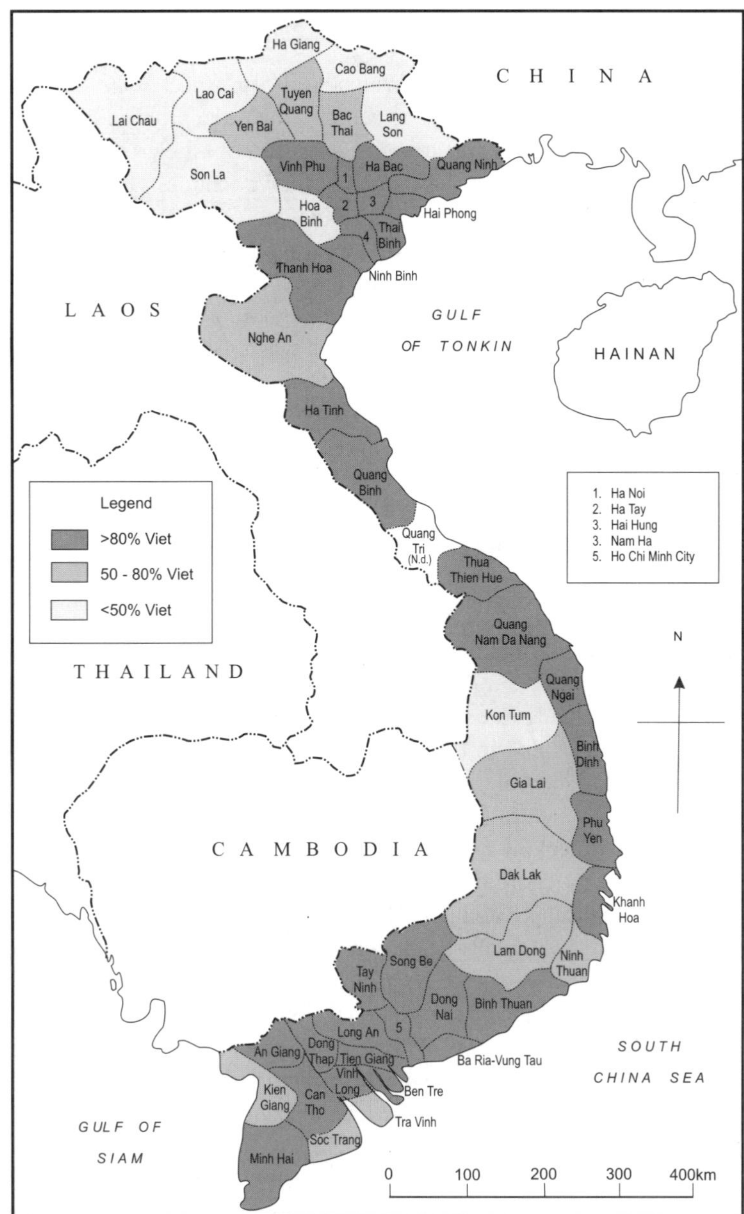

Map 7: Việt people in Vietnam's provinces, 1996
*By 1996, migration had caused Việt people to form a substantial proportion of the
population in midland and most highland provinces of the north and all provinces of the
central highlands (Dak Lak, Gia Lai, Kontum, Lâm Đồng).*
Source: Trần Thị Quê, Nguyễn Thị Hồng Phấn and Trần Đăng Tuấn, *Số liệu thống
kê các vùng thưa dân ở Việt Nam*, Hanoi: NXB Thống Kê, 1996, pp. 2–3. Map by
Lee Li Kheng.

ities. Some were people who had abandoned government-sponsored settlements in the hills.[16]

The boat people movement was, in some ways, an aspect of the same phenomenon of migration within Vietnam, as people sought the promise of a better life. The dynamism of migration was conveyed by titles of articles in the Vietnamese press, along with a sense of the loss of administrative control: 'The Urgent Problem of Free Migration', 'They Leave Their Home and Go ...', 'Internal Migration: An Urgent Social Problem'.[17] Some of the people who chose to stay within Vietnam's borders moved to centres of economic development in the plains, notably Hanoi and Ho Chi Minh City, but many were rural–rural migrants heading for the hills. The cities have grown, but their growth was relatively limited.* The highlands, on the other hand, have been both quantitatively and qualitatively transformed by these processes of migration. I determined to see how this transformation took place.

METHODOLOGY AND SOURCES

To this end, I enrolled in a PhD programme at the Australian National University. Reading through the available English language material on the subject, I observed that previous studies fell into two categories. A number of anthropological writers approached the problem from the perspective of Việt contact with ethnic minorities, particularly those in the central highlands.[19] Studies dealing with the country as a whole, meanwhile, made use of the specific tools of demographic or geographic analysis.[20] What I wanted to do, however, was to explore the social and economic dynamics of Việt migration, that is to say the way that Việt people went about settling a new area of land, the chaos and complexity of their experiences. As a result, readers seeking neatly constructed representative surveys of migrant households or nicely coordinated time-series of data on in-migration and out-migration will be disappointed here. I collected archival and interview material for qualitative analysis. Equally frustrated will be those who share Condominas's view of this story as an issue of contact between two peoples, with the ethnic minorities on the one hand and the Việt on the other. My approach may indeed be regarded as 'one hand clapping'. However, the scale of the subject of the one hand, and practical difficulties involved in researching the other rendered this limitation necessary. The ethnic minorities are not absent, but this is a story about Việt people.[21]

I arrived in Vietnam to research it in January 1995. Foreigners were now allowed to rent private accommodation, so I took a room with a Vietnamese family in Hanoi's old trading quarter. Before leaving Canberra, I had written to the Institute of Ethnology, at Vietnam's National Centre for Social Sciences and Humanities. They had agreed to arrange my visa, and now helped with letters of

---

*   Limited, that is, compared to growth rates of other cities in the region, such as Jakarta in Indonesia, and Tianjin in China. For sources, see note 18.

introduction to the National Archives and National Library. These two institutions would become my main places of work for the coming year and a half.*

The Vietnam National Library is an elegant building situated in a French-style formal garden off one of Hanoi's tree-lined boulevards. Its yellow colonial facade concealed indexes of books in French and Vietnamese, and provincial newspapers with many complete sets going back to the early 1960s. Next door, another colonial era building housed part of the National Archives of Vietnam.† Behind its more functional, but equally yellow facade, were stored two sorts of archives: colonial era documents left behind by the French, and post-1945 documents deposited by ministries of the Vietnamese government. Halfway through my stay, the post-1945 material was removed to a gleaming white new storehouse in the suburbs.‡ Archives, books and newspapers collected in these three buildings have become the main written sources of information for this history.

The distinguishing feature of French archives was the difference between the amount written on migration policy and the results achieved. Reading the plans churned out by the offices of provincial governors (Résident), by the government for the northern Vietnamese protectorate (Résidence Supérieur du Tonkin), or by the central government of French Indochina (Gouvernement Général de l'Indochine) one would have thought that vast programmes of organized migration had been set in motion.§ In fact, the contrary was the case. Other policies – relating to taxation, personal identification and security – directly and indirectly hindered the realization of such programmes. Contradictions within the French administration ensured that the French kept their attempts at organized migration on paper. While colonial administrators developed a theory about the religious and sentimental 'attachment' of Việt peasants to their native villages, the administrative system they were managing created ties that were stronger than sentiment. One colonial-era French academic complained: 'In sum, the results of Vietnamese colonization of the back country are very thin, especially if we compare them with the speeches delivered, the projects drawn up, the pages written on this subject.'[22]

As for the post-1945 Vietnamese archives, at the central government level comparatively few pages were written on migration policy, judging from the results

---

*   I did fieldwork during two stays in Vietnam, from January to December 1995, and April 1996 to February 1997. July to September 1996 was spent in the archives in France.

†   This was the National Archives of Vietnam, Centre No. 1 (hereafter NAV1).

‡   This became Centre No. 3 while Centre No. 2 is in Ho Chi Minh City (hereafter NAV2 and NAV3).

§   I consulted the following collections of French archives. Local documents on northern Vietnam up to the Résident Supérieur du Tonkin (RST) at NAV1. Documents of the Gouvernement Général de l'Indochine (GGI), and offices of the French Ministry of Colonies at the Centre des Archives d'Outre-Mer (CAOM) in Aix-en-Provence. Documents of the French army at the Service Historique de l'Armée de Terre (SHAT) in Vincennes.

of my research.* 1960s policy on migration was published in the Party news-paper, *Nhân Dân*, but not in the legislative record *Công Báo*. If detailed instruc-tions regarding its implementation were drawn up, I was not looking in the right place for them.† As far as I could tell, officials at the ministries responsible for migration policy limited their instructions to the setting of quantitative targets and general guidelines on how to fulfil them. Their subordinates in the provinces, meanwhile, reported back to Hanoi in detail. They presented their performance in formulaic terms. Good news about achievements was followed by bad news of failure, or what were termed 'shortcomings'. Shortcomings were, in turn, described with great delicacy. Migrants departing for the mountains were recorded in careful quantitative terms, while those returning, having abandoned their destination, were generalized into 'a number'. Unfitting behaviour on the part of Party members or officials was imputed, even, to 'a small number'. Details of individual mis-demeanour were recorded with care and regret as inadequacies, without meaning-ful indication of their frequency.

I was frustrated by this vagueness of instruction and report while reading through the archives. It was only when I started looking at the newspapers that I learnt how to interpret it. Newspaper articles had similar functions to many documents in the archives and employed similar formulae – indeed, these 'Party organs' were used by central and provincial authorities as a means of com-munication with local officials, and both legislation, guidelines on implementation and reports from districts, communes and cooperatives were to be found there. Policy guidelines, I learnt, were imprecise, allowing local authorities flexibility in the day-to-day business of putting the policy into practice. Reports about this practice were vague and euphemistic, but euphemism allowed officials to get away with saying a great deal without saying very much. And it was only in 'reading' the euphemism that I discovered that both archive and newspaper had a great deal of information to impart.

Newspapers, in particular, provided a wealth of detail about particular localities. One of the purposes of news was education. Specific case studies were used as focal points for emulation campaigns and while model villages or individuals were generally chosen for this purpose, learning from struggle and errors was often as important as conforming to a standard. One of the campaigns I came across, in the province of Thái Bình, combined the two techniques. The news-

---

* I consulted documents originating at central government offices in Hanoi and in a number of provinces. Most of them were in the collections of the Ministry of Labour (BLD), the General Statistical Office (TCTK), the State Planning Committee (UBKHNN), and the Bureau of State Farm Management, at the Ministry of Agriculture and Forestry (CQLNTQD). Few were written later than 1970. In 1995, under a sort of 'twenty-five year rule', post-1970 documents were withdrawn from consultation by foreign researchers.

† This is conceivable. Collections were being reclassified while I was reading at NAV3. Some were unavailable for consultation. Some ministries had not deposited their files, and jealously guarded access to their collections.

paper set up a model and then invited cooperatives and communes to send in self-critical summaries of lessons learnt. These articles, which were published in early 1964, made fascinating reading. They allowed leaders at the provincial level to speak to people and officials in the villages, and offered the latter a chance to pass messages back to 'higher levels'. Far from simply churning out Party propaganda, apparently useless for the purposes of historical scholarship, I discovered that newspaper 'debates' such as this offered detailed information which, if carefully interpreted, could be of great value.

I did not limit my sources to written materials, however. My intention instead was to collect a variety of data. Interpretation of one sort could be facilitated by comparison with another. I resolved therefore to interview some of the people who migrated, and some of the officials who organized their move. This required a rather different approach to the usual village study, for which I could not be sure of finding sufficient written materials. I settled on what Clifford has called 'multi-locale fieldwork', in an attempt to gain in breadth of focus what I would lose in depth.[23] My fieldwork was dispersed and I visited six provinces in all. I was interested primarily in the migration of people away from the Red River plains. Thái Bình, in the heart of the delta, was the province I chose in the sending region. As for destination areas, I worked in one province in the northern midlands (Thái Nguyên), two in the northern mountains (Hòa Bình, Sơn La) and one in the central highlands (Dak Lak).* Later I also made visits to the delta region of the province of Thanh Hóa. The situation of these provinces is illustrated in Map 8. In all, I carried out interviews with over 200 individuals, families and groups, including Việt and ethnic minority people and cadres at village, commune, district, province and central government levels.

For this, of course, I depended on the help of the Institute of Ethnology. Before each trip, which lasted no more than a fortnight, the Institute's director signed a letter of introduction addressed to the province. On my first trips, I went by car in the company of Diệp Đình Hoa, a friend and also professor at the Institute. I travelled later by motorbike with other friends, Đào Thế Đức, Nguyễn Tiến Đông and Trần Hà, younger researchers who agreed to help me out. In the countryside, over cups of tea with officials from each level in the administrative hierarchy, we sought permission to work. At the provincial People's Committee, we received a letter of introduction to the district. At the district, formalities varied: sometimes we were accompanied to the commune, sometimes another letter was written, signed and stamped. After stopping at the People's Committee of the

---

*   The following topographical terminology has been used. 'Mountains' refer to mountainous regions (over 200 m, approximately). 'Midlands' are foothill regions between the plains and the mountains. 'Hills' and 'highlands' are used as generic terms embracing both mountains and midlands (as in 'northern highlands'). See Plate 1 for a French demarcation between mountains and midlands. The demarcation mountain/midland/delta remains in use in Vietnam. For the Tây Nguyên plateaux in central Vietnam, the normal English name, 'central highlands', is used.

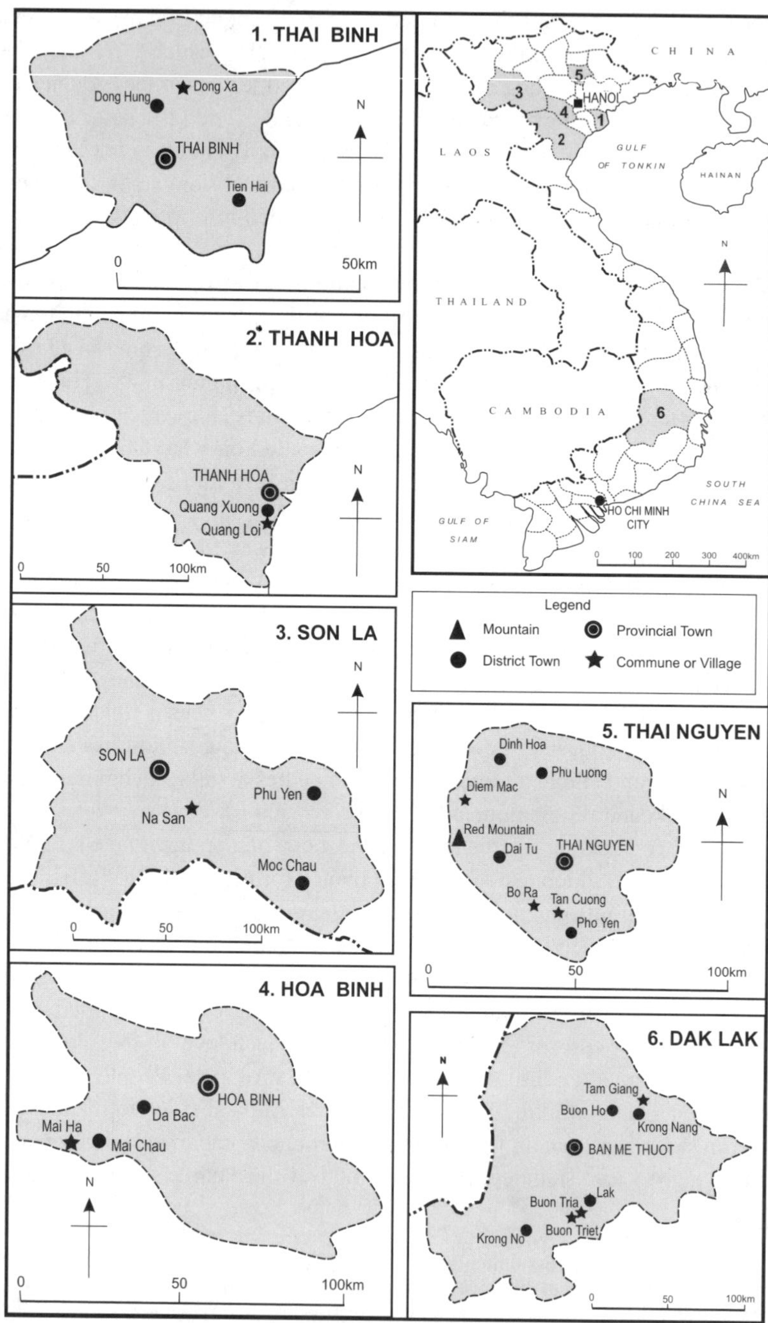

Map 8: Principal sites of fieldwork in Vietnam, 1995–2000
The main sites of my fieldwork for this book were grouped in the six provinces shown here.
Map by Lee Li Kheng.

commune, an administrative structure embracing a number of villages, we could proceed to interview in the villages themselves.*

This process indicates something of the ambiguity of the position of a foreigner working in the Vietnamese countryside. As far as the Institute was concerned, I was a guest of the Vietnamese state, invited to do research. However, people at the Institute told me (to remind me of the responsibilities of that position), I was also a 'state cadre'.† So that when I was accompanied to interview by local officials or police, in a security measure extended to foreign guests, my arrival there took the form of a 'delegation'. We didn't look like ordinary government officials, however, arriving out of the blue in outdated and unostentatious Russian-built vehicles: a clapped-out black Volga automobile, or Minsk motorbikes.‡ At least one person I interviewed seemed genuinely disappointed that I did not travel in a smart four-wheel-drive vehicle or a helicopter, like other foreigners he had met. Others were simply amused. These ambiguities tended to create spaces for interaction and communication, which although confusing for some people, could create confidence in others.

Local officials accompanying would at times join in the interview, helpfully contradicting people who distorted a story, or less constructively reminding them of an official line. At times they got bored, even fell asleep, hearing the same questions again and again. At times, we were left to interview alone – after a few days, when a relationship of confidence had been built up, or when there were more important things to do, like bring the harvest in. During the interviews I used a tape recorder at first, which created an atmosphere of formality which, after the stop button was pressed, could become a more intimate discussion. As my confidence in my language skills increased, I abandoned the machine and relied on written notes. At all times, I depended on my Vietnamese colleagues for help in making relationships both with officials and the people we interviewed,

---

* The following translations of administrative terms have been used: People's Committee for *Ủy Ban Nhân Dân* and its predecessor *Ủy Ban Hành Chính*, province for *tỉnh*, district for *huyện*, commune for *xã*, village for *thôn, bản, xóm*, and *làng*. The term 'commune' should not be confused with usage in China. The French rural administrative entity, from which the term is derived, more nearly corresponds to this Vietnamese structure embracing several villages. The translation 'village' captures the residential and sentimental connotations of the Vietnamese words better than the variant rendering 'hamlet'.

† Barnett's definition of the term 'cadre' in China can be applied to Vietnam: 'In its broadest usage, it includes all those, both Party members and non-Party cadres, who hold any post as a functionary in the bureaucratic hierarchies in China, from top to bottom.' See also note 24.

‡ These vehicles had clear connotations in Vietnam. The Volga, formally the smartest vehicle on the roads, was now the cheapest form of hire car and a bargain on the taxi run to the airport. The Minsk, a noisy 125cc two-stroke, was popular among highland motorbike taxi drivers for its robust frame and easily repaired engine, well suited to remote mountain tracks. This vehicle attracted derision on the streets of Hanoi, where Honda 'Dream II' motorbikes were the rage and a foreigner was perceived as having the means to follow the fashion.

and for their insights and understanding over rice wine in our end-of-day discussions.

WRITING

Data thus gathered required careful handling. The presence of officials at some interviews were one factor of interpretation; people's own agendas was another; the distortions of their memory a third; the limitations of my own understandings and memory a fourth. In my presentation of important interview information, therefore, I have communicated as much of the context surrounding its collection as was convenient within the text. I tried to set it against written source materials wherever possible. My aim was to convey the overlap implicit between the voice of the people I interviewed and my own voice and understanding (which impinges by means of language, fieldnotes, translation). Rather than seek an impartial objectivity, a scholarly distance from my sources, I sought to describe the details of my relationship with them. Inevitably the reader must rely on the judgement of the scholar. With a fuller understanding of the research process, however, one is better equipped to judge that judgement.

This is the purpose of the first chapter, which is an account of a week's fieldwork in the valley of the Công River, in Thái Nguyên province. Later chapters are concerned with questions of analysis, and will look in detail at processes of migration and settlement in the highlands. The first chaper, however, offers a portrait of a frontier region, presenting, at the same time, the materials and methodology used to represent it. To call an area of land a frontier is not a neutral act. This portrait aims to show how the idea of the frontier was constructed.

This open approach to writing is extended from the first chapter into the rest of the text. It takes the form, in the first instance, of a respect for landscape, micro-event and the stories of individual lives, going beyond the mere search for illustrative vignette. In a recent article enticingly entitled 'Braudel and China', Mark Elvin felt that image and evocation are valid modes of historical truth. He cited Braudel in support of this, where the French historian declared, in defence of his approach to the writing of the history of the Mediterranean, that 'images are not merely the picturesque aspect of a history rich in color but its principal verity.'[25]

Evocation – of landscape, lives and events – is a major preoccupation of my own approach. Landscapes are evoked, through my own observations, through the written and spoken observations of others, through maps. This history is ultimately about the land and the relationships of people to different parts of it. The shape and look of it and the impact of those relationships are an integral part of the story. In this respect I have been influenced by the work of Simon Schama, whose *Landscape and Memory* displayed the historical power not only of the landscape itself, but also of images – written, spoken and visual – of the land.[26]

Micro-events are evoked: a rickshaw robbery, a birth in a bus. Such happenings, of great importance to a small number of people, are mentioned for two reasons.

At times they carry the argument. The micro-data are used as building blocks in a larger edifice, as details in the broader picture of a twentieth-century historical process. But they also serve to remove and rescue people from that process – from 'histoire' – returning them to the arena of life and stories about it – to 'histoires'. Ordinary people's voices and stories are used not only in illustration of process, but also to advance complex arguments about the nature and history of migration.

With respect both to lives and landscape, I have been influenced by the philosophy that seems to me fundamental to the work of the artist Peter Bruegel the elder. The close relationship of people to their geographical and social surroundings is a recurrent theme in Bruegel's paintings, many of which are tableaux in which the detailed doings of men, women, children, animals even, contribute to the telling of some larger story. Bruegel, moreover, 'never separates man from the crowd of his fellows; he made no portraits', showing instead faces, bodies and actions within carefully constructed and highly chaotic social scenes.[27] I have sought in this study to set out such a tableau. No one is privileged, each life finding itself in context and relationship with others, every individual and every family making their own personal contribution. This is a reflection on the contradiction between chaos and construct.

In so writing, I sought to redress a balance. The study of migration has too often been set in terms of macro/micro, in the dry language of demographic trend or historical *longue durée*. What is required, as Halfacree and Boyle pointed out, is a biographical method which eschews 'an impersonal, dehumanized approach in which flows replace people' while avoiding the traps of parochialism, reliance on anecdote and bias into which historical biography often falls.[28] I have attempted such a synthesis, bringing an 'ethnographic-style holistic approach'[29] to the study of historical migration, setting information about individual lives in a framework informed by flows, not only of migration, but of time, landscape, bureaucracy, ideology – of history.

In his discussion of this approach to historical truth, however, Elvin pinpointed a number of difficulties. In particular, he quoted criticism of Annales history's tendency to tension between the evocative mode, an impulse to seize the 'pulse of the living', and the analytical mode, a contradictory impulse to follow 'science and scientific method'.[30] If there is a contradiction here – and, with Philippe Carrard, I doubt that one exists in any necessary sense – I have sought to counter it by developing my own 'pragmatics of scholarly writing'.[31] This takes the form of further evocation: evocation in this case not of land or story but of source. To allow the reader to judge the reliability of the sources, the origins of documents regularly escape from the footnotes, the contexts to interviews are made explicit in the text. Where possible, information of a rhetorical or deceptive nature is compared with more concrete instances and examples, or with contrasting rhetoric.

However, I have not always felt it necessary to decide, on behalf of the reader, on the acceptance or rejection of a particular perspective. Many people were involved in these migrations. They expressed their own points of view about them, manipulating in so doing both those of others and those of the state. I have provided the context necessary to understand where they are coming from. If I am judged to have too often given them the benefit of the doubt, my reply would be that it is not the benefit but the doubt which counts. Doubt is evoked by context. In presenting the sources in terms of doubt, moreover, I allow myself the illusion that I am among them.* My own voice, another source.

POLICY AND PRACTICE

My voice is, of course, more than just a source. But these personal and method-ological perspectives are important to the conceptual focus of my argument. At the outset, I wanted to research the historical experiences of Red River Delta farmers faced with the pressure of population on their land. I was less concerned to explore the region's human ecology and associated problems, than in reaching an understanding of how people reacted to those problems by leaving.[32] I started my enquiries, then, with an interest in the practice of migration from the delta, on peasant responses to population pressure.

Research reoriented this focus. From my initial discussions and reading of the archives, it became clear that government policy played an important role in stimulating population movement, that it was difficult to describe the experiences of many migrants without continual reference to the state. This was particularly the case after 1954, when the government of the DRV succeeded in organizing the mass relocation of delta dwellers to the highlands. It was inappropriate, however, to speak in black and white terms of forced migration, in the sense understood by Desbarats. In her study of migration under the SRV after 1975, the focus on compulsory rustication of urban inhabitants in the south unfortunately informed and deformed perceptions of much Vietnamese-organized migration.[33] Red River Delta people were persuaded to join the programme. Their departures were based on their decisions, however influenced, and could not be understood in policy terms alone. In Vietnam, organized migration was a phenomenon ill suited to conventional push–pull categorisation. A more complex and finely tuned apparatus for understanding was required.

I structured my analysis, therefore, in terms of policy and practice. The meaning of these terms was somewhat unstable over the twentieth century, but three periods and three corresponding structural configurations may be observed.

1. **Under the French**, policy was both crucial to highland settlement and quite irrelevant. The colonial administration drew up numerous detailed programmes to promote migration. But other policies over other matters contributed both to their non-realization and to a reduction in the mobility of the population. In

---

*   A migration official in Thái Bình encouraged me in this illusion: 'Only when you have got on the buses with the migrants and travelled to the south will you have a full under-standing of what it is about.' Interview (Thái Bình, July 1996).

this sense policy was crucial. It was irrelevant in that those families who did carry out successful migrations under the French did so with minimal reference to the state. Migration was practised without regard for policy.

2. **Under the DRV**, on the other hand, few people moved without seeking state permission and the majority of migrants took part in programmes of state-sponsored resettlement. This was despite the fact that few central government policies on migration were published. Those that existed were long on rhetoric and short on specific instruction. The way policy was put into practice was left to local authorities, and subject to negotiation according to local conditions. Practice thus influenced and defined the nature of policy.

3. **From the mid-1980s**, policy became increasingly unimportant as a determinant of migration. Peasants instead took advantage of changes in the system to make their own way and a significant movement of spontaneous migration developed. While migrant families enjoyed greater levels of choice in their relationship with the state, they did not practise migration in complete independence or isolation from policy. Some joined family or friends in the highlands who had arrived there under previous programmes. Some made use of the programme's resources. Others found that the state followed them into the forest, providing clinics and schools, demanding taxes. Policy thus acted in a relationship of interaction and support with migration practice.

Practice is thus defined in juxtaposition to policy. At times it describes the experiences of people who were putting a state policy into practice. It also describes those of people simply practising migration, with or without direct reference to the state. What is important, however, is to acknowledge that the two were inter-related. Policy in the 1960s had important effects on migration practice. In the 1990s, the independent behaviour of migrant families moving to the highlands had important effects on policy. I shall argue that it is in observing the interplay between policy and practice that we come closest to understanding the dynamics of migration to Vietnam's highlands.

HOME

A key interface between policy and practice is the concept of native place, or home. Linguistically, the concept centres on the emotionally charged Vietnamese term *quê hương*, and is symbolized by the bamboo hedge which surrounded and protected many villages in the Red River Delta. This was the focus of much discourse and discussion throughout the century. The hedge, in particular, was a powerful image invoked to give substance to elusive theories of corporate village solidarity and closed social systems.* I spent much time on field trips in the Red River Delta trying to spot one of these fabled bamboo barriers intact. Many of

---

* The term *quê hương* – or simply *quê* – carries the emotional charge of the English word 'home'. But its cultural connotations are different, focusing on ancestor worship, land and village, as well as house and family. I have translated it variously as native place, village of origin and home. For sources, see note 34.

these hedges were felled during collectivization, and as village residential areas spilled over onto agricultural land. But my failure to find one led me first to reflect that, in 1990s Vietnam, the major defensive wall was no longer around the village, but around the nation. The hedge was no longer necessary. Later on I began to wonder whether the ancient discourse of village, symbolized by the elusive hedge, was any more substantial than today's discourse of nation. Let us examine this classic case of imagined community for what it has to tell us about the practice of migration.

Colonial officials, and a majority of French and urban Vietnamese, shared and perpetuated a discourse that maintained that Vietnamese peasants were attached to their native place. One example of this way of thinking, illustrating the contribution of the idea to European orientalism, is offered by the following passage published in 1939:

> It is the very structure and basic meaning of Việt society which keeps the native at home and stifles the spirit of adventure. In general this is true of all the peoples of the Far East; the age-old influence of Chinese civilization hardly decreased the native's attachment to the village of his birth. Ancestor worship, whether or not it is considered as a subdivision of spirit worship, is very strong in the Việt heart. (…) To abandon one's birthplace without hope of return seems like a sacrilege which will harm not only the individual and his family but the entire community.[35]

This discourse, in which reference was invariably made to the Confucian practice of ancestor worship, blinded contemporary observers to the fact that many migrants and non-migrants maintained ambiguous relations with their village of origin. I share Kleinen's view that 'The colonial discourse has surely attributed reified elements to 'the Vietnamese village", but it would go too far to suggest that the Northern Vietnamese village serves as a reconstruction by the colonial state'.[36] Red River Delta villages certainly existed, as did their hedges. So did the cultural understandings and affinities surrounding these features of the society and landscape. The point is to unravel their meanings. Bryna Goodman noted, writing of the Chinese native place, the power of an ideology of home: 'The idea of the native place was imbued with different meanings at different times and by different historical actors and therefore (though undeniably an element of Chinese culture) cannot be divorced from changing political and ideological contexts or be understood merely as a cultural 'remnant".'[37] Or, as Thomas R. Gottschang and Diana Lary put it, in their study of migration to Manchuria, 'no place (…) is so poor, so barren, or so inconsequential that its inhabitants do not love it.'[38] What was that love built on? One aim of this book is to explore the nature of identification with home, among people living in – and leaving – the Red River Delta.

In many cases, villagers accepted or even actively sought a departure from home. They sought a departure though not necessarily a complete rupture. In other cases, they would have liked to leave but dared not, lacking the resources to do so. Many, of course, preferred to stay put. In a lucid analysis, which took no notice of the conventional view of *quê hương*, Nguyễn Văn Huyên noted the flexibility of these ties to home. The following is his definition of the Vietnamese village:

> It is formed not only by those who live there but also by all those who originated there and may return only once or twice in a lifetime, but have the tombs of their ancestors in the commune and their familial temple is maintained by a member of their clan. For a Vietnamese, it is always honourable to have a village of origin in a province. Otherwise one will be labelled by a rather derogatory term, in the eyes of the villagers, *người tứ xứ*, or people of the four corners of the world. With the facilities of movement, people can settle down elsewhere but will always claim to be a native of their original village; they pay their personal tax to the village, they contribute to the communal charges, even when they do not enjoy material advantages, they register their children and grandchildren in the village and try to possess at least a portion of land there, although they can give it to poor relatives. Quite a few make efforts to secure a plot and to erect a very humble hut for the installation of the altar of their ancestors.[39]

Nguyễn Văn Huyên confirmed that Việt peasants rarely left home 'without hope of return'. Return, however, was often conceived in terms of visit rather than move. He denied that village structures stifled their 'spirit of adventure'. In practice, relationships within the village often helped people leave it. And after departure relatives and acquaintances originating from the same place (known as *đồng hương*) appealed to each other in relationships of mutual aid and exploitation, based on the articulation of a shared origin. If they wished and were able to return, they returned. If not, they claimed to be too poor to go back. It was difficult, for example, for people to return to their village without presents and without boasted achievements to justify the absence. This is true of many parts of the world. What I found interesting in Vietnam was the way some people justified the fact that they had not yet returned in terms of poverty, when clearly they had no inclination to go back. The findings of Gottschang and Lary's research in China have resonance in Vietnam:

> Tradition held that the emigrant thought ceaselessly of the day when he could go home. The highest ideal was to 'return home wearing brocade' (...) Once a person had made money, he *had* to go home; the whole point of going away was to find the means to return in glory. Returning to one's home was as natural as 'the leaves of a tall tree falling close to its roots' (...). Any other outcome was a misfortune or a sign of bad character.[40]

Tradition here was clearly a Confucian value, based on respect to one's ancestors and by extension to the home community which had nourished their offspring. This was the ideal and those who wished to settle elsewhere paid respect to it, avoiding accusations of ill luck or bad behaviour. They manipulated the ideology of home in their own interest.

French officials failed to understand this. Many of the Vietnamese who informed them, moreover, were 'pure urbanites' – as described by Nguyễn Khắc Viện.[41] Whether in France or Vietnam, they used networks embracing other worlds than the village. Living far from the village, like Nguyễn Khắc Viện himself, they maintained an emotional and nostalgic interest in perpetuating the notion of an immutable *quê hương* to which all villagers were attached. Their nostalgia was not shared by communist and other advocates of independence. From before the Revolution there was a constant emphasis among activists on the need for urban people to study conditions in the countryside, and to disregard the myths surrounding village life current in the city. We may cite the example of Nghiêm Xuân Yêm, who completed his studies in Hanoi and then set up a small farm in Thái Nguyên, using it as a basis to write articles in the city press urging others to do the same.* And this was only the most public of a tendency, pronounced in the 1940s especially among members of the Indochina Communist Party, to stay in touch with the countryside.

As a result, after 1954, officials of the DRV harboured no illusions about the ties that bound people to their villages. Nghiêm Xuân Yêm became Minister of Agriculture, and many other officials had long, direct and bitter experience of village life. They may not have been able to articulate the idea of the *quê hương* as well as Nguyễn Văn Huyên, who became Minister of Education. But many shared his perception of its flexibility and were, above all, well equipped to manipulate it. The *quê hương* idea was reworked to persuade peasants to volunteer for migration. The birthplace was thus dubbed 'old home'. The new village became the 'second home' or 'new home'. A traditional saying, 'one destination, two homes', was taken up as a propaganda slogan.† Most significantly, the native place was put to work for the purposes of nationalism. In the 1960s peasants were told that the highlands were the 'home of revolution' and even that 'the whole country is your native place'.‡

Appeals to sacrifice feelings for home were not always greeted with enthusiasm, however. Among people for whom the native place was, in any case, of flexible value, arguments about it could only be of limited significance in people's decisions to stay or to leave. But the manipulation of this discourse is symptomatic of the dexterity with which policy was put into practice under the DRV. Cadres at all levels sought to base their implementation of migration policy on peasant practice. The essence of DRV administration in the 1960s was an ability to combine, in intense campaigns of persuasion, the idealistic energies of patriotism with the problem-solving energies of peasant need. Participation in highland migration

---

*   In his writings, he did not explicitly acknowledge Chinese influence. His work nevertheless echoed Mao Tse Tung's emphasis on the importance of the countryside, articulated in a 1926 article, 'The National Revolution and the Peasant Movement'. See also note 42.

†   This saying (*một chốn đôi quê*) referred to the practice of leaving home to make a living elsewhere, and returning on a sporadic basis, in the manner described by Nguyễn Văn Huyên above. For a fuller discussion of this type of migration, see Chapter 3. For discussion of how it was reworked under the DRV, see Chapter 6.

‡   Home of revolution: *quê hương cách mạng*. The whole country is your home: *đâu cũng là quê hương* (literally, everywhere is home).

was presented to people as a way out of the problems of overpopulation in the delta, whereby they could, at the same time, make a contribution to socialist development and the defence of the nation. Propaganda about the creation of new *quê hương* was, in this context, the icing on the cake.

By grafting the parochial to the national, and backing their rhetoric with a neo-Stalinist economic system and a tightly managed regime of household registration, the Party persuaded millions of people to leave their home villages in the 1960s and 1970s. Some were happy to seek a solution to economic problems, while others were wary and reluctant. But the same policy gave rise in the 1980s to a practice of spontaneous migration with its own momentum. By this time, there was no longer any need to persuade people to leave. Ideologies of patriotism and socialism became less powerful after the war. The planned economy and controls on residence were breaking down. Opportunities offered by the emerging market economy gave people both the freedom and desire to 'vote with their feet'. If they decided to head for the hills, it was less in the spirit of patriotic socialism than to seek prosperity in the fertile *terres rouges* of the central highlands.

This change was made clear in conversations with Mơ, a waitress at my hotel in Ban Mê Thuột city.[43] Her native place was a village in the Red River Delta. In her home province of Thái Bình, she told me, 'everyone wants to leave. Those who have the right conditions, leave. Those who don't, stay'. She made her first departure at the age of 21, to build roads in the upland province of Sơn La. Her parents, after hearing her talk of labour on the roads during a New Year visit home, refused to allow her to return to Sơn La. They hid her clothes to stop her leaving. A compromise was eventually reached, whereby she would join relatives near Ban Mê Thuột, and twelve months later, she came to live there. She rarely saw these people, who have a coffee farm out of town. She built her future prosperity on education, struggling to acquire language and other skills which would equip her for a job in Ho Chi Minh City. Mơ's story illustrates clearly the interplay of policy and practice in decisions of spontaneous migration in the 1990s. In Sơn La she chose a tough state job in the highlands, to fulfil her wish to get out. In Ban Mê Thuột, she used members of her family, who had themselves chosen to clear land on a state programme years before. The structures and networks she used were, in part, related to the state. But the decision to leave was her own.

This decision, put into practice with great determination, casts light on her relationship with her family and home. When I visited Ban Mê Thuột, her father had just left. He came, as she put it, to 'stabilize the marriage issue'. After speaking to her one evening, I wrote in my diary:

> She said she wants to sort out a decent job so that when she does get married she will not have a hard life. She's very independent. She said, 'if you have a hard life after marriage, it's better not to marry'. Marrying someone outside Thái Bình is better – she knows the hard life in Thái Bình.

Most of her friends back home have already got married. 'A girl has a season', her parents told her, persuading her to follow suit. But her parents can only advise, she said, 'they can't choose'. If Mơ gets her way, she will choose someone far from her native place. For her, home was no immutable concept. It stood for a tough life she wanted to escape. But, even from Ban Mê Thuột, she still goes home for New Year celebrations with her family. She will doubtless continue to do so for years to come.

OVERVIEW

In the chapters of this book, experiences of people like Mơ are presented in an exploration of the relationship of policy and practice in migration. The story starts with Thức's departure from his village in the Red River Delta in 1906. It ends in 1998, with a conference held by the Ministry of Agriculture in Hanoi to decide the future of Vietnam's migration policy. Over the intervening century, millions of people positioned themselves with regard to state policy, dodging, negotiating, obeying and using it to leave their native place and settle in the hills. At the same time, the state made use of these people to fulfil policy imperatives of its own.

This is a story about people from the Red River Delta. For that reason, it focuses on only two of the three major states that have existed in twentieth-century Vietnam: the French colonial administration and the communist government of the DRV/SRV. The majority of migrants who moved under the third state, the RVN, during the time of the country's partition (1954–75), were of southern or central origin and lie outside our subject. But we will meet some of them on the way, especially in the central highlands, where Việt people who moved up before 1975 form a substantial proportion of the population.[44]

Vietnam's political evolution also determined the geographical scope of this study. The organizational incapacity of the colonial administration ensured that most migration before 1945 was over relatively short distances. As a result, the early chapters on the French period deal with parts of the northern highlands quite near to the Red River Delta. With the war of resistance and establishment of an independent state in North Vietnam, our focus will broaden out to more distant parts of the northern highlands. And after the country's reunification, both the policy of migration and its practice were extended to the central highlands. Later chapters will deal with settlers there. Many of them, like Mơ, had indeed spent time in the northern highlands before moving to the central region.

The first chapter focuses, however, not on the delta of the Red River but on an obscure valley in the province of Thái Nguyên. The Công River valley lies behind the Tam Đảo mountain, which I visited on my first trip to the highlands in 1992. It is of no special significance in Vietnam's history but, like many other valleys in the hills, it forms a part of the upland frontier. In that capacity it figures as the subject for Chapter 1. 'The Road to Bờ Rạ: Portrait of a Highland Frontier' offers a historical overview of the Việt settlement of this part of the northern highlands and introduces some of the themes and personalities that emerge later on. After this introductory portrait, the remaining chapters are divided into four parts, each dealing with a specific period of time.

Part One, on the period 1906–45, is entitled *Attached to the Village? Policy and Practice of Migration, 1906–45*. It consists of three chapters. Chapter 2, 'Colonial Policy', argues that under the French, much migration policy was drawn up, but little was realized. Chapter 3, 'Colonial Practice', indicates that the little migration that did take place during the colonial period was generally the result of peasant initiative, moving along networks bearing little or no relation to the state. And Chapter 4, 'Peasants Attached to the Village' argues that if migration policy failed and little spontaneous migration took place, it was not as a result of a love of home and village by Việt peasants and their consequent refusal to leave it. Other policies of the colonial state – policies of taxation and identity control – inhibited the practice of migration, attaching the peasants to their native place.

Part Two, *Detached from their Villages? War and Migration, 1945–54*, consists of a single chapter, 'Green Forest, Red Hills'. Chapter 5 is a sort of 'hyphen' study, on which the argument of the book turns. It bridges the period of violent transition between the two states analysed in this study, the crumbling colonial regime and the DRV in its process of formation. From the point of view of the hills, the disruption of this decade was, moreover, of peculiar significance. War caused the movement of large numbers of Việt people from the Red River Delta into the remotest parts of the northern highlands. Forests provided cover for the revolution all the way to the valley of Điện Biên Phủ, near the border with Laos. These movements, and the acclimatization of both state and people to the hills which accompanied it, had repercussions which extended long after peace was restored. As a result, Việt people were no longer shy of moving beyond the delta. During this short war, a process was launched by which green forests would give way to red hills.

Part Three is entitled *Go and Build a New Village! Practice and Policy of Migration, 1954–89*. The nature of the Vietnamese state during this period caused me to inverse my analysis of policy and practice. The practice of migration, of which there was a very great deal, is dealt with first, in three chapters. Careful analysis of practice, in fact, offers more valuable information than documentation on policy. It allows us a close view of the realities of migration to the highlands, highlighting the flexibility of policy implementation. This flexibility meant that formal policy documents were of limited historical value. Much was left to individual cadres' initiative. Policy, as a result, is dealt with next, in a single chapter.

The nature of migration practice during this period was determined by the DRV's tools of administrative control, foremost among which was the technique of mobilization. Chapter 6, 'Deciding', shows how this technique of persuasion was applied to people living in the Red River Delta and examines the way in which people reached the decision to move. Chapter 7, 'Moving', sketches itineraries and situates the migration as an event in the lives and memories both of those who moved and those living in the places they moved to. Chapter 8, 'Settling' shifts the focus from event to process, examining the imperatives and experiences of settling in the hills, from the point of view both of the state and the migrants.

Reference is made, in particular, to the state's policy of identity control. Far from fixing people in their old village, as it had in the colonial period, identification policy worked to settle them in the new. Chapter 9, 'Policy', draws generalized conclusions about the nature of migration policy from the preceding discussion of practice and the documentation available. It concludes that migration policy aimed to overcome two problems – overpopulation in the delta and national defence in the highlands – with a single solution.

Part Four, *Beyond Village Society? The Practice of Free Migration, 1986–98*, consists of a single chapter. Chapter 10, 'Free Migrants to the Hills', examines the emergence, as a result of economic reforms, of a movement of free migration. Free migrants acted outside of immediate state control, but moved along networks and used resources made available by state policy. The scale and independence of this movement created considerable dilemmas for the state, and gave rise to unprecedented open debate on migration policy in the late 1990s. An international conference on the issue, held in Hanoi in May 1998, was informed of recommendations for radical change.

In February 2001, demonstrations were held by large numbers of ethnic minority inhabitants of the central highlands. Their demands, voiced peacefully on the streets of Ban Mê Thuột, Pleiku and other centres, touched directly on the issues raised here, as the highlanders lost their land to Việt settlers and their autonomy to the Vietnamese state. This book was researched and written before those events and I have not felt it necessary to modify its argument in the light of them. A forthcoming book will examine the background and current nature of the relationship of contact the demonstrations revealed. *Red Hills*, meanwhile, is an account of the past, and as such its *Conclusion* focuses instead on the implications of the study not only for the past hundred years but for the centuries before that. The Việt people's geo-political expansion to the south is not only a great frontier story, but also one of Vietnam's great historiographical frontiers. I suggest that this history can only be adequately approached via an analysis that examines not only the influence of the state on people's behaviour but also that of the people on the state.

NOTES

1 NAV1/RND 3175, Résident in Nam Định to RST, 20 March 1908.

2 Andrew Hardy, 'La politique économique française en Indochine de 1944 à 1948', Maîtrise d'histoire, Université de Paris 7, 1991.

3 For discussion of this debate, see Andrew Hardy, 'Les opinions de Paul Bernard (1892–1960) sur l'économie de l'Indochine coloniale et leur actualité', *Revue française d'histoire d'outre-mer*, vol. 82, no. 308, 1995, pp. 305–306. See below, Chapter 2.

4 CAOM/AgFOM 2666, 'Rapport Général sur le Premier Plan de Modernisation et d'Equipement de l'Indochine', Indochina Sub-Commission, General Commission for the Plan, Paris, 1948.

5 Andrew Hardy, 'La politique économique française', p. 214.

6 I am referring here to a discussion of the work of E. E. Evans-Pritchard's *The Nuer* and Emmanuel Le Roy Ladurie's *Montaillou* by Renato Rosaldo, 'From the Door of His Tent:

The Fieldworker and the Inquisitor'. In James Clifford (ed.), *Writing Culture*, Berkeley: University of California Press, 1986, pp. 77–97.

7   Paul Mus, *Sociologie d'une guerre*, Paris: Seuil, 1952, pp. 16–17.

8   Georges Condominas, 'Aspects of a Minority Problem in Indochina', *Pacific Affairs*, vol. XXIV, no. 1, 1951, pp. 77–82.

9   Grant Evans, 'Internal Colonialism in the Central Highlands of Vietnam', *Sojourn*, vol. 7, no. 2, 1992, pp. 274–304.

10 On DRV policy, see I. A. Mal'khanova, 'The Development of New Agricultural Lands in North Vietnam in 1961–65', *Soviet Geography*, vol. XI, no. 10, 1970, pp. 828–832. On RVN policy, see Gerald C. Hickey, *Some Recommendations Affecting the Role of Vietnamese Highlanders in Economic Development*, Santa Monica, California: Rand Corporation, 1974, pp. 5–9; Gerald C. Hickey, *Free in the Forest: Ethnohistory of the Vietnamese Central Highlands, 1954–1976*, New Haven and London: Yale University Press, 1982, pp. 17–20. For an overview of the central highlands' twentieth-century history, see Oscar Salemink, *The Ethnography of Vietnam's Central Highlanders: A Historical Contextualization, 1850–1990*, Richmond: Curzon Press, forthcoming.

11 Ngô Văn Lý and Nguyễn Văn Điêu, *Tây Nguyên Tiềm Năng và Triển Vọng*, Ho Chi Minh City: NXB Thành Phố Hồ Chí Minh, 1992.

12 Nguyễn Thế Huệ, 'Về di dân nông nghiệp vùng châu thổ Sông Hồng giai đoạn 1981–1990', *NCLS*, vol. 272, no. 1, 1994, p. 37.

13 Jacqueline Desbarats, 'Population Redistribution in the Socialist Republic of Vietnam', *Population and Development Review*, vol. 13, no. 1, 1987, pp. 43–76. For a contextualized overview of post-1975 migration, see Andrew Hardy, 'State Visions, Migrant Decisions: Population Movements since the End of the Vietnam War'. In Hy Van Luong (ed.), *Postwar Vietnam: Dynamics of a Transforming Society*, Rowman and Littlefield, forthcoming.

14 Rodolphe De Koninck, 'The Peasantry as the Territorial Spearhead of the State in Southeast Asia: The Case of Vietnam', *Sojourn*, vol. 11, no. 2, 1996, pp. 231–258; Dang Nguyen Anh, Sidney Goldstein and James McNally, 'Internal Migration and Development in Vietnam', *International Migration Review*, vol. 31, no. 2, 1997, pp. 312–337; Dang Nguyen Anh, 'Market Reforms and Internal Labour Migration in Vietnam', *Asian and Pacific Migration Journal*, vol. 8, no. 3, 1999, pp. 381–409; UNDP, *The Dynamics of Internal Migration in Viet Nam*, Hanoi: UNDP Discussion Paper, 1998.

15 The most comprehensive overview is W. Courtland Robinson, *Terms of Refuge: The Indochinese Exodus and the International Response*, London and New York: Zed Books, 1998.

16 Linda Hitchcox, 'Relocation in Vietnam and Outmigration: The Ideological and Economic Context'. In Judith M. Brown and Rosemary Foot (eds), *Migration: The Asian Experience*, Oxford: St Martin's Press, 1994, p. 204.

17 Ngô Tuấn, 'Bức xúc vấn đề di dân tự do', *Việt Nam Đầu Tư Nước Ngoài*, 26 February 1996, p. 74; Huynh Minh Vu, 'Họ bỏ quê ra đi', *Tuổi Trẻ Chủ Nhật*, 12 May 1996, p. 6; Khánh Bình, 'Di dân nội địa: Một vấn đề xã hội bức xúc', *Sài Gòn Giải Phóng*, 4 March 1998, p. 2. Note that where the original document uses three dots in a text or title, they are reproduced in my citation. I indicate text omitted from a citation with the symbol (…).

18 Dean Forbes, 'Urbanisation, Migration, and Vietnam's Spatial Structure', *Sojourn*, vol. 11, no. 1, 1996, pp. 38, 45. See also Li Tana, *Peasants on the Move, Rural–Urban Migration in the Hanoi Region*, Singapore: Institute of Southeast Asian Studies, 1996.

19 This was true of the following. Hickey, *Sons of the Mountains. Ethnohistory of the Vietnamese Central Highlands to 1954*, New Haven and London: Yale University Press, 1982. Evans, 'Internal Colonialism'. Oscar Salemink, 'The King of Fire and Vietnamese Ethnic Policy in the Central Highlands'. In Don McCaskil and Ken Kampe (eds), *Development or Domestication? Indigenous Peoples of Southeast Asia*, Chiang Mai: Silkworm Books, 1997, pp. 488–535.

20 This was true of the following. Dean Forbes and Nigel Thrift, 'Territorial Organization, Regional Development and the City in Vietnam'. In Dean Forbes and Nigel Thrift (eds), *The Socialist Third World: Urban Development and Territorial Planning*, Oxford: Blackwell, 1987, pp. 98–128. Gavin W. Jones, 'Population Trends and Policies in Vietnam', *Population and Development Review*, vol. 8, no. 4, 1982, pp. 783–810. Gavin W. Jones and H. V. Richter, *Population Resettlement Programs in Southeast Asia*, Canberra: ANU Press, 1982. Dang Nguyen Anh, Sidney Goldstein and James McNally, 'Internal Migration'. Dang Nguyen Anh, 'Market Reforms'.

21 A fuller account of 'both hands' – the contact between the Việt and the highlanders of central Vietnam – is, however, told in a forthcoming book by Andrew Hardy, Mathieu Guérin, Nguyễn Văn Chính and Stan B. H. Tan.

22 CAOM//INF 2282, 'Les causes de la répartition inégale des hommes en Indochine', article in *La Vie* by Charles Robequain, undated, c. 1941.

23 James Clifford, *Routes: Travel and Translation in the Late Twentieth Century*, Cambridge, Massachusetts: Harvard University Press, 1997, p. 57.

24 Barnett offered a typology of cadres, distinguishing state cadres (in the central government or Party bureaucracy) from local cadres (below this level). A. Doak Barnett, *Cadres, Bureaucracy and Political Power in Communist China*, Studies of the East Asian Institute, New York: Columbia University Press, 1967, pp. 39–41.

25 Cited by Mark Elvin, 'Braudel and China'. In John A. Marino (ed.), *History and the Social Sciences: Braudel's Mediterranean Fifty Years After*, Kirksville, Missouri: Thomas Jefferson University Press, forthcoming.

26 Simon Schama, *Landscape and Memory*, London: Fontana, 1995.

27 Bob Claessens and Jeanne Rousseau, *Our Bruegel*, Antwerp: Mercatorfonds, 1975, p. 196.

28 Keith H. Halfacree and Paul J. Boyle, 'The Challenge Facing Migration Research: the case for a biographical approach', *Progress in Human Geography*, vol. 17, no. 3, 1993, p. 344. This was a citation of C. Pooley and I. Whyte, 'Introduction: Approaches to the Study of Migration and Social Change'. In C. Pooley and I. Whyte (eds) *Migrants, Emigrants and Immigrants*, London: Routledge, 1991, pp. 4–5.

29 This phrase is Ronald Skeldon's, in his criticism of Halfacree and Boyle's call for a 'new paradigm' in migration research. Skeldon argued that in studies of migration in developing countries biographical techniques have a long and respectable tradition. Ronald Skeldon, 'The Challenge Facing Migration Research: a Case for Greater Awareness', *Progress in Human Geography*, vol. 19, no. 1, 1995, p. 92.

30 Elvin, 'Braudel and China'. Citations are from Philippe Carrard, *Poetics of the New History: French National Historical Discourse from Braudel to Chartier*, Baltimore and London: Johns Hopkins University Press, 1992, p. 218.

31 Carrard, *Poetics*, p. 220.

32 The ecological question was already treated in Le Trong Cuc and A. Terry Rambo (eds), 'Too Many People, Too Little Land: the human ecology of a wet rice-growing village in the Red River Delta of Vietnam', Honolulu: East–West Center, 1993.

33 Desbarats, 'Population Redistribution'.

34 Adam Fforde and Stefan de Vylder, *From Plan to Market, The Economic Transition in Vietnam*, Boulder, Colorado: Westview Press, 1996, pp. 49–50; John Kleinen, 'The Village as Pretext: Ethnographic Praxis and the Colonial State in Vietnam'. In Jan Breman, Peter Kloos and Ashwani Saith (eds), *The Village in Asia Revisited*, Delhi: Oxford University Press, 1997, pp. 384–385.

35 Charles Robequain, *The Economic Development of French Indochina*, London: Oxford University Press, 1944, p. 62. See Chapter 2 for more detailed analysis of this discourse.

36 Kleinen, 'The Village as Pretext', p. 384. This remark was made in qualification of the argument in Jan Breman, *The Shattered Image: Construction and Deconstruction of the Village in Colonial Asia*, Dordrecht, Holland: Foris Publications, 1988.

37 Bryna Goodman, *Native Place, City, and Nation. Regional Networks and Identities in*

Shanghai, 1853–1937, Berkeley, Los Angeles and London: University of California Press, 1995, p. 307.

38 Thomas R. Gottschang and Diana Lary, *Swallows and Settlers: The Great Migration from North China to Manchuria*, Ann Arbor: Center for Chinese Studies, University of Michigan, 2000, p. 95.

39 Nguyen Van Huyen, *La civilisation annamite*, Hanoi: Direction de l'Instruction Publique en Indochine, 1944, p. 71, translated into English as *The Ancient Civilisation of Vietnam*, Hanoi: The Gioi Publishers, 1995, pp. 70–71.

40 Gottschang and Lary, *Swallows and Settlers*, pp. 97–98.

41 Nguyen Khac Vien, 'Confucianism et Marxisme au Vietnam', 1962. In Nguyen Khac Vien, *Expériences vietnamiennes*, Paris: Editions Sociales, 1970, p. 225.

42 Nghiêm Xuân Yêm, 'Thanh niên trí thức với nghề nông ở xứ nhà', *Thanh Nghị*, no. 35, 16.4.43, pp. 194–198. Mao Tse Tung, '*Kuo-min ko-ming yü nung-min yun-tung*'. In Takeuchi Minoru (ed.), *Mao Tse Tung chi*, Tokyo: Hokubosha, 1970–1972, vol. 1, pp. 175–179. Quoted in John K. Fairbank and Albert Feuerwerker (eds), *The Cambridge History of China, Volume 13, Republican China 1912–1949, Part 2*, Cambridge: Cambridge University Press, 1986, p. 815.

43 Interviews (Dak Lak, May and November 1996).

44 Việt migration to the central highlands before 1975, and the role of the RVN state, is described in a forthcoming book. See note 21.

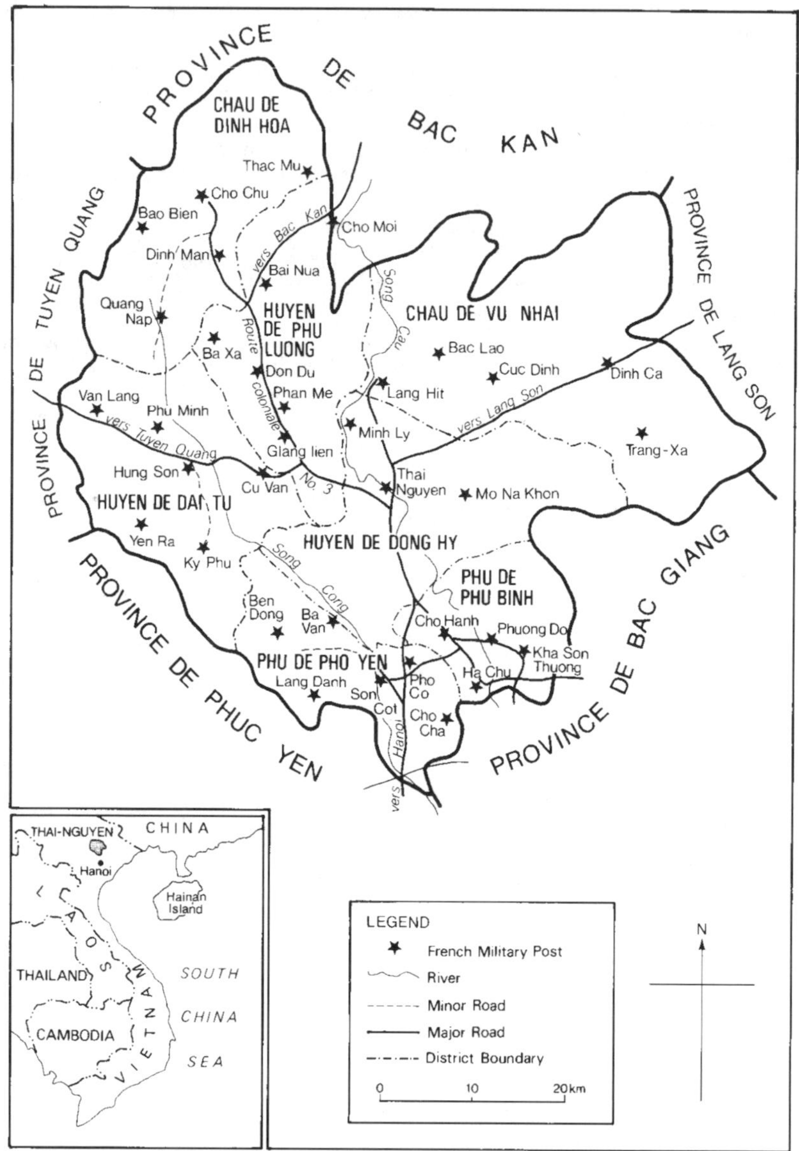

Map 9: The province of Thái Nguyên, 1934
A province on the edge of the Red River Delta about 100 km north of Hanoi, Thái Nguyên consisted of two lowland districts (Phổ Yên and Phú Bình), two midland districts (Đồng Hỷ and Đại Từ) and three highland districts (Định Hóa, Phú Lương and Vũ Nhai). It became well known in the 1930s for its resettlement initiatives. By the 1970s, it was no longer a destination for migrants, but a point of departure.
Source: Alfred Echinard, *Histoire politique et militaire de la province de Thai Nguyen, ses forces de police*, Hanoi: Imprimerie Trung Bac Tan Van, 1934. Redrawn by Chong Mui Gek.

The Road to Bờ Rạ
Portrait of a Highland Frontier

Figure 3: On the road to Bờ Rạ
Downstream from the Núi Cốc lake, in 1996 the Công River remained passable only by sampan or a rickety bamboo bridge. It was in this part of the northern highlands, the province of Thái Nguyên, that I set out to look for the village of Bờ Rạ.
Photograph by Andrew Hardy, October 1996.

'To see fieldwork as travel practice highlights embodied activities pursued in historically and politically defined places.' (James Clifford, *Routes, Travel and Translation in the Late Twentieth Century*, Cambridge, Massachusetts: Harvard University Press, 1997, p. 8)

'Now I found it and all such resting places for the imagination, are like shadows, which a man moving onwards cannot catch.' (Charles Darwin, *Journal of Researches into the Natural History and Geology of the countries visited during the voyage of H.M.S. Beagle etc.*, New York: 1896, p. 417)

'Alas! Wigan Pier has been demolished, and even the spot where it used to stand is no longer certain.' (George Orwell, *The Road to Wigan Pier*, London: Secker & Warburg, 1965 [1937], p. 75)

*T*his is an account of travel in the hill country of northern Vietnam. I made the trip to look for a village called Bờ Rạ. Before setting out I was told that this village was named after a French planter. I felt sure that the Frenchman had recruited labourers from the Red River Delta to work the plantation, and so I hoped to carry out interviews with former workers and their children. I anticipated that a few days' fieldwork in Bờ Rạ would increase my understanding of the processes of migration in colonial Vietnam, at the same time as satisfying my curiosity as to why a Vietnamese village 50 years after the revolution should bear the name of a Frenchman.

The valley in question was that of the Công River, which flows through the midland province of Thái Nguyên, about 100 km north of Hanoi (see Maps 9–10 and Plates 1–2). In the course of the twentieth century, the valley's geography underwent a number of administrative and topographical changes. These affected the lives and landmarks of many of its inhabitants. They also re-routed my research. As a result, a simple trip to a single village became a journey and took me upstream and downstream through four districts of the province, as I searched through the changes, first for the place, then the people and finally the origins of the name of Bờ Rạ.

I managed to interview some former workers on French plantations, as I had hoped. And on the way I met a number of other people, both 'locals' and more recently arrived migrants. As I got closer to Bờ Rạ, I realized that the information they gave me was forming itself into another narrative, a multi-layered story of the settlement of this place. Back in Hanoi, and in Australia where I wrote this account, I discovered accounts of other travellers and settlers there. Nowadays, few people move to the Công River valley. But in the first half of the twentieth century, it was a choice destination. People came here from the plains and from higher up in the hills, for all sorts of reasons impelled by all sorts of stimuli.

This chapter, then, is not only the tale of my travel; it is also my attempt to tell the story of other travellers and settlers. I set these experiences in two contexts. The geographical context receives attention for the light it sheds on the locality –

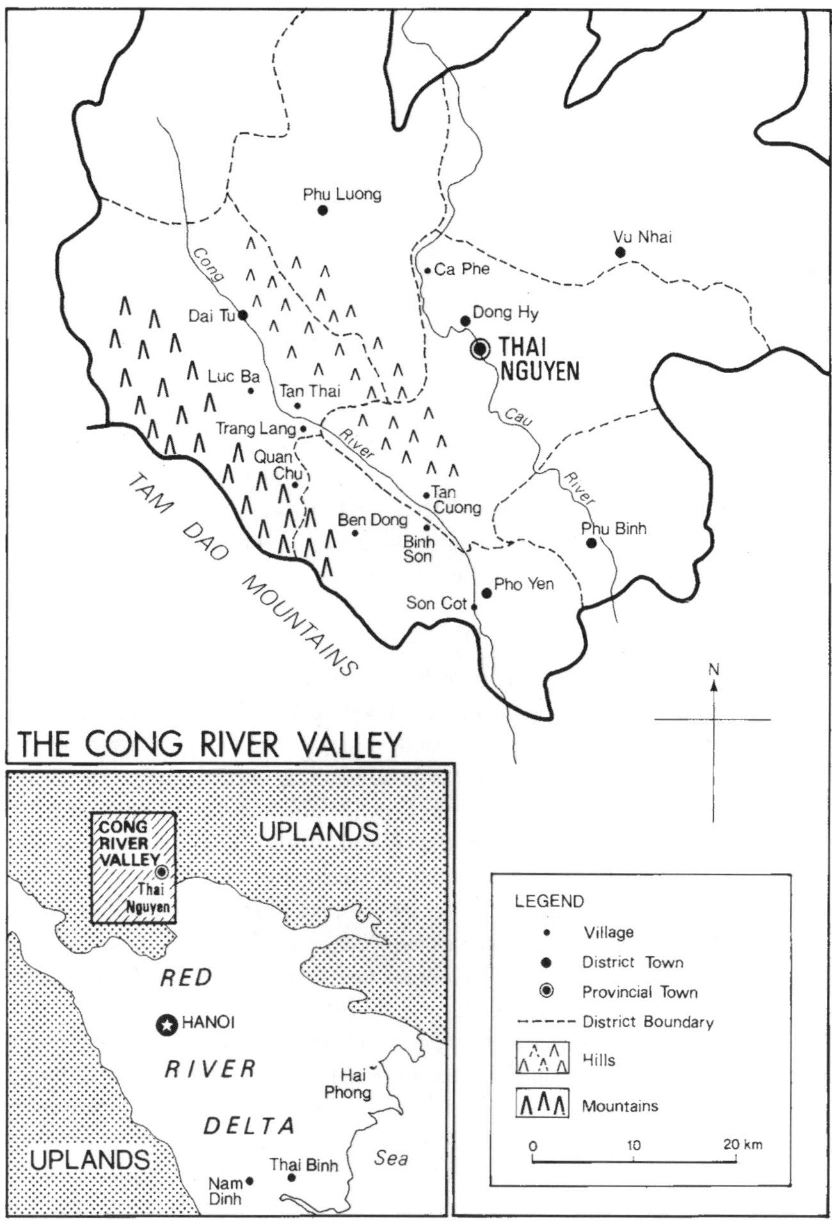

Map 10: The Công River valley
The Công River runs down the southwestern edge of the province of Thái Nguyên, in the shadow of the Tam Đảo mountain range. Scattered with small and unsuccessful French-owned plantations, it was earmarked in the 1930s for a 'massive transplantation' of migrants from the Red River Delta.
Map by Chong Mui Gek.

people's personal histories were intimately wrapped up in the landscape of the valley of the Công River, its slopes and forest, fields and roads. The administrative context – the influence of government on settlement – receives attention for the opposite reason. In terms of process, rather than experience, the Công River valley was similar to many other places in northern Vietnam. I try to convey a sense of the wider processes of settlement by reference to ways in which government attempted to promote and control migration. The history of the locality thus sheds light on what was happening in other parts of the country.

The story also offered me an opportunity for reflection on my own manner of historical research and writing. The journey was made in response to a conversation in Hanoi. My account of it was constructed from the notes and recordings I made on the way to Bờ Rạ, and documents written in Vietnamese, French and English collected in archives and libraries after I got back. These materials, and the manner of their collection, form an integral part of the narrative.

'The Road to Bờ Rạ' leads beyond the search for a name. It portrays a part of the upland frontier, and informs on the process of that portrayal. Its local history perspective aims to provoke reflection about what, on the ground, constituted a frontier in twentieth-century Vietnam.

HYPOTHESIS

The story starts with a hypothesis. A hypothesis which was first formed while I was reading colonial era documents in the National Archives of Vietnam. I came across a file entitled 'Dispatch of 3,000 coolies to Thái Nguyên for the development of certain pieces of land'. Inside was a letter addressed to the French Résident of the province and signed by the managing director of a plantation company, the SAFCAT (Société anonyme française de Colonisation Annam-Tonkin). The letter, written in 1932, is the company's reply to a request to provide land for former mineworkers.[1] Reading it, I noted that the workers, from the coal mines in Hồng Gai, faced redundancy at the onset of the Depression. The French, nervous after recent uprisings, were, I imagined, protecting themselves from further unrest; officials were trying to find something for the workers to do. The letter indicated that the SAFCAT agreed to receive one hundred workers and their families, on condition of what its director termed 'the verification of their origin and above all of the morality of their elements'. I could not discover whether the workers ever actually moved to the plantation. Nor did I pay much attention to the director's name – at this time I had never heard of André de Monpezat.

It was not long after this that I attended the forty-nine-day memorial of the death of Nguyễn Từ Chi, a renowned anthropologist. This was an occasion for his friends and colleagues in Hanoi to eat together and discuss the preservation of his papers. Over lunch, someone mentioned the same French name. He told me that Monpezat had been one of the biggest and best known planters in French Indochina, and added, 'during the war of resistance [1946–54] I spent some time at a village where Monpezat had owned land. It's in Thái Nguyên, a lovely shady spot beside the Công River.' The village, he said, was named after the planter. 'It's called Bờ Rạ'.[*]

His remarks roused my curiosity. Did this village become home to the miners I had recently read about? Why was it named after the Frenchman? I decided to go to Thái Nguyên and find out. Perhaps I could meet some former workers on the plantation. The village was apparently in Đồng Hỷ district. So, after a brief visit to the provincial authorities, together with Đào Thế Đức, my colleague from Hanoi, I arrived at the office of the People's Committee in Đồng Hỷ. I expected, after presenting my letter of introduction, to get to Bờ Rạ the same afternoon and start interviewing. Little did I imagine that it would take me two days merely to find the place, and even longer to locate its people.

SEARCH

No one at the office in Đồng Hỷ had heard of Bờ Rạ. But we were soon introduced to the official responsible for the Party's history in the locality. Mr Yêm sat us down in an office where there was a large map on the wall. Using a pointer, he described to us the settlement history of the district, outlining commune boundaries and underlining the names of villages within each commune. He pressed buttons, and government buildings, schools and clinics lit up in electric red and green. But careful scrutiny of the map revealed no village with the name Bờ Rạ. Yêm apologized. He wasn't brought up in the area, he said, he was from Thái Bình, in the Red River Delta. After training as a teacher in Hanoi, he had volunteered to live in the highlands. He was assigned to the university in Thái Nguyên, and a few years ago he transferred to the Party History Committee here. He couldn't tell us anything about this Bờ Rạ. Perhaps Bờ Rạ was in the next district, Phú Lương.

While Yêm was talking, a name on the map caught my colleague's eye. He pointed out a nearby commune where there was a place marked 'Xóm Cà Phê': coffee village. This may have been a French plantation, we thought. If we could not find Bờ Rạ, I could at least satisfy my curiosity about the plantation workers. The official agreed to take us there. The next morning we left our motorbikes at the People's Committee and set off in the district jeep. The dirt roads wound through a landscape of low tea-covered hills and wet-rice fields – I noticed the dark green colour of the tea trees contrasting with the yellow of ripening paddy (see Plate 3). Soon we stopped outside a house. We were introduced to Mr Hỷ, a man who had lived in the village since 1935. He confirmed that it had indeed been a French coffee plantation at that time.

Hỷ told us about the owner. Or rather owners, as there had been several.[†] The first was a Frenchman, known locally as *Anh Phét*.[‡] In 1937–8, *Anh Phét* sold the

---

[*] For this information, I am grateful to Đào Hùng, of the review *Tạp Chí Xưa & Nay*. The names of other informants, out of respect for their anonymity, have been changed.

[†] Six in all, over the plantation's 30-year history to 1944. V. H., 'Điều tra nhỏ: Một đồn điền lớn ở Thái Nguyên', *Thanh Nghị*, no. 83, 16 September 1944, p. 850.

[‡] This is a Vietnamese rendering. I could not find the original French name.

plantation to another Frenchman, one M. Jaillon, nicknamed *Chủ Què* – the 'Crippled Owner'. Then, in 1941–42, the land was bought by a trader from Haiphong, Nguyễn Thị Năm.* Hỷ remembered these dates and names without hesitation. Towards the end of the interview, I asked about Monpezat. It was only then that he remembered that Monpezat was the owner before *Anh Phét*. As with *Anh Phét*, he used a Vietnamese transliteration of the name, *Bông Bờ Rạ*. The way he said it, *Bông* sounds much as it would in English, while *Bờ* resembles the second syllable in the English word 'rubber'. He pronounced *Rạ* with the 'z' sound used by northern Vietnamese for the letter 'r', so that it sounded a bit like the English 'zap', without the 'p'. To a northern Vietnamese ear, *Bông Bờ Rạ* sounds like a plausible transliteration of Monpezat, which in French is pronounced with a hard 'p' and a silent 't'. *Bông Bờ Rạ* was, he told us, a friend of *Anh Phét* and gave the plantation to him. He could not say when this happened, nor what the nature of the 'gift' was.† But he was quite sure that there was no nearby village named after the Frenchman. *Bông Bờ Rạ* had land stretching all the way into the districts of Phú Lương to the north and Đại Từ to the west, he added (see Plate 4). We should look there.

Hỷ himself arrived after the gift had been made. He had family here, relatives from his home village in the delta.‡ His people were very poor, he said, so poor that his father used to go off to Bắc Giang for months of seasonal work and when presented with the opportunity of plantation work, he jumped at it. In the 1930s, middle region provinces like Bắc Giang were places 'where the more scattered population cannot alone carry out all the operations of transplanting, weeding and tenth month harvesting'.[2] Temporary migrants came up from villages in the Red River Delta to do these jobs. As Gourou explained,

> When the time came, those who had nothing urgent to keep them in the village, neither the need to watch their own harvest, nor any communal administrative responsibilities, and those who were too poor not to take the opportunity to earn a few cents, leave in groups of five or six, comprising generally more men than women. All they take with them is a coat made of leaves, a sickle, a *gánh* (shoulder carrying pole) and the suspension strings to tie on the bales. They leave with joy, as harvest time will ensure higher salaries than usual, and especially abundant food.[3]

---

*   In the 1990s Nguyễn Thị Năm remained a household name. She aided the 1945 revolution and her sons rose in the Việt Minh army. But during land reform, they were demoted. Their mother did not survive. One local remarked: 'there were possibly mistakes made at the time'. See Bui Tin, *Following Ho Chi Minh*, London: Hurst, 1995, p. 28.

†   Monpezat's company SAFCAT owned this land from 1924 to 1935. NAV1/RST 67475, 'Mouvement de la colonisation en 1935 (concessions européennes égales ou supérieures à 2000 ha)', Thái Nguyên, 1935.

‡   Hỷ was from Nông Quang commune (Gia Lộc district, Hai Dương). He was 67 at the time of my interviews for this chapter, all of which were conducted in Thái Nguyên province in October 1996.

Hỷ made no mention of any joy felt by his father at this prospect, saying only that in 1935 the whole family moved to neighbouring Thái Nguyên. Hỷ was 5 years old at the time, and remembered that there were about twenty people living on this part of the plantation. They grew rice and a few hectares of coffee.

Coffee is no longer grown at Cà Phê village. I asked why people now grow tea. Apparently a decision was taken after the revolution to stop growing coffee. Hỷ's neighbour explained that 'the coffee quality here was lower than in the south'. Other sources suggest, however, that by 1945 there was almost no coffee being harvested here at all. A journalist from Hanoi who visited this plantation at that time observed that

> the areas of coffee and hills of tea (…) were in fact a forest of grass. Looking carefully at it, you could see that the coffee plants were already very big, higher than your head, submerged under waves of dense grass; as for the tea trees, they had disappeared under dust and weeds.

A coffee processing factory, which used to keep hundreds of people busy, now provided work for ten. The journalist blamed the Pacific War: 'The price of these crops collapsed during wartime, as tea could not be exported; coffee consumption, there being no sugar, was also down'.[4]

The neighbour went on to say that after the revolution the village switched to growing sugar. A processing factory was built in 1961. People arrived in large numbers from the lowlands: some were demobilized soldiers; some came to build the factory; others came to set up agricultural cooperatives, which became from the early 1960s an important institution of Vietnamese farm production and a major vehicle for the migration of Việt people into the hills. Hỷ's neighbour, himself one of the factory group, moved in with more than a hundred families and young people, joining the thirty-six Việt and highlander families already there. The newcomers cleared large tracts of land for sugar, which along with rice became the area's main product.

During the 1960s, Cà Phê village was a place of opportunity. Another of Hỷ's neighbours, a woman of about 60 called Hảo, told us how her husband had worked for the state cereals office in Phổ Yên, a lowland district of Thái Nguyên. He travelled widely for his work and noticed that the land was good here, it was easy to make a living. To my ear, their story was similar to Hỷ's, thirty years earlier. 'Making a living in the lowlands was difficult', Hảo explained. The young couple found jobs, made the necessary arrangements and 'just upped and offed'. This was wartime, in 1966.

After reunification – Hỷ's neighbour said 'only a few years ago' – sugar was abandoned in favour of tea. He added proudly that tea now produced at Cà Phê village was just as good as Tân Cương tea, which is famous as Thái Nguyên's most delicious. He was adamant: 'It's very high quality. Wholesale purchasers come here, right to people's houses, to buy the tea'.

Tea is nowadays closely associated with the province of Thái Nguyên. In Hanoi, when you shop for it at the market or on Hàng Điếu street, merchants say that Thái Nguyên means quality. Tea was first grown there by French planters, although sources suggest that their plantations' potential was greater than their production. The Résident of Thái Nguyên found that 'results are mediocre on all the plantations and that tenant farming is the most common form of exploitation'.[5] In the 1930s, tea production was still in its infancy there and, as we have seen, was soon to be nipped in the bud by the Pacific War. After the departure of the French, the crop was withdrawn from the private sector. In the early 1950s, paddy fields were formally distributed to former tenants, who had taken de facto ownership of the land when the French fled, while land under crops like tea was farmed under state management.[6] Production of tea provided temporary employment during the war for people who moved from French-occupied areas into the 'liberated zones'. Cash crop land was later brought into Soviet-style collective agricultural enterprises, state farms which were set up in the late 1950s and for thirty years remained, alongside the cooperatives, a major institution of Vietnamese agriculture and a vehicle for Việt migration.

Curious to know more about the way these enterprises were organized, I asked if there was one nearby. Someone suggested we speak to Mr Khiêm, formerly an official at the local Sông Cầu state farm. So after a short drive, we arrived at Khiêm's house. He too was born in the delta.* He had worked as a security guard at the Thái Nguyên steelworks, and then in 1960 got a job at Sông Cầu. A relative newcomer to the area, he apologized for his ignorance of the farm's early history. He could only say it was formed from the merger of four smaller farms set up during the war against the French. In the 1960s the farm's activities expanded rapidly. When he arrived, there were 900 workers, but only four years later there were more than 2,000. Most were from Thái Bình, like Khiêm himself. His job, in the labour office, was to recruit them. Typically this meant three trips to Thái Bình. During the first he discussed the farm's labour requirements with local officials. During the second he persuaded volunteers to look forward to a future in Thái Nguyên. His encouragement helped them to overcome worries about the climate in the hills and the infamous 'terrifying forest and poisoned water' there. They enthusiastically filled in volunteer forms.† A fortnight later he returned, on his third trip, to take them up to the farm.

When I asked him about the early years, and what difficulties the farm had faced, he spoke of the war: 'Bombs meant we were constantly running, running meant productivity fell, which meant people's salary fell too'. But American bombs were not the only inconvenience. Accounts of the early days at other farms nearby suggest that the war was only one of many challenges. Quần Chu state farm, set up in 1966 further down the Công River valley, experienced numerous

---

* 63 years old when I met him, Khiêm was originally from Quỳnh Phụ district, Thái Bình.

† The saying 'terrifying forest and poisoned water' (*rừng thiêng nước độc*) powerfully expressed delta people's unfamiliarity with the upland climate and fear of water-related disease, which was often malaria.

teething troubles. Its workers were 200 people of Chinese origin, former residents of Hanoi and Haiphong, relocated there under a 1961 policy to move urban folk into rural areas, a policy which was accelerated after US bombing started in 1965. In 1968, two families were reported as giving the following reasons for abandoning the farm:

> We've been living in the State Farm for two years; our capital has just about run out; the income at the State Farm is [very low]; the system often fails to provide things like cloth ration cards, sugar ration cards, and foodstuffs; at the State Farm there is no shop, so people have to go as far as the Đại Từ district centre [about 15 km away] to buy things. Countless people have to go to and fro, wasting working time, maybe as many as five or six times and still cannot buy material or clothes; as for working tools and items for household use, these are even harder to get hold of because they are distributed according to the allocation system. We felt that our living is totally insecure, so we asked to leave.[7]

Not everyone on the farm felt this way, however. The farm official reporting this went on to offer some more positive images of the farm's development:

> A number of people have already dug ponds and put fish in; some are raising pigs and chickens, and around their houses they have planted different types of banana; certain families sell their bananas to get money for consumption purposes, so that while their living standard is not high, it is steady and good.[8]

The report was written by an official keen to get help from his superiors, to improve the situation on the farm. The good news – that workers on a state sector tea farm were living off their private cultivation of bananas – may have been even more persuasive than the bad.

This was the situation for a new farm in 1968. Before the bombings, however, things were hardly less difficult. At Tam Đảo farm in 1956, workers had to walk 5 km to buy food. They complained bitterly of the interminable diet of rice, water-spinach and fatty meat with salted water.[9] No doubt things had improved by the time of the Party's Third National Congress in 1960, when the farm was selected for a visit by delegates from abroad.[10] But documents sent to the Ministry of Labour from other areas described a general situation that was, in the early years at least, far from encouraging:

> At Yên Mỹ state farm some people sleep in cattle pens and low-lying areas – heavy rain brings water up to their pillows (...) at Sông Con state farm the housing is in the cattle raising area, a valley near the pens – often stinking smells come in. Sleeping quarters are usually makeshift bamboo arrangements, not beds. There is no eating house, people eat in the courtyard, or on their 'beds' when it rains.[11]

In his description to me, Khiêm was more circumspect than his contemporaries had been in their reports to superior authorities, stressing instead the rigorous virtues of communal living. 'On their arrival, people lived in collective accommodation immediately, they lived collectively and ate collectively, (...) even married couples lived collectively as well'.

When we left Khiêm's house it was already late afternoon. Outside his garden the tea trees spread in well-tended rows across the gently sloping hillside. Some children were picking leaves. We went to talk to them about life on the farm nowadays. Shy, they replied in monosyllables. But in the car on the way back to the district office, I learnt that a few years previously the farm's lands had been divided up among the families of former workers. These were children of the original farm workers. Each family now had their own plot of land, their own private share of the former state farm.

On our return to Thái Nguyên, I discussed our plans with my colleague Đức. We already understood a little about the colonial-era migration I had expected to find in Bờ Rạ. We even had some information on the state farms. Was it necessary to carry on looking for a place that might not exist? A Vietnamese village named after a Frenchman seemed an unlikely phenomenon. But its very strangeness prompted us to continue. So the following morning we returned to the provincial People's Committee. An elderly man at the gatehouse told us the names of some older people who might know about Bờ Rạ – the name meant nothing to him. But once beyond the gatehouse, an official vaguely recalled it. On the border between Đại Từ and Phú Lương districts, he figured. Remembering with some dismay Hỷ's remarks about the extent of Monpezat's lands, we accepted a paper of introduction to Phú Lương. The ride there is described in my field notes for that day:

We get 15 km down the road, stopping and asking people, 'where's Bờ Rạ?' No one knows, or they muddle it with Bờ Đậu at the junction with the Đại Từ road. Finally we meet an old man spreading hay on the road to dry. He thinks I am a Frenchman looking for my father's tomb, and hopes to make some money. He clearly doesn't believe a word of any story about 'historical research'. Eventually, free of charge, he informs us that Bờ Rạ isn't in Phú Lương. It's in Đại Từ. So back to the city to get a paper for Đại Từ. (…)

Another long ride later, and we arrive at Đại Từ People's Committee. It's nearly midday. Too late to meet officials, we have lunch in the main street and return to the office at half past one. A driver at the gatehouse knows Bờ Rạ, says it belongs to Phúc-something commune. The district vice-chairman remembers his mother going to the market at Bờ Rạ (known as Two Pine Tree Market) when he was a youngster. This was during the war against the French. The market, he says, is on the border of Đại Từ, Phổ Yên and Thái Nguyên city. Heads are scratched. We go back out to the gatehouse.

The conclusion is that in the 1970s, when the Núi Cốc reservoir was filled, part of Bờ Rạ was flooded. The remaining part was allocated to Phổ Yên district in an administrative boundary change in 1995. So we should go to Phổ Yên. 40 km away. Instead, we ask for a paper to go to one of the communes where Bờ Rạ's population was resettled. Tân Thái is mentioned, near the Núi Cốc lake tourist development.

We leave Đại Từ. It's past two. We miss the turn to Tân Thái and do a fair bit of mileage back to Thái Nguyên city before finding it. The track leads through rice fields, then skirts forested hillocks before the lake comes into view. Rice fields spread down to the water's edge; the paddy is green, ripening; the sun is high.[*] Three o'clock at Tân Thái People's Committee. We leave our bikes on the grass outside the office and state our problem to the officials. Yes Bờ Rạ was near here, but was flooded. But no, there are no people from Bờ Rạ resettled here. Most of them went to Phú Lạc 20 km away. The Vice-chairman eventually agrees to introduce us to an old man who lives nearby, formerly Party Secretary in the commune, knowledgeable about local history. He writes a note on the permission paper and it receives the commune stamp.[†]

The Party Secretary's house was beside the lake, and had wonderful views towards the mountains of Tam Đảo. But the Party Secretary was out. His wife Kim said he'd be back soon. We sat down to wait. She made tea. Times were hard after the river was dammed, she told us. The land was flooded, they had to leave their house for a time. Both she and her husband were born on this land; they're Việt people. Her home is here. But her husband was originally from the delta. 'His parents were so hungry living in Hà Bắc', she said. 'They were poor and hungry so were forced to wander, to run away, to clear land. They had no paddy fields or if they did, had to pay pay rent, open up a bit of land'. As she spoke she kept protesting that she knew nothing of historical matters, 'I don't know if what I'm saying is correct, but my husband, when he gets home, he knows it all. I really don't know at all'.

Between protestations she nevertheless gave us a clear outline of the Việt settlement of the valley. A Frenchman known as *Chủ Cụt* – the 'Amputated Owner' – had some scattered areas of land here. This man, whose French name was Garrigue (*Ga Ri* in Vietnamese transliteration), owned 207 hectares.[‡] In the 1930s a group of labourers from Thái Bình arrived to work on Garrigue's plantation. They were recruited and organized by a Vietnamese boss. The people paid their taxes to the boss. The boss paid Garrigue.[§] In the 1940s, refugees from the war in the delta evacuated here. Some settled, while others stayed a few years, then moved on. In the 1960s, finally, more Thái Bình people arrived.[¶]

---

[*] This section of the road, with its steeply wooded slopes on the left and green fields stretching out to the right, reminded me strangely of the valley where I grew up, in Haslemere, in the English county of Surrey. I later discovered that I was not the first foreigner in Đại Từ to find its landscape reminiscent of home. It was variously compared to the pastures of Normandy – by Auguste Darles, see below – and the rolling hills of the Australian bush – by Lorraine Salmon, *Pig Follows Dog*, Hanoi: Foreign Languages Publishing House, 1960, pp. 58–59.

[†] These notes, written on the evening of 26 October 1996, have been edited slightly for presentation here.

[‡] Like Hỷ's landlord at Cà Phê village, Garrigue was probably another amputee victim of the Great War. For source, see note 12.

[§] Garrigue acquired this land in the early 1940s, as his name does not appear on the 1939 cadastral register, nor on other records. In 1944 Garrigue fled, the Party Secretary's wife told us. The Vietnamese boss took the land and was jailed during land reform.

[¶] The Party Secretary's wife had only a vague memory for dates, but her account of the stages of Việt settlement was accurate. In this she was typical of many older women I met, an excellent informant.

What about Bờ Rạ? There was no plantation at Bờ Rạ, she told us, but there was one at Bình Thuận, the next village.* The plantation wasn't flooded by the lake. But Bờ Rạ was. 'Bờ Rạ is at the bottom of the lake', Kim said. 'Right at the lake's tummy button'.

PLACE

So this was Bờ Rạ, that shady spot by the Công River described by my colleague in Hanoi. Looking at the lake now, I found it hard to imagine that this expanse of water had not always been here (compare Plates 5, 6a and 6b). The name, Bờ Rạ, and the old lady's memory of the place at the lake's 'tummy button' persuaded me otherwise. But it was a discovery made with a bittersweet satisfaction. Bờ Rạ existed, was a place, had indeed shaded my resting colleague from the sun. But it turned out that, forty years on, Bờ Rạ could be a resting place for no more than my imagination.† If I wanted to know what the place was like before the water came, I would have to construct it in my mind's eye. The following is my attempt to do so, to 'catch' the shadow of the land around Bờ Rạ. Or, rather, to catch a number of shadows of the place. Travellers and settlers here looked at the land with their own desires, expressing them in Vietnamese, French and English, both for the valley as a whole and for this now submerged spot, bordering as it does three districts, Đại Từ, Đồng Hỷ and Phổ Yên.

A common feature of French writing on this part of the world, I found, is a sense of its situation as a natural frontier: an 'area of transition' between the 'vast, flat chequerboard' of the delta, and the 'alpine and wooded region' of the highlands.[13] Writing in 1907, planter Charles Rémery imagined the journey of a French traveller arriving at Haiphong, making the way up to Rémery's landholding in neighbouring Tuyên Quang province. Coming into this region from the delta:

> You no longer see the verdant expanses which, as the harvest approaches, wrinkle and tremble at the flap of the summer breeze's wings; you no longer see those uninterrupted twists and turns of the streams and canals which cut through the paddy fields in all directions, feeding them with their muddy water. Here stop the processions of coolies balancing their shoulders under the double load which they're carrying to market; rarer are the villages, more and more spaced out as you go up the valleys; more deserted appears the hinterland where diverse races, Tho, Man, Muong, Nhgiong [*sic*]‡ are scattered.[14]

---

* She mistook the name here. Her husband later confirmed that Garrigue's plantation was further upstream at Yên Thuận commune, Yên Lãng canton. In colonial times, the canton (*tổng*) was an administrative structure embracing a small number of communes. There were four communes in Yên Lãng canton: Yên Thuận, Yên Thái, Tràng Lang and Lục Ba. Bờ Rạ was a village in Tràng Lang commune.

† Darwin used this expression for place names on maps used during his Beagle voyage.

‡ These were the region's Tày (Thổ), Yao (Dao, Mán), Mường and Nùng inhabitants, now classified among Vietnam's fifty-three ethnic minorities.

An anonymous contemporary, writing in French, offered a closer vision of the landscape:

Already the countryside is losing its grace: to the west, like one of those strange monsters looming up all of a sudden in the bosom of calm and dormant waters, rises and bursts forth, in a swift and vigorous thrust, the imposing mass of Tam Đảo, a sort of symbolic dragon, throwing afar the folds and waves of its green carapace. You then enter an undulating country which spreads out at slow rhythm. No abrupt slope, only soft inclines of green grass, high and thick, which are coloured by the fires of the setting sun and which finish in the evening wind. In the hollows, long and narrow paddy fields have insinuated themselves, sometimes terraced in such a manner as to make irrigation easier: this is the district of Đồng Hỷ.[15]

By 1917, it was not the planter who was on the road, but the French tourist. Tourist development in these parts was proposed by the Résident of the province. Auguste Darles was better known for his harsh administration than his development initiatives, and was suspended from office after the Thái Nguyên prison revolt of 1917.[16] But the following passage, published the same year, conveys a rather sensitive vision of travel in the valley.

Truth to tell, this region, next to Tam Đảo, on the slopes of Thái Nguyên, is too little known: it's been barely two years since you could reach Hưng Sơn [Đại Từ district town] by automobile; but from there to the foot of the range with its vast plateaux – of which certain spots, dotted with groves of brilliant green trees, recall the landscapes of Normandy – you must not be afraid of a hard ride, across canals, along paths where the tall leaning reeds and the prickly bamboos sweep the face of the tourist or require a too often repeated wave. But the effort is rewarded by the picturesque elegance of the landscapes which rest the eye, as well as by the discovery of unexpected resources, waiting for human labour.[17]

Darles observed that some of this was empty land. Upstream from Bờ Rạ, for example:

On these plateaux and low knolls, between Lục Ba and Khôi Kỳ on the one hand, Lục Ba and Yên Rạ on the other, a progressive clearing of the land would give way to the cultivation of manioc, arrow-root, castor-oil and even coffee, a hilly area of two thousand hectares, with about a hundred hectares of paddy fields in the low-lying areas. This land, currently unoccupied, covered in bush, is still theoretically a part of the territory of Lục Ba and Yên Rạ; but, in fact, it is vacant state land on which no one pays tax and which Lục Ba and Yên Rạ could never bring under the plough.[18]

When Darles acknowledged the existence of a scattered population in the valley, he emphasized their precarious eking out of an existence, in full contrast to the rich potential of the land:

Despite the obstacle of the mountains, despite the sombre mystery of the insalubrious forests, man has found his living in the vast plains, made fat by the humus which the millenarian effort of torrential rains has dragged down from the mountain sides, cheerful plains which open suddenly their perspective of fresh greenery, as you come through the wild passes which seem to protect their riches. To the west, at the foot of

Tam Đảo, there is the plateau of Vân Lăng, criss-crossed with fifty canals which hasten their way towards the Công River, and there is the prosperous plain of Đại Từ which disappears towards Ký Phú and Cát Nê, between the main range and its long parallel buttress. In the middle of this tormented nature whose lush power seems to defy the fragility of human labour, the inhabitants, rare and dispersed in the clearings on the plains, have limited their effort of production to the strict satisfaction of their immediate subsistence.[19]

But precariousness was an adjunct to immobility:

Uninterested in luxury and even in improving their living, which would demand the addition of unnecessary activity to their daily tasks, they prefer the quiet of their happy isolation to the turbulent agitation of centres of civilization. Many are those who have never, in their life, covered the 25–30 kilometres which separate them from the provincial capital.[20]

The point here is not that Darles subscribed to an orientalist myth of the stagnant peasant society of Asia.* It is that the peasants described here were immobile by contrast to the mobility of the tourist. Or rather, the administrator, for one has a sneaking suspicion that Darles' tourist was none other than Darles himself. This impression is reinforced by a glance at a popular guidebook for colonial holiday-makers, where a map of the region leaves the Công River valley a blank.[21] Only those visitors to the Cascade d'Argent tourist resort on the peaks of Tam Đảo were in a position to appreciate the 'picturesque elegance' of these landscapes. But Darles' traveller, whoever he was, felt he was moving, by remarking the non-movement of the people in the landscape he appropriated to his own journey. And in his movement this traveller was used in the construction of a textual landscape, onto which Darles imposed a double fantasy – firstly the love of elegant views, reminiscent of Normandy, but secondly and more importantly, the bringing of land 'into value'. This was contemporary French parlance for economic development, a phrase in vogue in the colonies: the *mise en valeur* of France's overseas possessions.[22] The land was posited empty of all but an immobile and apathetic population; the traveller saw it as a duty to call attention to this.

In the following text, the traveller was a real tourist, a frequent visitor to the hill station resort of Tam Đảo, where he could enjoy the superb views of the Công River valley and surrounding hills:

I spend my summers in Tam Đảo. *Eh bien*! I can assure you that it hurts me to see, from my window, thousands and thousands of hectares of beautiful hilltops covered in unused pastures, without a single village, without a single farm.[23]

---

*   Gourou made a concise articulation of this orientalist self-other, mobile–immobile paradigm: 'In short, Tonkin presents the characteristics of a stabilized civilization in material and aesthetic accord with its natural conditions. Stagnant and retarded civilization, one might say; and certainly immobility has its defects, but are they much more serious that those which accompany the extreme mobility of European civilization?' Gourou, *Les paysans du delta*, p. 576.

The traveller lamented the absence of people. He called for a movement of people with livestock to make use of 'pasture', settlers to bring the land 'into value', to plant crops, reap harvests, graze cows and of course pay taxes, the payment of which defined the occupation of land. Their arrival was anticipated in the vicinity of Bờ Rạ:

> Joining itself in the east to that of Hưng-Sơn, the wide plain of Yên Thuận, Yên Thái and Lục Ba opens out on the banks of the Công River. At the middle of the land farmed by these three villages stretch out more than 400 hectares of former paddy fields, bordered with little knolls and cheerful copses. A digging over would suffice to obtain, from the first effort, a harvest which would feed the settlers put in.[24]

The land at Bờ Rạ and the Công River valley, moreover, was not unusually favoured. From the earliest days of colonial rule, French administrators looked at the land in all highland regions like this through the prism of their desire: the desire to settle people there. The first legislation granting free plots of land, called 'small concessions', in the midlands of northern Vietnam dates from three years after the conquest. In Thái Nguyên, Darles lost his job after the 1917 revolt and went, among other things, into the plantation business. But the publication of his article was followed by new grants of land, downstream at Tân Cương and two other villages to Vietnamese workers returning from First World War France.[25] The existence of empty land in the valley was posited again, but in this case it was previously cultivated land which had been abandoned during the French conquest, when roving bands of Chinese and Vietnamese 'pirates' made the region unsafe.[26] More than a hundred families settled there in 1918, all of them unskilled workers who had completed a three-year contract in the factories of wartime France.[*] Few of them stayed for long. In 1932, less than half were recorded as remaining.[27] Perception of failure in Tân Cương did not deter the colonial authorities. During the 1920s and 1930s, further laws were passed, encouraging migration to the hills. The most important of these policies involved grants of 5-hectare small concessions free of charge on submission of an application and a map of the land desired.[†] Few brought substantial results but the Résident of Thái Nguyên in the

---

[*]   These workers, known as ONS (*ouvriers non-spécialisés*, or unspecialized workers) were among the 100,000 soldiers, auxiliaries and factory workers who travelled to France during the 1914–18 war. Tân Cương, Tân Thành and Thịnh Đức villages were formally set up by RST decree of 18 December 1925. See Chapter 3.

[†]   Legislation included the following decrees: **7 June 1888**, allowing individuals to apply for five hectare 'small concessions'; **13 November 1925**, reproducing the 1888 legislation; **20 March 1936**, allowing enterprising individuals to organize 'settlement colonies', grouping several families on an area of land. For summaries of French settlement policy, see Charles Robequain, *The Economic Development of French Indochina*, London: Oxford University Press, 1944, pp. 59–73; Bureau International de Travail, *Problèmes de Travail en Indochine*, Geneva: Kundig, 1937, pp. 229–235; Services du Protectorat, 'Activité colonisatrice du Tonkin – Colonisation dans la haute et moyenne région du Tonkin', *BEI*, 1938, pp. 757–779; NAV1/RST 67470, 'Inventaire des terrains libres et fertiles pouvant être réservés à l'installation des excédents de population du delta', 7 January 1941.

1930s, Alfred Echinard, was unusually energetic in their promotion; two laws specifically concerning Thái Nguyên were enacted on his initiative.* The whole of Thái Nguyên was surveyed and mapped for settlement purposes, and had the best record of all the highland provinces for the small concessions programme (see Plates 7 and 8).

One would-be recipient of a smallholding in Thái Nguyên had recourse to a public scribe to make his request. The writer of his petition, like the French authors quoted above, laid emphasis on the contrast between delta and middle region:

> I beg to address to your excellency's understanding the following petition: on the land of Vĩnh Yên, Sơn Tây and Thái Nguyên, there remain many wild areas of paddy field as yet not entirely cleared, but in Nam Định there are frequent floods; anyone who can go to those other areas and make use of the land will be provided with one hundred piasters per person to make paddy fields. Currently in my area there are few paddy fields but many people, farmland is often flooded by water and lost; therefore I volunteer and request the provision of a living and a grant of land to go up to that other land and make use of it, so as later to become rich.[28]

The perspective here was not that of the travelling tourist or administrator, relating things seen. It was that of a potential settler, working his imagination, an imagination informed by contrast with home and by what he had heard – from officials, from relatives and friends, and possibly even from some of the workers who had abandoned the settlement at Tân Cương. His perspective was, of course, influenced by what the scribe thought the officials who would read the petition wanted to hear – there were large numbers of similar petitions in the file I consulted. But while perspectives differed, the petitioner's programme was ultimately the same as that of the official. This man was aiming to become an agent of the land's development. He was expressing an intention to put the land to use, to bring it into value. The settler hoped he could feed his family. The official hoped he would pay his salary.

The archives do not indicate whether this individual petitioned with success. But we know that some of his contemporaries fulfilled this dream, to clear and settle a small, rarely flooded, uncrowded plot of land. We owe this knowledge to the Great Depression. As we saw at the beginning of this chapter, in 1932 the Résident in Thái Nguyên received a request to provide land for miners from Hồng Gai. He sent his district mandarins across the province to survey for likely settlement spots. The mandarin in Phổ Yên reported on land just downstream from Tân Cương:

> In the region of Bến Đông, Làng Thang, Đầm Ban and the Sơn Cốt Plantation, while looking for areas of easily cultivable land I noted the fact that there are no new

---

* Decrees of **8 March 1938**, declassifying areas of Thái Nguyên forest reserve for use as small concessions and **5 December 1938**, allocating the area between the Công River and the foothills of Tam Đảo for use as small concessions. For details see NAV1/RST 67485, correspondence between Echinard and the Forestry Service, 1939.

inhabitants arriving; over by the plantation, there are a lot of places which are still uncleared, where there is thick forest, except that from Đầm Ban to the foothills [of Tam Đảo], while the land is wooded it is obvious that you can still cut it down and make rice-fields; there are some places where the trees are small, or where there are some muddy areas where the marsh is 40 or 50 cm deep; here on each side of the road from Đầm Ban to the provincial highway you can make rice-fields.[29]

The land was forested, marshy; but there remained large areas of uncultivated land in the valley, land rich only in potential. New settlers were not arriving then but, presumably before the Depression, there had been many of them. The key here was the road (Road 38), along the sides of which the former miners could be installed. Reference to the map attached to this report indicates that the road was only sparsely settled on the Phổ Yên side and deteriorated after crossing into Đại Từ (see Plate 9). The Phổ Yên mandarin knew the country too well to suggest that no one lived there, but further up settlement was more scattered. The Đại Từ mandarin, meanwhile, did not bother to visit his end of the valley. We may surmise that, in this area, poor roads were a hindrance to good government as well as to economic development.

The theme of slow settlement and economic development was taken up by later Vietnamese commentators. A Party historian, writing in the 1980s from a very different political perspective, described the district of Đại Từ, and regretted that this land remained sparsely populated right up to 1945. He blamed the lack of communications development under the French:

> The roads going to Phổ Yên and Định Hóa, not having received satisfactory invest-ment and as a result uncompleted, made travelling a very difficult matter. Because of this, although it is not far from the provincial capital, Đại Từ was [in 1945] still a remote place.[30]

A number of collaborators with the colonial government held the same view. Nguyễn Mạnh Hiền, of Thái Nguyên province's Chamber of the People's Repres-entatives, petitioned the provincial Résident about the same road:

> [To help] anyone wishing to request uncultivated land on either side of a road, and especially of Road 38, where there are thousands of hectares as yet not cleared: We request: (…) that you have Road 38 built immediately.[31]

The recipient of this petition, Alfred Echinard, who held the post of Résident in Thái Nguyên for the unusually long period of twelve years, was himself an energetic campaigner for the *mise en valeur* of his province, and notably for road building. Soon after coming into office, he complained that this road had been allowed to deteriorate, noting that 'the administration has neglected Road 38 along which people circulated ten years ago and which no longer exists from Bến Đông in Phổ Yên as far as Hưng Sơn, for a distance of 30 km'.[32] He stressed the benefit (calculated in terms of tax revenue, which had doubled) accruing from the construction of the northern section of the road towards Định Hóa district, urging his superiors in Hanoi to provide funds for the completion of the Đại Từ section to the south (see Plates 10–11). This would, he argued, allow the installation of 20,000 families in the Công River valley. Echinard's counterpart in the delta province of Nam Định, Lionel Lotzer, concurred, suggesting that a 'massive transplantation' of people could not happen before the road's construction.[33]

Echinard never received the funding he requested so persistently. The Japanese closed the road in the early 1940s, owing to its proximity to their new airport at Đa Phúc (now Hanoi's main airport at Nội Bài). The 1945 revolution soon ensured that no French administrator would implement the project. Revolution also gave new perspectives to the way the landscape was written about. In the following account, the lack of economic development at Phú Xuyên village (at the head of the Công River valley) was an unfortunate inconvenience for its few inhabitants but a distinct advantage for the effort of resistance against the French.'In the past, this place was a revolutionary resistance base surrounded by small hills and rolling mountains; most of it was empty land and barren hills, there was no intensive wet-rice farming'.[34] The benefits of this underdevelopment were made clear in a military history of the northern highlands:

> Roads here are all far from one another, so coordination and rescue will be extremely difficult, and forces may easily be isolated and cut off. Few roads and roads of poor quality, crossing complex topography and preventing turning, further hinder the mobile potential of the enemy.[35]

Hindrances to enemy mobility created room for revolutionary manoeuvre. But there were times, if we are to believe this historian, when the French may have preferred to forgo their mobility:

> On 12 December [1947], more than 600 soldiers in the French army withdrew towards Đại Từ along the Lục Ba–Ký Phú road, and reaching Sơn Cốt were ambushed. One hundred were wiped out and almost fifty were wounded. On the road from Sơn Cốt to Cầu Đuống [near Hanoi], the French army suffered from many landmine battles, in which around more than 200 were wounded.[36]

The road on which the above ambush took place was, of course, the same Road 38, for the construction of which Nguyễn Mạnh Hiền and Echinard had campaigned. The issue here is not the veracity of the events recorded. What the passage tells us is about the state of the roads, and the victories they allowed the historian to claim. Two confrontations were described in this text. The first took place on Road 38, where French failure to invest had left the area with large areas of forest cover and few inhabitants, highly suitable for ambush. It is not difficult to imagine victory in such a place, although we may doubt the casualty statistics offered in this account.* The second took place on the main highway from

---

*   This landscape was of strategic importance on a number of occasions during the twentieth century. **1917**. A French campaign against the rebel Đội Cấn, who fled to 'the Yao village of Quần Chu at the foot of Tam Đảo, in a particularly difficult region, crisscrossed by numerous streams swollen by strong rain, wooded with almost inextricable banks of bamboo.' Troops came from Thái Nguyên. 'We could not think of pursuing the group with

Hanoi to Thái Nguyên. Marsh and forest gave way to rice-fields and built-up areas. Daylight ambushes were dangerous. 'Battles' were carried out by landmine.

The non-realization of the Road 38 project had implications for the whole area around Bờ Rạ. In 1941, a report entitled 'Inventory of free and fertile lands which may be reserved for the installation of excess population from the delta' indicated that the settlement of the two cantons of Yên Lãng and Ký Phú remained 'subordinated to the construction of Road 38'.* The road was not built until the 1960s – in time for the arrival of more people from the delta, as Kim had told us. Even then it was passable by car only as far as the Quần Chu state farm. Vehicles from the farm travelling to Phổ Yên had to go back through Đại Từ, rather than over the Công River via Sơn Cốt.† But the presence of a state farm nearby gave the people at Bờ Rạ an advantage over other places.‡ Remoter spots had no roads at all. The author of a report on land clearance in the province, writing of the late 1970s, chafed against the priority given to state farms. He criticized the failure to promote development of small agricultural cooperatives in places like Bờ Rạ, cooperatives set up under a programme to build 'new economic zones' in the highlands with settlers from the Red River Delta. These new economic zone cooperatives were deemed strategically less important than the larger state farm organizations.

> The extension of the road network to small new economic zones has been organized too slowly, and to this day there are still no transport roads, so produce is lost and the cooperatives find it very difficult to receive materials and goods provided by the State. This situation is wasteful of manpower and heavily influences production.[38]

By the time this report was written, however, the new economic zone cooperatives of Bờ Rạ were already nothing more than a memory. The water level started

---

[*continued from previous page*] regular troops across the bamboo forest, nor make them attempt to climb Tam Đảo.' Đội Cấn escaped over Tam Đảo. **1945**. A Japanese campaign against the Việt Minh: 'On 9 April 1945, two Japanese with a group of Vietnamese traitors guiding them entered the liberated zone at Cát Nê-Ký Phú (Đại Từ) to sound out the strength of the revolution. Resolved to defend the liberated zone, our army and people killed the whole enemy group. This was the first gunshot which opened our people's anti-Fascist resistance in the southern districts of the province.' The Japanese retaliated with a pincer movement but were repulsed, leaving ten dead. **1982**. Precautions after the Chinese invasion, on this route to the delta: 'In the region of streams at the foot of Tam Đảo, in Mỹ Yên and Khôi Kỳ communes, a cooperative was established with a platoon of militia to defend the foothills of Tam Đảo and improve the defensive capability of the lake'. For sources, see note 37.

* Tràng Lang commune, where Bờ Rạ was situated, had 1,320 hectares of free land, on which 132 delta families might be settled. NAV1/RST 67470, 'Inventaire des terrains libres et fertiles', 7 January 1941.

† In 1996 the Công River could only be crossed at this point by sampan or by a rickety bamboo suspension bridge, on payment of a small toll. See Photo 3.

‡ A 1960 report indicated three priority destinations for road construction in Thái Nguyên: military rear-base areas, state farms and the city suburbs. NAV3/UBKHNN 1444(tt), Ministry of Communications and Post to State Planning Committee and Prime Minister, Hanoi, 12 July 1960.

rising in 1971. The road was cut by 1976. The lake flooded after heavy rains in 1978.* The project was completed in 1980. Bờ Rạ had become a reservoir.

The Party Secretary, when he got home, told me about this. He didn't mention the road, which was on the other side of the valley. But he did say that the land at Bờ Rạ was better than at spots downstream. There was ironwood forest there, tall *lim* trees which soldiers cut down before the village was submerged. I asked if there had been a French plantation there. He mentioned Garrigue, the 'Amputated Owner', whose plantation at Yên Thuận was remembered with a poem:

> The plantations Yên Thuận, Chàng Dương,
> As the stork flies with straight wings, must be ceded (*nhường*) to the French.

The poem conveyed the size of the plantation and the tenants' irritation at working for a foreigner, he said. He went on, saving me the trouble of questioning the historical value of such folk sayings: 'There's a problem with the poem. Chàng Dương plantation was owned by a Vietnamese, not a Frenchman. It's there to rhyme with *nhường*.' His point was that the only French plantation was at Yên Thuận. There had been no plantation at Bờ Rạ. As for Monpezat, he'd heard of the name, but not here. He didn't know the origin of the name Bờ Rạ. But he was adamant that people at Bờ Rạ did not cede their land to the French. They just had small plots of paddy, which they had cleared inside the forest.

Before I left, the Party Secretary, clearly bemused by my interest in this obscure place, told me another story. He related how, a year before my visit, a Japanese came to ask about Bờ Rạ. He thought there had been a Japanese unit stationed at Bờ Rạ during the Pacific War. He took lots of film. But, the old man added, the Japanese was wrong, there was no such unit. It wasn't until we were on the track back to Đại Từ that the story sunk home. Had I left the Party Secretary shaking his head at the spectacle of yet another foreigner chasing historical wild geese to Bờ Rạ?

PEOPLE

This moment of reflection did not put me off my chase, however. If I could do no more than imagine what Bờ Rạ – the place – was like, I was by now determined to meet some of its inhabitants. Kim had told us they were now living at Phú Lạc, at the top of the valley. My field notes take up the story:

> We ride back to Đại Từ office, to get a paper for Phú Lạc. But, it seems, after all, Phú Lạc has no Bờ Rạ people. The majority of them went to Phổ Yên … Then someone remembers that an official with the Labour Office, Mr Bình, is from Bờ Rạ. We rush to the Labour Office.
>
> 'Anh Bình đi học rồi' (Mr Bình has gone to a class) – 'Where?' – 'In Thái Nguyên city'. We ponder for a while, feeling through tea and small talk for a way forward. We can't abandon Bờ Rạ without meeting at least *one* person who lived there before it

---

*   Kim added later that twelve people died in this sudden flood.

became a lake. Finally the answer emerges. Bình's mother, Mrs Loan. She lives with Bình nearby. We finish our tea, then get on the bikes. At Bình's house, we meet his wife, but his mother's gone: walked to Bình's brother's house, 2 km away. It doesn't take long before we roll up in that courtyard.

'Bà đi chợ rồi' (She has gone to the market). Our hopes sink. The official accompanying us vocalises the image of the old lady busily making money and chatting to her friends. There's no water for tea while we wait. Eventually she returns. It's true. She is from Bờ Rạ. She did live there. But she only moved there in the 1960s, to a new economic zone, so she doesn't know much about its history.

Loan was originally from Hà Nam province in the delta, and in the 1960s she decided to 'follow the Party and state to clear land' in the mountains in doing so, she was part of a vast movement of people who came to Đại Từ and other parts of the northern uplands 'following the call of the Party and State who mobilized lowland compatriots to participate in the economic development of the mountains'.[39] The call is typically said to have come from Hồ Chí Minh, but the announcement of the migration policy was, in fact, first made by Lê Duẩn at the Party's Third Congress in September 1960:

> Stimulating their patriotism, we must organize the transfer of hundreds of thousands of people from the plains to the mountains to work in industry and agriculture, building industrial zones, state farms and state forest enterprises, devoting their strength and their talents to the cause of the Fatherland and its growing prosperity. If this work is carried out successfully, the development of socialist economy in the mountainous areas will certainly be guaranteed.[40]

This was the 'new economic zones'* programme, as it was later called. At the time of Loan's move, it was known simply as 'clearing the wilderness'† or 'highland economic and cultural development'‡. Along with the state farm and urban evacuation programmes, it was aimed at the development of the highlands. To participate, you had to fill in a form. Forms were difficult to get hold of because, Loan told us, so many people wanted to go. To be accepted, you had to have a good 'political record'.§ Some people who weren't accepted even made their own way to Thái Nguyên, applying at the reception centre there for the right to stay. They were refused, she said.¶ Loan herself arrived at Bờ Rạ on 24 February 1964, with twenty other families. They were given a welcome by others from the lowlands,

---

*   New economic zone: *vùng kinh tế mới.*

†   Clearing land: *khai hoang.*

‡   Highland economic and cultural development: *phát triển kinh tế văn hóa miền núi.*

§   CV: *lý lịch.*

¶   The programme's announcement triggered a movement of unauthorized migrants to Thái Nguyên just after the new year holiday in 1961, some wanting a permanent job, others after seasonal employment. Spontaneous migration was discouraged but never eradicated, even in the 1960s. Since the 1980s free migration to upland areas has become common, especially to the central highlands. NAV3/ BLD 1030(vv), 'Báo cáo tình hình người miền xuôi lên Thái Nguyên', Thái Nguyên, 23 February 1961.

who had been there for two years. Other Việt and some highlanders, Yao and Sán Dìu people, were also living there when she arrived. The other Việt had been there for generations, and spoke Sán Dìu fluently, 'just like the minorities', she said.

At this point in our conversation, the official with us leaned back in his chair and laughed. The story reminded him of an encounter he had once had while in the army at the China border. He himself was from Thái Bình, but on this occasion had been disguised as a minority – for strategic reasons, he said. He got talking to a woman dressed in minority clothes, and who had trouble speaking Vietnamese. It was only after asking about her background that he learned that she too was from the delta, from in fact the same district as him, Đông Hưng. She had just been away longer. She had 'lost her roots'.

The old lady went on with her story. Việt locals helped the newcomers settle in. But it was the Sán Dìu who taught them to cut down trees. 'There was a plantation 3 kilometres from Bờ Rạ, but at Bờ Rạ there was just forest and some old tombs. They were big trees, one of them could make a whole house. We had to do a really serious bit of land clearing.' In return for helping with this, the Sán Dìu set their new neighbours to work on the rice-fields, ploughing and harvesting. This was, perhaps, Loan's way of describing to us the 'loving solidarity between compatriots clearing land and compatriots from our brother ethnic groups' which excited Phạm Văn Đồng in a *Nhân Dân* article in 1962.[41] But when she started talking about this relationship, there was a note of ambivalence in her memory. The arrangement, she complained at first, was one day of teaching by the Sán Dìu, for three days of farm labour by the Việt. A few minutes later, after some thought, she cheered up, 'it was a fair deal. It was okay by us, we didn't mind'. But she went on to express her fear of the Sán Dìu, and how she kept relations with them to a minimum. She avoided going into their houses. 'They're really something else. They have strange practices, like purging.* If you steal from them, or get a girl into trouble and avoid marriage, they'll hate you, kill you. But if you have good relations with them, they might give you a wild pig, for free'.

Life as a Việt settler in 1960s Bờ Rạ was not an easy one, judging by the drop-out rate. Of the original twenty families who came up with Loan, only nine stayed on. Loan was silent as to why they left, though she did say that people suffered badly from malaria during the first year. Then, twelve years after they cleared it, the land was flooded. Some of the Việt people chose to move in with relatives elsewhere; her family was fortunate enough to go to the local town. The rest – Việt and Sán Dìu– did not go to Phú Lạc, as I had been led to understand. They moved a short distance down the Công River, she said, to Bình Sơn in Phổ Yên district. The people moved, the place disappeared, only the name remained, and even that was a matter of some doubt. When I asked her about the name, Bờ Rạ, her manner was dismissive; 'Old name. Must be the minority language'.

---

*   This was *tẩy*, a form of purging or fasting practised by some upland peoples.

We were at Bình Sơn first thing the following morning. I handed our paper of introduction to a young official with a certain feeling of trepidation. But my fears were unfounded. Loan was right, people from Bờ Rạ had indeed settled here. During the two days we spent there, the official introduced us to five people from Bờ Rạ and its neighbourhood. They were all men in their seventies or eighties. Three were Sán Dìu. Two were Việt. From them I was able to get an idea of the people and settlement of Bờ Rạ before the flood.

The first man we met was the former commune chairman, Mr Vượng, who lived in Bình Sơn's central village, Đình village. He confirmed that there had been four villages in what was then the commune of Tràng Lang.* He went on to sketch the commune for me, as follows (this is my reproduction of his rough sketch):

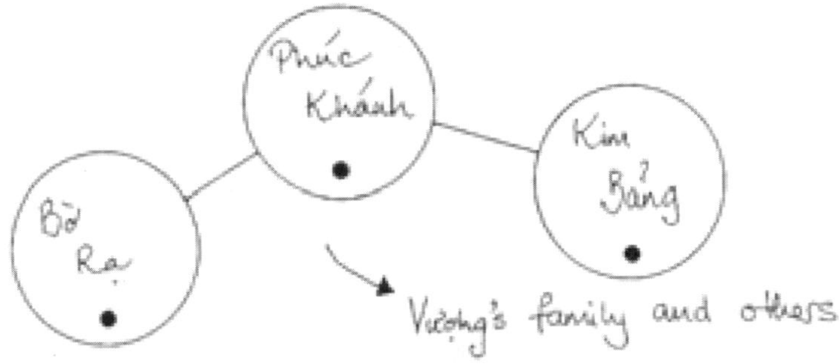

He then contradicted what I had heard from the old Party Secretary and from Loan: people in Bờ Rạ did cede land to the French. Not only in Bờ Rạ, either. Land in all three villages named on the sketch was owned by a Frenchman. Local people variously called him *Chủ Tây*, *Chủ Con* or *Chủ Sơn Cốt* after the name of his plantation (see Plate 12).† Vượng remembered his French name as *something-Nô*. Later, the name *Fê Rô* was mentioned.‡ As for *Bông Bờ Rạ* (Monpezat), he found the name vaguely familiar. The normal name, however, was *Chủ Con*. The fourth village, marked 'Vượng's family and others' on the sketch, was Long Hội, the most recently founded.

Vượng drew another sketch to show how his father and some other Sán Dìu families settled there.

---

* Tràng Lang's name changed to Phúc Thọ after 1945. Vượng was over 70 years old at the time of interview.

† Respectively: 'French Owner', 'Child Owner' and 'Sơn Cốt Owner'.

‡ *Fê Rô* is a transliteration of the French Féraud. Archives note that the Sơn Cốt plantation was owned by Reynaud & Féraud in 1939, and Reynaud & Reynaud a year later. Féraud may have been a partner brought in with additional capital to see the enterprise through the Depression. The other Reynaud was Reynaud's son, mentioned by Echinard as 'Reynaud père et fils, à Son Cot'. Echinard, *Notice sur la province de Thai Nguyen*, pp. 66–67; NAVI/RST 67475, 'Etat nominatif des concessions domaniales accordées à des français jusqu'au 31.12.1939', Thái Nguyên, 10 January 1941.

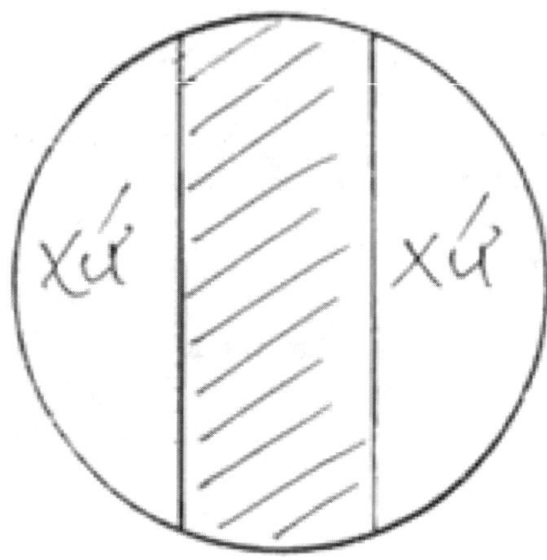

The central area was part of the plantation, while land surrounding it belonged to the state.* Vượng explained that anyone who wanted to clear state land could ask the French authorities for permission, at the office in Thái Nguyên, and then would be able to settle there. Long Hội was state land, and a certain Ôn Văn Tài had done the formalities. 'Ôn Văn Tài's wife was a member of the same family as my mother', Vượng related. He had never worked for the French, but he had an elder brother who was an NCO in the colonial army. This made things easier. He also had the advantage of possessing a head tax card, without which relations with officials were impossible. Ôn Văn Tài got the permission, but all five families paid for it together: 'After all, we were all relatives so Tài couldn't get any extra privileges. He was just an ordinary man'. But after the settlement went ahead – land tax was due after five years – Ôn Văn Tài was named village head.

The founders of Long Hội – Ôn Văn Tài and his relatives – were all Sán Dìu people, from nearby districts. People at Bờ Rạ were also Sán Dìu, but had been there for longer. The commune's former Party Secretary, Mr Ba, told us their story. Ba's family, Sán Dìu like the others, came from Lạng Sơn. Much like Vượng's father, his ancestors arrived, cleared land, planted rice. This was before the French; they did not ask for authorization. Ba said the family had lived there for two or three generations. Then, in his father's time, the French came; they brought maps and papers, which they showed the Sán Dìu; they employed Chinese people to supervise tenants; they pushed the Sán Dìu out from the valley floor, to the poorer land outside.† 'No one knew who the land belonged to. We fought them and sued

---

* He called this land *xứ*. This word was commonly used to denote a whole region – such as northern Vietnam – but here denoted areas of state-owned land, corresponding to the French term *domaine*.

† Compare Ba's account with Vượng's sketch. Ba, who was 76, confirmed my colleague's description of Bờ Rạ as a shady place beside the Công River.

them. We were chased away. In the end we had to live outside.* Living 'outside' cannot have been easy – the family moved twice while Ba was growing up: once to Kim Bảng, and then around 1940 back to Bờ Rạ. Kim Bảng was too crowded.'

'Kim Bảng was too crowded.' The comment was a thought-provoking one for an area of land earmarked at this time for a 'massive transplantation' of people from the delta. How had Ba's father wanted to make a living? How did the people already there use the land? What was their attitude towards the newly arrived family? What did 'crowded' mean in this context? One man who was able to answer some of these questions was Mr Hoài, who arrived in Kim Bảng from Thái Bình.† It was 1945. 'We were starving. Our family just had to leave, that's all. Me and my wife and our two children'. Hoài was more fortunate than many who fled the famine that year: at Đa Phúc, where the Cầu and Công Rivers join, he met a man called Lâm.‡ Lâm was a forester, floating wood down the river. He agreed to employ Hoài and sent him to Kim Bảng, a forest plantation, to cut down trees. There were only a few paddy fields at Kim Bảng, dry ones, as the water was poor. Both the forest and the fields belonged to the Frenchman Féraud, who let them to a plantation overseer. This man kept the fields to himself, sharing them with two Sán Dìu families; others were excluded.

If Kim Bảng had poor, jealously farmed land, the best fields were to be had Phúc Khánh.§ Listening to Mr Minh, who arrived there in 1918, I imagined the village to have been a little replica of his home in Thái Bình. There were Việt families there, and no Sán Dìu; there was a communal house, where the old men

---

* Later on Ba gave a different version of the family's departure from the valley floor. My notes record the following sequence of events: 'His father was village head for Féraud. He collected the taxes - but when the Vietnamese came from Féraud for the taxes, he beat them – then had to move to the state land (*xứ*).' A failed relationship of collaboration, rather than a heroic resistance is implied. French sources confirm his account of conflict of legalities. A report written by the French owners, Reynaud, Blanc & Co, contained the following passage: 'The native is increasingly turning against the colon, whom he considers as the usurper of lands which were nevertheless granted in the regular way. Under the intelligent and paternal management of the colons, they learned how to cultivate their soil and now, incited by people of bad faith, they want to take back the lands which used to belong to them.' Despite doubts over the legality of the grant, Reynaud was able to retain the land. J. Morel, *Les concessions de terre au Tonkin*, Paris: Pedone, 1912, p. 204.

† Hoài, from Nguyệt Lâm village (Vũ Bình commune, Vũ Thư district, Thái Bình), was 83 years old.

‡ Famine caused much migration in 1944–45. Motoo Furata estimated at 35/286 households (12 per cent), the number of families who left his sample village in Tiền Hải district (Thái Bình) to seek survival elsewhere. Of these, eighteen households (50 per cent), two thirds or more lost members in famine-related deaths. Hoài was one of the lucky ones. Motoo Furata, *Vietnam no Ichi sonraku ni okeru 1945 nen Kikin no Jittai Taibin-sho Tienhai-ken Tay Luong-mura Luong Phu-buraku ni Kansura Nichi Etsu Godo Chosa*, Tokyo: Tokyo University Research Report on History, 1994, vol. 22, p. 159.

§ Phúc Khánh was on low-lying land near Bờ Rạ. Probably the first settlement in the area, it figures in a nineteenth century list of communes here. Phúc Khánh was also the first to be inundated by the reservoir. Dương Thị The and Phạm Thị Thoa, *Tên làng xã Việt Nam đầu thế kỷ XIX (thuộc các tỉnh từ Nghệ Tĩnh trở ra)*, Hanoi: NXB Khoa Học Xã Hội, 1981, p. 474.

met; there was an opium-smoking landlord and a corrupt village head; there were wet rice fields, the only difference from home being the low population – eighteen families – which made it easy to get labour work. Minh never went back to Thái Bình: 'What's the point of going back? We came up here to make a living, there's nothing back there'.[*]

Few people, Việt or Sán Dìu, had their own land before the revolution. Vượng had some – land cleared by his father. Ba got his own plot in 1946. Hoài and Minh had to wait until land reform in the early 1950s, but they did not enjoy it for long. Cooperatives were set up in 1960 and the new economic zones people arrived in 1962. Before this, I was told, Việt people made up about a third of the commune. Afterwards, a Sán Dìu informant explained, there were more Việt than Sán Dìu. With the influx, the commune expanded from four villages to a total of twelve. First of all, Bờ Rạ split in two, creating a new village called Đông Lai. This was at the time the cooperatives were set up. Then the new economic zone villages were formed, seven of them. One of these, situated in the middle of the commune, was optimistically named Đoàn Kết (meaning 'solidarity').[†] But villagers were not together for long. When the lake flooded, the newcomers moved to Phúc Tân, further downstream, while those from the four original villages were evacuated to Bình Sơn (see Plates 13, 14 and 15).

At Bình Sơn they settled in two villages: Phúc Sơn and Đát Đá. So I was told by the young official who spoke to us on our arrival at the People's Committee. I was surprised then, when we went over to Vượng's house nearby, to hear the old man talking about Bờ Rạ in the present tense. He was recommending me to call on his 'old colleague Ba, who lives in Bờ Rạ'. Puzzled, I asked, 'he now lives in Bờ Rạ?' Vuong explained that before people moved from the lake bed, the land at this place was wild, they had to clear it. People now call the village they built there Bờ Rạ. 'New Bờ Rạ?' I ventured. 'No, just Bờ Rạ'.

A short ride took us there, but when we first arrived Ba was out; he'd gone to visit his daughter in the next village. While we were waiting I had time to write briefly about the place: 'We're now in 'new" Bờ Rạ: hilly, steep, terraced tea fields, some wet rice, vegetables, a bit of forest on the top of the hills. Nice place. Sun's gone in. It's cool'. The wait was fortuitous. It gave us time to drop in on Ba's neighbour, Mr Khoa. A Sán Dìu man in his early sixties, Khoa cleared up the confusion: the real name of the village is not Bờ Rạ but Đát Đá. He described how, when people arrived from the lake, 'the whole of this area was forest, nothing but wild forest'. The government gave land, but they had to fell trees,

---

[*]   Minh was 87 when I met him, and vague about his origins (probably Tiền Hải district, Thái Bình). Like Ba, his memory of relations with the French was subject to some negotiation. He initially commented that there were no French-owned lands at Phúc Khánh; later he corrected this, saying that *Chủ Sơn Cốt* (Reynaud) had employed Việt overseers to collect the rents on his land there.

[†]   The seven new villages were Đoàn Kết, Mạnh Phúc, Phúc Lương, Phúc An, Phúc Ninh, Phúc Tiến and Phúc Xá.

plant crops, channel water. It took five years for the place to look as it does now, ten before they stopped worrying about their livelihood. The experience left its mark, in a very concrete way, on the name they chose for their new home. '*Đất*', he said, 'means *many*. *Đá* means *rocks*. Đát Đá is the name people use', he insisted. 'Some people from outside call it Bờ Rạ, but only because the people are all from Bờ Rạ'. 'There's an official name as well', he added. In 1976, when the land was first settled, officials named it Tân Bình (New Peace): an aspiration for life after the war, or a variation on Bình Sơn. Whatever its inspiration, nowadays few people use this name or know it: even the taxes are collected from Đát Đá.*

It was late afternoon before we finally caught up with Ba. The long wait had convinced us that he had decided to stay with his daughter, so we set off to look for him. We bumped into him on the path; he was cycling home. But at the sight of a 'delegation' from the village People's Committee, from Hanoi and from overseas, he appeared quite terrified. It took a moment to reassure him that our business was nothing more than the history of a name; we went into a nearby house to talk. On the name, however – the name Bờ Rạ – he was insistent: it's a very old name, predating the French, it was even marked on the maps they brought. It was not named after any Frenchman; it's not a Sán Dìu name; in fact, he said, it's a Việt word. 'Bờ' is edge, 'Rạ' is stubble. When they harvested the rice in the old days, they used to cut the grain high off the stalk, which left a sort of bank of stubble. Or so he had heard the old men say, when he was young.

NAME

The place I thought of as 'new' Bờ Rạ, then, had three names – expressing associations of memory, experience, aspiration. 'Old' Bờ Rạ had, it appeared, just the one. If Ba was to be believed, it was named after a geographical feature, much like Đát Đá. But after getting back to Hanoi, I began to wonder quite how to interpret this former Party Secretary's story. Was it not possible that Ba's attribution of a 'stubble' meaning to the name Bờ Rạ was a later attempt, complete with the appropriate pronunciation of tones, to make sense of the Frenchman's name, 'Bông Bờ Rạ'? I returned to the archives. Two documents nudged me further in this direction.

The first was a decree, dated 19 June 1939, announcing the creation of two villages in the Công River valley, Bình Định and Văn Khúc. Brief geographical descriptions situated the newly created villages. In the case of Bình Định:

---

*   This is not an unusual process of popular renaming and existed even in Australia. The village of Major's Creek, where I wrote this account, was officially known as Elrington from its foundation in 1851 until the 1930s, after a Major Elrington. Usage, however, ensured that the popular name, Major's Creek, prevailed. Elrington, as a name for the village, is now unknown, although it persists as the name for the local pub. Interview with Brian Macdonald (Major's Creek, March 1998).

> To the north, the Công River,
> to the south, the forests of the 'Mạc Dynasty Citadel',
> to the east, the village of Bá Vân,
> to the west, the forests of Hồng Gia.[42]

This placed Bình Định in the present day commune of Bình Sơn, from which I had just returned (see Plate 16).

The inverted commas on the local, unofficial name 'Mạc Dynasty Citadel' gave me a clue to the interpretation of the second description, of the village of Văn Khúc:

> To the north, the village of Yên Thuận,
> to the south, the village of Lục Ba,
> to the east, the concession 'de Monpezat',
> to the west, the village of Bình Khang.[43]

The description situated this village slightly upstream of Bờ Rạ and the concession at Phúc Khánh. Its exact location was less important, however, than the description itself, which showed the existence nearby of a concession owned at some time by Monpezat. The concession, moreover, was used administratively as the name for a place. This was quite a normal procedure. Maps drawn by both French and Vietnamese bureaucrats in Thái Nguyên show that names of local origin were subsumed, in the eyes of the administration, by names from outside – usually names of planters. I noted that Monpezat's name was used in the decree to describe this place; I also observed that some official spellings of the name were unstable. Bi Ra appeared here, Bờ Rừc there. It began to appear that Ba's stubble explanation was not the whole story.*

The second document indicated that in the 1930s Monpezat's concession had a Vietnamese name. The document consists of two letters inside a folder entitled: 'Request made by Mr Trần Như Dũng, complaining that M. Olerte, purchaser of the concession De Monpezat, located at Go Gio, territory of the village of Yên Thái (Thái Nguyên) has seized the land which he cleared'. The first letter, hand-written and dated 10 March 1930, was a plea for justice from Trần Như Dũng, stating that he first came to Yên Thái in 1914, cleared some land, paid tax to the commune and could not understand 'why M. Olerte, purchaser of the concession de Monpezat, has come to seize my land'. The second letter, dated 22 April 1930, was signed by the recently appointed Résident, Alfred Echinard. Echinard was unsympathetic. He situated the disputed land as follows:

---

*   I researched no other examples of this naming process in Vietnam, although I heard of a number. In particular, a tantalizing couple of days before I left Vietnam, I was told that in Bắc Giang province there is a village named after a French planter, one Mr Hardy. Regrettably, I had no time to check this. I did, however, investigate a different example, in Myanmar. The resort of Ngapali beach is apparently named after an Italian who missed his home town of Naples (Napoli). In the local language, Arakanese, 'ngapali' is a type of fish. Interview (Thwandwe, July 1997). See Joe Cummings and Tony Wheeler, *Myanmar (Burma)*, Melbourne: Lonely Planet Publications, 1996, pp. 374–375.

The lands of the *xứ* of La Hô (or Na Hô) were sold to M. Olléac [*sic*] by the notables of the Yên Thái as communal land, in May 1918 ... The notables of Yên Thái committed the wrong of collecting taxes on lands which they had already sold ... There can be no doubt of the ownership of the lands under litigation 'Olléac property' ceded to M. de Monpezat.[44]

We should not allow ourselves to be distracted by Dũng's case here, and the conflicting legalities it raises, nor by the inconsistencies in spelling of Olerte/ Olléac and in timing of ownership by Monpezat/Olerte/Olléac (though we may wonder if Olerte was perhaps Hỷ's *Anh Phét*). The interest of this letter is two-fold. First, we may observe that the land under litigation, situated in close proximity to Bờ Rạ, had two Vietnamese names, both of which have since disappeared. A reason for the disappearance of the name La Hô may be surmised from the text. This was a *xứ* – an area of state land – and as such had not yet become a place, in any settled sense. Go Gio is obscure. Perhaps we should ask, rather, why the name Bờ Rạ persisted. How did the Frenchman's name survive the Revolution?

Trần Như Dũng's letter provides us with the elements of an answer to this question. He stressed that Monpezat/Olerte/Olléac did not make use of the land, and that he himself was able to farm it for years before the legal anomaly was discovered. The coming of the Depression, and consequent slump in plantation agriculture, makes it likely that Trần Như Dũng continued to use it for even longer. In any case, the plantation is not mentioned in provincial land registers for the 1930s. Perhaps the Sơn Cốt plantation acquired the land. But Monpezat clearly came nowhere near it. So that, in the minds of the people who lived there, Monpezat was nothing more than a name and, perhaps, a vague and distant threat of dispossession. The name was associated neither with ceding land to the French, nor with tax payment, nor with grain hoarding.* A place name recording the 'Amputated Owner' Garrigue's landholding at Yên Thuận, for example, could never have survived: the storming of his granary in 1945 to feed the famished was a memory sufficiently strong to reach the history books; name changes were integral to revolution.† By 1945 Bờ Rạ must have been a name bereft of associa-tion; an empty name among other names for the same place.

The lack of associations does not help us to understand how this spot came to be named after the Frenchman, although we may speculate that a process of informal administrative reference, enshrined in local cadastral maps and in usage contributed to this. How 'usage' settled upon Bờ Rạ, rather than La Hô or Go Gio, remains a mystery. But Bờ Rạ was an empty name, even the distant threat of foreign ownership dissolved by the revolution. And its very emptiness allowed

---

* Readers wishing to know more about Monpezat the man, rather than simply his name, are referred to the sources listed in note 45. André de Monpezat, managing director of SAFCAT in 1932, was a son of Henri de Monpezat, who died in 1929.

† This point is overlooked by Murzayev in his otherwise exhaustive study of Vietnamese place names. E. M. Murzayev, 'The Geographical Names of Vietnam', *Soviet Geography*, vol. 11, no. 10, 1970, p. 820. Vũ Ngọc Linh, *Lịch sử cách mạng tháng tám*, p. 108.

different people of different origins to invest it with their own associations. Ba and his ancestors, Sán Dìu people, gave it a Việt meaning. Loan, a Việt woman, saw it as a *minority language* name. An Englishman came to explore its associations with France.* Each gave Bờ Rạ an association with their Other in this relationship of contact – Việt with Sán Dìu, Sán Dìu with Việt. Associations of difference simply underline an absence of associations. The name Bờ Rạ is now little more than an echo, an echo that is perhaps appropriate to a place which no longer exists, except as misspellings on maps and as reminiscences.

Bờ Rạ does, of course, persist as an informal name for a place also known as Đát Đá and Tân Bình. It remains to be seen which of these three new names will survive, to animate, perhaps, the future research interests of a historian – Vietnamese, Japanese, English or other – in what remains of the Công River valley.

CONCLUSION

The Công River valley is but one part of the northern uplands which became home to Việt settlers from the Red River Delta during the twentieth century. Out of respect for the individuality both of the landscape and the lives of the people who inhabited it, I do not wish to say this was a typical part of the frontier. But it shared, with other parts of the uplands, common experiences of both policy and practice of migration and settlement. In the early decades of the century, the colonial authorities, here as elsewhere, sought to bring the land 'into value' and use it to relieve the delta's population problem. Sán Dìu and other groups moved down from the highlands bordering China. In mid century, famine and war brought refugees and resistance fighters to its forests. And, in the 1960s and 1970s, the Vietnamese government organized the settlement of this and many other valleys by people from the plains, for the purposes of economic construction and national defence.

Bờ Rạ's story ended, necessarily, in the late 1970s with the flooding of the lake. And this event coincided with the end of the Công River valley's historical significance as a frontier, an area of travel, settlement and contact between people of diverse origins. From the 1980s, the province of Thái Nguyên, along with the rest of the northern uplands region, lost its position as a destination of choice. Its people even started moving away. Some moved to the cities in search of work and education, but most moved south. In the 1990s a new upland frontier took shape on the plateaux of the central highlands.

Bờ Rạ's significance thus goes beyond the brief period during which it was the name for a shady spot in the Công River valley. It allows us to reflect, in microcosm, on the restructuring of the relationship between land and population which was taking place in numerous other places throughout Vietnam. The journeys people made to and through Bờ Rạ offer us multi-layered understand-

---

* We may only wonder what associations my Japanese precursor thought he could find in Bờ Rạ.

ings of this restructuring process, at a local level. But they also inform us of the ways by which this landscape was brought into value – both economic and cultural – and how these were historically defined. People travelling, settling and relating to one another around Bờ Rạ, whether – they were Việt or Sán Dìu, French or Australian, Japanese or English – used, viewed and expressed the land in different ways at different times. After the place disappeared, its site no longer certain, in these forms its shadows still linger.

NOTES

1   NAV1/RST 67478, SAFCAT to Résident in Thai Nguyen, 14 November 1932.

2   Pierre Gourou, *Les paysans du delta tonkinois: étude de géographie humaine*, Paris: Les Editions d'Art et d'Histoire, 1936, p. 220.

3   Gourou, *Les paysans du delta*, pp. 222–223.

4   V. H., 'Điều tra nhỏ: Một đồn điền lớn', p. 851.

5   NAV1/RST 67475, Résident in Thái Nguyên to RST, 22 February 1936.

6   NAV3/CQLNTQD 69(vv), 'Báo cáo tình hình hoạt động của các nông trường', 1959. See also Hoàng Quang Khánh, Lê Hồng and Hoàng Ngọc La, *Căn cứ địa Việt Bắc (trong cuộc Cách mạng tháng 8-1945)*, Thái Nguyên: NXB Việt Bắc, 1976, p. 317.

7   Tân Việt Hoa state farm, Report for the Fatherland Front, Thái Nguyên, 1968.

8   Ibid.

9   NAV3/BLD 383(vv), 'Báo cáo tình hình anh em miền Nam ở công trường, nông trường', 4 August 1956.

10 *Nhân Dân*, 'Các đoàn đại biểu các nước anh em thăm nhiều nơi ở Hà Nội, thăm Điện Biên Phủ và nông trường Tam Đảo', *Nhân Dân*, 10 September 1960, p. 1.

11 NAV3/BLD 383(vv), 'Báo cáo tình hình anh em miền Nam'.

12 NAV3/CQLNTQD 122(vv), 'Sổ thống kê các đồn điền của Pháp (ghi năm 1959)', Hanoi, 1959.

13 Charles Rémery, *Notice sur le repeuplement de la moyenne et haute région du Tonkin*, Hanoi-Haiphong: IDEO, 1908, p. 2.

14 Rémery, *Notice sur le repeuplement*, p. 2. For an early ethnography of the region, see Conrandy, *Les provinces du Tonkin: Thai Nguyen*, Paris: Maisonneuve, 1904.

15 NAV1/RST 55348, 'Monographie de la province de Thai Nguyen', 1901.

16 See Alfred Echinard, *Histoire politique et militaire de la province de Thai Nguyen, ses forces de police*, Hanoi: Imprimerie Trung Bac Tan Van, 1934.

17 Auguste Darles, *Les possibilités économiques de la province de Thai Nguyen et les conditions de son essor*, Hanoi-Haiphong: IDEO, 1917, pp. 7–8.

18 Darles, *Les possibilités économiques*, p. 7.

19 Ibid., p. 2.

20 Ibid.

21 Claudius Madrolle, *Indochine du Nord*, Paris: Librairie Hachette, 1932, p. 109.

22 See Jacques Marseille, *Empire colonial et capitalisme française, Historie d'un divorce*, Paris: Albin Michel, 1984.

23 Henri Cucherosset, *Le Tonkin est-il surpeuplé*, Hanoi: Imprimerie Tonkinoise, 1925, p. 26.

24 Darles, *Les possibilités économiques*, p. 6.

25 NAV1/GGI 7455, General Inspector of Labour and colonization to GGI, 1 August 1918.

26 Le Bo-Chanh, 'Notice sur la Province de Thai Nguyen', Thai Nguyen: unpublished monograph, 1933, p. 17.

27 Gourou, *Les paysans du delta*, p. 203.

28 NAV1/RND 3200, Mr Vũ Ưng (Cố Bản village) to Vụ Bản district mandarin (Nam Định), 4 September 1924.

29 NAV1/RST 67478, Phổ Yên district mandarin to Thái Nguyên mandarin, 31 October 1932.

30 Vũ Ngọc Linh (introduction), *Lịch sử cách mạng tháng tám tỉnh Bắc Thái*, Thái Nguyên: Ban Nghiên Cứu Lịch Sự Đảng, c1980, p. 114.

31 NAV1/RST 67498, 'Vœu No 37, Về việc di dân lên Thái Nguyên', 1938.

32 Alfred Echinard, 'Notice sur la province de Thai Nguyen', Thai Nguyen: unpublished monograph, 1932, p. 61.

33 NAV1/RST 67504, 'Mouvement de la colonisation à Thai Nguyen'. See NAV1/RST 74430, 'Rapport Economique, 1940'; L. E. Lotzer and G. Wormser, *La surpopulation du Tonkin et du Nord-Annam*, Hanoi: IDEO, 1941, p. 118.

34 Đoàn Thu, 'Ở một vùng chè', in Ministry of Labour, *30 năm sự nghiệp di dân khai hoang và xây dựng kinh tế mới 1961–1991*, Hanoi: Cục Điều Động Lao Động và Dân Cư, 1991, p. 62.

35 Đinh Trọng Hỷ, *Việt Bắc 30 năm chiến tranh cách mạng (1945–1975)*, Hanoi: NXB Quân Đội Nhân Dân, 1990, vol. 1, p. 81.

36 Ibid., p. 134.

37 Echinard, *Histoire politique et militaire*, p. 214; Vũ Ngọc Linh, *Lịch sử cách mạng tháng tám*, pp. 153–154. Hoàng Quang Khánh, Lê Hồng and Hoàng Ngọc La, *Căn cứ địa Việt Bắc*, p. 317; Trịnh Văn Đông, 'Báo cáo tổng kết công tác khai hoang xây dựng vùng kinh tế mới năm 1976–1981', Thái Nguyên: Bắc Thái Agricultural Office, 1982.

38 Trịnh Văn Đông, 'Báo cáo tổng kết công tác khai hoang'.

39 This is a typical presentation of the policy in official literature, and refers in this case to settlers at Phú Xuyên commune, Đại Từ district. Đoàn Thu, 'Ở một vùng chè', p. 62.

40 Le Duan, 'Political Report of the Central Committee of the Viet Nam Workers' Party, 5.9.1960' in *Third National Congress of the Viet Nam Workers' Party, Documents, Volume 1*, Hanoi: Foreign Languages Publishing House, c. 1961, p. 134.

41 Phạm Văn Đồng, 'Bài Ca Tây Bắc'. In Phạm Văn Đồng, *Tổ quốc ta, nhân dân ta, sự nghiệp ta và người nghệ sĩ*, Hanoi: Văn Học, 1969, p. 234.

42 NAV1/RST 67501, RST decree, Hanoi, 16 September 1939.

43 Ibid.

44 NAV1/RST 42402, Echinard to RST, 22 April 1930.

45 Gilles de Gantès, 'Coloniaux, gouverneurs et ministres. L'influence des Français sur l'évolution du pays à l'époque coloniale, 1902–1914', Paris: Doctorat d'histoire, University of Paris 7, 1994; Gilles de Gantès, 'Du rôle des "grands hommes" aux colonies: l'exemple d'Henri de Monpezat en Indochine', *Revue française d'histoire d'outre-mer*, vol. 80, no. 301, 1993, pp. 585–597.

Attached to the Village? The Policy and Practice of Migration, 1906–45

Figure 4: The French and the forest
The French faced the challenge of clearing the forest, settling migrants and creating new areas for crop production in the highlands. But other priorities stood in the way of this task, and by 1945 the forests became a refuge for revolutionaries led by Hồ Chí Minh.
Source: L. Girod, *Dix ans de Haut-Tonkin*, Tours, A. Mame, undated, p. 63.

OVERVIEW OF PART ONE

*I*n the three chapters that follow, we leave Bờ Rạ and travel downstream to the commune of Tân Cương, famous for its tea, before widening our focus to embrace the midlands province of Thái Nguyên as a whole, and the Third Military Territory (Hà Giang province) in the mountains to the north.* Case studies allow us to explore the relations between colonial policy and migration practice.

Chapter 2, 'Colonial Policy', catalogues French efforts to organize migration to the northern highlands – initially out of desire for development, but increasingly for fear of overpopulation in the delta. Attempts were sporadic; few succeeded. Their failure was explained in terms of cost, disease and a discourse of psychology. Bureaucrats saw peasants as inherently attached to their native soil, the land of their ancestors, the bamboo hedge of their village. Worries about demographic growth spurred them to overcome this psychology with organization. Few questioned the discourse itself.

Despite official attempts to organize settlement, the main motor of population movement under the French was spontaneous migration of families. Chapter 3, 'Colonial Practice', uses case studies to explore the dynamics of these movements. Processes of migration – how people moved – emerge in the settlement of Tân Cương (1919) and the application of a small concessions policy (1925) to the province of Thái Nguyên. Strategies of migration – why people moved – are examined. Evidence from the Red River Delta makes the case for a social dimension to departure decisions, in addition to the economic imperative. A survey of the province of Hà Giang (1938) is then used to show how a permanent migration often started as a temporary move. The chapter concludes with a typology of migration under the French.

Chapter 4, 'Peasants Attached to Villages', deals with the apparent paradox of a delta full of people and a low level of out-migration. Contemporaries explained this by reference to two key obstacles to settlement in the highlands: malaria and means of subsistence. There was a further obstacle, however. Peasants were indeed attached to their village, but not by their family or religion. The French administration required their incorporation into villages, making departure complicated and expensive. If the Vietnamese were attached to their village, the colonial government tied the knots.

---

*   What the French called the Third Military Territory is now Hà Giang province. For clarity, the modern name is used here.

2 *Colonial Policy*

Colonial Discourses

M onpezat owned land at Bờ Rạ. He never used it. At Cà Phê village, his plantation yielded coffee for a few years. Then he left it to *Anh Phét.** He had other interests, more profitable ones in the south. He let Thái Nguyên go.

His story was typical of French efforts at *mise en valeur* in the northern highlands. The planter could 'associate his interests' with Vietnamese tenants, people like Hỷ.† Or he could cut his losses and leave. Either way, there was no Eldorado in these hills. Within ten years of the first land grants, disgruntled articles started appearing in colonial reviews. One ambitious planter complained:

> Over the years millions have been swallowed up by these plantations, hundreds of verdant hectares have given birth to a good number of hopes. What remains? Nothing, or next to nothing. The colon is left the option of looking for some other project, if he has the means and the courage.[1]

The contemporary author of a doctoral thesis on the French concessions noted that 'wherever you come across a piece of waste land, you can say without much chance of mistake, that you are in the presence of a French concession'.[2] The administration was aware of the problem. The administration was also a model of bureaucratic inertia. In 1918, the RST proposed that these plantations, 'a weighty mistake we have inherited from the past', would have to be bought back.[3] Some land was returned after tenants intimidated French landlords. But most plantations were allowed to persist, passing from one undercapitalized owner to the next, farmed out to tenants. Alfred Echinard, Résident of Thái Nguyên during the 1930s, concluded that 'it is not too daring to say that European colonization has gone bankrupt'.‡

Echinard too was a Frenchman with ambitions. But he knew French planters would not fulfil them. Large scale-plantation could never turn Thái Nguyên from a forest backwater into the fully fledged farming province he desire: this required

---

*   See Chapter 1.

†   'Association of interests' was a euphemism for landlord–tenant relations.

‡   Alfred Echinard, 'Notice sur la province de Thai Nguyen', Thai Nguyen: unpublished monograph, 1932, p. 23. By 1939, less than a third of the 27,600 hectares of large-scale plantation was cultivated. CAOM/INF 2502, 'Etude de quelques remèdes au surpeuplement du delta tonkinois', M. de Carbon Ferrière, 6 June 1939.

Việt settlers. To Echinard's mind, their technology and knowledge of rice agriculture were indispensable, and he worked hard to bring them into the province. These exertions brought him into conflict with other departments in the administration notably the forestry service. A heated correspondence with a local forestry official, jealous of his forest reserves, led to the following outburst, where Echinard powerfully expressed his priorities for development:

> It suffices to travel on Colonial Road 3, towards Bắc Kạn, to note the poor quality of the forest which contains, here, no classified species. From the public health perspective, the existence of this scrub is particularly dangerous, and its removal is vital to ensure the good health of the settlers. But even from an aesthetic point of view, the sight of fields planted with paddy and tea would be far more agreeable to the eye than this form-less and tangled vegetation.[4]

He painted here an image of shaped and settled order, an order to replace the chaos of unbridled bush, with its threat to health and offence to good taste. The agent of Echinard's civilization was the Việt settler. The agenda, revealed in the reference to 'scrub', was to bring value where there was none. Poor forests, after all, pay no taxes.

There was nothing new about this. Since their conquest of northern Vietnam, the French tried to settle the hinterland with Việt people from the plains. The issue was subject to heated debate.

> Two conceptions took turns to enjoy the administration's favour. At times, it was con-sidered that colonization was an individual matter, and measures were taken to facilitate private initiatives. At other times, it was thought that colonization went beyond the realm of the individual and should be undertaken by the community.[5]

Thus an initial decree opened the northern highlands to free settlement by Việt families (1888). Its failure led to subsidized collective projects. In the highlands, Lieutenant Colonel Pennequin reported the failure of a project in the Điện Biên Phủ valley (1891): the settlers 'disappeared one by one'. In the midlands, General de Badens recruited poor people from Nam Định to live in Tuyên Quang (1895): 'straight after the first harvest, most of the workers disappeared, except an old, very old woman'. In the Mekong Delta, Inspector Ernest Outrey settled people in the province of Cần Thơ (1907): they all ran off, he said, because of their 'defective recruitment, communal authorities choosing unrecommendable people or people suffering from physiological miseries, to rid their villages of them'.[6] The project to settle former factory workers in Thái Nguyên (1919), as we shall see, was only slightly more successful.* Contemporary observers deplored the failure of these initiatives, and in the 1920s collective colonization was stopped. The 1888 law was reissued (1925), offering small concessions of land free of charge. Woodside described the policy succinctly:

---

* Workers (ONS) returning from France were offered land on the Công River. See Chapters 1 and 3.

Peasants who were willing to go to the highlands were allowed to claim small parcels of unowned land, of no more than five and one-half hectares, simply by submitting a petition and a map to the French province chief; by clearing at least twenty-five per cent of the lands within the first eighteen months of their settlement upon them; and by clearing and planting all these lands within a three-year deadline.[7]

As in 1888, few people took up the offer, and most land grants made in 1926–30 were regularisations of ownership by existing occupiers.[8]

The failure of project after project engendered, by the early 1930s, considerable scepticism about migration. This was reinforced in 1932 by a spectacular scandal on the island of Phú Quốc, where a whole colony of migrants from Nam Định 'had to be repatriated because the Phú Quốc Agricultural Company went bust in the great economic crisis'.[9] Việt people, it was thought, could not be moved. They suffered, apparently, from a 'pathological attachment to their native country'.* Theories emerged to explain this. They included the unhealthy highland climate, the cost of migration, the home-loving mentality of delta peasants. The mountains were indeed unhealthy – their mosquitoes were highly malarial. Moving was indeed expensive, for the administration and for migrant families. But the third explanation, popular among both French and Vietnamese, tells us more about perceptions of village society than it does about migration.

This was the so-called 'psychological explanation' for peasant immobility. As early as 1897, the Governor General of Indochina made reference to this 'indigenous population strongly attached to its native soil'.[10] And forty years later, the Résident Supérieur of Annam complained of 'the Việt people's attachment to their native commune'.[11] These ideas permeated the bureaucracy, and could be found under the pen not only of French officials but also their Việt counterparts. One member of the Sơn Tây province council of people's representatives felt that 'the Việt peasant only knows farming, he is attached to his village, which he will leave only with difficulty even if he suffers from poverty'.[12] The mandarin of the district of Ý Yên (Nam Định) was of the same opinion: 'pushed by hunger, they go to work in the mines and plantations, but they prefer to stay in the villages and live miserably'.[13] Even the most insightful and rigorous of intellectuals, Vũ Văn Hiền, was unable to see beyond these simplifications. There was an element of truth in his explanation for this perceived immobility, but like all such views it gave too much weight to generalized psychological factors, and not enough to socio-economic realities:

> The principal cause explaining the Tonkinese peasant's attachment to his village of origin is, in our opinion, purely psychological: used to living with the customs and traditions of his locality, he finds himself disoriented when he goes far; inside his commune, he has a well determined place; when he succeeds in whatever enterprise

---

* This was the view of Grégoire Khérian, Professor at Hanoi's Faculty of Law in the 1930s, as remembered by one of his former Vietnamese students. Khérian wrote opinions contrary to this one, but like many other observers, his ideas may have evolved during the debate on the issue. Interview, Paris, May 2000.

he undertakes, one of the first things he thinks about is to achieve a higher rank in the communal hierarchy. And this, within his village and not elsewhere. Why? Because that is where his ancestors rest, that is where his family members live, his neighbours and his friends; in a word, that is where he finds his 'public' and his 'judge'. Journeys frighten him because, among other risks, he exposes himself to the worst thing of all: the possibility of dying far from home.[14]

These essentialized notions of religious and family life created the image of a stagnant, immobilized society of villages. A process of bureaucratic simplification gave this perception the quality of discourse, a discourse of peasants irredeemably attached to villages. And this discourse had consequences. For the potential organizers of collective migration projects, it sapped the political will needed to overcome problems of malaria control and subsistence provision. And for potential free migrants, the structures of French rural administration, of which this was the legitimizing myth, locked them into their villages. As Breman observed on Java, 'the colonial state had an interest in a concentrated and permanently settled rural population'.[15]

In Vietnam, the colonialists did not create the village, as Breman imagined. Kleinen leaves us in no doubt that Breman took his conclusions too far.[16] The village did exist, but the colonial state established ideas and discourses around it. It mobilized to its own ends the 'well-worn cliché of "the Vietnamese village" as a somewhat "closed" society, "hidden behind thick bamboo hedges".'[17] These ideas were in themselves far older than the colonial state, and drew on the administrative tradition inherited by the French from the pre-colonial kings. The ideologies of Confucian government implemented in Vietnam since the fifteenth century had sought to attach people – through moral doctrines such as filial piety – to their ancestors, families and village communities, thereby ensuring the availability of a population providing taxes, corvée labour and military service to the state.[18] Under the French, the same ideology was backed up by new administrative structures, as we shall see in the next chapter. The result, for villagers who wished to leave, was disappointment and frustration.

The ideology did not emerge intact from contact with colonialism. There is no doubt that the religious and familial forms of Vietnamese society, when examined through the lens of European scholarship, took on some of the hues of western orientalism. The following lines were written by the geographer Charles Robequain:

It is the very structure and basic meaning of Việt society which keeps the native at home and stifles the spirit of adventure. In general this is true of all the peoples of the Far East; the age-old influence of Chinese civilization hardly decreased the native's attachment to the village of his birth. Ancestor worship, whether or not it is considered as a subdivision of spirit worship, is very strong in the Việt heart. Only the faithful observance of its rites can assure the happiness of both the dead and the living, whose deeply felt solidarity is expressed in a multitude of customs; for example, the 'hương hóa', a legal institution whereby an additional inheritance is provided, in principle, for the eldest son who is the priest of the cult. At least in certain circumstances, the cult gathers persons making up a family group much wider in scope than the family in

France. These rites cannot easily be performed far from the native's home where the written tablets are kept, or far from the soil where the bones of the dead lie buried. To abandon one's birthplace without hope of return seems like a sacrilege which will harm not only the individual and his family but the entire community.[19]

Robequain's explanation was interesting – and deceptive, as we shall see – for its capacity to draw categorical conclusions (in the last sentence) from vague statements of religious principle, rather than close observation of practice. Furthermore, his use of contrast with the French family concealed a certain similarity of suspicion with which certain 'traditional' types of French people could treat the 'uprooted', the 'unattached', the migrant. The following fictional description of post-1917 Russian émigrés indicates that Parisians with 'old-fashioned values' could hold the same view. 'For a Frenchwoman of the old school as was Miss Mesureux, that is to say inhabited more than anyone in the world by sentiment, *by the religion of the native land*, these people without a country became at a single stroke bodies poorly attached to the land, not quite human, whom one could not treat according to ordinary rules' (my emphasis).[20] Leaving home was blasphemy, an offence to good society.

This perspective was not exclusive to the French. As Robequain understood, it had roots in village philosophy and family religion. From these roots it found fresh life at the hands of many Vietnamese officials, in reinforcement of the values of their Confucian education – or that of their fathers – as well as nostalgia for the home and village they had left. Trần Văn Lý was the mandarin of the province of Haut Donnai, and observing the trickle of migrants moving to Dalat, observed that Việt people 'don't much like going far from their family and village. This is an atavistic character of the race, reinforced by moral precepts'.[21] One of these precepts insisted on the honourable nature of migration for education – the young scholar who succeeded in the Confucian exams and left for a job in the bureaucracy was feted on his return by the whole village. By contrast, those who left to earn an ordinary agricultural living were subject to insult: 'they would swear at each other, being proud of this, looking down on that, saying: don't leave the village'.[22] Those desiring to leave had to negotiate often violent social pressures to stay, while the mandarin – for whom departure was an ennobling experience – could wax lyrical on the morality and propriety of staying at home.

The idea that Việt people were immobile gave rise to an immobility of administration. A senior official voiced this inertia in 1918, saying that as a result of the peasants' attachment to their village, 'colonization will be destined for certain failure in Annam, and as a result it is useless now to find and divide into plots the land on which one would like to settle some of the returnees. The rather high cost of such an operation would be a pure loss'.[23] High costs and certain failure were prevailing bureaucratic perceptions of migration. Việt villagers were not to be moved.

Administrative inertia was not universal, however. There were those who, while maintaining that peasants were attached to their villages, made considerable efforts to detach them. Echinard was one of these. Provincial records show him mapping his province in the late 1920s, handing out small concessions in the early 1930s, setting up settlement colonies from 1936.[24] Energy earned him promotion – from Third Class Administrator when he came to the province, to First Class by the time he left. Even the Governor General, Jules Brévié, noted 'the activity and authority of Mr Echinard, who is one of the best Résidents in Tonkin'. He made these comments, moreover, in the context of a disciplinary investigation. Reading the file on this investigation, in the Ministry of Colonies archives at Aix-en-Province, I looked for clues as to who had complained about the Résident of Thái Nguyên. Why? I looked in vain. But I couldn't help remembering that forestry official whose letters I had read in Hanoi, helpless to protect his trees from Echinard's desire for development. Had he taken advantage of a passing commission of inquiry? If so, it was to no avail: Echinard's reputation, if anything, benefited from scrutiny. The inspector examined the budget, concluded that good governance creates enemies, and closed the case with a remark on his excellent migration initiatives.[25]

Echinard's small concessions policy won special attention. Brévié expressed his appreciation: 'the results – and this is all to the credit of the Résident, Mr Echinard, who has given himself to this project *for eleven years* – are already very considerable: more than 13,000 settlers on 6,100 hectares' (emphasis in original).[26] In the same year, Echinard revealed the cumulative total of settlers to be in excess of 15,000. Nearly 8,000 hectares had been granted to migrants. With an appropriate air of modesty, he noted his 'duty to continue and to seek to improve our methods' and looked to the future with optimism, declaring that, with 25,000 hectares of virgin land still available, 'some fine perspectives are opening up before us'.[27] Brévié shared this optimism. The previous year, as Governor General, he had presided with enthusiasm over the opening of a colonization Council.[28] And in 1942, as Secretary of State for Colonies, he approved the initial funding of five million piastres for a massive migration initiative throughout Indochina.[29]

THE OVERPOPULATION DEBATE

Brévié's efforts gained the gratitude of at least one settler in the south. In 1941, Bùi Văn Bích arrived from Thái Bình in Rạch Giá province in the Mekong Delta, and voiced his experiences in a poem of praise:

> To help the country's poor people,
> The government organized a migration
> Moving people there to make a living.
> Especially folk from Nam Định and Thái Bình could go.[30]

Brévié's enthusiasm and Echinard's activity indicate that some members of the administration were able to see beyond the prevailing discourse of peasants attached to villages.* Certainly the author of that poem didn't share the discourse, voicing his certainty that 'we won't lose our traditions, following the examples of

---

* Echinard paid lip service to the discourse but ignored it in his administrative actions. Alfred Echinard, *Histoire politique et militaire de la province de Thai Nguyen, ses forces de police*, Hanoi: Imprimerie Trung Bac Tan Van, 1934, p. 228.

Tiền Hải and Kim Sơn'.[31] Echinard and Brévié, however, were unusually imaginative administrators. Their colleagues were more cautious. Most officials expressed
pessimism or at best guarded optimism about the success of migration projects.
They made arrangements for migration if they were required to do so.

Their lack of enthusiasm was mirrored by many ordinary Vietnamese. Bùi Văn
Bích's views were far from universal, especially among people who had never
left the delta. Hùng told me that the French came to his village in the 1940s to
recruit the third son in each family for resettlement at Nam Tât Sơn, also in Rạch
Giá. He was selected, but managed to avoid going.* His reluctance may have been
informed by other stories from the south, as news in letters home, tales told by
returning migrants and memories of forced labour on mountain railways had created
an unhappy reputation for French migration initiatives. The plantations gave rise
to a sombre saying, that workers found it 'easy to leave, hard to return',† and in
1926, the harsh reality of life on the plantations – 'wholesale slaughter' as Lionel
Lotzer described it – sent ripples as far as the National Assembly in Paris. Many
delta villagers did not wish to leave their villages on colonial migration projects,
for the simple reason that they distrusted the French.[32]

French and Vietnamese at all levels of the administration regarded Việt farmers
as irredeemably attached to their villages. Many farmers, suspicious of French
motives, confirmed them in that opinion.

Echinard and Brévié did not lose heart before this inertia. It might seem, at first
glance, disingenuous to compare Echinard's energy in the 1930s with the caution
of administrators writing before the Depression. In the earlier period migration
responded to the administration's *mise en valeur* programme, in which calculations
about investment and returns were paramount. In the aftermath of the Depression,
however, it became involved in a debate about the direction of colonial policy at a
much deeper level, what one writer dubbed 'The Indochinese Economic Problem'.[33]
At the heart of this lay the question of overpopulation. As a result of the Depression, migration was evaluated, not only in terms of development, but also for
its success in facing up to the social, economic and political problems caused by
population pressure in the Red River Delta.

The comparison is valid, however. There was, in the 1930s, a new enthusiasm
for migration right to the top of the administration. Despite the atmosphere of
crisis, accentuated by uprisings in 1930–31, the political will to overturn the
attachment discourse never emerged. Individuals like Echinard disregarded it in
practice. In general, however, the debate about overpopulation was conducted
almost entirely within the paradigm of peasants attached to villages.

The terms of the debate were described in 1941 by the Résident of Nam Định,
Lionel Lotzer. A colleague of Echinard's, Lotzer wrote the following text in a
book on overpopulation: 'The symbolic bamboo hedge, limit to human settle-

---

*   Hùng's later experiences are related in Chapter 6.

†   Easy to leave, hard to return: *dễ đi khó về.*

ments, is overflowing; people build villages and farms in the middle of the paddy fields, further reducing the yields from farmland for mouths to feed'.[34] By the time he wrote these words, many French were losing faith in the 'bamboo hedge'. The hedge was a symbol of the security of Vietnamese villages, which were themselves the 'cornerstone' of Vietnamese society and a key element in the smooth functioning of French rule.[35] The delicate balance of political influence between the colonial administration and the village, what many French and Vietnamese saw as a self-regulating mini-state, found expression in a series of ill-fated reforms to local administration.[36] But the socio-economic basis of this relationship was under even more serious threat. The system of communal lands – object of much French admiration – was functioning poorly, if at all. The parcelling up of land, a factor of economic equality if not of efficiency, was yielding to large-scale ownership with losses on both counts. Individually these changes raised few eyebrows, and the existence of a large rural proletariat lacking any social insurance had long been taken for granted in the south. Taken together, however, they were seen as symptoms of an insidious threat to village stability in the deltas of northern and central Vietnam. This threat was usually called 'overpopulation'.

The northern delta's high population had been identified as a problem at the beginning of the century. But the Depression and political disturbances of the early 1930s concentrated French minds as never before. The election of the Popular Front government in 1936, and its reappraisal of the colonial project, ensured that overpopulation received almost obsessive attention. It was studied by officials, business people and academics in books and articles published in the late 1930s.[37] Businessman René Bouvier expressed vividly the mood of the time when he wrote: 'The problem of the growing overpopulation of the Tonkin delta is one of the most serious which France has ever had to face, throughout her colonising œuvre'.[38]

The most interesting account of the debate was published in 1937. A professor at the Faculty of Law in Hanoi tackled the controversy in clear and practical detail. His name was Grégoire Khérian, and a close look at the debate as he presented it allows us to understand the fears and priorities which shaped 1930s migration policy. Khérian's original plan was to look at the issue in a neat series of three articles – diagnosis, consequences, solutions. The first appeared under the title 'The Demographic Problem in Indochina'. It outlined a situation where population growth in the Red River Delta was creating a 'demographic disequilibrium' between north and south on the one hand, and between plains and highlands on the other. Of the twenty-two million people living in Indochina, seven million lived in the northern delta. A third of Indochina's people were packed into 2 per cent of its land – 14,500 km^2 of villages and paddy fields.* Khérian estimated this population to be growing at a rate of 100,000 per year, a perspective he qualified as 'horrifying'.[39]

---

* French Indochina covered 740,000 km^2; the Vietnamese territories (Tonkin, Annam, Cochinchina) 326,000 km^2. Of these areas, the Red River Delta made up 2 per cent and 4.5 per cent respectively. Pierre Gourou, *L'utilisation du sol en Indochine*, Paris: Hartmann, 1940, pp. 5, 8.

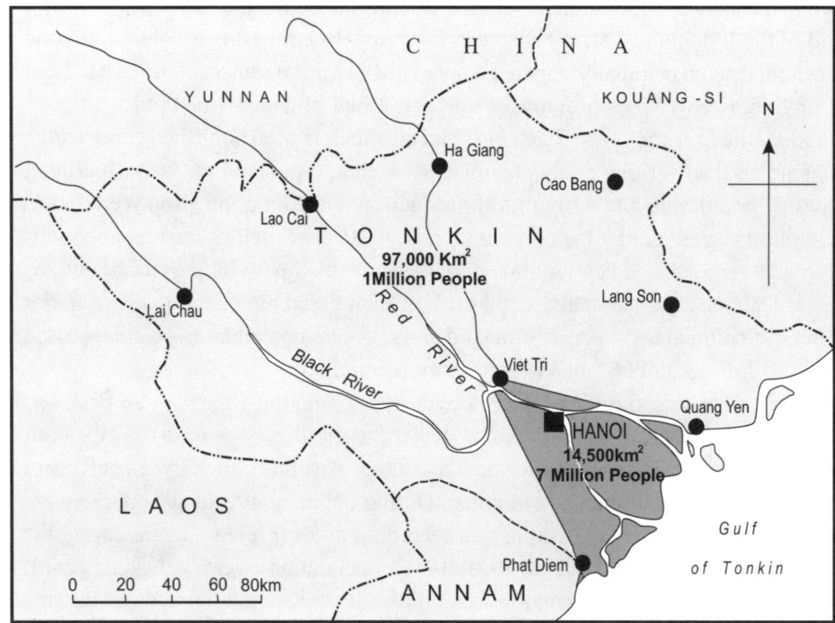

Map 11: Population distribution in northern Vietnam, 1934
Seven million people lived on 14,500 km2 in the Red River Delta, while one million lived on 97,000 km2 in the highlands. French analysts saw this as a major population 'disequilibrium'.
Source: Paul Bernard, *Le problème Economique Indochinois*, Paris: Nouvelles Editions Latines, 1934, p. 17. Redrawn by Lee Li Kheng.

The Red River Delta and its 'demographic disequilibrium' with the rest of Indochina is most clearly described in Ng Shui Meng's 1974 monograph on the colonial-era population. On disequilibrium, she quoted Gourou's estimate of the delta's average population density (430 people per km^2), noting that a 'a rural density of this magnitude was the highest to be found in all Southeast Asia'. By contrast, no more than 12 people per km^2 lived in the Tonkin highlands. On demographic growth, for Indochina she noted an annual average of 1.3 per cent in 1906–36 ('fairly low but not unreasonable') and 2.7 per cent in 1936–45 ('the figure might have been exaggerated'). Relative to this, Tonkin's population grew at the 'rather slow' rate of 0.9 per cent in 1906–36.[40]

We may conclude that the population was growing during the colonial period, though not perhaps at the spectacular rate imagined at the time. But the realities of population growth at the time faded in importance compared to the way they were perceived. While the overpopulation debate raised considerable passions, it was based on confusion about the basic questions of what the population level was, whether it was growing or not, and what 'overpopulation' actually meant.

On the actual population level, we can do no better than consult Smolski, head of the Indochina General Statistical Service. In a sobering article for anyone collecting data on colonial Vietnam, he noted in 1942 that a statistical office had been set up only twenty years previously, and that it had been abolished twice since.[41] The *Annuaire Statistique de l'Indochine* had nonetheless been published consistently, but Smolski had serious doubts about its contents, especially on the two crucial issues of population and agricultural production. Data on population were based on surveys carried out by the commune, relying on the 'intelligence and goodwill' of notables for its accuracy within a process of negotiation with provincial authorities.[42] Data on production also depended on such variables. Given that two major sources of colonial tax revenue – on land and registered population – were assessed from this information, Smolski found it most unreliable.

There were two further problems with the population figures. The first was that communes were only required to declare the numbers of *inscrits* – or adult males aged 18–60 registered for tax. This figure was multiplied by a coefficient to include women, children and old men. During population 'estimates' these were calculated by the provincial authorities according to local research, and during the five-yearly 'counts' (1921, 1926, 1931, 1936), declarations were 'adjusted according to an estimated per capita consumption of salt'.[43] Khérian pointed out that the choice of this coefficient (which fluctuated from three to eight from province to province) was a subjective, even arbitrary affair. Smolski concurred.[*] Population statistics thus became similarly arbitrary. But it was on the second problem, where the statistician disagreed with the demographer, that we get to the heart of the overpopulation debate.

This was the rate of growth. Khérian, distrusting the official figure of 21.5 million as the 'real' population of Indochina in 1931, felt comfortable with its use as 'an order of magnitude'. In a masterful display of the demographer's numerical agility, he compared the 'orders of magnitude' for 1921, 1926 and 1931 to show that while the size of the 'real' population was unknown, the 'legal' (ie. male, tax-paying) population had grown rapidly. To avoid the use of coefficients, he then generalized the more accurate birth rate figures for Cochinchina and the city of Hanoi, to the whole colony. His conclusion was that the population of Indochina was growing at a rate of 300,000 people per year (1.4 per cent), and the Red River Delta at 100,000 per year (1.5 per cent).[44] Without citing the professor directly, Smolski was sceptical, remarking coolly: 'It is regularly stated that the population of the Tonkin delta is growing by 100,000 to 120,000 individuals annually. This assertion requires verification.'[45] Gourou, who had estimated at 65–100,000 the 'surplus' population of the delta, admitted that his work sat on

---

*   Much variation was imputed to 'a very high number of absentees who have gone to seek a means of existence in Cochinchina, Laos, Cambodia and in the big centres of Tonkin'. CAOM/INF 2502, 'Etude de quelques remèdes au surpeuplement', 6 June 1939; Khérian, 'Le problème démographique', no. 1, p. 8; Smolski, 'Progrès et incertitude', p. 113.

very shaky foundations: 'the statistics are established with too much fantasy to give an exact idea of the evolution of the population.'[46]

When French observers wrote about overpopulation, they had little idea of what the population was, let alone what it was 'over'. Moreover, most writers failed to develop a concept, however vague, of optimum population against which the current population should be regarded as excessive.[47] And the one commentator who did come up with a measure of sorts – basing the idea of optimum on the amount of labour required for sustainable cultivation – concluded that the Red River Delta was not overpopulated. At times of 'important works' – harvest, dyke repair – villages hardly had enough labour.[48] In retrospect, it seems clear that there was a high and growing population in the Red River Delta in the 1930s. But to contemporaries, overpopulation was much more a euphemistic way of talking about immiseration. On this question there was little disagreement among French commentators: the people were poor and getting poorer.

Khérian himself employed a poverty study to measure overpopulation. Describing demographic measurement tools – nutritional density, minimum and optimum population levels – as excessively subjective, he pointed instead to indices of poverty, including undernourishment, underemployment and land shortage. These were concrete signs of an excessively high population. Their implications were alarming. Unrelieved poverty was dangerous, for its victims certainly, but also for the social stability of the colony.

The threat to rural stability gave the debate a strong sense of crisis. As Khérian put it:

> The crowds of people living in the Tonkin delta and northern provinces of Annam are in a sense doomed to poverty, failing a sizeable attenuation in the demographic disequilibrium, *sine qua non* condition for the improvement in living standards of the masses. As a result Progress – economic, social, physical or even cultural – is held back or even fundamentally prevented, and the worsening of the demographic malaise is likely to have tragic repercussions in the political sphere. Is it not in the midst of a starving and ignorant humanity that professional agitators and other troublemakers find the maximum of opportunity to carry off the crowds?[49]

Hồ Đắc Khải, a minister at the Huế court, expressed the same fear in 1938:

> The rhythm of births is much higher than that of deaths and there is no need for a prophet to predict that within fifteen years, we risk being overwhelmed by this starving multitude. *No political or social force will be able to resist such a tidal wave.* (emphasis in original).[50]

The overpopulation crisis fuelled extensive debate in the late 1930s. While communist leaders doubted the honesty of French concern for the people's welfare, colonial authorities worried about the opportunities opening up for 'communist intrigues'.[51] The problem was well understood – overpopulation caused poverty and poverty caused insurrection. Disagreement surrounded the solutions. In the midst of this, Khérian was due to publish his second article on the consequences of overpopulation. But he withdrew it at the last moment, because of the controversy. The third article, on solutions, was printed in its place, prefaced with the following apology:

> Numerous readers have kindly asked us not to put off until next July the problem of Remedies, [a] *problem of burning topicality* which is the subject of bitter controversy, while we are in general agreement as to the noxious effects of the delta's over-population. These circumstances have led us to *pass directly* to the analysis of possible solutions to the Indochinese demographic disequilibrium. In periodical publications, the author proposes but Topicality disposes. (emphasis in original).[52]

Topicality, in this case, demanded remedial action. Khérian's diagnosis spawned solutions to match. He saw the problem in terms of a population too large for the available resources. His solutions centred on ways to reduce this imbalance. He proposed measures to raise production and reduce population.

The article is fascinating for the range and vitality of solutions proposed. To raise production, physical limits would be overcome by means of dykes and dams, irrigation, canals and drains. Economic limits would also be overturned. To problems of tiny subdivided rice fields, unproductive communal lands and debt, Khérian proposed the abolition of communal land, cheap state provision of credit, and co-operatives. He also declared in favour of industrialization, a controversial position at the time.[53] To reduce population, he rejected 'direct solutions' – emigration to Madagascar and birth control – in favour of 'indirect solutions' involving internal population redistribution. While free migration was encouraged, Khérian felt that a 'bold policy of controlled collective colonization' was the only feasible means of rapid population reduction.[54]

This was an upbeat article, exuding faith in the search for solutions. But the optimism did not survive to his third article, 'The ravages of Indochinese over-population' (1938). In the intervening months his faith had been shaken. A passing mention of Malthus gave a clue to this, but it became clear in his attitude to birth control. He had rejected this idea in the previous article, observing a tendency of birth rates to fall only when living standards rise. He had relied instead on eco-nomic solutions – socio-economic reforms and migration – to raise the standard of living. But he came now to the following emphatic conclusion: 'It should be stated and repeated without respite that no remedy will be able bring any lasting improvement to the lives of the people of the Delta if they do not consent to bring a minimum of discipline to their production of men'.[55] Khérian now saw economic solutions as futile. He had retreated into 'neo-Malthusianism'.

This position was even more remarkable than his previous optimism. It was unfashionable and quite possibly illegal. Promotion of contraception and abortion, known as neo-Malthusianism, had been banned in France in 1920, by a birth pro-motion law aimed at making up for population losses during the Great War. Under French assimilation policy, the ban was extended to Indochina in 1933. Khérian called this absurd, but did not condemn the policy in France, although his silence may have owed much to the celebrated 1927 prosecution of Henriette Alquier for criticizing 'pronatalism'.[56] In any case birth control was rarely advocated in Vietnam.

Hồ Đắc Khải voiced the common view, which opposed the use of education programme teaching people to have 'fewer children to feed them them better',
because low demographic growth might weaken Indochina's defensive capability
(against Chinese, Japanese, Hindus). Above all, he doubted the people would
cooperate. He would have been surprised to learn that, while he was marshalling
his arguments, a district official in Nam Định was penning a proposal for 'mass
education to limit the birth rate'.[57] This was not lost on Khérian who noted that a
contraception policy, requiring female education, would entail investment in rural
schooling. For him to have voiced views so clearly ahead of their time was a sign
of desperation, a position of extreme ill-caution when all else seemed doomed.

Khérian had perhaps been overcome by late-colonial pessimism, described
by Fourniau as a 'colonial impasse'. This view holds that by the late 1930s the
colonial administration found itself in a corner. Political initiative was lost to the
communists; economic growth was lost to the Depression; poverty was causing
social dislocation.[58] Colonialism faced crisis in Indochina. Khérian and his contemporaries did not formulate the failures of the colonial project so neatly. But
there was a pervasive sense of things going fatally wrong. And in the absence of
reliable data, each commentator brought his own theoretical fantasies to bear, to
explain the situation and show how it was irredeemable.

Smolski founded his pessimism on the poor quality of the data, useless as a
basis for rational social or economic policy.[59] I initially imagined him as a cautious
statistician, unwilling to enter the fray without all the numbers. But an earlier
article put his pessimism in a rather different light. In 1929, he claimed that the
population of northern Vietnam was not growing at all and was, indeed, in a
'stationary state'.

> If it is confirmed that the population of these regions is limited in its extension by the
> impossibility of rapidly increasing, for the moment, its resources, no definitive advantage
> may be expected from the struggle undertaken by the administration against infant
> mortality and endemic disease, as the population gained thereby will be able to subsist
> only by means of greater and greater feats of frugality, and will find itself more than ever
> at the mercy of poor harvests and floods, always terrifying. It is advisable, therefore,
> in the current economic situation, to be extremely liberal in the granting of author-
> izations of recruitment, even to distant colonies, which will be followed by a general
> improvement of the welfare of the whole population, of those who stay as well as
> those who leave.[60]

We could not imagine a more succinct application of the ideas of Thomas Malthus.
The Depression can only have confirmed them for him.

Gourou's pessimism, by contrast, was based on too much data. Every page of
his 1936 book was 'an overwhelming witness to the misery which is rampant
throughout Tonkin'.[61] *Les Paysans du delta tonkinois* was indeed a monumental
work. For its vast details of socio-economic information, it still commands respect
today. But the work's very scale constituted both its strength and its weakness. It is
as if, by writing down this complex society of villages, Gourou created a towering
house of cards, fragile and immobile. As he put it in a later work:

> It is certain that the peasants of Tonkin are miserable and their misery must be alleviated.
>
> But the task is a delicate one, because the Tonkin Delta is an old country with limited but complex resources, where long years of human activity have forged a subtle and many-branched economic organism.
>
> We cannot cut into the flesh here, and any attack to one of the branches could have the most grievous consequences for the whole.[62]

We could not imagine a more depressing application of the theories of geographical determinism.

Pessimism was not completely universal. Paul Bernard described the conclusion to Gourou's *Les Paysans du delta tonkinois*, as 'a veritable abdication of the intelligence which we cannot accept'.[63] He was appalled by paragraphs of the book which denied the possibility that, one day, Vietnamese peasants might enjoy a higher standard of living. He rounded too on those who quoted Marx and Malthus, as well as the anti-capitalist ideologies of the Popular Front government. He offered instead a variety of economic plans for remedial action. By the early 1940s these centred around a programme of state-led industrialization.[64] But in the late 1930s industrial capitalism in Indochina was an idea before its time. It threatened to undermine crash-crippled French economic interests and risked to destabilize Vietnamese village society. Bernard was ignored.

The Popular Front's philosophy of social reform excluded the luxury of pessimism. It took refuge instead in politically safe policies of rural reform which were remarkable only in their conservatism, their distance from anything that smacked of substantial socio-economic change. The 'colonial impasse' was articulated by Justin Godart after his 1937 official visit from Paris:

> The Sûreté may well arrest all the communists, but that will not change the fact that the peasants' existence is of an inhuman precarity, that in overpopulated regions they do not eat their fill, and that, without external stimulation, they naturally aspire to improve their condition. We must not wait for demonstrations which, with the current police state mentality which dominates in Indochina, we will put down with machine guns. Profound agrarian reforms are needed. Peasant life must be based on small landownership and handicrafts.[65]

This combination of urgency (of discourse) and conservatism (of action) in the face of colonial crisis left the Popular Front little room for manoeuvre. In the implementation of a 'policy of the peasantry', centrepiece to a strategy of 'conservative reform', the solutions proposed had to be based on traditional practices.[66] In their respect for peasant tradition, indeed, lay the entire extent of the 'profound' nature of these reforms. But migration was an ancient practice in Vietnam, and as a result bureaucratic scepticism towards it began to crumble. Migration became, as Brévié's enthusiasm showed, among the most attractive options in the limited range available. It had the sanction of history. It preserved and reproduced the village, rather than breaking it up. It achieved immediate and tangible results which could be counted, in terms of numbers of families moved, numbers of new villages created. It might even make the administration a profit in tax. In the face of the overpopulation threat, migration policy underwent re-evaluation.

OVERPOPULATION AND MIGRATION

One symptom of this was that the first doubts began to be expressed over the attachment discourse. The evolution of Paul Bernard's thinking is illustrative:

1934: The Tonkinese, people say, does not like to expatriate himself. He is attached by tradition, by religion, by family spirit to the land which nourished him, to the village his ancestors inhabited. He fears the life which awaits him in different climates and prefers to vegetate in poverty where he was born rather than seek adventure elsewhere. No doubt there is an element of truth in this affirmation. But have we done anything up to now to encourage the Tonkinese to emigrate? Absolutely nothing.[67]

1937: We have no doubt greatly exaggerated the attachment of the Tonkinese to his village.[68]

Bernard's opposition to the discourse was rhetorical. Khérian's was more closely argued. In 1937, he told his readers that 'the majority of French in Indochina and many Vietnamese too show considerable scepticism as to the possibility of fixing, on the lands of the South, large numbers of men from the Delta'. Sceptics, he went on, invoked two arguments: the failure of past attempts and the psychology of the peasants.* The first was due to bad management: 'strongly directed', there was no reason why migration could not work. As for the second, while Khérian did not doubt the existence of sentimental and ritual ties to the village, he represented the villager above all as a pragmatist:

What have we generally offered to the poor '*inscrits*' of the commune? To work on a distant land as a *day labourer* or to accept the hard toil of a miner. But it is with difficulty that people resign themselves to leave their village *for that!* (Emphasis in original)

He gave examples of villagers who left home in hope of a better life: soldiers and subaltern officials, domestic servants. 'The Tonkinese', he noted, 'are not as fundamentally resistant to expatriation as people say.'[69]

One or two members of the administration took these ideas seriously. In 1938, the Nam Định mandarin published his analysis of the problem in the *Bulletin Economique de l'Indochine*:

Why then do these '*nhà quê*' pile up on this land which is too narrow and constantly exposed? It is not so much because they are attached to the tombs of their dead, to the pagoda and the bamboo hedge of their village or to their share in the communal rice land. It is quite simply because their material and physiological poverty does not allow them to go elsewhere.[70]

---

*   He referred specifically to the ONS project at Tân Cương in Thái Nguyên (1919) and the Phú Quốc fiasco (1932).

Such remarks, however, were no more than cracks in the edifice. In the same issue of the *Bulletin Economique de l'Indochine*, a fellow official reiterated the peasant psychology discourse.[71] Few bureaucrats found any need to question it. They spent their energy devising organizational forms to overcome the perceived psychology. Commissions were established. There was the Commission of colonization (1932);[72] the Commission on Tonkinese Immigration to Cochinchina (1935–36);[73] the Superior Council on the colonization of Indochina (1938);[74] and the Indochinese Federal Council (1941).[75] Discussions in commissions led to conclusions. And the consensus that emerged was that Việt people were better moved in villages rather than in families. Timeless village atmospheres and structures should be reconstituted, names, charters and tutelary spirits reproduced, identical communal houses constructed.[76] Attachment could be transferred from one village to another, without political disruption. The collective migration model was back in vogue.

Machines of French planning got to work. The 1932 discussions came up with the idea of 'settlement colonies', imitations of pre-colonial collective colonization.* The 1935–36 Commission invented the 'Tonkinese Box', an area of the Mekong Delta reserved for settlers from the north.[77] The 1938 Council proposed settlement projects inspired by the Dutch experience on Java and Sumatra as well as a colonization Office to organize them.[78] The 1941 Council resuscitated the Tonkinese Box which, the Governor General observed, 'has remained unused up to now'.[79] Inspiration was drawn from Mussolini's colonization of Libya, for the settlement of the entire highlands by a thousand French coffee planters each employing Việt workers 'capable of being transformed overnight into soldiers'.[80] The plateaux of Bolovens and Djiring, the foothills of Biên Hòa and the island of Phú Quốc were all earmarked for similar development. And even the province of Dak Lak, closed until the late 1920s to settlement by Việt or French, was to welcome its first contingents of people from the plains.†

Some of the plans were carried out. Three hundred railway workers settled their families in the hills of Khánh Hòa in 1936.[82] Some 3,000 Nam Định people moved to the midlands region of Tonkin in 1938–39,[83] and 100 Nam Định families moved to grow coffee at Blao (Bảo Lộc) in 1940–41.[84] But others never materialized. By 1942 the military coffee farm project was reported 'stagnant', the Tonkinese Box had filled up with settlers from the south, and the Office of colonization was still awaiting creation, 'due to a lack of personnel and funding'.[85] Personnel may have been a problem. The small successes obtained seem to have

---

*   These were the *colonies de peuplement*, approved by the decree of 20 March 1936. Services du Protectorat, 'Activité colonisatrice', p. 767.

†   The closure of Dak Lak was instituted by the Résident there, Léopold Sabatier. Hickey's statistics show twenty Việt people in Dak Lak in 1921 and 4,000 in 1940. Gerald C. Hickey, *Sons of the Mountains: Ethnohistory of the Vietnamese Central Highlands to 1954*, New Haven and London: Yale University Press, 1982, pp. 304, 439. For perspectives on colonial debates on Việt settlement in the central highlands, see note 81.

owed more to the energy of a single official, Lionel Lotzer, than to a concerted policy effort. With fifteen years' experience of the problem, Lotzer was recommended for the job of heading the colonization Office. His career suggests, however, that it was not so much personnel as political will that was lacking. Despite Brévié's approval of funding, the Colonization Office was never established. In August 1945, Lotzer was running Indochina's Credit Office.[86]

CONCLUSION

Policy on migration during the colonial period generated great energy of thought and debate. Energy that was inspired by the imperatives of development and the threat of overpopulation. But, in practice, little was realized. Even in the 1930s the urgency of land hunger in the delta was insufficient to create the political will to carry out more than a few experiments. Journalist Nghiêm Xuân Yêm put it in a nutshell:

> We have seen how the job of moving people to clear land in the mountains and middle region of the north and the provinces of the south has forced those holding power in our country to scratch their heads and tire out their brains for ages. Still today we are waiting for results; who knows when they will come?[87]

Nghiêm Xuân Yêm wrote these words in 1944. The colonial administation had almost run out of time to produce the results he sought. The following chapter will attempt to determine what was happening in the countryside while he was waiting.

NOTES

1 A. Bichot, 'Où en est la colonisation agricole au Tonkin', *Revue Indochinoise*, 15 February 1905, p. 197.

2 J. Morel, *Les concessions de terre au Tonkin*, Paris: Pedone, 1912, p. 2. See also the detailed analysis in Ta Thi Thuy, 'Les concessions agricoles françaises au Tonkin de 1884 à 1918'. Doctorat d'histoire, École des Hautes Etudes en Sciences Sociales, Paris, 1993.

3 NAV1/GGI 7455, RST to GGI, 2 November 1918.

4 NAV1/RST 67485, Echinard to RST, 3 July 1939.

5 Services du Protectorat, 'Activité colonisatrice du Tonkin – Colonisation dans la haute et moyenne région du Tonkin', *BEI*, 1938, p. 757.

6 CAOM/GGI 57168, Lt-Col. Pennequin to GGI, 22 November 1891; Charles Rémery, *Notice sur le repeuplement de la moyenne et haute région du Tonkin*, Hanoi-Haiphong: IDEO, 1908, pp. 9–10; NAV1/RND 3175, 'Note sur la colonisation des terres incultes de la Cochinchine par la main d'œuvre tonkinoise', Lt-Governor of Cochinchina, Saigon, 15 October 1907; Tran Van Thong, 'Mémoire sur la colonisation indigène en Indochine', *BEI*, 1938, p. 1123.

7 Alexander B. Woodside, *Community and Revolution in Modern Vietnam*, Boston: Houghton Mifflin Company, 1976, p. 154. For an example of such a map, see Plate 8.

8 NAV1/RST 67504, Echinard to Lotzer, Résident in Nam Định, 1 March 1939.

9 Tran Van Thong, 'Mémoire sur la colonisation indigène', p. 1123. NAV1/GGI 254, Governor of Cochinchina to GGI, 9 November 1932.

10 NAV1/RST 29792, Paul Doumer to Governor of Réunion, 27 March 1897.

11 M.G., 'Le paysannat en Annam', *BEI*, 1938, p. 13.

12 CAOM/Guernut 28, petition by Nguyễn Văn Đinh and Nguyễn Hưu Sinh, Sơn Tây province representatives (*nghị viên*), 1938.

13 CAOM/Guernut 92, 'Réponse au questionnaire no. 1C' by Duong Thieu Chi, mandarin at Ý Yên district (Nam Định), 16 April 1938.

14 Vu Van Hien, 1939, *La propriété communale au Tonkin*, Hanoi: IDEO, 1939, p. 170.

15 Jan Breman, 'The Village on Java and the Early Colonial State', *Journal of Peasant Studies*, vol. 9, no. 4, 1982, p. 226.

16 Jan Breman, *The Shattered Image: Construction and Deconstruction of the Village in Colonial Asia*, Dordrecht, Holland: Foris Publications, 1988. John G. Kleinen, 'The Village as Pretext: Ethnographic Praxis and the Colonial State in Vietnam'. In Jan Breman, Peter Kloos and Ashwani Saith (eds), *The Village in Asia Revisited*, Delhi: Oxford University Press, 1997, p. 384. See also Jeremy Kemp, *Seductive Mirage: The Search for the Village Community in Southeast Asia*, Amsterdam: Foris Publications, 1988.

17 Kleinen, 'The Village as Pretext', p. 384.

18 Insun Yu, *Luật và xã hội Việt Nam thế kỷ XVII-XVIII*, Hanoi, NXB Khoa Học Xã Hội, 1994, pp. 135, 304.

19 Charles Robequain, *The Economic Development of French Indochina*, London: Oxford University Press, 1944, p. 62.

20 Joseph Kessel, *Nuits des princes*, Paris: Editions Lidis, 1953 (first published 1927), p. 14.

21 CAOM/Guernut 96, 'Réponse à l'enquête sur les migration intérieures', 10 May 1938.

22 Interview, Thanh Hóa, February 2000.

23 NAV1/GGI 7455, RSA to GGI, 24 July 1918.

24 NAV1/RST 67504, Echinard to Lotzer, 1 March 1939.

25 CAOM/INF 2502, 'Vérification de M. Echinard', Inspector Pruvost, 6 July 1939. Born in 1883 in the Alps, at St Clair sur Galaure, Isère, Echinard arrived in Indochina in 1913. NAV1/RST 28373, 'Bulletin individuel de notes: M. Echinard Alfred Jean Baptiste', August 1914.

26 CAOM/INF 2502, 'Vérification de M. Echinard', 6 July 1939.

27 NAV1/RST 67504, Echinard to Lotzer, 1 March 1939.

28 Jules Brévié, 'Discours prononcé par M. le Gouverneur Général J. Brévié à l'ouverture de la session (séance inauguralee du Conseil Supérieur de la Colonisation de l'Indochine)', *BEI*, 1938, pp. 716–719.

29 CAOM/INF 2282, Brévié to Decoux, 20 June 1942.

30 Phạm Viết Hoàng, 'Bài ca di dân', *Tạp Chí Xưa & Nay*, no. 56, October 1998, p. 35.

31 Phạm Viết Hoàng, 'Bài ca di dân', p. 35. The settlement of Tiền Hải and Kim Sơn is related in Chapter 9.

32 NAV1/RND 3179, mandarin in Nam Định to the Résident there, 5 October 1926; Lotzer and Wormser, *La surpopulation du Tonkin*, p. 25; Le Fèvre, Georges, *Démolisseurs et Bâtisseurs*, Paris: André Delpuech, 1927, p.13.

33 Paul Bernard, *Le Problème economique indochinois*, Paris: Nouvelles Editions Latines, 1934.

34 L. E. Lotzer and G. Wormser, *La surpopulation du Tonkin et du Nord-Annam*, Hanoi: IDEO, 1941, p. 12.

35 Robequain, *The Economic Development*, p. 46.

36 Woodside, *Community and Revolution*, pp. 137–142; Nguyen Van Huyen, *La civilisation annamite*, Hanoi: Direction de l'Instruction Publique en Indochine, 1944, p. 81.

37 These included: Paul Bernard, *Nouveaux aspects du problème économique indochinois*, Paris: Fernand Sorlot, 1937; René Bouvier, *Richesse et misère du delta tonkinois*, Paris: Imprimerie André Tournon et Cie, 1937. Pierre Gourou, *Les paysans du delta tonkinois,*

étude de géographie humaine, Paris: Les Editions d'Art et d'Histoire, 1936; Grégoire Khérian, 'Le problème démographique en Indochine, Esquisse d'une politique démographique en Indochine': *RIJE*, extract from nos 1–2, Hanoi: IDEO, 1937. Bureau International du Travail, *Problèmes de travail en Indochine*, Geneva: Kundig, 1937; Robequain, Gourou and Lotzer dealt extensively with the issue in books published respectively in 1939, 1940 and 1941. Eight journal articles were written on the question (1936–37). They are listed in Bureau International du travail, *Problèmes de Travail*, p. 222, n. 1.

38 Bouvier, *Richesse et misère*, p. 65.

39 Khérian, 'Le problème démographique', no. 1, pp. 11, 38. See Map 11.

40 Ng Shui Meng, *The Population of Indochina*, Singapore, ISEAS, 1974, pp. 19–20, 23, 33. For further comments on population statistics in the colonial period, see the Appendix.

41 T. Smolski, 'Progrès et incertitude de la statistique en Indochine', *RIJE*, no. 17, 1942, p. 96.

42 Smolski, 'Progrès et incertitude', p. 108. For evidence of mistaken and manipulated declarations and calculations, see NAV1/RND 3135, 'Procès Verbal de la conférence des mandarins tenue à la Résidence le 21 février 1919'; NAV1/GGI 7456, GGI to Inspector of Colonies, 3 April 1923.

43 Ng Shui Meng, *The Population of Indochina*, pp. 16–18.

44 His independent estimate matched Gourou's. Khérian, 'Le problème démographique', no. 2, pp. 7–8, 25–26. Gourou, *Les paysans du delta*, p. 198.

45 Smolski, 'Progrès et incertitude', p. 110.

46 Gourou, *Les paysans du delta*, p. 179.

47 On the notion of optimum population, see Roland Pressat, *Population*, Baltimore: Penguin, 1970, p. 103.

48 Gourou, *L'utilisation du sol*, p. 431–2. NAV/RND 3175, Résident in Nam Định to RST, 20 March 1908.

49 Khérian, 'Le problème démographique', no. 1, pp. 4, 19–22.

50 Ho Dac Khai, 'Contribution à l'étude de la colonisation annamite', *RIJE*, no. 7, 1938, p. 414.

51 Truong Chinh and Vo Nguyen Giap, *The Peasant Question*, Ithaca, New York: Cornell University Southeast Asia Program, 1974, p. 73; Lotzer to Director of Economic Services, 22 November 1941. Lotzer's confidential memorandum found its way into a copy of his book (*La surpopulation du Tonkin*) at the National Library in Hanoi.

52 Khérian, 'Le problème démographique', no. 2, p. 5, n. 1.

53 Grégoire Khérian, 'La querelle de l'industrialisation de l'Indochine', *RIJE*, no. 8, 1938, p. 630.

54 Khérian, 'Le problème démographique', no. 2, p. 30.

55 Grégoire Khérian, 'Les méfaits de la surpopulation deltaïque', *RIJE*, no. 7, 1938, p. 503.

56 Khérian, 'Le problème démographique', no. 2, p. 31, n. 2. Khérian, 'Les méfaits de la surpopulation', p. 502–505. Siân Reynolds, *France between the Wars: Gender and Politics*, London: Routledge, 1996, p. 8–20. Ho Dac Khai, 'Contribution à l'étude', p. 415.

57 CAOM/Guernut 92, 'Réponse au questionnaire no. 1C destiné au fonctionnaires indigènes', Phạm Trọng Thiệu, Nam Trực district (Nam Định), 18 April 1938. CAOM/ AgFOM 229, 'Le malthusianisme peut-il résoudre le problème de la surpopulation?', *Việt Báo*, 27 November 1938.

58 Charles Fourniau, 'Les années 30 et l'impasse coloniale en Indochine'. In Justin Godart, *Rapport de Mission en Indochine, 1er janvier - 14 mars 1937*, Paris: L'Harmattan, 1994, p. 20.

59 Smolski, 'Progrès et incertitude', p. 102.

60 T. Smolski, 'Note sur le mouvement de la population en Indochine', *BEI*, 1929, pp. 99, 102.

61 Bernard, *Nouveaux aspects*, p. 159.

62 Gourou, *L'utilisation du sol*, p. 431.

63 Bernard, *Nouveaux aspects*, p. 159.

64 Andrew Hardy, 'La politique économique française en Indochine de 1944 à 1948', Maîtrise d'histoire, Université de Paris 7, 1991, p. 76–92; Andrew Hardy, 'Les opinions de Paul Bernard (1892–1960) sur l'économie de l'Indochine coloniale et leur actualité', *Revue française d'histoire d'outre-mer*, vol. 82, no. 308, 1995, p. 304.

65 Godart, *Rapport de mission*, p. 102.

66 Pierre Brocheux and Daniel Hémery, *Indochine, la colonisation ambigüe, 1858–1954*, Paris: La Découverte, 2001, p. 268.

67 Bernard, *Le problème économique*, p. 287.

68 Bernard, *Nouveaux aspects*, p. 72.

69 Khérian, 'Le problème démographique', no. 2, p. 38 and n. 1.

70 Tran Van Thong, 'Mémoire sur la colonisation indigène', p. 1118.

71 M.G., 'Le paysannat en Annam', pp. 11–29.

72 Services du Protectorat, 'Activité colonisatrice du Tonkin – Colonisation dans la haute et moyenne région du Tonkin', *BEI*, 1938, p. 759.

73 NAV1/RST 76109, 'Procès verbal de la Commission – Immigration Tonkinoise en Cochinchine', two sessions, held on 14 October 1935 and 2 June 1936.

74 Brévié, 'Discours prononcé', p. 716.

75 NAV1/GGI 1367, 'Le problème démographique, surpopulation et colonisation', December 1941.

76 Services du Protectorat, 'Activité colonisatrice', p. 774. See also NAV1/RST 76109, Lotzer to RST, 27 September 1936.

77 CAOM/INF 2502, 'Contestations foncières dans le Transbassac', M. de Carbon Ferrière, 2 May 1939; NAV1/RST 76109, 'Procès verbal de la Commission', 14 October 1935.

78 L. Réteaud, 'Office Indochinois de Colonisation et de propriété paysanne', *BEI* (1938), pp. 720–737.

79 CAOM/INF 2282, Decoux to Brévié, telegram no. 4512, 29 April 1942.

80 CAOM/AgFOM 229, 'Mille soldats-colons du Tran Ninh au Lang Bian. Le défense de l'Indochine et la question du café', 1938.

81 For perspectives on colonial debates on Việt settlement in the central highlands, see Emile Kemlin, *L'immigration Annamite en pays Moï, en particulier dans la province de Kontum*, Qui Nhon: Imprimerie de Qui Nhon, 1923. Paul Lechesme, *L'Indochine seconde, régions Moï (Kontoum-Darlac)*, Qui Nhon: Imprimerie de Qui Nhon, 1924. Oscar Salemink, '*Mois and Maquis:* The Invention and Appropriation of Vietnam's Montagnards from Sabatier to the CIA'. In George W. Stocky Jr. (ed.), *Colonial Situations; Essays on the Contextualisation of Ethnographic Knowledge*, Madison, Wisconsin: University of Wisconsin Press, 1991, pp. 243–260.

82 Louis Marty, 'Plan et modalités de l'action administrative locale pour déterminer l'installation progressive de colons indigènes dans les moyennes et hautes régions des pays annamites', *BEI*, 1938, p. 743.

83 CAOM/INF 2502, 'Etude de quelques remèdes au surpeuplement', 6 June 1939.

84 CAOM/INF 2282, Decoux to Brévié, telegram no. 4503, 29 April 1942. See also Lotzer and Wormser, *La surpopulation du Tonkin*, p. 85.

85 CAOM/INF 2282, Decoux to Brévié, telegram nos 4506–4507, 29 April 1942.

86 CAOM/INF 2502, 'Etude de quelques remèdes au surpeuplement', 6 June 1939; CAOM/AgFOM 218, 'Rapport sur la situation de l'office du crédit populaire au 31 December 1946'.

87 Nghiêm Xuân Yêm, 'Điều tra nhỏ – Những tá điền', *Thanh Nghị*, no. 55, 26 February 1944, pp. 64–67.

Colonial Practice

A closer look at the practice of colonial migration will give us a sense of how French official 'head scratching' related to events in the country-side. One of the better known failures of colonial migration policy was the settlement of three villages downstream from Bờ Rạ on the Công River. One of its lauded successes was Echinard's handling of the small concessions policy in Thái Nguyên. An examination of two case studies will serve as an introduction to the dynamics of migration in colonial Vietnam, showing how policy interacted with practice. Two questions will be addressed: first, how did people come to move from the delta to the highlands? Second, who were these people?

FAILURE AT TÂN CƯƠNG

During the First World War, Vietnamese were transported to France to work in military factories. Their return in 1919, and subsequent resettlement in Thái Nguyên, received a great deal of attention in the 1930s, during the debate on migration and overpopulation. The former workers, known as ONS,[*] were offered land on the left bank of the Công River, in reward for their contribution to the French war effort. A few accepted the offer; fewer settled there. The affair was publicized as an example of the inherent impossibility of moving Việt people away from home. Even Echinard managed to slip in, among the reasons for the failure, 'the attachment of Việt people to their native soil'.[1] To understand this episode, how-ever, we need to look carefully at how this reputation was produced. There are two sources of written information: correspondence generated by the project in 1919 and commentaries on its perceived failure in the 1930s. Close examination shows how the failure was constructed over a fifteen-year period. A mediocre project became a 'resounding failure which people like to blow out of all pro-portion'.[2]

First let us look at how this project was portrayed in the 1930s. Echinard described how the former ONS workers settled beside the Công River:

---

[*] ONS, *Ouvriers non-specialisés*: non-specialized workers.

The Administration's efforts were made on free land in Đồng Hỷ district, Thái Nguyên province. This was the former Metman concession which had been returned to state ownership, about 1,500 hectares. The road was upgraded and the site is only 12 km from Thái Nguyên [town].

138 lots were delimited, of an area varying between 10 and 15 hectares (…)

The Administration spent 40,000 piastres. In 1923, 108 lots had been *mis en valeur*. The Résident encountered considerable difficulties; one settler passed his lot to another; another installed a tenant; another purely and simply gave it away; another sold the buffalo and tools and disappeared.

Finally, on 1 July 1933, on the 138 lots, there remained forty-five former ONS settlers in three villages; with the indigenous people (Nùng and Thổ [Tày]) they occupy forty-eight lots, about 160 hectares.[3]

Two years later Gourou published his geography of the delta. The results obtained by Catholic missionaries maintained in the settlement of the Cháy River valley provided a point of comparison with government attempts at colonization in the Công River area.

Official colonization enterprises have not obtained the same success; the most important was attempted in 1919, to fix to the land some Tonkinese workers who had been sent to France during the war and who were now returning. At a favourable site in Thái Nguyên province, 138 families were given vast areas of land easy to transform into irrigated ricefields; the villages of Tân Cương, Tân Thành, Thịnh Đức (Túc Duyên canton, Đồng Hỷ district) were thus created. Besides the land, the settlers also received free tools, seeds, draft animals and a sum of 6 piastres, plus 1 piastre per child. Most settlers had no intention of making the necessary effort: left to themselves, not subject directly and daily to an authority capable of constraining them and helping them, many abandoned their land, which they sold on the cheap to Nùng people from Lạng Sơn; in 1932 there remained only forty-five official settlers. This attempt at colonization cost a total of 40,000 piastres, too large a sum for the size of the settler group, and totally excessive for the low number of settlers definitively established.[4]

Both writers accepted as the measure of failure a high drop-out rate – calculated at 67 and 49 per cent respectively. But what was the original purpose of the project, against which success or failure should be measured? In 1919, the RST established two objectives: 'to restore agriculture on abandoned land and to fix to the soil, by making them landowners, a certain number of Việt people having assisted with National Defence.'[5] Gourou and Echinard focused exclusively and rather bureaucratically on the second: the people. The investment was in 'official settlers', so the settlers' refusal to fix themselves made the project a failure. Agriculture there was, however, restored. This was a failure of migration, but not of development. Echinard should have known this. His own province mandarin wrote a monograph in 1933 stating that these three communes paid tax on more than 600 hectares of land (Echinard thought only 160 were *mises en valeur*).[6] Some of these hectares were farmed by Nùng migrants from Lạng Sơn (Echinard thought they were locals). Others were settled by Việt people from the delta. In terms of one original goal, development and taxation, the project succeeded. This achievement was a result of bureaucratic action. Bureaucratic assessment, however, led to a failure, not of development but of understanding.

The controversy deflected attention from the main story of this land's development. The three communes were settled by the ONS workers, certainly, but other people joined in as well. These other people contributed a great deal to the area's development, as I discovered when I visited Tân Cương. My field notes relate what an official there told me about the commune's foundation:

In 1922 Tân Cương was set up. Before that there was a village called Ỷ Na. Then some people went to France during World War One, and received land in Tân Cương. They came from all over the delta: Hà Nam, Nam Định, Thái Bình, Hải Dương, Hanoi, Hà Đông. Nine men went to France as soldiers. This official is himself descended from a soldier in the French army who originally came from Chèm village, Từ Liêm district, Hanoi. His grandfather went to France. His grandfather, who died in 1946, came up later than the others though, not in the first group. In that group there were only nine people. After that they brought other people up to work for wages.

Who were these 'other people'? To find out, I asked the official to take me to one of Tân Cương's constituant villages. The inhabitants of Nhà Thờ village were repairing their church when we arrived.* A group of older men took time off to talk. They were Catholics, all originally from Xuân Trường district (Nam Định). They arrived here before the revolution. We spent a couple of days discussing the foundation of their village. The official left us to it. My field notes again:

The Church was built in 1924. People cleared the land, set up the village and built the Church straight away. They came to work for wages at first, then were able to ask for land to farm as tenants. Landlords were all Việt people. These landlords had worked for the French, and got land here. They lived here. They used the labour of migrants from the delta to clear the land. They had large areas of land – one village, one landlord. The landlord's name here was Sergeant Nam. The landlords were from the same village and called them up to Tân Cương. They had been soldiers working for the French. They would then get land and bring poor people up to work on it. These people would then follow the soldier up.

There were twelve men who had served as soldiers for France. People came up to work for wages, then settled and called their family. There were small landlords and big landlords – many levels and sizes. The people all worked for wages. At home they could only work for wages, but here they could settle on land.

There was some confusion at Tân Cương over the 'official settlers'. Had they been soldiers or workers? Were there nine or twelve of them? But everyone agreed that the official settlers called their family and neighbours up to work and settle. One of these was Thân, who arrived at Nhà Thờ with his family in 1936.† I wrote down his story:

Mr Thân's father went to France as a soldier. But after one year (of a three-year contract) he missed home so much he came back. Because of this, he did not qualify for a land grant, and had to work for wages. If he had stayed on, he would have got land.

When his family first arrived here (one or two years after Thân's father), living with the landlord during the first year was no problem. They were close relatives. Big

---

*   Nhà Thờ means Church.

†   See Prologue.

landlords who had worked for the French gave the land to smaller people, and they shared it out to even smaller ones. Thân's family lived with the smallest kind of landlord, who fed the family in exchange for labour.

These stories point to two conclusions. The first is about French bureaucrats. Echinard was aware that other people – wage labourers, tenant farmers – were involved in settling the land. He published this information. But even Echinard, more open than most officials to the creative potential of migrants, missed their significance.* The official settlers had indeed liquidated their land and run off. But these were men who had spent years overseas. They were no longer farmers. French capital had made them rich, giving them the freedom to make choices. Focusing on these men, Echinard, Gourou and others cried failure. In so doing, they overlooked the poorer farming folk from their home villages who came to find work on the official settlers' land.

This leads us to a second conclusion, about processes of migration. Land ownership in Tân Cương, where people cleared, shared, sold and planted the land in a complex set of tenant relations, was highly chaotic. But from the chaos we may identify two types of settler. There were men who had worked for the French, and used their privilege to obtain land and capital. And then there were relatives, neighbours, highlanders – 'other people' – who cleared the land in exchange for food and wages. In Thân's view there were different layers of landlord, different layers of landless. This pattern did not respond to the French administration's desired outcome. But, ironically, it was a result of policy. French land grants facilitated both the settlement and its accompanying chaos.

SUCCESS IN THÁI NGUYÊN

To understand more clearly how this process worked, let us broaden the space of our analysis from the commune of Tân Cương to the whole province of Thái Nguyên. Let us return to Echinard's celebrated success in attracting free migrants into the province. Thái Nguyên was a popular destination at this time. In Đồng Hỷ during the 1930s and 1940s, Thân said there was a steady stream of migrants from the delta. In Định Hóa, I was told that 'many Việt people came from Hưng Yên, a few from Nam Định; they came to trade and work for wages'. In Đại Từ, Kim described a village head from Thái Bình bringing people up in the 1930s and settling on land now under the Núi Cốc lake. People came from Lạng Sơn too. At Tân Cương, Thức told of the arrival of Nùng and Tày people. Across the Công River at Bình Sơn, Ba's neighbour Khoa spoke of the comings and goings of the Sán Dìu: 'wherever our fathers liked to go and live, they'd just go'. This qualitative evidence of rapid population increase should allay any suspicion of the official

---

* In the initial project plans, however, the possibility of this sort of chain migration was envisaged. See NAV1/RST 67469, Rivet, General Inspector of Labour and colonization, to GGI, 1 August 1918.

statistics, which indicated an annual growth rate of 5 per cent.* When Echinard arrived in the province in 1929, there were about 80,000 people there. Eleven years later, just before leaving he boasted: '125,000 live in ease. The misery of the delta is unknown'.[7] We may be sceptical, but his boss was impressed. Not at the rate of growth *per se*. No, what pleased the Governor General was the image – Woodside called it a 'European hallucination' – offered by these figures: the image of frontier smallholders carving plots of farmland from the forest, planting crops to feed their families.[8]

Echinard left Thái Nguyên in March 1941. His successor may too have believed in these pioneers. But not for long. The first signs of something wrong came in May, with the arrival in the province of a Mr Godot. Godot was an inspector from the Land Registry Department. His visit revealed technical irregularities in the management of the small concessions. His report implicated the province registry official and, indirectly and in guarded language, Echinard himself.[9] By the end of the year the new Résident had uncovered other irregularities. They amounted to systematic and widespread fraud. Some of the 'pseudo-settlers' were wood traders. Others were 'men of straw' working for rich people building up land holdings. Still others were children, servants, relatives of the rich. There were false names and 'imaginary people'. The consequences were quite contrary to the spirit of the original legislation: deforestation without development, concentration of property, migration within the province rather than from the delta. New controls were instituted to eliminate abuses and protect the true pioneers. The new Résident sought 'a return to order'.[10]

The purpose here is not to work out the justice of allegations of impropriety against Echinard: that concessions had been granted 'with the primary objective of raising the total to an impressive level'.[11] Echinard certainly wanted to make his career in Thái Nguyên, he may also have wished to make a buck, but he wanted to leave his mark there as well.† His successor too no doubt. In this affair we can see two competing conceptions of bureaucratic order, at loggerheads over the same land.

For Echinard, deforestation and corruption were part and parcel of development. Any means of attracting settlers was good enough. The main thing was that the people should come, that taxes should rise. Echinard was aware of 'abuses'

---

*   For information on the population of Thái Nguyên, Thái Bình and Nam Định, see the Appendix.

†   The 1939 investigation into Echinard's administration criticized spending on photographs ('truly excessive'), all-night street lighting ('is it really necessary?'), flowers for the prison and football shirts for the local team. Echinard retorted that photos publicized improvements, flowers improved prisoners' daily life in winter, etc. The inspector concluded that 'it is impossible for an active Résident, desiring to leave a useful trace of his passage – and Mr Echinard is of this sort – to obtain results without breaking the budgetary rules.' The complaints that provoked the investigation were blamed on 'some solid enmities' acquired 'during his long stay in Thái Nguyên'. I could find no trace of Echinard after he left Thái Nguyên, nor any evidence of his financial status on departure. The war would hindered a return to France in 1941. CAOM/INF 2502, Report, Pruvost, 'Vérification de M. Echinard', 6 July 1939.

and did not regard them as such. In 1939 he dismissed a complaint that relatives of one Đào Văn Dương, a land registry official, had obtained concessions:

> Such a situation seems perfectly normal and in no manner contrary to the spirit of the decree of 13 November 1925 on small concessions. The latter have only been able to expand so rapidly in Thái Nguyên as a result of the constant promotion which, under my impulsion, all inhabitants of the province have been making to people around them, to their relatives and acquaintances in the delta.[12]

In his dismissal, he deflected attention away from Đào Văn Dương and other officials onto the whole population. Was this simply a nimble defence, or did he genuinely consider officials to be no different from other Vietnamese? Did he fail to identify the conflict of interest? Archival sources cannot answer these questions directly. But such documents as exist suggest that, whatever his ulterior motives, Echinard intended to 'do something' with the land and people under his charge. His was a pragmatic order. His corruption, if such it was, was the corruption of development.

His successor served a legalistic order. Development was not happening according to plan. The spirit of the legislation was violated.[13] His concern was not with the number of small concessions granted, but with the number planted with crops; not with the number of people who settled in the province, but with the number of formally registered concessionaries from the delta. It irked that forest destruction was bringing no profit to the administration. As he set about restoring his vision of order, he pointed out its fortuitous timing, as economic difficulties caused by the Pacific War reduced the demand for land.

> The right course seems to me, then, not of course to end a movement of which the principle is excellent, but to control it tightly and take all necessary precautions to avoid abuses: a new policy which, moreover, happily coincides with a considerable reduction – due to the present situation – in the recent infatuation for small concessions.[14]

Both men, however, insisted on fixing people. For Echinard, it didn't matter how. For his successor, the European hallucination was strictly applied. But while bureaucrats defended their respective orders, the situation in their province was far from orderly. One report on Thái Nguyên bluntly stated: 'We have to choose between the forest and the Việt people'. But this was a perspective of development. Its author failed to perceive that one form of chaos yielded not to order, but to another form of chaos. Forest, a 'formless and tangled vegetation', was giving way to the chaos of frontier.[15]

While chaos allows no rigid categorizations, in economic terms we may generalize these frontier folk into two types: people looking for land and people looking for work.

Economic Dynamics of Migration

Vietnamese looking for land found it easily in Thái Nguyên. Some, like Nguyễn Thị Năm, bought former French plantations. Some, like Echinard's officials, collected small concessions. Some took up the French offer of land grants to 'benefactors', migration leaders expected to recruit teams of workers and manage the settlement of the the land.[16] During my visits to Thái Nguyên, I was unable to meet any of these entrepreneurs but I heard a lot about them. Their former tenants remembered them well. A landlord in Đồng Hỷ, named Mỹ, left particularly vivid memories: 'Mỹ was from Nam Định, got rich and bought a lot of land. He had a lot of land. He was very cruel, beat people, forced people to do corvée. He took high taxes and rents. He made people hide their harvest from him'. How did he get the land? 'He'd worked for the French'.[*]

I was not the only foreign visitor to the province to find it hard to meet former landlords. American communist Joseph Starobin, who came here in 1954, also contented himself with hearsay about them. The story of one couple, related by a Việt Minh cadre, made a particular impression. He described what he had heard about their 1951 trial. They had made a fortune in Haiphong, before accumulating several hundred hectares in Thái Nguyên. Their land encompassed two communes. Starobin learnt that this couple, charged with usury, exaction and taxing the very leaves of the forest, as well as some thirty murders, were punished with five years' imprisonment. How did they make their fortune? 'They speculated in supplies to the French'.[17] In Đại Từ, there was no indication of how the village head I heard about came to organize the labour of a group of settlers from Thái Bình, but he met a similar fate. I was told in hushed tones: that he had been 'sent to prison'. In Đồng Hỷ, however, Mỹ was not so lucky.

These landlords had various ways of finding the labour to work the fields. Some recruited directly in the delta, like the village head from Thái Bình.[†] But moving generally involved a process of short-term wage work and village/family networks. Hỷ's father came to work on Monpezat's plantation in this way, having relatives at Cà Phê village. Thân's father came to work for relatives in Nhà Thờ village. Both men worked for a year or two before bringing up the family, limiting the risk of failure. The same strategy was described at a village in Định Hóa district. Đại was born in the delta but moved to this spot, Tân Tiến village, when he was 6 years old. There was a plantation there, owned by a Tày family, migrants from Lạng Sơn in the early years of the century. Đại had relatives (*anh em*). I asked what he meant by *anh em*. 'My mother's younger brother', he explained. 'He came up here before, with twelve other families from the village, to look for work'. Đại's parents, once word got back to the village, decided to follow. In 1936, the whole family made the move. They left just one elder daughter at home, to 'keep the house'. She joined them later.[‡]

---

* According to Thân, a former tenant. Interview (Thai Nguyen, October 1996).
† According to Kim, the Party Secretary's wife at Tân Thái. See Chapter 1.
‡ At the time of the family's move from Đao Lý commune (Lý Nhân district, Hà Nam), this plantation was called Tân Quảng. Interview (Thái Nguyên, January 1997).

Đại's story highlights a basic dynamic of Việt migration. An initial move was made by a member of the family or village. If this move succeeded, others would come and join. Hỷ, Thân and Đại were all children of second-stage settlers, as indeed were seven of the twenty pre-1945 settlers I interviewed in Thái Nguyên. The networks were very effective. But how was the initial move made? The variety of experiences thrown up by documents and interviews painted a messy picture, which seemed at first to defy any sort of coherent pattern. But discussions at Định Hóa district People's Committee, the evening after speaking to Đại, gave me a clue to their interpretation. There were two types of migrant, cadres said. Some people came from the delta after a disaster; they were usually very poor. Others came only for a short time. They were harvesters supplementing a delta income, live-in labourers sending their wages home, traders after a profit, soldiers on a temporary posting. Most planned to go home; some decided to stay.

Disasters caused considerable migration from the Red River Delta. In the eighteenth and nineteenth centuries, natural disasters and war had regularly provoked migration.[18] In 1922, a provincial mandarin recognized that the pattern continued to recur: 'With each catastrophe, hundreds of thousands of men emigrate and fall into poverty'. He proposed sweeping rural reforms to prevent it.[19] A French military officer, General Pennequin, made similar observations, and became, in the process, an early exponent of moral economy. In 1913, he characterized calamity in Vietnam as a fundamentally collective phenomenon:

> No one dies of hunger in Indochina. Every man who comes into the world is assured his material life, including procreation. He belongs in advance to a village, to the family of an *inscrit*. The latter feeds him, the former fulfils his moral needs, maintaining the pagoda where he prays. Solidarity provides everything. Which means that poverty here means public calamity, result of a shared misfortune: flood, tidal wave, banditry, seizure of property by Chetty or Chinese [moneylenders], or alas European administration.[20]

Pennequin's list of calamities was comprehensive: rising waters, social disorder, endebtedness from usury and taxation were disasters shared by many families in the Red River Delta.

Floods both from sea and river were a constant hazard. Floods were the reason given in 1924 by Nam Định peasants requesting resettlement to Thái Nguyên and Sơn Tây. Recruitment to the Hồng Gai mines fell that year, from the usual 16,000 to 1,000, as people were repairing the dykes. Floods chased people from Nam Định again in 1926; from Bắc Ninh, Hải Dương and Bắc Giang in 1937; from the whole delta in 1945.[21] In Tân Cương, Thân recalled the arrival of the refugees:

> In 1945 so many people came up from the famine. Mainly from Thái Bình and Nam Định. They begged, many died, when arriving, when leaving. People gave them work and rice at first, but then there were too many, we couldn't feed them. There were just too many.

Floods were regularly blamed on the administration, none more so than that of 1945. One account of the events of that summer closely associated the rising waters with insurrection, implying that Nature itself approved of the revolutionary turmoil.[22]

Social disorder presented a further danger. The *grande piraterie* of the late nineteenth century devastated the highlands and delta alike, as roaming bandits ruined many local economies. Localized rebellions periodically disrupted midland provinces until 1945.[23] Among the many dangers this presented, for women there was abduction for marriage in China. One official explained that during the French conquest: 'some pretty women from the delta [were] carried off by the Black Flags when they fled'. They were abandoned in Hà Giang during the retreat, stayed and married locally, later calling 'their brothers and sisters to come up and trade there'. But cross-border commerce in women continued long after the French conquest.* For men, the main fear was getting dragged into the fighting. French demands for labour to help the army were greatly resented, as Minh related when I interviewed him in Thái Nguyên. In 1918, his father had portered for troops fighting Đội Cấn, but fled his home town of Tiền Hải (Thái Bình) rather than go a second time, ironically ending up near where Đội Cấn himself sought refuge, at Phúc Khánh village near Bờ Rạ.[25]

Debt from taxation and the high price of credit caused major land loss for delta farmers.[26] By 1938, most land in Thái Bình belonged not to large numbers of smallholders, but to thirty moneylenders.[27] Trần Huy Liệu explained:

> Days of hunger between crops, years of harvest loss, seasons of tax collection, moments when there aren't enough tools or seeds, as well as occasions when contributions are due for feasts, for mandarins, for weddings, for funerals, for religious ceremonies, all these are times when peasant labourers have to mortgage their fields and pawn their houses to borrow money; these are the times when they lose their fields to creditors (...) The colonialists and feudalists pushed the peasants down one of two roads: one was to stay in the countryside, farm the fields and pay rent to a landlord; the other was to leave the village and sell their labour to the capitalists.'[28]

Pennequin predicted this: 'In this way, little by little, if we don't restore order promptly, our native subjects are being and will be dispossessed of their best land and will become, if they don't want to be errants and vagabonds, the agricultural serfs of these foreigners, new owners of their property'.[29] The people who picked up the land were Chinese, Indians and Việt landlords in the village.[30]

Calamity, then, might not only come by sudden event, a broken dyke, an armed attack. Disaster by debt was a slow and silent affair. A storm or corvée labour demand was often the last straw to families made vulnerable by borrowing. Pennequin recognized this but did not allow it to undermine his idealized image of community, of villagers held by village institutions in relationships of gentle mutual aid. Unlike other parts of Indochina, however, in the Red River Delta the lenders were not foreigners, but fellow villagers. And while the Chinese and Indian

---

* Việt women were still being sold across the northern border in 1999, when officials at Quảng Lợi commune (Quảng Xương district, Thanh Hóa) reported that more than ten young women of the commune were now living in China, with no means of return. Interview (Thanh Hóa, September 1999). For sources, see note 24.

sought profits, Việt lenders were after the land.[31] Pennequin understood the process whereby people fell into the hands of the usurers. A major expense, a short-term loan, a high rate of interest, a new loan to pay the interest: 'this is a ruined family'. His focus on foreigners and the corporate village blinded him, however, to the fact that there was nothing collective about this. James Scott in his *Moral Economy of the Peasant* was similarly distracted. He argued that the lack of north–south migration in Vietnam during the colonial period was evidence of village solidarity placing restraint on village lenders and landowners.* In fact, one villager inflicted ruin upon another. It was a lonely family calamity.

In the 1930s Pennequin's thinking was by no means outdated. But there was a growing understanding of the importance of the family – rather than the corporate village – in economic life. This was reflected in a fashion for collecting household budgets. Comparison of these budgets allows us a glimpse at the process of calamity on a family by family basis.

In 1939, a family of five described by Nguyễn Văn Huyên received most of of its annual income (204 piastres) from a small plot of communal paddy land and the sale of vegetables, pigs and poultry. But they could not live on this. Family members – husband, wife, and two teenage sons – had to go off for short periods of wage work. One third of the family's annual income came from this work.[32]

In 1938, the Guernut Commission recorded the budget of a family of three living in Nam Định. One fifth of its income of 100 piastres came from the sale of vegetables and paddy from a tiny plot, the rest from milling rice. They spent 114.70 piastres, mostly on food. An official noted: 'It appears clearly that this family is going into debt and has no hope of escaping from poverty. In most such cases, paddy fields are lost and each family member goes off elsewhere to get a job as a servant or coolie'.[33] Rice milling was a common practice among poorer families in Nam Định, being an itinerant profession practised between harvests.[34]

The Guernut Commission flinched from investigating peasants 'designated by local residents as truly poor'.[35] In 1937, Trường Chinh and Võ Nguyên Giáp had no such qualms. They estimated that if a male farmworker could find six months' work, he would earn a third of what he needed to spend on himself for a year. His family would cost extra. From this hypothetical budget they concluded that 'every year the agricultural worker must go hungry for seven or eight months, the poor peasant for five or six months, and a number of middle peasants are short of food for three or four months.' So, during the hungry months between harvests, 'the poor with bloodless faces carry a sickle looking for work'.[36]

The budgets outline a double process of mobility: downward socio-economic and outward spatial. This was not new in the 1930s. A decade earlier, the Nam Định mandarin calculated that a plot of five *sào* in the lower delta was enough to feed a family for three months, 'which is why, after the growing season, people

---

* North–south migration was low, but for other reasons, described below. James C. Scott, *The Moral Economy of the Peasant: Rebellion and Subsistence in Southeast Asia*, New Haven and London: Yale University Press, 1976, p. 82.

have to emigrate elsewhere to sell their labour, either in Laos or Saigon'. These were not the only destinations. Inhabitants from the provinces of Nam Định, Thái Bình, Hưng Yên and Ninh Bình regularly went off to other cities, to the mines and plantations, and to the highlands.[37]

Temporary wage work away from home was, then, a common and highly visible response to the cycle of debt and land loss. Inevitably, after a flood or a storm, when incomes were low, more people would leave. The decision to leave was made within the family. But if they had no relatives outside the village, no network, some members might join with other families, forming groups to make the move.* Rural proletarians wandering the roads could be seen by 'the most inobservant tourist'.[38] Wanderers became, indeed, potent symbols of poverty, constituting a call to action across a range of discourses – administrative, capitalist and revolutionary. Only the academics were satisfied with the status quo, if we can take the geographer Gourou as typical. He portrayed them as leaving their village with joy, at the prospect of work and a square meal for a few weeks, a brief holiday from poverty. For officials like the Nam Định mandarin and businessmen like Paul Bernard, there was nothing joyful about this migration, but the work represented nonetheless an opportunity – a problem solved.[39] For Nghiêm Xuân Yêm, they were people at their wits' end, victims of social and economic inequality, as his account conveys:

> Among these unemployed rural folk, there are those who resign themselves to leaving their home village to look for a living elsewhere. On the roads going to Phú Thọ, Vĩnh Yên, Tuyên Quang, Thái Nguyên … around January and February, we should look out for the gangs of people, from seven to eight, even fifteen to twenty of them, with blue faces and sunken cheeks, stumbling along, leading each other along the road into the forest to look for work. They go, wandering around, with no fixed address; their only goal is to come across a plantation with scrub to clear or a mine with ore to rinse, whereupon they stop, and without looking back go and ask to clear the scrub, rinse the ore, to earn a bite to eat.[40]

Nghiêm Xuân Yêm's portrayal was a potent form of protest.

Less visible was the process whereby a temporary move became, for one reason or another, a longer stay. Like the land ownership system, the wage-work situation was complex – employment was available by the day, month, season, year. Thân explained to me that in Tân Cương there were two basic types. You either did temporary work or live-in labour where you lodged with the landlord.[41] But the line between the two was blurred. The line between a temporary stay and a permanent move was equally so. In the commune of Hoàng Nông, at the head of the Công River valley, almost everyone had labourers from the delta working their land. Tuấn, whose family had lived there for nine generations, told me how some labourers came for a short stay, while others gradually settled.

---

*   This was the case for Thức in 1906 (see Prologue).

> Labourers, 80 to 90 per cent of people here employed them. Not like landlords, though; at the end of the harvest, the employers still had to borrow. There were many paddy fields, few inhabitants, everyone had people working. They came for a month or two, up from delta provinces like Nam Định, Thái Bình and Hà Nam; or as temporary residents, arriving in February, taking their earnings home in May [in time for their own harvest]. They'd be back again in May, returning home in December for the Tết festival. Then, one year, they would ask the village head for permission to bring their family up with them, clear some land.[42]

What started out as an attempt to supplement the family income at home became a definitive change of residence.

Let us summarize our findings so far. In Tân Cương we identified two sorts of migrant: those in search of land and those in search of work. Throughout Thái Nguyên, we found that people accumulated land in two ways, buying it from planters like Monpezat, or acquiring it by fiddling the small concessions system. Labourers, meanwhile, came to work the fields. Some were recruited directly from the delta. Others came after disaster struck. Still others came to work for a few weeks or months, and a temporary stay became permanent. The first settlers then called their relatives and neighbours, and networks came into being, moving people from all parts of the delta.

We have seen, then, how people came to settle in this middle region province. It remains for us to understand who these people were. Or, put another way, what were people looking for when they left their village?

SOCIAL STRATEGIES OF MIGRATION

The evidence presented thus far has tended towards the conclusion that migration was a poverty alleviation strategy. Few written sources contradict the impression that the people left to look for work because they were poor. Oral evidence is even more clear on the question. 'We were poor at home' was a phrase I heard again and again. But, throughout my fieldwork in Vietnam, I was niggled by a doubt planted on my first trip to the countryside by a district official in Thái Bình. 'People were not only moving because they were poor', he said, 'there was some other reason'.[43] He did not elaborate. But he led me to understand that in a society where the vast majority of peasants went hungry for long periods of the year, being poor in itself might not be a sufficient reason for departure. Poverty, I began to feel, was a sort of paradigm. In documentary sources, it fell neatly into the overpopulation mould. In interview, it dodged sensitive social questions, inviting sympathy rather than criticism.

Three stories evoke the social complexities of the poverty paradigm. The first is of Trần Tử Bình, who decided in 1927 to volunteer for plantation work in the central highlands. His refusal to accept discipline at school had led to expulsion:

> In a totally Catholic village, life was very hard for a family that had a child expelled from the seminary or excommunicated for 'rebelling against the will of God'. Neighbours and relatives said one thing and another – all manner of reproaches. There was no lack

of cruel words, insinuations, curses for the 'atheist' (…) If I went home, my family was too poor to support me. Actually, I could not have gone back even if I had wanted to. The village, including my family and friends, would have given me no peace.[44]

But signing up for the plantations was not a last resort. David Marr pointed out that Trần Tử Bình, with his knowledge of French, could have become a clerk, landlord's agent or shopkeeper's assistant. 'Instead he was determined to break away, to seek adventure, to test his physical and spiritual powers on totally unfamiliar terrain.'[45] Although from a poor family, Trần made his decision in a spirit of rebellion and adventure, not out of poverty.

The second is of Liên, the wife of a landlord in Định Hóa. Now in her eighties, she told me how she had arrived from the delta. 'In those days, we were poor at home, so I came up here to make a living. I came alone, married straight away, and by the age of 24, had a child'.* Her story fitted neatly into the grim saga of a delta with too many people, too much poverty, too many migrants. She was lucky, she married a Tày man, owner of a vast property (370 hectares of paddy land). Liên's story, however, did not fit with her son's version of events.

> She came here before 1945, when she was 21, about 1936. She came with an old lady, a trader. She had a marriage problem – her mother wanted to give her to some man she did not like, so she ran away. The old lady was not a member of the family, but agreed to take her along. Here, she met a big, rich man. She was very beautiful, like an actress …

When I met her, in her graceful old age, it was not hard to see how she had charmed the valley's biggest landlord. I checked, nevertheless, about her folks back home. Were they poor people? Did any relatives come and join her? 'They have come, but only to visit. My brothers and sisters are all still at home, no one went anywhere'.

This was an exceptional story, about someone whose courage and beauty – and the chance offered by a sympathetic trader – gave her the power to choose. Other women accepted the marriages imposed upon them.[46] But this story, like Trần Tử Bình's, raised a wider question. How many people, men and women, left home out of social frustration, which is now hidden – in statistics, in documents, in interview – under the socially acceptable and scientifically measurable label of poverty?

The third story, related in 1939 by Nguyễn Văn Huyên, reveals a different source of frustration:

> A peasant left his home four years ago, without sending any news back to his wife. She was forced to go to Hanoi for work, to raise money to feed their two children. She recently received a money order for 500 piastres. *Her husband sent her this money so that she could, on his behalf, pray to the village god and treat the village officials to a feast.* In that way, when the time came for him to return, he would have a small place at the village communal house. Only that was important! (…) Nothing for his wife, and after the day of the banquet, she will go back to live in the city. (Emphasis in original) [47]

---

* She was from Đại Vĩ village (Liên Hà commune, Đông Anh district, Bắc Ninh). I met her at Tân Tiến village (Tân Dương commune, Định Hóa district, Thái Nguyên). Interview (January 1997).

Here we glimpse two sides of the poverty coin. Her strategy was alleviation of economic poverty; his was of social. She left the village, too poor to feed the children. He left, too poor to join in 'society'. She (may we assume?) only left because he did, while his (male) goal was participation in village social life rather than escape from it. Nguyễn Văn Huyên offered no indication of where he went, what he did, nor indeed whether he ever managed to return. Nor do we hear how she made a living in the city.

Rather than speculate, let us turn these questions around. Let us ask in the highlands who the in-migrants were, rather than in the delta where the out-migrants went. This is not the place to examine in detail all the forms of migration from the Red River Delta. Certainly, men and women signed contracts to work on plantations in southern Vietnam and Cambodia, to go to the mines and plantations in the New Hebrides and New Caledonia. Private recruiting agents arranged labour export for construction and mine work in Laos. Companies employed tens of thousands in the mines and factories of Haiphong, Quảng Ninh, Nam Định and other parts of the north, as well as in Hanoi and Saigon. These itineraries are illustrated in Map 12. Men with education could get subaltern jobs in the colonial administration. Men without education could join the Native Guard. Men and women found jobs as servants. Men and women moved around the country buying, selling and playing itinerant theatre. But here, let us focus on those people who moved to the hills, bearing in mind that many of our conclusions could be applied to people going elsewhere.

Were they people seeking a definitive escape to a frontier freedom? Were they people who had left their lands in the hands of a creditor, looking to make enough money to buy them back? Were they, finally, people who had land but no status, and sought outside the village the capital to buy status at home? To answer these questions, we need access to the sorts of details that Nguyễn Văn Huyên left out. I rely here on a survey into spontaneous migration carried out in 1938 by the Guernut Commission. Two questionnaires were sent to the authorities in each province in the highlands – one for officials, the other for settler households. Thái Nguyên unfortunately was not covered by the survey. We shift our focus, instead, to a province further into the mountains.

Settlement Patterns in Hà Giang

Hà Giang is Vietnam's northwesternmost province. Part of what the French referred to as the High Region, it was topographically very different from the 'cheerful plains' and abandoned ricefields of Thái Nguyên. This was the landscape described, not without hyperbole, by Jean Marquet in his 1920 novel:

Mountains everywhere! They came down from the heights of heaven, like herds of giant, thirsty animals. They rushed, pushing, leaping, crushing each other before falling into the clear water of the river, as though to quench their thirst ... Between them, sombre shadows split the earth. The river's children came out from there, rivulets babbling and murmuring. From them, by contrast, you could see only a sharp fall into the stream;

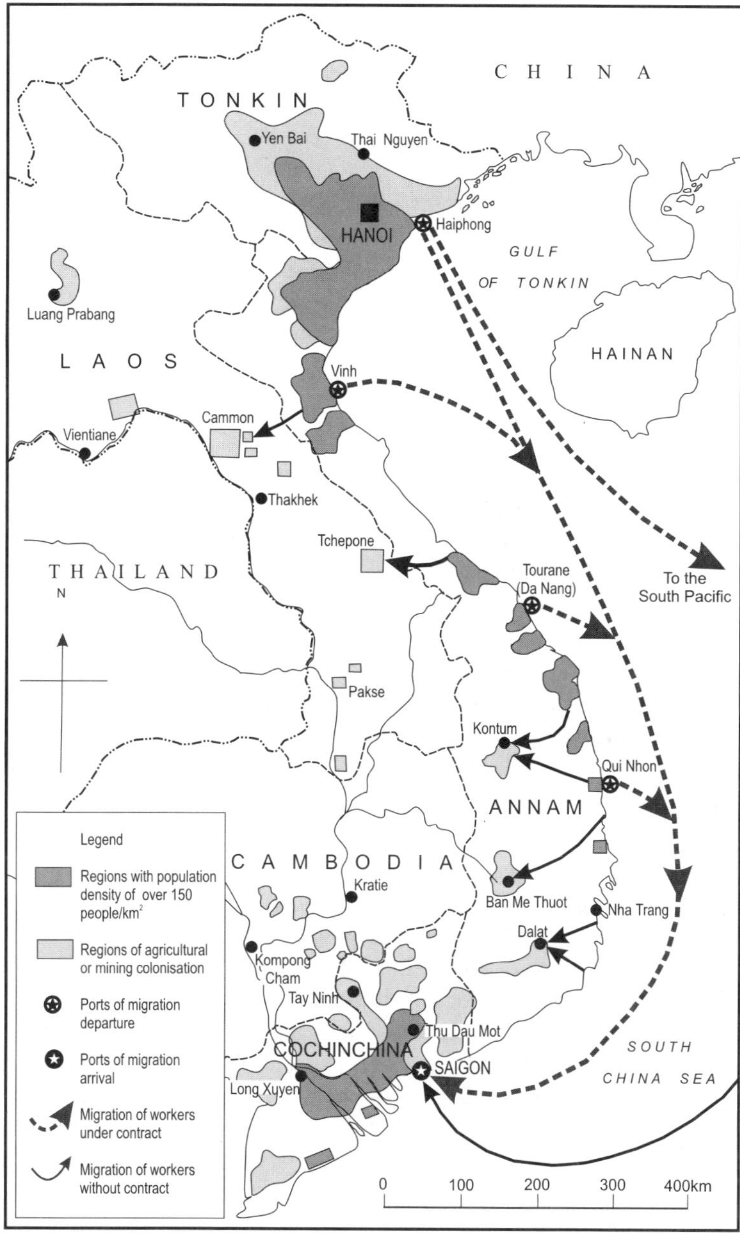

Map 12: Principal migration itineraries in colonial Vietnam
Contract labour migration was organised by the French authorities, to plantations in southern Vietnam (Cochinchina) and Cambodia, and to their possessions in the South Pacific. Spontaneous migrants also moved in small numbers to various points in the highlands.
Source: Emile Delamarre, *L'émigration et l'immigration ouvrière en Indo-Chine,* Paris: Felix Alcan, 1931. Redrawn by Lee Li Kheng.

their long, thin bodies, like reptiles, clothed with a tangle of creepers, trees and reeds. These narrow valleys were swept by chill winds, which froze the travellers with a penetrating humidity. Gusts tore down from the crests to the riverbanks, arching the white feathers of the reeds, breaking off dead branches and scattering splash from the waterfalls.

Ba was alarmed ...[48]

Ba, the novel's travelling hero, was on his way to find the remains of his brother, who had died at Hà Giang prison, and to earn some money for his family. In the story, he had no intention of settling there, and indeed returned to his village in Hà Đông after selling his sampan-load of tobacco, fish sauce and horseshoes.[49] In reality, few delta people settled. In 1933, the local military commander stated that there was no in-migration at all. He presumably meant none worth mentioning – for the 1938 survey counted over 1,200 Việt people living in eight centres. The reason he gave was the high incidence of malaria, especially in the valleys.[50] Hà Giang town itself, according to a leading malaria expert, well deserved its reputation as one of the least healthy places in Indochina: the 'town of fever and death'. In 1926, 80 per cent of the soldiers there went down with malaria, though by 1935 'de-contamination' measures and quinine use brought this figure down to 10 per cent.[51] Who were the people who chose to live in such a place?

To find out, the Guernut Commission organized forty-seven interviews with heads of household throughout the province. They were conducted not by sociologists but by mandarins and military officers who collected responses to a questionnaire dealing with the economic situation of all members of the family. Forty-five of these interviews figure in the analysis that follows. The small size of the survey (which reached around 7 per cent of Hà Giang's Việt population) means that the conclusions that follow are of qualitative value only.

Let us look first at respondents' professions. Reading through the survey forms, I was struck by how few people were involved in agriculture, either as farmers or plantation workers. Less than 10 per cent of the men and women interviewed put their profession in these two categories. With the exception of a Catholic woman, who sought to evangelize poor people from her province of Hà Nam by getting them to clear the forest, few came to Hà Giang to farm the land.[52] Indeed, two interviewees claimed to have left the delta to get away from the paddy fields. But to observe that 70 per cent of the Việt people interviewed in Hà Giang were traders and artisans is to say little about how they came to be there in the first place. The questionnaire did not require this information. To work it out, we must read reports describing the responses, and rely on the enthusiasm of officials who interpreted generously the survey instructions 'not to worry about saying more than the questionnaire asks for'.[53]

Officials painted a chaotic picture of the early Việt migrations. Before the First World War, the pioneers in the region were opium traders, adventurers, abducted women and their kidnappers, 'people who wanted to start a new life'. They were bandits in whose activities there was 'nothing insurrectionary', for whom the trade

Plate 1: Delta, midlands and highlands in northern Vietnam, 1914.
Northern Vietnam was divided into three geographical regions: delta, midlands (moyenne région) and highlands (haut région), indicated here with red dividing lines. The province of Thái Nguyên was situated in the midlands, to the north of Hanoi.
Source: Henri Brenier, *Essai d'atlas statistique de l'Indochine française*, Hanoi-Haiphong, 1914, pp. 27–28. Photograph by Coombs Photography Unit. Approximate scale 1/2,600,000.

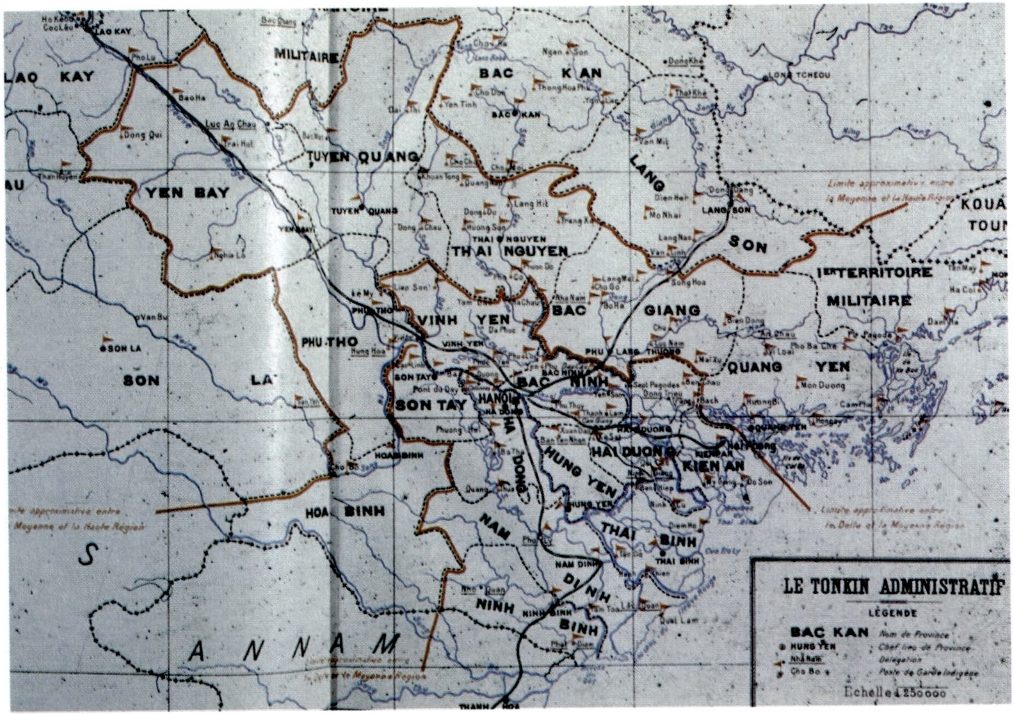

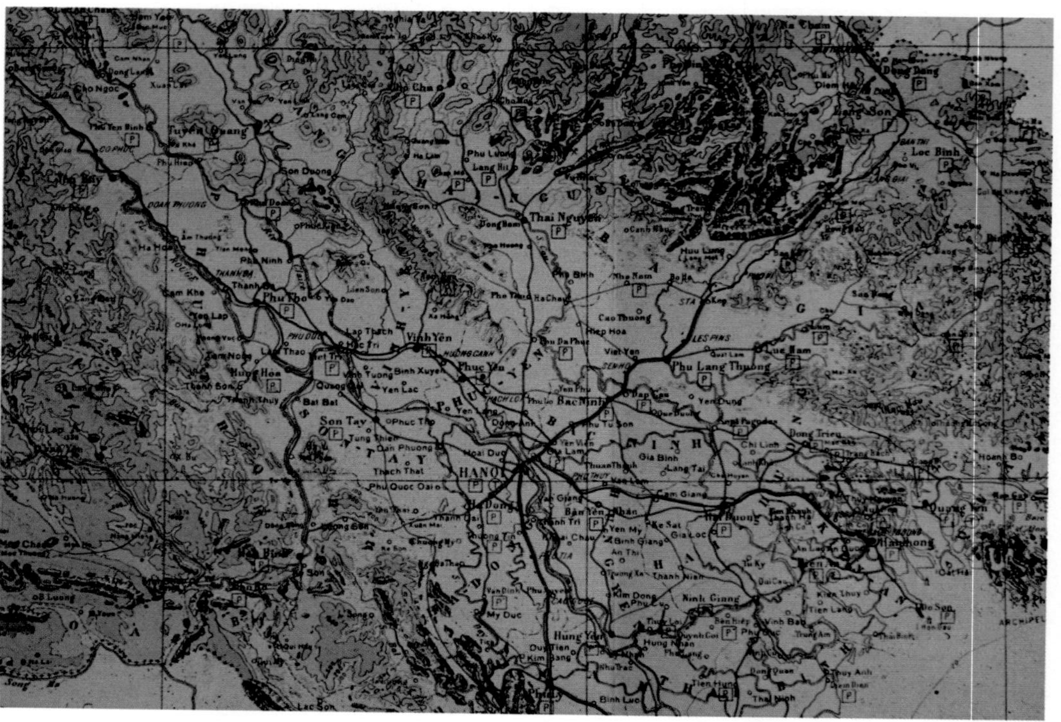

Plate 2: Relief of the Red River Delta and midlands, 1930.
The Công River flows to the west of Thái Nguyên town and east of the Tam Đảo mountain range, which extends into the Red River Delta from the hills to the north of Hanoi.
Source: Pierre Gourou, *Le Tonkin*, Paris: Exposition Coloniale Internationale, 1931. Photograph by Coombs Photography Unit. Approximate Scale 1/1,450,000.

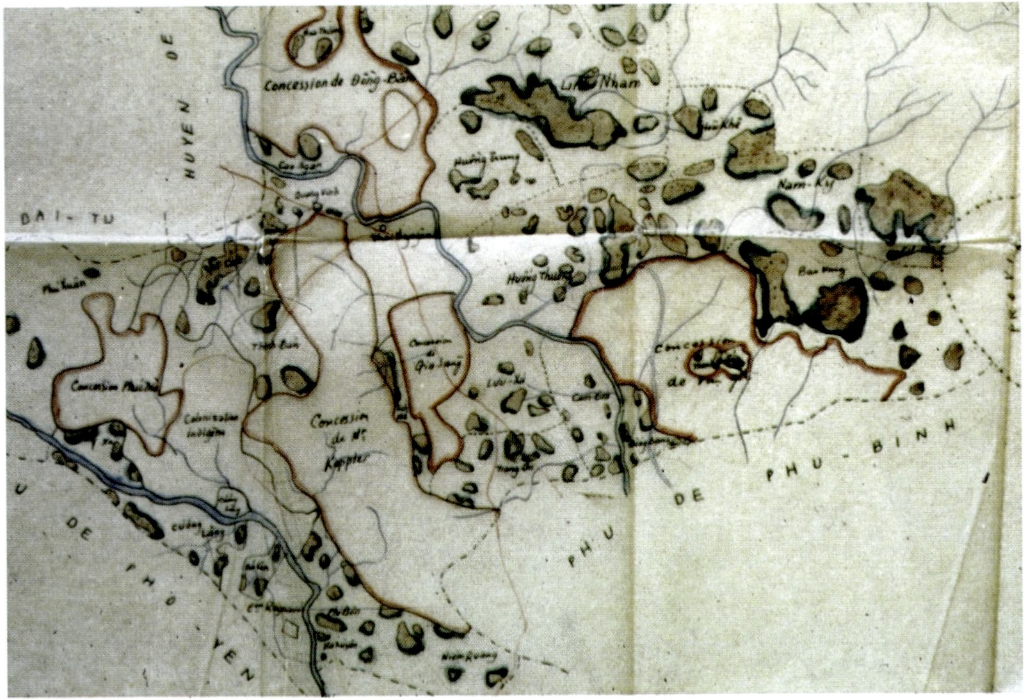

Plate 3: The landscape of Đồng Hỷ district, 1932.

The landscape of this part of Thái Nguyên province is clearly illustrated here. Areas of flat land suitable for wet rice are broken by small hills where other crops, especially tea, could be grown. Source: NAV1/RST 67478, Letter from Echinard, Résident in Thái Nguyên, to RST, 8 November 1932. Photograph by Đỗ Huy. Approximate scale, 1/220,000.

Plate 4: Plantations in Đồng Hỷ district, 1933.
Monpezat had extensive land holdings in Đồng Hỷ. Cà Phê village was on his Đồng Bẩm plantation (marked 1), in the northern part of the district near Minh Lý (2). Note the village of Tân Cương (3), on the left bank of the Công River (4).
Source: NAV/RST 67478, 'Thai Nguyen, Création de villages de colonisation', 3 April 1933. Photograph by Đỗ Huy. Approximate Scale 1/230,000.

Plate 5: Plantations in Đại Từ district, 1933

There were few French plantations in Đại Tù district and Garrigue's holdings are not marked here, as he acquired his land in the early 1940s. On the western edge of the district, there are some plantations belonging to Reynaud (marked 1) scattered along the Công River (2) in the vicinity of Bờ Rạ. The commune of Yên Thái (3) was later renamed Tân Thái.

Source: NAV/RST 67478, 'Thai Nguyen, Création de villages de colonisation', 3 April 1933. Photograph by Đỗ Huy.

Plates 6a–6b: The Núi Cốc lake, 1996.
The Công River was dammed in 1976, creating the Núi Cốc lake, a water reservoir and growing tourist resort. The above view, taken near Tân Thái commune, looks over Bờ Rạ towards the Tam Đảo mountain, picturing a fashionable island hotel submerged in a recent flood. Below, roofing materials transported along the bank of the Công River where it flows into the lake.
Photograph by Andrew Hardy, October 1996.

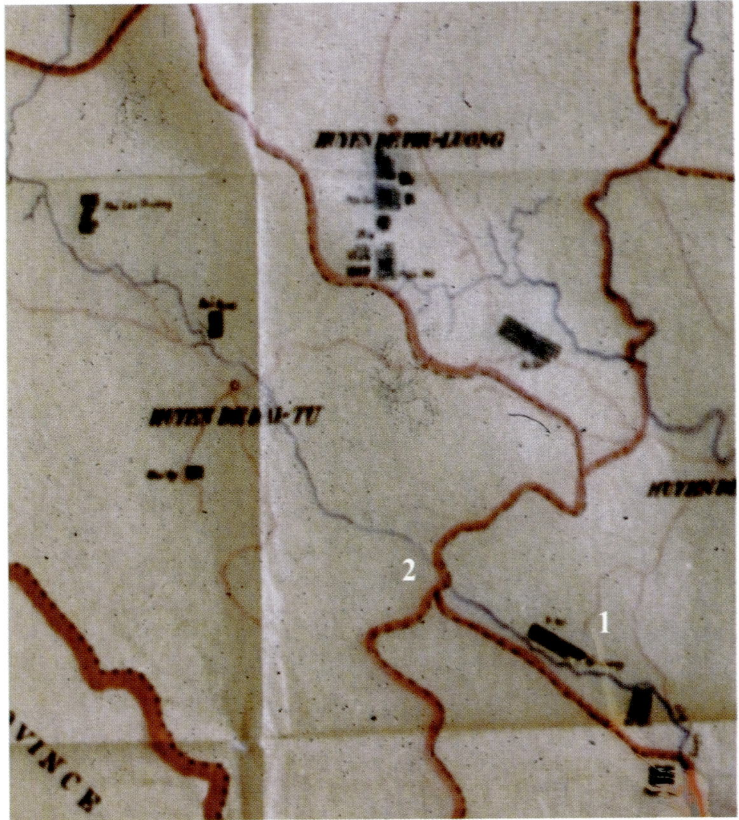

Plate 7: Small concessions in the Công River valley, 1933.
Proposed small concessions may be seen along the Công River valley, in the vicinity of Tân Cương (marked 1), where the boundary between the districts of Đồng Hỷ and Phổ Yên follows the river. Bờ Rạ was situated upstream, at the boundary with Đại Từ district (2).
Source: NAV1/47487, 'Thai Nguyen, Création de villages de colonisation', 3 April 1933. Photograph by Đỗ Huy. Approximate Scale 1/430,000

Plate 8: A small concession at the village of Yên Sơn, 1934.
*This map of a single village was drawn for a 'small concession' application.
Farmland was shaded yellow, forest brown. In 1997, local people said the
brown area was now entirely planted with tea.*
Source: NAV/RST 67499, 'Province de Thai Nguyen, Huyen de Dai Tu,
Village de Yen Son', 1934. Photograph by Đỗ Huy. Original map of scale 1/
4,000.

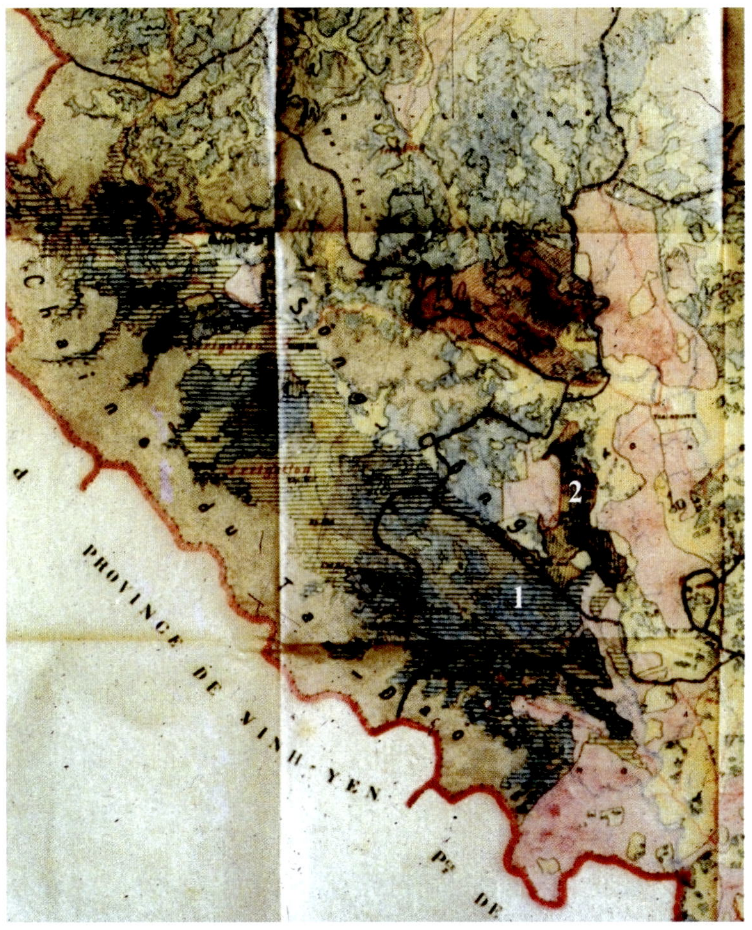

Plate 9: Land use in the Công River valley, 1941.
The modest ambitions for the valley's settlement of the early 1930s gave way by the 1940s to an extensive plan for its mise en valeur. Small concessions, shaded in green (marked 1), were set aside for Việt settlers on the right bank of the river. Land granted at Tân Cương in 1919 (2) lies between plantations, on the left bank.
Source: NAV1/RST 67470, 'Carte de la province de Thai Nguyen, 1938–41', 7 November 1941. Photograph by Đỗ Huy. Approximate scale 1/450,000.

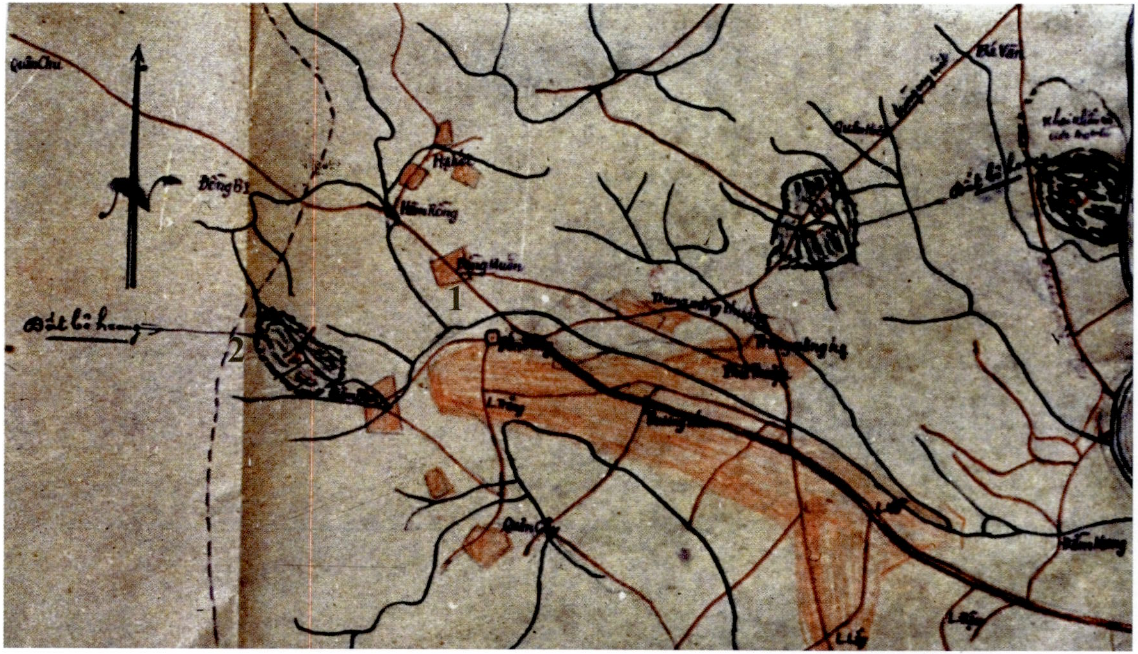

Plate 10: Road 38 in Phổ Yên district, 1938.

The road deteriorated beyond Bến Đồng, at the northwestern end of the Reynaud plantation (shaded pink and marked 1), after crossing the boundary with Đại Từ district (2). Areas shaded black were abandoned and unused land. Source: NAV1/RST 67478, 'Envoi de 3,000 coolies à Thai Nguyen pour la mise en valeur de certains terrains', 1932. Photograph by Đỗ Huy. Approximate scale 1/100,000

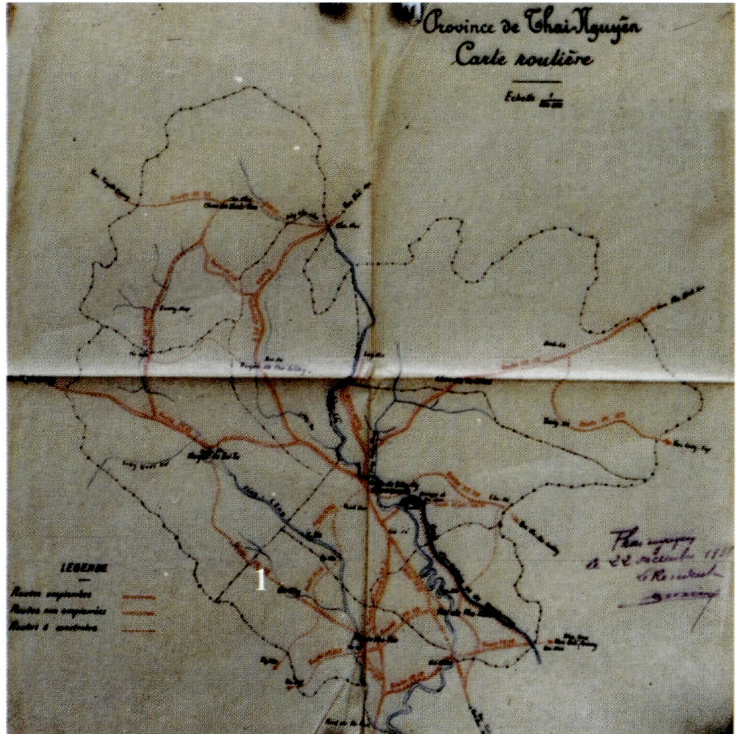

Plate 11: Roads in Thái Nguyên province, 1938.
The upgrading of Road 38 between Phổ Yên and Đại Từ districts (marked 1) was a pet project of the Résident of Thái Nguyên, Alfred Echinard.
Source: NAV1/RST 69048, 'Thai Nguyen – Redressement de l'Economie Rurale'. Photograph by Đỗ Huy. Approximate scale 1/630,000.

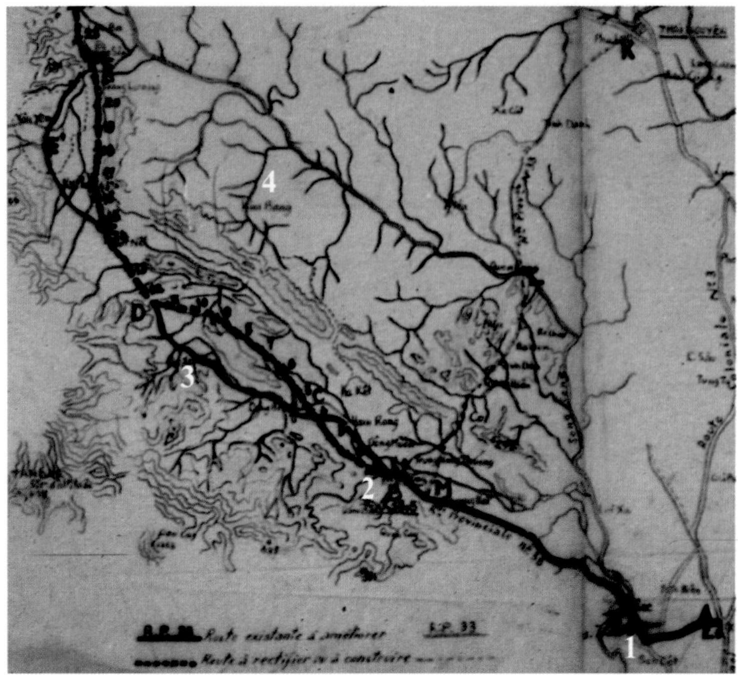

Plate 12: Proposed improvements to Road 38 in the Công River valley, 1939.
*This map shows Road 38 from Phổ Yên to Đại Từ, via Sơn Cốt (marked 1), Bến Đông
(2) and Quần Chu (3). The village of Kim Bảng (4), not far from Bờ Rạ, is marked on the
right bank of the Công River. The improvements proposed on this plan were never
carried out.*
Source: NAV1/RST 67504, 'Mouvement de la colonisation à Thai Nguyen', 1939. Photograph by Đỗ Huy. Approximate Scale 1/200,000.

Plate 13: The Sơn Cốt plantation in Phổ Yên district, 1933.

The plantation at Sơn Cốt (marked 1) was owned by Reynaud. Most of its holdings were centred around the district town of Phổ Yên, but it also consisted of scattered plots of land carved out of state land towards Đồng Hỷ and Đại Từ (2).

Source: NAV/RST 67478, 'Thai Nguyen, Création de villages de colonisation', 3 April 1933. Photograph by Đỗ Huy. Approximate Scale 1/230,000

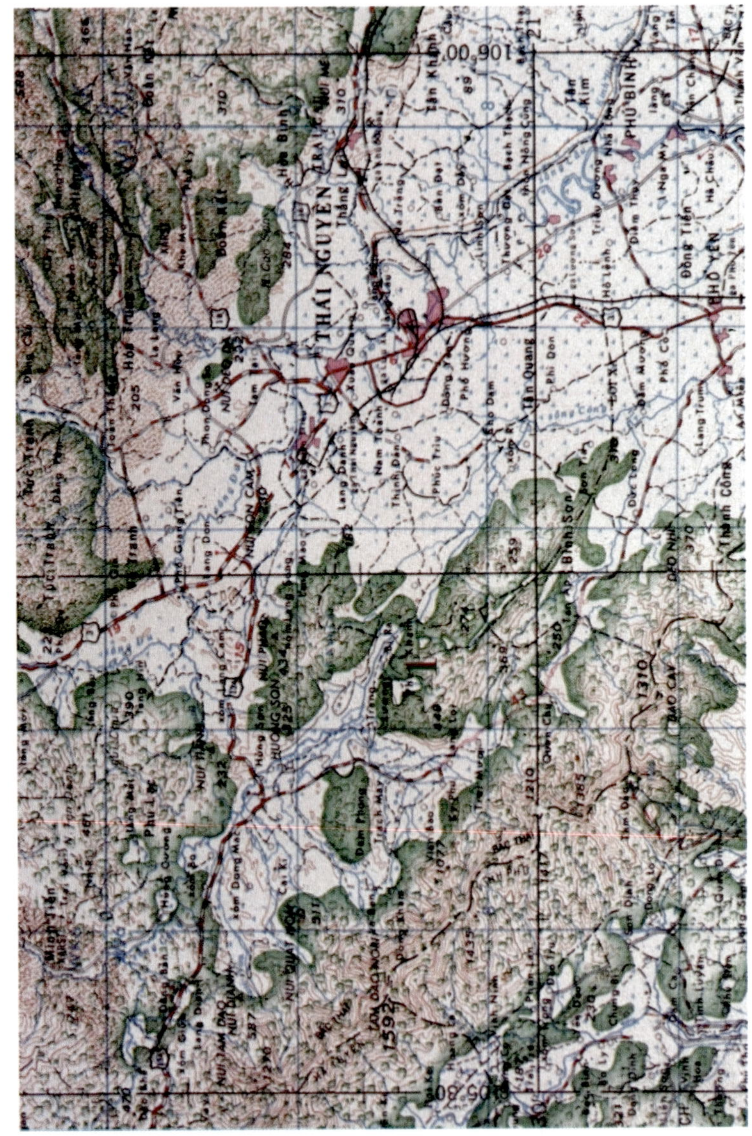

Plate 14: The Cống River valley, 1967. *The villages of Bi Ra (Bờ Rạ) and Phúc Khánh are marked here (1), a few years before the flood.* Source: Joint Operations Graphic (Air), Aeronautical Chart and Info Centre, US Air Force, 1967. National Library of Australia, map G3201 P6 s250, sheet NF 48-11. Photograph by National Library of Australia. Approximate Scale, 1/450,000.

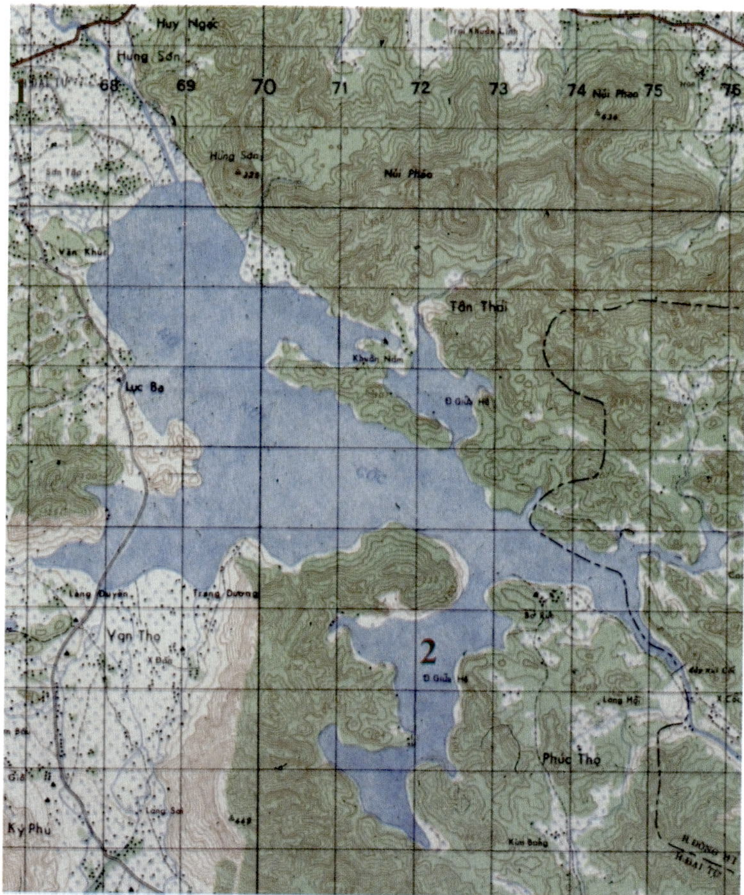

Plate 15: The Công River valley and the Núi Cốc lake, 1976.
Đại Từ town is visible at the head of the lake (1), and Road 38 along its western edge. Phúc Khánh village was already submerged, marked 'in the middle of the lake' (Đ. giữa hồ) (2). Bờ Rạ (marked Bờ Rực), Long Hội and Kim Bảng villages remained, for the moment, above water.
Source: Cục Bản Đồ, Bộ Tổng Tham Mưu, Quân Đội Nhân Dân Việt Nam (updated in 1976 from a 1964 United States original). National Library of Australia, map G 8020 s50, sheet 6152 III. Photograph by the National Library of Australia. Approximate scale 1/80,000.

Plate 16: The commune of Bình Sơn, 1976. *Downstream from the Núi Cốc lake, Tân Cương (1) lies on the Công River's left bank and Bình Sơn (2) on the right. The rigours of Bình Sơn's contoured landscape, where the people from Bờ Rạ were resettled, may easily be imagined.* Source: Cục Bản Đồ, Bộ Tổng Tham Mưu, Quân Đội Nhân Dân Việt Nam (updated in 1976 from a 1964 United States original). National Library of Australia, map G 8020 s50, sheet 6152 II. Photograph by the National Library of Australia. Approximate scale 1/80,000.

in drugs and the practice of violence were quite simply 'a means of existence'.[54] Henri Maître met some of these types in the central highlands, describing them as 'buccaneers of the frontier', people 'equipped only with a dark and agitated past, a complete absence of scruples and an audacity worthy of a better cause.'[55] By the 1930s these individuals were either dead, married with locals and integrated into highlander economies, or settled into regular trading with China and the delta. Data from the survey show, as we might expect, a well-ordered province in 1938, where migration remained within the structures of French rule. And while only 11 per cent recorded their profession as official or domestic service – activities directly linked to the presence of a colonial administrative or military post – most of the adult newcomers with a discernible network arrived as soldiers, servants for the French and subaltern administrators, or their wives.

Analysis of these networks turns up some interesting conclusions. From the response forms, I was able to identify networks for twenty-seven of the men interviewed. Eleven arrived in Hà Giang in the service of the colonial state (as soldiers, officials or servants), fifteen were there for family reasons (arriving with parents, joining relatives, or born there), and only one said he came up to practise trade. Of twenty-three women, one arrived as a result of the colonial presence in the province (as a child sold to an official there), while the others were either born in Hà Giang or arrived with their husband.

The profession of trader is conspicuously absent from these figures. This may be a function of the interviewers' assumptions. Focusing on what people do now rather than how they got there, survey officials simply assumed, as Marquet did in his story of Ba, that traders came to Hà Giang to practise trade. Trade was not mentioned as a motive or a method for moving: it was obvious. The following account of the crystallization of a Việt community around the military post at Phố Bảng supports this assumption: the French presence created commercial opportunities which were quickly seized.

> Throughout the Phố Bảng region, the migrations only concern the army post village itself. Until 1932, apart from the fonctionnaires, no Việt people seem to have fixed themselves at Phố Bảng, even briefly. Subsequently, the presence of the post and the security it offers, and the presence of a sizeable weekly [salt] market attracted a number of elements.
>
> In 1932 a Việt tailor from Bắc Ninh settled here with his wife. The next arrival was noted in 1936. There was a hairdresser in May, then another tailor in August. In March, May and December 1937, four traders settled at Phố Bảng to sell metal goods, cloth or soup.
>
> Besides these last, I note a number of servants (two) and cooks in full-time service of Europeans, or other village notabilities. For two years now, Thim-Siu has also had two young girls from the delta in his service.
>
> Finally, there are the Việt fonctionnaires, a writer, a post office official and a teacher. From 1933 to 1937, there was also Mr Thuyết, Secretary to the Assistant District Chief.[56]

But to get to places like Phố Bảng, to set up shop, to feed a family while establishing a reputation, traders and artisans needed a minimum of capital. In some cases, like Thân's in Tân Cương, family or friend networks acted as substitute. Cao Văn

Tịch, from Gia Hòa commune (Nam Trực district, Nam Định) was fortunate to have a brother with a business in Hà Giang. He got a job there. Trần Văn Cường also had a network. His father had lived in Hà Giang for three years in the 1920s. Indeed, he enjoyed a whole range of relationships when he arrived in Hà Giang. He too was from Gia Hòa. No fewer than seven of the eighty people covered by the survey were from this commune. It was often not enough simply to wish to trade – people followed networks which directed both their destination and their professional activity.

For those without such a network, there were jobs created by collaboration with the colonialists. Many of Hà Giang's traders were retired from such jobs, or married to men who held them. The first Việt settler in the small town of Đồng Văn, for example, was the widow of a sergeant in the Native Guard. Her 'little café' in 1902 developed into a 'rather rich commerce' by 1938. In Đồng Văn, in addition to a small garrison and six fonctionnaires, there were four retired soldiers or servants. One third of the Việt population interviewed at Đồng Văn lived off colonial salaries.

Đồng Văn was a remote place, however, and it is not difficult to identify the networks of all the members of its small Việt community. Most were traders or minor officials. But data for the whole province are less conclusive. I was unable to identify networks for seventeen of the men interviewed, and twelve of the women. How did these people come to be living in this distant province? A comparison of the population statistics of the town of Vị Xuyên and the survey compiled for the Guernut Commission helps to answer this question. According to population statistics, half of the 258 Việt adults whose profession was recorded were traders and artisans (131). Most of the other half were coolies or day labourers (109).[57] By contrast, the survey interviews throughout the province revealed the same story as the sample for Đồng Văn. Most of the forty-five people interviewed were traders. Only one fell into the category of labourer.

The absence of day labourers shows the major limitation of the Guernut survey data. As in Nam Định, survey officials in Hà Giang avoided speaking to the so-called 'truly poor', many of whom doubtless felt they were only there for a few months or years. They interviewed only those folk who were settled, established members of the community. The process whereby a temporary migration became a permanent settlement was obscured by the method of data collection. We may conclude, then, that colonial roads and buses – and the opportunites they created for profitable short-term trading or wage work – were more important than definitive decisions of permanent out-migration.* This indeed was Ba's experience, as Jean Marquet described him in his novel. Ba had already tried his hand at soldiering in the mountains – fighting rebels in Thái Nguyên 'in order to raise his social position'. Then he went off trading in Hà Giang, using his profits to bury

---

*   For bus routes in northern Vietnam, see Map 13.

his brother and pay his creditors when he got home.[58] Not everyone gambled on a short trip as successfully as this fictional Ba. Some found it hard to go back.

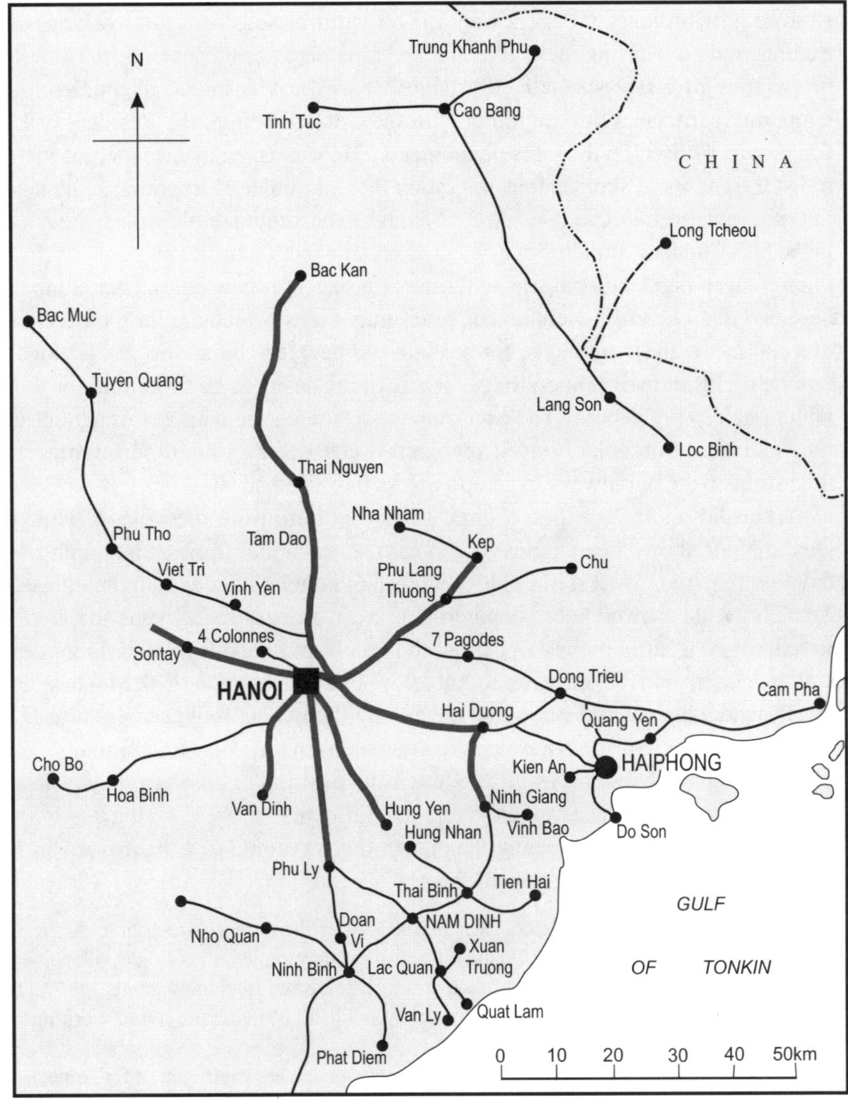

Map 13: Bus routes in northern Vietnam, 1931
Travel by public bus became popular in the 1920s. By 1930 a network of routes throughout the Red River Delta extended into the highlands. The route to Hà Giang which went via Tuyên Quang was established in the 1930s.
Source: Pierre Gourou, *Le Tonkin*, Paris: Exposition Coloniale Internationale, 1931, p. 247. Redrawn by Lee Li Kheng.

TEMPORARY/PERMANENT MIGRATION

The story of temporary migration is crucial, then, to understanding Việt settlement in the hills. And temporary migration had long been a feature of life in the Red River Delta's village society. In his book on trading villages, Nguyễn Quang Ngọc showed how ordinary villagers went off for short periods of wage work or petty trading, and how during the eighteenth and nineteenth centuries trade was not the prerogative of a few specialized villages. It was a widespread phenomenon of temporary/permanent out-migration.[59] In the colonial period, the Résident of Lào Cai province observed the same phenomenon. He was asked by the Guernut survey to list the causes of spontaneous migration there. In order of importance, he noted that migrants to Lào Cai consisted of paupers (destitute people trying their luck in the hills), traders (attracted to new commercial opportunities), opium-eaters (looking for cheap highland opium) and farmers (in search of new land). Last in his list, he stated that 'we must exclude temporary migrations, which are for the execution of a contract with an employer, for professional people to build up some savings to buy ricefields in their home village, or due to the desire to be forgotten, for those with troubled consciences.' The exclusion was made for the purposes of administrative statistics. But as he himself recognized elsewhere in the report, temporary migrations were not always as temporary as they seemed.[60]

What did migrants expect from a brief departure from the village? Nguyễn Quang Ngọc showed people leaving to earn some capital from trade, hoping one day to return and invest it in fields or a place of honour at the communal house.[61] Trần Huy Liệu showed poor people joining Native Guard for a livelihood, hoping to retire with a 'little money as capital to live off, or a modest mandarin grade as well which would be most honourable'.[62] Both ideals emerged in Marquet's novel, where the peasant Ba joined the colonial army and fought in the forests of Tam Đảo before returning, heroic, a man of status in the village community. Trần Văn Cường's father achieved this. He left the position of *chef de quartier* in Hà Giang to return to a place of wealth and honour in his village Gia Hòa.[63] Another who attempted it was Ta Quang Chieu. As the survey related, he arrived in Hà Giang in 1932 as 'second class rifleman':

> Having failed to renew his contract in 1935, after three years of service, due to his excessively bad conduct, Ta Quang Chieu, after ten months in his home village, with no paddy fields, no money, not much courage, preferred to come back in 1936 to the village near which he was garrisoned to try his hand at trade and avoid working the land …
>
> As a small shopkeeper and trader in groceries, haberdashery and a few objects of everyday utility such as machetes, horseshoes, small mirrors, little petrol lamps and ceremonial paper, Ta Quang Chieu manages to earn the 4 or 5 piastres a month, at most, which allow him and his family to subsist.
>
> Despite the mediocrity of his current situation, he has not despaired of one day being able to retire to his, and his wife's, place of origin.[64]

A man who manifestly failed was Trần Văn Đỗ, from Vĩnh Yên.

He was a servant to Europeans for six years. Then, having a little capital, he turned himself into a small trader for five years, travelling between Hanoi and Hà Giang to exchange highland products – tea, brown root dye – for products of necessity – soap, fish sauce, petrol – which he sold to the mountain people. But as his trade was going badly, and his health no longer permitted him to be constantly travelling, he acquired a land concession and has become a farmer.

He could not afford to return to his village, though the survey indicated that he wished to.[65]

These men saw their stay in Hà Giang as a temporary expedient, a way of earning money to take home. For the last two, the strategy failed. They were stuck. Not everyone intended to return, of course; the temporary stay was often used for risk limitation. This was the case for Thân's father, whose move to Tân Cương for a short period led to the discovery of higher earning power there. Once a settled job became available, he uprooted the whole family.[66]

Economic considerations were paramount in fixing Thân's family in the hills. But considerations of social status could also play a role. We are told that Nguyễn Văn Mạc, employee at Hà Giang post office, so enjoyed 'the jealousy of which he is the object from those around him', that he 'seems in no way disposed to envisage returning to his place of birth, when for him strikes the hour of retirement'.[67] For others, it was not money or status which fixed them, but love. Eight of the forty-four men interviewed married minority women from the locality. All but one of these voiced a desire to stay there. Love and money sometimes went hand in hand. Some men married women with commercial concerns. The wives of others developed trading networks in the highlands during the period of their husband's contract. They afterwards refused to abandon years of investment.[68] Still others, finally, were fixed in Hà Giang by the love of opium. Phạm Hữu Nguyên could not leave this region, Vietnam's drug capital, where his addiction was far cheaper than in the delta.[69]

Material and emotional ties linked people with their home in the delta. For traders, the home village was a market and a source of products. A return to the village was also a chance to stop in Hanoi and stock up. Other settlers went home while their parents were alive, stopping when they died. And some settlers never shed their ties to home. In Hà Giang, a 71–year-old Catholic, Nguyễn Ba Xa, had long lost his parents. He had ceased trading, and lived off his son. Yet after more than half his life in Hà Giang, he still returned to the delta every three years. This was 'to show the inhabitants of his village that he is still alive, to preserve his right to cultivate a share of the communal paddy fields'.[70] And in Phú Thọ province, trader Đỗ Văn Điên voiced the attachment discourse in his complaint about an obligation to pay head tax in the highlands. He objected to this transfer of payment place, arguing that it 'undermined the traditional scruple of the natives who have always seen the act of tax payment at the place of origin as an attachment to the land of their ancestors'.[71] Đỗ Văn Điên may have had other more down-to-earth reasons to resist a change in his tax situation. He nonetheless justified his request on the basis of this Confucian ideology of sentiment for home, which he may indeed have sincerely felt.

Settling processes may be discerned from the survey results. I use three measures to show how Viet heads of household came to stay in Hà Giang. The clearest measure is the place where they paid their head tax, indicating long residence in the hills. Twelve of the surveyed household heads paid tax in Hà Giang, two at their place of origin. The second is their expressed preference, as interviewers recorded where household heads said they wanted, ultimately, to live. Ten preferred Hà Giang, two their place of origin. Finally, there is the incidence of visits home. Twelve visited their home village annually.* To summarize these data, we may observe that half the male heads of household (26/44) either expressed a preference to live in Hà Giang, paid their tax there or never returned to their home village. They had settled.

These data by no means offer the last word on the issue. The measurement tools were crude. The sample was small. The bulk of Hà Giang's Việt population was excluded. One clear conclusion can be drawn, however. Some people nursed hopes of a return home. Others were happy to abandon the grind of delta farm work for good. But the return of all these people depended, ultimately, more on pragmatic considerations, contingent considerations – love, trade, income, opium – than on any 'attachment to their native soil'. For many, Hà Giang's mosquitoes would decide the issue first.

CULTURES OF MOBILITY

It was possible, during the colonial era, for people living in the Red River Delta to leave their village and settle elsewhere. What were the cultures of mobility that enabled them to do so?

First, some of the structures of delta village society promoted mobility away from it. This took the form of strongly articulated social distinctions within the village – analysed by Nguyễn Từ Chi in terms of 'insider'[†] and 'outsider'[‡]. He made the following observations about the status of outsiders:

> The object of contempt on the part of the insiders, they had to build their houses on the fringe of the hamlet, had no places in the *giáp* and at meetings of the insiders at the communal house, were not entitled to shares of public land, and had to hire themselves out for a living. They had to pay taxes, do corvée and answer conscription, and yet had not well-defined places in the village or hamlet.[72]

---

*   This is the a difficult measure, as economic factors determine the frequency of return, but also, as Diệp Đình Hoa noted, because return visits could be a sign of settlement success. While zero incidence of return might indicate settlement, therefore, we should be wary of attributing significance to actual returns. Diệp Đình Hoa, *Làng Nguyễn*, Hanoi: NXB Khoa Học Xã Hội, 1994, p. 71.

†   Insider: *inscrit*: *nội tịch*: *dân chính cư, dân làng xã.*

‡   Outsider: *non-inscrit*: *ngoại tịch*: *dân ngụ cư, dân hang xã.*

Decisions to leave were made in response to socio-economic exclusions within village society and the desire to overcome them.[73] They could be expressions of desire for escape from this society's closely regulated social and economic life. They could also reflect a wish to integrate more fully into these structures. As Georges Boudarel observed, villages were built on 'a class system of which the social cement is the passion to be someone'. A temporary departure from the village could be an effective strategy for a powerful return.

The decision might be made to feed the children at home or the notables at the communal house. In either case, it was a translation of internal social and economic mobility into terms of space. To leave the village was to hope, one day, to return to a better situation or to look for a better situation elsewhere.

Delta people were not, then, attached to their village in any inherent way. On the contrary, villages provided information and discourses which allowed them both to make the move in the first place and maintain contact for a long time thereafter. As Nguyễn Quang Ngọc showed, village-based networks providing resources for people to make a living far from home had long been the norm in the Red River Delta. In Hà Giang, members of Gia Hòa commune – people like Cao Văn Tịch and Trần Văn Cường mentioned above – moved along such networks. Families too formed the basis for mobility, as is clear from Diệp Đình Hoa's study of a village in Thái Bình and Philippe Papin's work on urban villages in Hanoi.[74] Diệp Đình Hoa's work is particularly interesting, as he used his study of the Cầu family records at Nguyễn village to show that people not only left the village, but also came there to live: 'Nguyễn village people went to other places to exercise their professions, but there were also people from elsewhere who came to Nguyễn village to make a living. This allows us to see that the village structure was not a closed system'.[75]

Networks extended beyond the delta. We saw this in Tân Cương, where Thân's family made use of relationships of mutual aid and exploitation in the midlands. Relatives offered a base for settlement in exchange for work. These networks were supported by a powerful discourse which maintained that by leaving, people had not lost their home. Traditional sayings, such as 'one destination, two homes'*, allowed even those who had been gone for decades, like the elderly Catholic Nguyễn Ba Xa mentioned above, to maintain a mental link with their native place.† At this level, if delta villagers were attached to their native place, they were tied only in a discourse of nostalgia which their social and economic behaviour belied.

---

* One destination, two homes: *một chốn đôi quê*.

† Diệp Đình Hoa acknowledged the importance of this discourse, reproducing in his book the following family poem: 'The Cầu family chronicle records - People go to Uông Bí and Hồng Gai - Individuals go to the south earning a dong a day - People go over to Thanh Hóa and Hàm Rồng - Individuals go up to Phú Thọ, Cao Bằng and Hà Giang - Folk leave in ten thousand directions - Still carrying with them the stamp of their home'. Diệp Đình Hoa, *Làng Nguyễn*, p. 33–34.

A second culture of mobility from the village was introduced by the colonial regime. Opportunities were created by the French, allowing people who wished to avoid using networks based on family and village relations a fast track to economic and social improvement. Those with a minimum of education took advantage of these opportunities to find work with colonial employers, as Nghiêm Xuân Yêm observed in 1943:

> In the village there is a small number of people who can read and write Vietnamese [*quốc ngữ*] or two or three words of French. Usually this group cannot stand to stay in the village. Proud of their knowledge of words, they have to go out to the town to work, so that out of ten people, seven or eight manoeuvre to get out to urban centres to find work: as traders' assistants, doing odd jobs, working as postmen, supervisors or artisans. Only when driven to extremity, unable to find any work at all, will they put up with living in the village.[76]

Nghiêm Xuân Yêm described these people as 'peasants off to town'.[*] Most hoped never to go home. But there were others who aspired – like Ba in Marquet's fictional account – to use the colonial system one day to come back to the village with a modicum of social and economic standing. Colonial employment thus both undermined and reinforced older patterns of out-migration from the village.

CONCLUSION

We can, therefore, conclude with a generalization. about cultures of mobility in northern Vietnam up to 1945. There existed, it seems, two such cultures – an ancient one based on networks of village and family relations, and a superimposed one, based on jobs created by the colonial military and administrative presence. Two questions nevertheless remain unsolved.

The first is the small number of people moving along these networks. In Hà Giang, Việt settlers could be counted in their hundreds; in Thái Nguyên in their thousands. But in the Red River Delta, as we saw in Chapter 2, overpopulation was measured in hundreds of thousands.[77]

The second is the absence of any large floating population, either in the delta or the highlands. This is strange when we consider the findings of Masaya Shiraishi's 1984 study, which identified a three-tier hierarchy to nineteenth-century Vietnamese society: state, villages and vagabonds.[78] It is even stranger when we read books published in the first decade of the twentieth century, such as Briffaut's monumental work *La cité annamite*. This recorded the existence of two classes of people in Vietnamese rural society: *sedentaires*, settled people living in villages, and *errants*, wanderers looking for villages to live in.[79] Thức, whom we met in the Prologue, spent a few years as a vagabond, at the beginning of the century.

---

*   Peasants off to town: *Nhà quê ra tỉnh.*

But by the 1930s, Thức was settled and the vagabonds – as a class – had disappeared from the sources.*

Was this because 1930s observers, blinded by discourses of attachment to the village, were unable to see the vagabonds? Or had the vagabonds ceased their wandering? These are the questions of the next chapter.

NOTES

1   Alfred Echinard, *Histoire politique et militaire de la province de Thai Nguyen, ses forces de police*, Hanoi: Imprimerie Trung Bac Tan Van, 1934, p. 228.

2   Grégoire Khérian, 'Le problème démographique en Indochine. Esquisse d'une politique démographique en Indochine', extract from *RIJE* nos 1–2, Hanoi: IDEO, 1937, no. 1, p. 35.

3   Echinard, *Histoire politique et militaire*, pp. 227–228.

4   Pierre Gourou, *Les paysans du delta tonkinois, étude de géographie humaine*, Paris: Les Editions d'Art et d'Histoire, 1936, p. 203.

5   NAV1/GGI 7455, RST to President of the Local Committee for the Repatriation of Vietnamese from France, 25 February 1919.

6   Le Bo-Chanh, *Notice sur la Province de Thai Nguyen*, Thai Nguyen: Unpublished monograph, 1933, p. 18.

7   Echinard, *Histoire politique et militaire*, p. 69. NAV1/RST 74431, 'Rapport Economique 1940'.

8   Alexander B. Woodside, *Community and Revolution in Modern Vietnam*, Boston: Houghton Mifflin Company, 1976, p. 154. The Tân Cương project was itself inspired by European experience of colonization – in New Zealand. NAV1/GGI 7454, Barthelemy, Government Commissioner, to RSL, 4 November 1918.

9   NAV1/RST 67486, Report by P. Godot, RST Land Registry and Topography Service, 21 May 1941.

10   NAV1/RST 67486, Michelot, Résident in Thái Nguyên, to RST, 5 May 1942; NAV1/ RST 74432, 'Rapport economique 1941'; Nghiêm Xuân Yêm, 'Điều tra nhỏ – Những tiểu đồn điền', *Thanh Nghị*, no. 62, 29 April 1944, p. 263.

11   NAV1/RST 67486, Michelot to RST, 5 May 1942.

12   NAV1/RST 67485, Echinard to RST, 4 August 1939.

13   NAV1/RST 67486, Michelot to RST, 5 May 1942.

14   Ibid.

15   CAOM/Guernut 28, 'Note sur la mise en valeur de la province de Thai Nguyen', 1938.

16   This model of 'settlement colonies' was introduced by RST decree of 20 March 1936. For details, see Bureau International du Travail, *Problèmes de Travail en Indochine*, Geneva: Kundig, 1937, pp. 233–234.

17   Joseph Starobin, *Eyewitness in Indochina*, New York: Cameron & Kahn, 1954, pp. 92–96.

---

*   The question of vagabonds, separate from that of seasonal migration, was addressed as a matter of course by French observers at the beginning of the century, but was no longer raised by the time Gourou and Robequain wrote their books on the rural society of northern Vietnam. My first thought was that the discourse on attachment to villages blinded later observers from the reality of their existence. But it is difficult to believe that seasoned observers like Gourou and Robequain would miss the existence of such a large-scale phenomenon. Diệp Đình Hoa's work on Nguyễn village provides evidence that the number of people leaving the village without a fixed destination declined during the colonial period. Diệp Đình Hoa, *Làng Nguyễn*, p. 33.

18 Yumio Sakurai, 'A Study of the Abandonment of Villages by Peasants in Vietnam during the Lê Dynasty (1)', *Tonan Ajia Kenkyu* [Southeast Asian Studies], vol. 15, no. 4, 1978, pp. 552–572.

19 NAV1/RST 71115, 'Pour le développement économique du Tonkin', report by Nghiêm Xuân Quang, mandarin in Ninh Bình, 1922.

20 CAOM/Guernut 26, Article by General Pennequin, *La Revue de Paris*, 1 December 1913.

21 1924: QNPM/uncatalogued report, 1924. NAV1/RND 3200, Mr Vũ Ưng (Cố Bản village) to Vụ Bản district mandarin (Nam Định), 4 September 1924; Giran, Résident in Sơn Tây, to RST, 17 January 1924. 1926: NAV1/RND 3179, RST to Résident in Nam Định, 20 September 1926. 1937: CAOM/Guernut 96, 'Réponse à l'enquête sur les migrations intérieures', Lạng Sơn, 30 April 1938. 1945: David G. Marr, *Vietnam 1945, The Quest for Power*, Berkeley: University of California Press, 1995, p. 101. In Thái Bình, I was told how people left the village to wander after the 1945 floods. In Thái Nguyên, Hoài was among the refugees. Interviews (Thái Nguyên, October 1996; Thái Bình, January 1997).

22 Phạm Quang Trung, 'Nạn lụt năm Ất dậu với cuộc tổng khởi nghĩa giành chính quyền ở đồng bằng Bắc Bộ năm 1945', *NCLS*, vol. 251, no. 4, 1990, pp. 56–60.

23 NAV1/A&G 233, Tôn Thất Phan, Foreign Affairs Minister, to Résident in Huế, 22 April 1884; NAV1/RST 1558, 'Notice sur la circonscription du poste administratif de Hung Son', 1901. Insurgencies included those of Đề Thám (Bắc Giang, 1914), Đội Cấn (Thái Nguyên, 1917) and Nguyễn Thái Học (Yên Bái, 1930).

24 CAOM/Guernut 96, 'Réponse à l'enquête sur les migrations intérieures', Bắc Quang, 25 April 1938; Truong Chinh and Vo Nguyen Giap, *The Peasant Question*, Ithaca, New York: Cornell University Southeast Asia Program, 1974, p. 12. For a fictional account of this trade, see Jean Marquet, *De la Rizière à la Montagne*, Paris: Librairie Delalain, 1926, pp. 114–141.

25 For French recognition of the 'deplorable' effects of forced labour, see NAV/RST 2437, Deputy Résident in Hải Ninh to RST, 17 April 1889.

26 CAOM/Guernut 26, 'Les solutions locales à apporter au problème du surpeuplement du delta tonkinois', Pierre Gourou, 1937. See also CAOM/Guernut 28, 'Le régime foncier au Tonkin', 1938.

27 CAOM/Guernut 26, 'Le Crédit dans la population rurale annamite', M. Bailly, 1938.

28 Trần Huy Liệu, *Lịch sử tám mươi năm chống Pháp*, Hanoi: Ban Nghiên Cứu Văn Sử Địa, 1956, vol. 1, p. 227.

29 CAOM/Guernut 26, 'Conférences du Général Pennequin sur la défense de l'Indochine', *L'Armee Coloniale*, 25 August 1912.

30 Vũ Đình Hòe, 'Vấn đề đi vay đối với dân quê', *Thanh Nghị*, no. 12, 1 May 1942, p. 14.

31 Grégoire Khérian, 'La position du problème du crédit dans l'Union Indochinoise', *RIJE*, no. 15, 1941, p. 377; Vũ Đình Hòe, 'Vấn đề đi vay', pp. 14–15; CAOM/Guernut 26, 'Le crédit dans la population', 1938.

32 Nguyễn Văn Huyên, 'Vấn đề nông dân Việt Nam ở Bắc Kỳ', 1939. In Hà Văn Tấn (ed.), *Góp Phần Nghiên Cứu Văn Hóa Việt Nam: Những Công Trình Nghiên Cứu Của Giáo Sư Tiến Sĩ Nguyễn Văn Huyên*, Hanoi: NXB Khoa Học Xã Hội, 1995, vol. 2, p. 34.

33 CAOM/Guernut 92, 'Réponse au questionnaire no. 1C destiné au fonctionnaires indigènes', Thanh Thế Vỹ, Vụ Bản school headmaster (Nam Định), 1938.

34 Nguyễn Quang Ngọc, *Về một số làng buôn ở đồng bằng Bắc Bộ thế kỷ XVIII-XIX*, Hanoi: Hội Sử Học Việt Nam, 1993, p. 60. Gourou, *Les paysans du delta*, pp. 473–476.

35 CAOM/Guernut 92, 'Réponse au questionnaire No. 1C', Thanh Thế Vỹ, 1938.

36 Truong Chinh and Vo Nguyen Giap, *The Peasant Question*, pp. 31–32.

37 NAV1/RND 3179, mandarin to Résident in Nam Định, 5 October 1926. See also Cao Văn Biên, 'Về dân số nông thôn Thái Bình trước Cách Mạng Tháng 8', *NCLS*, vol. 250, no. 3, 1990, p. 81.

38 Tran Van Thong, 'Mémoire sur la colonisation indigène en Indochine', *BEI*, 1938, p. 1117.

39 NAV1/RST 71115, 'Pour le développement économique', 1922; Paul Bernard, *Nouveaux aspects du problème économique indochinois*, Paris: Fernand Sorlot, 1937, p. 8; Tran Van Thong, 'Mémoire sur la colonisation', p. 1117.

40 Nghiêm Xuân Yêm, 'Cảnh nghèo ở thôn quê', *Thanh Nghị*, no. 47, 16 October 1943, p. 564. See also Truong Chinh and Vo Nguyen Giap, *The Peasant Question*, p. 12.

41 This distinction was made by Truong Chinh and Vo Nguyen Giap, *The Peasant Question*, pp. 29–30.

42 Tuấn was 78 when I met him. Interview (Thái Nguyên, January 1997).

43 Discussion at the People's Committee in Tiền Hải district (Thái Bình, May 1995).

44 Tran Tu Binh, *The Red Earth: A Vietnamese Memoir of Life on a Colonial Rubber Plantation*, Athens, Ohio: Center for Southeast Asian Studies, 1985, pp. 6–8.

45 David G. Marr, 'Introduction'. In Tran Tu Binh, *The Red Earth*, p. vii.

46 Truong Chinh and Vo Nguyen Giap, *The Peasant Question*, p. 101.

47 Nguyễn Văn Huyên, 'Vấn đề nông dân', p. 39.

48 Marquet, *De la Rizière à la Montagne*, pp. 148–149.

49 For non-fictional details of this sampan trade, see Gourou, *Les paysans du delta*, pp. 546–547, 552.

50 CAOM/Guernut 96, 'Réponse à l'enquête', Bắc Quang, 25 April 1938; NAV1/RST 56540, 'Bulletin d'information du commandant de 3e Territoire Militaire a.s. du paludisme et de la lutte anti-malarienne', 12 April 1933.

51 Henry G.-S. Morin, *Entretiens sur le paludisme et sa prévention en Indochine*, Hanoi: IDEO, 1935, p. 33; CAOM/Guernut 22, 'Contribution à l'étude du paludisme à Hà Giang de 1929 à 1935'.

52 CAOM/Guernut 96, 'Réponse à l'enquête', Bắc Quang, 25 April 1938.

53 CAOM/Guernut 96, 'Enquête No. 3 sur le problème des migrations intérieures. Note Introductive' by André Touzet, Secretary General of the Third Sub-Commission, Paris, 30 December 1937.

54 J.-L. de Lanessan, *La colonisation Française en Indo-Chine*, Paris: Felix Alcan, 1895, p. 313; Philippe Le Failler, 'Le mouvement international anti-opium et l'Indochine (1906–1940)', Doctorat nouveau régime, Université de Provence, 1993, p. 233; Hubert Lyautey, *Lettres du Tonkin et de Madagascar, 1894–1899*, Paris: Armand Colin, 1921, p. 159.

55 Henri Maître, *Les Régions Moï du Sud Indo-Chinois, Le Plateau du Darlac*, Paris: Librairie Plon, 1909, pp. 143, 147.

56 CAOM/Guernut 96, 'Réponse à l'enquête sur les migrations intérieures', Phố Bảng military post, (Đồng Văn district, Hà Giang), Lt. Prollemund, Chef de Poste, 10 April 1938.

57 CAOM/Guernut 96, 'Réponse à l'enquête sur les migrations intérieures', district mandarin, Vị Xuyên, 22 April 1938.

58 Marquet, *De la rizière*, pp. 157, 175.

59 Nguyễn Quang Ngọc, *Về một số làng buôn*, pp. 173, 294–295.

60 CAOM/Guernut 96, 'Réponses à l'enquête sur les migrations intérieures', Valençot, Administrateur Adjoint, Lào Cai, undated (1938).

61 Nguyễn Quang Ngọc, *Về một số làng buôn*, pp. 59–61, 151, 159.

62 Trần Huy Liệu, *Lịch sử tám mươi năm*, p. 190.

63 CAOM/Guernut 96, 'Réponse à l'enquête sur les migrations intérieures', Garnier, Chef de Poste, Yên Minh, 14 April 1938.

64 Ta Quang Chieu was a son of a village head in Nam Trực district (Nam Định). CAOM/Guernut 96, 'Réponse à l'enquête sur les migrations intérieures', Captain Lebret, Hoàng Su Phì, 20 April 1938.

65 CAOM/Guernut 96, 'Réponse à l'enquête', Vị Xuyên, 21 April 1938.

66 Interview with Thân (Thái Nguyên, October 1996).

67 CAOM/Guernut 96, 'Réponse à l'enquête', Hoàng Su Phì, 20 April 1938.

68 CAOM/Guernut 96, 'Réponses à l'enquête', Lào Cai, undated (1938).

69 CAOM/Guernut 96, 'Réponse à l'enquête', Hoàng Su Phì, 20 April 1938.

70 CAOM/Guernut 96, 'Réponse à l'enquête', Vị Xuyên, 22 April 1938.

71 CAOM/Guernut 28, 'Voeu de Do Van Dien, commerçant à Phu Tho', undated (1938).

72 Nguyen Tu Chi, 'The Traditional Viet Village in Bac Bo: Its Organizational Structure and Problems'. In *The Traditional Village in Vietnam*, Hanoi: The Gioi Publishers, 1993, pp. 97–98. Not all formal 'outsiders' suffered in this way, however: in some villagers, powerful people chose the formal status of 'outsider' to avoid paying taxes. Vu Van Hien, 'Les institutions annamites depuis l'arrivée des Français: L'impôt personnel et les corvées de 1862 à 1936', *RIJE*, no. 13, 1940, p. 88.

73 Georges Boudarel, 'L'insertion du pouvoir central dans les cultes villageois au Vietnam. Esquisse des problèmes à partir des écrits de Ngô Tât Tô'. In Alain Forest, Yoshiaki Ishizawa and Léon Vandermeersch (eds), *Cultes populaires et société Asiatiques*, Paris: L'Harmattan, 1991, p. 128.

74 Diệp Đình Hoa used family chronicles (*gia phả*) to show how a single family consisted of seventy-five households over ten generations, with forty-five of them in the village and thirty in other places. Philippe Papin showed how people used relatives to make the move. Diệp Đình Hoa, *Làng Nguyễn*, p. 32; Philippe Papin, 'Des "villages dans la ville" aux "villages urbains" – l'espace et les formes de pouvoir à Hanoi de 1805 à 1940', Doctorat d'histoire, Université de Paris 7, 1997, pp. 189–200.

75 Diệp Đình Hoa, *Làng Nguyễn*, p. 35.

76 Nghiêm Xuân Yêm, 'Thanh niên trí thức với nghề nông ở xứ nhà', *Thanh Nghị*, no. 35, 16 April 43, p. 196.

77 Gourou, *Les paysans du delta*, pp. 216–220.

78 Masaya Shiraishi, 'State, Villagers, and Vagabonds: Vietnamese Rural Society and the Phan Ba Vanh Rebellion', *Senri Ethnological Studies*, vol. 13, 1984, pp. 345–400.

79 Camille Briffaut, *La cité annamite*, Paris: Larose, 1909. See also Maurice Chautemps, *Le vagabondage en pays annamite*, Paris: A. Rousseau, 1908.

4

Peasants Attached to Villages

*T*he construct of the village, to which Red River Delta villagers were supposed to be 'attached', bore little relation to reality. As we saw in the previous chapter, there was a proportion of the population who had little to lose and much to gain by leaving the village. Some of these hoped one day to return. For them the very structures of village life – economic or social – created the need for departure. Others left without looking back. They understood, perhaps, the complaint of an old woman whom I met on a sandbank under the Chương Dương bridge in Hanoi: 'How can poor people have a home?'* At the heart of this comment was the idea that to have a home, to have a *quê hương*, you must have land. You must have a space not only to make a living, but to underwrite a position in village society, and above all to bury your ancestors. Those who propagated discourses of peasant attachment to the land failed to acknowledge the reality of political and economic relations in the village, and the fact that large numbers of people had no land there at all. It was not that they overlooked it exactly, for landlessness was a well-known problem by the 1930s. Victims/perpetrators of ancient and essentialized notions of Vietnamese culture, they failed to make the link.

A LOW LEVEL OF OUT-MIGRATION FROM THE RED RIVER DELTA

Landlessness offers us a measure of political and economic vulnerability in the village. It allows us a point of entry into the social structures which determined decisions to migrate – or, as the attachment discourse proposed, to stay in the village.

Quantifying landlessness in colonial Vietnam was a major challenge even at the time. Most estimates were based on Yves Henry's calculations, and even so gave rise to quite different views on the issue. Nghiêm Xuân Yêm and Đinh Gia Trinh came to (conservative) estimates of 200–300,000 landless. Khérian reckoned there were a million landless taxpayers in the delta. Trần Văn Giàu quoted Henry to affirm that two-thirds of the delta's eight million population were rural proletarians. Many of these figures are little more than guesses. The more prudent confined

---

* This Red River sandbank (called Bãi Giữa) has long been home to rootless people. The woman was 65 when I met her there. Interview (Hanoi, May 1996).

themselves to qualitative assessments. Trường Chinh and Võ Nguyên Giáp noted simply: 'there are so many landless peasants'.[1] The provincial mandarin in Hà Nam thought the landless formed a fifth class apart from the traditional scholar, farmer, artisan and trader (*sĩ, nông, công, thương*). He proposed grouping the population by class on a register and recruiting the landless to clear land in the highlands. A French pen annotated his comments on the landless, complaining with a bureau-cratic sense of the practical, that it was 'difficult to determine who they are'.[2]

Landless *inscrits*, by virtue of their registration on the tax roll, could cultivate a small plot of communal land. But not everyone figured on this roll, and not every-one feared losing this last mainstay against destitution, which René Dumont thought was a powerful incentive not to leave the village. But Dumont neglected all the people excluded from access to the commune's limited resources, when he observed that the landless *inscrits* constituted the 'most miserable part of the population'.[3] Marxist historians assumed that poverty from landlessness increased during the colonial period. Shiraishi showed that it was by no means negligible in the early nine-teenth century, but thought that the effects of economic and social differentiation were exacerbated in the colonial period by a lack of opportunity for out-migration.[4] And only the sort of socially differentiated approach employed by Shiraishi allows us to reflect upon the quality of the attachment discourse and the processes of migration in rural Vietnam. This chapter is my exploration of Shiraishi's hypothesis.

For landless people, a sense of attachment to a particular piece of land was no more than an ideal. Departure elsewhere might bring them closer to that ideal. But all the sources point to a low level of out-migration from Red River Delta villages during the colonial period. The number of landless in the delta was con-siderably higher than the number of out-migrants. If many aspired to social and economic upward mobility and if by leaving the village they felt they could achieve it – within the village or elsewhere – why did so few people leave?

There is no doubt that few people moved out of the Red River Delta during the half century to 1945. This is the case even if we allow for substantial unrecorded migration. There were, according to Gourou, seven million people living in rural areas of the delta in 1936.[5] Of these, he reckoned that a total of 50,000 left the delta definitively each year. But, as Gourou put it, 'the annual excess of births over deaths is at least 65,000 and is most probably in the region of 100,000'.[6] In Thái Nguyên, Echinard counted nearly 50,000 settlers over twelve years, of which over half were free migrants, 'settlers from all parts'.* His statistics for the middle region's most promising province amount to a low rate of in-migration, when compared to the numbers of people in the delta 'vegetating without hope'.[8] Statistics for other provinces in the highlands were lower still.†

---

* Not all were from the delta, however: only 1,632 out of the 2,674 families holding small concessions. Nghiêm Xuân Yêm thought that many came from nearby provinces like Vĩnh Yên and Bắc Giang. For sources, see note 7.

† See the Appendix.

All these figures are subject to the usual caution regarding colonial statistics. But even if they were hopeless underestimates, they would have made only the smallest dent in the delta's population. There was, furthermore, no significant movement of people to the south. The spontaneous migrations expected in 1936 on the opening of the Hanoi–Saigon railway never happened. People moving to the plantations in the south were counted only in thousands, rising from 3,486 in 1923 to a peak of 17,977 in 1928.[9] And many survivors of contract labour experiences in Cambodia and in New Caledonia and the New Hebrides went home after completing their term. Government-organized transfers to the Mekong Delta did not get under way before the early 1940s, and in a 1945 article Vũ Đình Hòe pulled no punches in his comment on them: 'People have talked a great deal about these experiments. We are still waiting for results.'[10]

Vũ Đình Hòe summarized the problem using the vocabulary of overpopulation. Using Gourou's figures, he estimated that 14,800 people left the Red River Delta annually. They went to the highlands, to land reclaimed from the sea, to mines, plantations and factories, to the cities, to the south. He described many of them as 'two white hands' people – people with nothing but their labour for capital.[11] One of them, indeed, described himself in such terms, saying he left Vietnam for the mines of New Caledonia in the 1930s with only his two white hands, adding 'You always hope, don't you?'[*] These people made up, Vũ Đình Hòe noted, 'in all one-eighth of the surplus population born every year. Which isn't counting all the "eternally" surplus, at least a million and a half people.' There were more than a million desperate people stuck in the delta, 'at their wits' end' for how to make a living.[12]

Vũ Đình Hòe also provided the elements of an explanation for the low rate of out-migration. He refused to draw on essentialized views of peasant psychology.

> Everyone comes up with plenty of explanations. But up to now people most commonly emphasize the psychological and social one. Vietnamese peasants do not like to leave their 'father's home, ancestors' land' where they have many ties to family and village; they must live by the paddy fields, by the particular rituals of their home village; they're frightened to go far, frightened to take risks, frightened of 'terrifying ghosts and poisoned water', etc.[†]
>
> I do not wish to say that this view is wrong and in fact I still think that this way of thinking usually makes every peasant doubt and hesitate when people go to recruit for the plantations. But I don't think this obstacle is enough to prevent people from leaving when they see that people who went before them are still healthy and able to make a comfortable living, while they themselves remain hungry at home, always worrying

---

[*] After his return in the 1950s, the capital he had earned there was soon gone – impossible to invest under the socialist system – and once again he was left, he said, with his 'two white hands' (*hai bàn tay trắng*). Interview (Hanoi, May 1996).

[†] Terrifying ghosts and poisoned water: *ma thiêng nước độc*. The full expression associates ghosts with the forest, from a specifically lowland perspective: *rừng thiêng nước độc chớ hề ở lâu* (terrifying forest and poisoned water, don't stay there long). Vương Trung Hiệu, *Tực ngữ Việt Nam chọn lọc*, Hanoi, NXB Văn Nghệ, 1996, p. 395.

about tomorrow's meal. Despite people's fondness for home there comes a point when 'the belly's hungry and the feet have to move'.[13]

Vũ Đình Hòe offered two reasons why people, despite their hunger, might decide not to move.

> Not only Vietnamese rural folk, but rural folk in any country (even if they are not afraid or like to take certain risks), if going to clear land means that i) they get sick, ii) they can't make a living, then they prefer to stay at home! This is a strong indication of the practical-minded spirit of country people.[14]

Malaria and a means of subsistence, then, were the main obstacles.

Let us look first at malaria.* Hà Giang was notorious as the 'town of fever and death'. But people got sick with malaria throughout the highlands. Even Đại Từ, Echinard's 'district of the future' was renowned for the disease. There was a folksong recording the malaria there: 'all the sick, sick people, if not in Đại Từ, then in Vũ Nhai'.[15] I was told by Tuấn, at Hoàng Nông commune, that because of malaria, 'many children were born, but few were raised. It was impossible to develop, many many children died'. Across the Công River, at Cà Phê village, Hỷ exclaimed, '*Ôi giời ôi!* So much malaria. Even people coming for one or two months got it. People got very sick, and died.' Downstream, at Tân Cương, Thân said people came to work but soon went away. 'They were frightened. Frightened of the terrifying forest and the poisoned water'. The fear of the disease was so prevalent, and its cause so little understood in the delta that bus drivers on mountain routes took bottles of water along, to avoid drinking from the streams.[16] One observer noted in the 1930s that a map of malaria corresponded closely to the map of the distribution of the Việt population, suggesting that the prevalence of the disease in an area was sufficient to deter all but the hardiest of settlers.† Gourou, indeed, saw malaria as the single major obstacle to mass settlement of the highlands.[18]

The other obstacle was finding a means of subsistence. There were malaria-free parts of the highlands. The dreaded *Anopheles minimus* could not survive in areas over 1,000 metres but these were areas with little land suitable for farming. And few people with capital to spare were inclined to invest it in the highlands; they moved to the towns,[19] or they lent their money at interest.‡ Migrants to the hills tended to be people looking for capital. They brought little with them. But to make a living from a small concession, they needed money for a house, for tools, for a buffalo or cow. To find wage work in the mountains they had to have the bus

---

* For the sake of clarity, the term malaria (*sốt rét*) is used throughout this discussion, but it is not necessarily the case that all fevers causing sickness and loss of life in the hills were malaria. For further discussion of the difficulty of diagnosing and identifying fevers, see Chapter 8.

† Compare Maps 3 and 5. See also note 17.

‡ Anyone with money immediately became a lender, as lending money at interest – which Vũ Đình Hoè called 'sitting and eating out of a golden bowl' (*ngồi mát ăn bát vàng*) – was better than work. Vũ Đình Hòe, 'Vấn đề đi vay', p. 15. See also Grégoire Khérian, 'La position du problème du crédit dans l'Union Indochinoise', *RIJE*, no. 15, 1941, p. 377.

fare, accommodation, food for a few days and money for implements and animals.[20] Unless, like Thức, they were so hungry that they left on foot, slept where they dropped, and lived from begging. Given the uncertainty of the venture, only the most adventurous or the most desperate took it on. Most people preferred, as Vũ Đình Hoè said, to stay at home.

There was, however, a further reason. This was the peasants' attachment to their village. This attachment was not, however, psychological and religious, as so many people thought. The strongest ties to the village, indeed, bore no relation to family, forefathers, festivals, fields; they were imposed by the French. The discourse on attachment to villages was not simply a misreading of peasant mentality. It sprang from the requirement, for purposes of colonial administration, that people be linked to villages. From the French point of view, the discourse served to legitimize this requirement. For many educated urban Vietnamese it played into an ideology of village nostalgia. If peasants were attached to villages in early twentieth-century Vietnam, it was because the colonial administration bound them there.

Shiraishi summed up this situation, in his analysis of nineteenth-century vagabonds:

> Under the new circumstances in which the colonial state increased its political and administrative control, the bandits and thieves could no longer act as freely as they had done in the traditional era. Furthermore, with more effective means of coercion and a strict identity card system, the authorities were in a better position to prevent people from becoming vagabonds. (…) Thus under a strict control system with insufficient social outlets, a majority of people were confined to the place where they lived.[21]

Three ties confined them: taxation, identity, security.

ATTACHMENT TO THE VILLAGE: TAXATION

The burden of colonial taxation has been analysed, albeit inadequately, elsewhere.[22] Here, the crucial factor was not the amount in fiscal terms, but the manner of its collection. Notably of head tax. Over the colonial period, there was a gradual shift in the manner of head tax collection, whereby the state, while recognizing the existence of individual men for tax purposes, refused to know exactly who they were. This knowledge was left to village authorities.

Vũ Văn Hiền explained the shift 'from the notion of *inscrit* to the notion of taxpayer'. *Inscrits* were, as we saw in Chapter 2, males over 18 registered for tax purposes. In the past, there had been large numbers of unregistered (*non-inscrit*) and tax-exempt people who were not officially required to pay. The French reduced the number of exemptions. They also obliged the unregistered, officially, to pay head tax. Initially they paid 0.4 piastres, while registered members paid 2.5 piastres (1897). Later, in taxation terms, the *inscrit/non-inscrit* distinction was abolished, and all men paid 2.5 piastres (1920). Finally a progressive head tax system was introduced (1937).[23] Under this equitable system, each man owed tax according to his means, although there are reasons to doubt the even-handedness of its implementation.[24]

The abolition of the *non-inscrit* was a purely fiscal measure. Unregistered men were still unable to enjoy the benefits of village membership (like the communal land), although some moves were made to encourage their participation in village government.[25] They often paid more than the tax amount stipulated. In this, there was no difference with previous generations. But while in previous generations – as far as the state was concerned – outsiders had not belonged to a village, they were now second-class people fixed to one. The 1937 legislation prescribed that villages keep five different tax rolls, counting men with their (a) origin in the village, (b) origin elsewhere in Tonkin, (c) origin elsewhere in Indochina (d) origin unknown, and (e) age under 18, although there is no evidence that this complex registration system was enforced. The refusal to abolish the formal distinction between *inscrit* and *non-inscrit* was deemed a concession to ancient forms of village administration, which maintained internal distinctions between the two categories. In a similar concession to Vietnamese tradition, women were neither taxed nor identified.[26] But the cumulative effect of French tinkering with the tax system offered no concessions to history, constituting instead a major social change. Floaters and drifters had formed a substantial section of the pre-colonial population. They were now, by state recognition, attached to villages.

ATTACHMENT TO THE VILLAGE: IDENTITY

State recognition of individual men – registered and unregistered – came in the form of personalized cards. Previously, when villages were taxed with limited reference to individual inhabitants, there was no need for this. But with the recognition of taxpayers, as the burden of taxation shifted from the village to the individual, it became necessary to issue identification. An 1897 law ordered that tax receipts take on the role of ID cards in Tonkin: 'for able bodied men, carrying a card is obligatory'. This 'external control' saved the trouble of state involvement in village administration. Men who failed to present valid tax cards risked fines and imprisonment if they ventured beyond the village. Cards were required for all business with the administration.[27] A 1937 law provided for their annual issue by the village head, on payment of tax. Each category (1, 2.5, 5 piastres, etc.) had a different coloured card. The village chop was placed on the card. The holder added fingerprints or a photograph.[28] Tax cards identified categories of taxpayer (1 piastre cardholders owned no property, 25 piastre cardholders voted in provincial elections, etc.).* They also, and more importantly, identified inhabitants of villages.

---

* Tuấn remembered that there were theoretically eight levels of tax payment: 1.2/2.5/5/ 7/12/15/20/25 piastres. In the legislation, however, I could not find his 12 nor his 20 piastre levels, which may have been local innovations. He said that 12 piastre cardholders could vote for district deputies (*hội viên*) and 25 piastre cardholders for provincial deputies (*nghị viên*). Tuan's 1.2 piastre card probably included a 0.2 piastre 'contribution' to officials. Interview (Thái Nguyên, January 1997). Pinto, 'Chronique législative', p. 435.

Identification with a particular village was not, however, immutable. A French legal expert interpreted it in significant terms: 'The taxpayer is not attached without remission to his village of origin. He can break this tie.' He could do so by writing a request to the Résident of the province where the village to which 'he desires to transfer his tax inscription' was situated.* But the principle was clear: a peasant must be attached to one village or another.

ATTACHMENT TO THE VILLAGE: SECURITY

Identification by attachment to a village was necessary not only for taxation, but also for security. A state identification service was created 'to fix the identity, filiation and birthplace of individuals who seek to escape justice by changing their name'.[30] In addition to the tax receipt, an ID card was invented – a sort of passport, required for border crossing and administrative tasks. The spirit of the legislation was expressed, albeit somewhat obliquely, in the following letter:

> As far as the identity card is concerned, I have already informed you that only natives leaving their country of origin (Tonkin, Annam, Cambodia etc.) are required to hold it. The Governor General, however, desires to come to a point at which the identity of each Vietnamese is established, and you will easily understand the reasons.[31]

Vagrancy laws restricted the circulation of suspect individuals. Beggars and drifters in towns, unable to justify their livelihood, were returned to their home village.[32] Individuals without identification outside their country of origin were imprisoned and expelled.† ID records helped track criminals and check up on soldiers.[34] State of the art methods of identification – anthropometric description, 'spoken portraits', fingerprinting, photography – were used for judicial and administrative purposes.

Anthropometry involved description of the human skeleton. An individual's height, chest, head, ears, and elbows were measured with meticulous precision with the aid of special instruments distributed to provincial authorities (Tonkin, 1919). The 'spoken portrait' was a means of classifying facial features. Nguyễn Văn Chi, acquitted for robbery in 1907, might have been surprised to recognize himself in the following *portrait parlé*: 'height – 1.52 m; hair – black; eyebrows – thick; forehead – small; eyes – brown; nose – spread; mouth – small; chin – pointed; beard – none; face – oval; colouring – yellow'. Techniques such as these were initially applied to people who infringed criminal laws (which could include vagrancy) or who worked in domestic service for French people. But on her 1940 identity card, Đỗ Thị Huế, a trader in Tuyên Quang, could read herself described (next to her photograph and right-hand fingerprints) as a woman of 'Tonkinese'

---

* Tuấn said a change of residence paper (*giấy chuyển cư*) cost 0.2 piastres. He equated it to the household residence (*hộ khẩu*) system instituted in the 1950s. See Chapter 8. Interview (Thái Nguyên, January 1997). See also note 29.

† For examples, see note 33.

race, 1.59 m in height, with a 'bulging forehead', 'a pointed chin' and a 'number of small hollow scars 0.5 cm above her left eyebrow'.[35] She was one of nearly 80,000 individuals placed on file that year, a total which had grown from 20,000 in 1928 and which allows us to calculate that around a million inhabitants of Tonkin carried ID cards by 1945, no mean achievement in an administrative region inhabited by around eight million people.[36]

Officials of the identification service aimed at scientific knowledge of individuals. But however scientifically processed, their knowledge depended on village authorities, who were responsible for acknowledging the existence of their villagers.[37] The system thus had two consequences. It increased the power of village authorities and prevented travel by people regarded as 'suspect'. Suspect meant, above all, without attachment to a village.

The identification of 'rootless' with 'suspect' was not merely institutional. No regular place of abode meant no regular income. Bandits lived outside villages and preyed on them. Outsiders also threatened the political security of the colonial state. Lionel Lotzer, on mission in the south, was surprised to find that 'almost all the southern subversive groups contain a majority of Tonkinese'. He was surprised, because he found the villagers of northern Vietnam uninterested in politics, easy to administrate. But his astonishment diminished when he realized the 'category' to which these people belonged:

> These are isolated people, errants, individuals who have broken with their family and village, subjects without any social attachment, and we know the deplorable effects, for Tonkinese people who remain community-orientated, of such an isolation, which deprives them of the necessary influence of the family group and village institutions.[38]

Lotzer, whose purpose for travelling in the south was to promote migration to the Mekong Delta, concluded that migrants should be sent in village groups:

> They will be grouped in organized communities; they will remain governed by village law; they will be supervised by their village head; they will keep their direct Tonkinese heads; they will aspire to attain to a position within the group; they will live in families; they will have their *đình* and the tutelary deities of the Tonkinese commune; they will continue to observe the customs which still weld the individual so strongly to the group.[39]

Lotzer worked under the illusion that village structures could simply be reproduced in a new environment. Central to this illusion was the issue of authority in the village.

The Role of Village Authorities

Village religion and family solidarity were important in the construction of the attachment discourse. But the agents of attachment in terms of taxation and ID were the village authorities. The state came to recognize the existence of individuals, but it did not know them. Village authorities knew them, and knowledge gave them power. Some people dodged the effects of this knowledge/power, and managed to survive outside of villages. But, since the nineteenth century, the numbers of such people had fallen dramatically. In their place was a new class of outsider, attached by law to a village, but effectively unable to make a living there. As Shiraishi put it, while 'social and economic differentiation in traditional rural society manifested itself as a struggle between those who remained in villages and those who were forced to leave, then differentiation in the colonial period tended to intensify tensions inside village society itself'.[40] In the colonial period, people depended on their village head (*lý trưởng*) for permission to leave, even for a short time. To obtain this permission they had to pay tax.

Thân explained to me how the system worked:

> There was a card. With this card, showing you'd paid tax, you could go everywhere. If you didn't have the card, you couldn't go anywhere. You'd have to stay at home. But if you stayed at home, you went hungry. With no income, you couldn't feed your family, they'd die of hunger. You had to go and work for wages.
>
> If you went out to Thái Nguyên town – only for fun, not for work – and they asked you 'Where's your card?', and you didn't have one, they'd put you straight into jail. Terrible! You stayed in jail until your relatives could buy the card. And you paid bribes to the police too.

Trường Chinh and Võ Nguyên Giáp described the effects of this regime at tax collection time:

> There is an uproar in the village. If destitute people cannot pay, then they must leave the village and flee elsewhere in order to escape cruel and savage mistreatment ... The government knows this, so every year after tax collection they organize very strict searches and checks everywhere in the cities and countryside. On the streets, at cross-roads, at markets, on boats, ferries, and in railroad stations travellers are stopped and asked for their identity cards. In the cities the police do this, in the countryside it is the guards. They organize round-ups to catch the people who have fled. During these searches and arrests, the poor of Indochina are treated like animals, not as human beings.[41]

The people who most needed to leave the village – those who had to look for wage work – were the least able to afford to. They were very vulnerable. Village authorities regularly demanded payment of more than the face value of the card.[42] Trafficking in cards started up. Fingerprints became 'formless inkstains'.[43] Photographs were removed and replaced.[44] Plantation recruitment, in particular, gave rise to numerous identity abuses. Recruiters paid village heads to provide identification for kidnap victims: in 1928, a young nun was abducted in this way. Recruitees bought cards from heads of villages other than their own: in 1927, a young man with 'sick eyes', dismissed from a plantation for medical reasons, paid 2 piastres for a fake one.[45] And procedures intended to prevent falsification proved useless. The following report on recruiting agents was compiled by the Sûreté in Nam Định, one of the few provinces where labour recruitment was authorized:

> Recruiting workers everywhere, they bring them to Nam Định and make arrangements with the *lý trưởng*. The *lý trưởng* looks on the village rolls for inhabitants whose age corresponds to that of the recruits; they are put through their paces and,

interrogated in my office, recite the name, age, place of origin, ancestors' names of the individual *inscrit* whose identity it has been decided to give them. Once the identity card is made, the *lý trưởng* certifies it and, except in special circumstances, it is impossible to suspect or detect the fraud.[46]

The French administration condoned the practice. While the Sûreté reported that several village heads had been taken to court for fraud, the RST warned that too many prosecutions would hinder the recruitment of these officials and prejudice village administration. The limit of the colonialists' control over their village collaborators was quickly reached. Or put another way, the power relation was reversed, as the French found themselves collaborating with village officials in their abuses of power.[47]

Abuses by village authorities did not make it impossible to leave the village; it was quite simply expensive. People could go in desperation and face the consequences. Or they could leave in full legality, after paying their tax, and going through complex procedures, both on departure and arrival.

Departure from the delta:

> The peasant must first speak to the head of the village. To get him to deal with his affairs, he has to pay a baksheesh. To get his identity papers, he goes next to the provincial town, accompanied by this village head. Of course, the latter's transport and food do not come free of charge. To issue the identity papers, the provincial administration's secretaries also require a small offering. As the unfortunate man who wishes to expatriate himself is precisely one who has nothing, we may understand that it is materially impossible for him to leave his village, despite the regime of liberty which authorises this.[48]

Arrival in the highlands:

> After Tết, they would ask the village head for permission to bring their family up with them, clear some land. There was no fixed fee. It depended on the year and the village. There were good men who only took 2 or 3 piastres. There were also others who (…)
> There were no rules, this is Vietnam. The land was empty, there were few people, the more the merrier. If you brought along a bottle of wine, then (…)[*]

The result, as the French observed, was overpopulation. People 'piled up' in their villages but not necessarily they liked living there. Quite simply because it was, practically and financially speaking, not worth leaving.

---

[*]   Interview with Tuấn (Thái Nguyên, January 1997). In 1918, Minh paid the village head 3 piastres to settle at Phúc Khánh village near Bờ Rạ (see Chapter 1). The high cost, he said, meant that 'few people came'. Interview (Thái Nguyên, October 1996). Those after small concessions faced other expenses: a request to be written; a map to be drawn; a village head's declaration to be made to the Verification Commission. NAV1/RST 67486, Michelot, Résident in Thái Nguyên, to RST, 5 May 1942; Nghiêm Xuân Yêm, 'Điều tra nhỏ – Những tiểu đồn điền', p. 263.

1945: A NEW PROGRAMME OF MIGRATION

Vũ Đình Hòe did not discuss the obstacle of corruption in his 1945 article.[*] But he was certainly aware of the others and called for a new programme of migration to overcome them. He thought that to help the people of the Red River Delta to leave, what was required was a strong programme of organization set up by the state. He proposed therefore the establishment of a Malaria Office to eliminate disease, a Land Office to prepare the terrain, and a Migration Office to coordinate the actual movement of people. His role models were Nguyễn Công Trứ, the nineteenth-century mandarin who founded two districts in the lower delta on land reclaimed from the sea, and the French missionaries of Kontum and Yên Bình, whose strong leadership he saw as essential to the success of their highland settlements.[†] He called for investment in organization rather than individuals. In 1935, the French had spent 73 piastres on digging ditches and building roads, and gave 400 piastres to the settlers. Vũ Đình Hòe proposed spending the latter sum on organization and the former on the settlers, who should be smallholders – not landless peasants. Recruitment should not be left to agents, nor even to volunteers:

> Government authority should be used. In overcrowded villages … all those families with a few *sào* up to a few hectares of land should be *forced* to leave their village and settle in migration areas where the state has prepared and built a base for them …
>
> They should go *for good*. They must not be allowed to think that they are there temporarily, that if they don't like it, they can go back. In this way they will get down to work and settle. Of course, the work of mobilizing and encouraging people should make them go with happiness and high hopes. The principle is to use state authority to take the place of personal discretion. The main thing is to use this authority to prepare carefully, so that settlers do not go down with malaria, to ensure they can make enough to eat, and to cater for any emergencies. If this is not done, but people are nevertheless forced to stay, then they've been pushed up, nothing less! (emphasis in original).[49]

Vũ Đình Hòe emphasized the need for sufficient resources – in terms of funding, personnel and determination – to implement a programme of migration on a national scale. In the past, migration had been promoted on a small scale, for purposes of overpopulation 'relief'. It should now become, as he put it, '*part of an expanded national economic programme*, as in the past a symbol of the expansionist strength of the Vietnamese nation' (emphasis in original). His ideas differed from past experiences in one significant way. The Vietnamese nation was now geographically defined, and colonization beyond this definition was ruled out. 'The southward march has stopped. Vietnam's borders must be regarded as fixed now. Overpopulation these days means uneven population distribution in the space within those fixed borders.'[50]

---

[*]   He certainly knew about these practices, having obtained a small concession in Thái Nguyên thanks to his father-in-law, Nguyễn Văn Khúc, the provincial mandarin there. In those days, he led me to understand in interview, such things were part of normal life. Interview (Hanoi, November 2000).

[†]   See Chapter 9 for discussion of Nguyễn Công Trứ. The Catholic settlement in Yên Bình is described by Gourou, *Les paysans du delta tonkinois*, pp. 202–203.

The obstacles to colonization could only be overcome with the sort of determination that a vast programme could generate. As the Đồng Hỷ district mandarin pointed out, in the matter of migration 'to want is to be able'.[51] Vũ Đình Hòe shared this perspective, suggesting that, 'over the last 50 years', the problem with migration was not so much a lack of ability, it was a lack of will. The French simply did not want the peasants to leave their villages.

Vũ Đình Hòe's article was prevented from publication by the colonial censor in January 1945. It was published in June, three months after the overthrow of French administration.[*] Fifteen years later, just six years after the French defeat at Điện Biên Phủ, migration from the Red River Delta became, as he proposed, a national project – a matter of state organization and orchestrated voluntarism.

CONCLUSION

We saw in Chapter 2 that much energy was spent on the promotion of migration, that little was achieved. In Chapter 3, we learnt that Việt people moved along networks based on the family, the village and the colonial state. At the beginning of the present chapter, we found that the number of people who moved along these networks was small.

Colonial observers explained this with a discourse about Việt people's attachment to home. But reality was less rosy. Malaria and a lack of means of subsistence were obstacles to settlement in the highlands. Movement from the plains was hampered by forms of administrative attachment to the village. As Vũ Đình Hòe noted on the eve of the August Revolution, only when those ties were broken would the state find the political will to organize the programmes of malaria control and cereals production necessary for highland colonization.

As we shall see in the next chapter, it took a war to install the sort of government with the political will to do this. And that war itself destroyed the administrative hindrances to migration, creating other incentives for movement. With the violent dismantling of colonial power structures in the countryside, Việt people were finally detached from their villages.

NOTES

1   Yves Henry, *Economie agricole de l'Indochine*, Hanoi: IDEO, 1932; Nghiêm Xuân Yêm, 'Điều tra nhỏ – Những tá điền', *Thanh Nghị*, no. 55, 26 February 1944, p. 64; Đình Gia Trinh, 'Dân số và các giai cấp xã hội ở Đông-Dương', *Thanh Nghị*, no. 7, 1941, p. 20; Grégoire Khérian, 'À propos de quelques ouvrages récents sur l'économie indochinoise', *RIJE*, 1939, p. 600; Truong Chinh and Vo Nguyen Giap, *The Peasant Question*, Ithaca, New York: Cornell University Southeast Asia Program, 1974, p. 19; Trần Văn Giàu, *Giai cấp công nhân Việt Nam*, Hanoi: NXB Sự Thật, 1958, p. 192.

---

*   Founder of the progressive review *Thanh Nghị*, Vũ Đình Hòe was, at this time, a member of the council charged with drafting a new constitution in the authority installed by the Japanese after their overthrow of the French on 9 March 1945. Although a member of Hồ Chí Minh's first cabinet, he never became involved in DRV migration planning. Phạm Khắc Hòe, *Từ Triều Đình Huế đến Chiến Khu Việt Bắc – Hồi ký*, Hanoi: NXB Hà Nội, 1983, p. 37. Interview with Vũ Đình Hòe (Hanoi, November 2000).

2   NAV/RST 71115, Trần Văn Đại, mandarin in Hà Nam, to RST, 11 July 1930.

3   René Dumont, *La culture du riz dans le delta du Tonkin*, Bangkok: Prince of Songkla University, 1995, first published 1935, p. 59.

4   Masaya Shiraishi, 'State, Villagers, and Vagabonds: Vietnamese Rural Society and the Phan Ba Vanh Rebellion', *Senri Ethnological Studies*, vol. 13, 1984, p. 394.

5   Pierre Gourou, *L'utilisation du sol en Indochine*, Paris: Hartmann, 1940, p. 105. See also Map 11.

6   Pierre Gourou, *Les paysans du delta tonkinois, étude de géographie humaine*, Paris: Les Editions d'Art et d'Histoire, 1936, p. 219.

7   NAV1/RST 67504, Echinard, Résident in Thái Nguyên, to Lotzer, Résident in Nam Định, 1 March 1939; NAV1/RST 69048, Echinard to RST, 22 December 1938; Nghiêm Xuân Yêm, 'Điều tra nhỏ – Những tiểu đồn điền', *Thanh Nghị*, no. 62, 29 April 1944, p. 266.

8   Jules Brévié, *Discours prononcé à l'occasion de l'ouverture de la session du Grand Conseil des Intérêts économiques et financiers, le 2 décembre 1937*, Hanoi: IDEO, 1937, p. 41.

9   Emile Delamarre, *L'émigration et l'immigration ouvrière en Indochine*, Hanoi: IDEO, 1931, p. 19.

10 Vũ Đình Hòe, 'Nạn nhân mãn và việc di dân', *Thanh Nghị*, no. 112, 9 June 1945, p. 359. See also L. E. Lotzer and G. Wormser, *La surpopulation du Tonkin et du Nord-Annam*, Hanoi: IDEO, 1941, pp. 14, 104.

11 Vũ Đình Hòe, 'Vấn đề đi vay đối với dân quê', *Thanh Nghị*, no. 12, 1 May 1942, p. 13.

12 Vũ Đình Hòe, 'Nạn nhân mãn', p. 343.

13 Ibid., p. 360.

14 Ibid.

15 Alfred Echinard, 'Notice sur la province de Thai Nguyen', Thai Nguyen: unpublished monograph, 1932, p. 60; Vũ Văn Cẩn, *Bệnh Sốt Rét Cơn*, NXB Vui Sống, 1947, p. 13. The same song emerged in the sources a decade later in a different version and a different context. See Chapter 8.

16 Henry G.-S. Morin, *Entretiens sur le paludisme et sa prévention en Indochine*, Hanoi: IDEO, 1935, p. 61.

17 G.B., 'Le problème de la population et des subsistances en Indochine', *BEI*, 1938, p. 1345.

18 Pierre Gourou, *L'utilisation du sol en Indochine*, pp. 165–77.

19 Nghiêm Xuân Yêm, 'Thanh niên trí thức với nghề nông ở xứ nhà', *Thanh Nghị*, no. 35, 16 April 1943, p. 195.

20 Nghiêm Xuân Yêm, 'Điều tra nhỏ – Những tiểu đồn điền', p. 264. See Thân's itinerary, described in the Prologue.

21 Shiraishi, 'State, Villagers, and Vagabonds', pp. 393–394.

22 The two best-known general accounts of colonial taxation are those of Ngo Vinh Long and Martin J. Murray. Both, however, take anti-colonial political perspectives which colour their analysis. There remains a glaring gap in the literature on French Indochina, namely a scholarly analysis of the structures of colonial taxation and their effects on the day-to-day existence of the peasants. Recent monographs by Kleinen and Le Failler must be seen as two tips to an immense iceberg. Ngo Vinh Long, *Before the Revolution: The Vietnamese Peasants under the French*, Cambridge, Massachusetts: MIT Press, 1973, p. 62. Martin J. Murray, *The Development of Capitalism in Colonial Indochina (1870–1940)*, Berkeley: University of California Press, 1980, p. 68. John G. Kleinen, "Do not pay taxes": The Anti-Tax Revolt in Central Vietnam, 1908'. In Leslie E. Bauzon (ed.), *A Comparative Study of Peasant Unrest in Southeast Asia*, Singapore: Institute of Southeast Asian Studies, 1991, pp. 74–94. Philippe Le Failler, 'Village Rebellions in the Tonkin Delta, 1900–1905'. In Gisèle Bousquet and Pierre Brocheux (eds), *Twentieth Century Vietnam: Essays on Vietnamese Society*, Ann Arbor: University of Michigan Press, forthcoming.

23 Vu Van Hien, 'Les institutions annamites depuis l'arrivée des Français: L'impôt personnel et les corvées de 1862 à 1936', *RIJE*, no. 13, 1940, pp. 86–92.

24 These are discussed in Nguyễn Khắc Đạm, *Những thủ đoạn bóc lột của tư bản Pháp ở Việt Nam*, Hanoi: NXB Văn Sử Địa, 1957, p. 241.

25 Henri Brenier, *Essai d'atlas statistique de l'Indochine française*, Hanoi-Haiphong: IDEO, 1914, p. 64.

26 R. Pinto, 'Chronique législative: La réforme des impôts personnels dans les pays de l'Union Indochinoise', *RIJE*, no. 10, 1939, pp. 432, n. 1, 437.

27 Vu Van Hien, 'Les institutions annamites', p. 92.

28 Decree of 23 December 1937. J. Obrecht, 'Le problème de l'identification et l'Organization des services d'identité en Indochine', *RIJE*, 17, 1942, p. 45.

29 Pinto, 'Chronique législative', p. 434.

30 NAV1/RST 12114, Tonkin Identity Service to Fort Bayard, Kouang Tcheou Wan, 27 November 16.

31 NAV1/RTQ 183, Résident in Tuyên Quang to Director of Trang Da mines, 5 August 1921.

32 NAV1/RST 67498, 'Voeu No 38, Việc lập làng ở những nơi hoang địa cho bọn cùng đinh', 1938.

33 See, for example: **1910**: Repatriation of migrants looking for construction work in South Annam; they were in 'a state of vagrancy'. NAV1/RND 3196, RST to province Résidents, 13 October 1910. **1911**: Repatriation of sixty people from Thanh Hóa, caught en route to Thái Nguyên, illegally crossing the Annam–Tonkin border without 'a pass issued by a *lý trưởng*'. NAV2/RSA 556, Résident of Thanh Hóa to RST, 16 June 1911; NAV1/RST 74609, correspondence, June 1911. **1921**: Strike threats by miners obliged to return to their village for identification. NAV1/RTQ 183, Director of Trang Da mine to Résident in Tuyên Quang, 25 August 1921. **1924**: Repatriation of Phạm Văn Hợp to Hà Đông, who came to Saigon 'a month ago, looking for work' and 'was recently arrested for not carrying an identity card'. There were four or five such repatriations weekly. NAV1/RST 81322, Governor of Cochinchina to RST, 27 December 1924.

34 Obrecht, 'Le problème de l'identification', p. 39.

35 NAV1/RST 12114, Tonkin Identity Service to RST, 18 March 1919; NAV1/RBG 5, 'Extrait de jugement, tribunal indigène de Bac Giang', 31 July 1907; Obrecht, 'Le problème de l'identification', pp. 4–8. My thanks to Pascal Bourdieu for allowing me to use his grandmother Đỗ Thị Huế's ID card.

36 Obrecht, 'Le problème de l'identification', p. 49.

37 Ibid., p. 38.

38 Lotzer and Wormser, *La surpopulation du Tonkin*, p. 67.

39 Ibid.

40 Shiraishi, 'State, Villagers, and Vagabonds', p. 394.

41 Truong Chinh and Vo Nguyen Giap, *The Peasant Question*, p. 47.

42 Vu Van Hien, 'Les institutions annamites', p. 91. Hoàng Đạo, 'Bùn Lầy Nước Đọng', 1938. Translated in Ngo Vinh Long, *Before the Revolution*, p. 212.

43 Obrecht, 'Le problème de l'identification', p. 46.

44 NAV1/RND 3240, Sûreté in Nam Định to RST, 6 September 1928.

45 NAV1/RND 3240, Nguyễn Văn Thách to Sûreté Service Head, undated (1927).

46 NAV1/RND 3240, Sûreté in Nam Định to RST, 28 December 1927.

47 NAV1/RND 3240, RST to Résident in Nam Định, 21 April 1928.

48 Paul Bernard, *Le problème economique Indochinois*, Paris: Nouvelles Editions Latines, 1934, pp. 287–288. See also Nghiêm Xuân Yêm, 'Nạn dân đói (Một vài nhân xét và thiên kiến về vấn đề thóc gạo)', *Thanh Nghị*, no. 107, 5 May 1945, p. 229.

49 Vũ Đình Hòe, 'Nạn nhân mãn', pp. 416–417.

50 Ibid., p. 431.

51 NAV1/RST 67478, Đồng Hỷ district mandarin to Thái Nguyên mandarin, 15 November 1932.

Detached from Their Villages?
War and Migration, 1945–54

Figure 5: Transformations at Điện Biên Phủ

As these commemorative cigarettes show, the battle of Điện Biên Phủ marked a turning point in the history of the highlands. Smoked by high ranking cadres from the 1950s, the older blue packet shows the raising of a victory flag, while on the newer green packet a flag bearing the slogan 'Fight with Determination, Win with Determination' is defended by vigilant soldiers. On the back of both packets, tractors turn the battlefield into farmland.

Cigarettes purchased in Hanoi in May 1998. Photograph by Coombs Photography Unit.

Overview of Part Two

*T*he single chapter of Part Two, Chapter 5, 'Green Forest, Red Hills', explores the effects of war on the Việt population of the highlands and the plains. Emphasizing the importance of the forested landscape in the history of the war, and with an initial digression to demonstrate this, it charts the disruptions to the structures of colonial administration and to everyday life in the Red River Delta of the eight years of resistance against the French. Anti-colonial resistance was based in the hills, where communist insurgents took advantage of difficult terrain to wage a guerrilla war. The war caused unprecented movements of the population. The chapter examines the effects of these movements on the practice and policy of migration after the war ended. In this sense, the chapter acts as a hyphen. It shows how the structural base of the colonial regime in the villages was destroyed and how, at the same time, some of the structures of the administration which followed it were formed.

Green Forest, Red Hills

A French Assault on Chợ Chu

12 January: 'A column of thirty officers, 478 European troops and 416 natives, with 1,200 coolies, is concentrated at Thái Nguyên, under the orders of General Borgnis-Desbordes. (…) The first objective of the column is Chợ Mới. (…) The second objective is Chợ Chu. (…) Chợ Chu is in a rocky cirque, difficult of approach and easily defended.

18 January: Captain Comte of the Third Marine Infantry Regiment is first to enter Chợ Mới, and the enemy flees in all directions after burning down the village.

20 January: General Borgnis-Desbordes sets out (…) for Chợ Chu; but the guides lose the way, and after seven hours' marching in excessively difficult terrain across unknown country, without a path, the column has to return to Chợ Mới (…) [and] Thái Nguyên, to resupply and attack from the south, via Hương Sơn.

1,200 coolies had to be requisitioned in Hanoi and Thái Nguyên to concentrate sufficient supplies at Hương Sơn and relieve those who went to Chợ Mới. Unfortunately the approach of Vietnamese new year festivals (Tết) made their recruitment extremely difficult and the resupplying operation was carried out in the worst conditions.

30 January: The column of 37 officers, 779 Europeans and 278 natives leaves Hương Sơn and camps for the night at Quan Thông.

2 February: The disposition of the terrain allows movement away from the hills which are the basis of defence and several villages southwest of Chợ Chu are successively taken. (…) At 4.10 pm Chợ Chu was occupied without resistance. The market and all the surrounding villages had been burnt.

*T*he year in this account is 1889. The place is Chợ Chu, the main town in Định Hóa, a district of narrow valleys enclosed by four mountain chains forming a natural fortress.* The 'enemy' is an exile from the Taiping rebellion in China, Lường Tam Kỳ, who in the late nineteenth century led a band of Chinese mercenaries around the northern highlands before settling in Định

---

* Chợ Chu is nowadays more commonly known as Định Hóa, Chợ Mới as Phú Lương, and Hương Sơn as Đại Từ.

Hóa. In the campaign described above, the colonialists captured Chợ Chu.[1] They were unable, however, to take the mercenary leader, who took refuge in the forests. 'The French couldn't defeat him, he was too difficult to find', I was told by Hoa, the son of one of his followers.* Lường Tam Kỳ described his situation in a letter to the French, written during subsequent negotiations:

> The thing is that I have many brothers and need these forests and mountains to give them a living. I do not intend to usurp the realm. Now that Annam has been conquered by France, the region of Chợ Chu, a single arm, remains; it is covered in high, wooded mountains; sparsely populated with men, its vegetation stretches as far as the eye can see. Here's a country![2]

Lường Tam Kỳ was true to his word. He struck a deal with the French, who paid him off with 'enormous annual subsidies' in silver.[3] He kept to the valleys of Định Hóa where his Chinese 'brothers' took land to farm and wives to marry from the local Tày people. He himself was often seen sitting in the market, 'dressed like a coolie', selling opium, collecting taxes, lending money and dispensing justice, running his 'state within a state.'[4]

Over the years the Chinese threat in Định Hóa faded. Guns were handed over (1897). A military post was set up (1908). Lường Tam Kỳ died (1924). While his 'family, his adopted sons and their countless kin' appropriated all the best land, the district reverted to regular taxpaying (1929).[5] But a monograph of the province, written in 1901 just after peace was restored, contained a warning to future generations of French officials in the region.

> We must never lose sight of the fact that the variety of ethnic elements and the divergence in the interests of the representatives of the different races could, at any time, become a cause of trouble and that the province of Thái Nguyên, by its situation halfway between the China border and the Tonkin delta, combines in a relatively confined space the characters of both zones, offering to ill-doers not only the bait of appreciable local resources and considerable circulation of money and goods but also the shelter of steep mountains and almost impenetrable forests, and remains from the point of view of piracy a sort of regulator. To ensure equilibrium, precautions will always be necessary and the indispensable counterweight will have to be, for a long time to come, the maintenance of a sizeable armed police force.[6]

The warning lost its urgency over the years of *la paix française*. Looking back on his experience of highland conquest, General Pennequin wrote in 1913 about the urgency of organizing the inhabitants of the hills into a 'defensive curtain'. More than two decades later, a French official referred to his dormant proposal: 'this article was written twenty-four years ago, but has nevertheless kept all its value'.

---

* Hoa was from Nam Định, and came to Định Hóa in 1926 (aged 4) with his aunt, who married a Chinese follower of Lường Tam Kỳ. He was brought up as their son and took a Chinese name. Interview (Thái Nguyên, January 1997).

Time passed was 'time lost'.* By the 1930s, time was beginning to catch up on the French strategic neglect of the hills. In February 1933, Nguyễn Văn Khúc, Echinard's provincial mandarin, described Thái Nguyên town as a '*coquette ville*' with its paved streets, its market of bricks and concrete, and the 'premises of the Native Guard lined up in perfect order like the soldiers on parade'. He then opened an outline of the province's history with the following prescient paragraph: 'Everything changes with time. The province of Thái Nguyên has not escaped from this rule. (…) Having gone through several successive transformations, it will perhaps see others with the passing of the years.'[7]

Only twelve years were to pass before Thái Nguyên's next transformation. And when it came, in the form of communist revolution, Nguyễn Văn Khúc's successor Cung Đình Vận was among its most ferocious opponents. This ferocity cost him his life in 1945.[8]

THE RED MOUNTAIN

One of the key agents of communist change in Vietnam was a native of Thái Nguyên. A Nùng man whose family had settled in Vũ Nhai (Thái Nguyên) after moving from China, Chu Văn Tấn was no stranger to the Công River valley. In the early 1940s, while he commanded the resistance army in his home region, his wife kept out of sight in the house of a Việt settler at the head of the valley, at Mới village (literally New village), on the road up to Định Hóa. And in February 1943, just ten years after Nguyễn Văn Khúc forecast transformations to the province, he received orders to open up a route from the resistance base in Cao Bằng province to the delta, via Thái Nguyên. He wrote in his memoirs:

> To carry out this resolution the AFNS [Army for National Salvation] Command Staff set forth as the task for the forthcoming phase of activities the establishment of a new base area in Định Hóa. We felt that with the favourable development of the movement at this time and the good terrain in this area which leaned against a vast mountain chain – the Hồng [Red] mountain – we could set up a large base camp.[9]

In April, he arrived at Mới village, on the eastern edge of the Red Mountain: 'an extensive and fairly high mountain range, where there are only Yao communities. Up there secrets can be kept'.[10] He met up with his wife and together they made preparations for the base. By December, he was able to picture the creation of a 'three-legged position' formed by small liberated zones in Cao Bằng, Vũ Nhai-Bắc Sơn and Định Hóa-Sơn Dương.[11] According to a later history of the region, these three centres 'gradually opened out, and are now unified, becoming

---

* David Marr noted a tendency among French observers to forget about the Vietnamese who chose to resist them. Regarding the highlands, this was the case even among the some members of the administration. David G. Marr, *Vietnamese Anticolonialism 1885–1925*, Berkeley: University of California Press, 1971, p. xvi. CAOM/Guernut 26, 'Conférences du Général Pennequin sur la défense de l'Indochine', extract from *L'Armée Coloniale*, 25 August 1912.

the largest revolutionary base in the country, the Việt Bắc Revolutionary Base'.[12] A tiny settlement at Kim Lũng in the heart of the Red Mountain range became the revolution's capital. Renamed as Tân Trào (New Tide), Hồ Chí Minh arrived there in May 1945.[13] Today, the (reconstructed) house he lived in there, set high on the slopes in an impenetrable thicket of bamboo, and the site of the revolutionary conference held just before the August Revolution, with its banyan tree now preserved in folds of concrete, have become one of Vietnam's prime sites of socialist pilgrimage, an icon to the revolution's home and haven in the forests.

Eighteen months later, with the Việt Minh return from Hanoi to armed struggle, Hồ Chí Minh chose not to return to Tân Trào. He settled instead in the nearby village of Điềm Mặc, at the headquarters of a newly establised 'security zone' (*An toàn khu*, or ATK).* Other government offices and ministries were scattered throughout districts of Định Hóa, Sơn Dương and Chiêm Hóa (Tuyên Quang), and Chợ Đồn (Bắc Kạn). When I visited Định Hóa in 1997, I asked the district Party Secretary about the war against the French. 'The town was very crowded then', he said.

WARTIME ITINERARIES

The mountains bordering Định Hóa became, once again, a stronghold for enemies of the French. But rather than causing an exodus of the Việt population living there, as in the time of Lường Tam Kỳ, the Việt Minh presence had the opposite effect.[15] In 1945, news of the uprising inspired hundreds of young patriots to walk to the resistance bases in the hills. They were less welcome even than the refugees from famine. Most were turned back, urged to organize revolution at home.[16] But after the war started, at the end of 1946, movement to the Việt Bắc zone was encouraged by communist leaders.

Hundreds of thousands of people moved to the highlands during the war.[17] This figure is not a statistic – more an order of magnitude. Drawn from a health manual for later migrants to the highlands, it warned them of the problem of 'poisonous water', recalling that 'during the resistance war, hundreds of thousands of lowland people went up to the Việt Bắc, but few suffered from 'water rash' [malaria]'. The migration figure, however, is more credible than the medical analysis, and there is no doubt that malaria was a dangerous enemy to both armies in the conflict. The Việt Minh opened classes for its soldiers, teaching them that mosquitoes, not bad water, were the cause of the fever. They also learnt to distinguish ordinary mosquitoes from the deadly *Anopheles minimus*, to keep a good diet and to kill mosquitoes as they killed Frenchmen – wherever they found them.[18]

Learning to live with malaria was only part of the process of adaptation to the hills. People from the plains had to adjust to the unfamiliar forested landscapes, the strange customs of the highlanders and the soporific effects of altitude. Yet,

---

*   Điềm Mặc is where the Công River rises. See also note 14.

whether they stayed only a few months or for the entire duration of the war, many people found the difficulties could be overcome, and the new environment even enjoyed. The writer Nam Cao, a man of delta origin who spent the war in a Việt Bắc minority village, wrote at the time about the shift in his own consciousness:

> We have also discovered many queer things and the queerest is that there is nothing queer. When I was in the plains my hair stood on end with terror whenever I heard raftsmen tell stories of jungle, tiger, panther, bear and boa. I believed that houses in the jungle had to be built on very high piles and strongly fenced, that people had to be in a great number when going out and they had to take with them gongs to frighten the tigers and at night time people dared not open the door and had to pass water right in their houses. Now we are living in the depth of the jungle and on top of very high mountains. The door is never closed because there is no door. Many nights there were only two of us. We go everywhere by ourselves and sometimes I am all alone. I had but a small stick, not to defend myself, but to climb the mountain. Yet I went out leisurely as if I were walking in my room or in my garden.[19]

In 1951, Nam Cao was killed in action in the plains. He expressed his sentiments more eloquently than most, but many others who survived the war saw their memories of combat in the hills transformed into nostalgia. This emotion was of course nourished by the patriotic ideology of the party's cult of heroes.[20] But before we look at the cumulative effects of these experiences on both the people and the party, let us consider briefly who moved to the hills during the war. Migrants were of three types: porters for the French, refugees from the war, and revolutionaries.

As in the past, the French used Việt people to work as porters. A group of them were captured by Colonel Đặng Văn Việt, during the Lạng Sơn campaign (1947–50). He described them as people arrested in the plains by the French, and other local people recruited for the task. The colonel, recruiting them for revolutionary labour, asked them: 'Now do you wish to return to your native provinces or stay in the liberated zone?' One replied, 'We were arrested by the French who falsely accused us of being guerrillas or Việt Minh soldiers (…) My native land is now in enemy hands.' In this uncomfortable situation, they had little choice but to stay.[21]

Many people fled the hostilities to the hills. Some of these refugees were 'turned into wanderers' by random French violence. In 1948 General Blaizot was obliged to warn his troops to learn the difference 'between Việt Minh and Vietnamese'. In the familiar language of 'attachment', he stressed that savagery was counter productive.

> Violence always strikes the 'country bumpkins' (*nhà quê*) who, like peasants throughout the world, are attached to their glebe and have to put up with the occupier. Burning their house, killing their animals, destroying their property cannot but throw them among the *errants* and drive them into the Việt Minh groups. (Parenthesis and emphasis in original)[22]

There were victims, too, of systematic violence. In 1952 a 'surveillance band' was drawn around a 'free circulation zone' between Hanoi and Haiphong. Several kilometres wide, it was designed as 'an absolute NOMANSLAND [*sic*] where nothing circulates, nothing works, nothing lives.'[23] The intention was to prevent 'leaks' of paddy and personnel to the Việt Minh. Villages were removed to 'free up fields of fire and observation' and 100,000 people were displaced. They should have been re-housed and re-employed but, unfortunately, the authorities responsible did not 'take their task to heart'.[24] One military report was bombastic in its assessment of the operation: 'The inhabitants of the prohibited zone will be invited to choose between Vietnam and the Việt Minh.'[25] Another was more realistic about the nature of this invitation: 'the population thus becomes an easy prey for the multiform propaganda of the Việt Minh.'[26]

The Việt Minh encouraged victims of French violence to join the flow of revolutionaries, the third type of wartime migrant to the hills. Distinctions between refugee and revolutionary were blurred, in experience as well as in propaganda. The Việt Minh newspaper *Cứu Quốc* encouraged these people 'not to see themselves as refugees, but as people with a long-term responsibility in the task of resistance'.[27] But, as French army sources acknowledged, the Việt Minh did not need to rely on enemy atrocities to fill their ranks. They had popular support, excellent mobilization capacity and a 'hemorrhage of personnel' was taking place to the liberated areas. However watertight, no French surveillance band could stem it, because the Việt Minh 'plunges its roots into the very heart of the masses'.[28]

What the French called 'hemorrhage' was known, in language of the revolution, as 'breaking away' (*thoát ly*). This came to describe a decision to leave home and join the revolution, as a cadre or a soldier. Implying a rejection of traditional values, the expression was used in association with the word 'forest' (*thoát ly vào rừng*), as before the revolution and during the war, revolutionary departure meant a journey into hills.[29] After the war ended in 1954, it became a 'lifestyle fashion' for rural youth: '*Thoát ly* was understood to mean "serving as a revolutionary" and becoming a revolutionary cadre, but [implied] seeking a better chance to improve the social standing and prospects of a peasant'.[30] This was as much a social and psychological move, the breaking away from obligations of family and village. One such tearaway, Chiến, told me how he left home to join the revolution, spending the years 1944–49 in the forests of central Vietnam, before walking north for training in Yunnan and Moscow and a political appointment at headquarters near the Red Mountain (1953). After listening to his detailed descriptions of various theatres of war – including Điện Biên Phủ (1954), the Hồ Chí Minh trail to Laos (1962), and the forest headquarters in the south near Tây Ninh (1964–73) – I felt inspired to write up an account of it. My Vietnamese colleague felt the same, adding with regret, 'But it's such a common story. How many others like this have we heard?'*

---

* By 1976, the Party had sponsored 82 memoirs on the years up to 1945. Others were published by the army. The 1945–75 period has received similar attention. David G. Marr, *Vietnamese Tradition on Trial, 1920–1945*, Berkeley, Los Angeles and London: University of California Press, 1981, p. 287, n. 114.

Chiến was unmarried when he got his first revolutionary assignment. He became a revolutionary group leader, in the highland district of Ba Tơ in his home province of Quảng Ngãi.* It was 1944 and Chiến was just 17. Many revolutionary leaders were similarly young. Gourou observed that 'since 1945 armed adolescents have replaced the peaceful councils of notables', adding drily that 'this is not necessarily an improvement'.[31] But for married people like Chu Văn Tấn, whose revolutionary activities took them away from home, the problem of their families arose. Chu Văn Tấn's wife managed to hide without her husband's help. Others called their families to join them. Bringing food, furniture, and of course their labour, these evacuees were welcome in the forests. Their presence, however, presented responsibilities. This was especially so in the months before the revolution when 'the army had to worry about defending the numbers of people who followed (mainly fathers, mothers, brothers and sisters and other relatives of the soldiers)'.[32] But during the war, in the Định Hóa zone at least, there were fewer concerns. Trịnh, a wartime resident there, pointed out that 'anyone with family here could come and find them'.[33]

Evacuees moved along family networks, which in addition to other advantages allowed for easy identification of potential infiltrators. But 'patriotic evacuation',† as such itineraries were called, was not restricted to networks of family. Trịnh referred to his brother's decision to leave Xuân Trường district and work in the Thái Nguyên wartime paper factory as an evacuation: 'he followed the factory', contributing to the supply of valuable paper used in the resistance base.[34] Employees of many other factories as well as cadres working for DRV government offices followed suit.‡

Evacuees put their labour to revolutionary use. Roads were repaired, land was cleared and farmed, goods and weapons were transported. A sergeant of the

---

* Chiến was from Bình Chánh commune, Bình Sơn district, on the plains. With its long-standing Việt settler population, Ba Tơ was an important resistance base. See Phạm Kiệt, *Từ núi rừng Ba Tơ*, Hanoi: NXB Quân Đội Nhân Dân, 1977.

† Patriotic evacuation: *sơ tán*.

‡ It is difficult to calculate how many people left their homes during the war. However, the amount of land abandoned offers a rough measure. A ministerial conference (December 1954) was informed that in twenty provinces of the DRV, 118,329 hectares (or 6 per cent of the pre-war cultivated total) were abandoned during the war. The Minister of Agriculture, Nghiêm Xuân Yêm, wished to know how many people were available to farm this land. No replies made it to the archives. Decisions to evacuate/remain in French areas had serious repercussions, especially at the end of the war. Competition over land caused chaos: 'people evacuating out to the free zone look down on people remaining in temporarily [French] occupied zones; people who remained to struggle scorn the evacuees; people hate the puppet government, the puppet government remained, so sometimes they hate even the families of those people [who remained]; some people were forced by the enemy to attack and seize the people's property, so the victims are angry and criticize; the enemy even created hostile contradictions between Buddhist compatriots, between this ethnic group and that, etc.' These tensions contributed to departures to the south, where nearly a million northerners moved in 1954–55. NAV3/UBKHNN 570(tt), 'Báo cáo tình hình ruộng hoang và kết quả của việc phục hồi ruộng hoang (nhất là từ khi hòa bình trở lại)', 10 December 1954, Minister of Agriculture and Forestry to provinces, 30 December 1954.

foreign legion, under fire at Điện Biên Phủ, paid unwitting tribute to the work of these porters and labourers* – men, women and children from both the delta and the hills – when he wrote the following:

> Totally surprised, we wonder where the Viets have been able to get so many guns, capable of unleashing artillery fire of such power. Shells rain down relentlessly, like a brusque shower of sleet on an autumn day. Blockhouse by blockhouse, trench by trench, everything collapses, burying men and arms.[35]

One of the people who contributed to this bitter achievement was Hà, a young woman from Thanh Hóa province. She was among the 'hundreds of thousands of porters, women as well as men' described in General Võ Nguyên Giáp's account of the battle, who 'surmounted perils and difficulties and spent more than three million work days in the service of the front, in an indescribable enthusiasm'.[36] This work took her from Thanh Hóa up the Mã River valley, on a trail known as Route Nine South Laos. She turned through Mai Châu district where a Thái inhabitant of one of the roadside villages remembered the porters' enthusiasm: the young women, he recalled, enjoyed teasing men on the way: 'Why don't you come and play with me'! Porters were not always in high spirits, however. On her winding way to Điện Biên Phủ, which took her to Nghĩa Lộ and Sơn La, Hà carried supplies to the battlefield at Nà Sản. A cadre organizing a group of Thái porters on the same road, set out from Phù Yên with 500 porters and reported that less than two-thirds of them arrived: the rest were killed or escaped before they reached Nà Sản.[†]

MOBILIZATION FOR WAR

This cadre's remark raises the issue of motivation for such movements. Many porters arrived from the delta as refugees, captured colonial soldiers or labourers. Others left home with the intention of helping out, recruited both in Việt Minh and French occupied parts of the country. In the early days they were given three days' training before hitting the road, learning the porters' code of conduct, the eight standards for being a 'good comrade', and the aims of the campaign.[37] Hà did not tell me why she left her village on the Thanh Hóa plain. She must have known that the work was arduous – in addition to the bombs and difficult terrain, living conditions were appalling. A Vietnamese army history described them in brutal terms. 'Lacking clothes, many people protected themselves from the sun and rain with nothing more than a conical hat; there was not enough food and medicine; erratic hot and cold weather took its toll on people's health'. If we believe this account, Hà and her colleagues were heroes: 'overcoming these subjective difficulties, cadres, soldiers and porters showed courage and determination in their

---

* Porters and labourers: *dân công*.

† This cadre, who was also Thái, was in his eighties when I met him. Interview (Sơn La, December 1996).

struggle against natural calamities and enemy destruction'.[38] American fellow-traveller Joseph Starobin could barely contain his admiration. Seeing the lines of people up from the French-occupied delta, he 'remembered General Giáp's account of how astonished the captured French officers always were by this system of portage – and all of it voluntary!'[39]

Thái porters recruited in the Việt Minh-controlled district of Phù Yên were less eager to volunteer. One might almost say they were volunteered for the task: their cadre told me the principle was one person from every family in the area. They set out with 20 kg of rice, but most of them arrived with only 5 or 10. Those, that is, who did arrive at Nà Sản – many ran away, and there were bombs.[40]

An army history confirmed the difficulty of the operation. The mobilization of porters in minority provinces was reported to have been a complicated and difficult task, requiring careful leadership and management.[41] Even displaced people from the delta needed persuasion and organization. But we cannot dismiss accounts of enthusiastic wartime labour as patriotic myth. Whether people stayed at home in the delta, fortifying their village against the French, or went to the hills, revolution and resistance undoubtedly inspired a spirit of self-sacrifice.[42] Some people ran off with the rice they were carrying, but others 'worked without a thought for themselves, with such a spirit that they repaired the road as though they were directly striking the enemy'.[43] When he described patriotism as 'a precious tradition of ours', Hồ Chí Minh was linking a present reality – which he acknowledged was only one of many present realities – to myths of past resistance: 'Every time our country is invaded, then this spirit rises, forming a huge and mighty wave, skimming over every danger and difficulty, sinking all those who sell and steal the country'. Starobin, who recorded these words, was impressed.[44]

EFFECTS OF THE WAR

The ideals of the maquis and resistance against the French, for those who fought in the hills and even for those who stayed behind, offered a new ideology to replace the Confucian value of 'attachment to the village'. Many people had first- or second-hand experiences of other places which they had formerly viewed with fear and trepidation. How these new ideals – and the wartime techniques of their mobilization – were put to use in civilian life is the subject of the coming chapters. But we must first consider some of the more immediate consequences of this decade of turmoil. As a result of the war, there were suddenly large numbers of Việt people in the highlands. How did this affect the geo-political position of the hills within Vietnam? How did the experience change people who had lived and fought in the forests? What was the cumulative effect of wartime migration to the hills?

For the colonial administration, the northern highlands had constituted a 'hinterland': a region on the margins, its nineteenth-century military significance forgotten in *la paix française*. The few colonial efforts at promoting migration aimed to help people escape the delta rather than occupy the hills. Overpopulation was the main stimulus for the administration's sporadic organization of settlement in the back country.[45] But for the government of the DRV this was, politically and militarily, a region of immense strategic importance. In 1954, its central government returned from Định Hóa to the delta. For officials in Hanoi, these forests and hills had been, for almost eight years, the nation's capital. While the city of Hanoi embodied the early success of seizing power, the resistance war was won, spectacularly, in the highlands. In constant reminder of the region's strategic importance, the cigarettes smoked by high-level cadres in the 1950s and 1960s – the prestige brand 'Điện Biên' – featured the Việt Minh flag flying amidst the mountains.[*]

Thus, for people who fought at home in the plains and for those who left to fight in the forests, the mountains underwent a change of image. They were the repair no longer of 'pirates' but of patriots. While the safe zone around Định Hóa was described as a symbol of the patriotic spirit of all the people in the highland Việt Bắc region, the Việt Bắc 'became known to compatriots throughout the country as the home of revolution'.[46] The idea of home (*quê hương*), in its articulation by DRV propaganda, was thus grafted away from the ancestors and the bamboo hedge of the village, and on to the story of the revolution and the forested landscape of the hills. There is no doubt that for many of those who lived through the war, the mountains took on a new mystique. They had survived the 'terrifying forest and poisoned water',[†] and many had learned to appreciate the beauty of the mountain slopes, the grandeur of the protective forest, as well as the hospitality of the highlander inhabitants. Above all, the hills were now imbued with an aura of heroism, rather than the mere menace of exile. In later years this imagery persisted, and military language was used to promote economic development. Việt and minority workers in highland cooperatives in the 1960s were described respectively as 'fighters in brown shirts, indigo shirts', working in solidarity as 'land clearance fighters'. In line with the contrasting images displayed on packets of Điện Biên cigarettes, DRV propaganda transformed the mountains and forests of the 'Việt Minh's resistance zone' into the 'nation's new economic zone'.[‡] The highlands had now become, in a very different way from that imagined by the ancient saying, the 'green forest and red hills' of Vietnam.[§]

For many individuals who served in these hills, the war was a crucial event in their lives. Some of them settled there during the war, after a spell of labour on

---

[*]   In 1997, Điện Biên cigarettes were still available, very cheaply, in parts of Nam Định and former state shops in Hanoi. See Photo 5.

[†]   Terrifying forest and poisoned water: *rừng thiêng nước độc*.

[‡]   *Khu căn cứ của Việt Minh* thus became *khu kinh tế mới của tổ quốc*. The term 'land clearance fighter' (*chiến sĩ khai hoang*) was used in the early 1960s in the Thái Bình newspaper's reports to emphasize highlander-lowlander solidarity in new economic zones. See especially Phan Khâm, 'Lấp sông Cài Đản', *Tiến Lên*, 25 August 1963, p. 4.

[§]   Green forest, red hills: *rừng xanh, núi đỏ*. This saying expressed the fear common among Việt people of the forests and mountains, which contrasted with the familiar landscape of the plains.

the roads, to produce food for the troops.[47] Some settled there after it ended.*
Others had their eyes opened to the long-term potential of this hitherto unknown
region, as one cadre explained to me. 'We knew land was plentiful here, the forest
far, because during the resistance war against the French, our people evacuated and
had already made a living here. After the liberation of the North, they returned of
their own accord'.† As Condominas observed, 'one of the great revelations of the
revolutionary struggle undertaken by the Vietnamese, lowland people *par excellence*,
was their acclimatization to the highland region'.[48] Many, no doubt, took their
wounds and their fever home and hoped never to return. For them the war was a time
of immense rupture, expressed in absence from home. But for others, including
Chiến who was to spend most of his career in the forests, acclimatization took
place almost without his knowing it. Somewhere en route to Điện Biên Phủ he
met a young porter, a woman called Hà. 'We fell in love on the road', he said.
Three years later, back in her home village, they were married. And in 1976
when he retired, the couple found nothing strange about a new move to the hills.
They live now in Dak Lak, in the central highlands. Chiến had a brother there.‡

CONCLUSION

The violent end to colonial rule in Vietnam had wide-reaching consequences.
There were consequences for migration practice. Disruption of life in the delta
destroyed the structures of power tying Việt villagers to their villages. Many left
to live or fight in the highlands. Those who stayed behind no longer simply
associated the hills with the dangers of forest and fever. The highlands now became a place of fighters for freedom, the forest a protective canopy against attacks
from the French. The revolution gradually extended its base in the Red Mountain
to all parts of the northern hills.

There were consequences too for policy, once the war had ended. The hills
were no longer regarded as a hinterland for half-hearted exploitation, a safety
valve for the delta's excess of population. They had become a place of strategic
importance. Migration there, as we shall see in the coming chapters, was organized
under the impetus of considerable political will. It aimed not only to relieve the
pressure of population in the plains but also to bolster the highland region's
defensive capacity against enemies from abroad. As Khổng Diễn pointed out, the

---

* There was a policy, after the battle at Điện Biên Phủ, to settle former soldiers and
porters in the valley rather than return them to the delta. One who stayed was Giang (see
Prologue). NAV3/BLD 343(vv), 'Báo cáo tình hình chỉ tiêu của Ban dân công'. Interview
with Giang (Hòa Bình, July 1995).

† This cadre, Dũng, was 68 when I met him. Interview (Hòa Bình, July 1995). The father
of a trader I met in Mộc Châu market followed a similar itinerary. Originally from the delta,
he fought at Điện Biên Phủ, and returned with his family to work for the state trading
company in Mộc Châu a year after the war ended. 'There were many people like that', his
son told me. Interview (Sơn La, September 1995).

‡ I met Chiến and Hà at their home in Lak district. Interviews (Dak Lak, May and
November 1996).

period after the war saw 'a new step in the country's migration history. This migration was not only for economic purposes, following traditional flows, but was suited to the laws of revolution and war'.[49]

The war of resistance against the French was led from the 'red hills' of northern Vietnam. And policy towards highland areas, after power had been seized, aimed to ensure that this revolution would be the last. The fulfilment of this aim was articulated to me by an official in Định Hóa. Speaking of the migration policy's impact on the environment, he smiled ironically as he pointed out the strategic role played by the forest: 'If we had the revolution now, Định Hóa would be a useless resistance base. There's no forest left for Hồ Chí Minh to hide in'.[*]

NOTES

1   This account of the campaign is extracted from Alfred Echinard, *Histoire politique et militaire de la province de Thai Nguyen, ses forces de police*, Hanoi: Imprimerie Trung Bac Tan Van, 1934, pp. 69–71.

2   Letter from Lường Tam Kỳ to RST, 19 March 1890. Reproduced in Echinard, *Histoire politique et militaire*, p. 79.

3   Hubert Lyautey, *Lettres du Tonkin et de Madagascar, 1894–1899*, Paris: Armand Colin, 1921, p. 158.

4   Ibid., p. 146.

5   Ibid., p. 146; Auguste Darles, *Les possibilités économiques de la province de Thai Nguyen et les conditions de son essor*, Hanoi–Haiphong: IDEO, 1917, p. 3.

6   NAV1/RST 55348, 'Monographie de la province de Thai Nguyen', 1901.

7   Le Bo-Chanh, 'Notice sur la Province de Thai Nguyen', Thai Nguyen: unpublished monograph, 1933, p. 3.

8   David G. Marr, *Vietnam 1945: The Quest for Power*, Berkeley, Los Angeles and London: University of California Press, 1995, pp. 124, 146, 518.

9   Chu Van Tan, *Reminiscences on the Army for National Salvation*, Ithaca: Department of Asian Studies, Cornell, 1974, p. 166.

10 Ngọc Tự, *Nguồn Vui Duy Nhất. Hồi ký cách mạng của đồng chí Dương Thì Ân*, Hanoi: NXB Phụ Nữ, 1974, p. 58.

11 Chu Van Tan, *Reminiscences*, pp. 167, 181.

12 Hoàng Quang Khánh, Lê Hồng, and Hoàng Ngọc La, *Căn cứ địa Việt Bắc (trong cuộc Cách mạng tháng 8-1945)*, Thái Nguyên: NXB Việt Bắc, 1976, p. 119.

13 Marr, *Vietnam 1945*, pp. 228, 418; Chu Van Tan, *Reminiscences*, pp. 201–202.

14 Đinh Trọng Hỷ, *Việt Bắc 30 năm chiến tranh cách mạng (1945–1975)*, Hanoi: NXB Quân Đội Nhân Dân, 1990, vol. 1, pp. 79, 81–82; Lại Văn Minh and Nguyễn Ba Cửu, *Đất Bắc Thái kèm theo bản đồ thổ nhưỡng tỷ lệ 1/100.000*, Ủy ban nông nghiệp Bắc Thái, c. 1970, p. 14.

15 NAV1/RST 1558, 'Notice sur la circonscription du poste administratif de Hưng Sơn', 1901.

16 Marr, *Vietnam 1945*, p. 230; Đinh Trọng Hỷ, *Việt Bắc 30 năm*, vol. 1, p. 69.

17 Hội Phổ Biến Khoa Học Kỹ Thuật Thành Phố Hà Nội, *Công tác vệ sinh phòng dịch đối với các gia đình đi tham gia xây dựng và phát triển kinh tế văn hóa miền núi*, Hanoi: Nhà in Báo Thủ Đô Hà Nội, 1965, p. 18.

---

[*]   This official was a Tày minority man in his late thirties. Interview (Thái Nguyên, January 1997).

18 Army Medical Office, *Chống sốt rét để tăng sức chiến đấu, Tài liệu học tập chiến sĩ*, Cục Quân Y xuất bản, 1952, p. 36. See also Andrew Hardy, 'One hundred years of malaria control in Vietnam: a regional retrospective. Part II, 1945–1999', *Mekong Malaria Forum* no. 6, April 2000, p. 102.

19 Nam Cao, 'In the Jungle'. In Nam Cao, *Chi Pheo and Other Stories*, Hanoi: Foreign Languages Publishing House, 1983, p. 163.

20 See the analysis of Tố Hữu's poem *Việt Bắc* in Patricia Pelley, '"Barbarians" and "Younger Brothers": The Remaking of Race in Post-Colonial Vietnam', *Journal of Southeast Asian Studies*, vol. 29, no. 2, September 1998, p. 377–8. Also Benoît de Tréglodé, *Héros et révolution au Viêt Nam*, Paris: L'Harmattan, 2001, p. 208.

21 Đặng Văn Việt, *Highway 4: The Border Campaign (1947–1950)*, Hanoi: Foreign Languages Publishing House, 1990, p. 51–52.

22 SHAT/10H 3727, 'Note de service. Objet: Pacification et représailles', General Blaizot, Commander in Chief, Armed Forces in the Far East, 24 August 1948.

23 SHAT/10H 3359, 'Dossier Blocus Economique (3e Bureau)', Report by Colonel de Saint Martin, 18 January 1953. A Vietnamese source estimated that this policy caused the abandonment of 70,000 hectares of paddy land.

24 SHAT/10H 901, 'Le blocus', undated report, 1952.

25 SHAT/10H 3359, 'Dossier Blocus Economique', 18 January 1953.

26 SHAT/10H 901, 'Le blocus', 1952.

27 Cited in Phạm Khắc Hoè, *Từ Triều Đình Huế đến Chiến Khu Việt Bắc – Hồi ký*, Hanoi: NXB Hà Nội, 1983, p. 153.

28 SHAT/10H 213, 'La guerre d'Indochine', lecture by Lt Colonel Boussarie, Paris, 24 January 1954; SHAT/10H 901, 'Fiche: mesures à prendre dans le delta par les autorités françaises ou vietnamiennes', 9 February 1952; 'Pacification du Delta Tonkinois', Hanoi, 9 February 1952.

29 Hoàng Quang Khánh, Lê Hồng, and Hoàng Ngọc La, *Căn cứ địa Việt Bắc*, p. 86.

30 Luu Dinh Nhan, 'The Migration Issue in Vietnam: A Case Study of Rural Migration from North to South', unpublished study, 1991, p. 8.

31 Quoted in Paul Mus, 'The Role of the Village in Vietnamese Politics', *Pacific Affairs*, vol. 22, no. 3, 1949, pp. 269–270.

32 Hoàng Quang Khánh, Lê Hồng, and Hoàng Ngọc La, *Căn cứ địa Việt Bắc*, p. 86.

33 Interview (Thái Nguyên, January 1997).

34 Đinh Trọng Hỷ, *Việt Bắc 30 năm*, vol. 1, p. 214.

35 SHAT/10H 1178, Sergeant Kubiak, diary of Operation Castor, Điện Biên Phủ, March–May 1954.

36 Quoted in Bernard B. Fall, *Hell in a Very Small Place: The Siege of Dien Bien Phu*, Philadelphia and New York: J. B. Lippincott, 1966, pp. 128–129.

37 NAV3/BLD 343(vv), 'Báo cáo tình hình chỉ tiêu của Ban dân công trong chiến dịch Điện Biên Phủ năm 1954'.

38 Đinh Trọng Hỷ, *Việt Bắc 30 năm*, vol. 1, pp. 239–241.

39 Joseph Starobin, *Eyewitness in Indochina*, New York: Cameron & Kahn, 1954, p. 79.

40 Interview (Sơn La, December 1996).

41 Đinh Trọng Hỷ, *Việt Bắc 30 năm*, vol. 1, p. 238. For a fuller discussion of the limits of the Việt Minh's mobilization of highlanders for revolution, see de Tréglodé, *Héros et révolution*, pp. 207–214.

42 For a description of the elaborate fortifications raised by certain delta villages against the French, see Diệp Đình Hoa, *Làng Nguyễn*, Hanoi: NXB Khoa Học Xã Hội, 1994, ch. 2.

43 NAV3/BLD 343(vv), 'Báo cáo tình hình chỉ tiêu của Ban dân công'; Đinh Trọng Hỷ, *Việt Bắc 30 năm*, vol. 1, p. 216.

44 Đinh Trọng Hỷ, *Việt Bắc 30 năm*, vol. 1, p. 361; Starobin, *Eyewitness in Indochina*, p. 79.

45 See the argument in Vũ Đình Hòe, 'Nạn nhân mãn và việc di dân', *Thanh Nghị*, nos 112–113, 9 June 1945–16 June 1945.

46 Đinh Trọng Hỷ, *Việt Bắc 30 năm*, vol. 1, pp. 137, 365. For a sentimental description of soldiers' feelings towards the mountains, see Phạm Văn Đồng, 'Bài Ca Tây Bắc'. In *Tổ quốc ta, nhân dân ta, sự nghiệp ta và người nghệ sĩ*, Hanoi: Văn Học, 1969, pp. 233–235.

47 Starobin, *Eyewitness*, pp. 77–78.

48 Georges Condominas, *L'espace sociale à propos de l'Asie du Sud-Est*, Paris: Flammarion, 1980, p. 217.

49 Khổng Diễn, *Dân số và tộc người ở Việt Nam*, Hanoi: NXB Khoa Học Xã Hội, 1995, p. 167.

Go and Build a New Village!
Practice and Policy of Migration,
1954–89

Figure 6: Travelling into the northern highlands
The road from into the mountains of Hòa Bình has its fair share of hairpin bends and for settlers from the Red River Delta, the bus ride would have been a strange, exciting and unnerving experience. Several million people on government migration programmes made journeys like this one, pictured on the road to Mai-Châu, in the second half of the twentieth century.
Source: Bùi Văn Kín, *Góp phần tìm hiểu tỉnh Hòa Bình*, Hòa Bình: Ty Văn Hóa Thông Tin Hòa Bình, 1972, p. 192a. Photograph by Coombs Photography Unit.

Overview of Part Three

*I*n the chapters that follow, we widen our geographical focus from northern Vietnam to embrace the country as a whole. Moving away from Thái Nguyên, we go first to the valleys of Mai Châu in Hòa Bình and Phù Yên in Sơn La, before moving back down to the Red River Delta provinces of Nam Định and Thái Bình. From there we go south to the central highlands, to the valleys and hillsides of the province of Dak Lak. In doing so, we explore the nature of migration to highland areas from the mid 1950s through to the late 1980s.

Unlike Part One, in which analysis was couched in terms of policy and practice, in the four chapters of Part Three the focus of attention is reversed. Chapters 6, 7 and 8 deal with issues of practice, while Chapter 9 reviews DRV and SRV migration policies over the period. This is because of the availability and, above all, the nature of the sources. At the time of my research (1995–97), policy documents for the DRV period in particular were not easily available. But more importantly, the way in which the migration programme was carried out – emphasizing local implementation over central policy-making – and the fact that it was carried out at all, present a stark contrast with the colonial period. While under the French many policies were published and little in practice was realized, under the DRV few policy statements were made and much was achived. In the first half of the century we learnt more about migration from colonial policy; in the second half we learn more about migration from its practice.

Part Three starts in the Red River Delta after 1954. The techniques of mobilization for migration from northern Vietnam's plains is the subject of Chapter 6, 'Deciding'. Focusing largely on the DRV period, this chapter catalogues the interaction of state imperatives and family strategies in the decision to move to the highlands. The role of local level cadres in this process is deemed crucial to the policy's success. More than a million people were persuaded to move to 'build a new home village' in the highlands between 1954 and 1975.[*]

In Chapter 7, 'Moving', I argue that the move to the highlands was, for many settlers, a defining moment in their lives. It was experienced in the stages of departure, travelling and arrival, and expressed in the successes and failures of mobilization which resulted in varied receptions from existing highland inhabitants.

Chapter 8, 'Settling' shifts the focus from the northern highlands under the DRV to the central highlands after 1975. Case studies from both regions are used to examine the meaning of 'settlement' to both the state and the migrants. For the state, settling implied staying and producing. The techniques by which these goals were met in practical terms are analysed. But the ways in which the settlers themselves negotiated these demands and sought to realize their own interests were often rather different.

---

[*] 'Go and build a new village!' (*đi xây dựng quê hương mới*) was a popular mobilization slogan in the 1960s.

Chapter 9, 'Policy' offers an overview of the migration policies of the DRV and SRV. We look into the aims of policy as understood at different levels of the administrative hierarchy. The goals which officials of the village, district, provincial and central administrations sought to attain provide a clearer sense of policy aims than do the statute books. Much policy, indeed, took shape as it was put into practice.

6 *Deciding*

On 26 October 1996, I was sitting in a house beside the Núi Cốc lake, under which the village of Bờ Rạ now lay. Night had just fallen. My Vietnamese colleague and I were drinking tea there. We had asked two elderly widows to tell us their story. The two women had moved to Thái Nguyên as part of the highland development programme launched by the DRV in 1960. They told of the difficulty of making a living now, after thirty years in Đại Từ district; of trees and rocks they'd moved when they arrived in 1965; highlanders they'd stayed with during the first three months; dilemmas of deciding to leave their village in Thái Bình; burning houses and flight from the village when the French came in 1951; death of family members in the famine of 1945. By this point, we had stopped asking questions. I was scribbling furiously. The younger woman recalled how she lost her mother in the famine. She herself had fled to the hills, to the tea fields of Phú Thọ, following relatives to work for wages. The older woman started crying, remembering the taste of banana roots in 1945. 'Like a cake', she said, adding, 'we were so miserable, so hungry. And then, she smiled and – to my great relief – the tears stopped: 'Thanks to the Party and government, we're not so hungry now'.

A day or two later I related this interview to some friends in Thái Nguyên city. A few days after that, back in Hanoi, I told other friends. Both times, at the end of the story, the slogan 'Thanks to the Party and government' raised a laugh. Young urban Vietnamese found it funny. But on the evening of 25 October, with the two elderly women – Phụng was 80, her sister-in-law ten years younger – this was no laughing matter. For the generation that had pioneered socialist construction in the decade after Điện Biên Phủ, memories of famine, of colonialism and war, and feelings of gratitude to the Party, even in the late 1990s, could still move people to tears. In the 1960s, they had been powerful forces for action.

In the 1960s, however, feelings such as these did not exist solely in a spontaneous way; they were also orchestrated. Many people felt loyalty to the Party and government. The Party and government constantly reminded them to feel loyal. This dialectic was the basis of the Việt Minh's mobilization capacity during wartime, and became highly effective after independence was established in the northern half of the country. After 1954, the DRV used techniques of population mobilization developed during the war to settle large numbers of lowland people in the hills. Up to 1975, more than a million people were moved from delta villages to the highlands, with the aim of securing these remote areas for the revolution.[*] This was a vast undertaking, carried out with the limited resources available to the newly independent state. To examine it, I ask the question: how were the villagers persuaded to move?

PERSUADING THE CADRES

Phụng and her sister-in-law helped me reach some answers when they talked of their decision to sign the form and volunteer to clear land in the hills. It was a hard choice, she said. 'to go was miserable, to stay was miserable'. When I asked Phụng who made the choice, she replied quickly that 'the whole family decided', adding that there were cases when the husband wanted to go and the wife didn't. She laughed then, saying 'the wife must follow the husband', but I couldn't tell whether her laughter indicated a joke or not.[†] It was clear from what she said that it took time for the family to decide. She described a process of mobilization[‡] whereby the village chose who could leave: out of three brothers, one had to go. She emphasized, however, that if the people didn't want to go, they'd mobilize more; if they still didn't want to go, they couldn't force you. It took six months of study and practice to mobilize Phụng's family.[§] Her husband was a Party member, and as such was required to be a model for other villagers. Once he had decided himself, he persuaded his younger brother to follow. They left Thái Bình at the end of 1965.[¶]

The timing of their move is significant. The land clearance programme, known as 'clearing the wilderness', had been launched four years earlier.[#] By 1964 it had failed to achieve satisfactory results. Communes throughout Thái Bình had consistently fallen short of their target quotas for migration to the highlands. By February

---

[*] For discussion of the difficulties of counting people who moved to the highlands, and for my attempt to do so from official figures, see the Appendix.

[†] This reaction was typical when I asked about family decision-making: realities were obscured behind jocular stereotypes of obedient wives and hen-pecked husbands. Only where anger was generated could I sense how choices were made. I learnt of a Thái Bình official, threatened with loss of position, who told his family he was going to Dak Lak, with or without them. The family followed and his son (Ngọc, see Prologue) was still furious twenty years on. By contrast, an industrial cadre, transferred to highland Ninh Bình, moved home after a son was attacked on the deserted mountain paths. The boy's mother understandably refused to raise a family in such a place. Rather than pursue his career, he followed his wife back to the plains.

[‡] Mobilization: *vận động*.

[§] The terms 'study-practice' (*học tập*) and 'education' (*giáo dục*) appeared regularly in DRV mobilization literature. Study-practice implied a process of organized learning and emulation (*thi đua*). Here the subject of study may have been the population–land ratio in the delta. Education implied informed persuasion, and was often used to describe cadres' attempts to bring into line someone unwilling to follow government policy.

[¶] They were from the coastal district Tiền Hải. Interview (Thái Nguyên, October 1996).

[#] In the early 1960s the usual administrative terms for the programme were 'clearing the wilderness' (*khai hoang*) and 'economic and cultural development of the mountains' (*phát triển kinh tế văn hóa miền núi*). People often referred to the policy as 'going to make the

of that year, only 58,206 people had left for the highlands (38.8 per cent of the plan for 1961–64).[1] This result – though considerable when compared with the colonial period – was lamented at a provincial conference on migration. The conference, held in January 1964 and attended by district officials from throughout Thái Bình and representatives of various ministries and highland provinces, was the first stage in a new mobilization campaign, intended to improve the ability of lower level cadres to implement the policy. The campaign was launched at the conference. But it reached a wider audience – of commune and cooperative leaders – through the provincial newspaper. Articles published in *Tiến Lên* in the first months of 1964 give us a unique insight into the process of mobilization. This tool of administration, used to persuade Phụng and her husband to move, was in constant use throughout the DRV countryside.

At the conference a single village was awarded a 'certificate of praise' for its successful implementation of policy, and throughout January and February readers of the newspaper were invited to focus on its mobilization campaign. The village in question, Trực Tâm (Trà Giang commune, Kiến Xương district), was held up as a model. In an exercise reminiscent of model collectivization, both in Vietnam (Đại Phong cooperative) and China (Dazhai commune), the Trực Tâm experience was minutely examined. Lessons were learnt by individual villages and the specific detail of those lessons gives these documents their historical interest. Lack of specificity was, indeed, one of the reasons for which mobilization had not worked well in the past – cadres tended to hold large and unwieldy meetings and pronounce 'generalities', rather than speak in concrete terms to individuals and families.[2] In a classic case of socialist emulation, the village of Trực Tâm gave them a standard against which to measure their own performance.[3]

The campaign to 'do like Trực Tâm' started with a call for debate. The debate was focused around four carefully worded newspaper articles.[4] They described the recent history of Trực Tâm village (nearly half its population died in 1945); its present situation (recent increases in production, even faster increases in population); reasons for the failure of the first mobilization campaign in 1961–62 (cadres' and people's lack of confidence in the programme); reasons for the success of the second campaign in 1963 (application of correct mobilization methods). That year, 109 people had moved to the hills, 80 per cent more than in 1962, bringing the total to 16 per cent of Trực Tâm's population.[5] The final article called on 'all cadres and Party members from the province to the commune, members of mass organizations, villagers and people to participate in the debate, especially comrade leaders in communes and cooperatives'. Payment was offered for articles published and discussion was invited on three topics:

[*continued from previous page*] economy' (*đi làm kinh tế*). This involved settlement in a cooperative, and was distinct from the state farm/state forestry enterprises programmes, though in the early years both were organized by the State Farm Ministry. By the 1970s, the term 'new economic zones' (*vùng kinh kế mới*) was in general use.

1. How is the highland development policy important to your locality?

2. What lessons from Trực Tâm can be applied to your locality? What did you do like Trực Tâm? What have you not yet done? Why?

3. What is the specific direction of your plan for 1964? [6]

The debate was set to end in May. Over the intervening months, each edition of the paper carried an article on Trực Tâm. Each article, headed 'Can we do like Trực Tâm?', was illustrated with a woodcut print showing three men sitting cross-legged deep in discussion, beside a bamboo forest waiting, presumably, to be cleared. In this forum seventeen local leaders aired their views and experiences.* They offer a fascinating glimpse into the workings of DRV local government. While at one level they read like advertisements for a miracle-cure product – before Trực Tâm/after Trực Tâm – at another level they allowed local leaders to voice real and specific concerns. They spoke to higher levels in the administrative hierarchy on behalf of fellow cadres and the people themselves.

The terms of debate ensured formal uniformity of response. The four articles that launched the debate acted, like Trực Tâm itself, as a model for emulation. Cadres structured their contributions accordingly, comparing their village to Trực Tâm, describing early difficulties in the campaign, applying Trực Tâm's experience to their own case, anticipating successful results. The articles' content was similarly choreographed. According to the newspaper's editorial board, contributors unanimously considered the lessons of Trực Tâm to be 'good'.[7] They agreed with the policy's revolutionary meaning and economic rationale. They agreed that cadres and Party members should volunteer first. They agreed that effective mobilization should be accompanied by efficient implementation. The language of the articles also seemed prompted: good cadres and Party members were 'mirrors', while poor mobilization depended on 'generalities'. Tố Hữu's dictum that the campaign should be 'hot like fire' was repeated, and even improved upon. The expression 'hotter than fire' appeared in one article.[8]

These were the formal parameters of debate. Within them, cadres enjoyed freedom to outline the way they overcame their difficulties, and the difficulties themselves. They did so in the spirit of self-criticism which underpinned bureaucratic education. At this time, Maoist methods of 'autoculpabilization' or self-criticism were current in Vietnam, whereby cadres transformed themselves into 'new men'.[9] This was often a matter for unspoken self-improvement, but in the case of Trực Tâm, public self-criticism by local collective leadership was used to educate all. Difficulties in implementing the policy were described in detail and fell into two types: people's difficulties and cadres' difficulties.

---

* *Tiến Lên* appeared every five days in 1964. The debate included three articles by district officials, six by commune Party members, two by commune officials, four by co-operative cadres, and two by commune cadres of unspecified position. Fifteen were written by cadres. Two were written by others 'according to the opinion' of a (possibly illiterate) cadre.

People had difficulty making a living. At home there was too little land and too little work. Chi Lăng commune could only offer its people seventy-two days of work annually, Hải An offered only sixty-five.[10] Many were forced to look elsewhere for a living: 300 people from Chi Lăng did so, as did an unspecified number from Đông Quang commune, heading 'to Vĩnh Phúc, Thái Nguyên, Tuyên Quang to saw timber and cut firewood'.* But these were temporary absences, journeys made during the hungry seasons between harvests, known in Vietnamese as *ngày 8 tháng 3*. People had more difficulty contemplating the risky venture of a definitive move to the highlands. They worried about losing property at home, fearful that the village authorities offered insufficient compensation.[12] They worried about leaving the land of their ancestors. They believed the 'unfounded rumour' about the 'terrifying forest and poisoned water' in the highlands. They worried that clearing land would present insurmountable practical problems. This fear was quickly confirmed in Thái Thuần commune, when an early group of settlers abandoned the highlands, bringing back stories that 'provoked doubts among people at home'.[13]

Contributors to the debate were unanimous that the people were nervous because their leaders were nervous. In Chi Lăng, there were apparently 'many people who really want to go, but they see that Party members are not going, so reluctantly put up with their poverty at home'. Cadres throughout the province failed to volunteer for the programme and failed to encourage their villagers to do so. There were personal reasons for this. At Đông Quang, cadres were 'shy of hardship', while at An Lập cooperative, they did not see participation in highland development as a duty. There were administrative reasons too. Comrades at Đông Quang worried that 'if many villagers left, there would be a lot of compensation to pay out, and no one knew when the debt to the Bank would be settled'. But the lessons of Trực Tầm were clear. Cadres had to have 'far-sighted eyes'. They had to allow others to leave. They had to sign up themselves. The key example was set at Hoa Lư village, where 'Comrade Quy, a Party member and concurrently secretary of the cooperative Party cell, came forward first; after that sixteen families of villagers, a total of sixty people, also asked to leave'.[14]

Local cadres had their chance to pass views back up to higher levels. And the newspaper debate allowed provincial authorities to gauge issues of concern in the villages. Communication worked in both directions. The debate's main message was underlined in a closing editorial which stressed the need 'to draw on Party members' and cadres' role as pioneers and mirrors'.[15] Cadres were persuaded to commit themselves to the programme and behave as examples for the people.†

---

* Đông Quang commune was in Đông Quân district (later Đông Hưng district). See also note 11.

† Edwin Moise stressed the role of newspapers in China in official communication with localities, though he played down their usefulness in Vietnam, a 'smaller country' with a 'better developed system for nonpublic communications'. The Trực Tầm debate shows how newspapers were used for the education and mobilization of cadres. Edwin E. Moise, *Land Reform in China and North Vietnam: Consolidating the Revolution at the Village Level*, Chapel Hill: University of North Carolina Press, 1983, pp. 87, 182.

Nguyễn Tiến Lộc described his experience of study-practice: 'We read in the news-paper *Tiến Lên* the article about Trực Tâm's experience in mobilizing people to go and clear land; our administrative committee and all the brigades studied the article, relating it to our locality.' Before doing this, he and his fellow cadres at An Lập cooperative had persuaded no more than forty people to go (over a period of three years), but after just one month of mobilization in the light of Trực Tâm, 115 people signed up.[16] There is no need to take these figures at face value to understand their significance. The key to successful mobilization was the village cadre.[*]

The Trực Tâm campaign placed tremendous pressure on village cadres to show results. Results were indeed forthcoming in 1964. By September the province had mobilized 15,541 people to go to highland cooperatives and state farms. This represented 67 per cent of the plan, double the previous year's result.[†] But the authorities were still dissatisfied. Despite the campaign, cadres remained the weak link; there were simply not enough 'mirrors'. In September 1964, Thái Bình pro-vincial authorities complained:

> The thinking of cadres and Party members has changed noticeably, but is still not yet high; a number of them go reluctantly, and there are even a number of cadres who were appointed to go and help for a short time and who are not truly acting as a nucleus for the movement (eight Party members have gone and since returned, including one Party Secretary); this shows that a spirit of responsibility is still lacking, that there is hesitation about getting involved in the mobilization of the masses.[18]

Pressure to get results does not seem to have translated into pressure to fabricate them – though this must have been tempting. Fabrication presented practical difficulties. Results could be measured tangibly in terms of trucks and trains full of settlers, although people returning could more easily be concealed.[19] It translated instead into expectations that cadres volunteer for migration themselves. Phụng unfortunately did not say how, in Tiền Hải district, her Party member husband was persuaded to sign up, mentioning only that the process took six months. But Hùng, one of the members of a village mobilization team in the neighbouring province of Nam Định, explained how this policy affected him: 'I went around mobilizing people, but few people went, so I had to come forward myself'.

A Village Cadre

When the programme was launched, Hùng was a cooperative official in the village of Xuân Hòa in the coastal district of Xuân Trường. I met him in the highland

---

[*]   As Douglas Pike observed of village cadres, 'The burden of the Revolution rested heavily on the cadre's shoulders'. Douglas Pike, *Viet Cong*, Cambridge, Massachusetts and London, MIT Press, 1966, p. 230.

[†]   This plan was the province's: 15,541 people was 74 per cent of the slightly lower central government's target. For source, see note 17.

district of Mai Châu, where he moved in 1963.* Before looking at the content of the education campaigns by which the people were mobilized to move, it is worth pausing to get to know one of the cadres who animated them. I enjoyed Hùng's hospitality three times when I visited his village, on two of those occasions staying for a week in his house. In the evenings, the first time in the light of the family's gas lamp, the second under a newly installed electric light bulb, I listened to his stories about home back in Nam Định and the early days in Mai Châu.

Hùng is a man full of avid enthusiasm. Forty years after leaving Xuân Hòa, he retains a keen sense of nostalgia for the place of his birth, describing with his hands the sea with its 'waves high as houses', the fish he caught 'big like that' which 'bite like pigs'. It felt strange to hear such stories of the sea up in the mountain valley of Mai Châu. But Hùng's enthusiasm was not limited to the ocean. As a young man, he was an expert buffalo trader ('I could always spot a good buffalo') and he used his knowledge to supplement the income from a 1.8 *sào* plot of communal land he received as a enrolled member of the village. In those days, he owned a she-buffalo and made money from renting it out. He also expressed pride that, later on, at the age of 50, he was still strong enough to slaughter such beasts ('two hundred kilograms it weighed, all on my own'). The expertise of his youth left its mark, moreover. Hitching a ride on my colleague's motorbike into the district town, he showed the way with sharp taps on the back, calling in the language used with buffalo in the fields: 'right! right!' (*vắt! vắt!*), 'stop! stop!' (*họ! họ!*).

He stayed in the fields during the war against the French. He did not leave for the Việt Bắc liberated zone. Instead, as leader of the local village militia, he guided cadres into nearby Catholic villages, finding his way across the night-time countryside, putting them in touch with reliable families inside. He was proud to have housed Việt Minh leaders. He dug a bunker for them, and of course expected no payment for food – 'where would the money have come from?' But his enthusiasm for fighting the French got him into trouble. 'In 1947 a group of French and Vietnamese soldiers came to the village, taunting "Hey, guerrillas! Hey, Việt Minh! Come and catch a Frenchman!"' Hùng rose to the challenge and actually managed to catch one, though he only mentioned later – to my colleague – that the unfortunate man died in his custody. That, he said, was the reason he never entered the Party.

He never entered the Party, but remained a committed Party man. When the country was divided after the war ended in 1954,

> Canada and Ngô Đình Diệm held a meeting in the village.† Each person had a card – to volunteer to go [to the south], they lifted the card in the air. But the Việt Minh were

---

*   Hùng was 73 when I first met him at his home at Tiền Phong village (Mai Hạ commune, Mai Châu district, Hòa Bình). Interviews (October 1995; June, December 1996; March 1999).

†   The Canadian government was a member of the International Control Commission, set up by the Geneva Agreements to oversee, among other things, the migration of northerners to the south (called in Vietnamese *di cư*), and southerners to the north (*tập kết*).

in the crowd. We were very crafty. Recognizing each other by two middle buttons of the shirt undone, we held down people's hands.

These and other tricks, he said laughing fiercely, ensured that no one in Xuân Hòa went to the south.[*] His fighting spirit survived even his experiences during land reform. Though jailed for four months, falsely accused of working for the Nationalist Party,[†] he recalled with tremendous pride the local land reform team's tough reputation in those days, clenching his fist in a 'guts pose'.

The team classified Hùng as a 'middle peasant'. He was sad to lose his buffalo, but his family got five *sào* of land. This, he said, was a lot but not enough to feed his wife and five children. He still had to work for wages. At the same time, he did the job of village policemen and when the land was collectivized in 1959 he was appointed Vice Chairman of the cooperative. Looking back, he was emphatic in his assessment of the cooperative system: '*Ôi giời ôi!* Things were difficult then. Hungry, everyone was hungry.' But he added – and his comment is significant given his position, 'We were hungry, but we still had to try and have confidence in the Party'.

His confidence was tested again over the migration policy. 'Cadres complained in their hearts, but outwardly, when talking to the people, we didn't complain'. But these doubts did not emerge until after arriving in Mai Châu, where Hùng continued as village policeman, and took on the job of village head for a short time. Back in Xuân Hòa before the move, people – as he told me in a vague phrase without noun – 'wanted to go'.

How were they mobilized? The commune received a plan and called a meeting: 'There were several evenings of village meetings. Cadres spoke. People didn't have to go to this meeting – everyone was there'. Then the village formed a mobilization team – there were women, young people, representatives of the cooperative (including Hùng), the Fatherland Front, the People's Committee, the police. This group then held meetings with individuals and families. The campaign took a month, 'it was very tiring', he said. Hùng recalled explaining the population problem: 'The land is scarce, there are so many people'. He told people how the government would help with money, clothes, and rice to live on for the first few years. He remembered that, as they went around the houses, 'If the husband hesitated, then we'd talk to the wife'. He thought, in fact, that it was the wives who made the decision. But he portrayed his own decision, to himself and to others, in terms of his children: 'Sacrifice the father's generation, strengthen the children's generation'. As for the children themselves, if Học, who was 12 when he moved to Thái Nguyên, is any guide, the upheaval was more an excitement than a sacrifice: 'All I knew was that my mother and father said they were taking us children to

---

[*]   I found no confirmation for this assertion, but Xuân Hòa did not have a high proportion of Catholics. Nearly everyone left the nearby Catholic village of Xuân Kiên.

[†]   Vietnam Nationalist Party: *Việt Nam Quốc Dân Đảng.*

clear land in the highlands. I couldn't imagine what mountains and forest would be like, so I really liked the idea of going'.[20]

Children may have been easy to persuade. But, one at least of the adults Hùng had to mobilize was more sceptical. This man told me that when the campaign started, no one went. But he was impressed by the prospect of an income of 18 đồng per month during the initial settlement period.[*] And Hùng and his colleagues managed to convince him that 'up there it is easy to make a living'. In the end, he decided to leave. He is now Hùng's neighbour in Mai Châu.

PERSUADING THE PEOPLE

The newspaper *Tiến Lên* reported that some people 'really did want to go'.[22] However, the whole point of the Trực Tâm campaign was that, initially, most were reluctant. Even Hùng, for all his enthusiasm, did not seem keen when he first heard of the programme. But once he volunteered, we can be sure he did so with his usual gusto. The example he set must have been an important element in confidence creation. Hùng said that poor 'mirrors' found themselves in trouble. In his village there was a Party member who mobilized people to go, then backed out himself, and lost his Party card as a result. In a nearby district, one Comrade Canh (Nam Giang commune, Nam Trực district) forestalled his expulsion, declaring 'If I have to go and clear land, then I ask to leave the Party.'[23] Hùng's neighbour, on the other hand, made no mention of the 'mirroring' influence Hùng's example had on his decision. But it was clear from his account, as indeed it was from Phụng's, that cadres' persuasive ability was crucial to the people's motivation.

Persuading the cadres was only the beginning of the task. Party member Nguyễn Duy Ngưu described how the campaign was presented to the people:

> Having resolved the situation within the Party, we then sent Party members and cadres around to mobilize and organize family by family, chatting sufficiently with the people, while on the other hand study sessions were organized in the production brigades and mass organizations, on the policy to build the highland economy.[24]

These discussions were used to appeal both to people's ideals – of patriotism and socialism, of confidence in the Party's leadership – and to their material interests. Evidence of cadres' actual working methods is scarce. Many of them operated, perhaps, like the illiterate Chinese village cadre Wang Fucheng: 'I keep everything in my head, and I work with my mouth'.[25] But the Trực Tâm debate gave cadres an opportunity for formal study on working practice. These form an important source, above all for what they tell us about DRV mobilization theory. The study tools tell us how mobilization should have worked, if cadres like Hùng were doing their job properly. Drawn up by the Kiến Xương district authorities and published in *Tiến Lên*, they came in the form of a psychological analysis of different types of villager. They detailed the reasons why different types of people avoided signing up:

---

[*]   18 đồng could buy 66 kg of paddy in 1963. For source, see note 21.

Cadres and Party members: 'They have strong family feelings, they are shy of hardship, and think that during the resistance war there was enough hardship, now in peacetime they prefer to stay quietly at home and work'.

Young people: 'They like to fly high, going off as soldiers or workers in factories or on state farms, rather than just clearing the wilderness'.

Women, especially older women: 'They have strong feelings for home, and say that wherever you live, you have to work and eat, so ask what crime they have committed that they have to leave; they prefer to stay at home and die in company rather than live alone'.

Old people: 'They have strong feelings for home and the land of their ancestors, and not only do not wish to go, but also want to keep back their children and grandchildren'.[26]

Psychological analysis was supported with suggestions for answering objections. The method often consisted of a reversal of the values expressed, or an integration of the objection into a positive context. Ancient concepts were rerouted. Everyday language was transformed into revolutionary slogans. For example, the common objection 'what crime?' was countered in an extraordinary speech printed in *Tiến Lên* in 1962. A resident of Trà Giang village explained why he had volunteered to clear the wilderness: 'What crime! A place where the land is vast, limitless and unused, without anyone farming it, [compared to] a place where even by squeezing you can't add another inch of land to cultivate. What crime have we committed that we cannot go!'.[27] Cadres were instructed to 'go deeply into the thinking of each category' when marshalling arguments for mobilization:

Party members: They should be reminded to 'act as mirrors for the masses to follow'. They were encouraged to see the revolutionary importance of the highland development programme: 'It is not that we are leading people into difficulties as some comrades believe. If there are difficulties, it is only at the outset. If there is sacrifice, it is sacrifice of feelings for home, which for us is not a great deal, as during the resistance war we had to suffer many more terrible sacrifices'. They were also invited to do some basic arithmetic, and understand that unless people went to clear land, the Party's economic development targets could not be met, and the standard of living would actually fall.

Young people: Appeal should be made to their enthusiasm for the Party. Hồ Chí Minh's saying should be quoted: 'Wherever needed, young people should be there; whatever difficult jobs there are, young people should do them'.

Women: They should be reminded 'of the spectacle of poverty and misery, of the spectacle of famine and death in 1945' and of their 'participation in the resistance war'. There was 'no reason why they should flinch now'. Cadres should tell them that feelings for home were precious, but a prosperous economy is more so. They should underline the fact that, now that Vietnam was an independent country, 'anywhere they go is home for the nation's compatriots' so people can go anywhere in groups from their place of origin, and make a living together.

Old people: The main thing was to convince them that 'now that the country is independent, everywhere is home', reminding them that in the past the village was not home, because 'the feudal landlords at home oppressed people, making them poor, forcing them to roam around to make a living'. They were likewise reminded of the famine, and of the resistance war, during which they had persuaded young people to sacrifice themselves. Now they were asked to urge young people to volunteer to 'go and build the country'.

The whole population: To calm worries provoked by news of settlers being 'crushed by falling trees, pounced on by tigers, sick with malaria', delegations should go to the highlands and highlanders should come to visit the plains, to show people that such reports were 'duck talk', to persuade them not to believe in misinformation and increase their confidence in cadres and Party members.[28]

It is impossible to say to what extent cadres actually implemented such a psychologically sensitive and nuanced approach. It may be that Hùng, who mobil-ized husband and wife in turn and in different ways, was typical. The following techniques, used in Đông Quang commune's campaign, may also have been common:

We also paid attention to propaganda: besides banners, posters and slogans, a map of Tây Bắc was drawn, showing the places where our compatriots were about to move to. We organized itinerant conversations, used projectors to show images of farming in land clearance cooperatives in Tây Bắc. There were continuous broadcasts of the names of families who had already volunteered to go. Party members and villagers who had already volunteered were used to mobilize other people. Above all, the Party used advantages here to roll back difficulties there, results in this village to persuade that village, calculations by this individual to make suggestions to that one ...[29]

Hùng, despite his flights of zeal – or perhaps because of them – was an effective local cadre. Đông Quang, meanwhile, was singled out for specific praise for its impressive campaign. Other people in other places were less energetic. The praise Đông Quang received indicates that its successes were by no means shared by all. A Thái Bình Statistical Office report complained that while Đông Quang had sent 661 people over a period of three years, similar communes with tight land–population ratios sent none at all.* The success of a village campaign clearly depended less on its concrete economic situation than on the ability of its cadres to muster arguments – many of them based on that situation – to persuade people to go. The report did concede that in 1964 the campaign had spread to more places, but reported that 'it is still not even', a problem that was also encountered in Nam Định and blamed on local cadres.[30] Different districts, different villages had different approaches to mobilization. Their campaigns, in effect, were only as good as the cadres who ran them. Trực Tầm was a model. Đông Quang was a worthy example. Hùng was an effective leader. None was typical.

As a result, I prefer not to attempt a detailed study of the mobilization experiences in a single lowland locality, asking why this individual left, why that family stayed. As in Chapter 3, I turn the question around, and try in a more

---

*   Tân Mỹ (Hưng Nhân district, Thái Bình) had a low land-population ratio: 1.7 *sào* per head. This was slightly higher than Đông Quang's 1.6 *sào*. But in 1961–64, Đông Quang sent 526 people to highland cooperatives, and 135 to state farms and factories. Tân Mỹ sent none. NAV3/TCTK 2399(vv), 'Báo cáo tình hình thực hiện kế hoạch', 23 September 1964.

general sense to piece together some of the decisions and calculations of those who actually moved to the highlands. Delta villagers did not have to leave; that was at least what I was told. A district official in Tiền Hải (Thái Bình) assured me that no one was forced to go.[31] Phụng, also from Tiền Hải, confirmed this in a more careful formulation, indicating a limited freedom of choice: 'If you didn't want to go, they'd mobilize more. If you still didn't want to go, they couldn't force you'. She and her husband clearly moved to the hills feeling that the family itself had made the (difficult) decision. On the basis of what calculations, then, did people come to their choice?

Long-term Calculations

The Party urged people to think long-term, both for the nation and for their family. Throughout the Trực Tâm debate, cadres urged one another to focus on both the 'revolutionary meaning' of the migration programme and the need for 'solutions to economic difficulties', when presenting it to the people.[32] While we cannot simply assume that propaganda brought 'revolutionary meaning' – shorthand for building socialism and fighting imperialism – into people's calculations, there is evidence that in the early days of the DRV socialist/patriotic motivations were important. The Director of Sông Con state farm, set up in 1955 on a French plantation in highland Nghệ An province, certainly believed this was so. During the farm's first year of operation, he reported: 'The workers were very eager, especially the former workers [under the French], and believed even more strongly in the Party's leadership, seeing clearly the progress made by the working class. As a result, during this period, they were very enthusiastic.'[33] There is no reason – particularly in the light of his later remarks on the demoralizing effect of the land reform on the workers – to imagine that the director was exaggerating. At Sông Con 2,000 workers, mostly young people from the plains and soldiers from the south, were involved in a vast project of agricultural development, with the aid of modern machinery and Soviet experts.* Despite the practical problems, in the immediate aftermath of Điện Biên Phủ and independence, this must have been an exciting venture.

Clearing land in areas where tractors, international attention, and large numbers of fellow Việt people were conspicuously absent was obviously a less exhilarating prospect. People were less spontaneously enthusiastic about getting involved in 'clearing the wilderness'. Some were nevertheless prepared to go: Nguyễn Văn Thế was one of these. A veteran of the resistance against the French, he had 'made his difficult way across the Nghĩa Lộ region, pushing through the gunsmoke of Điện Biên Phủ', before being wounded and returning to his village in Thái Bình. Once home, he joined the local cooperative where he 'always led the way in terms of

---

* The soldiers were among more than 130,000 southerners who rallied to the DRV, moving north according to the terms of the Geneva Agreements. Many went to work on state farms such as Sông Con. For sources, see note 34.

work days, in irrigation and manure shifting'. And when the migration programme was announced, Nguyễn Văn Thế went straight home to talk it over with his wife. She argued that 'staying at home, doing agricultural work in the cooperative, political work in the local area is quite enough ... After your seven or eight years of soldiering for the resistance, leave this responsibility now to the young people.' As for him, he thought very carefully about his wife's opinion, before replying: '*Mình ạ!* I know, I should stay with you and our child, we should live prosperously and happily. But we have to look beyond our own interests!' He went on to make a long speech to his wife about their duty to build the country, before signing up to clear land in the hills.[35]

Nguyễn Văn Thế's story appeared in the Thái Bình newspaper in October 1961. It was perhaps nothing more than the figment of a journalist's patriotic imagination. But people like him did exist. Giang, also from *Thái Bình*, told me a surprisingly similar story when I met him in the hills.[*]

> [At home] I was a policeman. If there were any bad elements I would threaten them, so they wouldn't do us any harm. That was the French time. Then I went as a soldier for the Việt Minh. In 1950, my health was not good and it was then possible to demobilize, so I came home. Then in 1952, there was a new recruitment campaign, so I came forward to go again.

Giang fought at Điện Biên Phủ, and volunteered to stay there and work on the roads. 'I came home in 1959, and in 1963 came up here [to Hòa Bình]'. He did not relate how he came to these decisions: to go to war, to work on the roads, to clear land in the highlands. But later in our conversation, an offhand remark – or was it a stock phrase? – gave me a clue: 'Wherever you are, you have to build the country and make a living'.[36]

Giang's remark put into a nutshell what Nguyễn Văn Thế's speech took several paragraphs to express: that calculations were made not only on the basis of nation building and socialist construction, but also faced the question of growing enough food to eat. Nguyễn Văn Thế reminded his wife: 'If we don't go and clear land to make new paddy fields and create new work to do, then our standard of living will never again be as high as it is now'. The national interest was presented in terms of the family's future. Those who were not yet fully committed to the national project could look for justification to more local, more concrete interests. A Tiền Hải district official told me how, during mobilization campaigns in the late 1970s, he would ask people to imagine 'what the village would be like in the year 2000 if the birth rate continued like that'. People took this seriously. Hùng certainly did – he was a father of ten by 1963. So did a certain Mr Tiêu, a villager at Minh Tân commune (Thái Bình), as a local cadre recorded in the provincial newspaper. After explaining the policy, cadres 'hinted that people could draw their own conclusions ... Mr Tiêu did so, calculating that at home land is scarce, people are

---

*   See Prologue. Giang was from Nam Bình commune (Kiến Xương district, Thái Bình).

crowded, not like in the highlands where land is plentiful and people are scarce. He has six sons, so he sent four of them to build a new home.'[37]

Tiêu's action should not, however, be viewed simply as the action of a patriotic old man who believed in the Party, worried about the economy and who loved his children. He sought, by this calculation, not only his children's interest but his own as well. This was an insurance policy for his old age. Similar calculations were reported by Giang, who told me that when he left for Hòa Bình, 'some men with six children, when they left, took half of them along, and three children stayed behind. That way, when they were old they could go back home to live with those that had stayed'.

Splitting the family was a religious calculation, giving parents the chance to return home to their ancestors' graves at the end of their days.[38] In Hòa Bình, Giang was keen to go back to the delta before he died:

> When I went home and saw the funerals they have there, I wanted to go back. That's how people think about old age and death: all the villagers will come in large numbers to attend a lavish funeral, so they want to go back. Up here there are few villagers, and not enough ceremonial clarinets and drums to serve the old people.

But in Định Hóa district, another elderly man articulated a more up-to-date view:

> Before, for a time, I missed home. But thanks to the Party's leadership I see now that everywhere is part of this land, wherever the child is the parents are there too, so I didn't have any more regrets, and mobilize my children to work hard and become prosperous. Thái Bình is the home of our ancestors, but wherever the children are, the parents are there too!

These were ways of calculating encouraged by the Party itself, which reworked an old proverb 'one destination, two native places'* into a mobilization slogan. The proverb, which traditionally described those who went to work for wages away from home for long periods, was now used to get people to move to the highlands. But as the idea of two homes – the 'old home' and the 'new home'† – entered the vocabulary of organized migration, the bridge between them remained the family. Families with many children particularly many sons were thus supposed to send some to the highlands. Phụng emphasized that 'if you had three sons, then one had to go', and her understanding was confirmed by many informants. State policy was tailored to suit strategies of family development and old age insurance.

The migration programme was not always used in ways intended by the state, however. Economic calculations legitimately spread the family's risks over two land areas. But as land recently acquired through agrarian reform (1953–56) was absorbed into the cooperatives (1958–60), some people saw participation on the highlands development programme as an opportunity to maintain or extend their

---

* One destination, two native places: *một chốn đôi quê*.

† Old home: *quê cũ*; new home: *quê mới*.

private plots of land. Cooperative regulations in the plains limited the amount of land a family could use for private production to 5 per cent. Migration, of course, was not the only way of avoiding the effects of collectivization. Two Catholic villages at Đông Xá in Thái Bình managed to dodge collectivization, and survived by building boats and learning how to fish.* But in the highlands there was more of the so-called 'percentage land' available, and a shortage of cadres meant that less attention was paid to abuses.

Authorities in Nam Định expressed their frustration about lax administration in the highlands which allowed this sort of situation to occur:

> The job of management has generally been lax, especially in the management of labour. There are families of three people who have only done 133 days' work a year, an average of forty-four days per person. The percentage land is still too high; in particular there are places where people all but make their living from private production, where the income from their family economy is four times that from the cooperative (Yên Hà cooperative, Bắc Quang district, Hà Giang province).[39]

Highland settlers not only had greater freedom of land use; they also enjoyed higher levels of mobility, which created opportunities for illegal trading. Collectivization was accompanied by strict controls on private trading. But even within the delta, these could not remove all forms of private exchange: the coop-busting Catholics at Đông Xá sold their fish on the black market. Trading in the delta, however, came with a price. One who found this, a Party member named Tiến from Đông Sơn commune (Đông Hưng district, Thái Bình), said he sold food in the market to make ends meet. He left the Party in 1959, before they threw him out, and in the late 1970s, he moved to the central highlands.[40]

The move to the hills was used by some as a one-off opportunity to make a little extra money. It gave them a chance to make a profit from the programme. This was almost certainly the case for a number of people whose activities came to the attention of authorities in Nam Định:

> The majority of people leaving have the right attitude, but there is also a small number who, because their thinking lacks prudence and their education lacks thought, go with the idea of taking advantage of opportunities for commerce, or have the intention of setting up in private trade. As a result, when they leave they usually come to the state and ask to liquidate their lamp oil immediately, exchanging it for cash, so as to buy goods to take with them to the mountains.[41]

For others, visits home created longer-term conditions by which they could supplement their income from agriculture. Cadres at the Quần Chu state farm in Thái Nguyên were suspected of such practices, when police stopped and searched their

---

* The two villages were Tân Hưng and Thịch Thủy (Đông Xá commune, Đông Hưng district, Thái Bình). In 1964, one of the villages was allocated a cooperative cadre, who moved there to mobilize them to join. They were frightened of the collective, this man told me, of losing their religion. Interviews (Thái Bình, January 1997).

car at a checkpoint on the way to Hanoi. An official of the farm complained about the difficulties this event entailed.

> According to a report from comrade the farm secretary, on 6 July 1968, the comrade drove a car to Hanoi to buy some raw materials and took with him 1 kg of dried tea to offer to some acquaintances in the central government, and comrade Tân, a cadre, accompanied him taking 2 kg of tea intended as gifts for his mother, his wife and a close friend. When they got to the junction at Bờ Đậu, they were stopped by the police who proceeded to confiscate the above mentioned tea, along with the driving licence of the driver. The comrade tried his hardest asking for the licence back, so that the driver could go back to the state farm and contribute to production, but to no avail. Two months later a new license was delivered, but meantime a number of jobs had to be cancelled, as there was no driver. On another occasion, on 9 July 1968 (...) comrade Lý Thành was heavily criticized, because the state farm was trafficking in tea.[42]

There were also 'professional smugglers'. In Hà Giang, where Việt people had traditionally carried out much of the local trade, as well as that between the delta and China, provincial officials were forced to admit that they were unable to stop more settled currents of exchange:

> Almost all the people who have come up to participate in economic development have carried out their duties well. However, in nearly every cooperative there is a small number of people who refuse to participate in production, but do all sorts of incorrect work, like: distil moonshine, buy here and sell there ...[43]

Some of the people whose trading activities were stopped did not return to land clearance duties. Their reason for moving had been specifically commercial. In Lai Châu province, two trading families from Nam Định abandoned the programme:

> There were two families who came to do highland economic development but took advantage of their situation to trade in goods from the delta, which they sold at below the market price. The local authorities discovered this and called them in for education, whereupon they left and went home.[44]

It is impossible to quantify these practices, particularly as many otherwise exemplary farmer-settlers made use of family visits to the delta to engage in trade. Provincial reports invariably referred to vague quantities like 'a small number'. But this was often a euphemism allowing negative news to be passed on to higher authorities. Where specific figures were given, as in the example above, they were very often so small as to be statistically meaningless. It is equally difficult to chart their development over time. Undoubtedly, as the programme gathered momentum, people became better informed of ways they could make use of it, and found ways of operating outside the formal structures of the cooperative system.

Whether migrants had 'the right attitude' towards the Party's policy, or exploited opportunities for 'trafficking' in the hills, there was a real element of long-term calculation in many decisions to leave. The highlands offered solutions to real problems, notably of subsistence. The Party pointed out the existence of those problems and articulated the solutions. Mobilization attempted to link the interests of families and individuals to the interest of the community. Propaganda aimed to reconcile the conflict, identified by Popkin, between peasant rationalities and the rationality of the community.* The context of the country's partition, the US presence in the south, and escalating war allowed the Party to give a sense of urgency and even heroism to otherwise ordinary tasks. Settlers were taught the 'revolutionary meaning' of what they were doing, and praised as 'land clearance fighters'.[45] Anthropologist Nguyễn Từ Chi described this phenomenon succinctly. In his view, the Party's achievement was not to present policy as patriotic, it was to make patriotic behaviour banal.[46] When mobilization worked, people actually believed patriotic behaviour was in their own interest, and made their calculations accordingly.

SHORT-TERM CALCULATIONS

There were many, however, who could not afford the luxury of long-term calculations. Propaganda presented many settlers as people who had enough to eat, and wanted to eat better still, or who wanted to serve their country. People like that certainly existed. But many of those who left came from the poorer sections of the community.[47] Their horizons were distinctly more limited.

Let us examine more closely the people who left provinces like Thái Bình. From information given to me by a migrant from Đông Hưng district who moved to a new economic zone in Gia Lai province in 1984, I worked out a rough typology of the people who left his village. As my notes show, there were four basic categories of out-migrant:

- Retired local cadres.
- People fed up with life in the village. ('Many very rich people went. They didn't like to stay in the village'). One family wanted to raise chickens, but neighbours complained. Another wanted to build a new house, but couldn't find materials. Others simply fell foul of village regulations.
- People implementing family strategies for economic survival or development: of two brothers, one might go to feed the rest of the family.
- Poor people.[48]

A cadre at Đông Hưng People's Committee confirmed the value of this information, identifying two types of out-migrant from the district:

- People who were hungry, without enough to eat (those without experience at making a living, with many children, usually in years of harvest loss).
- People with good economic situations, who knew that in new economic zones there were good conditions for development and hoped by moving there to get rich.[49]

---

* As Popkin noted, 'what is rational for an individual may be very different from what is rational for an entire village or collective'. Samuel L. Popkin, *The Rational Peasant: The Political Economy of Rural Society in Vietnam*, Berkeley: University of California Press, 1979, p. 31.

It is important to note, however, that neither man gave specific dates for these typologies. The central highlands were undoubtedly a more attractive destination than the northern highlands. They were also more attractive in the 1980s and 1990s than during the years immediately after reunification. For people moving south in the later period, a migration was more commonly a strategy for economic improvement or even enrichment. They gambled on making a fortune growing coffee on the rich red soils of the hills. Migrants in the 1960s were more likely to be either patriotic or poor.

Hunger was the problem at Đông Xá commune in Thái Bình in 1974. That year Đông Xá sent a group of families to set up a cooperative in highland Nghĩa Lộ province.* Kiệt, who was an official of that cooperative, told me about the terrible winter that year: 'It was February. It got really cold and the rice died on the stalks – the harvest was lost'.† Bùi, who went with him to Nghĩa Lộ, remembered the decision to leave: 'We didn't have enough to eat; the family wasn't cared for, so we had to go. Cadres came to the houses of poor people to encourage us to go, telling us about the policy, that anyone who wanted to go should fill in a form. We had nothing, so we went'.‡ The settlement in Nghĩa Lộ was unfortunately no more successful than the February harvest: 'The land there was poor'.§ By June, all but eleven of the original forty-seven families were back in Đông Xá. Kiệt was among them. 'We ate all the subsidies, then came back', he said.[50]

These subsidies were often crucial in people's decision-making. Hùng's neighbour was delighted with the 18 đồng a month he was promised for settling in Mai Châu. He was paid in cash and bought corn and cassava with it at the nearby district town. Others were happy to receive rice. Others were not paid at all. Like the results of mobilization, implementation of the subsidy policy was 'uneven', varying from place to place, from time to time. This was partly the intention of the policy itself.

In 1961, Deputy Prime Minister Phạm Hùng signed a provisional order, 'while waiting for the government to come up with a comprehensive policy on the people's land clearance campaign'. Instructions on capital investment were prefaced with the phrase: 'In the task of land clearance, the main thing is to rely on the strength of the people's solidarity and mutual aid'. Local self-reliance and initiative were paramount. Cooperatives were nevertheless authorized, in the event that local

---

* This was Tân Xá (New Village) cooperative (Tân Thịnh commune, Văn Chấn district, Nghĩa Lộ).

† Kiệt (aged 61) lived back at Đông Xá commune (Đông Hưng district, Thái Bình) when I met him. He had been chairman of the cooperative at Tân Xá. Interview (Thái Bình, January 1997).

‡ Bùi (aged 72) stayed in the hills, and was visiting Đông Xá for New Year when I met him. Interview (Thái Bình, January 1997).

§ This was a common oversight. It was reported, for example, in Hà Tĩnh province: 'Leadership and guidance of Party and ministries is still confused in the resolution of land selection'. NAV3/TCTK 2460(vv), 'Báo cáo số nhân khẩu di phát triển kinh tế văn hóa ở miền núi và trung du. Đi trong tỉnh', Hà Tĩnh Statistical Office, 20 September 1966.

resources were insufficient, to borrow from the state to buy the following items: tools, irrigation facilities, seeds and animals; cereals for consumption during the first months before harvest (three to nine months); a limited number of items for kitchen use. In addition, money was offered for transportation, food and medicine en route, and a year's medicine after arrival.[51]

In 1962, Phạm Hùng signed an amendment to the above. This extended loans to cover household items (blankets, mosquito nets, warm clothes), and set an 18 đồng ceiling on cereal subsidies for consumption during the first three months. The subsidy dropped to 15 đồng on the fourth month, and progressively until the first harvest, to a limit of two years. Provision was made for aged parents and children left at home, but the main principle of state aid was reiterated: 'The loan amount will depend on the actual concrete situation of each locality, combined with a spirit of utmost effort to mobilize self-sufficient mutual aid to resolve the issue appropriately.'[52]

In 1963, more generous amendments followed. Investment in roads, farm machinery, terraced paddy fields and cash crops was promised. The subsidy period was also extended by a year.[53] But the principle remained the same: 'Land clearance is a big task and must rely principally on the people's strength'.[54] These provisional laws formed the legislative basis for land clearance policy until the late 1970s and were published in books and newspapers by provincial authorities throughout the DRV. The legislation was sparse, deliberately leaving large areas of initiative to cadres at lower levels in the administrative hierarchy, stressing self-reliance and local resources, and underlining the partnership between the people and the state.*

But how did this partnership work out in practice? In 1961–66, state aid to new economic zones amounted to 57 million đồng. This represented an average of 16 đồng per capita in outright grants and 75 đồng in loans, a sum which permitted an upbeat conclusion: 'The problem of investment in mobilization was dealt with well'. The cost of clearing each hectare of land – 350 đồng – was regarded as a 'cheap price', which 'only our system is able to achieve, because we have actually relied on the people'.†

Hùng's neighbour was, therefore, right to be pleased with his 18 đồng. This sum was higher than the average, and in 1963 represented the maximum subsidy allowed. Ngô and his family, who moved from Thái Bình to Dak Lak in 1979, were equally pleased. Ngô signed up for the programme at a time of hungry gap between harvests. He was offered a total of 30 kg of paddy per family member and the right to buy state-subsidized rice for six months. This, he told me, coming as it

---

* Central government policy on aid to migrants changed continually, right up to the 1990s. But by contrast with DRV legislation, SRV laws on migration were extremely detailed. Interested readers are referred to the sources listed at note 55.

† Calculated at the 1963 average paddy price (0.27 đồng/kg) 15.80 đồng could buy 59 kg and 75 đồng could buy 278 kg. Most settlers received, in hand, a fraction of these sums. For sources, see note 56.

did in March when food was short, allowed him to feed his children well that season.

Not everyone was as fortunate. In Hà Tĩnh province, problems with the 1968 plan were blamed on American bombs and the fact that 'destination places do not want to receive our [land clearance] compatriots, because they increase the population there and various advantages like cereals, foodstuffs, draught power and state loans are insufficiently provided'.[57] Something like this must have happened to Phụng in 1965. All she got was the right to buy food at subsidized prices for six months. For her, there was no capital at all.

In circumstances of such local variation – over time and place – figures such as the 57 million đồng quoted above can have little specific meaning. Some people received a good share, others did not. The point was that for many families, when they were making their decisions to leave, the prospect of this capital investment was very attractive.

This was particularly true for Ngô, who had eight children and two aging parents to feed. His immediate needs were very pressing. Ngô's story is indicative of the way cadres presented migration as a solution to people's needs. There was, he said, 'a study session' in the village. There were different categories of people. There was a policy that 'whoever has many children should come forward'. Until that point he had enjoyed some preferential treatment at the cooperative. In recompense for the 'sacrifice' of a son in the war or simply because the family was poor, he had been able to borrow land and cereals from the cooperative. Without the loans, feeding a large family would have been impossible. And it was the withdrawal of this help that made him so relieved to receive 30 kg of paddy per person to move to the highlands. 'Not to go was not an option', he said. His wife added, 'it was very stupid of us to go but we had to, for economic reasons. So many mouths to feed – we couldn't make enough to eat. We weren't driven out, it was because of the system'.[*]

This solution must have seemed all the more attractive to Ngô, for whom the programme itself created new problems over and beyond simply feeding the family. According to the principle 'Divide up the people, divide up the property', the programme did not only affect those who left. People who stayed had to pay. Phạm Hùng had instructed cadres to 'mobilize people staying behind to help those who volunteer to leave'. He ordered that savings funds be set up, land be properly compensated, tools and seeds be provided by the village of origin.[58] In the case of Trực Tâm, most people agreed that each family should contribute 15 đồng and 32 kg of paddy into a 'land clearance fund'.[59] But even at Trực Tâm, some people complained at having to make such a sacrifice. A cadre at Đông Hưng district People's Committee described how the discussions were organized:

------

* Ngô and his family were from Lo Giang commune (Đông Hưng district, Thái Bình). They lived in Buôn Tría commune (Lak district, Dak Lak) when I met Ngô there. He was 65 at the time. Interview (Dak Lak, November 1996).

> We worked according to the principle of state and people doing it together, dividing up the people and the property. We argued with people staying behind to get them to understand the contribution to infrastructural construction of those who left; that they were leaving so those remaining had a responsibility to make a contribution towards the building of a new place for them, to guarantee them the basic conditions to start a new life. After that people remaining contributed more voluntarily.[60]

At these meetings, one official explained, the village 'discussed carefully the question of who should go, and who should stay, and fixed the responsibilities of those who go and those who stay'.[61] People like Ngô must have found such mobilization meetings distinctly uncomfortable experiences. Unable to afford the contribution, they must have been hard put to justify why they should not volunteer to go themselves.

Ngô was in a particularly tight spot. He was in debt. Unable to feed his family on the income he received from the cooperative (200 g of rice per day), he borrowed land. The first harvest failed, so he continued borrowing through to the next. This debt had to be returned before he moved to Dak Lak: 'We had to settle accounts with the cooperative; any man with a debt had to pay it all back'. Phụng confirmed his account. All outstanding taxes had to be paid before departure. And when I asked the policeman at Đông Xá commune whether anyone was prevented from leaving, his answer was significant: 'There was no discrimination by religion or any category. But there were cases where people were kept back because they owed money to the cooperative or the state, they hadn't carried out their citizen's duties, paid their taxes'. A former resident of Đông Hưng told me how the problem of her tax debt was 'resolved' on her departure. The allowance of subsidized rice she had enjoyed was withdrawn. She and her husband sold their house. They sat down with cooperative officials to count the tax they owed. From the price of the house added to the capital they were given on the programme, they were just able to pay off their debt. From her point of view, it meant they could go, even though they had to start again with nothing.* From the cooperative's point of view, a tax debt had been recovered. The policeman in Đông Xá was emphatic: if people couldn't pay back the tax, they couldn't leave. This, moreover, was the only reason for which people were kept back. For other misdemeanours, there was no discrimination: 'they could still go'.

Provincial authorities in Thái Bình were frustrated by local cadres' failure to be selective of settlers. Recruitment of people who were poor, sick or otherwise unsuitable had adverse effects on the mobilization campaign. In a self-critical article in the newspaper, the Đông Xuân commune Party Secretary admitted that in the past 'there were situations in which lazy workers, people in poor health and cripples were allowed to go, and met difficulties in the initial stages. These people have now abandoned the settlement and escaped back home creating puzzlement among the masses'.[62]

---

* She moved to Dak Lak in 1978. Houses and other property were sold to relatives and neighbours. Compensation was also supposed to be paid for land brought into the cooperative.

It is impossible to quantify the number of these people, even for the district of Đông Hưng. The district had a particularly successful migration programme and may well have 'topped up' its quota of volunteers.* But if we cannot quantify the question, we can say how the mobilization of particular individuals or families was carried out. Consider the following reconstruction:

> Tam was a Party member. He was quite well off. He lived at Liên Giang, a village in Đông Hưng district, which was introducing collectivization. Each village became a cooperative in the 1960s. Each commune became a cooperative in the late 1970s. In the 1980s the district itself aimed to organize collective production.† This rationalization policy affected the use of land in Đông Hưng. Some housing land was needed for agriculture. Some houses, on the outskirts of villages, were too far for services like water and electricity. Liên Giang village had houses like that. Tam lived in such a house. 'We were outside', he said.
>
> At Liên Giang, recruitment practice was coordinated with the rationalization policy. On the outskirts, there was more active mobilization. People living inside the village found it easier to stay. Outside, people were mobilized four times more than inside. No one was forced. But this team came round, that team came round, district cadres came round, commune cadres came round. Tam now lives in Dak Lak. He is chairman of a commune in Lak district.‡

A Đông Hưng district official explained the reason for this: 'Migration to new economic zones was a strategy to resolve the population pressure right here in our area'. He added that a number of communes transferred whole villages to the highlands. Hồng Việt commune moved all the one hundred families living in Bá Mai village to Lai Châu. Đông Phương commune moved the inhabitants of Phương Quan village to Lai Châu and Sông Bé. The official reported that 'at Hồng Việt, after the people had all left, we bulldozed the area to make land for farming'.[63]

Tam was not a debtor, nor was he a criminal. But he was 'outside' – in this case spatially so. His presence did not fit. The mobilization of this outsider was, in practice, approved and supported by district and perhaps higher authorities. But with regard to other types of outsiders, if officials I met in Hanoi are to be believed, the authorities did not intend the highlands to be filled with debtors, paupers, criminals, draft-dodgers, idlers and sick people. In the late 1970s, the central government felt it necessary to remind officials of this policy. Settler families should

---

*   During 1960–95, 10,573 families (60,092 people) left Đông Hưng on the government programme, not counting those who left without state assistance. Data provided by Đông Hưng People's Committee (Thái Bình, July 1995).

†   This involved district cadres giving detailed instructions to cooperatives by telephone, on what crops to plant, when to harvest, etc. For SRV policy on the primacy of the district in rural economic development, see Lê Thanh Nghị, *Xây dựng huyện thành đơn vị kinh tế nông công nghiệp*, Hanoi, NXB Sự Thật, 1979.

‡   Tam's experience at Liên Giang was not unique. In Đông Xá commune, Ngọc's family lived in an area which the cooperative wanted for agricultural development. They were visited by mobilization teams more regularly. Young people who had not joined the army received similar attention. I met Tam and Ngọc (aged 54 and 38 respectively) at Buôn Tría commune (Lak district). Interview (Dak Lak, November 1996).

have two people fit for work and not too many children. They should volunteer to go and possess some capital of their own. There was even a priority system, in case of over-subscription. The first in line were wounded soldiers with the strength to work, demobilized soldiers, assault youth, relatives of war heroes and people with appropriate technical qualifications. Criminal elements should not be sent to new economic zones, but should instead be handed over to the police.[64] The same policy had been expressed in a 1961 provincial document, stating that people should be mobilized according to five principles:

> **Economic situation**: population density and land availability in village of origin.
>
> **Political background**: no bad elements, politically suspect people, puppet sympathizers, cruel traitors, rascals, specialized petty criminals.
>
> **Age**: 65–80 per cent must be young people aged 18–26. No men over 45; no women over 40.
>
> **Health**: must be good.
>
> **Class background and current status**: 15 per cent must be Party members; 30–35 per cent members of mass organizations; 25–40 per cent young non-members of mass organizations; 15–20 per cent women.[65]

In reality these principles did not always translate into practice. Officials in different districts gave different versions of the policy. In Tiền Hải, for example, migration was regarded as a normal solution to people's problems with tax payment. One cadre told me frankly: 'We had to choose families with labourers, with difficulties (but no previous conviction or past history); families with at least two members; families who volunteered; families with many labourers, little land, and debts owed to the state'. Meanwhile cadres in Đông Hưng claimed not to collect outstanding debts: 'Many families had debts of paddy owed to the cooperative; we had to cancel the debts to encourage them to go (some families owed up to three to four tons of paddy)'. This may not have amounted to any more than a difference of presentation to a foreign researcher. It does seem, however, that practice varied between localities. Officials in Hanoi confirmed that large familes, poor families and families with few healthy adults were, in some places, allowed to go. They said this was regrettable and, as a result, Vietnam had received some bad press on the issue. I found myself agreeing politely that it was always possible to make good policy but that, in Vietnam as in any country, in practice, at the local level, good policy was not always implemented to the letter.[66]

POLICY AND PRACTICE

What these officials described went to the heart of the DRV's system of administration. With regard to migration as in other domains, the central government handed down policy to the provinces, districts, communes and villages. These took the form of guidelines, which were implemented at each level in accordance with local conditions. A retired migration official in Tiền Hải district told me how this worked:

Instructions were sent from the province to the district. The district had to check each village's population–land ratio. The district made its plans and decisions. These were transmitted to the villages; according to figures allocated to each village. People then volunteered.[67]

These figures formed the measure of local cadres' performance in mobilization. I was told this by Quốc, who moved from Đông Xá commune to Dak Lak province in 1977. He said that cadres had to mobilize the right number: 'More was okay. But if they mobilized less than the target, it was very terrible for the cadre'.[68] This was an administrative system which emphasized quantitative target fulfilment – an emphasis which could have unfortunate consequences. The Trực Tâm campaign, examined earlier in the chapter, aimed to increase the numbers of migrants leaving Thái Bình. It achieved some success in meeting the demands of the plan, as noted above. But behind every quantitative target fulfilled, there lurked some unfortunate practices:

> On the matter of choosing and approving people to go, a couple of places are still not doing their job well, and still get heavy on the numbers. As a result there are even cases where people who have lost the strength to work, chronically ill or lazy people, rascals, thieves, puppet soldiers and puppet officials who have committed serious crimes and have not yet been for re-education are also allowed to go, which creates difficulties for us.[69]

Formal attention to the plan led to negligence in the manner of its fulfilment. This was due to inadequate organization, as central government officials acknowledged:

> The Land Clearance Department is the office with direct responsibility for guiding the mobilization, but its organization still has many weak links. So the situation is still unstable, and little help is offered to lower levels for the resolution of their difficulties. (...) Since 1965, the new situation* has given rise to new requirements, but no concrete research has been carried out to find suitable policies.[70]

Local officials, meanwhile, complained of confusion and change in the guidelines they did receive. A district official in Đông Hưng made the following remarks about the policy of capital grants:

> The policy regime changed constantly. Before 1990 the state only gave money for the train, bus and food en route, and the transportation of people's property. Each locality had its own policy, sometimes giving cereals for the first six months, sometimes leaving families to provide it themselves. (...)
>
> The policies of the central government, province and district were also unstable, and based on each moment in time, so there could be several different policies. At times central government policy changed every two years; the district had a new policy every year. (...)
>
> The policy at the commune was based on decisions made by the locality in response to reality.[71]

---

* The 'new situation' was an allusion to US bombardment.

In these circumstances, higher levels in the administrative hierarchy paid attention to target fulfilment. Lower levels paid attention to local conditions. Little attention was paid to policy guidelines – which did not in any case provide detailed instructions for application to specific situations. Indeed, the Vietnamese word which normally translates as 'policy' (*chính sách*) seems closer in the above account to the English word 'implementation'. What counted was not policy, but practice. The important thing was the 'how' of cadres' implementation of the programme.

We can grasp here the significance of emulation exercises, like the Trực Tâm campaign. It was more important to train cadres on how to work, rather than instruct them on what work to do. And such training exercises gave authorities a second tool for evaluation. This was the administrative performance of cadres. When the numbers were not met, cadres were criticized for failing to meet them. When the numbers were met, their work was held up as an example for others to follow.

The quantitative results of mobilization were, as we have seen, highly uneven. They varied from commune to commune, district to district, and the quality of local leadership was seen as the determining factor in the variation. This was reported to be the case in Thái Bình in 1964, Nam Hà and Hải Dương in 1966, Thanh Hóa in 1967.[72] We have seen an example of good local leadership in the case of Hùng, though even Hùng was unable to recruit enough migrants to avoid going himself. Poor leadership, on the other hand, was blamed on two types of attitude. Some cadres, under pressure from other plans, resisted the policy. In Thái Bình, provincial authorities complained: 'Cadres, especially in the communes and co-operatives, tend to worry and are afraid to allow many members of their labour force to leave (especially young people), and feel that their locality will meet difficulties in production; as a result their tendency is to keep people back'.[73] Other cadres were simply incompetent. Authorities in Thanh Hóa observed:

> If the district and commune explain the problem positively, and carry out ideological work well with concrete methodology, the mobilization will have even better results. Party committees in Tĩnh Gia, Hoằng Hóa and Thiệu Hóa districts had a good way of explaining the problem and carried out good ideological work, showing as a result the best results of all the districts. By contrast, Quảng Xương district's way of explaining the problem lacked diligence from the beginning; no study sessions were organized to mobilize the thinking of the masses; the district's mobilization results have been the worst in the province.[74]

To get results, cadres had to do good 'ideological work'; it was not enough just to twist arms. Clear principles of good mobilization were stated:

> With regard to the masses, the questions 'to go or not to go', 'to welcome or not to welcome', 'to hold fast here or go back to the lowlands' are profound ideological struggles within each family and each production brigade, reflecting interests between the individual and the community, between the community and the state. Places should carry out ideological work thoroughly, from top to bottom, inside to out. People should be clearly shown both sides of the issue, both the duty and the advantage, but mainly the duty. The principle of 'true people, true work' should be used to persuade, and some mirror cadres and Party members should volunteer. In places like this, people

will see of their own accord that they have to go, that they have to welcome [people from the lowlands], that they have to build a new home without worrying.

On the other hand, places that use loudspeakers a lot, talk a lot about the advantages, emphasize in a one-sided way the interest of the project, promise things that cannot be delivered, even threaten 'to cut rice ration tickets', 'expel from the Party, or the mass organization' ... – in such places, the campaign cannot get under way, and difficulties will not reduce, but will increase instead.[75]

There were times when, of their own accord, people did not see that their own interests coincided with those of the community, as defined by the Party. In response to such moments, arm-twisting practices were used from time to time. The Trực Tâm campaign was intended to reduce their use, by educating cadres to improve the quality of their persuasion. If they learnt the lessons of the campaign, they should not have needed to use loudspeakers or threaten to cut ration tickets. But given the premium on quantitative results, and the personal consequences for failure, some cadres must have been tempted.

The implication of this assessment is that rule by mobilization worked well to the extent that people went voluntarily to the place assigned to them. Where they were browbeaten, where their arms were twisted because they failed to volunteer, mobilization had failed.

VOLUNTARISM

In these circumstances, the very conception of the volunteer is open to interpretation. This final section of the chapter will attempt to refine our idea of what it meant to volunteer in the DRV.

During the 1946–54 war, the ideals of an independent homeland and even the promise of a socialist future were beautiful in the midst of all the destruction. A journey to the hills of the Việt Bắc resistance zone was as much a statement of commitment to Hồ Chí Minh's red politics as it was an escape from the violence of the delta. With the return of peace, cadres of the DRV faced a challenge of a different order. The same techniques of mobilization were used in a different cause: the development and security of these highland margins of the communist state. In the villages of the Red River Delta mobilization meant, in practice, the creation of a minimal motivation necessary to ensure people's participation in projects of highland economic construction. Some people managed to avoid going to clear the wilderness. Some signed up enthusiastically at the start. A few were made to go. Many, however, were swayed by various forms of persuasion, and volunteered against their better judgement.

It is in this sense that we may understand the relationship of the state – with its projects relying essentially on the population for their realization – and the people themselves. The people's will to follow Party leadership was not always sufficient to ensure the immediate success of these projects. Huge energies were generated by the Revolution and a great fund of goodwill towards its leaders – still evident today among older people – was created. But the people could not always be expected spontaneously to obey 'the call of Uncle Hồ', where obedience involved sacrifice. And as we saw above, the sacrifices of clearing land for a cooperative in the hills could be less attractive than those of joining the army, or even of working on a state farm.

Yet the idea of spontaneity is a spurious one, in its implication that people can act independently of their social and political environment. The Party used this environment – by means of pressures exerted within it by officials, neighbours and relatives – to create will in the people. Ideals were presented – ideals of socialism, patriotism, home, hope for their children's future, desire for economic betterment – and these offered a rationale for volunteering for the government programmes of highland development. But the context of their presentation was a society in which room for independent manoeuvre was extremely limited.

I have attempted here to portray the context in which families made their decisions to volunteer. People believed in the ideals offered them to different extents, responded to the call of Party and country with differing degrees of enthusiasm, attempted to avoid it with different levels of resentment. But they were all described by the state – and by themselves – as volunteers. Volunteer has many meanings in this context. As a Đông Hưng cadre told me, people acted with degrees of voluntarism. If mobilization was carried out well, they contributed to the pro-gramme 'more voluntarily'. One writer invented the concept of 'semi-voluntary' to describe such decisions.[76] The central point here is that those who stepped forward contributed to the realization of the will of a government reluctant to strong-arm its people, which had to rely on subtle, more precarious methods of persuasion to obtain the results it wanted.

The precariousness of these methods was expressed, among many others, by Phụng who told me how cadres 'couldn't force people to go'. For some of them, there may have been an element of post facto justification in this sort of state-ment. They were, after all, reflecting on an important moment in their lives in the presence of a strange foreign man scribbling in a notebook. No one likes to have their arm twisted, or to admit to such. But this possibility does not detract from my argument. The point is that the use of mobilization allowed people to believe that they were not forced. Idealism, persuasion and various forms of economic and social pressure were certainly the only means at local cadres' disposal if they wished to rule in ways sanctioned by higher authorities. Yet there were cadres who overstepped the mark. In doing so, they jeopardized the major strength of DRV's administrative capacity. This was the reserve of goodwill and confidence in the Party's leadership which remained an important part of post-1945 popular consciousness.

For the villagers in the Red River Delta, this goodwill was not easily squandered. Most of those with very serious reservations about the communists had already made their choice, and left for the south after the Geneva Agreements. Many of those who remained had already reached some sort of internal accommodation with the new state. Even in 1996, Phụng and her sister-in-law, haunted by memories of the famine, found consolation in gratitude to the Party. Hùng, even during the dark days of settling in Mai Châu, refused to voice his doubts. But Hùng was a man of generous spirit. On another occasion, rather than complain to me that he had not been paid all the pension he was due, his response was to 'sympathize with the Party'. For Hùng, with his exuberant sense of description, we may imagine that he overcame his doubts about 'clearing the wilderness' with the sort of hyperbole expressed in the poem 'Going Up to the West':

> We build this place with magnificent hopes
> On this land in the west, like all of our Fatherland
> Our budding youth will always be green
> Like the green buds of the good green forest.[*]

Many of Hùng's contemporaries showed similar generosity. Few enjoyed his expressive imagination. But they all spent their youth cutting down the forest.

CONCLUSION

The DRV found the will to organize the movement of delta people into the highlands. The manner of this organization – rule by mobilization – was crucial to its success. Few people were forced. Few people really wanted to go. In a system allowing great flexibility of policy implementation by local authorities, there was considerable regional and local variation in mobilization practice.

In some villages people were persuaded to look both to their own interests and their country's future. Solutions were offered to the problem of population pressure and land hunger – very real concerns in the Red River Delta – and appeals were made for patriotic sacrifice. The essence of DRV administration, when it functioned correctly, was a grafting of family economic concerns on to patriotic sentiments of red nationalism. Convinced of this dual interest, some people volunteered for settlement in the hills.

In other villages more concrete forms of pressure were used to get individuals and families to sign up. Many of them lacked the economic and social resources to avoid going. They were placed in a situation where the offer of a few months' income on the government programme became an offer they simply could not refuse. In straitened circumstances, some people *were* volunteered to move to the hills.

NOTES

1 *Tiến Lên*, 'Trong công tác vận động nhân dân đi xây dựng kinh tế miền núi, chúng ta có thể làm được như Trực Tầm không? Tại sao?', *Tiến Lên*, 29 February 1964, p. 2.

2 *Tiến Lên*, 'Trong công tác vận động nhân dân', p. 2; Nguyễn Duy Ngưu, 'Cấp Ủy đi đầu, đảng viên gương mẫu xung phong là điều kiện tiên quyết của chúng tôi!', *Tiến Lên*, 15 March 1964, p. 2.

---

[*] The poem, written in 1958, was inspired by the movements of young people to state farms in the hills and made specific mention of farms at Mộc Châu and Điện Biên Phủ. Bùi Minh Quốc, 'Lên Miền Tây'. In *Tuyển tập thơ Việt Nam 1945–1960*, Hanoi: NXB Văn Hóa, 1960, p. 199.

3   Peter Seybolt offers insights into emulation campaigns in 1960s China, in his oral history portrait of village cadre, Wang Fucheng. Peter J. Seybolt, *Throwing the Emperor from his Horse: Portrait of a Village Leader in China, 1923–1995*, Boulder, Colorado: Westview Press, 1996, pp. 59–64, 72–73.

4   Tân Vũ, 'HTX Trực Tầm phấn đấu đưa một phần ba nhân khẩu đi các nơi xây dựng kinh tế', *Tiến Lên*, 1 January 1964, p. 3; Trực Tầm, 'Ra sức vận động nhân dân đi xây dựng kinh tế miền núi như HTX Trực Tầm', *Tiến Lên*, 25 February 1964, pp. 1, 4; Kiến Xương, 'Mấy kinh nghiệm vận động nhân dân đi xây dựng kinh tế miền núi của HTX Trực Tầm', *Tiến Lên*, 25 February 1964, p. 2; *Tiến Lên*, 'Trong công tác vận động nhân dân', p. 2.

5   Kiến Xương, *Báo cáo tổng kết công tác vận động chuyển dân đi tham gia phát triển kinh tế miền núi của hợp tác xã Trực-tầm, huyện Kiến-xương, tỉnh Thái-Bình*, Hanoi: Nhà In Báo Thủ Đô Hà Nội, 1964, p. 3.

6   *Tiến Lên*, 'Trong công tác vận động nhân dân', p. 2.

7   *Tiến Lên* Editorial Board, 'Chúng ta hoàn toàn có thể làm được như hợp tác xã Trực Tầm!', *Tiến Lên*, 5 May 1964, p. 2.

8   Nguyễn Văn Rương, 'Chúng tôi có thể vận động nhân dân đi xây dựng kinh tế miền núi như Trực Tầm!', *Tiến Lên*, 5 March 1964, p. 2; Đỗ Bá Các, 'HTX Hòa Bình quan tâm đến tình hình sản xuất của xã viên trên quê hương mới', *Tiến Lên*, 15 April 1964, p. 2.

9   Georges Boudarel, 'L'idéocratie importée au Vietnam avec le Maoïsme'. In Georges Boudarel, *La bureaucratie au Vietnam*, Paris: L'Harmattan, 1983, p. 31.

10 Nguyễn Duy Ngưu, 'Cấp Ủy đi đầu', p. 2. Ngọc Liên, 'HTX Hải An chúng tôi cũng sẽ chuyển một phần ba dân số đi xây dựng kinh tế miền núi', *Tiến Lên*, 15 April 1964, p. 2.

11 Phạm Xuân Điểm, 'Áp dụng kinh nghiệm của Trực tầm: trong một tháng xã Đông Quang chúng tôi vận động được 469 người đi khai hoang', *Tiến Lên*, 25 March 1964, p. 2.

12 Ngọc Liên, 'HTX Hải An chúng tôi', p. 2; Đặng Văn Sinh, 'Kinh nghiệm của Trực Tầm đã giúp cho Đông Xuân chúng tôi lối thoát', *Tiến Lên*, 30 March 1964, p. 2.

13 Ngọc Sơn, 'HTX Quyết Thắng gắn liền công tác xây dựng kinh tế miền núi với cuộc vận động cải tiến quản lý HTX đợt III', *Tiến Lên*, 20 April 1964, p. 2; Phạm Quang Khang, 'Chúng tôi đã làm như Trực Tầm: lãnh đạo quyết tâm, đảng viên gương mẫu', *Tiến Lên*, 10 March 1964, p. 2.

14 Nguyễn Duy Ngưu, 'Cấp Ủy đi đầu', p. 2; Nguyễn Văn Rương, 'Chúng tôi có thể vận động nhân dân', p. 2; Nguyễn Tiến Lộc, 'Chúng tôi đã đạt 97% kế hoạch cả năm', *Tiến Lên*, 1 May 1964, p. 2; Phạm Xuân Điểm, 'Áp dụng kinh nghiệm', p. 2; Ngọc Sơn, 'HTX Quyết Thắng', p. 2.

15 *Tiến Lên* Editorial Board, 'Chúng ta hoàn toàn có thể làm được', p. 2.

16 Nguyễn Tiến Lộc, 'Chúng tôi đã đạt 97%', p. 2.

17 NAV3/TCTK 2399(vv), 'Báo cáo tình hình thực hiện kế hoạch chuyển dân đi tham gia phát triển kinh tế miền núi 9 tháng đầu nam 1964', Thái Bình Statistical Office, 23 September 1964.

18 NAV3/TCTK 2399(vv), 'Báo cáo tình hình thực hiện kế hoạch', 23 September 1964.

19 For the effects at the village level in China of pressures to lie, see Seybolt, *Throwing the Emperor*, pp. 54–55.

20 Interview (Thái Nguyên, July 1995).

21 Đặng Phong, 'Thị trường và giá cả Việt Nam từ thế kỷ XIX đến nay', Hanoi: State Committee for Materials and Prices, 1992, p. 110.

22 Nguyễn Duy Ngưu, 'Cấp Ủy đi đầu', p. 2.

23 NAV3/TCTK 2474(vv), 'Tình hình thực hiện kế hoạch vận động đồng báo đi tham gia phát triển kinh tế, văn hóa miền núi 1966', Nam Hà Statistical Office, 19 December 1966.

24 Nguyễn Duy Ngưu, 'Cấp Ủy đi đầu', p. 2.

25 Seybolt, *Throwing the Emperor*, p. xv.

26 Kiến Xương, *Báo cáo tổng kết công tác vận động*. Excerpts also published in Kiến Xương, 'Mấy kinh nghiệm vận động nhân dân', p. 2.

27 Văn Hoa, 'Lòng những người đi khai hoang', *Tiến Lên*, 9 April 1962, p. 2.

28 These instructions may also be found in Kiến Xương, *Báo cáo tổng kết công tác vận động*.

29 Phạm Xuân Điềm, 'Áp dụng kinh nghiệm', p. 2.

30 NAV3/TCTK 2474(vv), 'Tình hình thực hiện kế hoạch vận động đồng báo đi tham gia phát triển kinh tế, văn hóa miền núi 1966', Nam Hà Statistical Office, 19 December 1966.

31 Interview (Thái Bình, May 1995).

32 See, for example, Đặng Văn Sinh, 'Kinh nghiệm của Trực Tầm', p. 2.

33 NAV3/CQLNTQD 140(vv), 'Báo cáo tổng hợp tình hình Nông Trường Sông Con', Report by the Director, Sông Con State Farm, 23 September 1960.

34 NAV3/CQLNTQD 140(vv), 'Báo cáo tổng hợp tình hình Nông Trường Sông Con', 23 September 1960; NAV3/CQLNTQD 69(vv), 'Báo cáo tình hình hoạt động của các nông trường quốc doanh nước Việt Nam Dân Chủ Cộng Hòa', Hanoi, 1959.

35 Bút Ngữ, 'Miền ngược, miền xuôi', *Thái Bình*, 16 October 1961, p. 2.

36 Interview (Hòa Bình, July 1995).

37 Nguyễn Phòng, 'Để cải thiện đời sống lâu dài cho nhân dân, chúng tôi tích cực chuyển người đi xây dựng kinh tế miền núi', *Tiến Lên*, 20 March 1964, p. 2. Minh Tân commune was in Kiến Xương district (Thái Bình).

38 Interviews (Hòa Bình, July 1995; Thái Nguyên, July 1995).

39 NAV3/TCTK 2474(vv), 'Tình hình thực hiện kế hoạch vận động', 19 December 1966.

40 Interview (Dak Lak, May 1996).

41 NAV3/TCTK 2474(vv), 'Tình hình thực hiện kế hoạch vận động đồng báo đi tham gia phát triển kinh tế miền núi 9 tháng đầu 1966', Nam Hà Statistical Office, 30 September 1966.

42 Tân Việt Hoa State Farm, Report for the Fatherland Front, Thái Nguyên, 1968.

43 NAV3/TCTK 2399(vv), Hà Giang Statistical Office to General Statistical Office, 22 December 1964.

44 NAV3/TCTK 2475(vv), 'Báo cáo tình hình nhân khẩu đến kinh tế văn hóa miền núi 9 tháng và ước tính cả năm 1967', Lai Châu Statistical Office, 22 December 1967.

45 Văn Khánh, 'Làm thủy lợi trên quê hương mới: Quỳnh Giáo ngăn suối làm sông biến đổi đất đỏ thành đồng lúa xanh', *Tiến Lên*, 1 January 1964, p. 2.

46 Interview (Hanoi, May 1995).

47 *Tiến Lên*, 'Đi xây dựng quê hương mới: Đảng bộ Vũ Thuận lãnh đạo tốt công tác khai hoang', *Tiến Lên*, 25 June 63, p. 4; Văn Hoa, 'Lòng những người đi', p. 2.

48 This man was 49 when I met him. Interview (Dak Lak, November 1996).

49 Interview (Thái Bình, July 1995).

50 Interview (Thái Bình, January 1997).

51 Prime Minister's Office Decision 491–TTg, 'Quy định tạm thời về việc Nhà nước giúp đỡ nhân dân đi khai hoang xa', Hanoi, 21 December 1961, reprinted in Cao Bằng, *Chính sách khai hoang thông tư số 491 TTg, 95 TTg, 31 TTg* Cao Bằng, Phòng khai hoang Cao Bằng, 1964, pp. 1–4.

52 Prime Minister's Office Circular to Ministries 95–TTg, Hanoi, 24 September 1962, reprinted in Cao Bằng, *Chính sách khai hoang*, pp. 5–7.

53 Prime Minister's Office Decision 31–TTg, 'Quy định bổ sung về chính sách nhân dân khai hoang', Hanoi, 24 April 1963. Reprinted in Cao Bằng, *Chính sách khai hoang*, pp. 8–12.

54 Thái Bình, *Chính sách nhân dân khai hoang*, Thái Bình: Ủy Ban Hành Chính, 1963, p. 4.

55 Policy documents on the early 1980s: Ministry of Agriculture, *Chính sách khuyến khích khai hoang xây dựng các vùng kinh tế mới*, Hanoi: NXB Nông Nghiệp, 1981. Reform in the mid 1980s: Nguyễn Văn Thanh, 'Đổi mới cơ chế quản lý công tác di dân xây dựng vùng kinh tế mới trong tình hình hiện nay', Hanoi: Trung Tâm Dân Số Nguồn Lao Động, 1990. Overview of the period 1976–90: Phạm Đỗ Nhật Tân, 'Hoàn thiện hơn nữa việc di dân nông nghiệp có tổ chức đi xây dựng các vùng kinh tế mới,' Luận án phó tiến sĩ khoa học kinh tế, Trường Đại Học Kinh Tế Quốc Dân, Hanoi, 1992, pp. 37–90.

56 General Department of Land Clearance, 'Báo cáo tổng kết cuộc vận động đồng báo miền xuôi tham gia phát triển kinh tế miền núi trong kế hoạch 5 năm lần thứ nhất và phương hướng nhiệm vụ những năm tới', Hanoi, July 1966. Calculations from Đặng Phong, 'Thị trường và giá cả Việt Nam', p. 110.

57 NAV3/TCTK 2494(vv), 'Báo cáo tình hình thực hiện kế hoạch vận động đồng báo đi xây dựng phát triển văn hóa miền núi, Báo cáo 9 tháng đầu 1968 và ước quy IV/68', Hà Tĩnh Statistical Office, 10 December 1968.

58 Cao Bằng, *Chính sách khai hoang*, p. 2; Thái Bình, *Chính sách nhân dân khai hoang*, pp. 13–15.

59 Kiến Xương, *Báo cáo tổng kết công tác vận động*, p. 10.

60 Interview (Thái Bình, July 1995).

61 Ngọc Liên, 'HTX Hải An chúng tôi', p. 2.

62 Đặng Văn Sinh, 'Kinh nghiệm của Trực Tầm', p. 2.

63 Interview (Thái Bình, July 1995).

64 Labour Ministry Circular 14–LD-TT, 21 June 1977; Government Council Decision 95–CP, 27 March 1980. Both reprinted in Ministry of Labour, *Chính sách chế độ về tổ chức điều động lao động và dân cư*, Hanoi: Cục Điều Động Lao Động, c. 1983. Interviews (Hanoi, July 1995).

65 NAV3/BLD 1030(vv), Hưng Yên Labour Office to district Party Committees and People's Committees, 5 July 1961.

66 Interviews (Thái Bình, June 1995; Hanoi, July 1995).

67 Interviews (Thái Bình, June 1996).

68 Quốc was 39 when I met him. Interview (Dak Lak, November 1996).

69 NAV3/TCTK 2399(vv), Thái Bình Statistical Office to General Statistical Office, 16 December 1964.

70 General Land Clearance Office, 'Báo cáo tổng kết cuộc vận động', July 1966.

71 Interview (Thái Bình, July 1995).

72 NAV3/TCTK 2399(vv), Thái Bình Statistical Office, 16 December 1964; NAV3/ TCTK 2474(vv), 'Báo cáo nhân khẩu di phát triển kinh tế văn hóa miền núi Quý 1 và Quý 2/1966', Nam Hà Statisical Office, 10 June 1966; NAV3/TCTK 2474(vv), 'Báo cáo lao động thời chiến năm 1966 của tỉnh Hải Dương', 9 December 1966; NAV3/TCTK 2460(vv), 'Báo cáo tình hình nhân khẩu đi tham gia phát triển kinh tế văn hóa ở miền núi, trung du. Quý 1 1967 và chính thức 1966', Thanh Hóa Statistical Office, 23 March 1967.

73 NAV3/TCTK 2432(vv), 'Báo cáo tình hình thực hiện kế hoạch chuyển dân đi tham gia phát triển kinh tế văn hóa miền núi 6 tháng đầu năm 1965', Thái Bình Statistical Office, 28 June 1965. See also NAV3/TCTK 2477(vv), 'Thống kê thực hiện di phát triển kinh tế miền núi 6 tháng đầu năm 1967', Vĩnh Phúc Statistical Office, 29 June 1967.

74 NAV3/TCTK 2460(vv), 'Báo cáo tình hình nhân khẩu di', 23 March 1967.

75 General Department of Land Clearance, 'Báo cáo tổng kết cuộc vận động', July 1966.

76 Hữu Mai, *Bưu ảnh từ những vùng đất mới*, Hanoi: NXB Quân Đội Nhân Dân, 1978, p. 3.

7 *Moving*

To maintain the people's goodwill, the Party informed them of the difficulties ahead. Prepared in advance, they would more cheerfully confront the challenge of clearing the land and making a living in the hills. A sense of the 'revolutionary meaning' of what they were doing would see them through. That, no doubt, was what kept Hùng going. And it was central to the experience of Trần Thị Đần, if we are to believe an article which appeared in *Tiến Lên* newspaper in December 1963. Her story was published under the rubric 'New People, New Work, Up in the New Home Village in Tây Bắc'.

> At the end of 1961, Mrs Trần Thị Đần left Hồng Hà commune, Hưng Nhân district and went, together with her son-in-law and two grandchildren, to build the economy of the highland forest region at Điện Biên Phủ. She travelled 600 km on a long and bumpy road in a jolty bus; the journey was tiring and the further she went into the rolling mountains, the more Mrs Đần missed her home village and worried about this strange land, these strange valleys. But seeing all the other people going with her gave her resolution; she started fretting less. Then she started to project her hopes onto Điện Biên Phủ, the place where our soldiers accomplished a glorious feat of arms, so that now she and the people of Thái Bình could go and contribute to the opening of a new economic area: the more she thought about it, the more the old lady saw herself as someone with a great honour and responsibility.
>
> She arrived at the new home. Difficulties appeared. The market was far away; the local compatriots' language was unfamiliar; clearing the land was hard work at first; she also missed her daughter and grandchildren back at their old home (…) There were times when, once again, she became worried and alarmed.[1]

Mrs Đần was one of hundreds of thousands of delta farmers to make such a trip in the 1960s. Not all of them stayed in the hills for long. Before we look at the process of settlement/abandonment of the 'new home' in the hills, it is worth considering for a moment the journey that brought them there. Whether they stayed or moved on from their new home, leaving the delta and travelling there was a moment of tremendous upheaval.

THE MOMENT

The article about Mrs Đần did not specify the exact date of her move: it was just 'at the end of 1961'. Many of her contemporaries, however, looking back on their journey thirty years later, were more precise. I was surprised at the accuracy of many people's recall. Loan, for example, remembered arriving at Bờ Rạ on 24 February 1964. This was also the time of year Hùng made his move, although he measured time by the lunar calendar. His journey took place a year before Loan's, on the eighteenth day after the lunar New Year (Tết). Học too had a clear memory of arrival at Điềm Mạc. By the western calendar it was 23 January 1963 but the year was still old in the lunar cycle. It was the twenty-third day of the twelfth month. Học remembered both dates.[2]

The slack season after Tết was a popular time for the move.[3] In Hà Nam at this time, Loan said, it was difficult to get the volunteer form and some applicants were rejected. A number of disappointed people left anyway, making their own way to Thái Nguyên where they were turned back by provincial authorities. The phenomenon was not unique to the year of Loan's move. Three years previously, Thái Nguyên Labour Office complained that 'especially at the moment, after New Year's Day, around the 19–20–21 February 1961, the number of people coming up is getting greater; every day between fifty and a hundred people arrive from every province: Hưng Yên, Hà Nam, Thái Bình, Bắc Ninh...'[4] Most of these New Year job seekers were sent home.

Sometimes the time of year was more readily recalled than the year itself. During discussions at Đông Xá commune, Kiệt, who abandoned a settlement in Nghĩa Lộ province, told me he left in 1972. Bùi, who still lived in Nghĩa Lộ, was adamant it was 1974. Bùi's account was eventually confirmed by other villagers. No one, however, argued about the season. They left one freezing February and most came back, after the subsidies were gone, in May and June.[5]

Sometimes the move was easier to date by use of the 'historical calendar', when its timing was set in the context of a memorable historical event.* Ngô said he arrived in Dak Lak 'in 1982, the year we fought the Chinese'. In fact, the war with China was fought three years before that, and neighbours confirmed that Ngô's family arrived at the same time as everyone else: in 1978. This was the year just before the Chinese invasion. Ngô also told me the day and month of arrival – 27 March – a date I was unable to check.[7]

The point, however, was not the accuracy of his recall of this date. It was rather that 27 March in the 'year we fought the Chinese' was, for Ngô, a moment important enough to remember – or mis-remember. This was true of most settlers. Whether they timed the event by the western, lunar or historical calendar, by the calendar of their family lives, by the year, the season or the weather, whether indeed they timed it 'wrong', when I asked about the date of their move it was commonly remembered with interest and alacrity. The journey was, indeed, added to other 'landmark moments' in their lives – weddings, births of children, funerals – and in the life of their country – reunification in 1975, collectivization in the

---

* The historical calendar has long been used by demographers as a method of estimating age. See also note 6.

late 1950s, land reform in the mid-1950s, the 1945 revolution.* This date itself became, like these circumstances of national signficance, an event against which they measured the passing of time. Moving to the hills was a moment of definition.

LEAVING

Mrs Đần, when she moved from her village in Thái Bình, left behind a daughter. She joined the family a while later, once they had settled. In this respect Đần resembled Đại, whom we saw earlier moving to Định Hóa district in the 1930s: Đại's family also left behind a daughter 'to keep the house'. But there was a subtle difference between temporary separation strategies in the 1930s and 1960s. In the earlier period, the daughter gave the family a chance to come home if things did not work out. But migrants on the DRV programme were not supposed to return. Dependants left behind were spared the tough early months of settling in. They were not meant to help families hedge their bets.[8]

This was explained before people left. The move was definitive. It was clear from the document they signed to volunteer for departure. I did not see a form from the 1960s, and it is possible that requests for inclusion on migration programmes were handwritten, as they had been in the 1920s. But by the 1990s, volunteers signed a form, pledging to 'carry out adequately the policy and duty which the state has determined', to 'build determinedly the New Economic Zone and settle there for the long term.' The form's final sentence was arresting: 'If I do not adequately carry out this duty or abandon it and come home, I agree to refund the expenditure that the state and community have made to help my family.' Few families could afford that after a failed venture in the hills. Once you signed the form there was no turning back.† Little wonder, then that people hesitated. Small surprise that, after signing, some got cold feet. Two stories – both written for purposes of propaganda – illustrate the dilemmas of departure.

The story of Phạm Thị Vân, a youth organization member in Kiến Xương district (Thái Bình), appeared in the Thái Bình newspaper in October 1961. On arrival in the highlands, she made friends with a young minority woman, a Mường, who consoled her in a moment of loneliness:

> You have come up to the west to live with us, certainly a long way from the sea, a long way from the wide expanses of paddy, a long way from your mother and father, but you will have a new home in addition to the old, in the high hills with the twittering birds, the good paddy terraces, the fresh green tubers, and with us and many other young Thái, Mèo, and Lào friends.[9]

---

*   The date which best illustrates this is 1954, a moment of multiple significance. Some saw 1954 as the time they got their own land, others as a time of return from war. Many made the decision to leave or stay in North or South Vietnam, according to provisions of the Geneva Agreements.

†   Considerable resources – financial, administrative, familial – were required for a return. See Chapter 8.

Phạm Thị Vân was frightened of losing her family. Her young Mường friend, holding her hand as they walked to the fields, gave her hope of new ties. Her story is beautifully stylized, inspirational. And back in Kiến Xương, its author affirmed that this sort of thinking inspired a young couple in Hồng Thái commune to marry quickly before signing up. Like Phạm Thị Vân, they thought to themselves, 'I'll miss mother, miss father, but already have a gentle friend by my side'. In the highlands, friends substituted for family, just as a new home would take the place of the old. The old home, the old family, moreover, would not be lost. The effort of moving to the highlands would be rewarded with a net gain, two home villages instead of one. As we have seen, a common slogan in 1960s migration propaganda – 'one destination, two native places' – played on traditional migration strategies, encouraging people to believe they were broadening rather than narrowing their options. Many people faced the dilemma of whether to believe this. Those who read the story about Phạm Thị Vân must have wondered if it were really true. By moving to the highlands, would they really be 'a long way from each other for a short time, only to build a future with each other for ever'?[10]

Hesitation before signing was one thing. Hesitation afterwards was quite another. A short story written in celebration of the New Year in 1964, entitled 'First Spring up at the New Home', related the dilemmas of a village school teacher and his wife, in Ý Yên district (Nam Định). The couple were 'the poorest of the poor' and the story opens with a description of their struggle to make a living. Then one day the teacher came home, and announced 'Darling! I've got it! Let's go and help build the mountain economy.' His wife, suspicious of the unfamiliar *Darling!*,* was appalled: 'What on earth are you imagining?' They argued. A week later, she came round. He resigned from the school and they sold the house. With the money from the sale, they bought clothes, blankets, scarves. For the first time she could afford 'a pair of rubber sandals with a red strap'. The departure date was set. Buses would come to the district town. A farewell ceremony was arranged with representatives from the district and province.

> The last thing she had to do was cross the bridge, go home and say goodbye to her relatives, in her parents' village. She was there for two days, and then carried her children back, with a sad and dismal face. No one knows who prompted her, who incited her, but she had changed her mind.

Her husband was furious.

> The house was sold and now to stay behind … their promise to the commune was clear, now how would they eat, how would they speak? Worst of all was his teaching, he'd already resigned, now if he stayed everyone would laugh and mock! The children would stare; so would their parents. The Party Secretary was sympathetic, advising him to stay and sort everything out, he could go next time round.

---

*   Darling: *mình này.*

Eventually, ignoring the Party Secretary, he split up with his wife and went alone. The rest of the story told of economic hardship on both sides, how they missed each other, and finally the arrival in the hills of a letter from the Party Secretary giving news and encouragement. The letter urged him to come home for a visit.

> She had just lit the kitchen fire, and went for a look out at the gate. That was how 'our old man' came home. Wow! He was really something. With his sun-helmet, his green cotton shirt, his soldier's shoes, and holding a glittering electric torch, he looked just like a district cadre.

In the story's final scene, convinced at last that life was possible in the hills, she followed him, red sandals and all, on the path to their new home.[11]

None of these stories need be taken as literal accounts of real experiences. They were idealized solutions to observed dilemmas. Such situations did exist, even if the denouement of the story was not always so neat and romantic. Some migrant workers to the Mộc Châu state farm (Sơn La) similarly found that their wives refused to follow them to the hills. By contrast with the hero of 'First Spring up at the New Home', many of these men later struck up relationships with young unmarried women, fellow migrants on the farm.[12] Yet these idealized stories played an important role in mobilization. If they were not read by the people themselves, they were intended for re-telling by cadres. They were also, as we saw in the previous chapter, intended for the education of cadres themselves. Indeed, a key figure in the story of the school teacher was the Party Secretary, whose subtle and sympathetic handling of the situation brought the estranged couple together again, at the same time as ensuring that they did actually leave the village and go to the mountains. Cadres were, in reality, faced with this sort of problem. I learnt this from Quảng, who in 1978 was preparing to leave his home village for a new economic zone in the central highlands. Then one of his children fell sick. He asked the head of the cooperative if he could stay. Quảng eventually left in a later group in 1984.*

Not everyone was as sensitively treated as Quảng, however. The central government complained about officials who 'do not make careful preparations, but "shift people out by the load" and "bring them in by the load"'.[13] Because of this bureaucratic 'fulfil the plan' mentality, or perhaps because he had fought for the South Vietnam army during the war, Bình, who moved from his village near Huế to Dak Lak in 1982, had to leave at a time his wife was heavily pregnant. He did not say whether he asked to delay the departure. But his wife gave birth on the bus.[14]

TRAVELLING

For Bình's wife, the trip to the hills must have been a highly traumatic experience. For others, like Mrs Đần, it was simply new and strange. It was the first time many

---

* Quảng was from Phú Lương commune, Đông Hưng district (Thái Bình). Interview (Dak Lak, November 1996).

of them had been far from home;* the trip was long and uncomfortable;† many
people had no idea where they were going;‡ and the scenery was unfamiliar. A
woman from Vũ Phong commune described the journey in a letter to her brother
written just after she arrived in Tây Bắc and published in *Tiến Lên*.

> Brother! (*Anh ạ!*) I have travelled such a great distance on these roads, hundreds of
> kilometres coming up here to the west. The day we left, there were eighteen buses in my
> group, taking 202 people. The buses went over Pha Đin pass, climbing high like a road
> to the sky. Such a long road, and all the way along it there were arches, posters and
> banners from our compatriots there welcoming us. We quite forgot our tiredness.[15]

This young woman expressed her excitement at the journey. But in a letter home
– in which she sent greetings both to her brother and to the Party committee at her
home village – she was under a certain amount of pressure. Học was less effusive
when, retrospectively, he described his journey to me.§ But like the woman above,
he was young, glad to be on the road, excited at the change of scene. The trip,
moreover, went according to plan. Other travellers had a harder time of it.

I found evidence of few major accidents on the road. What emerged from
people's accounts were the small and common things (car-sickness, loss of property)
or more rather significant events (childbirth, robbery) which interrupted smooth
travelling. One leader lost the group's introduction papers, which was a disaster in
those days of state subsidies. On another occasion, four pigs sent with accompanying baggage disappeared en route.[16] The one exception to this was the impact of
war. After American bombs started falling in 1965, this emerged clearly in archival
accounts as a major hindrance to the programme. A convoy of buses leaving Nam
Định in April 1966 was delayed for ten days on the road to Lào Cai. A few months
later another convoy had to wait for three weeks.[17] Delays were also caused by a
shortage of vehicles.¶ But at the end of 1966, the Nam Định provincial authorities
proudly claimed that since the bombing started, there had been not a single accident
due to war.[18] And the General Land Clearance Office praised those places which

---

*   Previous travel experience made the journey easier. Lộc moved to Dak Lak from Dong
Xa commune in 1977. He had regularly worked away from home (forestry in Nghĩa Lộ,
mining in Quảng Ninh) and aged 54 had no trouble with the seven day journey. His family,
he said, found it harder. Interview (Dak Lak, November 1996).

†   In the early 1960s, the bus journey from Thái Bình to Thái Nguyên took twelve hours.
Ten years later, travel to Nghĩa Lộ took two days. In the late 1970s, travel time to Dak Lak
was five to seven days.

‡   Tam left Thái Binh in 1978 (see Chapter 6). Before he arrived there, Dak Lak was just
a name. In 1963, migrants from Đông Quang commune (Đông Hưng district, Thái Bình)
could see a map of Tây Bắc before they left. The destination became a name on a map.
Phạm Xuân Điểm, 'Áp dụng kinh nghiệm của Trực Tâm: trong một tháng xã Đông Quang
chúng tôi vận động được 469 người đi khai hoang', *Tiến Lên*, 25 March 1964, p. 2.

§   His journey is described in the Prologue. Interview (Thái Nguyên, July 1995).

¶   Vehicle shortage was a problem in peacetime too, causing restrictions on luggage amounts.
In 1978, when Tam came to Dak Lak, only one lorry was provided to carry the luggage of
fifty-four families. Other groups indicated, however, that they could take with them as
much as they liked. Interviews (Dak Lak, November 1996).

'in wartime have organized people to leave in small groups, making use of means of transport ready to hand, setting up staging centres in safe places en route, making transport arrangements so that people do not have to wait a long time.'[19] One such success story was Phụng's trip from Thái Bình to Thái Nguyên in 1965. The bus did the round trip in twenty-four hours, and the migrants travelled at night, probably as much due to vehicle shortage as fear of bombs.[20]

There were, of course, places where arrangements were not properly made, and long waits caused 'the compatriots to be alarmed'.[21] But, even without delays, the long journey itself gave people plenty of time for worrying, particularly older people, like Mrs Đần. Before arriving, however, they could always – as Mrs Đần did – temper their nerves with the luxury of hopeful anticipation. Articles in *Tiến Lên* portrayed people combating anxiety in this time of transitory non-knowledge with fine thoughts about their responsibility for building the nation. Mrs Đần focused her hopes on the feat of arms at Điện Biên Phủ. She dreamed perhaps – as Bùi Minh Quốc did – of 'peacetime Điện Biên Phủ victories' in economic development.[22] But when people spoke to me of their anticipations, few used the words of duty, honour and responsibility quoted in the newspaper. One man looked forward to seeing the mountain bauhinia trees.[23] Hùng hoped to make a better life for his children. Quảng said he had no idea what it would be like, but just went. As for Hùng's neighbour: 'I didn't know anything of the future. But I hoped it would be alright'.

ARRIVING

Few people could take the bus directly to their new home. Usually, the place was remote and the last stretch was on foot by a path or poorly made road. When I visited Học's home at Điềm Mặc, it was July – rainy season – and the track was a morass of mud. I landed my motorbike in the ditch at one point, got stuck in a ford at another, none of which ruffled in the least the district official riding pillion, who had to leap to safety. Travelling, of course, had got easier since the new economic zone was set up thirty years before. Học said that, in particular, the fact that there were motorbikes now made easy work of the 10 km of 'forest road' to the highway. It didn't seem easy work to me. But in those days before the road, merely getting to the settlement site was no mean feat. As one local official put it, 'People moving to areas of uncleared land in Bắc Thái had to put up with major challenges: they climbed passes, fording streams on footpaths dozens of kilometres long'.[24] Fortunately for Học's family, when they reached the footpath in 1963, 'the minority people met us and gave us a hand carrying everything'. From there, they walked in.

At Bộc Nhiên, not far from Điềm Mặc, settlers also received a fine welcome: 'local compatriots received the Thái Bình people as they would greet their close friends'.[25] Downstream at Bờ Rạ, Loan was met by people from her home province who had moved there the previous year. At Phúc Linh commune, near Đại Từ district town, the first settlers must have been surprised to discover that Việt people

had been living there since the 1930s. They had joined local Tày and Nùng people
to walk the short distance out to the highway and help move their luggage back
in.[26] Speaking with Dũng, a retired district official in Mai Châu, revealed to me
that 'this was the first time our compatriots up here received Việt people'. The
arriving settlers were, nevertheless, greeted by the local Thái population, who
came out to welcome their compatriots and help them carry their luggage into the
temporary reception centre.[27]

But 'local compatriots' did not only extend a warm welcome on arrival. Học
went on to say how the Tày people in Điềm Mạc,

> showed us up to the stilt-houses where the minority people lived, and we stayed there
> for a short time, five or six people in each house. Then we went out to start clearing
> land. Once we'd finished building our houses we moved from the minorities' place
> out to the village here. That's how it was then!

At Bộc Nhiên, settlers from Thái Bình didn't stay with the locals. Both there
and at Phúc Linh, they found temporary housing already prepared for them. At
Tân Thái, Phụng stayed with local people for three months.* In Mai Châu, Dũng
told me that at Mai Hạ commune, 'six or seven families came up at first; they
were welcomed home and stayed with the local people. These families then built
a temporary shed, and when it was finished they moved out there'. Later arrivals
moved directly into the temporary accommodation.

Relations between the Thái inhabitants of Phù Yên valley (Sơn La) and a group
of Vietnamese recently repatriated from Thailand were particularly friendly. The
newcomers stayed in Thái houses for six months or more. One of them said she
found the Thái language spoken here to be quite different from that she had picked
up in Thailand, adding that 'living on top of one another, in constant contact, we
learnt this Thái quickly'.[28] This woman, who was 20 at the time, settled quickly
indeed – she fell in love with her new neighbour, a handsome Thái cadre twenty
years her senior. He told me one evening that her request to become his second
wife made for a rather awkward situation, as he was already married: 'I did not
accept, I couldn't marry her'. To justify his regret to a foreign visitor, he went on
to explain the practice of polygamy: 'This is the custom of people in Vietnam, in
Thailand, in Laos, in Indochina'. He then added, 'Unfortunately I am in the Party,
so it was different'.[29]

We can get a sense of the way some inhabitants of the highlands helped the
newcomers from the following account published in a provincial newspaper.

> When they first arrived, seeing the rolling, rolling mountains and the thick wild forest,
> many people found themselves worried and frightened: frightened of ghosts, frightened
> of tigers, frightened of terrifying forest and poisoned water, frightened of sickness and
> disease, etc. But after three months of living together with the local people, many of
> these fears have been gradually calmed, and emotional ties between the lowlands and

---

*   She did not specify who these people were. Interview (Thái Nguyên, October 1996).

highlands are getting closer. When our compatriots moved out to live on their own, many local households were sad to see them go; there were even families who stood and cried when they saw them off; some wrapped up sticky rice steamed with two eggs to give to the children; some gave chickens and dogs for breeding; there was one father who dug up the banana plant by his house and carried it on his shoulders round for his compatriots to plant. These feelings have made villagers from the lowlands see that there are great sources of consolation, so with enthusiasm and dedication they get down to work.[30]

Feelings of love and tears of sadness were, doubtless, exchanged from time to time between lowland and highland people. But the key currencies of exchange in those early days were material. In Hòa Bình in 1963 – as the article relates – rice, eggs, chickens, dogs and plants changed hands. Elsewhere people could be even more generous. Newspaper readers in Thái Bình thus learnt that in Tuần Giáo district (Tây Bắc, 1961), 'compatriots sold buffaloes, pigs and chickens to the land clearance group, and haven't asked for the money immediately.[31] In Phú Thọ (1962), it was reported that 'when the group from Đông Sơn commune had only just arrived, the people of Tự Cường came out to welcome them, and gave them houses to live in, as well as beds and mats. The very next morning, the whole commune of Tự Cường brought them four buffaloes, four ploughs, four rakes, 400 kg of paddy seeds, 8 tons of paddy and 18 tons of manioc for food, as well as many household utensils.'[32] A similar story was told of the settlement in Bắc Kạn (1964), where 'from the moment they [settlers from Thái Bình] arrived at the commune, the local people spent 1,360 work days moving luggage and helping with houses, offering chickens, rice, salt, corn and food for Tết, as well as capital, seeds, land and buffalo for production.'[33]

The size of the gift made to settlers in Phú Thọ – many tons of food for only sixty people – made front-page headline news in the Thái Bình newspaper. This must have been impressive reading for families still hesitating about whether to sign up themselves. We may imagine even that the figures were massaged for their benefit. But there is no doubt that highlanders did make considerable sacrifices to help the newcomers. In Mai Châu, in addition to help with temporary accommodation, building houses and various labour tasks, the local Thái inhabitants even gave Hùng and his fellow settlers some of their land. I asked a retired district official, a Thái man, about this: 'It was no problem at all, we felt for each other'.[34]

This official's generous spirit should not blind us to the fact that the welcome, in all its aspects, was the product of a process of mobilization. In Hanoi I was told that a successful migration programme was based on mobilizing three groups of people: lowland people to migrate, and both lowland people and 'ethnic minority compatriots' to help them. The situation in Mai Châu valley clearly showed how this worked. Dũng said: 'When we first started to receive people, everything was done in a relaxed and proper way; we mobilized each family up here to receive one or two families to come and stay with them and make a living together'.[35] This lasted only a short time, he told me, before temporary accommodation was quickly built.

Ordinary Thái residents of the valley remembered more longer-lasting sacrifices. In the commune of Chiềng Châu, I enjoyed some temporary hospitality in the house of one of them, Mr Vì. He told me – also in a relaxed and proper way – that when the new economic zone people came up, cadres came round to mobilize, explaining to people that they had to divide up the land. This, he confided with an air of cheerful resignation, was not the first time the Thái had lost their land to outsiders. In 1946 the French had confiscated large tracts of wet-rice land to build an airstrip in this strategic valley. At this point a neighbour, joining in the conversation, joked about the French: 'We weren't compensated, we even had to give them more money afterwards!' At first I thought it was a way of laughing things off which lay behind these men's cheerfulness about losing the land a second time. In the 1960s, when the mobilization started, someone said 'we didn't worry about it, we helped each other'.[36] But perhaps, I surmised later, it was because many of the Thái here have Việt ancestry. The leading family in Chiềng Châu, called Mạc, can trace their ancestry back to the royal dynasty ousted in the sixteenth century. Was I wrong to think that many of them remembered that they too arrived here from the plains, long ago?[*]

On one of my visits to Mai Châu, a spectacular festival was held – celebrating solidarity between ethnic groups in the northern highlands – and this, indirectly, gave me a new angle on Vì's attitude.[†] It was October, and the sun was still strong, so after watching the parades for a while, my colleague and I moved into the shade of a tea-stall. The woman serving tea was born in Nam Định. She had arrived in Mai Châu at the same time as Hùng. And as we drank her tea, she told us how, before she arrived, the locals were told that the Việt would be coming for three years, to help them with economic development, and would then go home. The Thái learned many things from the Việt: efficient wet-rice agriculture, vegetable farming, new food habits. But the Việt overstayed their welcome. When the three years were up, the Thái were told that 'the land is no one's, it belongs to the nation. We are all Vietnamese, so the Việt should stay here and cultivate it'.

At this point in the conversation, two men joined us in the tea stall. They too were Việt from the plains, and talked about their arrival there. The woman, however, had no more to say. One of the men, at the festival for a break from his duties as policeman at the commune of Vân Mại, invited us to continue our research in his village. When we did so, a few days later, no mention was made of an overstayed

---

[*]   The case of the Mạc in Chiềng Châu – whose family pride caused them to change their ethnic culture to preserve their name – is only the most illustrious of the Thái with Việt origins. Throughout the northern hills, there are people who can trace their ancestry to the plains, though their material and linguistic culture seems fully Thái. Their ancestors fled hunger (eighteenth century), received appointments as highland administrators (nineteenth century), or came as colonial soldiers to fight the Black Flags (late nineteenth century). See Andrew Hardy and Nguyễn Tiến Đông, 'Quelques intérrogations sur l'identité ethnique : le cas des Mạc de Mai Châu', *Tạp Chí Xưa & Nay*, no. 66, 1999, pp. I-III, 24–25.

[†]   This was the Thái-Tày festival, bringing together Thái and Tày people from all over the north, held on 17 October 1995.

welcome. But the tea-stall woman's account was confirmed by Việt people elsewhere in the district. I was told on one occasion that one or two Thái complained to the Việt: 'Such a long time, and we still haven't seen you go home'. On another occasion I heard that a few people said, 'Such a long time, why haven't you gone yet?' [37] A Việt man said that there had been incidents in the early days, usually fights between teenage men. A Thai man finally told me how these incidents were kept to a minimum: 'There was constant political work. People didn't cede their land straight away. There was constant arguing – we weren't allowed to argue'. He then added, laughing, 'Anyway, what's the point in keeping the land?'[38]

DIFFICULTIES

On the day the settlers arrived at their new home, none of this was yet apparent. It must have been an overwhelming experience – perhaps they were impressed and happy at the welcome they received, perhaps confused at the strangeness of the place and the people. For people in Mai Châu, as for Mrs Đần, this was the moment that anticipation ended and the challenges of settlement appeared. Hùng put it simply: 'We really ran into difficulties'. The first hours and days there were spent realizing what those difficulties would amount to. Dũng observed that when they first arrived, for the first month or two, many people went out to the stream to cry, missing their home. In Phù Yên valley, Vân, who had just arrived from Thailand, looked at the 'gloomy, foggy forests and cried and cried and cried'. Học expressed the disappointment he felt on arrival in the forests of Điềm Mặc with his usual equanimity:

> It was rather sad, coming up to those densely forested mountains. Many children cried and asked to go home, but they gradually got used to it. But since I was small I had felt I'd like to live in the highlands. Even now, I still find it suits me, even the environment.[39]

Học, in retrospect at least, set a good example of positive thinking towards this difficult situation. But the best example I came across was set by Mr Cách, a man from Nam Trực district (Nam Định), who settled on Cun Pass on the road to Mai Châu in 1961. His reaction, and those of the people who were with him, were recorded in the Hòa Bình provincial newspaper in 1963:

> The first time they set foot in the forested highlands, one major difficulty was that people did not understand the customs and living habits of the ethnic minority compatriots; wherever they went, all they saw was this strange forest, these strange mountains. In the first days, fresh off the road, no one could escape problems in their standard of living, and there was even a shortage of goods of everyday necessity. Faced with these initial difficulties, a number of 'weak-spirited' people wavered and lost heart. Some people cried, some people sighed. But only Mr Cách had a different way of thinking, and often said to people: more than fifty years I have been living in Nam Trực (…)

There is no need to repeat Cách's rousing speech here. The journalist, in fact, summarized it for us in a single phrase. Noting the old man's excitement at the extent of the land there, the potential for rich arable farming, the journalist observed that Cách felt like a 'mouse landed in a rice jar'. He was, as a result, certainly not going to be frightened of hunger. Cách's story, in its context as a newspaper item, gives us a clear and contrasting image of the arrival experience in terms of practice and policy. His fellow villagers demonstrated how people actually reacted when they arrived. Cách himself showed the way they were supposed to react. And as the personification of policy, we need not be surprised to discover, by the end of the article, that Cách – whose name itself means 'way' – had become a model for other people to emulate. Two years after arriving, we are informed, 'many villagers have already learnt from Cách's family about how to get rich'.[*]

CONCLUSION

In the delta, mobilization to move was carried out over time and accompanied by discussion, dilemma and decision. The move itself was an event. It constituted a major change in people's lives. Anticipation was followed by disillusionment and difficulty, a reality recognized in propaganda aimed at equipping people with the guts to overcome it. For the existing inhabitants of areas settled, this event marked the culmination of a process of mobilization, by which they were persuaded to offer land, shelter and practical help to the newcomers. In the short run, they made the sacrifices required of them, with good or bad grace. Many of them, indeed, were led to believe that these sacrifices would only be required for a short period.

In the long run, however, this event marked the lives and memories of those who moved and those who welcomed them. The next chapter looks at how the anticipations and apprehensions of this moment worked themselves out into the reality of settling the land.

NOTES

1   Nguyễn Sĩ Thưởng, 'Giỏi việc nhà, chậm việc hợp tác', *Tiến Lên*, 15 December 1963, p. 3.

2   Interviews (Thái Nguyên, July 1995, October 1996; Hòa Bình, October 1995).

3   This observation was made by migration programme officials in Thái Bình. NAV3/TCTK 2432(vv), 'Báo cáo tình hình thực hiện kế hoạch chuyển dân đi tham gia phát triển kinh tế văn hóa miền núi 6 tháng đầu năm 1965', Thái Bình Statistical Office, 28 June 1965.

4   NAV3/BLD 1030(vv), 'Báo cáo tình hình người miền xuôi lên Thái Nguyên', Thái Nguyên, 23 February 1961. Loan confirmed this in interview (Thái Nguyên, October 1996).

5   Interviews (Thái Bình, January 1997).

6   United Nations, *Handbook of Population Census Methods*, New York: 1959. For problems in its use, see J. C. Caldwell and A. A. Igun, 'An Experiment with Census-Type Enumeration in Nigeria', *Population Studies*, vol. 25, no. 2, 1971, p. 294.

7   Interview (Dak Lak, November 1996).

8   For legislation on dependants, see Prime Minister's Office Circular to Ministries 95–TTg, Hanoi, 24 September 1962. Reprinted in Cao Bằng, *Chính sách khai hoang thông tư số 491 TTg, 95 TTg, 31 TTg*, Cao Bằng: Phòng Khai Hoang Cao Bằng, 1964, p. 6.

---

[*]   The expression 'mouse landed in a rice jar' (*chuột sa chĩnh gạo*) is a metaphor for 'seizing a windfall'. Its negative connotations have been overlooked by the author of the article. Đăng Lân, 'Gia đình ông Cách trên quê hương mới', *Hòa Bình*, 12 July 1963, pp. 3–4.

9 Bút Ngữ, 'Miền ngược, miền xuôi', *Thái Bình*, 16 October 1961, p. 2.

10 Ibid.

11 Chu Văn (ed.), 'Mùa xuân đầu tiên trên quê mới', 1964. In *Hương cau hoa lim. Tập truyện ngắn*, Hanoi: NXB Văn Hóa, 1971, pp. 39–50.

12 Personal communication from Ingrid Schreiner (February 1998).

13 General Land Clearance Office, 'Báo cáo tổng kết cuộc vận động đồng báo miền xuôi tham gia phát triển kinh tế miền núi trong kế hoạch 5 năm lần thứ nhất và phương hướng nhiệm vụ những năm tới', Hanoi, July 1966.

14 Interview (Dak Lak, November 1996)

15 Đinh Công Thành, 'Những lá thư Tây Bắc gọi về', *Thái Bình*, 28 October 1961, p. 2.

16 Interviews (Dak Lak, May and November 1996).

17 NAV3/TCTK 2474(vv), 'Báo cáo nhân khẩu đi phát triển kinh tế văn hóa miền núi Quý 1 và Quý 2/1966', Nam Hà Statistical Office, 10 June 1966; 'Tình hình thực hiện kế hoạch vận động đồng báo đi tham gia phát triển kinh tế miền núi 9 tháng đầu 1966', Nam Hà Statistical Office, 30 September 1966.

18 NAV3/TCTK 2474(vv), 'Tình hình thực hiện kế hoạch vận động đồng báo đi tham gia phát triển kinh tế, văn hóa miền núi 1966', Nam Hà Statistical Office, 19 December 1966.

19 General Land Clearance Office, 'Báo cáo tổng kết cuộc vận động', July 1966.

20 Interview (Thái Nguyên, October 1996).

21 NAV3/TCTK 2474(vv), 'Tình hình thực hiện kế hoạch', 30 September 1966.

22 Bùi Minh Quốc, 'Lên Miền Tây'. In *Tuyển tập thơ Việt Nam 1945–1960*, Hanoi: NXB Văn Hóa, 1960, p. 198.

23 Interview (Sơn La, December 1996).

24 Trịnh Văn Đông, 'Báo cáo tổng kết công tác khai hoang xây dựng vùng kinh tế mới năm 1976–1981', Thái Nguyên: Bắc Thái Agricultural Office, 1982.

25 Hoàng Loan, 'Đồng báo Đông Quân trên quê hương Định Hóa', *Tiến Lên*, 15 October 1963, p. 3.

26 Interviews (Thái Nguyên, September 1995, October 1996).

27 Interview (Hòa Bình, June 1995).

28 Interview with Cầm, who arrived in Vietnam for the first time in 1963 (Sơn La, December 1996).

29 Interview (Sơn La, December 1996).

30 Trọng Hồng, 'HTX khai hoang Tân Ngọc sản xuất bước đầu có nhiều tiến bộ', *Hòa Bình*, 27 September 1963, p. 3.

31 Thanh Long, 'Đồng báo Tây Bắc tích cực giúp đỡ các đồi khai hoang tỉnh Thái Bình', *Thái Bình*, 30 October 1961, p. 1.

32 The group was from Đông Hưng district (Thái Bình). C. T., 'Nhân dân xã Tự Cường (Phú Thọ) giúp đoàn khai hoang 4 trâu, trên 8 tấn thóc, 18 tấn sắn. Đoàn khai hoang Đông Sơn phá hoang vượt kế hoạch', *Tiến Lên*, 10 December 1962, p. 1.

33 Ma Ngọc Cao, 'Xã Hùng Vương (Bắc Cạn) đón đồng báo xã Phúc Thành lên khai hoang', *Tiến Lên*, 10 March 1964, p. 4.

34 Interview (Hòa Bình, October 1995).

35 Interview (Hòa Bình, June 1995).

36 Interview (Hòa Bình, October 1995).

37 Interviews (Hòa Bình, October 1995).

38 Interview (Hòa Bình, July 1996).

39 Interview (Thái Nguyên, July 1995).

*B*ờ Rạ village lay on the banks of the Công River. Điềm Mạc commune lies at its source, by the Red Mountain. In the late 1940s, Hồ Chí Minh chose Điềm Mạc's forests for his headquarters. In the early 1960s, Học, his parents and forty-nine other families moved there from Thái Bình.* Before 1963, Học said, Điềm Mạc was covered with old forest, 'it was only when we came up that it was cut'. He spoke at length of how the great trees were brought down, and that day I had my tape recorder with me. I reproduce below some minutes of our conversation.

> *Hardy*: At the beginning, how was the forest cleared?
>
> *Học*: For the big trees we had to use axes to chop them down, then in the sunlight we'd set fire to them; we'd use whatever we could for firewood or to build houses. We couldn't sell the timber: there was no one to buy, because there was no road to carry it out. After that we hoed up the roots, then got down to planting. And we began to lay out areas, one by one. Each family staked out an area, men who did a lot of work got a big space, men who did little got a small space; it was then that it was all divided up.
>
> *Hardy*: And after the forest was cut?
>
> *Học*: We planted manioc, peanuts, potatoes and dry rice. We did three years of this work but got no results, so the state invested so we could plant tea. We planted tea, but there was no harvest straight away, so the state gave us rice to eat and guidance on farming techniques. When we started harvesting tea, started producing, the people's life stabilized.

I interrupt the conversation here, to introduce the theme of the present chapter. Học's arrival in the highlands – like that of many other people – was the beginning of a process of settling. Many settlers described this process using the word *ổn định*. This word is rendered in the dictionary simply as 'settled, stable'.[1] But when employed in the context of the highland frontier, it came to have a wider range of meanings. Học gave voice to a range of these:

> … the people's life stabilized (*ổn định*), of course not at a high level but there were fewer difficulties, everyone had enough to eat. Twenty families abandoned the settlement. They went one by one, in 1965–66–70; they went gradually. They went, one

---

* See Prologue.

because they found the work here wasn't suited to them; two because the climate didn't suit them. That's how they left.[2]

In the few moments it took him to say this, Học had expressed in a nutshell both the policy and the practice of settling in the Vietnamese highlands. For many cadres – those accompanying migrants to the forest and those in offices reporting on their results – *ổn định* meant ensuring that people did not abandon the settlement, and that they produced something from the land. For settlers, *ổn định* certainly implied making enough food to eat. But Học's other definition – 'fewer difficulties' – is indicative of the vague and shifting meaning people gave to the concept. Settling was a process of overcoming economic but also social difficulties in a new environment. Học, who as village head was both 'cadre' and 'people', was well placed to understand this. At one end of the process, settling meant survival and subsistence. At the other, it was the attainment of a life which 'lacked for nothing, materially or emotionally', a life 'like that at the old home'.[3] The present chapter charts the evolution of the settlement process, viewed in the light of the interest of both the state and the settlers.

STAYING

Cadres' first preoccupation was that people should stay. In the language of their reports, settlement was intimately and inversely associated with abandonment. 'We have not yet got our migrating compatriots to settle down contentedly to making a living and building their new home village' was a self-criticism made in 1964 by a provincial cadre in Thái Bình. He well knew what this implied: 'In the first six months of the year, 107 families – 491 people – abandoned the highlands on their own initiative'.[4] Given the persuasion effort that went into mobilizing them to go, not to mention the capital investment, administrative resistance to people giving up was only natural. But for many cadres non-abandonment became equated with settlement.

What made people refuse to stay? Certainly, as we saw in the case of Mrs Đần, this was a difficult experience.* I asked an official at Labour Office in Thái Nguyên about the difficulties they faced in the initial period.

> Firstly, there is the fact that although we are one country, the two regions are different in terms of climate, hydrography and border administration: the delta is different from our highland area here. In some ways people were unused to the customs and habits of both regions. But that was only for a short period, then they joined and became one. As for economic difficulties, the state provided a certain amount of aid. In the first five years, the state gave aid to maintain equilibrium in some villages, selling things at privileged prices. Generally speaking, in the first years there were not many difficulties.[5]

This official spoke in vague generalities about the process of acclimatization. But he also gave me a report on new economic zones compiled by the provincial Agricultural Office. This filled in some of the details he had passed over.

---

*   See Chapter 7.

People moving to areas of uncleared land in Bắc Thái had to put up with many challenges: they climbed passes, fording streams on footpaths dozens of kilometres long;
they were bitten by leeches and mosquitoes which, even when swatted at, would not go
away; they washed and bathed in water from streams and ravines; insects made their
whole body itch; they went to sleep in the evening only to wake up in the morning with
swollen eyes; after rain, everything got muddy and slippery like grease.

When clearing the land, they had to get straight down to using tools requiring strenu-
ous efforts, like knives and hammers for cutting down trees; they had to dig roots up with
mattocks and crow-bars; after two or three days, their hands were already swollen up.

In uncleared areas there were no vegetables to eat, no fish, no chickens, no ducks;
the market was a long way off and only met once every few weeks, so they just had
salt and a little fish sauce to eat. Their health deteriorated fast.

This is not to mention all the bad elements who influenced people's spirits and
thinking in all sorts of wicked ways: they feared 'terrifying ghosts and poisoned water',
poisonous snakes, places with ferocious wild animals, with goblins and elves, with
leprosy, etc.[6]

Even without the influence of 'bad elements' there were many reasons for
fear in the early stages, and fear led to abandonment. The first few months at Bờ
Rạ were no fond memory for Loan: 'We had to clear the land – it was terrible!
The trees were so big, one tree could make a whole house', she recalled, adding
that many people went down with malaria during that first year. Eleven out of the
twenty families in her group returned to the delta.[7] She did not specify exact
reasons for each departure. But, in Bờ Rạ as elsewhere, we may identify two
problems of survival which motivated people to go: problems with disease, and
problems with making a living.

MALARIA

Disease in the highlands above all meant malaria. Let us return for a moment to
my conversation with Học, where I picked up on his use of the word 'climate' as
a euphemism for sickness.

Học: … the climate didn't suit them. That's how they left.

Hardy: Did many people fall sick?

Học: When we first came up, there was a period when malaria was rife, the time when the
forest was still thick, and mosquitoes bit us, so we caught malaria. The state invested
to fight the epidemic by spraying and other means and then it stopped.*

---

* The expression 'the climate didn't suit' denoted a bewildering range of adaptation
problems. The highlands were cold. There was goitre, diarrhoea, pneumonia and scabies. But
people spoke most emphatically of fever (*sốt*). This was often malaria (*sốt rét*), though not
always. *Ngã nước* fever, traditionally associated with the hills, was blamed on 'poisoned
water'. Definitions were complex. The word for malaria is compounded from the words 'fever'
and 'cold'. One settler referred to his illness expressively but ambiguously as 'fever, cold fever,
forest cold fever!' (*sốt, sốt rét, sốt rét rừng!*). In 1960, medical workers were told to use care
in diagnosing malaria, to avoid confusion with other diseases (typhoid, flu, etc). Ultimately,
whatever these fevers were, they constituted a danger to life and settlement. Ministry of
Health, *Tài liệu huấn luyện cán bộ y tế xã về sốt rét*, Hanoi: NXB Y Học, 1960, p. 11.

Học managed again to encapsulate the issue. Where there was thick forest, people got malaria. Where the forest came down and the state sprayed DDT, the disease disappeared.

Malaria had been, before 1945, a major obstacle to settlement of the highlands. One of the DRV's achievements was its campaign against the disease, piloted in Thái Nguyên in 1957.[*] In an operation steeped in the language of military conflict, the 'work of fighting and eradicating malaria' was carried by 'anti-malaria teams' out to the villages, accompanied by Soviet advisers. There was a period of 'preparation' in 1957, of 'attack' in 1958–62, of 'reinforcement' in 1962–64.[9] Eradication techniques developed during the war were redeployed. Of these, education was paramount. Instruction formerly given to soldiers fighting the French was recycled now for the people clearing the land. They were taught not to fear ghosts in the highlands, not to fear the 'terrifying forest and poisoned water'. They were told that in the highlands 'the Anopheles is the ghost' and instructed to show vigilance towards it as they would towards 'an enemy with wicked plots'.[10] Cadres passed on concise, easily understood messages. Preventing mosquito bites was better than swallowing drugs. Living environments should be clear of plants and water where mosquitoes breed. Mosquitoes should be killed. People should sleep under nets. Citronella and strong alcohol should be used to lessen fever. Serious cases should be treated with quinine.[11]

The campaign in Thái Nguyên lasted eight years. During this time, 280 tons of DDT were sprayed in the province.[†] The Minister of Health boasted about the initial results. 'After spraying', he reported, 'there were very few mosquitoes compared with the cold season in previous years. Flies, bugs and insects all died. The people are elated.'[12] By 1959, in parts of Thái Nguyên – notably the 'foothills region of Đại Từ' – the authorities triumphantly announced that 'as regards the general distribution of the [plasmodium] parasite, in every age group from young to old, it is not to be found'.[13] Thái Nguyên's deputy Party Secretary, addressing a 1964 malaria conference celebrating 'eight years of victory', slickly reworked a local folklore poem about the disease. 'All the sick, sick people, if not in Đại Từ, then in Vũ Nhai' now became 'beautiful girls, handsome boys, not only in Đại Từ but also in Vũ Nhai.'[14]

---

[*] This was not the first time Thái Nguyên was used for the early phase of a major campaign. In 1953, Đại Từ district piloted land reform. In 1958, malaria eradication was extended to Bắc Kạn and Hà Giang, and in 1959 to Hòa Bình, Vĩnh Lĩnh, Mộc Châu and Điện Biên Phủ. By 1975, only 0.5 per cent of the DRV's population had the disease, though it was not clear what 'having' meant here. For sources, see note 8.

[†] The insecticide DDT (dichlorodiphenyltrichloroethane) was used against mosquitoes in Italy after 1945 and came to be seen as a miracle solution to malaria. Environmental damage caused by the poison was not immediately evident to policy makers. At Hoàng Nông commune (Đại Từ district), however, villagers cooked fish killed by DDT, but threw them out before eating, afraid of the toxic smell. The damage, in terms of loss of educational expertise caused by the increasingly reliance on this technology under the DRV, is not easily measured. Interview (Thái Nguyên, January 1997). Thái Nguyên Provincial Committee for Eradication of Malaria, *Báo cáo mừng Thắng lợi*, p. 20.

Học described how this campaign reached Điểm Mạc. But his comments were more ambiguous.

Hardy: What was the most important means of dealing with malaria?

Học: There were two methods. One, keeping the environment clean. Two, spraying DDT at correct intervals. Three, taking preventative medicine. (…) At that time there was a period in which as many as twenty to thirty people got fever. The state invested in containers of spray. Over the next two years or so, the disease was wiped out. When the forest was there, there was a lot of malaria; after it was cleared, the malaria abated. The state showed great concern, so the people were cured immediately. Since then, malaria has gone, no one gets fever any more.

Was malaria conquered by means of state sanitation? Or did it disappear with the forest? Học did not say clearly, and the same ambiguity emerges if we follow the situation down the Công River. At Hoàng Nông, Tuấn remembered that DDT was sprayed in the late 1950s – 'if we didn't have that spray, many people would have died' – adding that after the new economic zone people arrived, 'there was no more malaria'. At Tân Thái, Phụng remembered terrible mosquitoes while clearing the land, 'but after the forest came down, there were fewer mosquitoes'. At Bờ Rạ, Loan made only very vague associations, remembering that 'many people got malaria … mosquitoes … forest … the situation improved after a year or so'. At Tân Cương, my questions started an argument. Thức remembered things improving when the village set up a clinic. His neighbour recalled extensive spraying of houses in 1956 or 1957. Thức disagreed, saying that 'they only sprayed a little'. Whether they sprayed a little or a lot, health cadres in Tân Cương won a medal for their efforts – one of only two communes in the province to do so. But another neighbour, who moved there in the 1930s, emphasized his fear of malaria in the years before 1945. For him improvements in health were made at the expense of the forest, the destruction of which was closely linked with the action of the state. Back in those days, he said, Tân Cương was all 'forest and jungle – there was no Party yet!'[15]

The importance of these oral accounts is in their associations. They consistently implied that the reduced incidence of fevers was due not only to hygiene campaigns and education, but also to land clearance. At Cà Phê village, Hỷ was quite clear about this: 'They sprayed DDT a couple of times in 1957–58, that's all. After they cut down the forest, after six or seven years, the malaria got better. In the 1960s, they cut the forest and the mosquitoes disappeared'.[16] Agency is lost in Hỷ's account – the agency both of spraying and cutting trees – lost in impersonal pronouns I translate here as they. I assume that he saw actual people bringing down the forest and settling the land, though like others in the valley, he may have associated their arrival with Party policy.

The power of people, as agents to overcome the disease, was understood as early as 1947, when Dr Vũ Văn Cẩn published a malaria manual. He made the following observation:

A small number of people moving into a region with poisoned water only acts as a bait for the mosquitoes (because the population there is not increased). But, on the contrary, a mass migration into that region is one excellent method to turn the disease around. Our people, as far as migration is concerned, are often suspicious or fearful, but they don't know that migration in large numbers is not frightening and will turn the disease around (especially nowadays that we know methods of avoiding malaria).[17]

Dr Cẩn's point was that an influx of people – cutting trees, ploughing land, raising animals, killing mosquitoes, and adjusting thereby the ecological balance – could result in a reduction of malaria. From a scientific perspective, as we have seen, his analysis was borne out in villages like Bờ Rạ, Tân Thái, Hoàng Nông and Điềm Mặc. Scientific perspectives – despite education from cadres – were of little comfort to newly arrived settlers. As we have seen, they were faced not only with the low hum of deadly mosquitoes but also with the work of forest clearance, the prospect of accidents from falling trees, the discomforts of temporary accommodation, and the attentions of leeches, snakes and tigers. Few had the patience to wait for malaria, a disease about which vast bodies of superstition had existed for generations, to be 'turned around'.* Even Học, an optimist on most issues, gave me an inkling of this. Later on when I enquired again about matters of health, he spontaneously associated illness with abandonment.

Hardy: Was people's health checked before they came to the highlands?

Học: No. If you got sick, you would just go for treatment. There were cases of people coming up for a year, then abandoning because they found it sad and remote. Five families. After one or two months they went home straight away.

Five families was 10 per cent of Học's group. This was slightly above Định Hóa district's average abandonment rate during the first year of settlement, according to official figures. In 1995, when I met Học, only thirty of the fifty original settler families lived at Điềm Mặc. The others had gone gradually over the first ten years. But by then malaria was down. Apart from a brief epidemic in 1969, people in Điềm Mặc have suffered little since the land was cleared.† The other families went for other reasons, mainly the difficulty of farming the land.

FARMING

In the *Hòa Bình* newspaper, an article appeared in December 1963, describing the worries of a recent migrant to the province. Dương Văn Sừng used to live in Thailand, and had recently returned to the country of his birth. After years away, the article's author asked with rhetorical relish, 'who would not be happy and elated?'

---

* Superstitions associated with malaria are described in A. Sallet, 'Les esprits malfaisants dans les Affections épidémiques au Bình Thuận', *BAVH*, 1926, pp. 81–88.

† Malaria later returned to the northern highlands. The homecoming of soldiers from the south after 1975 and Cambodia after 1989 caused a recrudescence of the disease in the north. A major epidemic occurred in the early 1990s. The epidemic did not affect Điềm Mặc, however.

But elation dispersed on arrival, as he was resettled in the highlands. The writing took a philosophical turn:

> with a change of place, there's no way of avoiding worries about how to make a living, especially in this region of forests and mountains. A few people thought that, though land on these wooded hills of Tân Lạc is plentiful, it must be hard to live off, that the water is poisonous … Many have become pessimistic.[18]

In this situation Dương Văn Sừng did not despair. The article ended on an upbeat note, as he was awarded a 'certificate of praise' for his positive thinking. No doubt fellow returnees from Thailand needed an optimist among them. In this part of hills there was no market for their skills, no obvious way to make a living. It was not only that the population was small, offering little demand for their services, though this was a problem for Anh, who returned from Thailand in 1961 and settled in Phù Yên district (Sơn La). He scraped a living mending bicycles. His only customers were other returnees who had arrived in Phù Yên at the same time. Every now and then he sold a household object to make ends meet. The main trouble was that markets were run by the state, as Anh's neighbour Đức found out. A self-employed blacksmith, in the early 1960s, he earned 100 đồng a month. When I asked the price of rice then, he replied that there wasn't any to buy. Working for himself, he couldn't get the coupons he needed to buy from the state and the 'outside' market was poorly supplied. After a couple of years, he was offered a job with the state cereals office and jumped at the opportunity to 'stabilise'. Working there, he earned just 37 đồng a month, but with plenty of coupons and stamps, he said he was comfortably off. His former colleague at the forge was too old for state employ, and struggled to get by. His wife, Vân, bowed to the inevitable. For the first time in her life, she went down to the farm.*

I asked Vân how it was, at the age of 50, to learn how to grow things. Inexperience, she replied, caused some unfortunate accidents. Once when she was preparing sesame seeds for planting, she took them to the stream to wash and somehow washed them all away. Another time, her neighbours obtained some peanut bushes, planted them and waited patiently for harvest. They waited and waited until eventually someone said they were not peanut bushes after all. Vân complained, 'There was no one at the cooperative to teach us. We had gardens; we did it by ourselves'. I asked her if she would have liked to grow paddy rather than vegetables. 'Liked?' she replied, in a revealing misunderstanding of my inadequate Vietnamese 'I had never done rice farming so didn't know whether I liked it or not'.

A former neighbour of Vân's had stronger views on the subject. I met him in the garage where he worked in Đồng Hỷ district, on the outskirts of the city of Thái Nguyên. He moved to this growing industrial centre just one year after returning

---

* In Thailand there were restrictions on what the Vietnamese could do for a living. They were not allowed to run large trading enterprises or own paddy fields. Most small town occupations, becoming hairdressers, tailors, petty traders, mechanics. Few farmed the land. Interviews (Sơn La, November–December 1996).

from Thailand. He couldn't stay in the remote valley of Phù Yên, he told me. Farming was not for him.[*]

These difficulties were shared by two migrants to Dak Lak in 1976. Chiến was a political commissar, recently retired from the army. His wife Hà had worked in an office in the town of Thanh Hóa. Neither of them were farmers. Hà said they chose poor land for their crops, low-lying and often flooded: 'We didn't know where was where'. Chiến said farming hurt his hands and he got terrible blisters. But proud cadres, they felt even in their retirement they had to show an example and 'lay the foundations for the campaign'. Neighbours – farmers from Quảng Ngãi – must have been bemused by Chiến's attempt at leading the way. They referred to him jocularly as 'Soldier Chiến'. Hà said, 'No one helped us at all'.[19]

Agriculture was new to some people, these former small-town folk from Thailand, career soldiers and officials who retired to the hills, and the people sent out of southern cities after 1975.[20] But the problem for most settlers was not inexperience, but adaptation. They knew how to farm the fertile paddies of the plains, but the slopes and valleys of the highlands required different skills. People in different places faced different challenges, but they amounted to issues of land use. Could the land be used, and how could it be used? Responses varied greatly, but they depended basically on the physical and administrative environments in which they found themselves.[21]

PHYSICAL ENVIRONMENTS

Land use was a problem at Điềm Mạc, as I learnt from Học. He was a teenager during these years, and continued his studies while his parents cleared the land.

Hardy: What about the process of clearing the land?

Học: The first year we planted corn and peanuts, right up to 1970–72 when we started growing tea, cash crops.[†] At first the state invested, giving knives and hoes to clear the land for burning; we used all types of labour to get the roots up. Then some families planted manioc, some planted corn, some grew dry rice and peanuts. After a while we realized that from an economic point of view this wasn't suitable, so the state invested in tea. The state handed out seeds, and gave the people rice for the first months of tea planting. Every month each main labourer received an allowance of 18 kg of husked rice from the state, each dependant got 10 kg. And each month, according to the number of work points done, people would receive rice from the state warehouse, until we could harvest the tea, which we sold to the state and slowly repaid the debt. (...)

Hardy: While you went to school, how did you help your parents?

Học: 'It was very tiring in those days, *anh ạ!* In the morning I'd go to school, then in the afternoon come home and concentrate on working to help my mother and father.

---

[*] Vân's former neighbour was 53 when I met him. Interview (Thái Nguyên, December 1995).

[†] Học contradicted himself on the date here; previously he said that tea was planted after three years, in 1966. The earlier date appears correct: he had already joined the army in 1971.

Some days I'd plant tea, some days I'd transplant rice, or collect firewood, all sorts of work. My parents couldn't do it all, because our standard of living was very low. If you compare it with now, it's changed a hundred times. Then we really struggled, even riding a bicycle was difficult!'

In Điềm Mạc, it was three years before people realized that their land was ill-suited to cereals and switched to tea. This learning process was widespread throughout the 1960s and 1970s. It was also the consequence of a specific policy giving priority to cereals, over so-called 'industrial crops' like tea, coffee, tobacco, ramie (china grass) and sugar cane. This was a time of food shortages throughout the hills, and the policy was implemented with a certain voluntarism in the use of technology. Yields were seen as depending entirely on the way the land was used. Fertile valleys such as that at Phù Yên, with its excellent wet rice harvests, were presented as emulation models for less productive parts of the highlands. Production of rice had clear priority, as officials in Hanoi noted in 1966:

> As regards production, our compatriots should be involved in comprehensive activities, including clearing land, agriculture, forestry, local industry, irrigation, roadwork (...) That is correct but emphasis on intensive cereals farming, to improve harvests and develop agriculture is appropriate at the present time.[22]

Three decades later, looking back on the northern highlands in 1961–75, a different official came to a different conclusion:

> Almost all areas failed to survey and plan, and did not define a basis for migration for each region and locality, corresponding to the needs of large-scale migration. In receiving areas, production focused on cereals. Over 70 per cent of cooperatives gave priority to cereals, and only 10 per cent of cleared land was planted with industrial crops. The natural strength of the midlands and highlands – planting and exploiting forest – was ignored. We may say that, during this period, the state organized the movement of a large proportion of the lowland population to the highlands for the purpose of clearing new land for production and that population endured a situation of self-sufficiency. That was the consequence of applying policies unsuited to the scale and form of production organization in new lands, when there was insufficient preparation.[23]

Specific and erroneous policies were only partly to blame, however. The co-operative system itself tended to discourage risky moves towards non-food crops: 'The combination of high climatic risks with poorly developed markets resulted in unreliable supplies and outlets for goods, creating strong disincentives for diversification away from staples production'.[24]

As a result, where authorities did try to adapt production to the environment, they commonly met with resistance. Delta farmers were accustomed to growing rice and other cereals. New crops were alien and unwelcome. At the village of Tân Tiến (Tân Lạc district, Hòa Bình) the struggle was long and acrimonious. The cooperative management committee decided in 1963 to start growing a crop deemed 'useful for industry'. This was ramie, or china grass, a plant prized for its tough fibres. The village had been set up only two years before. Settlers were suspicious of innovation. Their reactions were detailed in the provincial newspaper:

When the project was taken up for discussion with villagers, some of them did not want to grow ramie. Even a number of cadres were not unanimous, maintaining that there would be no harvest if you planted ramie in the hill country, and much work would be wasted. Some villagers said: 'All these years up here, no one has seen ramie grown on this land; in the lowlands we never grew it; everyone says that hilly land is poor; the seeds are expensive.' The comrade specialist cadre showed how to sow ramie seeds for seedlings, and when people heard that ramie seeds required more work than ramie roots, some of them raised more objections, but eventually the management committee's decision received a warm response from a majority of villagers.

The ramie was planted, but the committee's troubles were not yet over.

In the process of growing ramie, some difficulties emerged. The cooperative had just finished planting three *mẫu* and sowing three *sào* of seeds, when drought struck and lasted nearly two months, so people had to carry water out to the ramie day and night. Faced with this problem, a number of people showed pessimism, reproaching cadres. Some people spoke with a tone of irony: 'Our cooperative will have to hire three trucks to move all this ramie out for sale.'

Only when the harvest was finally brought in were people persuaded of the crop's value.[25]

Poor planning and peasant conservatism combined to maintain the predominance of cereals. As late as 1989, over 80 per cent of the cultivated area of the northern highlands was growing cereals. Sixty-six per cent was planted with wet and dry paddy. Mistakes in crop choice damaged the environment.[26] They also slowed up the process of settlement. At Tân Tiến village, the newspaper reported how progress ultimately triumphed over pessimism. No mention was made, however, of the people who left the project before the victory was won, the ramie was harvested and the village 'climbed onto the road to happiness and prosperity'.[27] Học recalled that Điềm Mặc lost five families in the first twelve months and fifteen more over the next ten years, during the switch to tea. He did not say, however, what became of them, limiting his remarks to his own folk: 'Now my family is stable for the moment (*tạm ổn định*), thanks to the concern of the Party and state '.

ADMINISTRATIVE ENVIRONMENTS

Hoc expressed his appreciation of the Party and state's concern in a familiar formula. Others who enjoyed a favourable administrative environment included settlers at Mai Hoàng Thung village (Mai Châu district, Hòa Bình). The village was part of Thung Khe commune, through which the road from Hanoi passes, and where minibuses heading for the popular tourist destination of Mai Châu stop for people to photograph the valley below.[28] For visitors breaking their journey, the view is stunning, as the following account tries to suggest:

The road climbs far up the Thung Khe slope, a tiring trip but also truly interesting. The road goes up a steep slope, on one side a standing wall, on the other a deep abyss, dense forests growing from top to bottom. (...)

The higher you go, the thicker the fog. (…)

And suddenly there appears a bauhinia tree. You can find the virgin white colour of the flowers at all historical ruins throughout the Tây Bắc region, but we've already met it at Thung Khe. (…)

The wind whistles around the Thung Khe peak. We have a quiet time to contemplate the whole scenery of Mai Châu. Below, in the valley, the fields show the sweet green of the seedling paddies. The tiny dikes edging the paddy fields cling and twist together like cords. Vãng street [the district town centre] is the red colour of roof-tiles, one-storey red roof-tiles. Please, dear tourist, come along Vãng street, along the stone-laid road running smoothly under two rows of Hưng Yên longan trees. (…)

This road will take us to Văn village, Lác village, and going further we'll get to Mai Hạ, Mai Hịch, then Hồi Xuân in Thanh Hóa. You'll see the Mã river flowing swiftly between the rocks.

The people arriving there to live must have found it unforgettable in other ways. An official at Mai Châu People's Committee told me about their less exhilarating experience:

> They were right next to the road on the peak of the mountains, looking down. The land there is cultivable, but there's very little water, so they had difficulties making a living. They planted corn, peanuts and tubers. At the same time they cut the forest down to use the firewood and collect forest products. They realized that this didn't make them a living. Eventually they came to the district office, and we requested the provincial authorities that they should be moved over to Lạc Sơn district.[29]

These settlers were from the province of Hà Tây. The official did not say when they arrived in Mai Châu, but it can have been no earlier than the late 1980s, by which time most of the district's cultivable land was already settled. The necessary arrangements for a transfer were made. Six out of the original twenty families chose to stay put at Mai Hoàng Thung, to 'wait for a harvest of vegetables', and were still there two years later. The water problems had probably been solved, at least on a small scale. But the majority of them accepted the authorities' offer of new land in a neighbouring district, and moved there in 1993.

Practical help from cadres was often crucial to a settlement's success. Villagers at Điềm Mạc were helped to find a suitable use for their land, at Mai Hoàng Thung to find more suitable land. Without cadres' problem-solving skills, more of them may have abandoned the project. This at least was Dũng's opinion, a retired district official responsible for migration to Mai Châu. He explained what he had to do to stop people leaving. In his experience, the main problem in the 1960s was not the land itself, but the organization of production from it. Settlers, he told me, were organized in cooperatives of two types, independent or merged with the local Thái people.

> At the beginning there were ten independent settlements and seventeen merged settlements, merged with local cooperatives (with production brigades and teams). But then the number of merged settlements dwindled; people asked to join independent settlements and not stay in the merged ones, because of language difficulties and different working customs. Because up here we had at that time seven ethnic groups, later six, and now there are only five; this village has three.

By 'this village' he meant Mai Hạ commune, on the Mai Châu valley floor, where he lived. At this point in the interview Dũng gave me information about the ethnic groups in Mai Châu, saying that Thái made up 60 per cent of the population, Việt 20 per cent, Hmong 19, Mường 15, Chinese and Tày a negligible number.[*] He then went on to explain the problems the Việt settlers had communicating with the other highlanders they were meant to work with: 'The compatriots up here had never had Việt compatriots come in before. When Việt people came and asked about something, they would all just shake their heads'. He concluded that the settlers' greatest difficulty was language differences. Dũng did not indicate whether the minorities were unable to speak Vietnamese, or simply did not wish to. Instead he pressed on with his account of his reaction to these problems.

> So, because of people's wavering, I got in touch with the higher authorities who, after making a concrete analysis of the situation, allowed people to move from those merged settlements. They then formed twelve independent settlements. If they hadn't been allowed to do that, our compatriots would have left. Because the effort of moving compatriots up was so difficult, to let them go home would have been tough not only for them, but also for local authorities down there, turning the plan on its head, making it impossible to implement.[30]

He told me proudly that the rate of abandonment from Mai Châu, unlike other districts in the province, was not even as high as 1 per cent. The comparison with other districts may simply reflect his sense of achievement, but the terms in which it was boasted were revealing:

> I'd like to report to you comrades that only in Mai Châu was the programme pursued persistently, pursued constantly. If you go up to Tây Bắc or Đông Bắc their final results were not worth the paper they were written on. When speaking to the people, cadres only knew how to say 'no', leaving them to get on with life on their own. But I was constantly on the move.

If we accept that, according to his own account, Dũng was a model cadre, constantly travelling to solve problems, and that Mai Châu was a model district, where problems were solved quickly and efficiently, then the new economic zone village of Tiền Phong, where I met him, was a model pioneer settlement.[†] It was literally so, Dũng told me. A miniature replica of the village was made for exhibition at the provincial Cultural Office in 1967. Tiền Phong village had a low rate of abandonment and a good record for cereals' production. How were these results achieved?

A MODEL VILLAGE

Tiền Phong was set up in March 1963, with settlers from the commune of Xuân Hòa (Xuân Trường district, Nam Định). It was one of five villages in Mai Hạ, a place long inhabited by Thái people.[31] When I visited in 1995, I found Kha village

---

[*] Hao Tá was the seventh group, now counted as Mường. Most of the Chinese left in 1979.

[†] Tiền Phong means 'pioneer' or 'vanguard'.

a short distance into the hills, its stilt-legged houses scattered across the landscape. The others were concentrated at the valley edge, in a grid pattern with fenced gardens and beaten earth streets. Tiền Phong was in this area and it was here, forty years before, that the thirty-six settler families had built their houses. They lived alongside the Thái people but had their own separate cooperative.* Hùng and his neighbour, who were among the settlers there, lived down one street. Thái and Mường villagers lived down the next. Dũng described the place: 'When people arrived they were given places to live here, at the foot of the hill. Over there, out on the valley floor, they had land to farm'.

Compared with Học at Điềm Mạc commune, their situation was highly favourable. There was no malaria. The district was first sprayed with DDT in 1959 and Mai Hạ was sprayed again in 1963.[32] No one got malaria, Dũng said. They were afraid of it, though, and dug wells to avoid drinking the 'poisoned' water of the streams. The streams were also blamed for goitre (caused by iodine deficiency), which posed a more immediate threat to the community.

> The main medical problem here was goitre. Many people, in the first one or two months after arriving, went out to the stream to sit and cry, missing home. Then they came up and told us that for old people it didn't matter, but how could young people with goitre find someone to marry? So we had to do our medical work thoroughly, consoling and persuading people; if it was neglected they'd just go home'.

Their main fear, however, was tigers. Thái informants told me chilling stories of the dreaded beast roaming under people's houses at night, even as late as the 1950s. Dũng, however, responded with bravado: 'of course, there weren't any'.

Making a living at Tiền Phong also posed few problems. Mai Hạ was situated at the widest part of the valley, with good access to water and plentiful land. Some of this land was provided by the locals. The rest was cleared from the wartime airstrip, built by the French on fields of wet rice and now covered in tall grass. A local Thái man said, that 'the Việt didn't clear any land'. Another was emphatic that' at Tiền Phong the land was fields, not wild; the Việt only improved it'.[33] No time, then, was wasted on felling forest. 'There were no big trees to clear', according to Hùng's neighbour. Hùng himself spent those first days working on the fields, in the evenings building his house. Within six months the settlers had planted 8 hectares of corn and peanuts, 2.5 hectares of wet rice, 3.5 hectares of manioc. They had harvested enough to feed themselves for seven months.[34] These data are subject to caution – they were announced in the newspaper as the good news preceding some 'shortcomings' – but such achievements were at least conceivable here. Hùng himself remembered that they grew manioc; that the first two or three

---

* Dũng said that the commune's five constituent villages each had their own cooperative. The villages were named, respectively Lồ, Đông Uống, Tiền Phong, Chiêng Hạ and Kha. The inhabitants were white Thái, with a few Mường at Chiêng Hạ and Lồ villages. Tiền Phong people were all Việt from Nam Định. In 1982 the organization of production was merged into a single cooperative. Cooperative land was divided up in 1995.

years were hard work; that he grumbled about the hardship in his heart, but outwardly just put up with it.[35]

At first glance, these conditions – no malaria, tolerable labour and tangible results – offer sufficient explanation of Tiền Phong's low rate of abandonment – two families out of thirty-six.* Yet the 'shortcomings' mentioned in the article above pointed to a much less rosy beginning to the process of settlement. They offer, above all, a different explanation for its success. Its author, Trọng Hồng, an official at the provincial Land Clearance Office, lamented that, at Tiền Phong:

> Party members and cadres have worked without unanimity, and are not yet mirrors for the villagers; some comrades have only done five days' work in six months. Cadres have not gone deeply into the fields, have organized production without planning, have no concrete production orientation; things are managed undemocratically, the finances are not run publicly. On the other hand, the villagers still depend passively on their leaders; they are disorganized and some of them are still ill-disciplined.

He exposed these shortcomings in justification of his initial comment, that:

> After mobilizing our lowland compatriots to move to the highlands, after setting up the cooperatives, the work of leadership as regards people's thinking and the actual running of the cooperatives is a problem every bit as difficult and complicated as mobilizing people to come up in the first place.

Settling, then, was a work of mobilization. Trọng Hồng's article, indeed, did not come out of the blue. It was written in support of a campaign to 'step up people's production and stabilize their living even faster'.[36]

Dũng took much of the credit for the strength of mobilization in the district. But its success at Tiền Phong village was neither Dũng's nor even Hùng's achievement. Hùng resigned from the position of village head after a few months. 'No one wanted to do that job, you couldn't direct', he told me. Villagers were unanimous that the credit should go instead to the head of the local Party cell, a man by the name of Đàn. This emerged in a conversation about village religion. I asked a fellow Party member and contemporary of Đàn's about why there was no communal house (*đình*) at Tiền Phong. One of the answers he gave was the lack of a clear village founder there. The only person it could be was Đàn – but everyone hated him. Đàn was a poor figure for a village deity. 'Everyone fought Đàn', Hùng said, 'he was a difficult character'.[37] Eventually, after several years living alone at Tiền Phong, the detested Mr Đàn decided to leave. His was one of only two households to abandon the village. No one in Tiền Phong seemed to care where he went.

---

* I rely on Hùng for this figure, compiled over several days of repeated remembering. After counting off the names of twenty or so household heads, he would suddenly say: 'Ah, but I have forgotten one, there was Mr...' Settlers came in three groups, two in 1963, one in 1964. The newspaper recorded that twenty-six families arrived at Tiền Phong in November 1963. It did not of course report the departures. Trọng Hồng, 'Qua cuộc vận động', p. 2.

BUREAUCRATISM AND MOBILIZATION

Đàn was the sort of cadre Dũng deplored, who knew only how to say 'no'. He was in no way a model, according the standards expected by Trọng Hồng. If we apply these standards, we can conclude that if he managed to raise such strong feelings of antipathy among the people, it was because he failed to console them when they suffered from goitre, failed to 'go deeply into the fields', failed to seek unanimity and democracy in management. In short, he failed to mobilize. Tiền Phong was a difficult place to be a cadre in the 1960s. Hùng kept his head down. Đàn went for the other option: he neglected mobilization and applied the rules.

In this he exhibited signs of 'bureaucratism', as defined by Gareth Porter who quoted in the following account of tax and corvée collection in the early 1950s:

> In 'very many places,' however, the DRV admitted that cadres had not 'explained and propagandized' but had 'compelled by bureaucratism and commandism'. The problem of bureaucratism (*quan liêu*), defined as using commands rather than persuasion to obtain compliance, was described as 'rather serious within our government, from top to bottom.'[38]

Porter placed a rather doubtful interpretation on these remarks – that the existence of bureaucratism implied that Vietnam was a fundamentally authoritarian state. On the contrary, their significance lay in Phạm Văn Đồng's recognition of these abuses, rather than in the abuses themselves. For Phạm Văn Đồng, cadres were not supposed to behave like Đàn. They were, as he put it in a 1975 article on highland development, supposed to be 'young, healthy, capable, experienced, having already been tried and tested, inspiring of trust and confidence'.[39]

Phạm Văn Đồng wrote this, not to describe an idealized reality that did not exist – he was well aware of behaviour like Đàn's – but to reform the flawed and chaotic reality that did. To the above paragraph, he added: 'We have already paid a very high price to learn these valuable lessons. They should inspire us to make great efforts for improvement in the future'. Porter concluded that this constituted an 'admission' of the existence of a situation opposite to the ideal. He failed as a result to understand its significance as education. Rather than draw the sorts of polarized conclusions which Porter's oppositional methodology throws up, let us examine the situation in its details. What was the administrative reality Phạm Văn Đồng sought to improve?

He saw local level administration in terms of a scale. Bureaucratism and commandism existed at one end, explanation and persuasion – good mobilization, that is – at the other. If we are to understand the way the system worked, we must not pick up on one or two instances of malfunction, but should analyse both ends of the scale, as well as the grey areas in between. A close look at the administration of settlement in new economic zone villages – at the rules cadres like Đàn had to apply – gives us the opportunity to do this.

Đàn had many responsibilities as head of the village Party cell. But the issue that elicited most resentment was that of residence. He was remembered for refusing to allow anyone to leave. For the four years Đàn was there, no settler at Tiền Phong could get permission, for themselves or their children, to go to the plains – for work, for study, or for medical treatment.[40] Đàn strictly implemented the law, by which once settled in one place, a family could not move to another without permission. We can place him at one end of the scale. Somewhere towards the other end, we should find a cadre described by Vân, who arrived from Thailand to settle in the valley of Phù Yên. She told me of the following conversation, when the cadre visited her house soon after her arrival there. He found her crying by the window, looking out at the rain.*

Cadre: Why are you crying so?

Vân: There's no one here, just forest, so far from the city. It's so sad.

Cadre: But we're very near to Hanoi here. When you hear the sound of dynamite, they'll make roads, and trains and ships will come. Hanoi will be very near.

Vân: When?

Cadre: Only two weeks' time.

Looking back on this story, she laughed at her own credulity. Ascribing it to her upbringing – 'Girls and women don't know anything; we didn't think about anything' – she acknowledged a certain respect for the cadre who cheered her up with his empty promises, saying that he did a good job: 'After a few months of crying, I got used to it'. When I visited in 1996, Phù Yên remained a good day's drive from Hanoi, on rough roads. In the meantime, Vân had stopped waiting for the sound of dynamite.

In Mai Châu, Đàn applied the rules rigidly. In Phù Yên, Vân's cadre applied them with skilful sensitivity. He bothered to listen to Vân. He made her feel she was doing the right thing. He persuaded her to put up with the difficulties for the sake of the future. Despite his embellishment of the truth, he was a very different type of cadre from Đàn. At one end of the scale, Đàn practised bureaucratism. Towards the other, this imaginative cadre practised rule by mobilization. The stumbling block of Porter's argument is his failure to distinguish authoritarianism, a term which accurately describes behaviour like Đàn's, from rule by mobilization. The flexible and interactive nature of this form of government was described by Benedict Kerkvliet in his 1995 study of agricultural cooperatives, when he wrote that 'a prominent theme in the recent history of rural Vietnam is debate, bargaining and interaction between the state and villages to the point that most peasant households who opposed or disliked collectivization have had their way'.[41] It is true that in the case under consideration here – highland settlement – not everyone got their way. This was not, however, because of something fundamentally authoritarian

---

* Vân was not alone among tearful returnees from Thailand. In Vĩnh Phú, a woman cried when told she was going to the countryside, complaining 'if you take people and leave them in the forest, then I will just drink some poison and die now on the spot and be done with it'. There is no record of official reaction to her threat, nor of whether she carried it out. NAV3/BLD 1017(vv), Vĩnh Phú Labour Service to Ministry of Labour, 18 May 1961.

about the system of administration. The point is not that people were unable to pursue their own interests, but the manner by which limitations on their pursuits were imposed. In this sense, as Phạm Văn Đồng pointed out, authoritarianism and rule by mobilization were conceptually opposed.

But what were the rules applied so differently by Đàn and Vân's cadre? The key here was the household registration system, by means of which population movement was quite effectively controlled from the 1950s to the 1980s. Household registration was an important key to the success of Vietnam's migration programme.

THE POLICY OF HOUSEHOLD REGISTRATION

What was household registration? It was explained to me in Đại Từ district as a modern equivalent of the colonial system, whereby a tax card permitted travel and a village-issued transfer of residence paper allowed a permanent move.[42] The comparison is interesting, especially coming from a villager whose memory of 1930s legislation was second to none. But in terms of administrative technology, it is an uneasy one. Under the DRV, village-issued transfer papers persisted from previous decades. But its most important legislation on residence – the regime of household registration, or *hộ khẩu* – was new. Imported from China, where it was known as the *hukou*, it provided the state with a far superior tool than had existed under the French.

The *hukou* system was developed in China in the early 1950s, receiving definitive legislative enactment in 1958 and rigorous implementation across the country in the 1960s.* It was introduced to urban areas of the DRV in 1955, and extended to the countryside in 1960.[44] As in China, registration was initially intended to restrict population movement to cities and border areas and curb the activities of 'counter revolutionaries and criminals'. It also serviced the implementation of various state policies.[45] But in Vietnam the extension of the *hộ khẩu* system to the countryside coincided with the announcement of the highland development programme.† The *hộ khẩu* was to become a crucial element in the programme's management. Before examining its impact on settlement in the highlands, let us look briefly at how the system worked.

There were, from 1960, two distinct types of registration, *hộ tịch* and *hộ khẩu*. The *hộ tịch* – a statistical register of births, marriages and deaths – little concerns us here. The *hộ khẩu*, on the other hand, recorded and restricted people's movement. The population unit was the household (*hộ*), defined as a group of people (*khẩu*) living and eating together. Households were of two types, family and collective.

---

* This was the Population and Household Registration Regulation of the People's Republic of China (9 January 1958). In the USSR, Stalin introduced a system of internal passports in 1932. The main difference between the two was that in China the population unit was the family, not the individual. For sources, see note 43.

† The extension of the *hộ khẩu* to the countryside was announced in March 1960. The highlands development programme was announced the following September, at the Third Party Congress.

Families in urban areas kept their own registration booklet. In the countryside, village authorities kept records on families' behalf. Collectivities like factories, hospitals, state farms and forestry enterprises maintained a single booklet for all their members. This booklet recorded each person's usual place of residence. This was the vital piece of information. In addition, it noted all migrations (in-migration, out-migration or temporary stay) as well as births, deaths, marriages, divorces and other changes in household composition. It also indicated each member's name, age, profession, ethnic group and place of origin.[46]

The implications of the system were made clear in a 1958 manual:

> *Hộ tịch* and *hộ khẩu* should not be confused. To maintain law and order and protect the people's life and property, as well as to grasp the population situation, in cities there are regulations on *hộ khẩu*. Every household, that is every family, must go to the police post where they live and formally declare how many people their household has. They will receive a booklet, called a *hộ tịch* [*sic*] booklet,[*] in which all the individuals in the household are recorded as well as every change in the household, like moving to another place, the departure of a household member, the arrival of family or friends to stay for a while, etc. This is booklet not to be confused with the *hộ tịch* booklet, used for the registration of births, deaths and marriages.[47]

People wishing to change their place of residence were subject to onerous procedures. They had to get a 'moving certificate'[†] from the place they wished to leave. The police authority competent to issue this certificate varied according to destination. Movements within the same province were authorized by the village police, to another province by the district police, to border or urban areas by the province police. In the latter case the request had to be supported by a letter from a labour office, university or police authority at the place of destination.[48] In a clear example of the system's operation, at Cà Phê village Hảo explained the formalities of her move from Phổ Yên district up to Đồng Hỷ (Thái Nguyên). Registering at Đồng Hỷ was easy then, she said. She asked her employer for permission. She then signed up with authorities in Đồng Hỷ, returning finally to Phổ Yên to cancel her registration there. By the 1990s, however, Đồng Hỷ was a densely populated area where registration was difficult to obtain.[49]

In practice, the system aimed at channelling migration in two directions, to rural areas and to the highlands. Country folk found it hard to obtain permission to live in urban areas, but city people moved easily to the countryside. Highland residents found it hard to move to the plains – as the inhabitants of Mai Hạ discovered – but delta dwellers moved easily to the hills.

---

* It appears that, despite his own advice, the author confused the two booklets: this should read '*hộ khẩu* booklet'.

† Moving certificate: *Giấy chứng nhận chuyển đi.*

THE PRACTICE OF HOUSEHOLD REGISTRATION

How effectively did the system work? Law prescribed penalties for fraud, which could mean forging or lending *hộ khẩu* booklets, and making false declarations. The legislation, however, made no mention of punishment for people who changed their place of residence without obtaining permission on departure and arrival.* Consequences existed, nonetheless, and mainly affected the offender's economic situation. These were spelled out to me by a policeman at the commune of Đông Xá (Đông Hưng district, Thái Bình). This was the time of the state supply economy, he said. There were no free markets and people depended on state supplies for their subsistence. If you weren't registered at the village, the state was not obliged to look after you. Without proper registration, you could not be employed at the cooperative where payment was made in work points. Without payment in work points, you could not get tickets and stamps to buy meat, cereals and consumer goods at state outlets, or a ration booklet to buy rice†. 'If you queued up but had no ration booklet, you couldn't buy; whatever you wanted to buy, you had to have tickets and stamps.' If people settled in a place without transferring their *hộ khẩu*, the policeman concluded, they 'couldn't work on the paddies (which belonged to the cooperative), couldn't do trading (it was illegal), couldn't work for wages (nobody hired wageworkers). They had to rely on other people for everything. They could live, but only very miserably.'[50]

This last remark indicates the limits of the system's effectiveness. In practice, there were ways of getting round these difficulties. The policeman here referred specifically to the people who abandoned a new economic zone in Nghĩa Lộ, set up in 1974 after frost destroyed the harvest at Đông Xá. Their experience in Nghĩa Lộ had not been a happy one. The land there was poor, malaria was endemic, the settlement had been hastily prepared. 'No one went up to Nghĩa Lộ to see the land first', I was told by Kiệt, the head of the cooperative set up there, a man who was now living back in Thái Bình. 'People ate all the subsidies and then came straight back'.[51] Bùi, who still lived in Nghĩa Lộ, pointed out that some people wanted to come back but couldn't. Why not? 'They had no money', he said. 'There was nowhere for them to live', added a woman sitting nearby. 'They weren't in the system', chipped in the policeman.[52]

Problems with money, with housing, with papers: how did people negotiate them? They had to have some sort of resource. Leaving Nghĩa Lộ itself was not a problem. No one asked for permission. 'People chose for themselves, and went back to Thái Bình', said Kiệt. They walked the 40 km to the station at Yên Bái. They paid for their own tickets, which could be bought only after a long queue and presentation of valid travel papers or, in this case, at a high price on the black market. 'This was wartime', I was told. Once back home they tried to fit in, as

---

*   Departure and arrival transactions were called, respectively, *cắt khẩu* and *nhập khẩu*.
†   Rice ration booklet: *sổ gạo*.

the policeman explained: 'When they got back from Nghĩa Lộ, they lived with relatives, but the relatives had to look after them. Everyone got poorer'.[53] As Ngọc, who was among the returnees, put it: 'Authorities in Thái Bình accepted the people back from Nghĩa Lộ, because everyone came back, even the head of the cooperative. It was impossible up there. Terrible!'[54] Their survival back home depended very much on the support they could muster – in terms of money for the journey home, help from family and friends, and sympathetic treatment from the local authorities.

Availability of resources depended from family to family and from place to place. At Đông Xá, three years after people returned from Nghĩa Lộ, the authorities found a solution for their future. A new settlement was created in the central highlands' province of Dak Lak. They were all expected to volunteer. Ngọc saw red. He recalled this second move, in 1977, with an oath: 'Damned a second time! It was horrible the first time round, we didn't want to go again'. He was 19 and had to follow his family, but soon joined the army, serving in Cambodia. Even after that, Dak Lak held no attraction: 'I didn't want to go home. My family was too hard up'.[55] He went home nonetheless. I met him there in November 1996, at Buôn Tría commune in the district of Lak (see Map 14).

Ngọc complained, but in actual fact it seems that the authorities in Đông Hưng district dealt with returnees quite sensitively. This at least was the opinion of another resident of Lak district, Tiến, who lived in the neighbouring commune of Buôn Triết. Some Thái Bình people could not stand life in Dak Lak and went home, he said. When they got back, 'the cooperative didn't supply them with anything. Well, a little. We are all compatriots, they could not throw them away, so they gave them some supplies.'* Elsewhere in Thái Bình, a former cadre responsible for organizing migration explained that in his district of Tiền Hải, the rules were applied strictly. 'Twenty-five familes came back', he said. 'They had to accept that if they came back, they would meet difficulties. Otherwise people would just come and go.' Of the twenty-five families, three eventually returned to the south and the other twenty-two were sent to a new economic zone on reclaimed land by the sea.†

Bình was another settler in Dak Lak who hoped to negotiate the rules. He sought help from both relatives and local authorities, and his attempt to do so gives us a good indication of both the strength and limitations of the *hộ khẩu* system. Consider the following reconstruction.

Bình, his wife and his four children left their village near Huế in 1978. They arrived at the new economic zone commune of Tam Giang (then Krông Buk district, Dak Lak). There was a serious malaria epidemic. Within two years, his wife and five children

---

* Tiến was from the commune of Đông Sơn (Đông Hưng district, Thái Bình). Interview (Dak Lak, May 1996).

† These families went to Sông Bé, in the south, in the late 1970s. The settlement on reclaimed land was Đông Hải village, set up in 1970, the second of Tiền Hải's coastal new economic zones. The first was Nam Cường, set up in 1960 and visited by Hồ Chí Minh on 26 March 1962. For source, see note 56.

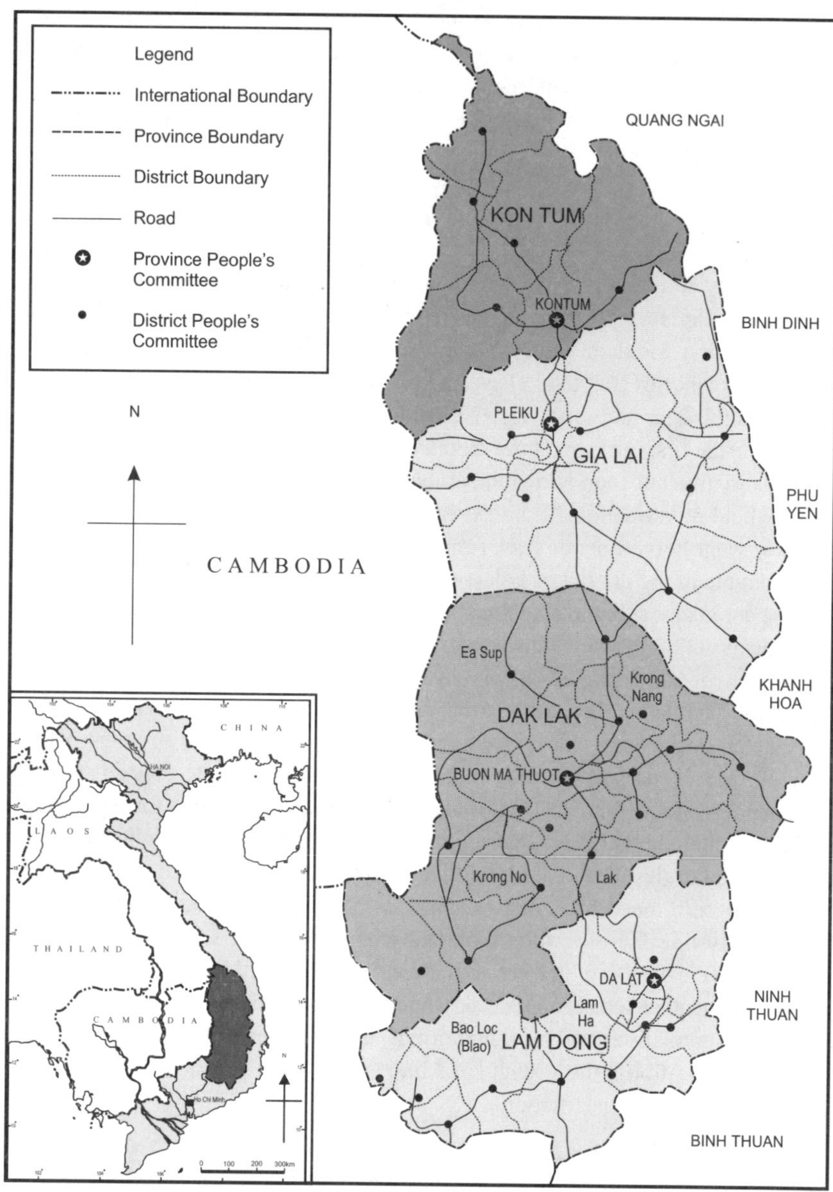

Map 14: Provinces and districts of the central highlands, 1996

In the decades after Vietnam's reunification in 1975, the central highlands became a major destination for Việt settlers from the Red River Delta and the central coastal plains. The largest province in this region is Dak Lak, with its capital at Buôn Ma Thuột (Ban Mê Thuột). Principal districts discussed in this account are marked on the map.

Source: Trần An Phong (ed.), *Nghiên cứu xây dựng luận cư khoa học cho định hướng phát triển kinh tế-xã hội các tỉnh Tây Nguyên*, Hanoi: NXB Nông Nghiệp, 1996, p. 7. Redrawn by Lee Li Kheng.

went down with malaria. Bình got frightened. He wrote to relatives at his old village. They had connections who could arrange the *hộ khẩu* transfer. He decided to take the family home.

They left in 1982, Bình, his wife and six children. The journey was tough – they had no papers, as they had 'run off'. They travelled by bus in 'frog leaps': from Tam Giang to the district centre Buôn Hồ, to the provincial town of Pleiku, down the mountains to the port of Qui Nhơn, up the coast to Đà Nẵng, then finally to Huế and home. It took a week, mostly spent waiting for transport. It cost a fortune – borrowed from his sister – in black market tickets, food and accommodation.

Back home, they stayed with his parents. Relatives helped with money and rice. But arrangements for the *hộ khẩu* proved more difficult than he had hoped. Local authorities 'refused to register us, but they sympathized with our situation and allowed us to stay'. He survived on this basis for two years.

In 1984, they started dividing up the cooperative land. Without a *hộ khẩu*, he was not a cooperative member and had no right to a share. He had no capital and no land, at a time of economic change. The future looked grim. He decided to return to Tam Giang, where at least there was land and where the malaria now had abated. There were, of course, no objections to this. When he got back to Tam Giang, with his wife and seven children, his *hộ khẩu* was waiting for him there.

Bình's story is revealing, as it indicates the freedom he found to negotiate the system. He chose to leave Tam Giang and face the consequences. Two years later he chose to return there – and the decision was based on economic rather than directly administrative difficulties. But this room for manoeuvre is indicative not only of the system's weakness, but also of its strength. In China, this strength was described as residing in:

> its integration with the rural collective economy and system of state employment, which, one way and another, touches virtually the entire population. Only through registration can one be legally part of a collective and partake of its economic benefits – grain allocations, private plots, cotton and other rations. Unlike other countries where registration defines legal residence, in China it defines livelihood as well.

Its limitations were also recognized in the same context:

> But the linkage between registration and the availability of economic benefits provided by the team, such as rations and private plots, is probably not as strict as intended because such internal allocations are decided by the team.[57]

In other words, the people who made decisions about household registration (police) were not the same as those responsible for allocation of economic benefits (cooperative officials). If you had the resources, this administrative space could be negotiated. In Bình's case, this situation lasted as long as the cooperative did. The redistribution of the land reduced his access to economic goods. It is ironic that the measure which destroyed the link between household registration and economic benefits, creating vast possibilities for free movement in the late 1980s and early 1990s, should have increased his dependence on the *hộ khẩu*. Registration gave access to land, which after its privatization at home, was available to Bình only in Dak Lak. He packed his bags again.

Bình's case shows the extent to which the *hộ khẩu* system effectively limited population movement. Quantification of that effectiveness is difficult. At Mai Hạ, for example, was Đàn's strict application of the rules responsible for the settlement's success? Was it due to the lack of malaria and availability of good farmland? Or was it simply that Hùng and his neighbours could not muster the resources to negotiate the system? This last factor seems in many cases to have been crucial. In Phù Yên, it is clear that the Vietnamese who returned from Thailand waited until they found the resources – in terms of money, family support, administrative contacts – to leave. For most people, this took no more than three years. They then just upped and offed. Those without resources stayed put. As I was told by An, who stayed put: 'People with a good economic situation left a few years after arriving; the families that stayed were all the poor families'.[58] The same was true in Nghĩa Lộ, where only those families who were very poor stayed there and didn't come back.[59] And in Dak Lak where Ngô, who had serious debts, three times intended to leave. But, he said, it was impossible to go: 'Without economic resources, how could you go back home?'[60]

VOLUNTARISM

The story, unfortunately, does not only consist of those able to find resources (who left) and those unable to (who stayed). There was a third category: those unable to find resources, but who left anyway. The experiences of these people tell us about the difference between settlement perceived by the state and settlement perceived by settlers. They were described by Lê Khánh, a journalist commissioned to write about new economic zones for people from Hanoi. Writing in the 1980s, he looked back to 1963, when more than one hundred families had moved to Thái Nguyên, noting that if they had stayed there, Hanoi would have found a new way of resolving its problems. He continued:

> Regrettably, reality did not develop according to our wishes. Anyone who was in Hanoi at that time will take a long time to forget a phenomenon which stung everyone deep in their hearts. In a general atmosphere of enthusiastic labour, there inexplicably appeared on the roads and streets numerous families carrying their children, shouldering poles, looking truly pitiful. They lived like vagabonds, like disaster victims out on the pavements or pitching canvas tents under bridges, in narrow alleyways ... like people staging a sit-down protest.* People whispered to each other: 'Are they the new economic zone people coming back?' If you spoke to them, that clinched it: 'Either place is difficult,' they said, 'so we'd rather return to the city we know, where it's easier to live!' Each family had its own heart-rending story, but one thing emerged: they did not have a basis for mutual aid to rely on while they got used to life in their new home, a time full of difficulty and adversity; the city did not assume its responsibilities; cadres accompanying them all withdrew to the plains; local authorities accepted the new labourers but lacked sufficient means for their support.[61]

---

* These people had returned from new economic zones in Tân Cương, Đại Từ and Phú Bình.

He went on to indicate that officials currently running the programme agreed with this perspective.

> One comrade at the New Economic Zone Committee told me that when they reviewed the work done at that time, the city's leaders clearly pointed out that this had been an irresponsible population reduction exercise which achieved results amounting to three zeros: in economic terms, in political terms and in terms of the fact that some compatriots ended up worse off than before.[62]

This opinion was published in 1983, a low point in the programme when migration plans suffered annual downward revisions. Ten years later, another official made an even more detailed study of the highland settlement programmes of 1954–75. His analysis, summarized below, highlighted three basic problems in the organization of migration:

Voluntarism: 'Simplistic and one-dimensional thinking on the part of the State'. Emphasis on administrative factors, at the expense of social and economic issues. Excessive attention to 'the number of people moving, the area of land to be cleared, the number of production teams set up'. Neglect of basic questions like 'How will people live? How is the actual organization of production and development going to be organized?' This amounted to simplistic thinking, caused by 'subjective consciousness' and 'voluntarism'.

Poor planning: 'Little attention to preparation and confusion in the organization of production, provoking long-term instability in new settlement areas'. Insufficient survey work; inappropriate crop choices. This resulted in production for subsistence, not development.

Errors of investment: 'Lack of (…) incentives to migrants, to attract people to volunteer, and stabilise their living conditions within the overall development of the whole community in the new area'. There was a clear distinction between official and popular conceptions of stability: 'The programme only provided direct help to migrants during the initial stages. Indirect measures to step up production, settle living conditions, provide for children, give people the assurance of receiving the fruits of their family's labour … were not implemented in accordance with the development of each new settlement place. This has had negative consequences right up to the present day'.[63]

The main motor of settlement was the principle of state–people cooperation, according to the slogan 'State and people do it together'.* This relationship was underpinned up to the 1980s by a philosophy of voluntarism. Voluntarism, in this context, took the form of an assumption among state cadres that the people could be relied upon to build their own new homes, out of pure zeal for the revolution and socialist construction. As we saw in earlier chapters, migration policy was implemented 'at a "cheap price" which only our system is able to achieve, because we

---

* This slogan recurred in reports on highland settlement. Here it was used alongside a slogan drawing on military imagery: 'Scout and engage battle at the same time'. General Land Clearance Office, 'Báo cáo tổng kết cuộc vận động', July 1966. Variations on this theme were still popular in the 1980s. Lê Khánh, *Quê mới người Hà Nội*, p. 21.

have actually relied on the people.'[64] Reliance on the people's revolutionary zeal led to neglect of investment, a neglect concealed behind pronouncements about the need to overcome initial difficulties. Trần Duy Dương, Vice President of Hanoi's People's Committee, made a typical such pronouncement with respect to the new economic zones in Lâm Đồng: 'Of course, the future in these places will be better, but there will be more than a few difficulties in the early stages'.[65]

For the people, however, getting beyond the initial stages was only part of the difficulty. Some gave up. Others stuck it out, and for them settling no longer meant just staying put. They strove, as Trần Duy Dương suggested, to reach a better future, a more concrete stability. We look now at the perspective of the people who decided to stay. For these families, what did stability entail?

Settlement at Buôn Tría

This perspective emerged clearly in interviews at a new economic zone in Dak Lak. This was Buôn Tría commune which, as we saw earlier, was where returnees from Nghĩa Lộ to Đông Xá commune were sent in 1977.[*] We arrived at the house of one family from Đông Xá, in the middle of an afternoon drinking party. The host, Quốc, invited us to pull up a stool and join in. He got quite animated when he realized we wanted to interview him about his experiences as a settler. After pouring us cups of rice wine, he tapped vigorously the wooden stool he was sitting on, boasting: 'We've built our new home, isn't it great!' He then added, and I couldn't tell if he was using irony or not, 'we even have stools to sit on now'.[66]

Quốc's house was situated in what had been, in 1975, a wide and deserted valley, stretching down from the small district town of Lak (see Map 15).[†] During the war, this valley was 'a no man's land', I was told by one of the Mnong people who lived there until 1963.[‡] He explained how they had moved away: 'The Americans

---

[*] Some 383 families of organized migrants (1,878 people) arrived there from Thái Bình; 580 families (3,177 people), also from Thái Bình, settled at nearby Buôn Triết. Data from Lak district People's Committee (Dak Lak, May 1996).

[†] Before 1975, both town and district were named Lạc Thiện, a Việt rendering of the local name. The province is named after the lake here, Dak Lak (or 'the lake of Lak', mistransliterated by the French as Darlac). After 1975, the town took the Việt name Liên Sơn and the district became, simply, Lak. This followed an SRV tendency to give larger administrative units minority names, while smaller ones kept names of Việt origin. In the 1980s, Dak Lak portrayed itself as the 'Ede province' (the name of the province's main indigenous group, Ede (Rhadé), came into usage there meaning 'ethnic minority'), camouflaging the presence of Việt settlers. This policy was dropped in the 1990s, when the province preferred to recognize its migrants and seek funding for the problems they caused. The local name for Ban Mê Thuột city (Buôn Ma Thuột) persisted into the 1990s, as did variant spellings for the province's name (Dak Lak, Đắc Lắc, Daklak, Đăklăk).

[‡] There was some confusion at Buôn Tría about this group. Some said they were Ede people, others Mnong. The village head stressed they were Mnong Bih, a sub-group of Mnong; there also existed an Ede sub-group called Bih. A 1930 ethnographic map of the province showed the Bih as a separate ethnic group. It appears that, during a process of post-colonial ethnic reclassification, groups of Bih were subsumed into Mnong and Ede. I am grateful to Dr Thu Nhung Mlo at the University of Tây Nguyên for helping me unravel this issue. A. Monfleur, *Monographie de la province du Darlac (1930)*, Hanoi: IDEO, 1931, p. 48.

were frightened we'd have contact with the Việt Cộng, so they moved us into a strategic hamlet. American soldiers burned down our houses. Long, old houses they were'. The Mnong returned after the war, but there was no longer room in the valley to graze their 500 mountain buffalo: 'in the old days, there was plenty of land. Lots of land, few people. Then, when the Thái Bình people came, land got scarce. There are so many of them!'[67] The Mnong sold and sacrificed their mountain buffalo, buying lowland cattle which could feed beside the road. The Thái Bình people cleared the grass and small trees which had grown up during the war. Quốc, who arrived there in October 1977, complained, using a slang expression common in northern Vietnam, that 'clearing the land was rather tough'.[*]

The results of Quốc's labour were celebrated in a poem, 'Meeting the Plains Again', written about the transformation of the Lak landscape a couple of months after his arrival. The valleys of Lak were portrayed as a new Thái Bình:

Wet rice beside the hills, fields of summer rice
Fields of highland corn, on the banks of the Luộc river
Buffalo in the mountain's shadow still go down to the cooperative fields
Villages and hamlets now familiar with the accent of Thái Bình
Blue smoke in the exhausted afternoon rises from thatched roofs.

Meeting the plains again on a quiet afternoon
Lak district – Đông Hưng, how are they so close?
Warm village of blue smoke, green afternoon of forest leaves
Gentle afternoon in the plains, in the middle of the central highlands.[†]

Quốc's account of this transformation was less ideal, less romantically pastoral. The accent was on exhausting afternoons at Buôn Tría rather than gentle ones. He repeated his favourite northern Vietnamese slang expression, which I have translated somewhat inadequately as 'rather'. In those days, he said, 'mosquitoes were rather numerous!'[‡] But medical services[§] were 'rather poor!'[¶] The same was true for educational services. There was a school, but few classes were held and, as the commune chairman told me, 'quality was not guaranteed'. Water, both for drinking and farming, presented further problems. Wells were sunk, a large irrigation dam was built, but in the dry season there was still no water, and in the

---

[*]   Clearing the land was rather tough: *khai phá hơi bị ác.*

[†]   Compare this poem with Map 15. Buôn Tría and Buôn Triết are on the southern edge of the valley. An earlier spelling of Buôn Triết's name (Triek) figures on the map, later adapted to the needs of Việt pronunciation. Buôn Tría was the name of the original Mnong Bih village there. After people came from Thái Bình, this name was used for the commune, Việt villages were given names reminiscent of home and the Mnong village was renamed Tân Tiến, a Việt word meaning 'new progress'. Văn Thành, 'Gặp lại đồng bằng'. In Dương Thanh Từng (ed.), *Dak Lak tập sáng tác văn nghệ,* Ban Mê Thuột: Ty Văn Hóa và Thông Tin Dak Lak, 1977, p. 39.

[‡]   Rather numerous: *hơi bị nhiều.*

[§]   A village clinic was built in 1980, saving people the 15 km trip to the district town.

[¶]   Rather poor: *hơi bị kém.*

The Krông Ana River runs from the lake of Dak Lak through a wide valley, home up to the 1960s to Mnong and Bih people. Displaced by the Americans during the war, the ethnic minority inhabitants of Buôn Tría and Buôn Triết (Buôn Triek) villages now share their land with Việt migrants from the Red River Delta province of Thái Bình.

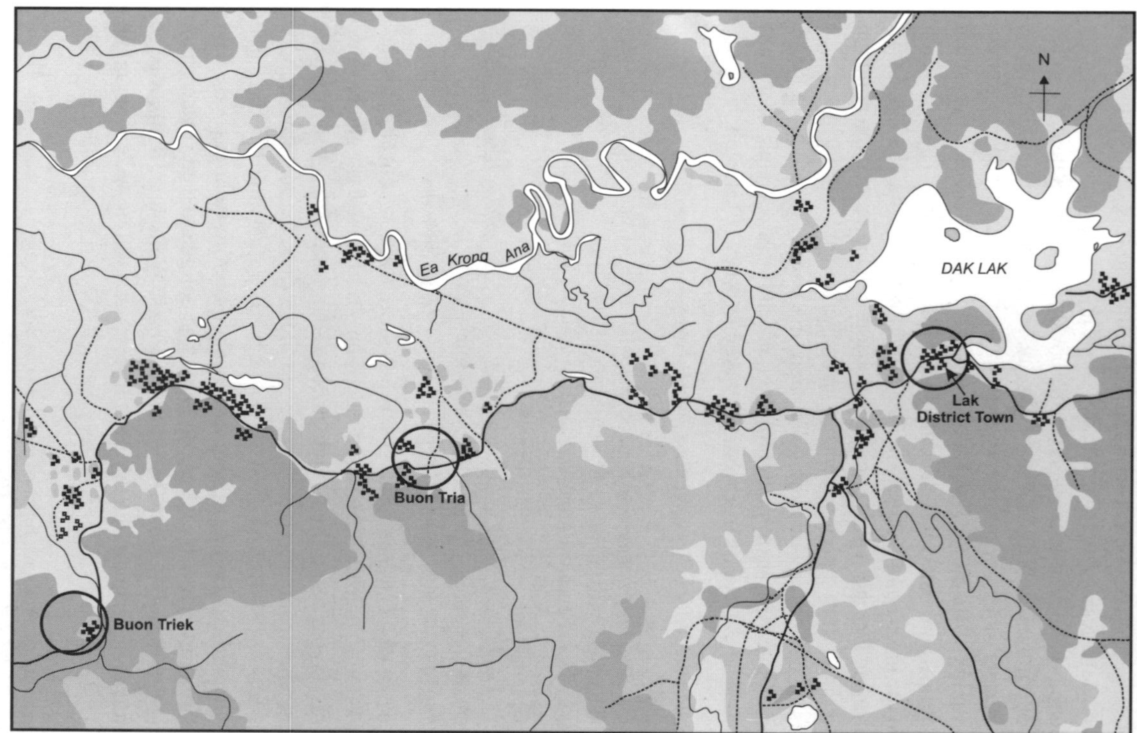

Map 15: The Krông Ana River valley in Lak district, 1964
Source: Cục Bản Đồ, Bộ Tổng Tham Mưu, Quân Đội Nhân Dân Việt Nam (updated in 1976 from a 1967 United States original). National Library of Australia, map G8020 s50, sheet 6633 IV, approximate scale 1/65,000. Redrawn by Lee Li Kheng.

wet there was too much.[68] In such circumstances, making a living from the land was not an easy business. Quốc said it took five years before they could produce enough to eat: 'Development here was rather slow!'* His conclusion was downbeat: 'There were so many difficulties then, people's lives were rather miserable!'†

Quốc's recollections were slurred and strongly coloured. They complement a more sober version of events published in the provincial newspaper. The results of the hard work in Lak were reported by a journalist writing under the by-line PV: 'People's lives have, step by step, settled down'.[69] The significance of this phrase lies in its narrow conception of stability. Settling down implied that people would not move on, that their primary economic needs were satisfied. Wider issues, the sorts of thing Quốc was concerned with, were set aside. PV elaborated on this two weeks later, in an article on new economic zones across the province:

> Besides the work of developing the economy and stabilizing the lives of the people, economic zones have attached great importance to cultural development, education, health, and the opening up of a network of rural transportation. New economic zones have built schools for levels I and II,‡ kindergartens, village clinics, shops and other services for the people; hundreds of kilometres of rural roads have been built and convenient means of transport made available.[70]

PV did not indicate either the quality or the quantity of the social, cultural and medical services, beyond mentioning their 'great importance'. But he did note that they were 'beside' the basic goals of stability and development, which were economic in content.

In many places, however, even the economic content was a long time in the coming. According to the usual formula, the passage quoted above constituted the good news before the bad, and preceded the following sobering announcement: 'Despite this there are a small number of places which do not yet produce enough to eat'.[71]

Buôn Tría was one of these places. Quốc's neighbour Ngô told me that, in the early 1980s, the people there survived off gleanings left on inefficiently harvested fields at the nearby state farm.§ He was one of many who noted the distance between the discourse they heard on the television, about giving priority to remote highland areas, and the experience of living in one. He used a proverb to tell me how he felt when they first arrived: that here it really was a case of 'taking the

---

* Rather slow: *hơi bị chậm*.

† Rather miserable: *hơi bị thiệt thòi*. Interviews (Dak Lak, November 1996).

‡ These correspond to primary and lower middle schools. Students at level III had to go to the district town.

§ The local newspaper described this state farm as being 'in the Buôn Triết area, with land of 10–15,000 hectares, taking the name '8.4 Construction Project' to mark the day [in April 1978] when comrade General Secretary of the Party [Lê Duẩn] visited the province'. *Dak Lak* editorial, 'Phấn khởi, tự hào cả Dak Lak mở "Công Trường 8.4"', *Dak Lak*, 24 August 1978, p. 1; Nguyễn Văn Nhi, 'Vài nét về công trường 8–4', *Dak Lak*, Tết issue 1979, p. 7.

children and abandoning them in the market'.* This saying reflected the traditional practice among impoverished parents of abandoning unwanted children out in the market. The idea was that the authorities organized the migration but made inadequate provision for migrants' needs.

There were, then, quite different conceptions of the idea of stability – of settling – from the perspectives of settlers and those managing the settlement. One retired cadre I met in Thái Bình, responsible in the late 1970s for organizing migration to the central highlands, smiled as he tried to persuade me that people were generally stable within three months. This meant, as he put it, 'making a living without worrying; producing, and producing well'. Not every cadre exuded such confidence. Later the same morning, another retired official down the road gravely assured me that it took a good five years before people were properly stabilized, before they had enough work to make a living, and their livelihood was assured.† Their timeframes differed, but both cadres shared a fundamentally economic perspective with an exclusive emphasis on production.

Phạm Đỗ Nhật Tân saw this as a major shortcoming in migration management:

> organization of migration paid attention only to the formation of production regions but neglected the formation of the basis for a new society. As a result, it is difficult to point to a model by which a new economic zone has been created according to a process of beginning with the fixing of people's place of residence, and ending up with the moment they are properly settled. What are the indicators that show that a new economic zone is properly settled? What does this actually mean? As yet, no government department has made clear and concrete definitions.

If government departments organizing migration to the central highlands did not work out what they meant by 'properly settled', it would be wrong to imagine that the people had a firmly fixed sense of this themselves. As Phạm Đỗ Nhật Tân pointed out to me, migrants to new economic zones had a shifting perspective on the idea of stability – both in terms of meaning and of time.

This emerged in my interviews at Buôn Tría. Quốc did not tell me when he thought he was settled. But when I asked his neighbour – who gave a more measured account of his experiences – he said it took ten years.‡ He did not say exactly what he meant by *ổn định* here. But later in our conversation he answered my question a second time, in a different, unsolicited context. The first time he went home to his village in Thái Bình, he told me, was at the end of 1980. This was after he had 'settled' the family here, a year after they had arrived in Dak Lak. Again, he didn't elaborate on the meaning of 'settled', but it was clearly quite

---

*   Taking the children and abandoning them in the market: *đem con bỏ chợ*.

†   The two cadres gave quite different timeframes for settlement. This may be because one only made periodic visits to the highlands, while the other lived in Sông Bé and Dak Lak as Thái Bình's representative. The first, of course, may simply have been feeding me a line. Interviews (Thái Bình, June 1996).

‡   He was 76 when I met him (Dak Lak, November 1996).

different. It implied little more than the initial arrangements for shelter and getting farm production under way.

Quốc's neighbour's way of remembering confirmed Phạm Đỗ Nhật Tân's view that settling was process. As some needs were satisfied, others were created. The perceived meaning of settlement thus underwent constant extension. The decision to stay, not to abandon the settlement in the first instance, would stand at one end of the process, along with building shelter, surviving malaria, reaping the first harvest. Ensuring a steady subsistence and access to good medical and educational facilities would be further along. Building a fine house and planting profitable crops would be next. And beyond the idea of settlement was that of development, opening up possibilities of improving one's livelihood to a level above that of the old village in the lowlands, of growing rich. Beyond this, in social and environmental terms, there was the idea of adaptation, which involved extensive changes in the procedures both for production and living.

DEVELOPMENT AT TAM GIANG

To examine more closely the processes of settlement, development and adaptation, we need to leave Buôn Tría. The unique geography of Lak, which had allowed the Mnong people to grow wet rice for generations, lent itself to the illusion of recreating Thái Bình in the highlands. The Lak valleys were adapted to the needs of the lowland people, rather than vice versa.

For a landscape which in no way resembled the plains, we go instead to the commune of Tam Giang (now part of Krông Năng district, Dak Lak). In 1978, 1,000 families from the coastal region settled in this area of forested hills. With its shallow slopes and narrow valleys, this was a rolling landscape typical of the central highlands. The trees they felled were small. Highlanders who had once cut swiddens from the forest had long since left – in the 1960s, one settler said vaguely, because of the war. In this, Tam Giang was also a more typical settlement. Most new economic zones set up in Dak Lak in the 1970s had little direct contact with local minority inhabitants.* In fact, this region was bombed early in the war. On US army maps published in 1964, highlander villages – as well as those of migrants settled there in the late 1950s by Ngô Đình Diệm – already appeared as 'destroyed' or 'destroyed area'.[72] In a better-known highland war zone, Khe Sanh, one observer expressed a similar legacy of war on the enviroment in words of bitter hyperbole: 'They turned the green of the forest into red'.[73] The new economic zone migrants were given the task of repairing the damage.

Tam Giang's new inhabitants came from the district of Hương Điền, near Huế. Their new village was named after the beautiful lagoon near their home, the Tam

---

* Of thirty-five cooperatives established in 1976–79, only four resembled Buôn Tría in their close physical and administrative proximity with a minority village. PV, 'Qua tổng kết công tác', p. 1.

Giang lake. Settlers at Buôn Tría 'enjoyed the plains again' in the valleys of Lak. At Tam Giang they contented themselves with a nostalgic name.

I visited Tam Giang in May 1996, at the end of the dry season. The red earth had caked dust into the wooden houses lining the main street. Lanes either side led to houses set back in gardens of vegetables and coffee. We stopped at the social centre of the commune, a pub which doubled as restaurant/karaoke/billiards bar, and also turned out to be the home of the commune's chairman, Thành, and his entrepreneurial wife. From discussions with Thành and other villagers, I came to the conclusion that Tam Giang's short history can be written in four chapters. These cover malaria, agriculture, social services, and population.[74]

Malaria almost brought the settlement to a premature close, within just a few years of its creation. The disease was negligible in 1978–79 – diarrhoea and plague posed a greater threat. But an epidemic started in 1980, peaking in 1981–82. Over those three years, at least sixty people died of the disease. Thành said that in a single year there were forty deaths, while many others fell sick. Thành said that 95 per cent of the population was affected. Some lost children as infant mortality rose and everyone got very frightened. As much as half the population chose to abandon the settlement altogether.[*] After 1983, the original settlers ceased to suffer seriously from symptoms of the disease, although new arrivals continued to be vulnerable. The last deaths from malaria were in 1992 and 1995.[75] As in the northern highlands, the disease was blamed as much on the stream water as on mosquitoes – though with more justification. There was evidence here of the sorts of sickness – birth defects, mental illnesses – associated with wartime defoliant poisoning of the environment.

Tam Giang's agricultural history was less traumatic. Six months before people arrived, the land was cleared by teams of soldiers and 'assault youth'.[†] These teams built houses in anticipation of their arrival and planted the first rice, potatoes and manioc.[76] Cereals remained the principal crops until the mid 1980s. In those days production was organized by the cooperative. One former cooperative member, Doanh, remembered this as a time of terrible hard work: getting up in the dark to avoid the midday heat, taking lunch out to the fields, resting at times dictated by the plan.[77] This version of events concurs with an account published in the provincial newspaper:

---

* Nguyên, another resident of Tam Giang, lost four of his eleven children shortly after their birth in the early 1980s, two from malaria. He was 45 when I met him (Dak Lak, May 1996).

† Assault youth (*thanh niên xung phong*) were young people mobilized to do arduous physical tasks, though in Tam Giang they used earth-moving machinery. The military term 'assault' was by the 1980s closely associated with clearing land – one dictionary defined it as follows: '*xung phong đi khai hoang*: to volunteer to go and reclaim virgin land'. In Tam Giang, each family volunteered one child for this work. Among them was Thành, now commune chairman, who became one of forty (out of 1,000) to stay on afterwards. Interview (Dak Lak, May 1996). Đặng Chấn Liêu, *Từ điển Việt Anh*, p. 792.

> The people of Tam Giang commune (…) along with units of assault youth have focused on clearing land and building rice fields wherever the land has potential for wet rice. (…) Every day more than 500 labourers join in clearing the land, building fields with hand tools, and have already completed nearly 2 hectares. Teams of assault youth organize themselves to go to work early, come back late; they take rice for lunch at the site, make the most of their time, work ten to twelve hours a day, and always meet targets set by the commune. In a short time, Tam Giang has cleared and built fields amounting to 30 hectares of land.[78]

Bình, however, had rather different memories:

> No one knew how to farm this land; there were wet and dry seasons and no one knew how to react to them. But even if they did, it wouldn't have made any difference, because the work programme was arranged by the cooperative. So the people would go out to the fields and spend eight hours there, doing a bit of work, but talking and having fun, so work wasn't hard as it is now.

Under this regime, Bình added, 'no one ate till they were full'. Back in the pub, Thành confirmed this. For the first three years, the government helped if there was not enough food. Rice and corn were provided, as in 1981 when the harvest failed. But after that people were on their own if they couldn't make a living. 1983 was a bad year, he said, but people just had to put up with it.[79] One of those people, Nguyên, had bitter memories of those times: 'At the beginning, there was enough rice and corn because the state helped, but after that there were many difficulties. We never reached the next harvest before our rice had run out'. He fed his family during the hungry gap by going off to other parts of the district for a few days' carpentry work every now and then. He couldn't go for long though, because of the threat from FULRO minority insurgents, and because cooperative rules required him to work on the fields.[*]

The cooperative was dismantled in 1985. Each labourer was allocated three *sào* of land. It was only then, according to Thành, that their livelihoods stabilized: 'After the cooperatives were broken up, people had more freedom, so their economic situation improved'. The economic situation was given a further boost the following year, with the upgrading of the road to town. Speaking of this, Thành defined stabilization in economic terms: 'People were guaranteed enough cereals to eat and the road meant it was easier to get to market – both to buy and sell'.

The unravelling of the cooperatives allowed households to choose their crops. Investment in cash crops, particularly coffee, became profitable. The production of cereals fell. Dak Lak, in the meantime, had nonetheless vastly increased the land area planted with wet rice: from 200 hectares on reunification, to 10,000 in 1980 and 12,000 by 1991.[81] Nguyên pointed out to me that growing rice was fine for consumption purposes but, that compared to coffee, it was uneconomical.

---

[*]   FULRO was the minority insurgency in the central highlands – the acronym is from the original French name, Front Uni pour la Libération [or Lutte] des Races Opprimées. See also note 80.

With rice, you make enough to eat but with coffee you could make money. The benefits of diversification were clear. By 1986, Thành said, the commune was economically over the worst. In 1989, it was stable. After 1989, the economy started developing.

In Nguyên's experience, the process took a little longer. He was initially given poor land, only good for rice and beans. It was later re-divided more equitably and he obtained a better plot. In 1996 he had wet rice fields enough to feed his family of nine. He also had seven *sào* of coffee. He stated, when I met him, that things were 'stable for the moment (*tạm ổn định*). We have enough to eat, but for other expenses, it's still tight.'[*]

I heard the phrase 'stable for the moment' a great deal in Tam Giang. Initially I imagined it was used by those who had not yet reached any level of development. But Nguyên, despite his large family and multiple complaints, was clearly doing rather well with his coffee. The previous year, he let drop, he felt confident enough to borrow 10 million đồng.[†] On reflection, I realized that 'stable for the moment' also situated the speaker in a process. The process embraced both settlement and development, conveying as it did the sense that while some needs were fulfilled, others remained outstanding. It evoked, moreover, a precariousness to the process, a sense that all could be reversed if the rains did not come, if insects did, if the harvest were lost. The expression was, in this sense, a Vietnamese equivalent of the ritual phrase 'God willing', uttered to avoid offending fate or the elements.

Doanh's story epitomized the use of this expression and, with it, the settlement process. He was not settled, he told me at the beginning of our conversation, until 1980–81. After that, harvests of wet rice made his livelihood stable for the moment, even though wild pigs from the forest regularly destroyed his manioc farm. When I asked about his situation now, he described it in the same terms: 'for the last three or so years, stable for the moment'. It was not that his situation in 1996 was unchanged from 1981. His ritualized use of the expression 'for the moment' left room for further changes to come. Stability, previously implying only a very basic living, now became a matter of decent food, housing and clothing. Who could tell what it would become in the future?

Interestingly, Doanh did not define stability in 1996 in terms of the social services he received. This may be because he felt they were adequate to his needs. A school was set up in September 1979, a clinic soon after. But the inability of the medical service – despite DDT spraying and prophylactic drug use – to prevent the malaria catastrophe would indicate the contrary. In the days of the epidemic, Bình remembered taking his children along the narrow path to the nearest hospital at Buôn Hồ, as medicine was short in the village. Doanh confirmed this when we started talking about malaria: 'Medicine was always lacking, you could

---

[*]	Nguyên was 45 when I met him (Dak Lak, May 1996).

[†]	About US$ 900 at that time.

get it in the district or provincial centre, but the roads were hard going'. He added that now all you need is money to buy it. In those days, it was free of charge but unavailable.

The case of educational services – investment in future development, rather than present survival – was not so clear-cut. Thành told me that the first school was staffed with teachers from their home village and from the district town. He noted with pride that each cooperative had an elementary school, and the commune centre boasted both elementary and lower middle schools, with a total of twenty class-rooms. But few others in Tam Giang spoke of education with any animation. This may, again, reflect the adequacy of its provision. It may, on the other hand, indicate the lower priority given by settler families to investment in education. The malaria threat provoked an exodus from Tam Giang in the early 1980s. Survival was para-mount in the decisions of families who left. Bình justified his departure entirely in terms of his family's health, saying 'there were no economic reasons for going back home, the same system existed there'. By the late 1980s these settlers had different concerns. They worried about making a living from the plot of land which the cooperative had handed them. The more immediate imperatives of survival from malaria and subsistence from agriculture had, to be dealt with before the children's education could be properly addressed.

The place of education in the settling process varied from one place to the next. Back in Điểm Mặc, Học indicated that education was of great importance to his family from the earliest stages of settlement. Through the early years (1963–70) he continued to study – walking 6 km daily to primary school, 16 km to middle school, getting up at four in the morning, getting home at two in the afternoon, then helping on the farm. He stopped his studies for a single year during the switch to tea cultivation and completed seventh grade, before joining the army when he was 18. For many families, education (of at least one male child) and subsistence (for the family) were priorities to be balanced and negotiated. Only in very difficult times would the child be brought home for full-time work on the farm.[82] This supports Phạm Xuân Đại's contention:

> From the initial period, even though cereals are supplied, more attention needs to be paid to the organization of cultural life, so that people are not caught off-balance in their new life. Reality shows very regularly that they abandon the settlement in the early stages if they feel themselves abandoned, victims of the practice of 'taking the children and abandoning them in the market.[83]

The importance of education was clearly demonstrated at Ea Lê commune (in nearby Ea Súp district), where a newspaper report in 1986 looked back on five years of settlement:

> Once material life was satisfactorily [settled] and the people had enough food to eat and clothes to wear, Ea Lê had the conditions to worry about cultural, medical and educational services as well as maintaining order and safety throughout the commune. With its own capital, the commune built a clinic with fifteen beds, set up a 'popular' medicine chest, and a basic school where this year the commune has 732 pupils.[84]

Demands for educational and other services, met fairly quickly in Ea Lê if we can believe this report, arose further along in the process of stabilization and development.

The final chapter in Tam Giang's history concerns its population. The table tells the story:

Table 1: Population of Tam Giang commune, 1978–96

Year	Families	People
1978	1,015	5,624
1979	1,104	5,558
1984	533	3,295
1990	930	5,146
1996	1,558	8,009

Source: For this data (except 1979) I am grateful to cadres at Tam Giang People's Committee. For 1979, see Hoàng Nguyễn Vẹn, 'Xã Tam Giang (Krông Buk) hoàn thành công tác tổng điều tra số dân trước thời hạn 4 ngày', *Dak Lak*, 25 October 1979, p. 3.

The population story is a simple one. In 1979–84, the malaria epidemic caused a nearly 50 per cent fall in the commune's population, partly from mortality but mainly from migration. In 1984–90, the numbers were made up by people like Bình, who came back after finding life difficult at his home village, and also by newcomers. Over the final period, Thành explained to me how the commune's population increased by a further 50 per cent: 'Since 1990, about 100 families per year have come up and settle here. Usually they have relatives here, so have already been to visit'. These free migrants were quite different from the original settlers. They heard from relatives about opportunities for development. They brought with them capital to invest, or relied on family resources to start them off. They hoped to get rich at Tam Giang.

SETTLEMENT, DEVELOPMENT AND ADAPTATION

Processes of settlement and development similar to those of Buôn Tría and of Tam Giang may be observed throughout the central highlands. But what about adaptation?

As we have seen, many settlers suffered from malaria. Tam Giang was not the only commune whose future was jeopardized in this way.[*] The disease was among

---

[*] Phạm Đỗ Nhật Tân noted an example of a similarly affected new economic zone settlement in Krông Pa district (Gia Lai). Phạm Đỗ Nhật Tân, 'Hoàn thiện hơn nữa việc di dân', p. 66.

the principal threats to the settlers' attempts, under the cooperative system, to transform the highland landscape to suit agricultural technologies imported from the plains. Their project was to adapt the landscape to the people, epitomized in spirit by Lê Duẩn's stirring dictum that 'All Dak Lak must become one huge construction project'.[85] Later analysts noted the voluntarist philosophy that informed this ideal:

> It seems that no small number of people follow the economic way of thinking which maintains: if you have labour and land, then you can do anything! As for capital, management capability, infrastructure, these factors receive less emphasis. It must be because of this that 'new economic zone' communities, now scattered throughout the mountain plateaux, were created with only one important condition: they must have agricultural land, and especially land for growing rice![86]

This attempt to adapt the highland environment to lowland techniques of agriculture prolonged the process of settlement as much as malaria did. But malaria levels dropped, generally due to forest clearance and acquired immunity to the disease. As far as their health was concerned, settlers simultaneously adapted the environment to themselves and themselves to their environment. The same process was discernible in the economic sphere, after the reforms of the late 1980s. Changes in economic organization contributed to the stability of food provision and improvements in social services. Settlers could plant coffee and other crops better suited to highland soils and to market opportunities. With the adaptation of farming methods to the local environment, their family economy developed accordingly.[87]

Generally, however, the process of adaptation stopped with these basic environmental and economic factors, if adaptation is defined as 'making changes in production methods, changes in crop choice, changes in customs and habits, changes in appearance, etc.'[88] I found the perspective of Dương, a Tày minority cadre in Định Hóa district, to be applicable throughout the Vietnamese highlands: 'Việt settlers are of two sorts: those who come in small groups, who absorb local customs and adapt, and those who come in big groups, who don't change at all'.[89] In the past, Việt people who settled as individuals or families in the highlands tended to merge into the majority populations there, the people now known as Vietnam's ethnic minorities. Throughout the northern highlands, I met people who dress, talk and live like Tày, Nùng and Thái people but who claimed to have Việt parents and ancestors from the lowlands.[90]

In the mid-twentieth century, the settlement process changed. New economic zone settlers arrived in large groups. They did not have to adapt, and their presence there was intended to bring progress to the highlands, to encourage adaptation on the part of the highlanders. Most of them looked no further than the immediate goals of settlement and development. Ngọc, who so resented coming to Dak Lak after his experiences in Nghĩa Lộ, gave a very tangible indication of this. 'When we first arrived, going back to Thái Bình was impossible, it was too far. If it was near, we'd have gone back straight away.' His situation had changed over the years, however. 'Things have got better since 1991. Now, if they let me go back north, I wouldn't go'.[91]

The policeman accompanying us that day added his own conclusion to Ngọc's comment: 'He's settled', he said.

CONCLUSION

We understood in the preceding chapters how the Vietnamese state broke the administrative 'attachment' of Red River Delta people to their village. We saw how techniques of mobilization were used to shift the ideological basis of rule from the village to the nation. We saw how many villagers were willing, under this regime, to leave their village in the plains and contribute to the building both of the nation and their own economy in the highlands. And the present chapter showed how the state fulfilled this precondition of successful migration policy – a favourable administrative environment – and dealt with the other basic practical problems of settlement – control of malaria and provision of a means of subsistence. These achievements ensured that many of the people who moved to the highlands also settled there for the long term.

However, large numbers of people failed to settle. Others who settled were unable to express satisfaction at having done so. Their experiences illustrate the limitations inherent in the state's conception of settlement, which amounted essentially to staying, surviving and subsisting. The settlers themselves had higher goals. As the case of Tam Giang demonstrated, they sought to develop a new and vibrant society and economy in the highlands. They saw settlement in terms of a long-term process of improvement in their standard of living.

There were limits to the settlers' conception of this process, however. The society and economy they sought to build on the new land was a fundamentally Việt one. Some adaptation to both the environment and the population into which they had moved did take place, and the existing inhabitants of the highlands did enjoy a measure of influence over the newcomers. But most of the adaptation went the other way around. The highlands were, after all, expected to 'catch up with the plains'.[92]

NOTES

1   Đặng Chấn Liêu, *Từ Điển Việt Anh*, Hanoi: NXB Khoa Học Xã Hội, 1987, p. 545.

2   Interview (Thái Nguyên, July 1995).

3   Interview (Thái Nguyên, September 1995).

4   NAV3/TCTK 2399(vv), Thái Bình Statistical Office to General Statistical Office, 16 December 1964.

5   Interview (Thái Nguyên, July 1995).

6   Trịnh Văn Đông, 'Báo cáo tổng kết công tác khai hoang xây dựng vùng kinh tế mới năm 1976–1981', Thái Nguyên: Bắc Thái Agricultural Office, 1982.

7   Interview (Thái Nguyên, October 1996).

8   NAV3/SYTKTTVB 58(vv), 'Báo cáo sơ kết điều tra sốt rét cơn đợt 2, huyện Vị Xuyên', Hà Giang Medical Office, Anti-Malaria Team, 1959; Hòa Bình Committee for Eradication of Malaria, 'Giải đáp khoa học về công tác tiêu diệt sốt rét', *Hòa Bình*, 26 April 1963, p. 2; NAV3/UBKHNN 1820(tt), Director of Malaria Institute to Health

Ministry, 1 November 1958; Lê Khánh Thuận, 'Muỗi Anopheles Meigen chuyển bệnh sốt rét ở miền Trung, Việt Nam', Luận án phó tiến sĩ y học, Trường Đại Học Y, Hanoi, 1988, p. 2.

9   Thái Nguyên Provincial Committee for Eradication of Malaria, *Báo cáo mừng Thắng lợi tám năm tiêu diệt sốt rét (1957–1964) của tỉnh Thái Nguyên*, Thái Nguyên, 1965, pp. 13–14; NAV3/UBKHNN 1820(tt), 'Dự tính viện trợ về chuyên gia Liên Xô', Malaria Institute, Hanoi, 9 October 1957.

10 Army Medical Office, *Chống sốt rét để tăng sức chiến đấu, Tài liệu học tập chiến sĩ*, Cục Quân Y xuất bản, 1952; Thái Nguyên Provincial Committee for Eradication of Malaria, *Báo cáo mừng Thắng lợi*, p. 5.

11 Ministry of Health, *Tài liệu huấn luyện càn bộ*, p. 35; Thái Mèo Autonomous Zone Health Service, *Chống và tiêu diệt bệnh sốt rét ở miền núi*, Hanoi: Nhà in Tiến Long, 1959; Trần Nam Hưng, *Tự chữa sốt rét (kinh nghiệm trong kháng chiến)*, Hanoi: NXB Phổ Thông, 1958.

12 NAV3/UBKHNN 1820(tt), Minister of Health to Prime Minister, Hanoi, 26 February 1958.

13 NAV3/SYTKTTVB 59(vv), 'Báo cáo tình hình sốt rét trong toàn tỉnh Thái Nguyên trong 3 năm 1957–59', 1959.

14 Thái Nguyên Provincial Committee for Eradication of Malaria, *Báo cáo mừng Thắng lợi*, p. 20.

15 Interviews (Thái Nguyên, October 1996, January 1997). Thái Nguyên Provincial Committee for Eradication of Malaria, *Báo cáo mừng Thắng lợi*, p. 19.

16 Interview (Thái Nguyên, October 1996).

17 Vũ Văn Cẩn, *Bệnh Sốt Rét Cơn*, NXB Vui Sống, 1947, p. 25.

18 Dương Văn Đao, 'Người Việt Kiều hồi hương ở đất Tân Lạc', *Hòa Bình*, 17 December 1963, p. 2.

19 Interview (Dak Lak, November 1996).

20 For discussion of difficulties faced by folk rusticated from southern cities after 1975, see Jacqueline Desbarats, 'Population Redistribution in the Socialist Republic of Vietnam', *Population and Development Review* vol. 13, no. 1, 1987, p. 35.

21 Diệp Đình Hoa, *Sự biến động của cộng đồng dân tộc do tác động của hồ Hòa Bình*, Hanoi: NXB Khoa Học Xã Hội, 1995, p. 69.

22 General Land Clearance Office, 'Báo cáo tổng kết cuộc vận động đồng báo miền xuôi tham gia phát triển kinh tế miền núi trong kế hoạch 5 năm lần thứ nhất và phương hướng nhiệm vụ những năm tới', Hanoi, July 1966; Hoàng Bắc, *Tìm hiểu cuộc vận động cải tiến quản lý hợp tác xã nông nghiệp miền núi*, Hanoi: NXB Phổ Thông, 1965, pp. 8–10.

23 Phạm Đỗ Nhật Tân, 'Hoàn thiện hơn nữa việc di dân nông nghiệp có tổ chức đi xây dựng các vùng kinh tế mới', Luận àn phó tiến sĩ khoa học kinh tế, Trường Đại Học Kinh Tế Quốc Dân, Hanoi, 1992, pp. 46–47.

24 Adam Fforde and Stefan de Vylder, *From Plan to Market, The Economic Transition in Vietnam*, Boulder, Colorado: Westview Press, 1996, p. 184.

25 Thanh Xương, 'Hợp tác xã khai hoang Tân Tiến thu hoạch lúa gai đầu tiên trên đất đồi', *Hòa Bình*, 1 October 1963, pp. 2–3.

26 State Scientific Committee, Vietnam Scientific Institute, Geological Institute, Geography and Resources Centre and National Economics University, 'Chương trình tiến bộ khoa học kỹ thuật: Đánh giá tổng hợp tự nhiên kinh tế xã hội 9 tỉnh miền núi phía Bắc', Programme Summary Report, Hanoi, 1990.

27 Trọng Hồng, 'HTX khai hoang Tân Ngọc sản xuất bước đầu có nhiều tiến bộ', *Hòa Bình*, 27 September 1963, p. 3.

28 Phan Quế, 'Mai Châu'. In Phạm Quốc Bang, *Hà Sơn Bình Di Tích và Danh Thắng*, Xí nghiệp in Hà Sơn Bình, 1985, pp. 49–50.

29 Interview (Hòa Bình, July 1995).

30 Interview (Hòa Bình, July 1995).

31 Diệp Đình Hoa, *Sự biến động của cộng đồng dân tộc*, p. 86; Dương Thị The and Phạm Thị Thoa, *Tên làng xã Việt Nam đầu thế kỷ XIX (thuộc các tỉnh từ Nghệ Tĩnh trở ra)*, Hanoi: NXB Khoa Học Xa Hội, 1981, p. 86.

32 Interview (Hòa Bình, October 1995). Mai Châu Medical Service, 'Xã Mai Hạ rời chuồng trâu xa nhà', *Hòa Bình*, 23 April 1963, p. 2; Hòa Bình Committee for Eradication of Malaria, 'Giải đáp khoa học', p. 2.

33 Interviews (Hòa Bình, July 1996).

34 Trọng Hồng, 'Qua cuộc vận động thí điểm 'củng cố HTX khai hoang'', *Hòa Bình*, 19 November 1963, p. 2.

35 Interviews (Hòa Bình, October 1995, July 1996).

36 Trọng Hồng, 'Qua cuộc vận động', p. 2.

37 Interview (Hòa Bình, July 1996).

38 Gareth Porter, *The Politics of Bureaucratic Socialism*, Ithaca and London: Cornell University Press, 1993, p. 73.

39 Phạm Văn Đồng, *Tổ chức lại sản xuất và cải tiến quản lý Nông Nghiệp và Lâm Nghiệp trung du và miền núi*, Hanoi: NXB Sự Thật, 1975, p. 55.

40 Interview (Hòa Bình, July 1996).

41 Benedict J. Tria Kerkvliet, 'Village–State Relations in Vietnam: The Effect of Everyday Politics on Decollectivization', *JAS*, vol. 54, no. 2, 1995, p. 415.

42 Interview with Tuấn (Thái Nguyên, January 1997). For comparison of colonial and post-colonial identity laws, see Ministry of Interior, *Một số điểm chính về công tác hộ tịch*, Hanoi: Bộ Nội Vụ, 1960, p. 7.

43 Mervyn Matthews, *The Passport Society: Controlling Movement in Russia and the USSR*, Boulder, Colorado: Westview Press, 1993, pp. 27, 99; Y. C. Yu, 'The Demographic Situation in China', *Population Studies* vol. 32, no. 3, 1978, p. 431; Cheng Tiejun and Mark Selden, 'The Origins And Social Consequences of China's Hukou System', *The China Quarterly*, vol. 139, 1994, pp. 644–668.

44 'Circular for explanation and guidance on the implementation of regulations for the management of household registration', Ministry of Police Circular 1005–P3, 24 September 1964. Reprinted in Yên Bái Police Service, *Tài liệu học tập về công tác quản lý hộ tịch, hộ khẩu*, Yên Bái, 1973, p. 12. Ministry of Culture, *Những điều cần biết về hộ tịch (sinh, tử, giá thú)*, Hanoi: NXB Phổ Thông, 1958, p. 6.

45 Yên Bái Police Service, *Tài liệu học tập*, p. 13; Hein Mallee, 'China's Household Registration System under Reform', *Development and Change*, vol. 26, no. 1, 1995, p. 2.

46 'Regulations on the management of household registration', Council of Ministers' Decision 104, 27 June 1964. Reprinted in Thái Bình Police Service, *Tài liệu học tập về công tác kiểm tra đổi sổ hộ khẩu và cấp giấy chứng nhận căn cước cho các khu phố, xã, hộ tập thể*, Hanoi: Xí nghiệp in Thái Bình, 1972, pp. 18–21.

47 Ministry of Culture, *Những điều cần biết*, pp. 5–6.

48 This legislation was signed by Phạm Văn Đồng in 1964. Thái Bình Police Service, *Tài liệu học tập*, p. 20.

49 Interview (Thái Nguyên, October 1996).

50 Interview (Thái Bình, January 1997). The same situation existed in China: the *hukou* was described as resting on three pillars, its links to: a) access to food rations and coupons, b) access to state employment, c) access to social services. Wang Feng, 'The Breakdown of a Great Wall: Recent Changes in the Household Registration System of China'. In Thomas Scharping (ed.), *Floating Population and Migration in China: The Impact of Economic Reforms*, Hamburg: Institut für Asienkunde, 1997, pp. 149–150.

51 Interviews (Thái Bình, January 1997).

52 Interview with Bùi (aged 72) and others (Thái Bình, January 1997).

53 Interviews (Thái Bình, January 1997).

54 Ngọc was 38 when I met him. Interview (Dak Lak, November 1996).

55 Interview (Dak Lak, November 1996).

56 Nam Cường commune: 'Tham luận hội thảo khoa học nhận dịp 19-5-1995 ngày sinh chủ tịch Hồ Chí Minh, về một miền quê đón Bác và làm theo lời Bác dậy', 1995. My thanks to officials at Nam Cường for this document.

57 William R. Lavely, 'China's Rural Population Statistics at the Local Level', *Population Index*, vol. 48, no. 4, 1982, pp. 665–677. Quoted in Penny Kane, *The Second Billion: Population and Family Planning in China*, Ringwood, Victoria: Penguin, 1987, p. 64.

58 Interview (Sơn La, December 1996).

59 Interview (Thái Bình, January 1997).

60 Interview (Dak Lak, November 1996).

61 Lê Khánh, *Quê mới người Hà Nội ở Lâm Đồng*, Hanoi: NXB Nông Nghiệp, 1983, p. 18.

62 Ibid., pp. 18–19.

63 Phạm Đỗ Nhật Tân, 'Hoàn thiện hơn nữa việc di dân', pp. 46–47.

64 General Land Clearance Office, 'Báo cáo tổng kết cuộc vận động', July 1966.

65 Lê Khánh, *Quê mới người Hà Nội*, p. 20.

66 Interview (Dak Lak, November 1996).

67 Interview with a 57–year-old Mnong man (Dak Lak, November 1996).

68 Nguyễn Thanh Sơn, 'Đoàn thanh niên trong phong trào 'Ba xung kích làm chủ tập thể'', *Dak Lak*, 27 September 1979, p. 3; Nguyễn Pháp, *Nông-lâm nghiệp Đắc Lắc, 1975–1995*, Hanoi: NXB Nông Nghiệp, 1995, p. 15.

69 PV, 'Huyện Lak tổng kết công tác dân vận, mặt trận và tổ chức học tập chính sách dân tộc của Đảng trong giai đoạn mới', *Dak Lak*, 4 October 1979, p. 1.

70 PV, 'Qua tổng kết công tác xây dựng kinh tế mới', *Dak Lak*, 18 October 1979, pp. 1, 4.

71 Ibid., p. 4.

72 See Cục Bản Đồ, Bộ Tổng Tham Mưu, Quân Đội Nhân Dân Việt Nam (maps updated in 1976 from a 1964 US Army original), National Library of Australia, map G8020 s50, sheet 6634 I, approximate scale 1/65,000.

73 Hữu Mai, *Bưu ảnh từ những vùng đất mới*, Hanoi: NXB Quân Dội Nhân Dân, 1978, p. 76.

74 Interviews (Dak Lak, May 1996).

75 I am grateful to officials at Tam Giang commune clinic for these data. Interview (Dak Lak, May 1996).

76 Interview (Dak Lak, May 1996). Hải Dương, 'Trên vùng kinh tế mới Krông Buk, Trung đoàn Tam Giang khai hoang đất năng xuất lao động cao', *Dak Lak*, 20 April 1978, p. 4.

77 Doanh was 45 when I met him. Interviews (Dak Lak, May 1996).

78 Hoàng Vũ Lâm, 'Xã Tam Giang khai phà 30 héc-ta ruộng nước', *Dak Lak,* 1 November 1979, p. 1.

79 Interview (Dak Lak, May 1996).

80 For details on the FULRO (including its links with 'reactionaries disguised as religious elements' and 'Polpot and Ieng Sary's gang') and a periodization of the conflict (1975–77 post-liberation period; 1978–79 link with Cambodia period; 1980–92 guerrilla warfare period) see Ngô Văn Lý and Nguyễn Văn Điêu, *Tây Nguyên Tiềm Năng và Triển Vọng*, Ho Chi Minh City: NXB Thành Phố Hồ Chí Minh, 1992, pp. 205–209. The insurgency ended in the early 1990s, but a curious magazine article appeared in April 1998 announcing the surrender of the 'last FULRO group' along with the startling information that, after so long in the forest the guerrillas did not know how to eat rice. This seemed to symbolize a recent shift in the practice of journalism in Vietnam, from education to

sensationalism. This item was clearly not so much edifying as exciting and bizarre. Nguyễn Khương, 'Đoạn kết có hậu cho toàn FULRO cuối cùng', *Thế Giới Mới*, 27 April 1998, pp. 77–81. For discussion of FULRO in English see Gerald Cannon Hickey, *Free in the Forest. Ethnohistory of the Vietnamese Central Highlands, 1954–1976*, New Haven and London: Yale University Press, 1982, ch. 3.

81 Ministry of Labour, Invalids and Social Affairs, *30 năm sự nghiệp di dân khai hoang và xây dựng kinh tế mới 1961–91*, Hanoi: Cục Điều Động Lao Động và Dân Cư, 1991, p. 8; Ministry of Agriculture, 'Báo cáo tình hình khai hoang và phân bố lao động, dân cư đi khai hoang xây dựng vùng kinh tế mới 5 năm 1976–89', Hanoi: Bộ Nông Nghiệp, January 1982.

82 Interview (Thái Nguyên, July 1995).

83 Phạm Xuân Đại, 'Khả năng hòa nhập và mức độ ổn định của các cộng đồng di dân tại Đông Nam Bộ', *XHH*, vol. 12, no. 4, 1985, p. 90.

84 Bùi Đức Thịnh, 'Ea Lê – vùng quê mới – nhiều hứa hẹn', *Dak Lak*, 24 October 1986, p. 3.

85 This declaration was made by Lê Duẩn on his visit to Dak Lak in 1978. Dak Lak editorial, 'Phấn khởi, tự hào cả Dak Lak mở 'Công Trường 8.4', p. 1; Nguyễn Văn Nhi, 'Vài nét về công trường 8–4', p. 7. Interview (Dak Lak, November 1996).

86 Tương Lai and Phạm Bích San, 'Khao sát xã hội học về những cộng đồng người Kinh sinh tử và phát triển tại Tây Nguyên', *XHH*, vol. 27, no. 3, 1989, p. 40.

87 For analysis of the importance of coffee and markets in the development of the central highlands, see Stan B.-H. Tan, 'Coffee Frontiers in the Central Highlands of Vietnam: Networks of Connectivity between New Productive Spaces and Global Markets', *Asia Pacific Viewpoint*, vol. 41, no. 1, 2000, pp. 51–67.

88 Diệp Đình Hoa, *Sự biến động của cộng đồng dân tộc do tác động của hồ Hòa Bình*, Hanoi: NXB Khoa Học Xã Hội, 1995, p. 53.

89 Interview (Thái Nguyên, January 1997).

90 For preliminary analysis of the T'ai-ization of Việt residents of the highlands, see Andrew Hardy and Nguyễn Tiến Đông, 'Quelques intérrogations sur l'identité ethnique: le cas des Mạc de Mai Châu', *Tạp Chí Xưa & Nay*, no. 66, 1999, pp. 24–25, I–III.

91 Interview (Dak Lak, November 1996).

92 Lê Duẩn, 'Báo cáo chính trị của Ban chấp hành trung ương Đảng ở Đại hội toàn quốc lần thứ ba', *Nhân Dân*, 6 September 1960, p. 6.

9 *Policy*

*I*n the four decades after 1960, several million people were persuaded to 'go and build a new home village', under the government migration policy.* We saw in the previous chapters how this took place, looking at people's experiences of decision-making, moving and settlement. But what was the purpose of this vast programme of organized migration? In this chapter, shifting our focus from practice to policy, we examine this question from the points of view of both the migrants and the officials running the programme.

As we saw in the previous chapter, one of those who volunteered to go was Quốc. I asked him why he had felt the need to move. He made quite a speech in response. He started with three reasons: 'One because the Party and state called; two because of my family economy; three because that was the duty of a citizen of the Vietnamese state'. He paused for a moment, before adding quietly, 'otherwise I would not have volunteered to do this'. There was a short silence before he recovered his momentum. Then he went on to conclude with a neat and patriotic formula, that the purpose of moving was twofold: 'to defend both myself and my fatherland'.

This, at least, I thought was the conclusion. But there was more: 'Uncle [Hồ Chí Minh] taught us that "there is nothing more precious than independence and freedom". The Party applies his teaching, so we must implement it too, following Uncle's call'.† During mobilization sessions back at home in Đông Xá commune, Quốc had evidently received sound teaching on the 'revolutionary meaning' of the migration programme.‡

POLICY AND PEOPLE

Quốc's understanding of the national significance of his decision is a tribute to the mobilization capacity of cadres at Đông Xá. But for people living in Thái Bình, what exactly was the meaning of this policy? Quốc understood it as a double

---

* For closer analysis of the numbers, see the Appendix.

† Quốc moved from Đông Xá (Đông Hưng district, Thái Bình) to Buôn Tría commune (Lak district, Dak Lak) in 1977. Interview (Dak Lak, November 1996).

‡ Phrases like 'revolutionary meaning' and 'revolutionary character' appeared often during the Trực Tâm debate, discussed in Chapter 6. For sources, see note 1.

benefit, for himself and his country. Articles in the Trực Tâm debate, written to explain the policy to the people, explored the relationship between local and national imperatives, couching them in economic and strategic terms.

Economically, the programme eased the pressure of population on the land. Most contributors to the debate pointed to the tight land–population ratio in their village. Thus, at Trường Xuân cooperative: 'the average paddy land area per head is only 1.9 *sào*'. This caused chronic underemployment: 'Labourers only do sixty to seventy days' work at the cooperative, then there's no more work'. Which, in turn, boded ill for the future: 'Living standards improve slowly, or even get worse, as the population increases by forty people every year'.[2] Migration was shown to be in the economic interest of all cooperative members, families staying as well as those going.

Highland development, moreover, was important for the national economy. A Trực Tâm article explained: 'Starting from the aims and meaning of highland economic construction, we made it clear to Party members that land clearance was not only intended to provide rice to eat and work to do, but was a matter of national welfare policy for the whole people'.[3] In the first instance, welfare implied agricultural development. But the production of food was itself necessary, as Hiệp Hòa commune inhabitants were led to understand, for the development of industry.[4]

Strategic and political factors also entered the Trực Tâm debate. At Minh Tân commune, the land–population ratio had been explained. People already recognized the local economic benefits of the programme. But the commune's chairman emphasized that its purpose went beyond both the parochial and, even, the merely economic: 'We tried to ensure that cadres, Party members and people all understood that going to build the highland economy serves the construction of socialism and the struggle for the fatherland's reunification.'[5]

The war with the French had underlined the strategic importance of the highlands. And in the 1960s, Hồ Chí Minh's ability to lead the resistance from his mountain fortress in Định Hóa had not been forgotten. Nor later on, after the war in the south, were the implications lost of the victories at Pleiku and Ban Mê Thuột, which in March 1975 helped open the road to Saigon.* French and American forces, moreover, posed only the most immediate dangers to Vietnam's security. China, to the north, despite a relationship of aid and alliance during the 1950s and 1960s, always posed a potential threat. Memories of 1945–46, when Chinese troops ransacked northern Vietnam on the pretext of disarming the Japanese, had barely faded by 1979, when Chinese troops crossed the border again.[7] And China's close relationship with the Khmer Rouge regime in Cambodia gave incidents along Vietnam's southern border a more menacing meaning. Ethnic minorities in border areas, moreover, were not regarded as reliable bulwarks against infiltration from

---

*   This was explained in a study of the border village new economic zone Tân Đông (Tân Châu district, Tây Ninh). For sources, see note 6. For an impression of the distribution of new economic zones throughout Vietnam, see Map 16.

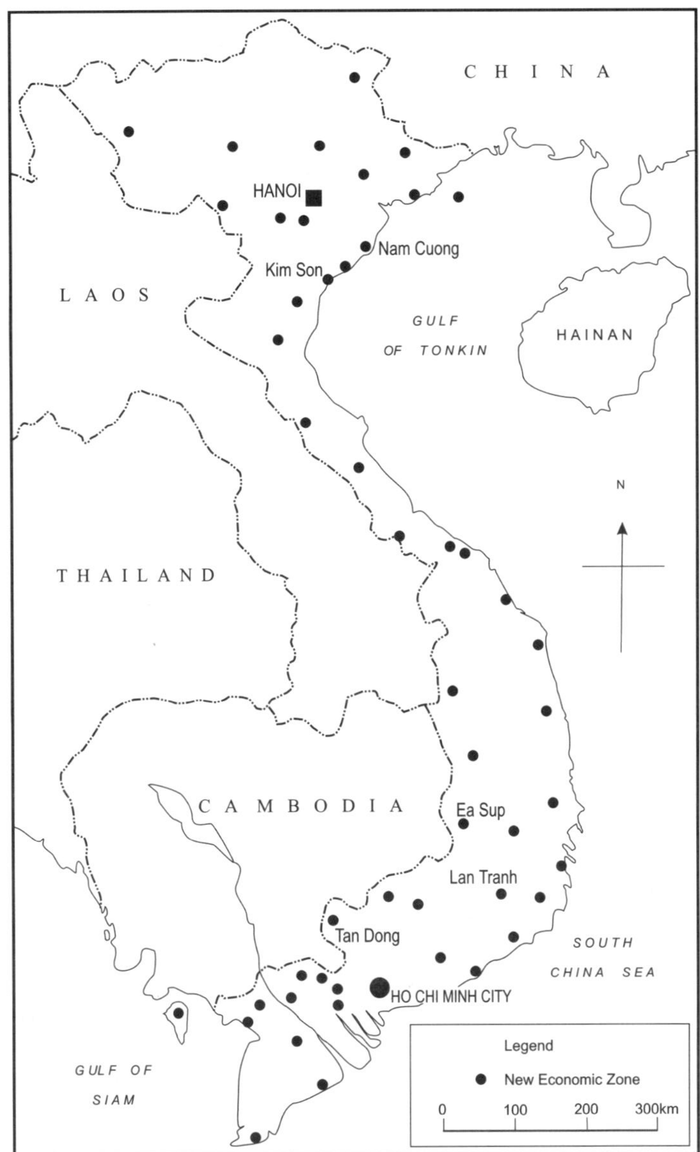

Map 16: Number of new economic zones, 1995

New economic zones were established throughout Vietnam. The following appear in the text: Kim Sơn district on land reclaimed from the sea in Ninh Bình; Nam Cường commune on land reclaimed from the sea in Thái Bình; Ea Súp commune, on the Cambodian border in the central highlands province of Dak Lak; Lán Tranh, in the new economic zone district of Lâm Hà, in the province of Lâm Đồng; Tân Đông commune, on the Cambodian border in Tây Ninh.

Source: 'Một số vùng kinh tế mới đã định hình và phát triển', QĐND, 4 July 1995, p. 3. Redrawn by Lee Li Kheng.

abroad, quite the contrary. The Việt Minh's own seizure of power in 1945, with the help of highlanders in the Việt Bắc region, underlined this. So did the subsequent opposition of groups like the Nùng during and after the war with the French.[8] Quốc was not alone in understanding that the defence of the fatherland required his presence, and that of other Việt people, in the highlands.[9]

The military importance of settlers would have been clear to readers of *Dak Lak* newspaper in January 1978. A 'young people's regiment from Thái Bình', comprising 800 men and women, was described as participating in economic construction in the border area. 'Along with their production work, the regiment has organized and reinforced self-defence teams, increased the number of patrols and the level of security; in coordination with the commune of Ea Súp (Ea Súp district), they fight when necessary, to protect the borders of the Fatherland.' The border in question was that with Cambodia, and a photograph published later that year gave some indication of the need for increased security. A small arsenal captured from invading Khmer Rouge troops was pictured with the modest caption: 'War booty recovered'.

Threats to security, moreover, did not always come from abroad. In 1978, *Dak Lak* reported victories against internal enemies:

> Village militia and self-defence teams often go on patrol and pursue gangs of reactionaries. Since the beginning of the year, they have chased the enemy out into the forest seventy-four times, meeting the enemy fourteen times, killing seventeen, capturing eight, recovering thirty-four guns of all kinds and other important materials.[10]

This action took place in Krông Buk district, not far from Tam Giang commune. Settlers at Tam Giang were not involved in this fighting. The commune was set up in the same month as this article was published. They too set up their own militia and self-defence teams. I did not like to ask about security matters there, however. Some of Tam Giang's settlers had fought for the opposing regime before 1975. They too had been 'reactionaries'. I felt more comfortable discussing the forest and asked whether people found it frightening when they first arrived. One man was emphatic: 'The forest wasn't frightening – the snakes were afraid of us! But we were afraid of malaria, and the FULRO'. Minority insurgents were active nearby, and nearly as deadly as the mosquitoes. Another settler remarked: 'The local security situation did not allow us to leave the village for long periods or travel around a lot'.[11]

Settlers were frightened of insurgents but also posed a threat to them. A central government report later praised their contribution to internal security: 'The people who came to build new economic zones in the central highlands helped, along with compatriots of all ethnic groups, to drive back the activities of the FULRO gang in many areas, creating regions of political stability'. Referring to the invasion of the 'Chinese reactionary gang and their lackeys' in Cambodia, the same report added: 'because of this, the organization and mobilization of people to move and open up agricultural and forestry land over the last five years has a very deep meaning, not only in economic terms but also in terms of politics, society and defence'.[12]

POLICY AND CADRES

People understood the policy in terms of two complementary sets of interests: personal and collective, economic and strategic. They may or may not have acted on these understandings, though in Quốc's case they featured in later self-justifications, which may have been important in his decision not to abandon the settlement. And if these understandings were important for the people, they were doubly so for their leaders. Cadres were expected to have a clear grasp of the 'revolutionary meaning' of the policy, to convince both themselves and everyone else of the importance of what they were doing. This was, of course, particularly true for those accompanying settlers to new economic zones.

Some cadres needed no convincing. Dũng, who left Nam Định province for the district of Mai Châu in 1963, was one of these. He barely paused for breath when he explained to me what the programme was for. It was clearly not the first time he had made this speech:

> The Party and state had a policy to implement the Third [Party Congress] resolution, providing for the harmonization of manpower, the redistribution of the labour force, the reinforcement of the revolutionary base, the reinforcement of national defence, the successful construction of socialism in the North, to create a firm basis for the struggle to reunify the country.[13]

Dũng had a firm grasp on 'revolutionary meaning'.[14] But how far were cadres convinced by the rhetoric they repeated? While in 1964 the Thái Bình newspaper told readers that the land–population ratio 'made the Thái Bình campaign leaders think a great deal', it published few indications of open policy debate.[15] Debate of the Trực Tâm variety was about the implementation rather the content of the policy. At this time, the threat of war and the context of socialist construction must have focused doubts on the policy's immediate consequences, for the individual cadre as well as the community, rather than its intentions. Down in the plains, indeed, it must have been hard to voice counter-arguments to the prevailing discourse on the highlands, eloquently expressed in the following passage:

> In the North, the highlands are the rearguard resistance base. They make up two-thirds of the land area of the North, contain abundant natural resources, and represent a safe rearguard zone in which the development of agriculture and the construction of industry may be continued. Thus, now more than ever before, efforts must be concentrated on the development of the highland economy, especially highland agriculture. Only that way will the highlands be able to provide for its own cereals and other needs, without depending on the lowlands. Only that way will the highlands achieve economic prosperity, political stability, defensive strength and reinforcement, and turn into a truly solid resistance base, ready to face any wartime trick from the American imperialists. Only that way will the highland economy be strong enough to supplement the lowlands, allowing each ethnic group to make its own appropriate contribution to the revolution of the people of the whole country.[16]

In this account of highland development, the participation of lowland people was an essential condition.[17] The condition did not, however, go without saying.

The text directly addressed concerns of ethnic minorities who 'do not want to accept lowland compatriots' into their cooperatives, offering both local and collective reasons for reassurance. Lowlanders, apparently, would contribute to the 'particular interest of every ethnic group in the highlands, as well as the general interest of the revolution'. Highland cooperatives, apparently, would be unable to fulfil production and development targets without their labour. It is unlikely that all the ethnic minorities were reassured. But the message was, at least, accepted by regional leaders. Indeed, Cầm Liên, a member of the Thái Mèo (Tây Bắc) Autonomous Zone Executive Committee, displayed considerable enthusiasm about it on an official visit to Thái Bình in 1961.[18] In his arrival speech he waxed lyrical about the future of Thái Bình–Tây Bắc relations:

> Though this is the first time we have been to the lowland part of our fatherland, we regard it as our own family. Tây Bắc–Thái Bình fought hand in hand to liberate our beloved North, and are struggling now to secure the country's reunification. Tây Bắc–Thái Bình are also struggling together for a new happy and prosperous life. Tây Bắc is an vast area of our fatherland, and is waiting for Thái Bình's courageous hands to come and clear it. With the strength of Thái Bình and Tây Bắc we are determined to win victory over nature, to produce large quantities of white rice and fresh vegetables,[*] to raise the standard of living and enrich the whole country.

Cầm Liên's visit was celebrated in the provincial newspaper. The journalist covering it commented astutely that his 'speech was short, but its meaning was long'. For a reporter in Thái Bình, writing in 1961 at the very beginning of the programme, it must have been difficult indeed to resist the ideals of a 'tomorrow, [in which] Tây Bắc's forested hills and grassy expanses will be flattened and immense fields of rice, fields of corn will be opened up'.[19]

This of course was one side of the coin. The other was noted in 1959 by the Minister of Labour, who focused on the economic needs of the Red River Delta.

> In the delta today there is a shortage of land for cultivation, and the labour force is too abundant. The population increases every year. According to documents from the Central Rural Affairs Committee, in the coming five-year plan, in order to improve the welfare of the people and develop the economy, it will be necessary to organize the migration of over 1.5 million people to go up to new economic zones.

Migration to the highlands was important for the future development of the plains.

It was easy to talk big about the future – less so, the past. After twenty years of implementation, the new economic zones programme received the attention of a more down-to-earth newsman. Lê Khánh introduced an account of the policy's vicissitudes with a comment on what he called the 'curiosity' of journalists in the capital: 'From Hanoi, there comes the sound of many different bells, the majority of them sing [the policy's] praises, seeing it as the appearance of a flower, full of

---

* These types of farm produce are associated with Việt people. Interviews (Hòa Bình, October 1995).

fragrance and colour. So what is the truth?' Lê Khánh did not elaborate directly on other, less laudative points of view. But he went on report a fascinating interview with a migration official in Hanoi, during which he brought up the policy's past record.

> When he gave us an outline of the current new economic zones in Lâm Đồng, comrade Trần Duy Dương, Vice Chairman of the city's People's Committee, did not once bring up the past. I was curious to know more, so I asked: 'Compared with the organization of migration in the past, what new noteworthy aspects does the plan to build new economic areas in Lâm Đồng contain?'
>
> Sitting and listening attentively, Mr Dương's face showed clearly that he took no pleasure in this question. I suddenly realized how tactless I was, how lacking in delicacy. Normally in a situation like this, one ought not to put him in an embarrassing position, especially with respect to comparisons. The previous plan was someone else's responsibility, even though the leadership community had approved it. But just a moment later, he returned to his cheerful and flexible manner, smiling sympathetically: 'I will tell you our way of thinking in this matter, so you can understand clearly'. Then with a very open tone of voice, he spoke as though telling a confidence (…)[20]

Trần Duy Dương confided the policy at some length. He told how it reversed the normal 'laws of migration' by which people move to seek an easier life. The purpose of building new economic zones, he explained, was 'different from that of spontaneous migrants. It is the redistribution of labour around the country to be carried out in every locality, combining the needs of society with the voluntary decisions of each family'. He was aware that 'there are people who disparage us for formalism and not concentrating on getting down to producing', adding that 'that is a point of view'. But his opinion remained that as long as the 'state and people see to it together', the new economic zones policy would 'create areas with a varied and abundant economic life, and a bright and developing social life'.[21]

The early 1980s, when this interview took place, were a time of difficulty for the migration programme. People throughout the highlands were abandoning their settlements. In a situation of national economic crisis, both the budget, targets and journey distance for migration were revised downwards. Administrative confidence in the policy was low and there is evidence of a debate about its future.[22] Trần Duy Dương was in no position to entertain direct criticisms. Doubts about the policy, such as Lê Khánh's, could only be voiced obliquely. But changes in the economic system, recognized in 1986 under the slogan 'renovation' (Đổi Mới), created a new space within which officials could reappraise their attitude to the past. In a 1995 interview with a Vietnamese journalist, Hoàng Đông, director of the department responsible for new economic zones, spoke of debate within the government on 'renovation in the way of doing migration', and singled out education, health and transportation as areas for improvement.[23] And in a 1996 interview with a foreign researcher, officials at the People's Committee in Thái Bình were similarly frank. They acknowledged that, before the 1980s, migration had been a matter of 'taking the children and abandoning them in the market', by which they meant there had been no infrastructural support, 'no clinics, no schools, no roads, just clearing land'. They then contrasted this unhappy but former situation with the current reality. Migration since 1989 had been managed with more success.[24]

In their conversations with me, officials in Thái Bình talked mostly about policy implementation. Few questioned the actual aims of the programme, although I overheard their colleagues, during lunch at the cadres' canteen, discuss them with some animation. Nor was controversy limited to Thái Bình. The purpose of the programme underwent discussion in Hanoi too, as the following comment from a Labour Ministry leader illustrated: 'There was a time, even up to the present, when managers and researchers in different fields, in evaluating organized migration during the period 1961–91, were not united in their point of view, and even held opposite ideas'.[25] Forest destruction and environmental impact were particular concerns of central government officials I spoke to in 1995–97. Their concerns mirrored those of officials in destination provinces. In Dak Lak I heard frequent complaints about the cost of settlers – to the environment and to the provincial budget. Settlers, however, continued to be recruited. The administrative momentum remained. The programme was maintained.

By the late 1990s, however, the policy was becoming an issue of increasing irrelevance. Organized migration was no longer the main motor of highland settlement at all. The crux had become free migration, by which vast numbers of people had been, for ten years or more, moving to the central highlands without reference to the government. Debate and controversy within the leadership found a new and urgent focus on the relationship between free and organized migration. They faced the difficult task of bringing free migrants under government supervision.

This question was the subject of two conferences in early 1998 organized jointly by the UNDP, the Population Council and Vietnam's Ministry of Agriculture and Rural Development. The conferences – a national one in February to stimulate debate and an international one in May to learn from neighbouring countries' experiences – were intended to influence future migration policy. Their results were later to be submitted to the National Assembly. This was first occasion for international debate on migration policy in Vietnam, and was a historical event in itself. A central government official set the tone at the May conference, which I attended, with a formal request for opinions on how to organize migration in Vietnam 'in a good and rational way'.

Discussion at the conference was lively. One Vietnamese participant suggested that Dak Lak province no longer needed in-migrants, who damaged the environment and destroyed the forest, and that the programme needed a rethink. A young American aid worker wanted it stopped immediately. Dak Lak's Vice President, resigned to receiving further settlers, asked for increased funding to cope with them. A Vietnamese participant called for a new policy; 'a policy to promote development, a policy to prevent destruction'. This contribution eloquently described the atmosphere of research and reorientation among those managing migration which emerged during the conference. Officials appeared to be seeking a way forward,

a way commensurate with old priorities of highland settlement, the newer imperatives of environmental protection, and above all the desire to bring free migration
under closer administrative supervision. The central government official's reaction
to most issues was to call for more discussion.

There remained, of course, clear limits to the discussion, as this official's call
signified. These were most in evidence around the underlying aims of migration
policy. To a question from British academic Ronald Skeldon about the political
and strategic purposes of the migration programme, the official replied that 'it
seems that some of our foreign friends have not yet understood clearly'. He went
on to say that the programme existed to help poor people in the plains and raise
the living standards of minorities in the highlands. If the rationale for migration
policy were in reality restricted to economic and philanthropic issues, then
Skeldon might not be alone among Vietnam's confused foreign friends. But the
limits, such as those described here, did not spoil the discussion.

POLICY AND POLICY STATEMENTS

The people understood this policy as a single stone intended to kill the two birds
of economic development and national defence. Cadres, at different levels of the
administration, implemented these aims with varying levels of conviction. As we
saw in previous chapters, much policy took shape as it was put into practice. But
it is worth examining actual statements of policy – legislation and commentary
on it – for what they can tell us about its aims, values and evolution.

After our analysis of migration practice, legislative statements of policy aims
hold few surprises. The 'clearing the wilderness' programme was launched at the
Third Party Congress in 1960. In his speech, Lê Duẩn made reference to the
contribution of migration to economic development and national defence. He
voiced the principle that the Party and state 'should help the highlands catch up
with the plains, the highlands and border areas catch up with the heartlands, the
ethnic minorities catch up with the Việt, aiding each ethnic group to develop its
revolutionary spirit and its great capability, so as together in close solidarity to
make progress on the road to socialism'.[26] He had not tired of these principles
fifteen years later. In his speech to the Fourth Party Congress, in 1976, the same
goals were reiterated: 'The construction of the country must go together with the
protection of the country, these are the survival requirements of the nation'.[27]
The goals remained unchanged. Their implementation, indeed, was stepped up,
as Phạm Văn Đồng noted: 'From the beginning of 1977 a redistribution of manpower should be implemented with a scale of four million people in four years,
which will increase in subsequent years'.[28] Little more of concrete interest was said.
Legislated policy aims differed little from the implementation targets received in
instructions by cadres or the 'revolutionary meanings' received in education by
the people.

The programme's origins are less easily discernible, however. Formal policy
statements focused on aims and implementation rather than origins. I had to pick

through some of the more general, and often retrospective official discussions to find clues as to where the policy came from.

In 1991 the policy celebrated its thirtieth anniversary. The Minister of Labour, Trần Đình Hoan, took the opportunity to write the introduction to a commemorative volume. I expected to find some description of the inspiration for the policy and an assessment of its achievements. The article did not disappoint my latter hope, but my curiosity about the policy's origins remained unsatisfied. I had to content myself with some generalized opening remarks, which – in contrast to those of Trần Duy Dương in 1983 – showed no hesitation in drawing comparisons with the past. Recent organized migration was likened to the founding myth of the Vietnamese nation:

> According to the flow of our country's history, we can see that migration has always been linked to the history of building and keeping the country. Migration in history was set under way many generations ago as we know from the legend of Âu Cơ – Lạc Long Quân, who opened up the frontier and first formed our wet rice civilization.[29]

The first sentence here, with its twin formulation of the purpose of migration, gave no cause for surprise. Quốc had told me as much. But its legitimation by Vietnamese legend seemed more unusual. Looking further into the issue, I discovered that Trần Đình Hoan's commemorative remarks reproduced the argument of an earlier and more extensive article. Here he noted that: 'the process of migration in our country has always been linked to the history of the national group's building and keeping of the country, to the history of border defence and the step by step opening up of the border to the south'.[30] He found legitimacy for a nationalist conception for twentieth-century migration not only in the Vietnamese founding myth, but also in their epic settlement of the south.

In the same article Trần Đình Hoan also invoked Marx and Lenin. This also gave no cause for surprise. The language of Marxism-Leninism remained into the 1990s a discourse of legitimation in Vietnam, albeit an increasingly hackneyed one. What was interesting was the flexible way it was worked into the discussion. Lenin, in an unreferenced work, was quoted as having identified a natural law of migration: 'People will move from places with low standards of living to places with a high standard of living'. Trần Đình Hoan pointed out that Vietnam's experience, seen in this light, had 'distinct particularities', by which he meant that Vietnam's experience did not correspond to the law. This perspective was elaborated by another contributor to the same volume, Phạm Đỗ Nhật Tân, who observed that migrants in Vietnam, contrary to Lenin's law, did not initially find higher living standards at their new home. He called for a re-interpretation of the law, which focused on economic factors, to take account of the specific situation in Vietnam:

> In our country, laws of organized agricultural migration have always been closely connected to particularities of a historical nature: the history of building and keeping the country. Consequently the aims of migration do not only follow economic requirements but also bear the imprint of a higher and nobler goal: the interest of building and keeping the country. This is the spirit of patriotism which, together with the spirit

of volunteering to go, has created the conditions for the land clearance and new economic zones programme, to open up the country and defend the borders of socialism.[31]

These references to the founders of socialism and the history of Vietnam were, of course, post factum legitimating discourses. As such they offered little concrete evidence of the origins of the policy. However, in the absence of documentation conclusively outlining a process of policy formulation, I consider such discourses, which provide a basis for speculation, to be of some limited use. In the hope that more detailed sources on this subject will in the future come to light, I suggest that policy on migration to highland areas was inspired by influences from other socialist countries, from history, and from practical challenges of immediate import.

The influence of Soviet bloc aid on 1950s policy in Vietnam has been well documented. In the elaboration of programmes of land reform, industrialization, state-run agriculture and cooperativization, inputs from both the Soviet Union and China were crucial.[32] Soviet and Chinese inputs into development of the Vietnamese highlands are less well known. Contemporary western writers such as Fall failed even to record the existence of the migration policy. Soviet writers such as Mal'khanova, who in 1969 documented the programme in the Soviet journal *Geografiya*, gave no indication of where it came from.[33] Vietnamese policy statements and published sources made scant reference to foreign influence. More recent foreign language studies, such as that of Desbarats, were concerned with effects rather than causes.[34]

The late 1950s was the great period of land clearance in the Soviet Union. In 1954, Khruschev launched his Virgin Land Programme, an ambitious attempt to get migrants to bring into cultivation huge areas of the steppes of central Russia and Kazakhstan.[35] The Chinese leadership, meanwhile, started experimenting with techniques of mass mobilization for the purposes of national development. The best known of these was the Great Leap Forward,* but there was also, from the mid-1950s, a programme of agricultural settlement of frontier areas.[36] Both Soviet and Chinese movements influenced migration policy in Vietnam.

I found no archival evidence of direct Soviet input into Vietnam's land clearance initiatives, with the exception of the state farm policy. The energies created by Khruschev's programme were, however, felt in Hanoi, as in other capitals of the Soviet bloc. Later observers recorded the influence of developments in socialist Europe:

---

* The Great Leap Forward was well known in Vietnam. State farm workers in highland Nghệ An were reported as excited by its initial successes, though doubtless the cadre who described them thus was more excited than they were. He reported that, after the demoralizing events of land reform, 'successive victories in Vietnam and abroad, especially the Chinese people's Great Leap Forward, have had a strong effect on the thinking of workers and cadres at the State Farm, and their thinking as a result is gradually stabilizing'. He made no mention of the effects of the Great Leap Forward's disastrous aftermath. NAV3/CQLNTQD 140(vv), 'Báo cáo tổng hợp tình hình Nông Trường Sông Con', Director, Sông Con State Farm, 23 September 1960.

Clearing the wilderness is one method of using land in a sufficient and rational way. Clearing the wilderness is one of the great projects of socialism. In the Soviet Union today, as during the early years of the collectivization movement, the area of agricultural land collectively farmed has been opened up by 30, 40 and 60 per cent. In 1929–33, using the strength of men, cattle and horses, the Soviet Union brought 11.7 million hectares of new land into production. In 1954–62, the Soviet Union made advances in a great project of clearing the wilderness. (…) In total, during the eight years from 1954–62, the Soviet Union cleared 42 million hectares. After the Second World War, Poland also opened up 5 million hectares in four years. Nowadays and in the near future, clearing the wilderness is a spearhead of agricultural development in our country.[37]

In the case of China, archival sources are clearer, as advisers from over the border offered specific advice to Vietnamese officials on highland settlement and development. Welcoming a delegation visiting Hanoi for this purpose, a Vietnamese official made the following speech:

Nowadays, the Chinese Party is calling people to 'Go to the Highlands' for long-term settlement to exploit highland resources, because the highlands in China are also a revolutionary base, as in Vietnam. As far as we are concerned, highland development is very important in both economic and political terms. If we can develop the hills, our rearguard base will be much strengthened. In Vietnam's highlands there are many rich mines. If we want to develop industry, we also have to rely on the highlands, as indeed in agriculture. The highland people are all minorities. We have to help our brother ethnic groups to open up the highlands. Nowadays, there are many Chinese cadres and party members who have long moved to the highlands to develop production, planting coffee, fruit trees, raising rabbits etc.[38]

I was unable, however, to find direct supporting evidence for a contention that the new economic zone policy was formed and managed with direct Soviet or Chinese support. The most we can say from the documentation currently available is that 'brother countries' were pursuing similar policies on the road to 'socialist construction'.

It is equally, if not more difficult to demonstrate a historical influence on Vietnamese policy-making. The few legislative documents available make no reference to migration policy or practice under the French or the pre-colonial Vietnamese kings. Yet the ambiguous position, in the writings of the DRV as well as in its pantheon of heroes and saints, of a figure like Nguyễn Công Trứ would suggest that the historical lessons of Vietnamese geo-political expansion were by no means lost. An examination of the status of this nineteenth-century mandarin offers us some idea of the historical influences over the decisions of twentieth-century officials. Nguyễn Công Trứ, a mandarin at the emperor Minh Mạng's court, organized the settlement of land reclaimed from the coast of northern Vietnam, creating two new districts: Tiền Hải (Thái Bình) and Kim Sơn (Ninh Bình). In a 1928 account of this land extension programme, written in the centenary year of Tiền Hải's foundation, Lê Thước portrayed Nguyễn Công Trứ in glowing terms:

To my mind, if the then king had known how to employ and respect a man of his capability – controlling the people with law, making plans with method – rather than distrust and hinder him; if he had been left to make land arrangements at his discretion, to organize agriculture at his will, then perhaps not only Tiền Hải and Kim Sơn districts would have been put to the plough, but other land in our country too, places which are still unfarmed, fallow fields, thick forests; our people would no longer have to grow water-ferns and floating flowers as they do now.[39]

Hanoi's later historians were similarly kind to the mandarin. Nguyễn Khắc Đạm, commissioned in 1962 to write a history of organized migration, concluded that 'the land clearance project led by Nguyễn Công Trứ in the coastal region in the past, was for those times a noble project, and as a result many people, including the colonial capitalists, have praised it'. He placed Nguyễn Công Trứ, moreover, in a migration chronology that included the efforts of nineteenth-century French administrators in the Mekong Delta, and culminated with the First Five Year Plan of 1960. This latter was also characterized as a 'noble land clearance plan'. No comment was made on the French.[40] In 1993, Phan Đại Doãn found no reason to disagree with Nguyễn Khắc Đạm's assessment of Nguyễn Công Trứ. The mandarin was characterized as a responsible and caring servant of the feudal court, and contrasted with 'many of his colleagues who only thought of repressing the peasant movement'.[41]

If historians were generous in their judgements, other published sources were more restrained. Official accounts of land reclamation projects showed little interest in historical precedent and passed over the role of Nguyễn Công Trứ. Neither contemporary newspaper articles nor official commemorative literature on the foundation of Nam Cường commune in Tiền Hải, set up in 1960 on land reclaimed from the sea, deemed it necessary to remember the mandarin.[42] A retrospective account of the army's reclamation of agricultural land at Kim Sơn, published by the military authorities, also managed to compile a section on the project's historical background without once mentioning his name.[43] Yet this last book is also significant. Its frontispiece photograph shows a temple to the mandarin's memory.* His presence was acknowledged, if only indirectly. The same situation held true in Hanoi. With a few exceptions, central government policy documents make little mention of Nguyễn Công Trứ in legislation or commentary. But his importance was acknowledged by the nation's leaders in their organization of the city's space. One of Hanoi's main streets is named after him.

Neither Nguyễn Công Trứ's presence in DRV/SRV historiography nor on the streets of Hanoi, give him a role in the formulation of policy. Accounts such as that of Nguyễn Trần Trọng and Nguyễn Đặng Kiêu, which make mention of the mandarin, as well as of land clearance as 'a national policy of strategic significance' for the Lý, Trần, Lê and Tây Sơn rulers of pre-colonial Vietnam,

---

* Cadres in Tiền Hải were keen to show me a similar memorial. The temple, in the middle of a small lake, had recently been restored when I visited in July 1996.

may only be understood in retrospective terms.* The question of historical influence on the actual formation of policy remains open at present, a matter for speculation. If pre-colonial, or indeed French policy did in any way provide concrete models for emulation by those drawing up migration plans in the late 1950s, I have not found the documents that allow us to assess this. The most convincing conclusion may be that of Phạm Đỗ Nhật Tân, for whom the migration programme was implemented without attention to other models from the past or other countries in the region.[44] It is clear that the nature of any emulation was no more than inspirational. The DRV did not follow the example of Indonesia's leaders in Java and Sumatra, who simply picked up the previous regime's transmigration programme and perpetuated it. The poor quality of the French programme and a decade of war ensured a firm rupture. The past was, at most, a point of reference. It was never a model.

IDEALISM AND PRAGMATISM

Historical experience and foreign advice played a part in the formation of DRV migration policy. Their influence, however, was never direct. It was mediated, rather, by application to the particular situation in Vietnam. This created a hybrid and often chaotic process of policy-making, described as 'a characteristic combination of pragmatism and idealism'.[45] This was true of legitimating discourse, as was demonstrated in the rewriting of Lenin's law noted above. It was also true of the formulation and implementation of the migration programme. This was, one analyst reported,

> a system based on bureaucratism and subsidies, where objective laws were replaced by subjective will, by desire with no basis in reality, no analysis, no consideration, no learning from the experience of history or from that of other countries in the region. This reason encompasses and governs all other reasons, giving rise to the very specific nature of migration organized by the Vietnamese state.[46]

The contingency of this system may be seen in the most formal of policy documents. Lê Duẩn, in his 1960 speech – a key statement of DRV policy towards the highlands – characterized relations between the ethnic minorities and the majority Việt people in historical terms:

> In the North of our country there are many ethnic minorities. In the process of history over the several thousands of years, ethnic minorities have shown solidarity with Việt people to struggle against foreign invaders, to build and defend the country. Over the last thirty years, especially during the Second World War and the nine years of resistance war, under the leadership of our Party, the minorities have heroically struggled side by side with Việt people against imperialism, to liberate the country. Today they are

---

*   Out of respect for the politically correct line of the day, this account describes nineteenth- and twentieth-century land clearance initiatives in the Mekong Delta and the highlands without a word on the Nguyễn dynasty. The French appear briefly as 'oppressors'. Nguyễn Trần Trọng and Nguyễn Đặng Kiêu, *Những vấn đề kinh tế chủ yếu*, pp. 18–20.

putting their strength into socialist construction and the struggle for reunification. The minorities have clearly made a worthy contribution to our people's revolution.[47]

History here was tailored to suit circumstances. The story of highlander relations with Việt people passed on many lessons for posterity. In the above account some were selected, others discarded. The selection served to create an idealized image of patriotic minorities, an ideal which suited a highly practical purpose. The circumstances that determined this choice were those of Vietnam's particular historical situation. As Fall observed, with the notable exception of the Long March, communists in China never had to rely on the goodwill of non-Han peoples as the Việt Minh had to rely on the ethnic minorities.[48]

Vietnam's historical situation also shaped and transformed policy imported from abroad. Fforde demonstrated that, in the years after Điện Biên Phủ, the implementability of the ideals of socialist construction was limited by a variety of social, economic and historical factors. He described the tensions this gave rise to:

> After 1954–55 the post-independence DRV government adopted essentially foreign institutional forms (…) [which] did not, in practice, provide a strict guide to the realities of Vietnamese socialism, for those controlling the DRV's leading institutions naturally operated both in and through the existing society and economy of North Vietnam. Strong constraints operated to limit the possibilities for Socialist Transformation and Socialist Construction along the lines prescribed, which stressed the extraction of surplus from agriculture and the rapid creation of an industrial base. Consequently, local interests routinely adapted socialist institutions. This meant that for many years the Party's public pronouncements about social and economic development could not begin to reflect day-to-day reality, and Party theoreticians had to cope with the massive non-implementability of the Party Line, which was, on the contrary, deemed to be both correct and realisable. This resulted in a characteristic combination of pragmatism and idealism.[49]

Migration policy imported from Soviet bloc countries was similarly adapted to Vietnamese circumstances. In 1960, the programme to clear uncultivated areas in the highlands was an extension of earlier moves to bring abandoned land back into agriculture – land in both the highlands and the northern deltas abandoned by French planters in 1945, by refugees from the war in 1946–54 and people moving south at Vietnam's partition in 1954–55.[50] Beyond these problems, the policy also responded to the demographic problem in the northern delta and the political and strategic concerns we have already noted.

These goals were addressed with a combination of idealistic discourse and pragmatic implementation. The following passage, for example, was published in *Tiến Lên* to launch the Trực Tâm debate.

> This mobilization project has an important meaning in many respects. It will contribute to the construction of a material and technological base for socialism, to the balanced development of the people's economy, to the utilization of the multiple potential of the highlands, increasing the economic strength of the entire country, improving the living conditions of the people both in the highlands and the lowlands, ensuring that brother ethnic groups are able to make the most of their revolutionary spirit and creative cap-

ability; pooling our strength in the construction of socialism will enable us to implement ethnic solidarity and equality. This mobilization project will provide political and social bases for rapid highland development, contributing to the implementation of the reinforcement of defence, the reinforcement of the revolutionary base, increasing the protection of political order and the protection of the border.[51]

The language of this statement was that of universally applicable socialist construction. The programme, however, remained a pragmatic adaptation to the situation in Vietnam.

The same tension between idealism and pragmatism was apparent in the policy's evolution. The Minister of Labour, in a retrospective analysis of migration practice, divided this evolution into three periods, summarized below.

1961–75: Most people moved to the northern highlands, according to the formula 'mainly rely on the cooperatives' strength, with help from the state'.

1976–80: The same principle applied, but the main migrations were north to south and urban to rural; people moved in large groups (to cooperatives or state farms); but results were not commensurate with expectations or investment.

1981–90: Policy changed direction and its implementation slowed down; most movement took place in-province, rather than over long distances; a proportion of migrants moved as families rather than in larger social units.[52]

We might add a fourth period to his analysis, 1990–98, during which methods of implementation again shifted significantly, becoming characterized by increased capital investment and greater emphasis on the movement of individual families rather than large groups. The key turning points were not reunification, which essentially saw a reorientation of DRV policies towards the south, or the announcement of the Đổi Mới reforms in 1986. They were, instead, 1980 and 1990, when the programme's results were perceived as failing to correspond to the investment made. In 1980, in the context of generalized economic crisis, the significance of large numbers of abandonments – of people voting with their feet – was recognized. In 1990, in the context of generalized economic reforms, a government decision announced the 'renovation in the way of doing and organizing agricultural migration'.[53]

This periodization was recognized by officials lower down the administrative hierarchy. A cadre at the People's Committee in Đông Hưng district gave me an account of the history of migration policy. For him, 1979 and 1988 were the key turning points. From 1960 to 1979, the example of cadres was used to 'build a campaign to move people to those areas'. After 1979, economic arguments were used in the persuasion process. After 1988, 'there was a policy to set up facilities: roads for communication; infrastructural development for the people; the resolution of economic problems'. Đổi Mới impacted directly on the implementation of the policy at the local level.[54]

The evolution of migration policy thus corresponds to changes in the economic sphere. But throughout the period, the policy itself was regarded as basically correct, if not by all those implementing it, at least by enough members of the 'leadership community' to ensure its continued implementation.[55] Even after 1990, its aims remained unchallenged. In the context of an idealized and voluntaristic policy framework, implementation responded pragmatically to situations at the local level. This phenomenon was described in the preceding chapters, where provinces, districts, communes and cooperatives received plans and targets to fulfil, but few specific instructions as to how to do so. Implementation took place in an environment of local administrative bricolage, of managed chaos. In times of crisis – and the key moments in the process of transition to the market economy were indeed 1980 and 1990 – chaos prevailed over command. The programme in its contemporaneous form became unimplementable. Reforms were inevitable.

Reforms in 1980 and 1990 aimed at improving the practical implementability of the policy. Policy aims remained the same. Implementation was reoriented on both occasions towards a system placing greater emphasis on investment in destination areas and the creation of regional development projects.[56] The point was to set up areas of socio-economic development which would attract people to move on the basis of their family economy. Elements of persuasion based on patriotic motivation, cadre emulation and belief in the Party became significantly less important. Migration was no longer managed by means of mobilization; indeed a cadre at Đông Xá commune remarked to me in 1997 that 'if we mobilized people now, no one would want to go'.[57] This was not a sudden change, but emerged out of the interrelation of policy and practice dating from the early 1980s, when families were encouraged to join relatives or friends in existing highland cooperatives.[58] As I was informed by a cadre at the People's Committee in Đông Hưng district; since the 1980s cadres 'persuaded people that conditions for economic development and enrichment were more difficult in Đông Hưng. Aware of this, the people volunteered to leave. We organized their migration in conjunction with policies of stimulating the economy'. The perception of new economic zone settlers as motivated by patriotic idealism and fundamentally different from free migrants (expressed, for example, by Trần Duy Dương at the People's Committee in Hanoi) was gradually abandoned.

This process of gradual change found its first formal expression in the migration conferences of 1998. By this time, organized migration had come increasingly to resemble free migration. Delegates recommended the abolition of a policy distinction between organized and free migrants. They proposed that the role of government should be reoriented from that of developing land and organizing migration to a role of facilitating free migration. The provision of necessary infrastructure and administration would then ensure the governability of communities of free migrants.[59] This implied the direction of state funding towards the development of roads, markets, schools and health centres in highland project zones. These zones would act to attract migrants who would otherwise fell the forest or dispossess ethnic minorities of their land. Those who wished to move there would make their own arrangements for travel, initial subsistence, etc. The state would thus have the benefit of projects it was able to govern and tax, peopled by families with their own capital endowment and a strong will to settle. From the state's point of view, the negative consequences of unsupervised free migration would also be avoided.

These recommendations, themselves a pragmatic state response to individual peasant decisions, were made for presentation to the National Assembly in June 1998. They have not yet been ratified, and subsequent research suggested that the old programme remained alive and well.[*] In the event that the changes are approved and traditional forms of organized migration are abandoned, will the tension between idealism and pragmatism dissolve into pure pragmatism?

ACHIEVEMENTS AND COSTS

We have examined perceptions of policy by migrants and cadres, as well as its aims, origins and the history of its evolution. In conclusion to this chapter, let us reflect in a more general sense on the achievements of organized migration under the DRV and SRV. These achievements may, in particular, be compared with the results of migration policy during the first half of the century. If we can generalize this comparison in terms of colonial failure and communist success, we should ask the following questions. What does this comparison imply? How far does it hold? What were the limits and costs of this success?

As we saw at the end of Chapter 4, Vũ Đình Hòe published an article on migration in 1945. I found no evidence that either Vũ Đình Hòe or his proposals had a direct influence on subsequent policy formation. But we can measure the results of that policy with his tools. Basing his programme on a criticism of French-organized migration, he insisted on strong state involvement at all stages – recruitment, preparation, settlement, production. He insisted also on a redirection of investment from individuals into organization. Let us examine these two spheres in turn.

State organization after 1954 enjoyed considerable superiority over the colonial administration. The history of migration policy and practice clearly highlights the fact that the independent Vietnamese state was better able to organize than its colonial predecessor. In particular, it enjoyed crucial advantages in terms of technology and legitimacy.

Key technological advances, many of them imported from abroad, were in place by 1960. Despite French attempts to identify and fix villagers by means of tax and ID cards, they had no tool comparable to the *hộ khẩu* system and the state supply economy. These regimes were undoubtedly inefficient in economic terms. But with the enforcement of a link between place of residence and source of income, they provided an administrative foundation to organized migration. Policy-makers were able to go against the grain of Lenin's 'law', by which people move to eco-

---

[*]   In March 1999, authorities in Quảng Xương district (Thanh Hóa) recruited eighty fishing families to set up a new economic zone on Cô Tô, an island off Haiphong which lost most of its population as boat people. Interview (Thanh Hóa, September 1999); UNHCR, 'Insight into the Return of the "Boat People": UNHCR's monitoring experience in Vietnam, 1989–98', Hanoi: UNHCR, 1998, p. 22.

nomically advantageous areas, allowing the transformation of short-run advantageous areas (home villages) into relatively disadvantageous ones. Bình was one of many to find out that, without the economic benefits provided by household registration, it was hard to make a living back at home. With its complementary regimes of household registration and neo-Stalinist economy, the DRV succeeded in fulfilling one of Vũ Đình Hòe's conditions for policy success: '[Settlers] should go *for good*. They must not be allowed to think that they are there temporarily, that if they don't like it, they can go back. In this way they will get down to work and settle.' *

Imported technology was also crucial in the control of malaria. Here, again, the DRV enjoyed superior technology. The application in the 1950s and 1960s of methods of fighting the disease drawn from experience during the war of resistance, the use of DDT and the migration programme itself allowed the authorities to bring the disease under control in many parts of the north. Reunification in 1975 unfortunately reversed these achievements. Soldiers returning north from the central highlands brought plasmodium parasites with them, which once again became endemic among the non-migrant population. International setbacks in the effectiveness of anti-malaria technology made a repeat of the 1950s campaign against the disease impossible. In the future, this situation may, ironically, necessitate a return to artisanal methods of prevention learnt during the resistance war, and even colonial-era environmental methods of malaria control.[60] As Vũ Đình Hòe put it: 'Malaria is the major hindrance – we can say the enemy number one – to land clearance'.[61] This hindrance was, at a crucial moment in the process of highland settlement, removed by the DRV.

A further element of DRV/SRV organizational superiority was its capacity for mobilization. The process of persuasion whereby cadres explained to peasants their needs before presenting the solution was, when it worked properly, a highly effective one. This, moreover, was not simply an achievement of administrative technology. Psychological factors were of tremendous importance in mobilization, particularly the confidence of the people in their leaders.[62] As observed in Chapter 6, stock phrases along the lines of 'Hồ Chí Minh called and I followed' cannot be dismissed as mere propaganda. These phrases had psychological and administrative power. In a climate of confidence – nurtured by the Party but founded in the legitimacy created by the revolution of August 1945 and in memories of famine and war – those who resented the policy were encouraged, like Hùng, to keep their doubts to themselves. Others followed the example of Hùng's neighbour, trusting in the Party's leadership, hoping things would turn out right. As Vũ Đình Hòe suggested: 'The work of mobilizing and encouraging people should make them go with happiness and high hopes. The principle is to use state authority to take the place of personal discretion.'[63]

---

* In this section, quotations from Vũ Đình Hòe's 1945 article are reproduced from the discussion in Chapter 4, and unless otherwise noted were referenced there.

This environment of confidence contrasted vividly with the situation under colonial rule. The Résident of Nam Định reported, in 1908, that: 'There is a rumour running already that, under the guise of a colonisation œuvre, we wish, in reality, to reduce the population of Tonkin so as to be stronger ourselves and meet less resistance on the day of reckoning'.[64] The rumour was doubtless still running in 1941 when a report to the Indochina Federal Council made the following dismal observation:

> Among the most direct causes of the overpopulation of Tonkin and North-Annam, we must mention the manifest repugnance of the Vietnamese to go far from their village. This suspicion, it must be said, manifests itself much more with regard to administrative recruitment than to private recruitment.[65]

When they heard propositions for migration, Vietnamese peasants were quite clearly not prepared to believe that their colonial rulers had their best interests in mind. Under the leadership of the Party, however, people allowed themselves to be persuaded to make short-term sacrifices for what they could believe was a long-term good.*

Animating technological and psychological factors in DRV and SRV policy was the will to succeed. This too was identified by Vũ Đình Hòe, in his analysis of the failure of colonial policy. The French administration lacked determination in the organization of highland settlement. Energetic officials like Lionel Lotzer in Nam Định and Alfred Echinard in Thái Nguyên were the exception rather than the rule. Contradictions between branches of the administration detracted from the realization of any significant project.[66] Such contradictions did not affect the implementation of DRV/SRV policy, which was above all characterized by its determination.

In Vũ Đình Hòe's analysis, however, determination was not sufficient in itself. The migration programme should be well funded, and that funding should be well directed. Here subsequent policy failed to meet his standards. What little capital was available was spent on the subsistence needs of settler families during the first few months in the highlands. Investment in infrastructure and long term development was neglected. Vũ Đình Hòe predicted the likely consequences of this shortcoming in his discussion of the importance of government authority:

> The main thing is to use this authority to prepare carefully, so that settlers do not go down with malaria, to ensure that they can make enough to eat, and to cater for any emergencies. If this is not done, but people are nevertheless forced to stay, then they've been pushed up, nothing less.

---

* By the 1990s this 'revolutionary spirit' seemed a thing of the past. One of my friends in Hanoi, who grew up during the war, indicated as much when she pointed to her 20-something-year-old children during a conversation in December 1995: 'this is not a generation for making sacrifices'.

In reality, as we have seen, large numbers of settlers abandoned the highlands. Among those who stayed, I heard no one say anything about being 'pushed'. There were ambiguous comments containing the word 'obliged', but the ambiguity turned around the fact that their economic situation – or the economic system – obliged them to leave. Clearer complaints were more often couched in terms of 'taking the children and abandoning them in the market'. This amounted to failures of investment in the destination area. There were insufficient resources. Limited funding was not always spent in the most efficient way.

This understanding highlights the limitations of the policy. In 1954 the DRV leadership inherited a country that enjoyed 'relatively low levels of actual and potential economic surplus', and attempted 'by using apparently proven neo-Stalinist institutions, to extract resources from the economy'.[67] The migration programme was integrated into this strategy. It was not only launched to deal with overpopulation and national defence, but was part and parcel of a development drive. Resources were not only unavailable, but the programme was intended to create them. People, of which there was no shortage, were the main strength in this strategy for economic growth, its main raw material. A slogan published in the late 1970s expressed this vividly: 'With the strength of the people, even stones turn into rice'.[68] The policy was thus constrained by what the people – even people fired up with determination to build and keep their country – could achieve.

With such raw materials, the policy's first costs were, of course, human. The above slogan was, indeed, written in recognition of this. Referring to the settlement of 3,000 families from the north on virgin land in the south, the writer pointed out:

> Everyone knows very clearly that life at the beginning will undoubtedly be full of terrible hardship and exhaustion; but because of our revered and beloved Party's call and for the future of the Fatherland and their own and their children's splendid happiness, precious people and communities have decided to use determination to overcome the difficulties, to fulfil for everyone [the ideal that]: 'with the strength of the people, even stones turn into rice'. Many examples of victory over difficulty, of endurance, have contributed to production and construction, allowing the dignified, beautiful and rapid establishment of sources of agricultural produce, which are not only enough to supply people's own needs but are beginning to become agricultural commodities for tax payment or sale to the State.

For some people who moved to the highlands, many of whom I met during my field trips, these costs were short-lived. After some years they observed that they lived better than their relatives in the plains. Some complained that the opposite was the case. And there were, of course, others who did not wait for the stones to turn into rice. These people were more difficult to meet, having left the highlands and moved on. Costs to them were far higher, and correspondingly difficult to quantify.

The other major cost was on the 'stones' in this metaphor – the environment. It is not possible here to carry out exhaustive analysis of the environmental impact of highland settlement. But the effects of the clearing of land are illustrative. Emphasis on meeting targets for forest clearance, and a corresponding neglect of cultivation, caused forest destruction and soil degradation.[69] Where land was cultivated, unsuitable crop choice, an emphasis on cereals and the preference for rice caused further damage.[70] This contributed to the extension of areas of barren land and 'bald hills'. As one 1989 report observed, 'The need to solve the question of cereals at any price led to weighty consequences for the destruction of the environment and ecology, thus limiting, often very greatly, the northern highlands' strengths in forest and industrial crops, livestock and water sources.'[71] The influx of Việt people to the northern highlands in the 1960s, where land suitable for agriculture was limited, created great pressure of population.[72]

Among those moving to the central highlands in recent years were both Việt from the delta and minority inhabitants from the northern highlands. Both groups were suffering from a shortage of cultivable land. In the central highlands, moreover, no local's observation could sum up the cost of migration to the highland eco-system better than that made by a district cadre in Krông Nô, a 40-year-old Ede man. In the context of a discussion about the settlers, he pointed out to me that previously, 'the rainy season was six months, now it's shorter, it's only three'. His sense of time was challenged by Việt farmers I met elsewhere, who said that the wet season was only a month shorter than in the past. But all agreed that the climatic change was due to forest loss. We may greet these conclusions with scepticism. But, in the Krông Nô district office that day, no one disagreed with that cadre's judgement, made in specific reference to free migration, that 'there's only one way to protect the forest, and that is stop the people coming'. His colleague added simply, 'Of course, there's no way to stop people coming'.[73] As we saw earlier in this chapter, even the Vice President of the province had to accept this reality: 'Like it or not, we will certainly continue to receive settlers in the province of Dak Lak'.

This last remark points to a further consequence – and cost – of the migration policy. The settlement of large numbers of Việt people in the highlands and the process of economic reform created, by the mid 1980s, the social and administrative basis for a large-scale movement of free migration. This had been an intention of the makers of French migration policy – to set up an initial 'kernel of attraction' which would create an influx of other settlers.[74] The French failed in this purpose. The fact that by the 1990s the authorities were unable to control the influx of free migrants is an indication of the importance of the achievements of policy since the 1960s. With the institution of free market refoms, the central highlands became Vietnam's latest agricultural frontier, with all the chaos that that implied.

This was one of the major costs of the policy – the emergence in the hills of an uncontrolled movement of population of vast economic, social and environmental importance. The 'kernel' had been created, and over it the government enjoyed increasingly limited regulatory power. The migration policy was, in this respect, overwhelmed by its own achievements.

Conclusion

We saw in the preceding chapters how the highlands were settled under a policy of migration organized by the Vietnamese state. We noted that there was, by contrast to the colonial period, considerably more practice of migration than policy. Policy took the form of general guidelines for flexible implementation and quantitative target fulfilment.

In the present chapter we explored the rationale for the policy. This was a programme which aimed to kill two birds with one stone, resolving the problem of land shortage in the delta at the same time as reinforcing national defence in the strategically important highlands. The policy drew inspiration from the experiences of China and the Soviet Union and from the lessons of Vietnam's precolonial past. It represented a rupture with policy during the French period, which aimed only at the first of these two imperatives and conflicted with the colonial state's main security interest, which was internal.

Where the French administration failed, the government of the DRV/SRV succeeded. Policy success brought with it unforeseen costs, in both human and environmental terms. But the most unexpected cost of all was the creation, with the changes in the economic system of the 1980s, of a practice of free migration to the central highlands. The actions of free settlers became, by the 1990s, the major factor in the development of Vietnam's highland areas. The state, indeed, found itself in a new situation, tailoring policy to migration practice, rather than putting migration policy into practice. The emergence of this situation is the subject of the coming chapter.

Notes

1   Trực Tâm, 'Ra sức vận động nhân dân đi xây dựng kinh tế miền núi như HTX Trực Tâm', *Tiến Lên*, 25 February 1964, pp. 1, 4; Nguyễn Văn Rương, 'Chúng tôi có thể vận động nhân dân đi xây dựng kinh tế miền núi như Trực Tâm!', *Tiến Lên*, 5 March 1964, p. 2; Phạm Quang Khang, 'Chúng tôi đã làm như Trực Tâm: lãnh đạo quyết tâm, đảng viên gương mẫu', *Tiến Lên*, 10 March 1964, p. 2.

2   Nguyễn Văn Rương, 'Chúng tôi có thể vận động nhân dân', p. 2.

3   Phạm Quang Khang, 'Chúng tôi đã làm như Trực Tâm', p. 2.

4   *Thái Bình*, 'Xã Hiệp Hòa đã tổ chức học tập Nghị quyết 5 cho cán bộ, đảng viên và xã viên', *Thái Bình*, 25 September 1961, p. 1.

5   Nguyễn Phòng, 'Để cải thiện đời sống lâu dài cho nhân dân, chúng tôi tích cực chuyển người đi xây dựng kinh tế miền núi', *Tiến Lên*, 20 March 1964, p. 2.

6   Hoàng Hải, 'Khía cạnh quốc phòng – an ninh trong công tác di dân phát triển kinh tế mới', *Lao động và Xã hội*, no. 4, 1995, pp. 22–23. See also Dak Lak, 'Từ Buôn Ma Thuột tiến về Sài Gòn', *Dak Lak*, Ban Mê Thuột victory commemorative issue, 1990, p. 3.

7   See Stephen J. Morris, *Why Vietnam Invaded Cambodia: Political Culture and the Causes of War*, Stanford, California: Stanford University Press, 1999, ch. 7; Grant Evans and Kelvin Rowley, *Red Brotherhood at War: Vietnam, Cambodia and Laos since 1975*, London and New York: Verso, 1984, pp. 116–117.

8   SHAT/10H 1040, 'La question Nùng', 1954.

9   Vũ Quang, 'Trung đoàn II (thanh niên Thái Bình) ra quân đầu năm, khai hoang xây dựng vùng kinh tế mới Ea Súp', *Dak Lak*, 12 January 1978, p. 1; Hồng Mai, 'Chiến đấu, sẵn sàng chiến đấu tốt', *Dak Lak*, 19 October 1978, p. 3.

10 Văn Hồng, 'Huyện Krông Buk củng cố lực lượng dân quân du kích vững mạnh', *Dak Lak*, 23 November 1978, p. 4. At that time Tam Giang was in Krông Buk district, which later divided to form Krông Năng.

11 Interviews (Dak Lak, May 1996).

12 Ministry of Agriculture, 'Báo cáo tình hình khai hoang và phân bố lao động, dân cư đi khai hoang xây dựng vùng kinh tế mới 5 năm 1976–1989', Hanoi: Bộ Nông Nghiệp, January 1982.

13 Interview (Hòa Bình, July 1995).

14 This meaning is set out in detail in instructions issued to cadres by the authorities in Nam Định. NAV3/UBKHNN 504(vv), 'Phương hướng nhiệm vu kế hoạch 1965', Nam Định, 1965.

15 Quang Chất, 'Phá rừng, lấn biển bắt dất quay nhiều vòng', *Thái Bình*, 9 October 1961, p. 2.

16 Hoàng Bắc, *Tìm hiểu cuộc vận động cải tiến quản lý hợp tác xã nông nghiệp miền núi*, Hanoi: NXB Phổ Thông, 1965, pp. 3–4.

17 NAV3/BLD 961(vv), Minister of Labour to Prime Minister, 22 August 1959.

18 The DRV set up three highland autonomous zones: 1955, the Thái Mèo Autonomous Zone (the name changed to Tây Bắc in 1962); 1956, the Việt Bắc Autonomous Zone, its capital at Thái Nguyên; 1957, the Lào Hà Yên Autonomous Zone, in the upper Red River (abolished in 1959). Bernard B. Fall, *The Two Vietnams: A Political and Military Analysis*, New York: Praeger, 1963, pp. 148–152.

19 KD, 'Thái Bình – Tây Bắc một nhà', *Thái Bình*, 11 September 1961, p. 1.

20 Lê Khánh, *Quê mới người Hà Nội ở Lâm Đồng*, Hanoi: NXB Nông Nghiệp, 1983, p. 19. Hanoi's new economic zone in the 1980s was Lâm Hà district (Lâm Đồng).

21 Ibid., pp. 19–21.

22 Trần Đình Hoan, '30 năm di dan phăt triển vùng kinh tế mới và những đổi mới cơ bản trong giai đoạn tới' in Ministry of Labour, Committee for Information on Labour Allocation, *30 năm sự nghiệp di dân khai hoang và xây dựng kinh tế mới 1961–1991*, Hanoi: Cục Điều Động Lao Động và Dân Cư, 1991, p. 8.

23 Phạm Minh, 'Đổi mới công tác di dân phát triển vùng kinh tế mới', *QDND*, 4 July 1995, p. 3.

24 Interview (Thái Bình, June 1996).

25 Labour Ministry document, Hanoi, 1992.

26 This quotation is my translation of the Vietnamese published text: Lê Duẩn, 'Báo cáo chính trị của Ban chấp hành trung ương Đảng ở Đại hội toàn quốc lần thứ ba', *Nhân Dân*, 6 September 1960, p. 6. The English version was nuanced differently, with discussion of defence restricted to the south and greater emphasis on economic imperatives. Le Duan, 'Political Report of the Central Committee of the Việt Nam Workers' Party, 5.9.1960', in *Third National Congress of the Viet Nam Workers' Party, Documents, Volume 1,* Hanoi: Foreign Languages Publishing House, c. 1961, p. 131.

27 Lê Duẩn, *Báo cáo chính trị của Ban chấp hành trung ương Đảng tại Đại hội đại biểu toàn quốc lần thứ IV (do đồng chí Lê Duẩn, Tổng bí thư Ban chấp hành trung ương Đảng, trình bày)*, Hanoi: NXB Sự Thật, 1977, p. 58.

28 Communist Party of Vietnam, *Phương hướng, nhiệm vụ, và mục tiêu chủ yếu của kế hoạch 5 năm 1976–1980 (Báo cáo của Ban chấp hành trung ương Đảng tại Đại hội đại biểu toàn quốc lần thứ IV do đồng chí Phàm Văn Đồng, Ủy viên Bộ chính trị trung ương Đảng Thủ tướng Chính phủ, trình bày)*, Hanoi: NXB Sự Thật, 1977, p. 84.

29 Ministry of Labour, *30 năm sự nghiệp di dân*, p. 7.

30 Ibid.

31 Phạm Đỗ Nhật Tân, 'Tìm hiểu một số quy luật di dân nông nghiệp đi xây dựng vùng kinh tế mới ở Việt Nam'. In Nguyễn Văn Thanh, *Đổi mới cơ chế quản lý*, pp. 27–28.

32 For discussion of aid to the DRV, see Fall, *The Two Vietnams*, pp. 175–179; P. J. Honey, *Communism in North Vietnam: Its Role in the Sino-Soviet Dispute*, Cambridge, Massachusetts: MIT Press, 1963, p. 42. For land reform, see Edwin E. Moise, *Land Reform in China and North Vietnam: Consolidating the Revolution at the Village Level*, Chapel Hill: University of North Carolina Press, 1983. For state farms, see Fall, *The Two Vietnams*, p. 161. For collectivization, see Benedict J. Tria Kerkvliet, *State–Village Relations in Vietnam: Contested Cooperatives and collectivisation*, Clayton: Monash University, 1993, p. 3.

33 I.A. Mal'khanova, 'The Development of New Agricultural Lands in North Vietnam in 1961–65', *Soviet Geography*, vol. XI, no. 10, 1970, pp. 828–832.

34 Jacqueline Desbarats, 'Population Redistribution in the Socialist Republic of Vietnam', *Population and Development Review*, vol. 13, no. 1, 1987, pp. 43–76.

35 For an account of Khruschev's programme, see Martin McCauley, *Khruschev and the Development of Soviet Agriculture: The Virgin Land Programme 1953–1964*, New York: Holmes & Meier, 1976. See also Frank A. Durgin, 'The Relationship of the Death of Stalin to the Economic Changes of the Post-Stalin Era'. In Robert C. Stuart (ed.), *The Soviet Rural Economy*, New Jersey: Rowman & Allanheld, 1984, pp. 128–131.

36 On organized migration in China, see Yan Hao, 'Population Distribution and Internal Migration in China since the early 1950s'. In Wang Jiye and Terry H. Hull (eds), *Population and Development Planning in China*, Sydney: Allen & Unwin, 1991, pp. 212–234.

37 Nguyễn Trần Trọng and Nguyễn Đặng Kiêu, *Những vấn đề kinh tế chủ yếu về khai hoang xây dựng vùng kinh tế mới ở nước ta*, Hanoi, NXB Nông Nghiệp, 1982, pp. 21–22.

38 NAV3/UBKHNN 267(vv), 'Ý kiến chuyên gia về kế hoạch Miền Núi (Đồng chí Vượng phát biểu, ngày 5.3.1958)'.

39 Lê Thước, *Sự nghiệp và thi văn của Ủy viên tự íng công Nguyễn Công Trứ*, Hanoi: Nhà in Lê Văn Tân, 1928, p. 45, cited in Mai Khắc Ứng, *Chinh sách khuyến nông dưới thời Minh Mạng*, Hanoi: NXB Văn Hóa Thông Tin, 1996, p. 146. Tiền Hải was created in 1828, Kim Sơn in 1829.

40 Nguyễn Khắc Đạm, 'Vai trò của nhà nước về vấn đề khai hoang trong lịch sử Việt Nam', *NCLS,* vol. 39, 1962, pp. 40, 52.

41 Phan Dai Doan, 'Tien Hai and Kim Son Districts in the 19th Century'. In *The Traditional Village in Vietnam*, Hanoi: The Gioi Publishers, 1993, p. 248.

42 Quang Chất, 'Phà rừng, lấn biển', p. 2; Nam Cường commune: 'Tham luận hội thảo khoa học nhân dịp 19.5.1995 ngày sinh chủ tịch Hồ Chí Minh, về một miền quê đón Bác và làm theo lời Bác dạy'.

43 Khuất Quang Thụy, *Mười năm lấn biển và xây dựng vùng kinh tế mới*, Hanoi: NXB Quân Đội Nhân Dân, 1990.

44 Phạm Đỗ Nhật Tân, 'Hoàn thiện hơn nữa việc di dân', p. 69.

45 Adam Fforde and Suzanne H. Paine, *The Limits of National Liberation: Problems Of Economic Management in the Democratic Republic of Vietnam*, London: Croom Helm, 1987, p. 28.

46 Phạm Đỗ Nhật Tân, 'Hoàn thiện hơn nữa việc di dân', p. 69.

47 Le Duan, 'Political Report of the Central Committee', p. 158.

48 Fall, *The Two Vietnams*, p. 112.

49 Fforde and Paine, *The Limits of National Liberation*, pp. 27–28.

50 A conference on abandoned land was held in Hanoi (December 1954) to return to cultivation 120,000 hectares of land (6 per cent of pre-war land cultivated before the war, according to data excluding the Tây Bắc highlands). One solution was 'to mobilize people to migrate'. By mid-1956 a number of projects had been completed, for example in Hồng Quang, where authorities 'mobilized a number of compatriots from three communes in the Hà Nam area to move to Bình Khê (Đông Triều)'. NAV3/UBKHNN 570(tt), 'Báo cáo tình hình phục hồi ruộng hoang', Ministry of Agriculture and Forestry, 26 May 1956; 'Báo cáo tình hình ruộng hoang và kết quả của việc phục hồi ruộng hoang

(nhất là từ khi hòa bình trở lại)', Ministry of Agriculture and Forestry to Government Economic Committee, 10 December 1954; Minister of Agriculture and Forestry, Nghiêm Xuân Yêm, to provinces, 30 December 1954.

51 *Tiến Lên*, 'Trong công tác vận động nhân dân đi xây dựng kinh tế miền núi, chúng ta có thể làm được như Trực Tầm không? Tại sao?', *Tiến Lên*, 29 February 1964, p. 2.

52 Trần Đình Hoan, 'Về những quan điểm cơ bản', p. 4.

53 This was decision 116/HDBT of 9 April 1990. Phạm Đỗ Nhật Tân, 'Hoàn thiện hơn nữa việc di dân', p. 91.

54 Interview (Thái Bình, May 1995).

55 Phạm Đỗ Nhật Tân, 'Hoàn thiện hơn nữa việc di dân', p. 91.

56 Ibid.

57 Interview (Thái Bình, January 1997).

58 Council of Ministers' Decision 254–CP, 16 June 1981, reprinted in Ministry of Labour, *Chính sách chế độ về tổ chức điều động lao động và dân cư*, Hanoi: Cục Điều Đọng Lao Động, c1983, p. 34.

59 'The Future of Migration in Vietnam. Recommendations of the International Seminar on Internal Migration: Implications for Migration Policy in Vietnam', Recommendations of the Conference, Hanoi, 6–8 May 1998.

60 This has been convincingly argued in the case of Indonesia. See W. Takken, W. B. Snellen, J. P. Verhave, B. G. J. Knols and S. Atmosoedjono, *Environmental Measures for Malaria Control in Indonesia – an Historical Review on Species Sanitation*, Wageningen, The Netherlands: Agricultural University Wageningen, 1990.

61 Vũ Đình Hòe, 'Nạn nhân mãn và việc di dân', *Thanh Nghị*, no. 113, 16 June 1945, p. 370.

62 More research on colonial period Catholic settlements, as in Yên Bái, may reveal similar strengths. See Pierre Gourou, *Les paysans du delta tonkinois, étude de géographie*, Paris: Les Editions d'Art et d'Histoire, 1936, pp. 202–203.

63 Vũ Đình Hòe, 'Nạn nhân mãn và việc di dân', p. 416.

64 NAV1/RND 3175, Résident in Nam Định to RST, 20 March 1908.

65 NAV1/GGI 1367, 'Rapport No. 5. Le problème démographique, surpopulation et colonisation', December 1941.

66 L. E. Lotzer and G. Wormser, *La surpopulation du Tonkin et du Nord-Annam*, Hanoi: IDEO, 1941, p. 104.

67 Adam Fforde and Stefan de Vylder, *From Plan to Market: the Economic Transition in Vietnam*, Boulder, Colorado: Westview Press, 1996, p. 13.

68 *Chế độ đối với lao động đi xây dựng vùng kinh tế mới*, Hanoi: NXB Lao Động, 1978, p. 6.

69 NAV3/UBNNTW 99(vv), 'Chỉ thị của Ủy ban nông nghiệp trung ương – lập kế hoạch xây dựng các vùng KTM và phát triển các Nông trường Quốc doanh năm 1974', Central Agricultural Committee, Hanoi, 30 August 1974.

70 State Scientific Committee, Vietnam Scientific Institute, Geological Institute, Geography and Resources Centre, and National Economics University, 'Chương trình tiến bộ khoa học kỹ thuật: đánh giá tổng hợp tự nhiên kinh tế xã hội 9 tỉnh miền núi phía Bắc', Programme Summary Report, Hanoi, 1990, p. 89.

71 Ministry of Labour, 'Báo cáo sơ kết công tác điều động lao động dân cư xây dựng kinh tế mới 1981-1988', undated draft, c. 1989.

72 N. J. Jamieson, Le Trong Cuc and A. T. Rambo, *The Development Crisis in Vietnam's Mountains*, Honolulu: East–West Center, 1998, p. 9.

73 Interview (Dak Lak, May 1996).

74 NAV1/RST 76109, 'Procès verbal de la commission – Immigration Tonkinoise en Cochinchine', Minutes of the session on 14 October 1935; Charles Robequain, *Le Thanh Hoa: Etude géographique d'une province annamite*, Paris and Brussels: Editions G. Van Oest, 1929, vol. 2, p. 294.

Beyond Village Society?
The Practice of Free Migration, 1986–98

Figure 7: Fares for bus travel advertised at Ban Mê Thuột, 1996
From the 1980s, communist restrictions on internal travel in Vietnam were lifted, and people were able to move around the country without obtaining transport coupons, petrol rations and permission papers from the police. All you needed was the money for a ticket on one of the buses that plied the routes between the hills and the plains. In 1996, a one-way ride between the central highlands (Ban Mê Thuột) and the Red River Delta (Thái Bình) cost 102,000 đồng (US$9). Photograph by Andrew Hardy, November 1996.

Overview of Part Four

*P*art Four consists of a single chapter which explores the recent history of non-organized migration in Vietnam. The socialist system did not prevent all unauthorized and unorganized movement during the 1960s and 1970s. But the economic reforms of the 1980s, and the perceived opportunities for enrichment in the south, allowed many inhabitants of the Red River Delta to leave their villages in search of a better life. Many moved to join family members, fellow villagers and acquaintances who had already built new homes in the hills, under the government programme. In contrast to their predecessors on the programme, these migrants enjoyed great freedom of choice in their relationship with the state. Some made use of the programme to finance their venture. Some sought permission for their move, but otherwise acted independently of the state. Others avoided the authorities, and moved without any reference to the state whatsoever.

In the late 1990s, the scale of this movement, its consequences for the receiving area – the central highlands – and the erosion of administrative control over the migrants, reoriented central government thinking about migration. The way in which free migration practice forced a rethink in migration policy is the subject of Chapter 10, 'Free Migrants to the Hills'.

Free Migrants to the Hills

TIGERS IN TÂN CƯƠNG

*T*ân Cương commune, 27 October 1996. I was asking about life in the village before the revolution. The room was crowded, the conversation chaotic. I had trouble making sense of the old man's accent: 'Three o'clock in the afternoon – that was late! We didn't dare go out after three or four. Tigers. People were afraid, so they'd stay in'. With these remarks, he caught the attention of his neighbours. They were sitting around, talking, drinking tea, staring out of the window, half-listening to our interview. But on the subject of tigers, everyone had a contribution to make.

> 'Mister *Cọp!*' exclaimed one man.
> 'Mister *Thirty!*' called another.
> 'Mister *Hùm!*' growled a third.

These were nicknames for the beast who had terrorized the settlers of this forest. Both beast and forest were long gone, but memories too were long. 'People who went out at night, some of them were killed by Mister *Hùm*. Dogs too. From here to the church, it was all forest then. Big trees – big as a well or a bicycle wheel', one man recalled. 'But after 1945, things changed', added another.[1]

Before 1945, Tân Cương was an area of new settlement. At the beginning of the century the landscape was described in the purple prose of a French monograph. Settlers were portrayed as:

> struggling against the devouring bush of this exuberant vegetation which seems to want to erase all trace of human activity. Victory in this combat is with man, however, who hems in with the mesh of his road network the inextricable massif of Nhui-Chúa, throws the long ribbon of his paths across the savage poetry of the Thanh Mục gorges where, in the depths of the chasm below, rumbles the clear and seething water of the Ta Ma river, revealing the secrets of the mountain and violating the sacred horror and profound peace of the forest.[2]

It was after the victory over nature had been won that Mr Hợp, whose house I was sitting in, arrived at Tân Cương, in the 1930s. His account was more down-to-earth. 'People called each other up continuously during the 1930s. The biggest stream came in 1945. They came up to work for wages, then settled and called their family'. One of the younger men sitting around spoke up at this point. He asked me if I had heard of all the people now moving to Gia Lai – Kon Tum, in the central highlands. I sat up and told him I had just been to the neighbouring province of Dak Lak. 'Just like that', he said – Hợp and the others moved 'just like that'.[3]

This man's remark caught my attention for two reasons. The first was in its implication of a break in the process of free migration. His comment suggested that before the mid 1980s, when the movement to the central highlands got under way, people were unable to up and off, to work for wages, to join their family, as they had done under the French. He compared the French era with the last ten years. The second was in the nature of his comparison. Was Hợp's move really similar to the recent settlement of hundreds of thousands of people in the central highlands? A look at these two issues will help us understand the workings of free migration to the hills.

FREE MIGRATION, 1954–86

A few days before this conversation, I had met Yêm, the official historian of the district of Đồng Hỷ. He confirmed my impression that free movement of the population was quite limited in the years after Điện Biên Phủ. It was no longer possible, as it had been before 1945, simply to pay your head tax, leave the village and settle elsewhere. There were formalities to complete, and these required considerable negotiation. Yêm spelled out for me a three-point typology of migration in this era. Some people moved without any reference to the authorities – movement described as 'illegal', 'clandestine' or 'secret'.[4] Of this type, Yêm said, 'there was virtually none'. Others made their own arrangements but asked permission from the authorities – 'free' or 'spontaneous' migration. Third, there was migration under the government programme – 'organized migration'. Lê Bạch Dương identified a fourth type of movement during the socialist period, organized and approved by the government but not part of a specific resettlement programme. This included both employment posting and migration for family reunion.[5]

Many Vietnamese sources label the first two of these types 'free migration'. Here 'free migration' is used as a generic term for people moving outside the government programme. 'Spontaneous migration' distinguishes a declared change of residence from an undeclared 'secret migration'.

The relationship between these types of migration is clear from the situation in Thái Nguyên in the early 1960s. As Loan told me, when she moved to Bờ Rạ in 1964, she felt lucky to be included on the programme organized by her home province of Hà Nam: 'Some wanted to go, and couldn't; they still came to the reception centre in Thái Nguyên, unofficially, to ask to go'.[6] Officials described this as a substantial movement of 'spontaneous' migrants sparked off by the announcement of the migration programme.[7] But they turned up not only in Thái Nguyên but at destinations across the northern highlands, throughout the early 1960s. Authorities back in Hà Nam soon received complaints from Thái Nguyên about these unplanned and unwanted arrivals. They in turn instructed districts and communes to stick to the plan, warning them that 'if people freely go off to look for work, they will run into difficulties, which can only be resolved at great expense in term of labour and money for their return fare.' In an apparent throwback to the ways of the past, village cadres had been signing papers of introduction for people wanting to look for work. They were rebuked for failing to 'grasp thoroughly and implement the principle of manpower policy management'. Migrants should move according to the plan, not of their own volition.[8]

Uncontrolled mobility was limited by the plan but could not abolished. Despite legal obstacles, there were numbers of free migrants moving around, making use of a variety of 'interstitial liberties'.[9] In the 1960s, they could take advantage of flexible implementation of the rules. After 1975, they increasingly exploited opportunities afforded by the existence of two parallel markets, one organized by the state, with a fixed price system, and another informal market operating according the laws of supply and demand.[10] Individuals and groups managed to obtain tickets for travel throughout the country, by bus or train, to look for work away from home.

Some intended only a short stay. In a time-honoured tradition, villagers from Thái Bình and other provinces of the Red River Delta went off looking for woodcutting and other temporary work during the slack season between harvests.[11] This continued into the 1980s. Several men from Xuân Trường district (Nam Định) told me how they took a bus to the hills, sawing timber for sale at high prices to smugglers. In his short story 'The Sawyers', Nguyễn Huy Thiệp described how a group of woodcutters worked the system. After concluding a verbal contract with the tough vice-director of a state farm, his character Bường is criticized by a local woman:

> 'You are a real soft touch. Does anyone go to work felling trees in the forest for the same wage as the sawmill workers on the state farm? The state farm workers are supplied with rice, but you are free people, so how are you going to eat?'
>
> Bường replied, 'If you're tricked, you just have to accept it. I'm actually not a soft touch at all. Pulling the saw, tricking the blade, but ...'

In the end, of course, the trick was turned. Bường supplemented his wage with cash payments from truck drivers, who bought the wood for resale in the delta.[12]

In the 1980s the widespread development of this trade gave rise to an unusual phenomenon: woodcutters travelling by aeroplane along the politically significant but economically marginal air routes to Nà Sản and Điện Biên Phủ, sites of major battles in the 1946–54 war. Government officials tended to travel to these places by car. Unable or unwilling to afford the flight, they sometimes used the trip to carry goods back for sale on the black market. Woodcutters, by contrast, were paid handsomely and had the resources to fly, preferring if possible to avoid the gruelling ride in the bus, which might take a week to reach Điện Biên Phủ. But these men tended to return home after their stint in the hills, or moved on to seek work elsewhere, in the central highlands, in the south, and increasingly in urban centres like Hanoi. With their families remaining in the delta, they returned from time to time for festivals and to help with the harvest. The men departed as sojourners, temporary migrants living off their labour and regularly remitting their earnings.[13]

Some sojourners settled. This was the case of Hải, a young woman from a village near Haiphong. Hải told me how in 1967 she left home 'to go and work around, to go and work for wages, in a group of seven women'. They had no financial incentive from the state, as they left at their own initiative. These young women had heard from a group of road workers that it was possible to make a living in the hills. In a pattern of wandering labour reminiscent of colonial times, they took a paper of introduction from the commune authorities, rode the train as far as Yên Bái, and then set off on foot. They walked over 100 km, reaching a certain distance, then asking locals for a place to sleep, until three days later they arrived in the valley of Phù Yên. Hải was able to find casual work and survived for two years, until she was offered employment at the district cereals office. At this point she was able to transfer her household registration from her home village to Phù Yên. A year later she married a local man, and what had begun as a sojourning experience became a permanent move.[14]

Phù Yên was a remote farming community, and Hoa had to wait two years for her job. But Thái Nguyên, a burgeoning industrial centre in the early 1960s, was known to be a place of opportunity. The town was rebuilding at this time.[15] And the result was that in a single month – March 1961 – authorities in Thái Nguyên complained of an influx of nearly four thousand people:

> Every day from fifty to one hundred people come from every province: Hưng Yên, Hà Nam, Thái Bình, Bắc Ninh (…) and as far as their papers are concerned, they only have travel passes or letters of introduction from their cooperative, though a few have letters from the district Administrative Committee: Most arrive in Thái Nguyên having spent all their money, and request work, creating problems here in many respects.[16]

As we have seen, this was not simply a one-off occurrence, although it was influenced by the recent announcement of the migration programme (September 1960). Loan testified to the same phenomenon three years later, when she moved to Thái Nguyên just after New Year.

Different provinces reacted to the influx in different ways. Employers in the Thái Mèo Autonomous Zone were instructed to give migrants any available short-term work, if only for their immediate food needs. In Lào Cai, cooperatives were encouraged to find room for the new arrivals to stay.[17] In Thái Nguyên, however, provincial authorities worked by the book:

> It would be against the principles if we employed the people with insufficient papers, so our Department firmly sends them back to their locality to obtain legal papers. Apart from exceptional cases, when we offer employment for five or seven days so they can earn enough money for the train fare back.[18]

This sort of practice was described by some lowland officials as 'mechanical' and liable to give rise to 'worries'* among the population.[19] Loan was sharper in her account of the same story. 'People were refused', she said.

Even with its policy of rigid application of the rules, Thái Nguyên remained a choice destination. Provincial statistics indicate that nearly 5,000 free migrants managed to settle there in 1964, as well as a further 10,000 cadres and workers and their families.† Indeed, at lower levels of the administration, the rules were applied only sporadically. Yêm said that 'after 1954, people came up freely, asking permission from the village, reporting to the district later'. The policy of strict enforcement allowed cadres to pick and choose. Exceptions could be made for migrants with skills. Statistics did not, of course, record numbers of 'secret migrants' to the highlands. But the ease with which people could get letters of introduction from the lowlands and the readiness of most highland provinces to accept them, combined with the difficulties faced by people without household registration, lend plausibility to Yêm's assessment of secret migration – 'There was virtually none'. This view was confirmed by Phạm Đỗ Nhật Tân: the *hộ khẩu* system was systematically enforced before 1986; secret migration to the hills was negligible; those who flouted the rules remained poor for long periods.[20]

Secret migration was more common in the other direction, from highlands to lowlands, or within the highlands. We have already examined cases of people abandoning new economic zones and returning to their home villages or to the cities. Others, however, found it expedient to move on to new and better land, as the following extract from a Ministry of Labour report shows:

> In many past years (1976–85), according to policy, new economic zones were formed according to the line 'easy ones first, difficult ones later', but in practice the organization of new economic zones' formation and settlement started with difficult places and distant places, which contributed to localized free migration (…) This type of spontaneous 'redistribution' of population entirely depended or was formed on foundations laid by organized migration groups.[21]

By comparison with migration into the cities, this type of localized second move – usually to better land near roads or small towns – was described as more common. One source estimated that as many as 20 per cent of migrants in 1976–80 were of this type, as were 10 per cent of migrants from 1984–93.[22] These figures are high, but they are more interesting for what they leave out. In the 1976–80 period, most of the remaining 80 per cent of migrants were on government programmes, although the years 1975–77 did see the arrival in the central highlands of free migrants from the plains, moving for both economic and political reasons.[23] In 1984–93, by contrast, a significant proportion of the remaining 90 per cent were free migrants.‡ This shift was a symptom of the wider change in the economic

---

*   Worries: *thắc mắc.*

†   One of these was Hảo, whose moved is related in Chapter 1.

‡   For a discussion of statistical information on migrants to the central highlands, see the Appendix.

system which took place during the 1980s. It is to an analysis of this change that we now turn.

THE IMPACT OF ĐỔI MỚI

Prior to the 1980s, the system of employment, residence control and restriction of non-state economic activity had the effect of controlling and channelling movements of the population. In the preceding section, it was shown that this system was far from watertight, even in the DRV before 1975. After reunification, it became progressively less so. As Philippe Papin observed, in April 1975, 'To the military and political victory of the north was superimposed the triumph – ideological and commercial – of the liberal economy of the south'.[24] How did this transition, formalized in the Đổi Mới legislation of 1986, take shape in practice?

The existence of an informal market sector has already been noted. And the symbiotic relationship between this sector and the state distribution system, theoretically contradictory but which actually complemented and reinforced each other, created opportunities for migration outside of state control.[25] In the examples above, the young woman who left Haiphong in the 1960s found it easier to join a state organization, and did so when the chance arose. But the woodcutters of Xuân Trường who in the 1980s travelled across the country in search of work, exemplify the sort of people who preferred, over long periods, to take advantage of opportunities in the informal sector. Others obliged to seek their survival in these spaces were the frightened families who returned from the new economic zones, fleeing poverty or malaria. Some of these people returned to their villages to become the dependants of their relatives. Some of them left Vietnam as boat people. Many subsisted in the informal economy. As Nguyễn Huy Thiệp observed in his story about Bường and the woodcutters, they were 'free people'.* The informal sector constituted a powerful limit to the effectiveness of the state's control over population mobility.

Development of informal economic activities accompanied the land decollectivization process, which lay at the heart of the Đổi Mới transition. Decollectivization proceeded from its seeds in the 'sneaky contracts' of the 1960s and 1970s, through to the legalization of contract relations between cooperatives and families (Directive 100, 1981), to the important Directive 10 of 1988. This law 'destroyed the rural basis of the command economy' by leaving the cooperatives a wide margin of freedom in their economic activity. Benedict Kerkvliet observed that discontent in the mid 1980s had manifested itself in 'reports of people refusing to pay quotas, peasants quitting their fields in disgust, and villagers continuing "sneaky contracts" that went beyond the new system'. This rejection of the system in the villages and the opening of new 'sneaky' spaces for activity led to a carve-up of use rights to cooperative land, which took place from the late 1980s at different times in different communes.[26]

---

* 'Free people': *dân tự do*. Nguyễn Huy Thiệp, 'Những người thợ xẻ', p. 259.

As rural families' discontent with the cooperative system grew, so did migration. Use rights over land, distributed to people for a period of twenty years, could now be bought, sold and mortgaged. Owners became free to dispose of the land's product – over and above their duty to pay taxes – as they wished. They could, above all, sell their rights in the free market.[27] In short, by the 1990s farmers were legally entitled to sell up and leave, temporarily or for good. Indeed, the structure of the Vietnamese economy of the 1990s, offering low profits and imposing high taxes on agricultural production – in particular that of rice – promoted this option. As one analyst put it:

> Strong fiscal pressure and weak profits came together to favorize rural migration and the informal economy. Three forms of behaviour clearly emerged. Either the peasants moved towards production which paid, and fed the urban markets by transporting goods on shoulder poles, or they left the countryside and went to join the cohorts of day-labourers working in the cities (...), or they turned directly to the informal economy.[28]

The removal of restrictions on private sector commerce, approved at the Sixth Party Congress in 1986, offered further impulsion to uncontrolled mobility of the population. This came in the form of private transportation companies which sprang up throughout Vietnam.[29] It is difficult nowadays to imagine the difficulties faced in the past by people wishing to travel privately, that is without documentation and funding supplied by the state. The existence of bus companies and the removal of the need for papers to buy seats greatly facilitated the act of travel. By the 1990s, it was possible, even in provincial centres in the central highlands, to buy tickets for travel on direct bus routes, not only to the nearby towns of the coastal plains and urban centres of Hanoi and Ho Chi Minh City, but also to more distant destinations in northern Vietnam such as Thái Bình, Hải Dương and Cao Bằng.*

The dismantling of the cooperatives, the break in the link between economic benefits and residence status enshrined in the *hộ khẩu*, the opening up of new opportunities – of travel and of livelihood – provided not by the state, but by market mechanisms: these were the major elements in Đổi Mới affecting migration. The 'free people' found themselves freer, and many of them seized opportunities to move. As government control over mobility lessened, what forms did this mobility take? How did people organize themselves to take advantage of the new opportunities?

RESOURCES FOR MIGRATION

By the 1980s, Thái Nguyên was no longer a favoured destination. When I visited, delta people no longer thought of looking there for land; it was already settled. Reactions to an old French map I took to a remote village at the head of the Công River valley were revealing. In the sunlit courtyard, the old men pored over the map of their village, talking with animation, recognizing landmarks. I thought

---

* For prices and destinations of such bus services, see Photo 7.

they had forgotten me, but one of them finally turned round, and pointed out the large areas of woodland on the map: 'Nowadays this isn't forest anymore, it's all tea'.* The forest had gone, and with it the tigers: 'If there are any left', he said, 'they're all hiding'. Further down the valley, at Tân Thái, a young woman I spoke to laughed loudly at the idea of tigers. 'Tigers? In the past there were tigers. Now there's just Tiger beer!' And further downstream still, back at Tân Cương, I discovered that it is not only the tigers that have gone away. Far from being a frontier, the village that Hợp and his neighbours founded in the early part of the century now sends settlers elsewhere. 'Since 1975', Hợp told me, 'many people have left for the central highlands; it's easier to make a living there'. An official in Thái Nguyên confirmed the fact: 'We have no programme to move people out of the province. They go of their own accord'.[30]

Hợp's neighbour compared these people to Hợp himself and other migrants of the colonial era. But Hợp disagreed:

> We were poor people who cleared the land at Tân Cương. But nowadays, if you're poor, you can't leave. Now you need capital to leave. Now if you want to work for wages, you go for a short time and you don't go far.

No one challenged this observation. And I found it confirmed in a conversation with a Tày free migrant at Buôn Tría commune in Dak Lak, about the costs of migration. Mr La brought his wife and four children to Buôn Tría in 1992, to join his brothers who already lived there. The journey took three days and three nights from their home in Cao Bằng to the provincial centre at Ban Mê Thuột. For each passenger, the bus fare was 140,000 đồng. For the whole family, he calculated that total travel costs came to 2 million đồng (slightly less than US$200 at the time). Food and luggage fees cost extra. La may have exaggerated this sum, and certainly his family lived off relatives during the first few months at Buôn Tría. But he was clearly well off before he left. The travel costs alone were beyond the means of any 'two white hands' peasant going off to work for wages.[31]

La went to Dak Lak to join relatives. In this, despite Hợp's comments to the contrary, the comparison with pre-1945 migration was apt. As I was told at the labour office in Thái Nguyên, the most important resource used for the move was the family.

> *Cadre*: They go of their own accord. In cases where they have relatives in the south, they go south on holiday visits and see that conditions for making a living are better than here in the north, so they just move south. (...)

> *Hardy*: These people moving south, are they mainly Việt or ethnic minority people?

> *Cadre*: Mainly Việt.[32]

---

* This was Yên Sơn village (Hoàng Nông commune, Đại Từ district, Thái Nguyên), settled under Echinard's 'small concessions' scheme. NAV1/RST 67499, correspondence, Thái Nguyên, 1934. See Plate 8.

For Việt people, 'relatives' (*anh em*) here should be understood in the broadest sense.* I asked a cadre at Đông Hưng district People's Committee to tell me what 'relatives' might mean in this context.

> People who went twenty or thirty years ago took their [immediate] family with them on the programme, but now those who want to follow are just their more distant relatives, nephews and nieces, aunts and uncles, brothers and sisters on the wife's side and on the husband's side (…)
>
> There are also cases where people went south to work or as soldiers, and raised a family there. If conditions there were good, they would bring their whole family, all their relations down. There are many cases like this.[33]

A 1993 Ministry of Labour report gave an even broader definition, emphazing migrants' pragmatic approach to the networks they used: 'they rely on the knowledge and relatives *available* to them'.[34] The knowledge might be gleaned from experiences as a soldier or official in the south before or after 1975. It might come from relatives or neighbours who settled a new economic zone. It might simply be a word of advice from a friend or acquaintance who had spent time in the south, or had relatives there. The relatives, as noted above, could well be very distant. They might not even be relatives at all, but close friends, former colleagues or fellow war veterans incorporated into family structures.

Fictive kinship was a major feature of migration networking. The case of two soldiers stationed in highland Thái Nguyên during the 1940s shows how these relationships worked. One was a local man, the other from the lowland province of Nam Định. They became firm friends during their military service. They agreed to swear brotherhood.† The Nam Định man eventually moved to Thái Nguyên, in 1966, to be close to his new found 'brother'. The local man's son, who told me about this relationship, referred to this former soldier from the plains as his 'extended family uncle'.‡ This distinguished him from an immediate 'flesh and blood uncle'§ but included him in the wider family network. Membership of this network, as he explained it to me, was an open and flexible affair. Family relations were as much invented as inherited.[35]

Family membership was flexible, and the functioning of family networks was organic.[36] Benefits, in terms of financial and emotional support as well as information, were available to members. These benefits, however, did not come free. Despite much discourse to the contrary – centred around a concept of sentiment (*tình cảm*) – Vietnamese families operate on a basis of negotiated reciprocity. Reciprocal favour-seeking, justified by appeals to *tình cảm*, could involve both mutual aid and mutual exploitation. Particularly in circumstances of distant kinship, power

---

* For comment on the use of the expression *anh em* with reference to colonial era migration, see Chapter 3.

† Swear brotherhood: *kết nghĩa*.

‡ Extended family uncle: *bác họ*.

§ Flesh and blood uncle: *bác ruột*.

relations – articulated in languages of exchange, concern about welfare and friendly but heavily loaded banter – are rarely absent. Indeed, the idea of *tình cảm*, so prominent in many perceptions about family- and village-based relationships, is commonly subject to deliberate manipulation for gain.

In the light of this, we should be wary of any view stressing the unconditional nature of family solidarity. Family networks were as negotiated as any other, and perhaps – given the appeal to discourses of *tình cảm* – more so. To illustrate this tension, we might contrast two traditional Vietnamese proverbs:

> *Một giọt máu đào hơn ao nước lã*: 'A single drop of pink blood is better than a pond full of water'. Family relationships are permanent and reliable.

> *Bán anh em xa, mua láng giềng gần*: 'Sell your distant relatives, buy your close-by neighbours'. Human relationships are contractual. Residential proximity is a better basis for contract than ties of kinship.

It was common for people to find it advantageous to deal with people from outside the family. This was the choice of a young woman from Thái Bình, who moved to Dak Lak in November 1996 with her husband and young child. This family did not have the resources to build a fine brick house by the road. They lived in a small mud and bamboo dwelling in a rather remote village. A 'distant uncle' had told them about the place, but they did not know him well enough to ask for more concrete help. The land they lived on and the fields they farmed were rented from acquaintances. The family member thus provided information (and possibly a hope of help in case of trouble, which might come with strings attached), while land was contracted from outsiders.[37]

We are cautioned, then, against a rosy view of relatives as a never-failing source of support. Our reticence, moreover, is confirmed in Lê Thi's recent study of the family.

> The family is a unit of close ties. But its structure is varied because its members differ from one another in age, gender, profession, hobby, character, educational and cultural standard and way of life, etc. The Vietnamese family has traditionally been extended (at least, two generations) therefore contradictions between generations are inevitable. This situation seems to be graver in Vietnam at this period of economic transition and all-round Renovation.
>
> In the old-type family, patriarchy was a great power in unconditionally subjecting children to their parents. This 'parental dictatorship' cannot exist in the present society imbued with democracy and equality. On the contrary, there should be discussion, exchange of views and mutual respect in considering family affairs. However, we should also admit that in a number of families, the contradictions between generations are so profound that sometimes they require a lot of energy to be resolved (due to the conservatism of the elderly and the immorality of the children).[38]

This view of the family, with its emphasis on energy for successful functioning, responds closely to the realities observed in migrant networking. Close-knit family relationships do not simply exist, in Vietnam as elsewhere. As Lê Thi suggests, they require considerable investment.

Let us take a closer look at migrants' use of networks. A Ministry of Labour official described their use of family resources:

> They rely on the knowledge and relatives available to them; one healthy family member or the household head will go south first, as an advance party. They have the responsibility of preparing the material base: a place to live, land to farm (…) for the whole family. Usually they put their own or the whole family's savings into this preparation. With the help of close friends and family, they create an initial material base for the whole family. Once settled at a certain level, after discussion, verification, consideration even (…) they decide to move the whole family south. Or each member will gradually come south in turn, according to the model of *gradually swelling the destination place and gradually narrowing the departure place. This process usually lasts two or three years, from the original intention to the arrival of the last person at the new place of residence. This form of migration happens among all residents of northern provinces who migrate freely to the south.*[39]

This text was written with reference to Việt people. Ethnic minorities, such as the Tày and Nùng people who moved from Lạng Sơn and Cao Bằng, also moved in this way, as in the case of La described above. But they also tended to move in larger groups, even whole villages.* Apocryphal stories circulated of village leaders carrying their stamps of authority, and even faked letters from Nông Đức Mạnh, then President of the National Assembly, with which to impress local authorities in the south. Highlanders' migratory practices were highly varied, differing from one group to the next. A detailed examination of such practices lies outside the scope of this study. Việt people, on the other hand, moved in whole families and groups if displaced by war (on the Chinese border, for example) or lake-fill (from the Đà River hydroelectric scheme in Hòa Bình, or Núi Cốc lake in Thái Nguyên). But the most common method was that described above. Family and related networks were used in pragmatic and opportunistic ways.

This point was made by Hein Mallee in his study of rural mobility in China. Emphasizing the role of 'expanded families', defined as families that are 'spatially dispersed, but functionally united', he suggested that the availability of networks might be as powerful a stimulation for migration as traditionally identified 'push' factors.[40] His argument is an important counterbalance to an assumption observed in China, and certainly prevalent in the Red River Delta, that 'rural under employment ('surplus labour') almost automatically and directly leads to out-migration'. In Tân Cương, Hợp made the same point. It was not the poor who migrated. Migrants were people who found a resource, got into a network, saw their chance.

FREE MIGRANTS AND THE STATE

Many people found this resource in the state. In 1977, Ngọc moved to Dak Lak on the government programme. He had to follow his family, and he was furious

---

* This was true of the Hmong and Yao people, in particular, who moved in villages. See Diep Dinh Hoa, 'Dynamics of Yao Genealogy (A Case Study of a Yen Stream Village)', *South Pacific Study*, vol. 17, no. 1, 1996, pp. 109–110.

about it. Twenty years later, however, he had settled and was better off than before. Not long after meeting him, I visited his home village he had left back in Thái Bình. I met an older man who saw the pioneers board the buses in 1977. Seeing them head off towards the new economic zones, he may have heaved a sigh of relief. He was not among them. But in recent years, he told me, he had heard that they were doing rather well. Initially sceptical ('I didn't believe a word of it') curiosity got the better of him, and he made the long trip down to visit his relatives at Buôn Tría. 'Amazing!' he exclaimed. 'The coffee, it's so profitable! They are incredible, they're all rich!' He was palpably jealous.[41]

One of his younger neighbours, moreover, refused to sit around and nurse feelings of jealousy. Her husband had already left for Dak Lak. She was waiting at home, looking after their house, and their one hectare of paddy land. She had been waiting for a year when I met her. She told me, simply, that they wanted 'to develop the family economy, so freely migrated to the south'. Her husband and two eldest children were growing tobacco. She and the youngest child would join them later, when they was settled.

I asked the Đông Hưng district authorities how many people moved in this way. The reply was revealing, not of the numbers involved, which are difficult to assess even at district level, but of the reasons for this difficulty.

> In cases like these we have no statistics. There are years when people like this go south correctly according to the programme, in which case the state provides some financial support. There are years though when they don't do this. When the state provides support they have to come and see us to carry out formalities for the support. But when there is no support, they don't come and see us, only doing formalities for the change of household registration. We don't have accurate statistics on this.[42]

Authorities' control over free migrants was contingent. People effectively chose the relationship they wanted with officials. As I found out at the Labour Office in Thái Nguyên, some were nervous of the reaction they might receive: 'Many families here in the highlands go without even telling the local authorities; they're afraid they won't be allowed to go.'[43] They became secret migrants. Others – spontaneous migrants – preferred to remain within the law. To do so, they had to write a letter of request to the district authorities. Phạm Xuân Hải and his brother-in-law, from Tiền Hải district (Thái Bình), signed the following handwritten letter on 20 June 1993, asking permission to move to the south.

> Our two families are writing this letter to make a request of our dear leadership about the following matter. Respectfully, in 1992 our families went south to visit a brother at the commune of Buôn Triết, district of Lak, province of Dak Lak, and have already asked the local authorites to allow us to settle and live there. Until now we have not had the opportunity to return to our home village to transfer our household registration and carry out other formalities, so we now respectfully request our dear leadership to consider and make the necessary arrangements for our families to follow our aspirations and settle down to production.[44]

Phạm Xuân Hải had nothing to fear. His request was approved in November the same year and he now lives at Buôn Triết. He was one of 1,350 free migrants to settle in that commune up to 1995, according to an official at Lak district People's Committee. This official indicated that people came to Lak from every one of Vietnam's fifty-three provinces and cities, with the single and significant exception of Ho Chi Minh City. Many of these individual families settled in Lak district town, following the example of Mr Lăng, one of the earliest Việt settlers in the region. Lăng was an electrician whose brother worked for Emperor Bảo Đại at his hunting lodge by the lake. On his brother's recommendation, he arrived in Lak in 1950 to look after the imperial refrigerator, a walk-in freezer which 'could hold four or five deer'.* More recent arrivals had more mundane professions, but followed the same networks based on state settlement and family relationship. At Buôn Tría, the majority were relatives of previous migrants there, people from Quảng Ngãi who moved there under the RVN land development programme in 1959 (like Chiến's brother) or from Thái Bình on a new economic zone scheme in 1977 (like Ngọc).

When they joined existing towns or village settlements, they were generally welcomed by local authorities. This was particularly so at Tam Giang, where they made up the numbers lost by abandoning families. It was also the case at Ea Lê commune, as revealed in the *Dak Lak* newspaper:

> 'On lush land, birds alight.'† Now Ea Lê is not only a place for people from Hòa Vang district.‡ Many families from other districts have already come to ask to 'settle' at Ea Lê to make a living.§ The families who abandoned a few years ago have now returned. Many families with homes in Thanh Hóa, Thái Bình, Hà Nam Ninh and even Cao Bằng, Lạng Sơn (…) have also arrived to seek their fortune.
>
> Ea Lê is becoming an area of good earth peopled by farmers from every home region.[46]

The official in Lak gave me a specific example of their welcome, mentioning fourteen families who turned up one day in 1985 at the commune of Dak Liêng. He did not say how they found the land there, nor whether they asked permission to settle. But when local authorities found the place was suitable, they asked the province People's Committee to provide the settlers with capital and include them in the programme. In the district statistics, these free migrants appeared under the category 'planned'.[47]

---

* Lăng arrived at Lak in 1950, aged 38, and brought his family up three years later. The only Việt people there were soldiers, elephant trainers and servants for the Emperor's hunts. The fridge was destroyed in 1975. See also note 45.

† On lush land, birds alight: *đất lành chim đậu*. A fuller version of the saying voices both steps in a migration process: 'On lush land, birds stop. On poor land, birds fly' (*Đất lành chim đỗ đất ngộ chim bay*). Vương Trung Hiệu, *Tục ngữ Việt Nam chọn lọc*, Hanoi: NXB Văn Nghệ, 1996, p. 391.

‡ Hòa Vang district (Quảng Nam) was the origin of new economic zone settlers at Ea Lê (Ea Súp district, Dak Lak).

§ The word I translated as 'settle' is '*nhập khẩu*', used here as a pun meaning both 'import' and 'register your arrival at a place of destination'.

For the migrants to Dak Liêng, this state support was a stroke of luck, a wind-fall. Others left nothing to chance. Thắng was one of these, a settler from Nam Định in the neighbouring district of Krông Nô. He first arrived there just after the district's creation in 1987, on his own, to choose some land and build a house. Seven months later, he returned to Nam Định. While he was away, his wife had volunteered the family for the new economic zones programme, intending to benefit from a 1981 law which stipulated;

> If there are labourers who themselves have chosen a place with land and have asked to go and clear it, then they should be positively encouraged. If there are people wanting to go to places they know or places where they have relatives to clear land, they should not be forced to go to other regions.[48]

Thắng's family was duly accepted onto the programme. They moved in 1988. Their household registration, of course, was immediately transferred, and they received the statutory three months' supply of rice before departure from Nam Định. Unfortunately, Thắng's planning did not prevent a stroke of unforeseeable ill-fortune. En route for the south, the papers of introduction to Dak Lak provincial authorities were lost and a further three months' supply of rice could not be granted. Looking back, Thắng can laugh at this. He has a small coffee plantation and a prosperous milling and grocery business. He has given up growing rice. For him, Dak Lak has indeed proved a 'promised land'.[*]

FAMILY NETWORKS, STATE RESOURCES

Thắng's story highlights the relationship of interdependence between free migrants and the Vietnamese state. Since the 1980s, settlers in the hills have enjoyed con-siderable freedom of choice in their relationship with the authorities, both at the place of departure and destination. Officials, when discussing this freedom, focused on instances where migrants chose to avoid contact with local authorities. At Krông Nô, for instance, a district cadre complained that secret migrants arrived in the forest, and were discovered only months later by a passing ranger. 'The state wants people to be here [he tapped the table] but they move here [he tapped again elsewhere] and forcing them to move back here [a further tap] is very difficult'. When they arrived in the district, it was quite impossible to turn them away. The cadre explained:

> If their bus was turned back, they'd rent a *tuk tuk*. If their *tuk tuk* was turned back, they'd rent motorbike taxis. If their motorbike was turned back, they'd just come in on foot. And once they'd cleared the forest, if they were forced to move, they'd just go and clear more forest, somewhere else.[49]

---

[*]   The term 'promised land' was used in a 1996 article on free migration. The land's promise lay in migrants' hopes of finding 'a place where people are few, where land is plentiful, where life will be more liveable'. Ngô Tuấn, 'Bức xúc vấn đề di dân tự do', *Việt Nam Đầu Tư Nước Ngoài*, 26 February 1996, p. 74.

This failure of administration on the frontier created many problems for officials, especially in newly created and fast growing districts like Krông Nô. Officials' focus on the fact that they 'want to manage, but can't manage' was, in the circumstances, quite natural. For the purposes of analysis, however, it is more useful to examine those moments when migrants chose to declare their decisions to the authorities. This was, in a sense, nothing more than the conscientious act of a law-abiding citizen. In the case of Phạm Xuân Hải, whose letter to Tiền Hải district authorities was reproduced above, formal registration of residence was required by the authorities at Buôn Triết. It was of course possible, in the mid 1990s, to dodge this sort of requirement. Phạm Xuân Hải had done so for a year before he wrote his letter. It presumably suited him to do the paperwork correctly. Without it, he could not legally buy land, send his children to school, or enjoy other services provided to new economic zone settlers there. While law-abiding citizens had to pay tax, they also enjoyed benefits denied to those who moved without reference to the state.

The case of Thắng's family is more significant still. Thắng chose not only to obey the law, but also to turn it to material advantage. In volunteering for the new economic zone programme after he had already moved, he was implementing a strategy of free migration in which resources provided by the state played a significant part. The programme of organized migration by the late 1980s differed from the 1960s. Poor people continued to sign up as in the past, but state migration funding was increasingly used to supplement the capital of families of free migrants. It was no longer simply a situation in which the state 'relied on the people' to serve its interests in a selfless and patriotic programme of nation-building. People now were relying on the state, using the state programme to serve their interests of family-based economic development in the highlands.

MIGRATION: A SOCIAL EVIL?

The distinction, in practice, between organized and free migration became increasingly blurred, as free migrants joined the programme to gain access to its resources. Policy debates took this into account. The 1998 conference recommended that the policy distinction between organized and free migration be abolished. State investment could then be redirected into project zones to attract free migrants. In this vision, free migrants were presented in a positive light, and the recommendation aimed, by attracting and directing their energies, to avoid negative impacts traditionally associated with their arrival.

In the past, free migration had had a bad press. Forest loss and reduction in biodiversity, difficulties of administration and disputes over resources, as well as 'social evils' such as gambling, drug addiction and theft were all imputed to free (hence undisciplined) migrants.[50] Land was the most important point of conflict, and the most serious reported clash between local minority residents and incoming settlers took place in Dak Lak, in a remote area far from the possibility of immediate government intervention:

The case of Ea Phê – Krông Pach (Đắc Lắc) – is symbolic, where in July 1991 the people of six old villages took sticks, knives and spades to fight and chase away the residents of a new village, who had recently arrived from Cao Bằng. They laid claim to their land and their forest. As a result, thirty-two houses were burnt down, one person died and damage worth over 8 million đồng was caused.[51]

This incident was incorrectly reported in a more recent study as having happened in 1980.[52] The error is significant, involving a distancing not only in terms of ethnic group (the newcomers in the second account are implied to be Tày or Nùng people from the northern hills, and not lowland Việt), but also in terms of time. In the absence of detailed and difficult research on the issue, it is hard to present a fuller analysis, especially on the basis of this single 'symbolic' event repeatedly invoked to bring attention to a problem rather than comprehend its dynamics and extent. There is no doubt, however, that competition over land became, as a result of migration to the central highlands, one of the region's most complex problems.

Among officials in the central highlands, the desire to avoid detailed discussion of issues such as land was mirrored by a corresponding tendency to scapegoat free migrants for other problems. During my visits to Ban Mê Thuột I observed this at almost every turn. At the Malaria Control Office, the increase in malaria was imputed to the free migrants. At the Agricultural Office, forest loss was 'mainly caused' by free migrants. And many ordinary people felt it necessary to explain the growth in 'social evils' in the same terms. Free migration started to seem something of a social evil itself. The urgency of all these problems seemed to stand in the way of a more satisfying but also more challenging, multi-dimensional perspective.

The very distinction between 'organized' and 'free' migration, enshrined in Vietnamese law, tended to promote both the fact and the image of such negative impacts. One participant at the 1998 conference expressed the hope that government policy would recognize the blurring of this distinction. Policy should no longer be used to move people, but would instead 'act as a catalyst' to draw migrants into designated places of destination. There the people would benefit from infrastructural investment, while the administration could maintain higher levels of management and control. Free migrants could hope to lose their negative reputation. The state and the people would work together and the highland environment would, to some extent and for some time, be spared.

This policy recommendation has not yet been ratified. Implying an end to the programme of organized migration in its existing form, it remains controversial. But in the event of ratification, how effective could it be in controlling and channelling the flow of free migrants to the central highlands? The aim – to tempt people to choose state-funded project zones rather than a patch of land cleared from the forest – is admirable. This, indeed, is a migration policy based on migration practice. But practice has a tendency to overflow the constraints placed upon it by policy. And the itinerary of one settler in Dak Lak should give us pause for thought before we leap into expressions of optimism. In 1990, Mr Bắc came to Buôn Tría on holiday from Thái Bình. He stopped off to visit his brother there on his way back from the seaside resort of Nha Trang. During a brief stay with his brother, he found land to farm and a woman to love, a woman from his home province who had lived in Dak Lak for some time. Imagine his mother's surprise when he returned to the village, announcing his marriage and a decision to move to Dak Lak. Respective formalities were completed quickly. Bắc soon returned to Dak Lak, where he bought land with money borrowed from his mother-in-law.[53]

This sort of pragmatic approach to migration, where opportunity and obligation play a big role in the orientation of people's lives and livelihoods, is ill suited for channelling into state-organized settlement zones. However well funded these zones might be, they would not offer the conveniences of the social and sentimental networks Bắc enjoyed.

Bắc was not the only one to respond, on a pragmatic basis, to his social environment. I asked him who sold him the land on which he built the house we were sitting in, the land from which he harvested his crop of rice. 'From another Thái Bình man', he said. But the head of the Mnong village, where Bắc's land was situated, told me a different story. 'That land belonged to a minority family', this Mnong man reported, after we took our leave of Bắc. 'Where do they live now?', I asked. 'I don't know', he replied. 'They took the money and went away.' According to people I spoke to in Dak Lak, highlanders who sold their lands and left in this way tended to take one of two paths. One was to Ban Mê Thuột or another urban area, where they tried trading or some other traditionally 'Việt' activity. The other was to the forest, where they cleared a plot in their traditional style, to farm the land further from the interlopers.[54] In so doing, they reinforced Viet stereotypes of 'minorities destroying the forests'.

CONCLUSION

In Part One we saw how the free migration of Việt people functioned during the colonial period. We noted in Chapter 3, in our case study of Tân Cương village, how a government programme, even a poorly organized and unsuccessful one, could give rise to networks and currents of spontaneous migration. In Part Three, we saw how comparatively well-organized programmes of migration created large settlements of Việt people in highland areas. And in the current chapter, we have examined the ways in which the existence of these settlements gave rise to a powerful movement of free migration in the 1980s and 1990s.

Free migrants paid no attention to discourses aimed at creating attachment to the village. Nor did they act in response to policies drawn up by the authorities. And their actions created dilemmas for the state. On the one hand, they fulfilled an objective of policy at no cost to the budget, establishing a population loyal to the red flag in this area of recent ethnic insurgency. On the other, free migrants in remoter areas operated outside of state control, generating costs to both physical, social and administrative environments. In 1998 this dilemma was the focus of debate in Hanoi during a conference on internal migration. From a security point of view, the central highlands no longer posed a threat to the communist government. The *terres rouges* of the region generated vast coffee incomes on the global export market. But Hanoi's control there was far from even. As the century closed, policy on the region was confused and contradictory. The question remained unanswered: will migration policy be reorientated to take account of migration practice?

NOTES

1   Interviews (Thái Nguyên, October 1996).

2   NAV1/RST 55348, 'Monographie de la province de Thai Nguyen', 1901.

3   Interviews (Thái Nguyên, October 1996).

4   Nguyễn Hồng Minh, 'Di dân tự do, tổng luận khoa học', Hanoi: Bộ Lao Động Thương Binh và Xã Hội, 1993, p. 3; Rodolphe De Koninck, *Deforestation in Viet Nam*, Ottawa: International Development Research Centre, 1999, p. 81.

5   Interview (Thái Nguyên, October 1996). Nguyễn Hồng Minh, 'Di dân tự do', p. 5. Le Bach Duong, 'State, Economic Development and Internal Migration in Vietnam', PhD thesis, Binghamton University, New York, p. 34.

6   Interview (Thái Nguyên, October 1996).

7   NAV3/BLD 1030(vv), Thái Mèo Autonomous Zone Labour Office to Minstry of Labour, 15 March 1961.

8   NAV3/BLD 1030(vv), Hà Nam People's Committee to districts and communes, 9 March 1961.

9   Philippe Papin, *Vietnam, parcours d'une nation*, Paris: La Documentation francaise, 1999, p. 134.

10 Lê Bạch Dương, 'State, Economic Development and Internal Migration', p. 30.

11 Phạm Xuân Điếm, 'Á dụng kinh nghiệm của Trực tầm: trong một tháng xã Đông Quang chúng tôi vận động được 469 người đi khai hoang', *Tiến Lên*, 25 March 1964, p. 2.

12 Nguyễn Huy Thiệp, 'Những người thợ xẻ'. In Nguyễn Huy Thiệp, *Như những ngon gió*, Hanoi: NXB Văn Học, 1999, pp. 259–260. See Vương Đức's superb film of this story, *Những người thợ xẻ*, Hanoi, 1999.

13 Interviews (Hanoi, May 1998, September 1999).

14 Interview (Sơn La, December 1996).

15 NAV3/BLD 1030(vv), 'Báo cáo tình hình người miền xuôi lên Thái Nguyên', Thái Nguyên, 23 February 1961.

16 NAV3/BLD 1030(vv), Thái Nguyên Labour Office to Ministry of Labour, 29 February 1961; 'Báo cáo tình hình số người các tỉnh miền xuôi lên, chi tiết sẽ Báo cáo sau', Thái Nguyên Labour Office, 19 April 1961.

17 NAV3/BLD 1030(vv), Thái Mèo Autonomous Zone Labour Office, 15 March 1961: 'Báo cáo tình hình nhân dân miền xuôi lên thị-xã Lào-Cai trong năm 1960 và từ tháng 1-1961 đến 4–1961', Lào Cai Labour Office, 5 May 1961.

18 NAV3/BLD 1030(vv), 'Báo cáo tình hình người miền xuôi lên Thái Nguyên', 23 February 1961.

19 NAV3/BLD 1030, Hà Đông Labour Office to Yên Bái Labour Office, 24.3.1961.

20 Interview (Hanoi, April 1996).

21 Nguyễn Hồng Minh, 'Di dân tự do', p. 12.

22 Ibid., p. 21.

23 Interview (Dak Lak, May 1996).

24 Papin, *Vietnam parcours d'une nation*, p. 147.

25 Dang Phong, 'Opening the Door: Two Centuries of Markets in Vietnam', unpublished manuscript, Hanoi, 1998.

26 Benedict J. Tria Kerkvliet, 'Village–State Relations in Vietnam: The Effect of Everyday Politics on Decollectivization', *JAS*, vol. 54, no. 2, 1995, pp. 410–411. See also Adam Fforde and Stefan de Vylder, *From Plan to Market*, Boulder, Colorado: Westview Press, 1996, p. 157.

27 Ibid., p. 412.

28 Papin, *Vietnam; parcours d'une nation*, pp. 156–157.

29 Li Tana, *Peasants on the Move, Rural–Urban Migration in the Hanoi Region*, Singapore: Institute of Southeast Asian Studies, 1996, p. 4.

30 Interviews (Thái Nguyên, July 1995, October 1996, January 1997).

31 La was 47 when I met him. Interview (Dak Lak, November 1996).

32 Interview (Thái Nguyên, July 1995).

33 Interview (Thái Bình, June 1995).

34 Nguyễn Hồng Minh, 'Di dân tự do', p. 11 (my emphasis).

35 Interview (Thái Nguyên, January 1997).

36 On the organic nature of family networking, see Hy Van Luong, 'Vietnamese Kinship: Structural Principles and the Socialist Transformation in Northern Vietnam', *JAS*, vol. 48, no. 4, 1989, p. 749; Hy Van Luong, *Revolution in the Village: Tradition and Transformation in North Vietnam, 1935–1988*, Honolulu: East-West Centre, 1992, p. 60.

37 Interview (Dak Lak, November 1996).

38 Le Thi, *The Role of the Family in the Formation of the Vietnamese Personality*, Hanoi: The Gioi Publishers, 1999, p. 84.

39 Nguyễn Hồng Minh, 'Di dân tự do', p. 11 (emphasis in original).

40 Hein Mallee, 'Rural Household Dynamics and Spatial Mobility in China'. In Thomas Scharping (ed.), *Floating Population and Migration in China: The Impact of Economic Reforms*, Hamburg: Institut für Asienkunde, 1997, pp. 283, 295–296.

41 Interview, Đông Xá commune, Đông Hưng district (Thái Bình, January 1997).

42 Interview (Thái Bình, June 1995).

43 Interview (Thái Nguyên, July 1995).

44 I am grateful to authorities at Tiền Hải district People's Committee (Thái Bình) for this document.

45 Interview (Dak Lak, November 1996). For description of the hunting lodge, see Gerald C. Hickey, *Free in the Forest: Ethnohistory of the Vietnamese Central Highlands, 1954–76*, New Haven and London: Yale University Press, 1982, pp. 30–31.

46 Bùi Đức Thịnh, 'Ea Lê – vùng quê mới – nhiều hứa hẹn', *Dak Lak*, 24 October 1986, p. 3.

47 For fuller analysis of this case, see the Appendix. See also Andrew Hardy, 'Strategies of Migration to Upland Areas in Contemporary Vietnam', *Asia Pacific Viewpoint*, vol. 41, no. 1, 2000, p. 26. Interview (Dak Lak, May 1996).

48 Council of Ministers Decision 254–CP, 16 June 1981, reproduced in Ministry of Labour, *Chính sách chế độ về tổ chực điều động lao động và dân cư*, Hanoi: Cục Điều Động Lao Động, c. 1983, p. 34.

49 Interview (Dak Lak, May 1996). See Andrew Hardy, 'Phát triển và phát rừngăă vài điểm trong lịch sử hiện đại của quá trình di dân tới Dak Lak', *Tạp Chí Xưa & Nay*, no. 29, 1996, p. 24.

50 Interviews (Dak Lak, November 1996); Ministry of Labour, Invalids and Social Affairs, 'Report on the Result of the Survey on Rural Migration in Dak Lak Province', Hanoi: Project VIE/95/004, 1997, p. 7; N. J. Jamieson, Le Trong Cuc and A. T. Rambo, *The Development Crisis in Vietnam's Mountains*, Honolulu: East-West Center, 1998, p. 15; De Koninck, *Deforestation*, p. 81.

51 Nguyễn Hồng Minh, 'Di dân tự do', p. 27.
52 Ministry of Labour, 'Report on the Result of the Survey on Rural Migration', p. 7.
53 Interview (Dak Lak, November 1996). See Prologue.
54 Interviews (Dak Lak, May and November 1996).

Migrants to the Red Hills

Figures 8 and 9: Settling in the central highlands
By the 1990s, villages of Việt people from the plains could be found through-out the central highlands, as here at Tam Giang commune, in Dak Lak province. Villages established by government organised settlers (above) were used by spontaneous migrants (below) who took to heart the Party's slogan to see the entire country as their home. As for the forest, as one ethnic minority official put it, there could be no further revolution now: 'there's no forest left for Hồ Chí Minh to hide in'.
Photographs by Andrew Hardy, May 1996.

Policy and Practice

*T*he twentieth century saw the formation of a frontier in the Vietnamese highlands. Where the hilly terrain – with its difficulties for rice agriculture, danger from malaria, hostility from local inhabitants – had in the past kept Việt people in the plains, it became in the course of the century home for many of them. Policies of migration and the free movement of farming families combined to create a stream of settlers. This combination of organized and free migration shaped the place they settled.

Policy, under the French, had little effect in stimulating migration. Attempts to encourage farmers of the Red River Delta to live in the hills were poorly planned, insufficiently supported, confused and often aborted. Other policies – policies of taxation and identity – conspired to limit and obstruct internal migration. Indeed, by contrast with the late nineteenth-century settlement of the Mekong Delta, where the French authorities played an active role in opening up the country, the structures of colonial administration in the twentieth century conspired to prevent it.[1] Small numbers of free migrants nevertheless found their way along French-built roads to the valleys and small towns of the highlands. They were, for the most part, poor people and people who, for one reason or another, sought to distance themselves from village society in the plains.

Revolution and war gave the highlands a new geo-political importance. In 1945, Hồ Chí Minh arrived in Hanoi from the hills, and a year later returned there to lead the resistance against the French from his base near the Red Mountain. No longer a region peripheral to a core society of lowland villages, the highlands became – in the calculations of communist leaders – strategically crucial to that society's independence. In the short term, large numbers of lowland people moved there, to fight first the French, then the American-backed regime in Saigon. Key battles were won there, first at Điện Biên Phủ, then at Ban Mê Thuột and Pleiku. And the newly independent state made plans to settle the strategic hills with a loyal population from the lowlands.

This was a nationalist programme, intended to secure the borders of the Vietnamese nation with Việt people, first in the northern hills, and after 1975 in the central highlands. The state relied on settlers from the Red River Delta to make a contribution not only to their own economic wellbeing, but also to the security of their now communist 'fatherland'. From the late 1950s, a neo-Stalinist economic system, a regime of household registration imported from China and campaigns of malaria control provided technological support to this programme of settlement. The main motivation of these settlers, if state propaganda is to be believed, was red patriotism. At the same time, while existing inhabitants of the highlands became 'ethnic minority compatriots', citizens of an independent nation, they were deemed to need reminding of their ties to the Fatherland. Việt settlers from the lowlands provided the necessary reminder. The key question, which lay at the heart of the highland settlement policy, was 'whose fatherland is it?'

The transition to a free-market economic system in the 1980s had far-reaching implications for this process. State-organized migration to the central highlands continued, but the development of free migration loosened state control over patterns of settlement. Systems of control over population movement – notably the link between economic welfare and place of residence – fell foul of the free market. Free migrants instead developed pragmatic networks of knowledge, support and capital provision to move to the *terres rouges* of the central highlands, to clear land, grow crops, and make their fortunes. Many of them did indeed achieve prosperity. But many networks existed because of prior state migration policy. People who had moved on the programme called their families and friends to join them. Some of these later settlers made use of the programme. People were increasingly able to determine their own relationship to it. In this context, officials found it increasingly difficult to maintain control, or even knowledge over the movement. Frontier formation found a momentum of its own.

This momentum created dilemmas for the state, dilemmas which emerged in two 1998 conferences on internal migration. The practice of free migration to provinces such as Dak Lak, fulfilling state imperatives at little financial cost to the national budget, was seen as bearing clear advantages. Officials nevertheless baulked at its costs in terms of environmental degradation and loss of administrative control. The dilemmas raised by this contradiction inform us about the negotiated nature of the highland frontier. On the one hand, Party General Secretary Lê Duẩn's desire that 'all Dak Lak must become one huge construction project' was in the process of fulfilment. On the other, the Party was by the 1990s no longer the project's main architect. Its control became increasingly uneven, almost like a Gruyère cheese. Key decisions were made on the basis of individual negotiations and small-scale boundary demarcations by settler families, in relation with previous settlers, indigenous inhabitants, local officials and the land/forest itself.

CONTINUITY AND CHANGE

Viewed from the metropole – situated in this story in the delta of the Red River - the highland frontier shifted south in the course of the century. Peasants of this delta, moving in the first instance to destinations in the northern and western hills, began after 1975 heading south to the central highlands. And over the century there also came a change of migrant. No longer poor people fleeing hunger (people like Thức and his mother), a number of migrants in the 1920s and 1930s had small capital sums to invest (people like Thân and his family). They sought opportunities to improve their family economy that were lacking in the overcrowded delta. Later, people moved to join the army (people like Giang). And mobilization techniques developed during the war were redeployed, to persuade people to contribute to nation building and the country's defence. The motivation of people (like the families of Học and Ngọc) in their 'semi-voluntary' decision to move was ideological rather than economic. Not all of these migrations were successful (as in the case of Mẫu). However with the reforms of the 1980s, increasing numbers of migrants were people with the capital and determination to grow rich (people like Bắc).*

A comparison of Vietnamese and American frontier mythology highlights this change. This comparison was made by Nguyễn Đăng Thục in an article on Vietnam's 1,000 year southward advance (*nam tiến*) published in Saigon in 1970:

> The truth about the southward migration and expansion of Vietnam is different from the westward advance of the American people, which was a venture, a satisfying adventure, responding to desires for authority and extraordinary greatness. But for our Việt people, this was a matter of survival, of the very existence of the nation, an attempt to remain a nation with a more or less traditional character; it is distinct in this respect.[2]

If we accept Nguyễn Đăng Thục's terms of reference, then the change effected for 'our Việt people' in the course of the twentieth century was that they moved increasingly in the manner of Americans, with capital, contacts and a buoyant sense of optimism.[3] As we saw at the beginning of this study, by the 1990s some of them – such as Mẫu with his 'Cow-Boy' cigarettes – consumed and appropriated symbols of American frontier culture.† But Nguyễn Đăng Thục's terms of reference are doubtful. The Turnerian image of the frontier in America's west – risk, adventure, grandeur and derring-do, shaping the very course of American history – was reproduced by Nguyễn Đăng Thục in this article. But this has been shown to be a caricature, a myth, even if the myth was created out of reality and in turn influenced that reality. This was understood by Henry Nash Smith who, as early as 1950, was able 'to compare and contrast that agrarian myth with the real world of agriculture and to show the agrarian myth at work in shaping and sometimes distorting legislation, party politics, and sectional rivalry'.[4] In Vietnam, a Social Darwinian language of survival and retention of tradition is clearly inadequate. The conceptualization of Vietnam's historical frontier remains an open field.

Recent research in English has started to respond to Michael Cotter's call for a study of the social and economic dynamics of Vietnam's southward expansion.[5] Keith Taylor, Li Tana and Nola Cooke have provided glimpses into the workings of Việt settlement in the 'Đăng Trong' region of central and southern Vietnam.[6] Choi Byung Wook offers insights into the 'Vietnamization' of people living in the Gia Định area of the south.[7] Keith Taylor went as far as to abolish the term *nam tiến* ('I do not believe any such event took place'). He proposed an alternative reading, previously couched in terms of an inexorable march to the south of Việt armies and their accompanying settlers, now seen as a series of episodes of regional conflict over the centuries.[8] Yet these are only the beginnings of a reinterpretation of this complex historical process, and we remain ignorant even of its historiography. When did the concept of a 'southward advance' first enter the vocabulary of Vietnamese history? The continuities remain a mystery, the changes unexplained.

---

*   See Prologue.

†   See Prologue.

The argument of this book is that, in twentieth-century Vietnam, interplays between the people moving and the state were crucial to the process of frontier formation. Migrants may have been risk-taking entrepreneurs or famished flood victims, but the key relationship on the frontier was that between these individuals and the state; this even influenced the nature of contact between the migrants and the indigenous population of the frontier areas. If, as we saw in Chapter 9, Việt people moving in small numbers assimilated into the local destination culture, and those moving in large groups assimilated local culture into their own, the determining factor was a relationship of social and political dominance, a relationship implying the support of some sort of authority at local or state level. The relationship of state policy to migratory practice moulded the nature of the contact from which the frontier was formed.

This relationship was by no means a new feature of Vietnam's history, nor of its historiography. This was underlined by a study published in Hanoi. In his 'History of Việt People's Migration from the Tenth to the Nineteenth Century', Đặng Thu rightly stressed the diversity of migration form in the process of geo-political expansion towards the south.[9] The book is packed with stories of soldiers, traders, paupers and wanderers; families, villagers, individuals and roving gangs; kings, mandarins, convicts and Chinese. And in its conclusion, it stressed the links between free migration and settlement projects organized by the state:

> This was the redistribution of part of the population by natural and spontaneous means, following the model of 'on lush land, birds will alight'. The phenomenon of spontaneous migration was carried out *reluctantly*, especially in the context of Vietnamese farmers who essentially have a psychology of attachment to their village, and do not want to go far from the home of their fathers and the land of their ancestors.
>
> Alongside spontaneous migration there was migration organized by the state. This phenomenon was particularly prevalent during Nguyễn times, for the opening up and development of the country. Is it true to say that this was in part the Nguyễn dynasty's method of controlling spontaneous migration?
>
> The main direction of migration under the Nguyễn was to encourage migrants to go to the South, where land was plentiful, fertile and the border was not yet stable.[10]

In this account, the policy of migration was in constant interactive relationship with its practice. Yet, some interpretations of those relations are open to question. In reproducing the discourse about peasants' attachment to their village, Đặng Thu showed some of the blocks that went into building the myth of a reluctant expansion, already signalled in Nguyễn Đăng Thục's article above. The coin of the reluctant peasant, meanwhile, could be turned over to reveal an aggressive state: 'in the occupation of a new area of land, usually the army went first, the people followed later'.[11] This conclusion is contrary to a vastly more diverse historical record. For example, Diệp Đình Hoa made mention, in his study of a village in the southern province of Đồng Nai, of the seventeenth-century establishment of administrative structures in this region, formerly the territory of the kingdom of Champa. There were, he observed, 'Việt people living as foreign nationals alongside other ethnic groups who now became subjects of the Nguyễn lords in this area of land'. This was presumably an example of what Nguyễn Thế Anh described as 'peaceful infiltration by an avant-garde of settlers who cleared land abandoned by the Cham'.[12]

Đặng Thu's conclusion looks like an inherited orientalism of feudal despots and stagnant peasants, distorted under the lens of revolutionary nationalism. What I wish to highlight here is the pragmatism of the Nguyễn rulers. The Emperor Minh Mạng, we learn in a study by Mai Khắc Ứng, 'used every method available' to encourage the cultivation of new fields of rice. These included 'permitting any individual who cleared land himself to use it as his own private field, or encouraging rich people to come forward and recruit tenants to set up new village settlements'.[13] The state's principal aim was the maintenance of control over the population. Vagrancy was discouraged and displaced people were fixed to a plot of land, where they could be turned into reliable sources of taxation, corvée labour and military service.[14] Of equal importance were the dynamism, mobility and pragmatism of the people themselves, whose attachment to their village of origin was far more a result of state policy than much of the literature cares, or dares, to acknowledge.

With respect, then, to the history of Vietnam's southward expansion, I add my voice to those of historians such as Michael Cotter and Claudine Lombard-Salmon in calling for new and detailed research on socio-economic aspects of frontier formation.[15] The present account catalogues that frontier's turn to the hills of the north and west, and its incorporation into the structures and boundaries of a twentieth-century nation state. It will, I trust, offer some guidance to hardy pioneers prepared to open up such a difficult field of scholarship, and throw up ideas of practical research value concerning the continuities in settlement and migration over Vietnam's *longue duree*. We need to have access to detailed, local studies of individual steps and processes in the southward advance, monographs outlining its policy and practice in specific contexts. We need also a certain perspective on the creation of myths and discourses surrounding that movement. How was it was that the term 'southward advance' (*nam tiến*) came into being; that the expansion of the Vietnamese nation came to be seen as 'reluctant'; that Viet peasants came to be described, by Vietnamese as well as by French, as attached to their home village (*quê hương*)? Finally, we need close-grained analysis of the relations of contact between the Việt and neighbouring peoples, mediated above all by the settlers on the frontier.

Given the current momentum of migration to the hills, by the time such studies emerge, the population map of Vietnam will have changed considerably. This point was made by a Vietnamese participant at the International Seminar on Internal Migration held in Hanoi in May 1998 who posed the question:

> When will the province of Dak Lak become a sending province, sending migrants to other regions? Because we have already seen that the provinces of the north, like Bắc Kạn, Tuyên Quang and Thái Nguyên which used to receive settlers, now send them elsewhere in increasing numbers.

The question was rhetorical and received no answer. The silence that followed it concealed, however, a question far more intriguing for anyone concerned with migration in Vietnam. When Dak Lak will send migrants out is an issue of academic interest – five years or ten years? The Vice President of the province implied as much in her call for increased funding from the state: 'The people keep having children. People in Dak Lak are developing too fast. There's no coffee land left.' But the question of where people can go from Dak Lak is altogether more problematic. We may hope that the family planning policies will contain the rate of population growth rate. We may anticipate that the factories of Ho Chi Minh City, Hanoi, Ban Mê Thuột and elsewhere will provide employment enough to attract people to areas of urban development. We may hope that such policies can keep the Vietnamese frontier within its frontiers.

If it does not, we should take careful note of a joke I shared with an old man in the highlands. He was from Thái Bình. We were sitting on the verandah outside his house in Dak Lak. Crowds of excited children were playing and fighting around us as we talked. Unable to hear himself think, the old man chased them away, remarking: 'In five years' time, there'll be no more land, if people have so many children. We must implement family planning'. Then he laughed. 'Otherwise', he added, 'we'll have to go and clear land in Cambodia'.

NOTES

1   Pierre Brocheux, 'L'économie et la société dans l'ouest de la Cochinchine pendant la période coloniale, 1898–1940', Université de Paris, Faculté des Lettres, 1969. Parts of this thesis have been published, as follows: 'Grands propriétaires et fermiers dans l'ouest de la Cochinchine pendant la période coloniale', *Revue Historique*, no. 499, 1971, pp. 59–77; *The Mekong Delta: Ecology, Economy and Revolution, 1860–1960*, Madison: University of Wisconsin-Madison, Center for Southeast Asian Studies, 1995.

2   Nguyễn Đăng Thục, 'Nam Tiến Việt Nam', *Sử Địa*, nos 19–20, 1970, p. 25.

3   For an account of American optimism and doubt about migration to the west, see John D. Unruh, *The Plains Across, The Overland Emigrants and the Trans-Mississippi West, 1840–1860*, Urbana and Chicago: University of Illinois Press, 1993, p. 29.

4   Henry Nash Smith, *Virgin Land: The American West as Symbol and Myth*, Cambridge, Ma.: Harvard University Press, 1950. Discussed by Patricia Nelson Limerick, 'Making the Most of Words – Verbal activity and Western America'. In William Cronon, George Miles and Jay Gitlin (eds), *Under an Open Sky – Rethinking America's Western Past*, New York: W. W. Norton & Company, 1992, p. 173.

5   Michael Cotter, 'Towards a Social History of the Vietnamese Southward Movement', *JSAH*, vol. 9, no. 1, 1968, pp. 12–24.

6   Keith W. Taylor, 'Nguyen Hoang and the Beginnings of Vietnam's Southward Expansion'. In Anthony Reid (ed.), *Southeast Asia in the Early Modern Era: Trade, Power, Belief*, Ithaca, New York: Cornell University Press, 1993, pp. 42–65. Li Tana, *Nguyen Cochinchina: Southern Vietnam in the Seventeenth and Eighteenth Centuries*, Ithaca, New York: Cornell Southeast Asia Program, 1998; Li Tana, 'An Alternative Vietnam? The Nguyen Kingdom in the Seventeenth and Eighteenth Centuries', *JSAS*, vol. 29, no. 1, 1998, pp. 111–121; Nola Cooke, 'Regionalism and the Nature of Nguyen rule in Seventeenth-Century Dang Trong (Cochinchina)', *JSAS*, vol. 29, no. 1, 1998, pp. 122–161.

7   Choi Byung Wook, 'Southern Vietnam under the Reign of Minh Mang (1820–1841): Central Policies and Local Response', PhD thesis, Australian National University, Canberra, 1999.

8   Keith W. Taylor, 'Surface Orientations in Vietnam: Beyond Histories of Nation and Region', *Journal of Asian Studies*, vol. 57, no. 4, 1998, p. 951.

9   Đặng Thu (ed.), *Nghiên cứu lịch sử di dân của người Việt thế kỷ X đến giữa thế kỷ XIX*, Hanoi: Viện Sử Học, 1994, p. 167.

10   Ibid., p. 164.

11   Ibid., p. 167.

12   Diệp Đình Hoa, *Làng Bến Gỗ*, Đồng Nai: NXB Đồng Nai, 1995, p. 50; Nguyễn Thế Anh, 'Le Nam Tiến dans les textes vietnamiens'. In P.B. Lafont, (ed.), *Les frontières du Vietnam: Histoire des frontières de la péninsule Indochinoise*, Paris: L'Harmattan, 1989, p. 121.

13   Mai Khắc Ứng, *Chính sách khuyến nông dưới thời Minh Mạng*, Hanoi: NXB Văn Hóa Thông Tin, 1996, p. 6.

14   Masaya Shiraishi, 'State, Villagers and Vagabonds: Vietnamese Rural Society and the Phan Ba Vanh Rebellion', *Senri Ethnological Studies*, vol. 13, 1984, pp. 345–400; Yumio Sakurai, 'Peasant Drain and Abandoned Villages in the Red River Delta between 1750 and 1850'. In Anthony Reid (ed.), *The Last Stand of Asian Autonomies: Responses to Modernity in the Diverse States of Southeast Asia and Korea, 1750–1900*, New York: St. Martin's Press, 1997, pp. 144–145; Yumio Sakurai, *Betonamu Sonraku no Keisei*, Tokyo: Soubunsha, 1987, pp. 233–238.

15   Michael Cotter, 'Towards a Social History', p. 12–24; Claudine Lombard-Salmon, *Un exemple d'acculturation chinoise: la province de Gui Zhou au XVIII siècle*, Paris: École française d'Extrême-Orient, 1972, p. 286.

Statistical Essay
'The name is there but the body is not': Interpreting the Figures on Migration in Twentieth-Century Vietnam

*M*igrants are difficult people to count. Unlike folk of fixed abode, whose numbers, fertility, mortality and other demographic characteristics can more easily be measured, migrants do not remain still. This appendix aims to explore the numbers involved in the story of migration from Vietnam's Red River Delta over the twentieth century. These numbers had their own culture, and an idea of how they were produced and consumed will contribute to our understanding both of the data themselves and of the story they tell. The bottom line to this enquiry is that it is very difficult, as a result of the different statistical cultures involved, to answer the question of how many people migrated in twentieth-century Vietnam. An attempt must nonetheless be made.

Officials of the census and other data-collecting bodies face the challenge of people's mobility. This compounds the difficulty of interpreting normal statistical inaccuracies and misrepresentations. In a country like Vietnam, where the reach of such bodies over the twentieth century has been subject to considerable logistical variations (historical, geographical and organizational), the challenge is all the greater. This was particularly the case after 1954, when these bodies' responsibilites were vastly expanded. Greater volumes of information were generated but administrative arrangements and categories changed over time, along with the implications for families of provision of certain data. It was for this reason that I opted, in researching *Red Hills*, for a qualitative approach, aimed at a portrait of the dynamics of migration rather than analysis of migrant 'flows'. Flow analysis can lead the researcher into abstracted approximations that obscure the nature of the reality being described. I do not wish here to deny the importance of quantitative work. The purpose of this essay is, rather, to offer an introduction to the difficulties of quantitative measurement of migration in Vietnam. In doing so, I hope to point to some of the traps which future analysts of the figures may wish to avoid. I also aim to provide some specific statistical background to this study. Those seeking more general population data are referred to the books by Ng Shui Meng and Khổng Diễn, which remain the best sources in English for the historical demography of twentieth-century Vietnam.[1]

COLONIAL ERA

Pierre Gourou opens his analysis of population change in the Red River Delta with a sober reflection entitled 'Difficulties of the Study': 'It is unfortunately very difficult to study the evolution of the population, as the documents available show no rigour at all. As a result, we must above all examine our sources of information.'[2] There is no need to reproduce Gourou's findings here, as we examined some of the issues he raised in the discussion of 'overpopulation' in Chapter 2. His conclusion was pessimistic, interpreted bluntly by Ng Shui Meng in terms of the 'gross deficiencies of the population data'.[3] These data were compiled from declarations made by village authorities. The declarations were, moreover, structurally incomplete. They counted only registered males of the village, and used coefficients to include children, women and old men. Coefficients varied from place to place, reflecting local circumstances and the calculation methods used by local authorities. Ng Shui Meng noted the distinction in Tonkin between 'estimates', based on village tax returns multiplied by a coefficient, and 'counts', whereby population 'was estimated from the village returns and then adjusted according to an estimated per capita consumption of salt'. Counts were made in 1921, 1926, 1931 and 1936.[4] No census comparable to that of the Netherlands Indies was ever carried out.

The quality of the data relied, as a result, on the 'goodwill and intelligence' of the village authorities.[5] Villages had historically under-declared their populations, on the basis of which taxation was calculated. And while the colonial authorities gradually freed tax revenue from dependence on population rolls, the culture of under-declaration remained. Indeed, it extended up to the mandarin administration at the province level, as the senior French official in Nam Định province discovered. The minutes of his meeting with the mandarins on 21 February 1919 recorded how 'the Résident noted with surprise that the information provided showed a gradual reduction in the population, while outward signs tended to show the contrary'.[6] Accidental calculation errors were also reported, as for example in 1923 by an Economic Services Department official, who concluded that although the population had probably grown, it would be 'entirely vain to seek to put figures to the increase'.[7]

Table 2: Population of Thái Bình, 1921–43

Year	Population	Growth (%)
1921	689,000	
1931	960,000	3.3
1936	1,027,000	1.3
1943	1,139,800	1.4

Source: *ASI*, quoted in Nguyễn Thế Huệ, 'Về dân số Việt Nam từ thập kỷ 20 đến trước Cách Mạng Tháng Tám', *NCLS*, vol. 265, no. 6, 1994, pp. 49–52, 64.

Figures were put on the increase, however. Available data for the densely settled provinces of the Red River Delta suggest population growth was considerable. See Tables 2 and 3.

Table 3: Population of Nam Định, 1921–43

Year	Population	Growth (%)
1921	826,000	
1931	1,013,000	2.0
1936	1,056,000	2.0
1943	1,233,400	2.2

Source: *ASI*, quoted in Nguyễn Thế Huệ, 'Về dân số Việt Nam', pp. 49–52, 64.

These data, from the *Annuaire Statistique de l'Indochine*, remain the best we have for this era. Ng Shui Meng urged caution. 'Although one should not give too much weight to these results, they nonetheless form the most "accurate" basis for the analysis of the demographic growth pattern for this period and, to a certain extent, do indicate the major demographic trends.'[8] I share this view. But there remains a further question. If these were the difficulties involved in estimating the settled populations of villages, then what problems lay in store for those wanting to count migrants?

We may start by comparing data for provinces of out- and in-migration. Thái Bình and Nam Định were provinces of out-migration, though curiously Nam Định (with transport communications offering easy access to labour recruiters) shows higher growth than Thái Bình. Thái Nguyên in the northern midlands was a province of in-migration. Changes in Thái Nguyên's population are shown in Table 4.

Growth rates vary in the above table, reflecting 'normal' inaccuracies which also manifested themselves in the data for Nam Định and Thái Bình. But the persistently high levels of growth warrant attention. If these figures are to be believed, Thái Nguyên's population growth was at least double and perhaps up to four times that of the lower delta.

Examination of these data in the light of archival evidence raises a number of questions. These figures necessarily passed through the office of the province Résident. It was related in Chapter 2 that during the 1930s the Résident, Alfred Echinard, had an interest in inflating the statistics of in-migration, in support of his policy of granting small concessions. As his successors discovered, many concession holders turned out to be 'pseudo-settlers' and 'men of straw'.[9] How far were Thái Nguyên's population figures subject to manipulation, not only in the village but at the provincial Résidence as well? There are no easy answers to this question, although there is ethnographic evidence of in-migration to in the

                    Red Hills

Table 4: Population of Thái Nguyên, 1902–43

Year	Population	Growth (%)
1902*	70,000	
1905*	35,879	
1905	70,000	
1916	45,000	
1920	67,018	4.1 (since 1905)
1921	69,524	
1926	69,341	
1931	84,685	2.0 (since 1921)
1932	90,508	
1936	100,000	3.3 (since 1931)
1939	120,000	6.0 (since 1936)
1940	125,000	4.0 (since 1939)
1943	153,500	6.8 (since 1940)

***Note**: The accuracy of the 1902 and 1905 figures are particularly doubtful

Sources: Data on **1902**: NAV1/RST 39055, Telegram, 5 February 1902. On **1905**: CAOM/Madrolle 42PA/3, Résident's report, 13 April 1905; *ASI*, quoted in Alfred Echinard, 'Notice sur la province de Thai Nguyen', Thai Nguyen: unpublished monograph, 1932, p. 69. On **1916**: Darles (former Résident), quoted in Echinard, 'Notice', p. 69. On **1920**: *ASI*, quoted in Echinard, 'Notice', p. 69. On **1921–32**: census, quoted in Echinard, 'Notice', p. 69. On **1936**: *ASI*, quoted in p. 50. On **1939**: NAV1/RST 69048, Echinard correspondence, 22 December 1938. On **1940**: NAV1/RST 74431, Economic report, 1940. On **1943**: *ASI*, quoted in Nguyễn Thế Huệ, 'Về dân số Việt Nam', p. 50.

1920s and 1930s. We may say that Thái Nguyên's population grew rapidly up to 1943, and owed much of that growth to in-migrants.

Comparison of Thái Nguyên with other provinces indicates that high growth was an exception rather than the rule. Figures for the Việt population in highland regions of Indochina at the end of the colonial period show a relatively low level of in-migration.

Population statistics for these regions desert us in the middle of the Pacific War (1943) and re-emerge only with the restoration of peace (1954). It is clear from the qualitative evidence that during these years, Thái Nguyên enjoyed a substantial influx of migrants. There were refugees from famine in 1944–45 and from the war thereafter, as well as soldiers and cadres who moved to the communist resistance capital in the mountains bordering Tuyên Quang province.

Table 5: The Việt population in the highland regions of colonial Indochina

Province	Year	Population
Northern Highlands		
Bắc Kạn	1938	2,815
Lạng Sơn	1938	7,000
Hà Giang	1938	1,200
Lào Cai	1938	5,143
Điện Biên Phủ	1938	46
Total		16,204
Other parts of Highland Indochina		
Pleiku	1938	4,000
Kontum	c. 1941	15,000
	1943	7,000
	1943	7,000
Dak Lak	1943	4,000
Haut Donnai	1938	12,427
	1943	10,000
Vientiane, Laos	1938	6,500
Whole of Laos	c. 1941	27,000
	1939	39,500

Sources:
Northern Highlands CAOM/Guernut 96, 'Réponses à l'enquête sur les migrations intérieures'. Reports by provincial administrators.
Other parts of Highland Indochina On **Pleiku**: CAOM/Guernut 96, 'Réponses à l'enquête'. On **Kontum**: CAOM/INF 2282, 'Les causes de la répartition inégale des hommes en Indochine', article in *La Vie* by Charles Robequain, undated (c. 1941); Gerald C. Hickey, *Sons of the Mountains. Ethnohistory of the Vietnamese Central Highlands to 1954*, New Haven and London: Yale University Press, 1982, p. 439. On **Dak Lak**: Hickey, *Sons of the Mountains*, p. 439. On **Haut Donnai**: CAOM/Guernut 96, 'Réponses à l'enquête'; Hickey, *Sons of the Mountains*, p. 439. On **Vientiane**: CAOM/Guernut 96, 'Réponses à l'enquête'. On **Laos**: CAOM/INF 2282, Robequain, 'Les causes de la répartition'; Eric Pietrantoni, 'La Population du Laos de 1912 à 1945', *BSEI*, vol. 28, no. 1, 1953, p. 34.

Thái Bình and Nam Định suffered population loss. Some of these movements are described in Chapter 5. Only a close combing of war-related archival documents would allow any quantitative estimate of their numbers. Hostilities prevented the collection of more traditional forms of demographic data.

THE DEMOCRATIC REPUBLIC OF VIETNAM, 1954–76

After 1954, a statistics collection apparatus was established by the DRV. In many ways, this greatly facilitates quantitative analysis of the population and its movements. In reality, however, the way these data were collected, the manner of their reporting and changes in administrative arrangements pose numerous difficulties of interpretation.

If we restrict our study to data on organized migration, we are struck by the variety of sources from which statistics may be gleaned. That is to say, there was no single body from which all the necessary statistics may be obtained. We must digress briefly from an analysis of the figures to an examination of the bodies responsible for migration policy and the generation of data about it. There were two main policies (state farms and migrant cooperatives), though some administrative overlap existed at certain periods. The following chronology is my attempt to chart their administrative evolution.

State Farms[10]

1945–51	Bureau of Land Clearance and Migration (*Nha Khẩn Hoang Di Dân*), under the Ministry of Farms (*Bộ Canh Nông*).*
1951–54	Office of Resettlement and Land Reclamation (*Sở Doanh Điền*), Ministry of Farms.†
1955–60	Several offices had responsibility for state farms, including: Department of National Agricultural Enterprise Management (*Cục Quản Lý Quốc Doanh Nông Nghiệp*); Ministry of Agriculture and Forestry (*Bộ Nông Lâm*); Ministry of Defence (*Bộ Quốc Phòng*); Central Reunification Committee (*Ban Thống Nhất Trung Ương*).*
1960–75	Ministry of State Farms (*Bộ Nông Trường*).* Ministry of Agriculture (*Bộ Nông Nghiệp*).*

Migrant Cooperatives in New Economic Zones[11]

1961–63	Department of Land Clearance (*Cục Khai Hoang*), Ministry of State Farms.
1963–66	General Land Clearance Office (*Tổng Cục Khai Hoang*), Ministry of State Farms.
1967–70	Highlands Department (*Vụ Miền Núi*), Ministry of Agriculture.
1971–74	Committee for Highlands Economy and New Economic Zones (*Ban Kinh Tế Miền Núi và Vùng Kinh Tế Mới*).
1975–76	General Office of State Farms and National Enterprise (*Tổng Cục Nông Trường Quốc Doanh*), Ministry of Agriculture.
1977–81	General Office for Land Clearance and the Building of New Economic Zones (*Tổng Cục Khai Hoang và Xây Dựng Vùng Kinh Tế Mới*), Ministry of Agriculture.
1981–84	Two offices had responsibility for policy and implementation respectively: Central Steering Committee on Labour and Population Dis-

tribution (*Ban Chỉ Đạo Phân Bố Lao Động và Dân Cư Trung Ương*), under the Government Council (*Hội Đồng Chính Phủ*); and the Office of Labour Appointments (*Cục Điều Động Lao Động*), under the Ministry of Labour (*Bộ Lao Động*), later Ministry of Labour, Invalids and Social Affairs (*Bộ Lao Động Thương Binh và Xã Hội*).

Five offices had responsibility for planning, budgets, land clearance, implementation and sedentarization of highlanders, respectively, after 1984: State Planning Committee (*Ủy Ban Kế Hoạch Nhà Nước*); Ministry of Finance (*Bộ Tài Chính*); Ministry of Agriculture and Food Industries (*Bộ Nông Nghiệp và Công Nghiệp Thực Phẩm*) and Ministry of Forestry (*Bộ Lâm Nghiệp*); Department of Labour Appointments organization (*Cục Tổ Chức Điều Động Lao Động*) under the Ministry of Labour, Invalids and Social Affairs (this department moved to the Ministry for Agriculture and Rural Development in 1996); Committee for Sedentarization (*Ban Định Canh Định Cư*), previously under the Committee for Highlands Economy and New Economic Zones, later under the Ministry of Forestry.[12]

The frequency of change in government office responsible for migration influenced the availability of data. During my research in the mid 1990s, I found that documents from the Department of State Agricultural Enterprise Management (for the 1950s), the State Planning Committee and the General Statistical Office (for the 1960s), and the Central Agricultural Committee (for the early 1970s) were available in the National Archives of Vietnam (Centre No. 3). However, these by no means covered all the relevant government departments during those periods. Documents on the 1980s had not yet been passed to the archive depot. They had to be sought directly from the ministries responsible, notably the Ministry of Labour, Invalids and Social Affairs. Since the latest change in the management of migration, in 1996, these documents are now at the Ministry for Agriculture and Rural Development.

As Phạm Đỗ Nhật Tân commented in his 1992 doctoral thesis on the issue, these changes also had an impact on the quality of policy implementation:

> On average every three years, an organization was formed with a new name on top of that of an old organization, even though the work itself did not change. This allows us to conclude that this is a difficult and complex business, as the old forms of organization were unable to obtain results or satisfy the demands of migration targets set.[13]

Poor implementation meant poor data, particularly at the province and district levels where the availability of information often depended on the memory of the cadres responsible. More than once I heard the apologetic euphemism, that historical data were not available because of the difficulty of keeping records owing to the war, storms, floods, etc. At this level, however, organizational instability was most strongly felt in terms of personnel changes. In the countryside, I met few cadres who had more than ten or even five years' experience of organizing migration. The only provincial or district cadres who could remember anything about the policy in 1980 had already retired. They were often happy to share their experience with me, and sometimes perhaps with their successors in office. This problem was less frequent in Hanoi, however, where I met cadres who had worked on migration for fifteen or more years and where the institutional memory was considerably longer.

Statistics drawn from the government department responsible for organized migration had to be complemented by reference to other data. Newspapers were a surprisingly good source of figures at the provincial and district levels, while interviews with officials, locals and migrants generated figures at the commune and village level. While these could, on occasion, be cross-checked, many of these semi-official or non-official statistics are subject to caveats. Let us turn first to the manner of their reporting.

Sometimes reporting of numbers was vague. This, of course, was true for interview information, though less often than I imagined. The recall of migrants could often be surprisingly accurate. Vagueness also plagued figures in newspaper articles, which were designed to promote policy rather than report on it. *Nhân Dân* stated, for example, in 1958–61, that 'tens of thousands of cadres and soldiers', and 'more than 14,000 lowland families and youth' moved to state farms in the northern highlands.[14] Both of these figures were orders of magnitude rather than statistics.

Sometimes data on migrant departures were given, while numbers of people who returned home or abandoned the settlement were ignored or underreported. A 1966 General Land Clearance Office report stated that in 1961–66, 1,050,000 people moved (630,000 to cooperatives, 420,000 to state farms, forestry enterprises and factories in the highlands), while only 3 per cent went home.[15] This last figure was a vast understatement, even for that time.

Scattered references to short periods are more readily available than detailed statistics on decades. In this way we learn that, in 1971–74, 24,000 people moved to state farms and new economic zones in the highlands.[16] This statistic, considerably lower than that for the early 1960s, suggests that after the American bombing started and urban areas were evacuated, the numbers of migrants to highland areas dropped off, an impression confirmed by Phạm Đỗ Nhật Tân.[17]

Data on the country and the period as a whole tend to be excessively generalized. For example, 'during the fifteen years from 1960–75, nearly 1 million people migrated within northern Vietnam'.[18] Khổng Diễn's more carefully assembled figure of 384,000 may be closer to the truth, taking into account a rate of abandonment estimated at over 50 per cent during this period.[19]

When figures are reported in sufficient detail, other problems become immediately apparent. One of the most obvious is the administrative boundary change. Anyone researching the history of Vietnam's countryside during the second half of the twentieth century will have come across the periodic mergers and separations that characterize the administrative geography of many provinces, districts and communes. These changes seriously compromise the quality of time series statistics. The complexity of boundary changes in the province of Nam Định, which merged and separated with two neighbouring provinces (Nam Hà and Ninh Bình) several times between 1965 and 1997, got the better of my attempts to establish continuous data.

Table 6: Population of Thái Bình, 1954–89

Year	People (000s)	Year	People (000s)	Year	People (000s)
1954	952	1964	1,254	1969	1,254
1960	1,184	1965	1,250	1970	1,285
1961	1,201	1966	1,222	1979	1,506
1962	1,221	1967	1,210	1989	1,632
1963	1,236	1968	1,224	1999	1,786

Sources: Data on **1954–70**: NAV3/TCTK 2548(vv), 'Báo cáo một số chỉ tiêu dân số từ 1954 đến 1970', Thái Bình Statistical Office, 19 March 1970. On **1979**: *Dân số Việt Nam*, 1-10-1979, Ban Chỉ Đạo Tổng Điều Tra Dân Số Trung Ương, Hanoi, 1979. On **1989**: Central Census Steering Committee, *Vietnam Population Census - 1989, Completed Census Results*. Hanoi, 1991, vol. 1. On **1999**: Central Census Steering Committee, *1999 Population and Housing Census: Sample Results*, Hanoi: Thế Giới Publishers, 2000, p. 99.

. The province of Thái Bình is unusual in that its administrative boundary did not change at all. It owed this stability to its geographical situation as a sort of island, accessible only by crossing one of the waterways of the Red River Delta. Thái Bình's continuity of boundary allows us to establish data continuity for population growth, out-migration from the province, and migrant destinations (see Tables 6, 7 and 8). These are drawn from a variety of sources, and provide a fairly good picture of organized migration from a province reputed for its successful policy implementation. Note that Vietnamese officials used three measures when counting migrants: numbers of families, numbers of people, numbers of people able to work (labourers).

Note that the reduction in Thái Bình's population in 1965–67 was due not only to the implementation of the migration policy (29,217 people left for highland areas in 1966), but also to the war. American bombs were falling. An article, fairly common of its type, in the provincial newspaper in 1966 entitled 'Setting off to fight America and save the country,' reported that young people were enthusiastically leaving to join the fighting.[20] But see the discussion of Vĩnh Phú's population data below, for a further interpretative dimension to figures for this period.

The data in Table 8 were drawn from the same source, the Migration Office in Thái Bình, but on two different occasions. In addition to some rather obvious omissions – data for the provinces of Sơn La and Hòa Bình, and the city of Hanoi

Table 7: Migration from Thái Bình to new economic zones, 1961–94

Date	Families	People	Labourers
1961		9,800	
1962		10,700	
1963		23,900	
1964		20,400	
1961–65	16,500	82,367	33,500
1966–70	9,600	70,700	24,200
1971–75	8,800	38,900	15,500
1961–75	34,900	192,000	73,300
1976–80	13,500	70,100	32,300
1981–85	14,000	68,100	30,700
1986–90	6,400	25,400	14,800
1991–92	2,40	10,400	5,900
1961–92	71,200	366,000	157,000
1990–94	4,400	16,100	10,000
1961–94	76,900	378,900	192,300

Note: These figures, where comparison is possible from one document to another, are frequently inconsistent. I have rounded them to the nearest hundred.
Sources: On **1961–62**: NAV3/TCTK 2399(vv), Thái Bình Statistical Office to General Statistical Office, 16 December 1964. On **1963**: calculations from NAV3/TCTK 2399(vv), 'Báo cáo tình hình thực hiện kế hoạch chuyển dân đi tham gia phát triển kinh tế miền núi năm 1964', Thái Bình Statistical Office, 20 December 1964. On **1964**: NAV1/TCTK 2399(vv), Thái Bình Statistical Office to General Statistical Office, 25 January 1965. On **1961–92**: Thái Bình, 'Báo cáo tình hình thực hiện nhiệm vụ chuyển dân đi xây dựng các vùng KTM qua các năm', Ban Điều Động Lao Động và Kinh Tế Mới, Thái Bình, c1992. On **1990–94**: data provided by Thái Bình People's Committee (July 1995).

– there are some striking discrepancies between the figures for migrants going to Lạng Sơn, Kiên Giang, Quảng Ninh and those moving within the province. How did these discrepancies arise?

Before attempting to answer this question, it is worth looking at the statistics for a more typical province than the unusually stable Thái Bình. Thái Nguyên's experience was relatively normal. It merged with neighbouring Bắc Kạn in 1965 and redivided in 1997. Population and in-migration statistics for the province are presented in Tables 9 and 10.

Table 8: Destinations for out-migrants from Thái Bình, 1961–95

Province	Families	People	Labourers
Dak Lak*	7,800	38,800	17,000
Gia Lai-Kon Tum*	5,600	28,100	12,400
Sông Bé*	5,300	24,000	11,700
Lai Châu*	5,600	20,000	14,000
Hoàng Liên Sơn*	3,700	18,600	9,300
Bắc Thái*	3,100	15,300	7,000
Quảng Ninh*	2,160	10,800	4,320
Quảng Ninh †	488	2,025	1,189
Lạng Sơn*	200	600	400
Lạng Sơn †	325	1,286	800
Kiên Giang*	2,500	12,400	4,900
Kiên Giang†	4,800	25,806	9,708
within Thái Bình*	3,200	15,100	8,100
within Thái Bình†	16,722	87,126	35,181
Lâm Đồng†	1,121	5,663	2,609
Minh Hải†	4,982	24,772	11,016
Tây Ninh†	2,518	10,300	5,608
Đồng Nai†	786	4,095	1,717
Cao Bằng†	1,230	6,486	2,708
Tuyên Quang†	815	4,006	2,010
Lào Cai†	1,082	9,866	3,920
Ninh Thuận (1995)†	102	397	243
Yên Bái (1995)†	10	32	22
In small groups, throughout the country *(xen ghép toàn quốc)*†	9,674	44,458	14,491

Note: Figures marked * are for the period 1961–94, and were gathered in July 1995. Figures marked † were collected in June 1996 and relate to the whole period 1961–95, except where other periods are noted.

Source: Data provided by Thái Bình People's Committee. Interview (Thái Bình, July 1995).

Table 9: Population of Thái Nguyên/Bắc Kạn/Bắc Thái, 1955–89

Province	Year	People (000s)
Thái Nguyên	1955	230
	1964	400
Bắc Kạn	1965	113
Bắc Thái	1966	571
	1967	577
	1968	586
	1972	667
	1974	714
	1979	815
	1989	1,030
Thái Nguyên	1999	1,046
Bắc Kạn	1999	275

Sources: On **1955 and 1964**: Thái Nguyên Provincial Committee for Eradication of Malaria, *Báo cáo mừng Thắng lợi tám năm tiêu diệt sốt rét (1957–1964) của tỉnh Thái Nguyên*, Thái Nguyên, 1965. On **1965**: Lèng Văn Tý, Phạm Tất Quynh and Triệu Quang Tiến (eds), *Lịch sự đảng bộ thị xã Bắc Cạn*, NXB Chính Trị Quốc Gia, Hanoi, 1996, p. 12. On **1966–68**, NAV3/TCTK 2497(vv), 'Báo cáo dân số 1966–1967–1968', Bắc Thái Statistical Office, 13 December 1968. On **1972**: Nguyễn Hồng Minh, 'Di dân tự do, tổng luận khoa học', Hanoi: Bộ Lao Động Thương Binh và Xã Hội, 1993, p. 14. On **1974**: Hà Văn Phụng and Nông Văn Phách (eds), *Lịch sử đảng bộ tỉnh Bắc Thái*, Bắc Thái: Ban Nghiên Cứu Lịch Sử Đảng Tỉnh Bắc Thái, 1980, p. 16. On **1979**: *Dân số Việt Nam, 1-10-1979*, Ban Chỉ Đạo Tổng Điều Tra Dân Số Trung Ương, Hanoi, 1979. On **1989**: Central Census Steering Committee, *Vietnam Population Census - 1989, Completed Census Results*, vol. 1. On **1999**: Central Census Steering Committee, *1999 Population and Housing Census*, pp. 102, 104.

Table 9 counts in-migrants who were registered by the government on the various migation programmes.

For the period 1962–66 detailed statistics of in-migration to Bắc Thái (split between Bắc Kạn and Thái Nguyên for most of these years) were available. They present a picture of high in-migration and high population growth. The population of Thái Nguyên was more than 70 per cent higher in 1964 than it had been on independence in 1955. Arrivals in Bắc Thái over the four years of the new economic zone programme from 1962 amounted to 50,000 people. To this we may add the figures for free migration recorded by the Thái Nguyên Statistical Office in 1964 (many of whom appeared to come from Thái Bình – one quarter of those

Table 10: In-Migration to Thái Nguyên/Bắc Thái, 1962–94

Province	Year	In-migrants
Thái Nguyên	1962	1,756
	1963	10,184
	1964	5,106
Bắc Thái	1965	30,000
	1962–June 1966	49,043
	1976–80	11,450
	1982	145*
	1983	411*
	1984	2,187*
	1985	2,069
	1986	1,755
	1987	689*
	1988	1,110*
	1989	1,186*
	1990	1.270*
	1991	1,833*
	1992	1,032*
	1993	1,629*
	1994	1,325*

***Note**: Indicates migrants within the province.

Sources: On **1962–64**: NAV3/TCTK 2399(vv), 'Báo cáo số liệu đồng báo miền xuôi lên xây dựng kinh tế miền núi và tình hình biến động nhân khẩu ở thành phố Thái Nguyên', Thái Nguyên Statistical Office, 26 December 1964. On **1965**: NAV3/UBKHNN 564(vv), 'Dự àn chỉ tiêu kế hoạch phát triển kinh tế (hai năm 1966–7) của tỉnh Bắc Thái', Bắc Thái People's Committee, 22 September 1965. On **1962–66**: NAV3/TCTK 2474(vv), 'Báo cáo tổng hợp về tình hình nhân khẩu khai hoang', Thái Nguyên, 25 July 1966. On **1976–80**: Trịnh Văn Đông, *Báo cáo tổng kết công tác khai hoang xây dựng vùng kinh tế mới năm 1976–1981*, Thái Nguyên: Bắc Thái Agricultural Office, 1982. On **1982–94**: data provided by Bắc Thái Labour Office (Thái Nguyên, July 1995).

Table 11: Numbers of free migrants to Thái Nguyên, 1964

Free migrant destinations	Numbers
Phổ Yên district	609
Phú Bình district	99
Phú Lương, Định Hóa, Đại Từ, Đồng Hỷ and Vũ Nhai districts	4,089
Thái Nguyên city	7,716
Thái Nguyên province: cadres and workers bringing families up	10,388
Total	22,901

Source: NAV3/TCTK 2399(vv), 'Báo cáo số liệu đồng báo miền xuôi lên xây dựng kinh tế miền núi và tình hình biến động nhân khẩu ở thành phố Thái Nguyên', Thái Nguyên Statistical Office, 26 December 1964.

who arrived in early 1961).[21] It is unclear from the source whether these arrivals actually took place in 1964, or during the two or three years up to that date. Either way, the numbers are high. They are reproduced in Table 11.

I could not find data on in-migration to Bắc Thái during 1967–75, and was unable to compare the rate of population growth there to that of in-migration. But for the period 1976–80, the available statistics are more illuminating. The population rose by 100,000, of whom about 10 per cent were migrants on the government programme. The remainder, I thought, could be accounted for by a proportion of free migrants (lower than in the early 1960s, at a time of diminishing economic opportunities) and by natural increase.

However, my discovery of a rather unusual document in the archives denied the possibility of so easy an interpretation of these statistics. This document, produced by the Statistical Office in Vĩnh Phú province (1970), presented a far more complex picture of the demographic situation in highland provinces such as Bắc Thái. Its analysis casts light on the origin of the discrepancies observed in our earlier discussion of statistics generated in Thái Bình. I was forced to conclude that it was not only necessary to make allowance for the manner of data reporting and for administrative boundary shifts. It was important also to account for the highly frequent changes in the way population statistics were calculated. The document was unique to Vĩnh Phú province, as no other provincial reports described their counting methods. But the methods described were widespread throughout the provinces of the DRV and persisted to some extent into the SRV.

In 1970, responding to a request from the General Statistical Office in Hanoi, provinces sent in retrospective statistical series of their population growth from 1954 to 1970. Vĩnh Phú Statistical Office sent in the series reproduced in Table 12.

The National Archives contain figures like these for most provinces of the DRV, compiled at the same time in response to the same request. Only the officials in

Table 12: Population of Vĩnh Phú province, 1954–70

Year	Total population	Agricultural population
1954	826,274	755,578
1955	855,194	782,024
1956	885,126	809,396
1957	915,294	836,969
1958	947,097	866,046
1959	979,299	895,493
1960	1,013,343	926,638
1961	1,048,930	958,842
1962	1,092,350	998,591
1963	1,137,660	1,040,044
1964	1,134,951	1,083,274
1965	1,234,302	1,128,361
1966	1,259,752	1,138,785
1967	1,287,078	1,149,615
1968	1,315,326	1,160,580
1969	1,352,888	1,177,685
1970	1,381,990	1,198,363

Source: NAV3/TCTK 2548(vv), 'Báo cáo một số chỉ tiêu dân số từ 1954 đến 1970', Vĩnh Phú Statistical Office, 20 August 1970.

Vĩnh Phú, however, took the trouble to compile a report, attached to these statistics, explaining their empirical inaccuracies and structural inconsistencies. The contents of this report, which amount to a blow-by-blow account of how the goalposts were shifted, offer a unique insight into the workings of province-level data collection, calculation and compilation. They cast doubt on the usefulness of the statistics sent in. These would otherwise lead to the conclusion that the province's population grew rapidly from 1954 to 1963, fell slightly in 1964, grew in 1965 and continued to grow less rapidly thereafter. The report is, therefore, essential reading for all those wishing to base conclusions on quantitative data generated in the DRV countryside, on which General Statistical Office statistics were themselves based. The document is so interesting that I felt it worth reproducing a translation here in full.

Report on a Number of Population Norms, 1954–70
Explanation of Population Statistics (Vĩnh Phú, 20 August 1970.)

These historical statistics of average population were re-compiled in August 1970. Compared with historical statistics of average population calculated in the past and printed in the thirteen-year book of basic statistics (1955–67) circulated by the Vĩnh Phú Statistical Office, there are various inconsistencies. This is for the following reasons:

1. Changes in the method of calculating historical population statistics made during the process of re-compilation.
2. Changes in regulations concerning the population categories counted as local inhabitants.
3. Historical changes in the nature of inhabitants influenced the quantity and structure of the population.

We wish to explain clearly the situation and method of calculation as follows:

<u>1. Changes in the method of calculation:</u>

From 1960 to 1967, all Statistical Offices had guidelines on the methods of calculation of historical statistics of average population. These methods usually took the annual rate of natural population growth (births and deaths) and the average speed of this growth to make the calculation.

Use of the Natural Calculation Method is only suitable for situations where the change in the population is natural (births and deaths). It is unsuitable for populations with large changes of a mechanical nature (in-migration and out-migration). Use of the Average Speed Method of calculation will not give a result corresponding with the actual population existing every year, because this depends on mechanical population change over time, the very large increases and decreases which occur unobserved. It is impossible for absolute statistics to record these annual mechanical changes in the population, changes to its quantity as well as its structure. If historical statistics of the population calculated before recompilation are used, then they will be limited in their value by the objective situation of the current population. They will also influence other aspects of research and calculation. As a result, the process of recompilation of population statistics changes constantly, in terms of calculation method.

<u>2. Changes in regulations concerning population categories counted as local inhabitants</u>

In the past, the total number of regulated individuals included soldiers, police, militia, defence workers and convicts in re-education camps [henceforth abbreviated in the original to 'soldiers, etc.']. At this time, these types of individual were no longer counted as belonging to the locality.

In March 1960 (during the population census), the Central Government reallocated the soldiers, etc. counting them as belonging to the population of Vĩnh Phú province – 20,833 individuals. In October 1963 (during the survey into the supply of cloth vouchers for 1964), the Central Government re-allocated the soldiers, etc. again. They counted them now as individuals belonging to the General Statistical Office. As a result, the statistics of the province counted the total number of individuals in the locality.

Later there was a further change, due to General Statistical Office circular number 366/TCTK-VX, of 4.5.1966. This circular provided guidelines for the recompilation of population statistics, which decided on the reduction of the number of soldiers, etc. from the category of local population from 1961 to 1965. This took place on the principle that every year a quarter of the total should be removed: that is in 1961, reduction by a quarter; 1962, reduction by half; 1963, reduction by three quarters; 1964, removal of the entire number of soldiers, etc. re-allocated to the locality in 1960 and still unchanged, for the reason that population survey materials had been published publicly.

On the basis of the above methods, in 1966 historical population statistics were re-calculated and re-edited (dealing with the period 1955–66). In reality at that time, Vĩnh Phú was still not merged, so each province made its calculations in a different way. Phú Thọ province did not count soldiers, etc. in the local population from 1955 to 1965. Vĩnh Phúc, on the other hand, counted the entire body of soldiers, etc. from 1955 to 1960 in the population; from 1961 a part of the force of soldiers remained counted in this number; in the period up to 1965 they only withdrew the part re-allocated to Vĩnh Phúc province after 1963, while the part re-allocated after 1960 was not withdrawn from the population.

The changes in categorisation of individuals influenced the method of calculation. But the method of calculation described above had a further shortcoming. This was as follows. While in one period, from 1955 to 1960, there was a policy to include the soldiers, etc. in the local population, in a later period, from 1961 to 1964, there was a policy to withdraw the soldiers, etc. from the population. The number withdrawn was small in one year, large in another. In addition, while calculation methods were not yet coordinated, the two regions also calculated and re-compiled the statistics in uncoordinated ways, as mentioned above. As a result, historical statistics of average population calculated in the past, when considered nowadays, are still not yet rational.

3. <u>Historical changes in the nature of inhabitants influenced the quantity and structure of the population</u>

Natural changes in the population (births and deaths) are very great each year, but mechanical changes in the population (in-migration and out-migration) are even more complex. From 1962 to 1966 compatriots from provinces in the lowlands arrived to build and develop Vĩnh Phúc province's economy, as many as 43,734 people. In recent years the American enemy's war of destruction has been happening, and from 1965 to 1968 many Central Government offices have evacuated in large numbers to the localities. At that time they were considered as temporary residents; later they were allowed to register officially under the household registration system, and were counted as permanent residents of Vĩnh Phúc province. Also at the present time, because of the need to service the military struggle, every year quite large numbers of people leave the locality to go and clear the wilderness. And the number of compatriots who left to clear the wilderness and then abandoned that project and returned to their home village is quite large. Changes in the population are related to the definition of the annual population level and the methods of calculation using the average speed of growth.

Let us take an example from the time historical population statistics were recompiled for the period up to 1966. During the period 1962–65 the number of compatriots who came to clear land and still remained in Vĩnh Phúc had to be counted as local inhabitants. But from 1965 to 1968 they left and returned to their home village. If the calculation was not redefined, with regard to the average over those years, then in reality that quantity of population actually existed, but is useless for the purposes of calculation of average economic expenditure per head, as *the name is there but the body is not* [my emphasis].

On the other hand, also in this period, a large number of people from Central Government offices evacuated to Vĩnh Phúc province. While they were still temporary residents, they were not counted as local inhabitants. Later they were officially registered under the household registration system as permanent residents and had to be counted as belonging to the average population of the locality during those years.

From the above situation, [we can see] the requirements of calculation and recompilation historical statistics of average population of the years 1954–69.

The method of calculating historical statistics of average population on this occasion is based on circular 186/TCTK-VX, of 26.2.1970 issued by the General Statistical Office:

Principles of calculation

Withdrawal of the entire body of soldiers, people's police, militia, people's gendarmerie, defence workers and convicts in re-education camps from the local population. Statistics of the population [are recorded] according to currently existing administrative units. Readjustment of statistics is considered not to be rational.

Period of calculation and re-editing

From 1954 to 1969 the average population calculation is made from 1 July every year.

Method of calculation

From the beginning of 1960 and 1963, the force of soldiers, etc. allocated by the Central government will be withdrawn entirely and in a unified manner, and removed from the category of local population. After withdrawal of the force of soldiers, etc. the calculation of the average population for each period is carried out.

From 1954 to 1960: the population at 3/1960 (population census) is taken as the base, and using that year's proportion of natural growth the average population is calculated to 1 July. This acts as a standard for calculation of previous years with the coefficient of population for each year, caused by the rate of qualitatively calculated natural increase. In cases of years where there is no available rate of natural population increase, then the following years's rate is used (in 1954, 1955 and 1956 there was no survey, so the growth rate for 1957 is used, for 1958 the rate for 1959 is used). (…)

Urban inhabitants

In 1960, according to General Statistical Office regulations concerning urban inhabitants, people in the suburbs of the cities and towns were included. Nowadays, only inhabitants of the city centre are counted.

Statistics of the total number of inhabitants and the number of agricultural inhabitants from 1962 to 1965 show that the speed of increase is faster than in other years. This is because of the large numbers of people coming to clear land and the people from Central Government offices coming to reside permanently in the localities. In 1966–68 the slow increase is due, on the one hand, to the need to service the military struggle and, on the other, to the rather large number of inhabitants in general and agricultural inhabitants in particular who moved away and left the locality. Non-agricultural inhabitants from 1966 to 1968 increased rapidly because of the evacuees working for the schools and offices of the Central government, who became permanent residents of the locality.

This fascinating and profoundly confusing document takes us through the full range of statistical calculation traps. It may be summarized as follows. The calculation of a historical 'average population' for the province was based on extrapolation from natural increase rates. The statistics were periodically 'recompiled', counting in or out categories such as soldiers, police, militia, defence workers, convicts, evacuated officials and their families, as well as in-migrants to new economic zones, out-migrants to new economic zones, and migrants who secretly returned from new economic zones. Changes in administrative boundary took place twice, once on the merger of Phú Thọ and Vĩnh Phúc provinces and again on the revision of urban boundaries. The provincial authorities of Phú Thọ and Vĩnh Phúc had used different methods of calculation, causing difficulties on merger. Without a full and chronological understanding of these administrative matters, it is difficult to draw conclusions from the recompiled population figures provided by the province. Above all, we must ask why the recorded population fell in 1964. This was a time of high in-migration to the province's new economic zones (43,734 people in 1962–66). The document suggests it was because, during recompilation, the category of 'soldiers, etc.' was removed from the population statistics. This is plausible, but ultimately we cannot be sure. The only interpretation we may place on Vĩnh Phú's population statistics over the period 1955–70 is that the population grew by an indeterminate amount. The same, by extension, must be true of other provinces of the DRV, where officials revealed no concerns about these sorts of discrepancies in their data collection methods.

THE SOCIALIST REPUBLIC OF VIETNAM, 1976–

Estimates of the growth in population and the numbers of people moving during the years after 1975 are no more available or credible than before that date. The same caveats therefore apply, and should be borne in mind during the discussion that follows. During the 1980s, however, two new factors entered the equation. The first, of course, was Đổi Mới, which effected a number of changes in the government's ability to manage the population, reducing its control (and therefore knowledge) over people's place of residence. The second was the inclusion in 1989, for the first time, of a question about migration in the census. Both these changes affect our quantitative understanding of migration in Vietnam. During this period, the northern highlands ceased to be a major migration destination, and that position was increasingly taken over by the central highlands. We shall confine our discussion on this period to the available figures for central highlands, a region of high demographic growth. Tables 13 and 14 record that growth, for the central highlands as a whole and for the province of Dak Lak.

The high level of population growth during the 1990s, which in Dak Lak reached an annual level of 4 per cent and probably more, was largely a function of in-migration from other parts of Vietnam. After reunification, the SRV government initiated a programme of organized migration to this region, an extension of the programme implemented since the early 1960s in the north. One strategy report referred

Table 13: Population of the central highlands

Year	People (000s)
1976	1,522
1995	3,099

Source: Trần An Phong (ed.), *Nghiên cứu xây dựng luận cứ khoa học cho định hướng phát triển kinh tế-xã hội các tỉnh Tây Nguyên*, Hanoi: NXB Nông Nghiệp, 1996, p. 50.

to the two provinces of Dak Lak and Gia Lai-Kon Tum in 1975 in the following terms: 'At present our lowland compatriots are moving up to the central highlands for the purposes of highland construction and forecasts for the coming five years indicate that the two provinces' population will increase to 2,000,000 people'.[22] State organized migration was followed, from the 1980s, with a flow of free migrants, both Việt people from the plains and Tày, Nùng and other ethnic groups from the northern highlands.[23] Free migration presented major problems of administration, not least in terms of population data collection. On occasions, migrants arrived to clear an area of land in the forest, and authorities did not discover their presence there for months. The difficulty of putting a figure on the population in such circumstances was directly acknowledged by the then Vice President of the Dak Lak People's Committee, Huỳnh Thị Xuân, as demonstrated by the 1998 statistic in Table 14. All recent population statistics for this region should thus be regarded as underestimates of reality.

The influence of migration on the region's population is reflected in the change in its ethnic structure, presented in Table 15. In the 1940s, the overwhelming majority of people in the central highlands were local highlander people, Ede, Jarai, Mnong, etc. By the 1990s, these people formed minorities in their own provinces. Việt people formed more than half the population, and there was a substantial number of migrants from the northern highlands. Most sources suggest that by the mid-1990s the Tày, Nùng, Thái, Mường, Yao and Hmong population of Dak Lak made up approximately 10 per cent of the province's population (103,000 arrivals between 1976 and 1996, according to one official report). But a monograph of Dak Lak province published in 1990 suggested that northern highlanders made up the vast majority of free migrants to the province:

> In addition to those people who moved to Dak Lak to build the new economy according to the annual plan, over the last few years about 30,000 people have arrived outside the plan, of whom more than 22,000 are Tày and Nùng compatriots from Cao Bằng and Lạng Sơn who moved spontaneously to settle there.[24]

In this way, the perceived negative impact of migrants and the presence of northern highlanders added a further layer of interpretative difficulty to the statistics: an ethnic factor of political importance. Up to the mid 1990s, official statements tended to characterize free migrants to the central highlands as 'ethnic minority

Table 14: Population of Dak Lak province

Year	People (000s)
1944	83
1973	379
1975	346
1976	363
1979	490
1989	975
1990	1,026
1991	1,114
1992	1,126
1993	1,175
1994	1,211
1995	1,242
1997	1,304
1998	'more than 1,500'
1999	1,776

Source: On **1944**: B. Y. Jouin, *Enquête démographique au Darlac, 1943–44*, extract from *BSEI*, vol. XXV, no. 3, 1950, p. 11. On **1973**: Lê Duy Đại, 'Bước đầu nghiên cứu những đặc điểm biến động dân cư tự nhiên tỉnh Đắc Lắc', *DTH*, no. 3, 1982, p. 50. On **1975**: NAV3/UBKHNN 12(tt), 'Báo cáo kết quả khảo sát khả năng đất nông nghiệp tỉnh Gia Lai Công Tum Đắc Lắc năm 1957 [*sic*] của Bộ Tư Lệnh 559, Quân Đội Nhân Dân Việt Nam', 12 December 1975. On **1976**: Nguyễn Pháp, *Nông-lâm nghiệp Đắc Lắc, 1975–1995*, Hanoi: NXB Nông Nghiệp, 1995, p. 6. On **1979**: *Dân số Việt Nam, 1-10-1979*. On **1989**: *Vietnam Population Census – 1989, Completed Census Results*, vol. 1. On **1990–95**: Trần An Phong, *Nghiên cứu xây dựng luận cứ khoa học*, p. 51. On **1997**: Ministry of Labour, Invalids and Social Affairs, 'Report on the Result of the Survey on Rural Migration in Dak Lak Province', Hanoi, Project VIE/95/004, 1997, p. 9. On **1998**: Huỳnh Thị Xuân, 'The Impact of Rural–Rural Migration to Resettlement Areas in Dak Lak Province', Proceedings of the International Seminar on Internal Migration, held in Hanoi, 6–8 May 1998, Hanoi: Population Council Research Report No 9, p. 98. On **1999**: Central Census Steering Committee, *1999 Population and Housing Census: Sample Results*, Hanoi: Thế Giới Publishers, 2000, p. 118.

compatriots' from the north, rather than as Việt from the plains. In the late 1990s, increasing recognition of the problem, the impossibility of hiding the large numbers of Việt arrivals, and the need for practical solutions, put an end to this tendency. But historical statistics on the ethnic issue remain of doubtful value.

Table 15: Ethnicity of inhabitants of Dak Lak province (%)

Year	Việt people	Highlanders (local & other)	Highlanders (local)	Highlanders (other)
1944	4		96	
1974	44		56	
1975	40		59	1
1979	60			
1989	70		29	1
1994	65	35	25	10
1995		29		
1996				9

Sources: On **1944**: Jouin, *Enquête démographique*, p. 11. On **1974**: Interview with Dak Lak Population and Family Planning Committee (May 1996). On 1975: NAV3/UBKHNN 12(tt), 'Báo cáo kết quả khảo sát'. This statistic covers the two provinces of Dak Lak and Gia Lai-Kon Tum. On **1979**: Lê Duy Đại, 'Những vấn đề đặt ra xung quanh việc bố sung thêm lao động để phát triển kinh tế xã hội ở Tây Nguyên hiện nay', *DTH*, no. 3, 1983, p. 30. On **1989**: *Vietnam Population Census – 1989, Completed Census Results* vol. 1. On **1994**: Interview with Dak Lak Population and Family Planning Committee (May 1996). On **1995**: p. 53. On **1996**: Huỳnh Thị Xuân, 'Báo cáo những ảnh hưởng của vấn đề di dân từ nông thôn ra nông thôn lên những vùng dân đến định cư ở tỉnh Daklak', Chi Cục Định Canh Định Cư và Vùng Kinh Tế Mới Daklak, 1998.

Vietnamese statistics on migration make a distinction between migrants on the programme and those moving with their own resources. This became particularly noticeable by the 1990s, as free migration began to overtake organized migration in numerical importance.

Organized migration during 1976–83 totalled 400,000 people.[25] During 1976–93, it totalled 666,300.[26] The largest province in the region for most of the latter period, Gia Lai-Kon Tum, received 129,287 of these people.[27] This province was divided in 1991, whereupon Dak Lak became the province with the largest land area. Dak Lak was also the destination for the most sizeable contingents of organized migrants. Statistics on organized migration during this period are subject to similar difficulties as before 1975 (discussed above), as well as some additional ones which will be raised below. Data on organized migration to Dak Lak are presented in Table 16.

Regarding spontaneous migration, during 1990–93 official statistics estimated at 201,206 the number of people who moved freely – that is without state aid – to the central highlands.[28] Over the eighteen years from 1976–93, the region became home to at least 419,000 such migrants. Of these, 300,000 were supposed to be highland minorities from the north.[29] These figures are subject to caution, parti-

Table 16: Organized migration to Dak Lak, 1976–97

Period	People
1976–80	127,000
1976–85	214,279
1986–95	87,500
1976–97	311,764

Sources: On **1976–80**: Ministry of Agriculture, 'Báo cáo tình hình khai hoang và phân bố lao động, dân cư di khai hoang xây dựng vùng kinh tế mới 5 năm 1976–1989', Hanoi: Bộ Nông Nghiệp, January 1982. On **1976–85**: Huỳnh Thị Xuân, 'The Impact of Rural–Rural Migration', p. 99. On **1986–95**: Ministry of Labour, Invalids and Social Affairs, 'Report on the Result of the Survey on Rural Migration'. On **1976–96**:, 'The Impact of Rural–Rural Migration', p. 99.

cularly given the problems involved in measuring movements of this nature, and the reluctance many free migrants show towards announcing their move to the authorities, either on departure or on arrival. They are almost certainly underestimates.

The 1990s was a period of high growth in free migration, and statistics reporting it were often contradictory and based more on estimates than counts. The difficulty of using official figures for spontaneous migration is evident in the following confusing data for Dak Lak province, summarized from government reports compiled during the 1990s.

- A 1993 study estimated that over a twelve year period, 1980–91, Dak Lak became home to a total of 72,050 free migrants from other provinces. The same study noted that in the thirteen years from 1980 a total of 82,245 people arrived in the province. It then stated elsewhere that 'over 100,000 people' moved there in 1980–93.[30]

- A 1996 report, on the other hand, estimated at just less than 100,000 people the number of free migrants who settled in Dak Lak in four years alone, 1990–93.[31]

- A 1997 report counted 166,000 free migrants to Dak Lak over twenty years, 1976–96.[32]

Data published in 1998 by Dak Lak provincial authorities come closest to a clear picture of free migration trends into the province. They are reproduced in Table 17. But even these figures, regularly more than double those that appear in previous sources, remain subject to caution. The downturn recorded in 1997 is particularly doubtful; the 'abrupt decline' was explained as resulting from 'government orders 267/CP and 268/CP and the Premier's message 1157/DPI (14 April 1997) on forest conservation, calling for serious measures to deal with spontaneous settlers who destroy forest land and refuse to follow regulations.'[33] Interview sources suggest that this was a serious underestimate, owing to the limited sample studied.

Table 17: Free migration to Dak Lak, 1976–96

Period	Migrants	Migrant families
1976–80	14,693	2,656
1981–85	10,689	7,602
1986–90	91,658	18,338
1991–95	166,227	35,580
1996	29,577	6,081
1997	7,284	1,728
1976–97	350,128	71,985

Source: Huỳnh Thị Xuân, 'The Impact of Rural–Rural Migration', p. 100.

It was possibly made for political reasons, being the findings of a paper given to an International Conference on Internal Migration in Hanoi, in May 1998. Certainly it gave participants the impression that the problem was now, thanks to forward-thinking government policy, well under control. This was contrary to much of the conference discussion.

A comparison of statistics of organized and free migration becomes all the more interesting – and difficult to interprete – as one goes down the administrative hierarchy. At the district level, there emerges considerable statistical overlap between the two categories, particularly of free migration into organized migration. The case of Lak district (Dak Lak) illustrates this point well. Tables 18–23 offer a profile of the population and migration characteristics of the district.

Table 18: Population growth in Lak district, 1975–95

Year	Population
1975	14,616
1985	38,376
1995	39,626

Source: Committee for Minorities and Highlands, 'Báo cáo về di dân tự do', pp. 38–39.

Note that Lak district was split in 1987. A large section of its territory became the district of Krông Nô. This boundary change hides a considerable increase in the population, invisible in the data for 1995.

Lak district statistics are interesting not for what they reveal (a high rate of in-migration, both organized and free) but for what they conceal. It was mentioned in Chapter 10 that one day in 1985, fourteen migrant families arrived at Dak Liêng

Table 19: Typology of inhabitants of Lak district, 1995

Type	People
Local born	26,776
New economic zone	5,115
Free migrants	7,735

Source: Committee for Minorities and Highlands, 'Báo cáo về di dân tự do', pp. 39.

commune, coming from Hải Hưng province in the Red River Delta. District authorities were informed of their arrival, and arranged for them to receive funding as part of the province's new economic zone programme. Since then they have been counted as 'planned migrants', in Tables 20 and 21. This is administratively true, in that they benefited from some of the structures and funding of the plan. But sociologically it is deceptive, as their migration as far as Dak Liêng was entirely self-funded and self-organized. It is likely that this was one of many such cases of flexibility and generosity on the part of local authorities. All statistics on organized migration must be analysed with this sort of situation in mind.

Such examples could be multiplied and further caveats added. It is not necessary to do so – the evidence presented points clearly to a situation in which both the statistics and their categorisation require immense interpretation. Vietnam's administrative culture, with its short institutional memory and its flexible approach to problem-solving, contributed in no small part to this situation. And even at the level of the commune, where memories are much longer, the researcher who makes the effort to enquire will soon find gaps and distortions. At Tam Giang commune (Krông Năng district, Dak Lak), the People's Committee chairman was quite frank in his evaluation of the local population statistics (reported in Chapter 8). Population figures for 1978 and 1996 were accurate to within 2 per cent, he said. Figures for the intervening years, when the majority of the commune's free migrants arrived, were much less so.

All authorities face difficulties in keeping track of the numbers. The particular challenge in Vietnam, as one of my friends in Hanoi explained to me, is that figures

Table 20: Planned/free migration to Lak district, 1976–95

Migration	Families	People
Planned	1,088	5,115
Free	1,556	8,322
Total	2,644	13,437

Source: Data provided by Lak People's Committee. Interview, May 1996.

Table 21: Planned migration to Lak district, by commune, 1977–85

Commune	Origin of in-migrants	Migration Date	Families	People
Buôn Tría	Thái Bình	since 1977	383	1,878
Buôn Triết	Thái Bình	since 1977	580	3,177
Dak Liêng	Hải Hưng	1985	14	62
total			977	5,117

Note: Data in Tables 18 and 19 do not tally. The margin of error is small, however, and I present them here as provided by officials in Lak.

Source: Data provided by Lak People's Committee. Interview, May 1996.

are very often 'exact' (faithfully recording a reality according to historically specific bureaucratic norms) but not 'accurate' (recording only partially that reality). The researcher is left to rely on personal resources and qualitative methods to work out what happened.

There is of course a new tool. This is the National Census carried out in April 1989 (and repeated in April 1999). Collecting a far broader range of data than the 1979 census, it has undoubtedly increased our knowledge of a whole variety of demographic variables. For the first time in 1989, there was a question on internal migration, whereby respondents were asked about their place of usual residence five years before the census date. If this place was situated across an administrative boundary (district or province), a migration was observed.[34]

Table 22: Free migration to Lak district by commune, 1977–96

Commune	Migrants' ethnicity (& origin)	Families	People
Bông Krăng	including some Thái	222	1,254
Buôn Tría	Việt (Thái Bình and Quảng Ngãi)	149	809
Buôn Triết	Việt (Thái Bình & Quảng Nam Đà Nẵng)	269	1,350
Dak Liêng	Việt and Tày	348	1,743
Dak Nuê	Việt (Nghệ An and Hà Tĩnh) and Tày (Cao Bằng)	229	1,060
Dak Phơi	Tày (Cao Bằng)	53	261
Giang Tao	Việt (Huế, An Giang and Quảng Trị)	44	192
Liên Sơn (town)	Việt (diverse origins) and Tày (Cao Bằng)	353	1,653
Total		1,667	8,322

Source: Data provided by Lak People's Committee. Interview, May 1996.

Table 23: Migration to Krông Nô district, 1987–94

Migration	Migrants' ethnicity (& origin)	Date	Families	People
planned	Việt from Xuân Thủy district (Nam Định)	1987 1988	187 89	432 350
free	At least 15 ethnic groups mainly from the northern highlands (Cao Bằng, Bắc Thái, Lạng Sơn, Thanh Hóa, Tây Ninh and Sông Bé*); Việt (Nam Định)	1991–94	2000	9600
total			2,276	10,382

***Note**: These settlers were northern highlanders who moved first to Sông Bé, then, after two or three years, to Dak Lak.

Yet even this tool leaves much mobility unrecorded. One migration recorded in Table 23 above offers a good example. One group of people moved to Sông Bé and then after two or three years to Dak Lak. Only the latter move would have shown up in the census. In addition, certain features of the old counting system remained problematic. The basis for the census was a household of usual residence. As its organizers noted,

> An important principle was to ensure that all persons in Viet Nam at the time of the census, other than temporary visitors, were assigned to a household of usual residence. In most cases this was an easy task, but where people had moved frequently or had moved recently, special rules were required to ensure that the proper location was assigned.[35]

Attempts were made to ensure that migrants were counted, but those attempts were based on interview questions and the responses depended on the good-will and interest of the informants. In addition, some tables in the sample results of the 1989 census 'exclude certain groups of persons such as the military, the police and Vietnamese diplomats serving overseas', and hence 'some caution is needed in using the data as representative of the entire country.[36] Despite these difficulties, however, the census represents a considerable advance on previously available statistics. The full results of the April 1999 census should make fascinating reading, particularly as they will allow us finally put a figure on the high levels of spontaneous migration to the central highlands over the last decade of the twentieth century.

CONCLUSION

The difficulties of statistical analysis of migration in Vietnam need no further emphasis. But the reader may wish for an impression, drawn from among these disparate and discrepant data, of the scale of migration in twentieth-century Vietnam. I propose, in conclusion, to make a brief comparison of the situation before and since 1945.

Before 1945, we may base our comparison on the following figures. The population of Indochina (including Laos and Cambodia) was estimated at 16 million in 1906 (of which possibly 14 million lived in Vietnam). It grew to 27 million by 1943. In 1936, Vietnam was home to 19 million people.[37]

After 1945, the population grew more quickly. By partition in 1955, the population had grown to 25 million, reaching 30 million in 1960 and 49 million on reunification in 1975.[38] A total of 64 million people lived in Vietnam by the time of the 1989 census.

Thus, if we compare the two periods, we can see that over the five decades up to 1955, Vietnam's population grew by 11 million. Then, over the thirty-four years up to 1989, it grew by a further 39 million. A low rate of demographic growth in the first half of the century contrasted with a rapidly growing population during the second half.

A similar pattern may be observed in the statistics of migration. During the colonial period, the rate of migration was low. Gourou, whose statistics are the most complete in this regard, estimated at 35,000 the nett annual organized out-migration from the Red River Delta, and at 15,000 the number of free migrants. At the time his statistics were published (1936), the population of the delta was 6.5 million.[39] For this highly populated region, we may calculate a migration rate of less than 1 per cent.

In the thirty years after the Vietnamese government launched its migration programme in 1960, several million people moved from their home province to other parts of the country. For reasons that will be clear from this essay, it is no easier to obtain an accurate idea of exactly how many million than it is to accept Gourou's figures as more than estimates. For the purposes of argument, I accept here the total of more than 6 million migrants to new economic zones in 1960–97.[40] This figure includes migrants to lowland areas (principally the Mekong delta) and highlands. The figure is certainly inflated, possibly by calculation methods, and certainly by the failure to subtract the numbers of people who abandoned their settlement, many of whom were counted twice as they moved to a second new economic zone. In addition, many slipped out of the statistics as boat people.[41]

Even if this figure for organized migration during 1960–93 is overestimated by one-third, it implies an annual average rate of migration of about 100,000 people. Annual population growth in 1960–89 averaged 750,000. So for the country as a whole, we may calculate a migration rate averaging more than 13 per cent. The figure would be far higher for the Red River Delta, which remained the country's principal region of out-migration up to the end of the century. We would have to add to this statistic of organized migration an estimate of free migration, which became of great significance in the last decade of the century.

These calculations, with their incompatible categories and poor statistical foundations, must inevitably be regarded as neither accurate, nor perhaps even exact. Figures were calculated from lists of people's names, as the Vĩnh Phú Statistical Office informed us. And when we speak of migration in Vietnam, we all too often find that cultures of statistics concur with cultures of human behaviour. As the Vĩnh Phú officials observed: 'the name is there but the body is not'. In such circumstances, it is better to focus on the names.[*]

NOTES

1 Ng Shui Meng, *The Population of Indochina: Some Preliminary Observations*, Singapore: Institute of Southeast Asian Studies, 1974; Khổng Diễn, *Dân số và tộc ngươi ở Việt Nam*, Hanoi: NXB Khoa Học Xã Hội, 1995.

2 Pierre Gourou, *Les paysans du delta tonkinois: étude de géographie humaine*, Paris: Les Editions d'Art et d'Histoire, 1936, p. 173.

3 Ng Shui Meng, *The Population of Indochina*, p. 16.

4 Ibid., pp. 17–18.

5 Smolski, 'Progrès et incertitude de la statistique en Indochine', *RIJE*, no. 17, 1942, p. 108.

6 NAV1/RND 3135, 'Procès verbal de la conférence des mandarins tenue à la Résidence le 21 février 1919'.

7 NAV1/GGI 7456, GGI to Inspector of Colonies, 3 April 1923.

8 Ng Shui Meng, *The Population of Indochina*, p. 18.

9 NAV1/RST 67486, Michelot, Résident in Thái Nguyên, to RST, 5 May 1942.

10 Sources. Items marked * from: Đường Hồng Đật (ed.), *Lịch sử nông nghiệp Việt Nam*, Ho Chi Minh City: Xưởng in Học Viên, 1994, p. 212. Item marked † from NAV3/CQLNTQD 69(vv), 'Báo cáo tình hình hoạt động của các nông trường quốc doanh nước Việt Nam Cộng Hòa Dân Chủ', 1959.

11 NAV3/CQLNTQD 69(vv), 'Báo cáo tình hình hoạt động của các nông trường quốc doanh nước Việt Nam Cộng Hòa Dân Chủ', 1959.

12 Phạm Đỗ Nhật Tân, 'Hoàn thiện hơn nữa việc di dân nông nghiệp có tổ chức đi xây dựng các vùng kinh tế mới', Luận án phó tiến sĩ khoa học kinh tế, Trường Đại Học Kinh Tế Quốc Dân, Hanoi: 1992, pp. 85–86.

13 Ibid., p. 85.

14 VNTTX, 'Trong ba năm các nông trường quân đội đã vỡ hoang 18,482 mẫu đất, thu hoạch 43,609 tấn nông phẩm', *Nhân Dân*, 18 June 1961, p. 1.

15 General Land Clearance Office, 'Báo cáo tổng kết cuộc vận động đồng báo miền xuôi tham gia phát triển kinh tế miền núi trong kế hoạch 5 năm lần thứ nhất và phương hướng nhiệm vụ những năm tới', Hanoi, July 1966.

16 NAV3/UBNNTW 99(vv), 'Chỉ thị của Ủy Ban Nông Nghiệp Trung Ương – lập kế hoạch xây dựng các vùng KTM và phát triển các nông trường quốc doanh năm 1974', Hanoi, 30 August 1974.

17 Phạm Đỗ Nhật Tân, 'Hoàn thiện hơn nữa việc di dân', p. 44.

18 Kim Dung, 'Một số kết quả 30 năm di dân và xây dựng KTM'. In Ministry of Labour, Invalids and Social Affairs, *30 năm sự nghiệp di dân khai hoang và xây dựng kinh tế mới 1961–1991*, Hanoi: Cục Điều Động Lao Động và Dân Cư, 1991, p. 55.

19 Khổng Diễn, *Dân số và tộc người ở Việt Nam*, Hanoi: NXB Khoa Học Xã Hội, 1995, p. 172; Phạm Đỗ Nhật Tân, 'Hoàn thiện hơn nữa việc di dân', p. 46.

20 Lý Văn Nghĩa, 'Lên đường chống Mỹ, cứu nước', *Tiến Lên*, 19 February 1966, p. 4.

21 NAV3/BLD 1030(vv), 'Báo cáo tình hình số người các tỉnh miền xuôi lên, chi tiết sẽ Báo cáo sau', Thái Nguyên Labour Office, 19 April 1961.

---

[*] A list of the names of people interviewed during the research of this book, including a short migration biography and page references for their appearances in the story of Red Hills, is included in the Biographical Index.

22 NAV3/UBKHNN 12(tt), 'Báo cáo kết quả khảo sát'.

23 Vietnam Social Science Committee, Party and People's Committees of Dak Lak Province, *Vấn đề phát triển kinh tế xã hội các dân tộc thiểu số ở Đắc Lắc*, Hanoi: NXB Khoa Học Xã Hội, 1990, p. 12.

24 Ủy Ban Khoa Học Xã Hội Việt Nam, Vấn đề phát triển kinh tế xã hội các dân tộc thiểu số ở Đắc Lắc, p. 12.

25 Lê Duy Đại, 'Những vấn đề đặt ra', p. 30.

26 Phạm Đỗ Nhật Tân, 'Luận cứ khoa học cho xây dựng các chính sách di dân trên các địa bàn nông thôn Việt Nam', Đề tài KX-08–04, Hanoi, December 1994.

27 Gia Lai People's Committee, 'Báo cáo tổng kết công tác di dân xây dựng vùng kinh tế mới theo dự án – phương hướng nhiệm vụ di dân trong những năm tới', Pleiku, 5 April 1994.

28 Committee for Minorities and Highlands, 'Báo cáo về di dân tự do ở miền núi Việt Nam', Hanoi: Centre for Population, Labour and Society, 1996, p. 11.

29 Trần An Phong, Nghiên cứu xây dựng luận cứ, p. 56.

30 Nguyễn Hồng Minh, 'Di dân tự do, tổng luận khoa học', pp. 8, 13, 16.

31 Committee for Minorities and Highlands, 'Báo cáo về di dân tự do', p. 11.

32 Ministry of Labour, Invalids and Social Affairs, 'Report on the Result of the Survey on Rural Migration', p. 10.

33 Huỳnh Thị Xuân, 'The Impact of Rural–Rural Migration', p. 100.

34 *Vietnam Population Census 1989, Sample Results*, Hanoi: Central Census Steering Committee, 1990, pp. 40–41. *Vietnam Population Census 1989, Completed Census Results,* Hanoi: Central Census Steering Committee, 1991, vol. 1.

35 *Vietnam Population Census 1989, Sample Results*, p. 6.

36 Ibid., p. 26.

37 Ng Shui Meng, *The Population of Indochina*, p. 24, 35. Pierre Gourou, *L'utilisation du sol en Indochine*, Paris: l'Hartmann, 1940.

38 General Statistical Office, *Số liệu thống kê 1930–1984*, Hanoi: NXB Thống Kê, 1985, p. 12.

39 Pierre Gourou, *Les paysans du delta*, pp. 7, 217, 219.

40 Francis Gendreau, Do Tien Dung and Pham Do Nhat Tan, 'Les migrations internes', in Patrick Gubry (ed.) *Population et développement au Viêt-Nam*, Paris: Karthala-CEPED, 2000, pp. 200–201.

41 Linda Hitchcox, 'Relocation in Vietnam and Outmigration: The Ideological and Economic Context', in Judith M. Brown and Rosemary Foot (eds), *Migration: The Asian Experience*, Oxford: St Martin's Press, 1994, p. 204.

Bibliography

Works in Vietnamese

Army Medical Office (Cục Quân Y), *Chống sốt rét để tăng sức chiến đấu, Tài liệu học tập chiến sĩ* [Combatting malaria to increase fighting strength. Study-practice documents for soldiers], Cục Quân Y xuất bản, 1952.

Bắc Thái province, *Bắc Thái 2010* [Bắc Thái 2010], Hanoi: *Tạp Chí* Công Nghiệp, c. 1996.

Bùi Đức Thịnh, 'Ea Lê – vùng quê mới – nhiều hứa hẹn' [Ea Lê – new home region – great promise], *Dak Lak*, 24 October 1986, p. 3.

Bùi Minh Quốc, 'Lên Miền Tây' [Going up to the west]. In *Tuyển tập thơ Việt Nam 1945–1960* [Selected Vietnamese Poetry 1945–1960], Hanoi: NXB Văn Hóa, 1960, pp. 197–199.

Bùi Văn Kín, *Góp phần tìm hiểu tỉnh Hòa Bình* [Contribution to research on Hòa Bình province], Hòa Bình: Ty Văn Hóa Thông Tin Hòa Bình, 1972.

Bút Ngữ, 'Miền ngược, miền xuôi' [Uplands, lowlands], *Thái Bình*, 16 October 1961, p. 2.

Cao Bằng, *Chính sách khai hoang thông tư số 491 TTg, 95 TTg, 31 TTg* [Land clearance policy circular nos 491 TTg, 95 TTg, 31 TTg], Cao Bằng: Phòng Khai Hoang Cao Bằng, 1964.

Cao Văn Biền, 'Về dân số nông thôn Thái Bình trước Cách Mạng Tháng 8' [On the rural population of Thái Bình before the August Revolution], *NCLS*, vol. 250, no. 3, 1990, pp. 80–84, 95.

Chế độ đối với lao động đi xây dựng vùng kinh tế mới [The system for labour going to build new economic zones], Hanoi: NXB Lao Động, 1978.

Chu Văn (ed.), 'Mùa xuân đầu tiên trên quê mới' [First spring up at the new home] (1964). In *Hương cau hoa lim. Tập truyện ngắn* [Scent of betel-nut, flower of limwood. Collection of short stories], Hanoi: NXB Văn Hóa, 1971, pp. 39–50.

Committee for Minorities and Highlands (Ủy Ban Dân Tộc Miền Núi), 'Báo cáo về di dân tự do ở miền núi Việt Nam' [Report on free migration in the highlands of Vietnam], Hanoi: Centre for Population, Labour and Society (Trung Tâm Dân Số Lao Động và Xã Hội), 1996.

Communist Party of Vietnam (Đảng Cộng Sản Việt Nam), *Phương hướng, nhiệm vụ, và mục tiêu chủ yếu của kế hoạch 5 năm 1976–1980 (Báo cáo của Ban chấp hành trung ương Đảng tại Đại hội đại biểu toàn quốc lần thứ IV do đồng chí Phạm Văn Đồng, Ủy viên bộ chính trị trung ương Đảng Thủ tướng Chính phủ, trình bày)* [Essential lines, tasks and targets for the five year plan 1976–80 (Report by the Central Party Committee to the Fourth Whole Nation Congress of Delegates presented by comrade Phạm Văn Đồng, member of the Central Party Politburo, Prime Minister of the Government)], Hanoi: NXB Sự Thật, 1977.

C.T., 'Nhân dân xã Tự Cường (Phú Thọ) giúp đoàn khai hoang 4 trâu, trên 8 tấn thóc, 18 tấn sắn. Đoàn khai hoang Đông Sơn phà hoang vượt kế hoạch' [The people of Tự Cường commune (Phú Thọ) have helped the land clearance group with four buffaloes, over 8 tons of paddy, 18 tons of manioc. The Đông Sơn land clearance group have cleared more land than planned], *Tiến Lên*, 10 December 1962, p. 1.

Dak Lak, 'Từ Buôn Ma Thuột tiến về Sài Gòn' [From Buôn Ma Thuột advancing on Saigon], *Dak Lak*, Ban Mê Thuột victory fifteen year commemorative issue, 1990, p. 3.

Dak Lak editorial, 'Phấn khởi, tự hào cả Dak Lak mở 'Công Trường 8.4'' [All Dak Lak is enthusiastic and proud at the opening of 'Project 8.4'], *Dak Lak*, 24 August 1978, p. 1.

Dân số Việt Nam, 1-10-1979 [The Population of Vietnam, 1 October 1979], Ban Chỉ Đạo Tổng Điều Tra Dân Số Trung Ương, Hanoi, 1979.

Diệp Đình Hoa, *Làng Nguyễn* [Nguyễn village], Hanoi: NXB Khoa Học Xã Hội, 1994.

——, *Làng Bến Gỗ* [Bến Gỗ village], Đồng Nai: NXB Đồng Nai, 1995.

——, *Sự biến động của cộng đồng dân tộc do tác động của hồ Hòa Bình* [Changes in ethnic communities under the impact of Hòa Bình lake], Hanoi: NXB Khoa Học Xã Hội, 1995.

——, *Người Việt ở đồng bằng Bắc Bộ* [Việt people of the northern delta], Hanoi: NXB Khoa Học Xã Hội, 2000.

Dương Thanh Từng (ed.), *Dak Lak tập sáng tác văn nghệ* [Dak Lak collection of artistic compositions], Ban Mê Thuột: Ty Văn Hóa và Thông Tin Dak Lak, 1977.

Dương Thị The and Phạm Thị Thoa, *Tên làng xã Việt Nam đầu thế kỷ XIX (thuộc các tỉnh từ Nghệ Tĩnh trở ra)* [Names of villages and communes in Vietnam at the beginning of the nineteenth century (in provinces north of Nghệ Tĩnh)], Hanoi: NXB Khoa Học Xã Hội, 1981.

Dương Văn Đao, 'Người Việt Kiều hồi hương ở đất Tân Lạc' [Việt Kiều people who have returned home to live in Tân Lạc], *Hòa Bình*, 17 December 1963, p. 2.

Đặng Chấn Liêu, *Từ Điển Việt Anh* [Vietnamese-English Dictionary], Hanoi: NXB Khoa Học Xã Hội, 1987.

Đặng Lân, 'Gia đình ông Cách trên quê hương mới' [Mr Cách's family up at their new home village], *Hòa Bình*, 12 July 1963, pp. 3, 4.

Đặng Phong, 'Thị trường và giá cả Việt Nam từ thế kỷ XIX đến nay' [Markets and prices in Vietnam from the nineteenth century to the present], Report for the State Committee for Materials Prices (Ủy Ban Vật Giá Nhà Nước), Hanoi, 1992.

Đặng Thu, *Nghiên cứu lịch sử di dân của người Việt thế kỷ X đến giữa thế kỷ XIX* [Research into the history of Việt people's migration from the tenth century to the mid nineteenth century], Hanoi: Viện Sử Học, 1994.

Đặng Văn Sinh, 'Kinh nghiệm của Trực Tầm đã giúp cho Đông Xuân chúng tôi lối thoát' [Trực Tầm's experience has already helped us at Đông Xuân find a way out], *Tiến Lên*, 30 March 64, p. 2.

Đinh Công Thành, 'Những lá thư Tây Bắc gọi về' [Letters sent back from Tây Bắc], *Thái Bình*, 28 October 1961, p. 2.

Đinh Gia Trinh, 'Dân số và các giai cấp xã hội ở Đông-Dương' [Population and social classes in Indochina], *Thanh Nghị*, no. 7, 1941, pp. 18–20.

Đinh Trọng Hỷ, *Việt Bắc 30 năm chiến tranh cách mạng (1945–1975)* [Việt Bắc, thirty years of revolutionary war (1945–75)], Hanoi: NXB Quân Đội Nhân Dân, 1990.

Đỗ Bá Các, 'HTX Hòa Bình quan tâm đến tình hình sản xuất của xã viên trên quê hương mới' [Hòa Bình cooperative attends to the production situation of villagers up in their new home village], *Tiến Lên*, 15 April 1964, p. 2.

Đoàn Thu, 'Ở một vùng chè' [In a tea region], in Ministry of Labour, Invalids and Social Affairs, *30 năm sự nghiệp di dân khai hoang và xây dựng kinh tế mới 1961–1991*, Hanoi: Cục Điều Động Lao Động và Dân Cư, 1991, p.62.

Đường Hồng Đật (ed.), *Lịch sử nông nghiệp Việt Nam* [A history of agriculture in Vietnam], Ho Chi Minh City: Xưởng in Học Viên, 1994.

General Land Clearance Office (Tổng Cục Khai Hoang), 'Báo cáo tổng kết cuộc vận động đồng báo miền xuôi tham gia phát triển kinh tế miền núi trong kế hoạch 5 năm lần thứ nhất và phương hướng nhiệm vụ những năm tới' [Summary report on the mobilization of lowland compatriots to participate in upland economic development in the first five year plan and the line and tasks for the coming years], Hanoi, July 1966.

General Statistical Office (Tổng Cục Thống Kê), *Số liệu thống kê 1930–1984* [Population statistics, 1930–1984], Hanoi: NXB Thống Kê, 1985.

——, 'Báo cáo phân tích thống kê 30 năm hợp tác hóa nông nghiệp (1958–1988)' [Report analysing statistics of thirty years of agricultural collectivization (1958–88)], Hanoi, 1989.

Gia Lai People's Committee, 'Báo cáo tổng kết công tác di dân xây dựng vùng kinh tế mới theo dự án – phương hướng nhiệm vụ di dân trong những năm tới' [Summary report on the work of migration to build new economic zones according to projects – guidelines for the task of migration in the years ahead], Pleiku, 5 April 1994.

Hà Văn Phụng and Nông Văn Phách (eds), *Lịch sử đảng bộ tỉnh Bắc Thái* [History of the Party organization in the province of Bắc Thái], Bắc Thái: Ban Nghiên Cứu Lịch Sử Đảng tỉnh Bắc Thái, 1980.

Hải Dương, 'Trên vùng kinh tế mới Krông Buk, Trung đoàn Tam Giang khai hoang đất năng xuất lao động cao' [Up at the Krông Buk new economic zone, Tam Giang's regiment clears land with high productivity of labour], *Dak Lak*, 20 April 1978, pp. 1, 4.

Hardy, Andrew, 'Phát triển và phát rừng: vài điểm trong lịch sử hiện đại của quá trình di dân tới Dak Lak' [Development and deforestation: Aspects of contemporary history in the process of migration to Dak Lak], *Tạp Chí Xưa & Nay*, no. 2, 1996, pp. 24–25.

Hòa Bình Committee for Eradication of Malaria (Ban Tiêu Diệt Sốt Rét), 'Giải đáp khoa học về công tác tiêu diệt sốt rét' [Answering scientific questions about malaria eradication], *Hòa Bình*, 26 April1963, p. 2.

Hoàng Bắc, *Tìm hiểu cuộc vận động cải tiến quản lý hợp tác xã nông nghiệp miền núi* [Investigating the mobilization of management improvements in upland agricultural cooperatives], Hanoi: NXB Phổ Thông, 1965.

Hoàng Hải, 'Khía cạnh quốc phòng – an ninh trong công tác di dân phát triển kinh tế mới' [The defence and security aspects of migration for development of the new economy], *Lao Động & Xã Hội*, no. 4, 1995, pp. 22–23.

Hoàng Loan, 'Đồng báo Đông Quân trên quê hương Định Hóa' [Compatriots from Đông Quân up at their home in Định Hóa], *Tiến Lên*, 15 October 1963, p. 3.

Hoàng Nguyễn Vẹn, 'Xã Tam Giang (Krông Buk) hoàn thành công tác tổng điều tra số dân trước thời hạn 4 ngày' [Tam Giang commune (Krông Buk) completed the general population census four days before the deadline], *Dak Lak,* 25 October 1979, p. 3.

Hoàng Quang Khánh, Lê Hồng, and Hoàng Ngọc La, *Căn cứ địa Việt Bắc (trong cuộc Cách mạng tháng 8-1945)* [Việt Bắc resistance base (in the August Revolution)], Thái Nguyên: NXB Việt Bắc, 1976.

Hoàng Vũ Lâm, 'Xã Tam Giang khai phá 30 héc-ta ruộng nước' [Tam Giang commune has cleared 30 hectares of wet rice land], *Dak Lak*, 1 November 1979, p. 1.

Hồng Mai, 'Chiến đấu, sẵn sàng chiến đấu tốt' [Fighting, ready to fight well], *Dak Lak*, 19 October 1978, p. 3.

Hữu Mai, *Bưu ảnh từ những vùng đất mới* [Postcard from regions of new land], Hanoi: NXB Quân Đội Nhân Dân, 1978.

Huynh Minh Vu, 'Họ bỏ quê ra đi' [They leave their home village and go], *Tuổi Trẻ Chủ Nhật*, 12 May 1996, p. 6.

Huỳnh Thị Xuân, 'Báo cáo những ảnh hưởng của vấn đề di dân từ nông thôn ra nông thôn lên những vùng dân đến định cư ở tỉnh Daklak' [Report on the impact of rural–rural migration into destination residential areas of the province of Dak Lak], Chi Cục Định Canh Định Cư và Vùng Kinh Tế Mới Daklak, 1998.

Insun Yu, *Luật và xã hội Việt Nam thế kỷ XVII–XVIII* [Law and society in Vietnam in the seventeenth and eighteenth centuries], Hanoi, NXB Khoa Học Xã Hội, 1994.

K.D., 'Thái Bình–Tây Bắc một nhà' [Thái Bình–Tây Bắc one family], *Thái Bình*, 11 September 1961, p. 1.

Khánh Bình, 'Di dân nội địa: Một vấn đề xã hội bức xúc' [Internal migration: an urgent social problem], *Sài Gòn Giải Phóng*, 4 March 1998, p. 2.

Khổng Diễn, *Dân số và tộc người ở Việt Nam* [Population and people in Vietnam], Hanoi: NXB Khoa Học Xã Hội, 1995.

Khuất Quang Thụy, *Mười năm lấn biển và xây dựng vùng kinh tế mới* [Ten years of land reclamation from the sea and new economic zone construction], Đảng Ủy Đoàn 500, Hanoi: NXB Quân Đội Nhân Dân, 1990.

Kiến Xương district, 'Mấy kinh nghiệm vận động nhân dân đi xây dựng kinh tế miền núi của HTX Trực Tầm' [Trực Tầm cooperative's experiences in the mobilization of people to go and build the upland economy], *Tiến Lên*, 25 February 1964, p. 2.

——, *Báo cáo tổng kết công tác vận động chuyển dân đi tham gia phát triển kinh tế miền núi của hợp tác xã Trực-tầm, huyện Kiến-Xương, tỉnh Thái-Bình* [Summary report on the mobilization and transfer of people to participate in the development of the upland economy in Trực Tầm village, Kiến Xương district, Thái Bình province], Hanoi: Nhà in Báo Thủ Đô, 1964.

Kim Dung, 'Một số kết quả 30 năm di dân và xây dựng KTM' [Some results from 30 years of migration and building the new economy]. In Ministry of Labour, Invalids and Social Affairs, *30 năm sự nghiệp di dân khai hoang và xây dựng kinh tế mới 1961–1991*, Hanoi: Cục Điều Động Lao Động và Dân Cư, 1991, pp. 55–56.

Lại Văn Minh and Nguyễn Bá Cửu, *Đất Bắc Thái kèm theo bản đồ thổ nhưỡng tỷ lệ 1/100.000* [The land in Bắc Thái, with a map of its soils attached, 1:100,000], Ủy Ban Nông Nghiệp Bắc Thái, c. 1970.

Lê Duẩn, 'Báo cáo chính trị của Ban chấp hành trung ương Đảng ở Đại hội toàn quốc lần thứ ba' [Political report of the Central Party Administrative Committee at the Third Whole Nation Congress of Delegates], *Nhân Dân*, 6 September 1960, pp. 3–12.

——, *Báo cáo chính trị của Ban chấp hành trung ương Đảng tại Đại hội đại biểu toàn quốc lần thứ IV (do đồng chí Lê Duẩn, Tổng bí thư Ban chấp hành trung ương Đảng, trình bày)* [Political report of the Central Party Administrative Committee to the Fourth Whole Nation Congress of Delegates (presented by comrade Lê Duẩn, General Secretary of the Central Party Administrative Committee)], Hanoi: NXB Sự Thật, 1977.

Lê Duy Đại, 'Bước đầu nghiên cứu những đặc điểm biến động dân cư tự nhiên tỉnh Đắc Lắc' [First steps in the research of some aspects of natural population change in Dak Lak province], *DTH*, no. 3, 1982, pp. 50–61.

——, 'Những vấn đề đặt ra xung quanh việc bổ sung thêm lao động để phát triển kinh tế xã hội ở Tây Nguyên hiện nay' [Problems relating to the additional labour destined for the socio-economic development of the present-day central highlands], *DTH*, no. 3, 1983, pp. 30–37.

Lê Khánh, *Quê mới người Hà Nội ở Lâm Đồng* [New home for Hanoi people in Lâm Đồng], Hanoi: NXB Nông Nghiệp, 1983.

Lê Khánh Thuận, 'Muỗi Anopheles Meigen chuyển bệnh sốt rét ở miền Trung, Việt Nam' [The mosquito Anopheles Meigen carries malaria in central Vietnam], Luận án phó tiến sĩ y học, Trường Đại Học Y, Hanoi, 1988.

Lê Thanh Nghị, *Xây dựng huyện thành đơn vị kinh tế nông công nghiệp* [Building the district to become the economic unit of industry and agriculture], Hanoi: NXB Sự Thật, 1979.

Lê Thước, *Sự nghiệp và thi văn của Ủy viên tướng công Nguyễn Công Trứ* [The work and writings of His Excellency Nguyễn Công Trứ], Hanoi: Nhà In Lê Văn Tân, 1928.

Lèng Văn Tý, Phạm Tất Quynh and Triệu Quang Tiến (eds), *Lịch sử đảng bộ thị xã Bắc Cạn* [History of the Party organization in the town of Bắc Cạn], Hanoi: NXB Chính Trị Quốc Gia, 1996.

Lý Văn Nghĩa, 'Lên đường chống Mỹ, cứu nước' [Setting off on the road to fight the USA and save the country], *Tiến Lên,* 19 February 1966, p. 4.

Ma Ngọc Cao, 'Xã Hùng Vương (Bắc Cạn) đón đồng báo xã Phúc Thành lên khai hoang' [Hùng Vương commune (Bắc Cạn) welcomes compatriots from Phúc Thành commune coming up to clear land], *Tiến Lên*, 10 March 1964, p. 4.

Mai Chau Medical Service (Phòng Y Tế Mai Châu), 'Xã Mai Hạ rời chuồng trâu xa nhà' [Mai Hạ commune puts buffalo pens far from houses], *Hòa Bình*, 23 April 1963, p. 2.

Mai Khắc Ứng, *Chính sách khuyến nông dưới thời Minh Mạng* [Emperor Ming Mạng's agriculture promotion policy], Hanoi: NXB Văn Hóa Thông Tin, 1996.

Ministry of Agriculture (Bộ Nông Nghiệp), *Chính sách khuyến khích khai hoang xây dựng các vùng kinh tế mới* [Policy to encourage land clearing and the building of new economic zones], Hanoi: NXB Nông Nghiệp, 1981.

——, 'Báo cáo tình hình khai hoang và phân bố lao động, dân cư đi khai hoang xây dựng vùng kinh tế mới 5 năm 1976–1989' [Report on land clearance and the redistribution of labour and population to clear land and build new economic zones, during the five years 1976–80]. Hanoi: Bộ Nông Nghiệp, January 1982.

Ministry of Culture (Bộ Văn Hóa), *Những điều cần biết về hộ tịch (sinh, tử, giá thú)* [Necessary things to know about civil status (births, deaths, marriages)], Hanoi: NXB Phổ Thông, 1958.

Ministry of Health (Bộ Y Tế), *Tài liệu huấn luyện cán bộ y tế xã về sốt rét* [Materials for training commune medical cadres about malaria], Hanoi: NXB Y Học, 1960.

Ministry of Interior (Bộ Nội Vụ), *Một số điểm chính về công tác hộ tịch* [Some important points about civil status adminstration], Hanoi: Bộ Nội Vụ, 1960.

Ministry of Labour (Bộ Lao Động), *Chính sách chế độ về tổ chức điều động lao động & dân cư* [The policy regime concerning the organization of allocation of labour and population], Hanoi: Cục Điều Động Lao Động, c1983.

——, 'Báo cáo sơ kết công tác điều động lao động dân cư xây dựng kinh tế mới 1981–1988' [Report on the distribution of labour and population to build the new economy, 1981–88], undated draft, c. 1989.

——, 'Tờ trình về việc cải tiến tổ chức bộ máy chỉ đạo phân bố điều động lao động-dân cư xây dựng vùng kinh tế mới' [Report on reform to the organizational apparatus for the distribution of labour and population and the building of new economic zones], 1989.

Ministry of Labour, Invalids and Social Affairs, (Bộ Lao Động Thương Binh và Xã Hội), *30 năm sự nghiệp di dân khai hoang và xây dựng kinh tế mới 1961–1991* [Thirty years of migration to clear land and build the new economy 1961–91], Hanoi: Cục Điều Động Lao Động và Dân Cư, 1991.

'Một số vùng kinh tế mới đã định hình và phát triển' [A number of new economic zones already established and developing], map, *QDND*, 4 July 1995, p. 3.

Nam Cường commune: 'Tham luận hội thảo khoa học nhân dịp 19-5-1995 ngày sinh chủ tịch Hồ Chí Minh, về một miền quê đón Bác và làm theo lời Bác dạy' [Speech at a conference on 19 May 1995, on the occasion of chairman Hồ Chí Minh's birthday, about a home area which once welcomed Uncle [Hồ Chí Minh] and follows his teaching]. An earlier version was published by Đỗ Mạn and Bùi Đức Thắng, 'Nam Cường – nơi Bác Hồ đã về thăm' [Nam Cường – a place Uncle Ho visited]. In Ministry of Labour, *30 năm sự nghiệp di dân khai hoang và xây dựng kinh tế mới 1961–1991*, Hanoi: Cục Điều Động Lao Động và Dân Cư, 1991, pp. 23–26.

Nghiêm Xuân Yêm, 'Thanh niên trí thức với nghề nông ở xứ nhà' [Young intellectuals and the agricultural profession in our country], *Thanh Nghị*, no. 35, 16 April 1943, pp. 194–198.

——, 'Cảnh nghèo ở thôn quê' [Poverty in the countryside], *Thanh Nghị*, no. 47, 16 October 1943, pp. 574–576, 564.

——, 'Điều tra nhỏ – Những tá điền' [Small survey – The tenant farmers], *Thanh Nghị*, no. 55, 26 February 1944, pp. 64–67.

——, 'Điều tra nhỏ – Những tiểu đồn diền' [Small survey – The small concessions], *Thanh Nghị*, no. 62, 29 April 1944, pp. 263–266.

——, 'Nạn dân đói (Một vài nhận xét và thiên kiến về vấn đề thóc gạo)' [Famine (A few comments and prejudices concerning the rice problem)], *Thanh Nghị*, no. 107, 5 May 1945, pp. 225–229.

Ngô Tuấn, 'Bức xúc vấn đề di dân tự do' [The urgent problem of free migration], *Việt Nam Đầu Từ Nước Ngoài*, no. 6, 26 February 1996, p. 74.

Ngô Văn Lý and Nguyễn Văn Diêu, *Tây Nguyên Tiềm Năng và Triển Vọng* [The central highlands, potential and prospects], Ho Chi Minh City: NXB Thành phố Hồ Chí Minh, 1992.

Ngọc Liên, 'HTX Hải An chúng tôi cũng sẽ chuyển một phần ba dân số đi xây dựng kinh tế miền núi' [Our cooperative Hải An will also transfer one third of the population to build the upland economy], *Tiến Lên*, 15 April 1964, p. 2.

Ngọc Sơn, 'HTX Quyết Thắng gắn liền công tác xây dựng kinh tế miền núi với cuộc vận động cải tiến quản lý HTX đợt III' [Quyết Thắng cooperative has linked the building of upland economy with the mobilization of improvements in cooperative management stage III], *Tiến Lên*, 20 April 1964, p. 2.

Ngọc Tự, *Nguồn Vui Duy Nhất. Hồi ký cách mạng của đồng chí Dương Thị Ân* [Unique source of happiness. Revolutionary memoirs of comrade Dương Thị Ân], Hanoi: NXB Phụ Nữ, 1974.

Nguyễn Duy Ngưu, 'Cấp Ủy đi đầu, Đảng viên gương mẫu xung phong là điều kiện tiên quyết của chúng tôi!' [The Party Committee goes first, Party members assault as mirrors, this is our prerequisite condition!], *Tiến Lên*, 15 March 1964, p. 2.

Nguyễn Đăng Thục, 'Nam Tiến Việt Nam' [Vietnam's southward advance], *Sử Địa*, no. 19–20, July 1970, pp. 25–43.

Nguyễn Hồng Minh, 'Di dân tự do, tổng luận khoa học' [Free migration, a general scientific conclusion], Hanoi: Bộ Lao Động Thương Binh và Xã Hội, Trung Tâm Thông Tin Khoa Học Lao Động và Xã Hội, 1993.

Nguyễn Huy Thiệp, 'Những người thợ xẻ' [The sawyers]. In Nguyễn Huy Thiệp, *Như những ngọn gió*, Hanoi: NXB Văn Học, 1999, pp. 245–289.

Nguyễn Khắc Đạm, 'Những thủ đoạn bóc lột của tư bản Pháp ở Việt Nam' [The means of oppression of French capital in Vietnam], Hanoi: NXB Văn Sử Địa, 1957.

——, 'Vai trò của nhà nước về vấn đề khai hoang trong lịch sử Việt Nam' [The role of the state in the question of clearing land in Vietnamese history], *NCLS*, vol. 39, 1962, pp. 5–40, 52.

Nguyễn Khương, 'Đoạn kết có hậu cho toàn FULRO cuối cùng' [A decisive solution for the last group of FULRO], *Thế Giới Mới*, 27 April 1998, pp. 77–81.

Nguyễn Pháp, *Nông-lâm nghiệp Đắc Lắc, 1975–1995* [Agriculture and forestry in Dak Lak, 1975–95], Hanoi: NXB Nông Nghiệp, 1995.

Nguyễn Phòng, 'Để cải thiện đời sống lâu dài cho nhân dân, chúng tôi tích cực chuyển người đi xây dựng kinh tế miền núi' [In order to raise the long-term standard of living of the people, we diligently transfer people to go and build the upland economy], *Tiến Lên*, 20 March 1964, p. 2.

Nguyễn Quang Ngọc, *Về một số làng buôn ở đồng bằng Bắc Bộ thế kỷ XVIII–XIX* [Trading villages in the northern delta, eighteenth to nineteenth centuries], Hanoi: Hội Sử Học Việt Nam, 1993.

Nguyễn Sĩ Thưởng, 'Giỏi việc nhà, chậm việc hợp tác' [Skilful at home, slow at the cooperative], *Tiến Lên*, 15 December 1963, p. 3.

Nguyễn Thanh Sơn, 'Đoàn thanh niên trong phong trào "Ba xung kích làm chủ tập thể"' [The youth team in the campaign 'Three assaults to achieve collective mastery'], *Dak Lak*, 27 September 1979, p. 3.

Nguyễn Thế Huệ, 'Về dân số Việt Nam từ thập kỷ 20 đến trước Cách Mạng Tháng Tám' [Vietnam's population from the second decade of the twentieth century to the eve of the August Revolution], *NCLS*, vol. 265, no. 6, 1992, pp. 49–52, 64.

——, 'Về di dân nông nghiệp vùng châu thổ Sông Hồng giai đoạn 1981-1990' [Agricultural migration in the Red River delta in the period 1981–90], *NCLS*, 272, no. 1, 1994, pp. 35–38.

Nguyễn Tiến Lộc, 'Chúng tôi đã đạt 97% kế hoạch cả năm' [We have already fulfilled 97 per cent of the annual plan], *Tiến Lên*, 1 May 1964, p. 2.

Nguyễn Trần Trọng and Nguyễn Đặng Kiêu, *Những vấn đề kinh tế chủ yếu về khai hoang xây dựng vùng kinh tế mới ở nước ta* [Important economic issues concerning land clearance and the building of new economic zones in our country], Hanoi: NXB Nông Nghiệp, 1982.

Nguyễn Văn Huyên, 'Vấn đề nông dân Việt Nam ở Bắc Kỳ' [The problem of the Việt peasantry in northern Vietnam] (first published in French as 'Le problème de la paysannerie annamite au Tonkin', 1939). In Hà Văn Tấn (ed.), *Góp Phần Nghiên Cứu Văn Hóa Việt Nam: Những Công Trình Nghiên Cứu Của Giáo Sư Tiến Sĩ Nguyễn Văn Huyên*, Hanoi: NXB Khoa Học Xã Hội, 1995, vol. 2, pp. 27–44.

Nguyễn Văn Nhi, 'Vài nét về công trường 8–4' [Some aspects of project 8–4], *Dak Lak*, Tết issue 1979, p. 7.

Nguyễn Văn Rương, 'Chúng tôi có thể vận động nhân dân đi xây dựng kinh tế miền núi như Trực Tầm!' [We can mobilize people to go and build the up-land economy like Trực Tầm!], *Tiến Lên*, 5 March 1964, p. 2.

Nguyễn Văn Thanh (ed.), 'Đổi mới cơ chế quản lý công tác di dân xây dựng vùng kinh tế mới trong tình hình hiện nay' [Renovation in the management mechanism for migration to build new economic zones in the current situation], Hanoi: Trung Tâm Dân Số Nguồn Lao Động, 1990.

Nhân Dân, 'Các đoàn đại biểu các nước anh em thăm nhiều nơi ở Hà Nội, thăm Điện Biên Phủ và nông trường Tam Đảo' [Groups of delegates from brother countries visit many places in Hanoi, visit Điện Biên Phủ and Tam Đảo state farm], *Nhân Dân*, 10 September 1960, p. 1.

Phạm Đỗ Nhật Tân, 'Tìm hiểu một số quy luật di dân nông nghiệp đi xây dựng vùng kinh tế mới ở Việt Nam' [Research into a number of laws of agricultural migration for building new economic zones in Vietnam], in Nguyễn Văn Thanh (ed.), 'Đổi mới cơ chế quản lý công tác di dân xây dựng vùng kinh tế mới trong tình hình hiện nay', Hanoi: Trung Tâm Dân Số Nguồn Lao Động, 1990.

——, 'Hoàn thiện hơn nữa việc di dân nông nghiệp có tổ chức đi xây dựng các vùng kinh tế mới' [Further improving organized agricultural migration to go and build new economic zones], Luận án phó tiến sĩ khoa học kinh tế, Trường Đại Học Kinh Tế Quốc Dân, Hanoi, 1992.

——, 'Luận cứ khoa học cho xây dựng các chính sách di dân trên các địa bàn nông thôn Việt Nam' [Scientific discussion for the construction of a migration policy for the whole rural area of Vietnam], Đề tài KX-08–04, Hanoi, December 1994.

Phạm Khắc Hòe, *Từ Triều Đình Huế đến Chiến Khu Việt Bắc – Hồi ký* [From the Huế Court to the Việt Bắc War Zone – Memoirs], Hanoi: NXB Hà Nội, 1983.

Phạm Kiệt, *Từ núi rừng Ba Tơ* [From the hills and forests of Ba Tơ], Hanoi: NXB Quân Đội Nhân Dân, 1977.

Phạm Minh, 'Đổi mới công tác di dân phát triển vùng kinh tế mới' [Reform in migration and the development of new economic zones], *QĐND*, 4 July 1995, p. 3.

Phạm Quang Khang, 'Chúng tôi đã làm như Trực Tầm: lãnh đạo quyết tâm, Đảng viên gương mẫu' [We have already done as Trực Tầm: determined leaders, mirror Party members], *Tiến Lên*, 10 March 1964, p. 2.

Phạm Quang Trung, 'Nạn lụt năm Ất dậu với cuộc tổng khởi nghĩa giành chính quyền ở đồng bằng Bắc Bộ năm 1945' [The 1945 inundation and the general insurrection for power in the plain of northern Vietnam in 1945], *NCLS*, vol. 251, no. 4, 1990, pp. 56–60.

Phạm Văn Đồng, 'Bài ca Tây Bắc' [Song of Tây Bắc]. In Phạm Văn Đồng, *Tổ quốc ta, nhân dân ta, sự nghiệp ta và người nghệ sĩ* [Our fatherland, our people, our work and our artists], Hanoi: Văn Học, 1969.

——, *Tổ chức lại sản xuất và cải tiến quản lý Nông Nghiệp và Lâm Nghiệp trung du và miền núi* [Production reorganization and management improvement in agriculture and forestry in the midlands and highlands], Hanoi: NXB Sự Thật, 1975.

Phạm Viết Hoàng, 'Bài ca di dân' [Migration song], *Tạp Chí Xưa & Nay*, no. 56, October 1998, p. 35.

Phạm Xuân Đại, 'Khả năng hòa nhập và mức độ ổn định của các cộng đồng di dân tại Đông Nam Bộ' [Potential for assimilation and level of stability of migrant communities in southeastern Vietnam], *XHH*, vol. 12, no. 4, 1985, pp. 85–90.

Phạm Xuân Điểm, 'Áp dụng kinh nghiệm của Trực Tầm: trong một tháng xã Đông Quang chúng tôi vận động được 469 người đi khai hoang' [Applying the experience of Trực Tầm: in one month our commune Đông Quang has mobilized 469 people to go and clear land], *Tiến Lên*, 25 March 1964, p. 2.

Phan Khâm, 'Lấp sông Cài Đản' [Filling in the Cài Đản river], *Tiến Lên*, 25 August 63, p. 4.

Phan Quế, 'Mai Châu' [Mai Châu]. In Phạm Quốc Bang (ed.), *Hà Sơn Bình Di Tích và Danh Thắng* [Hà Sơn Bình, vestiges and landscapes], Xí nghiệp in Hà Sơn Bình, 1985, pp. 49–57.

P.V., 'Huyện Lak tổng kết công tác dân vận, mặt trận và tổ chức học tập chính sách dân tộc của Đảng trong giai đoạn mới' [Lak district sums up propaganda work, front and Party ethnic policy study-practice sessions in the new period], *Dak Lak*, 4 October 1979, p. 1.

——, 'Qua tổng kết công tác xây dựng kinh tế mới' [Through a summary of new economic zone constrution], *Dak Lak*, 18 October 1979, pp. 1, 4.

Quang Chất, 'Phá rừng, lấn biển bắt đất quay nhiều vọng' [Destroy the forest and reclaim land from the sea to avoid land degradation], *Thái Bình*, 9 October 1961, p. 2.

State Scientific Committee, Vietnam Scientific Institute, Geological Institute, Geography and Resources Centre, and National Economics University, 'Chương trình tiến bộ khoa học kỹ thuật: đánh giá tổng hợp tự nhiên kinh tế xã hội 9 tỉnh miền núi phía Bắc' [Technological improvement programme: General evaluation of the natural, social and economic environment of the nine provinces of the northern uplands], Programme Summary Report, Hanoi, 1990.

Tân Việt Hoa state farm, *Report for the Fatherland Front* (Mặt Trận Tổ Quốc), Thái Nguyên, 1968.

Tân Vũ, 'HTX Trực Tầm phấn đấu đưa một phần ba nhân khẩu đi các nơi xây dựng kinh tế' [Trực Tầm cooperative struggles to take one third of its people to places for economic construction], *Tiến Lên*, 1 January 1964, p. 3.

Thái Bình, *Chính Sách Nhân Dân Khai Hoang. Tài liệu học tập* [Policy for people clearing land. Study-practice document], Thái Bình: Ủy Ban Hành Chính tỉnh Thái Bình, 1963.

——, 'Báo cáo tình hình thực hiện nhiệm vụ chuyển dân đi xây dựng các vùng KTM qua các năm' [Report on the implementation of population transfers to build new economic zones over the years], Committee for Labour and Population Appointments and New Economy (Ban Điều Động Lao Động và Kinh Tế Mới), Thái Bình, c. 1992.

Thái Bình, 'Xã Hiệp Hòa đã tổ chức học tập Nghị quyết 5 cho cán bộ, Đảng viên và xã viên' [Hiệp Hòa commune has organized study-practice of Resolution 5 for cadres, Party member and villagers], *Thái Bình*, 25 September 1961, p. 1.

Thái Bình tự giới thiệu [This is Thái Bình], Sở Văn Hóa Thông Tin và Thể Thao Thái Bình, 1996.

Thái Bình Police Service (Ty Công An Thái Bình), *Tài liệu học tập về công tác kiểm tra đổi sổ hộ khẩu và cấp giấy chứng nhận căn cước cho các khu phố, xã, hộ tập thể* [Study practice document concerning the verification of changes to household registration booklets and the issue of identification papers to zones, streets, villages and collective households], Hanoi: Xí Nghiệp In Thái Bình, 1972.

Thái Mèo Autonomous Zone Health Service (Ty Y Tế Khu Tự Trị Thái Mèo), *Chống và tiêu diệt bệnh sốt rét ở miền núi* [Fighting and eradicating malaria in the uplands], Hanoi: Nhà in Tiến Long, 1959.

Thái Nguyên Provincial Committee for Eradication of Malaria (Ủy Ban Tiêu Diệt Sốt Rét Tỉnh Thái Nguyên), *Báo cáo mừng Thắng lời i tám năm tiêu diệt sốt rét (1957–1964) của tỉnh Thái Nguyên* [Report celebrating the eight year victory in malaria eradication (1957–64) in Thái Nguyên province], Thái Nguyên 1965.

Thanh Long, 'Đồng báo Tây Bắc tích cực giúp đỡ các đội khai hoang tỉnh Thái Bình' [Tây Bắc compatriots positively help land clearance teams from Thái Bình province], *Thái Bình*, 30 October 1961, p. 1.

Thanh Xương, 'Hợp tác xã khai hoang Tân Tiến thu hoạch lúa gai đầu tiên trên đất đồi' [Land clearance cooperative Tân Tiến harvests its first crop of ramie on hilly land], *Hòa Bình*, 1 October 1963, pp. 2, 3.

Tiến Lên, 'Đi xây dựng quê hương mới: Đảng bộ Vũ Thuận lãnh đạo tốt công tác khai hoang' [Going to build a new home village: Vũ Thuận Party apparatus leads well in the work of land clearance], *Tiến Lên*, 25 June 63, p. 4.

——, 'Trong công tác vận động nhân dân đi xây dựng kinh tế miền núi, chúng ta có thể làm được như Trực Tầm không? Tại sao?' [In the mobilization of people to go and build the upland economy, can we do like Trực Tầm? Why?], *Tiến Lên*, 29 February 1964, p. 2.

Tiến Lên Editorial Committee (Ban Biên Tập), 'Chúng ta hoàn toàn có thể làm được như hợp tác xã Trực Tầm!' [We definitely can do like Trực Tầm co-operative!], *Tiến Lên*, 5 May 1964, p. 2.

Trần An Phong (ed.), *Nghiên cứu xây dựng luận cứ khoa học cho định hướng phát triển kinh tế-xã hội các tỉnh Tây Nguyên* [Research towards a scientific approach to the socio-economic development of the provinces of Tây Nguyên], Hanoi: NXB Nông Nghiệp, 1996.

Trần Đình Hoan, 'Về những quan điểm cơ bản trong công tác di dân ở Việt Nam' [Some basic concepts in the work of migration in Vietnam]. In Nguyễn Văn Thanh (ed.), 'Đổi mới cơ chế quản lý công tác di dân xây dựng vùng kinh tế mới trong tình hình hiện nay', Hanoi: Trung Tâm Dân Số Nguồn Lao Động, 1990.

——, '30 năm di dân phát triển vùng kinh tế mới và những đổi mới cơ bản trong giai đoạn tới' [Thirty years of migration to develop new economic zones and basic renovations in the period to come]. In Ministry of Labour, *30 năm sự nghiệp di dân khai hoang và xây dựng kinh tế mới 1961–1991*, Hanoi: Cục Điều Động Lao Động và Dân Cư, 1991, pp. 7–12.

Trần Huy Liệu, *Lịch sử tám mươi năm chống Pháp* [History of eighty years fighting the French], Hanoi: Ban Nghiên Cứu Văn Sử Địa, 1956.

Trần Nam Hưng, *Tự chữa sốt rét (kinh nghiệm trong kháng chiến)* [Self-treatment of malaria (experience during the war of resistance)], Hanoi: NXB Phổ Thông, 1958.

Trần Thị Quế, Nguyễn Thị Hồng Phấn and Trần Đăng Tuấn, *Số liệu thống kê các vùng thưa dân ở Việt Nam* [Population data of sparsely populated areas in Vietnam], Hanoi: NXB Thống Kê, 1996.

Trần Văn Giàu, *Giai cấp công nhân Việt Nam* [The Vietnamese working class], Hanoi: NXB Sự Thật, 1958.

Trịnh Văn Đông, 'Báo cáo tổng kết công tác khai hoang xây dựng vùng kinh tế mới năm 1976–1981' [Summary report on land clearance and the building of new economic zones, 1976–81], Thái Nguyên: Sở Nông Nghiệp Bắc Thái, 1982.

Trọng Hồng, 'HTX khai hoang Tân Ngọc sản xuất bước đầu có nhiều tiến bộ' [Land clearance cooperative Tân Ngọc has made much progress in its initial production], *Hòa Bình*, 27 September 1963, p. 3.

——, 'Qua cuộc vận động thí điểm "củng cố HTX khai hoang"' [Through the mobilization by experimental place 'reinforcing land clearance cooperatives'], *Hòa Bình*, 19 November 1963, p. 2.

Trực Tầm commune, 'Ra sức vận động nhân dân đi xây dựng kinh tế miền núi như HTX Trực Tầm' [Strive to mobilize people to build the upland economy like Trực Tầm cooperative], *Tiến Lên*, 25 February 1964, pp. 1, 4.

Tương Lai and Phạm Bích San, 'Khảo sát xã hội học về những cộng đồng người Kinh sinh tử và phát triển tại Tây Nguyên' [Sociological investigation into Việt communities in the process of living and developing in the central highlands], *XHH*, vol. 27, no. 3, 1989, pp. 34–48, 66.

Văn Hoa, 'Lòng những người đi khai hoang' [The spirit of people going to clear land], *Tiến Lên*, 9 April 1962, p. 2.

Văn Hồng, 'Huyện Krông Buk củng cố lực lượng dân quân du kích vững mạnh' [Krông Buk district reinforces the strength of its militia guerrilla unit], *Dak Lak*, 23 November 1978, p. 1, 4.

Văn Khánh, 'Làm thủy lợi trên quê hương mới: Quỳnh Giáo ngăn suối làm sông biến đổi đất đỏ thành đồng lúa xanh' [Irrigation work up in the new home village: Quỳnh Giáo dams streams and makes canals, turning red land of hills into green fields of paddy], *Tiến Lên*, 1 January 1964, p. 2.

Văn Thảnh, 'Gặp lại đồng bằng' [Meeting the plains again]. In Dương Thanh Từng (ed.), *Dak Lak tập sáng tác văn nghệ* [Dak Lak collection of artistic compositions], Ban Mê Thuột: Ty Văn Hóa và Thông Tin Dak Lak, 1977, p. 39.

V. H. [Vũ Đình Hòe], 'Điều tra nhỏ: Một đồn điền lớn ở Thái Nguyên' [Small survey: A large plantation in Thái Nguyên], *Thanh Nghị*, no. 83, 16 September 1944, pp. 850–852, 870–871.

Vietnam Social Science Committee, Party and People's Committees of Dak Lak Province (Ủy Ban Khoa Học Xã Hội Việt Nam, Tỉnh Ủy, Ủy Ban Nhân Dân Đắc Lắc), *Vấn đề phát triển kinh tế xã hội các dân tộc thiểu số ở Đắc Lắc* [The problem of socio-economic development among ethnic minorities in Dak Lak], Hanoi: NXB Khoa Học Xã Hội, 1990.

VNTTX, 'Trong ba năm, các nông trường quân đội đã vỡ hoang 18,482 mẫu đất, thu hoạch 43,609 tấn nông phẩm' [In three years, the military state farms have cleared 18,482 *mẫu* of land, and harvested 43,609 tons of agricultural produce], *Nhân Dân*, 18 June 1961, p. 1.

Vũ Đình Hòe, 'Vấn đề đi vay đối với dân quê' [The debt problem among the country people], *Thanh Nghị*, no. 12, 1 May 1942, p. 13–15.

——, 'Nạn nhân mãn và việc di dân' [The problem of overpopulation and the work of migration], *Thanh Nghị*, nos 112–113, 115, 9 June 1945, 16 June 1945, 7 July 1945, pp. 342–343, 358–360, 370–373, 378, 414–417, 431.

Vũ Ngọc Linh (introduction), *Lịch sử cách mạng tháng tám tỉnh Bắc Thái* [History of the August revolution in Bắc Thái province], Thái Nguyên: Ban Nghiên Cứu Lịch Sử Đảng, c. 1980.

Vũ Quang, 'Trung đoàn II (thanh niên Thái Bình) ra quân đầu năm, khai hoang xây dựng vùng kinh tế mới Ea Súp' [Regiment II (Thái Bình young people) left the army at the beginning of the year, clearing land and building Ea Súp new economic zone], *Dak Lak*, 12 January 1978, p. 1.

Vũ Văn Cẩn, *Bệnh Sốt Rét Cơn* [Malaria], NXB Vui Sống, 1947.

Vương Trung Hiệu, *Tục ngữ Việt Nam chọn lọc* [Selected Vietnamese proverbs], Hanoi: NXB Văn Nghệ, 1996.

Yên Bái Police Service (Ty Công An Yên Bái), *Tài liệu học tập về công tác quản lý hộ tịch, hộ khẩu* [Study-practice material concerning the administration of civil status and household registration], Yên Bái, 1973.

WORKS IN OTHER LANGUAGES

Barnett, A. Doak, *Cadres, Bureaucracy and Political Power in Communist China*, New York: Columbia University Press, 1967.

Bernard, Paul, *Le problème économique' Indochinois*, Paris: Nouvelles Editions Latines, 1934.

———, *Nouveaux aspects du problème économique indochinois*, Paris: Fernand Sorlot, 1937.

Bichot, A., 'Où en est la colonisation agricole au Tonkin?', *Revue Indochinoise*, 15 February 1905, pp. 196–198.

Boudarel, Georges, 'L'idéocratie importée au Vietnam avec le Maoïsme'. In Georges Boudarel (ed.), *La bureaucratie au Vietnam*, Paris: L'Harmattan, 1983.

———, 'L'insertion du pouvoir central dans les cultes villageois au Vietnam. Esquisse des problèmes à partir des écrits de Ngô Tât Tô'. In Alain Forest, Yoshiaki Ishizawa and Léon Vandermeersch (eds), *Cultes populaires et société asiatique*, Paris: L'Harmattan, 1991, pp. 87–146.

Bouvier, René, *Richesse et misère du delta tonkinois*, Paris: Imprimerie André Tournon et Cie, 1937.

Breman, Jan, 'The Village on Java and the Early Colonial State', *Journal of Peasant Studies*, vol. 9, no. 4, 1982, pp. 189–240.

———, *The Shattered Image: Construction and Deconstruction of the Village in Colonial Asia*, Dordrecht: Foris Publications, 1988.

Brenier, Henri, *Essai d'atlas statistique de l'Indochine française*, Hanoi-Haiphong: IDEO, 1914.

Brévié, Jules, *Discours prononcé à l'occasion de l'ouverture de la session du Grand Conseil des Intérêts économiques et financiers, le 2 décembre 1937*, Hanoi: IDEO, 1937.

———, 'Discours prononcé par M. le Gouverneur Général J. Brévié à l'ouverture de la session (séance inaugurale du Conseil Supérieur de la Colonisation de l'Indochine)', *BEI*, 1938, pp. 716–719.

Briffaut, Camille, *La cité annamite*, Paris: Larose, 1909.

Brocheux, Pierre, 'L'économie et la société dans l'ouest de la Cochinchine pendant la période coloniale, 1898–1940', Thèse de 3e cycle, Université de Paris, Faculté des Lettres, 1969.

———, 'Grands propriétaires et fermiers dans l'ouest de la Cochinchine pendant la période coloniale', *Revue Historique*, no. 499, 1971, pp. 59–77.

——, *The Mekong Delta: Ecology, Economy and Revolution, 1860–1960*, Madison: University of Wisconsin-Madison, 1995.

Brocheux, Pierre and Daniel Hémery, *Indochine, la colonisation ambigüe, 1858–1954*, Paris: La Découverte, 2001 (first published 1995).

Bui Tin, *Following Ho Chi Minh*, London: Hurst, 1995.

Bureau International du Travail, *Problèmes de travail en Indochine*. Geneva: Imprimerie Kundig, 1937.

Caldwell, J. C. and A. A. Igun, 'An Experiment with Census-Type Enumeration in Nigeria', *Population Studies*, vol. 25, no. 2, 1971, pp. 287–302.

Carrard, Philippe, *Poetics of the New History. French National Historical Discourse from Braudel to Chartier*, Baltimore and London: Johns Hopkins University Press, 1992.

Carter, Paul, *The Road to Botany Bay*, London: Faber & Faber, 1987.

Central Census Steering Committee, *Vietnam Population Census 1989, Sample Results*, Hanoi, 1990.

——, *Vietnam Population Census 1989, Completed Census Results*, Hanoi, 1991.

——, *1999 Population and Housing Census: Sample Results*, Hanoi: Thế Giới Publishers, 2000.

Chautemps, Maurice, *Le vagabondage en pays annamite*, Paris: A. Rousseau, 1908.

Cheng Tiejun and Mark Selden, 'The Origins and Social Consequences of China's *Hukou* System', *The China Quarterly*, vol. 139, 1994, pp. 644–668.

Choi Byung Wook, 'Southern Vietnam under the Reign of Minh Mang (1820–1841): Central Policies and Local Response', PhD thesis, Australian National University, Canberra, 1999.

Chu Van Tan, *Reminiscences on the Army for National Salvation* (Mai Elliott trans.), Ithaca: Department of Asian Studies, Cornell, 1974.

Claessens, Bob, and Jeanne Rousseau, *Our Bruegel*, Antwerp: Mercatorfonds, 1975.

Clifford, James, *Routes: Travel and Translation in the Late Twentieth Century*, Cambridge, Massachusetts: Harvard University Press, 1997.

Condominas, Georges, 'Aspects of a Minority Problem in Indochina', *Pacific Affairs*, vol. XXIV, no. 1, 1951, pp. 77–82.

——, *L'espace sociale à propos de l'Asie du Sud-Est*, Paris: Flammarion, 1980.

Conrandy, *Les provinces du Tonkin: Thai Nguyen,* extract from *Revue Indochinoise*, 1904, Paris: Maisonneuve, 1904.

Cooke, Nola, 'Regionalism and the Nature of Nguyen rule in Seventeenth-Century Dang Trong (Cochinchina)', *JSAS*, vol. 29, no. 1, 1998, pp. 122–161.

Cotter, Michael, 'Towards a Social History of the Vietnamese Southward Movement', *JSAH*, vol. 9, no. 1, 1968, pp. 12–24.

Cucherousset, Henri, *Le Tonkin est-il surpeuplé?*, Hanoi: Imprimerie Tonkinoise, 1925.

Cummings, Joe and Tony Wheeler, *Myanmar (Burma)*, Melbourne: Lonely Planet Publications, 1996.

Dang Nguyen Anh, Sidney Goldstein and James McNally, 'Internal Migration and Development in Vietnam', *International Migration Review*, vol. 31, no. 2, 1997, pp. 312–337.

——, 'Market Reforms and Internal Labour Migration in Vietnam', *Asian and Pacific Migration Journal*, vol. 8, no. 3, 1999, pp. 381–409.

Dang Phong, 'Opening the Door: Two Centuries of Markets in Vietnam', unpublished manuscript, Hanoi, 1998.

Dang Van Viet, *Highway 4: The Border Campaign (1947–1950)*, Hanoi: Foreign Languages Publishing House, 1990.

Darles, Auguste, *Les possibilités économiques de la province de Thai Nguyen et les conditions de son essor*, extract from *BEI*, 1917, Hanoi-Haiphong: IDEO, 1917.

Darwin, Charles, *Journal of Researches into the Natural History and Geology of the Countries Visited during the Voyage of H.M.S. Beagle etc.*, New York, 1896.

De Gantès, Gilles, 'Du rôle des 'grands hommes' aux colonies: l'exemple d'Henri de Monpezat en Indochine', *Revue française d'histoire d'outre-mer*, vol. LXXX, no. 301, 1993, pp. 585–597.

——, 'Coloniaux, gouverneurs et ministres. L'influence des Français sur l'évolution du pays à l'époque coloniale, 1902–1914', Doctorat d'histoire, University of Paris 7, 1994.

De Koninck, Rodolphe, 'The Peasantry as the Territorial Spearhead of the State in Southeast Asia: The Case of Vietnam', *Sojourn*, vol. 11, no. 2, 1996, pp. 231–258.

——, *Deforestation in Viet Nam*, Ottawa: International Development Research Centre, 1999.

De Lanessan, J.-L., *La colonisation française en Indo-Chine*, Paris: Felix Alcan, 1895.

Delamarre, Emile, *L'émigration et l'immigration ouvrière en Indochine*, Hanoi: IDEO, 1931.

Department of Mines and Technical Surveys, *Indo-China, a Geographical Appreciation*, Ottawa, 1953.

Desbarats, Jacqueline, 'Population Redistribution in the Socialist Republic of Vietnam', *Population and Development Review*, vol. 13, no. 1, 1987, pp. 43–76.

De Tréglodé, Benoît, *Héros et révolution au Viêt Nam*, Paris: L'Harmattan, 2001.

Diep Dinh Hoa, 'Dynamics of Yao Genealogy (A Case Study of a Yen Stream Village)', *South Pacific Study*, vol. 17, no. 1, 1996, pp. 103–111.

Dumont, René, *La culture du riz dans le delta du Tonkin*, Bangkok: Prince of Songkla University, 1995 (first published 1935).

Durgin, Frank A., 'The Relationship of the Death of Stalin to the Economic Changes of the Post-Stalin Era'. In Robert C. Stuart (ed.), *The Soviet Rural Economy*, New Jersey: Rowman & Allanheld, 1984, pp. 118–142.

Echinard, Alfred, 'Notice sur la province de Thai Nguyen', Thai Nguyen: unpublished monograph (available at the National Library of Vietnam, Hanoi), 1932.

——, *Histoire politique et militaire de la province de Thai Nguyen: ses forces de police*, Hanoi: Imprimerie Trung Bac Tan Van, 1934.

Elvin, Mark, 'Braudel and China'. In John A. Marino (ed.), *History and the Social Sciences: Braudel's Mediterranean Fifty Years After*, Kirksville, Missouri: Thomas Jefferson University Press, forthcoming.

Evans, Grant, 'Internal Colonialism in the Central Highlands of Vietnam', *Sojourn*, vol. 7, no. 2, 1992, pp. 274–304.

Evans, Grant and Kelvin Rowley, *Red Brotherhood at War: Vietnam, Cambodia and Laos since 1975*, London and New York: Verso, 1984.

Fall, Bernard B., *The Two Vietnams: A Political and Military Analysis*, New York: Praeger, 1963.

——, *Hell in a Very Small Place: The Siege of Dien Bien Phu*, Philadelphia and New York: J. B. Lippincott, 1966.

Fforde, Adam and Suzanne H. Paine, *The Limits of National Liberation. Problems of Economic Management in the Democratic Republic of Vietnam*, London: Croom Helm, 1987.

Fforde, Adam and Stefan de Vylder, *From Plan to Market: The Economic Transition in Vietnam*, Boulder, Colorado: Westview Press, 1996.

Forbes, Dean, 'Urbanisation, Migration, and Vietnam's Spatial Structure', *Sojourn*, vol. 11, no. 1, 1996, pp. 24–51.

Forbes, Dean and Nigel Thrift, 'Territorial Organisation, Regional Development and the City in Vietnam'. In Dean Forbes and Nigel Thrift (eds), *The Socialist Third World: Urban Development and Territorial Planning*, Oxford: Blackwell, 1987, pp. 98–128.

Fourniau, Charles, 'Les années 30 et l'impasse coloniale en Indochine'. In J. Godart (ed.), *Rapport de mission en Indochine, 1er janvier–14 mars 1937*, Paris: L'Harmattan, 1994.

Furata, Motoo, *Vietnam no Ichi sonraku ni okeru 1945 nen Kikin no Jittai Taibinsho Tienhai-ken Tay Luong-mura Luong Phu-buraku ni Kansuru Nichi Etsu Godo Chosa* [The reality of the 1945 famine in a village in Vietnam. Japan Vietnam joint research report in Thái Bình province, Tiền Hải district, Tây Lương commune, Lương Phú village], Tokyo: Tokyo University Research Report on History, vol. 22, 1994.

'The Future of Migration in Vietnam. Recommendations of the International Seminar on Internal Migration: Implications for Migration Policy in Vietnam'. Recommendations of the conference, Hanoi, 6–8 May 1998.

G. B., 'Le problème de la population et des subsistances en Indochine', *BEI*, 1938, pp. 1339–1349.

Gendreau, Francis, Do Tien Dung and Pham Do Nhat Tan, 'Les migrations internes'. In Patrick Gubry (ed.) *Population et développement au Viêt-Nam*, Paris: Karthala-CEPED, 2000, pp. 195–217.

Girod, L., *Dix ans de Haut-Tonkin*, Tours: A. Mame, undated.

Godart, Justin, *Rapport de mission en Indochine, 1er janvier–14 mars 1937*, Paris: L'Harmattan, 1994.

Goodman, Bryna, *Native Place, City, and Nation. Regional Networks and Identities in Shanghai, 1853–1937*, Berkeley, Los Angeles and London: University of California Press, 1995.

Gottschang, Thomas R., and Diana Lary, *Swallows and Settlers: The Great Migration from North China to Manchuria*, Ann Arbor: Center for Chinese Studies, University of Michigan, 2000.

Gourou, Pierre, *Le Tonkin*, Paris: Exposition Coloniale Internationale, 1931.

——, *Les paysans du delta tonkinois: étude de géographie humaine*, Paris: Les Editions d'Art et d'Histoire, 1936.

——, *L'utilisation du sol en Indochine*, Paris: Hartmann, 1940.

Halfacree, Keith H. and Paul J. Boyle, 'The Challenge Facing Migration Research: the case for a Biographical Approach', *Progress in Human Geography*, vol. 17, no. 3, 1993, pp. 333–348.

Hardy, Andrew, 'La politique économique française en Indochine de 1944 à 1948', Maîtrise d'histoire, University of Paris 7, 1991.

——, 'Les opinions de Paul Bernard (1892–1960) sur l'économie de l'Indochine coloniale et leur actualité', *Revue française d'histoire d'outre-mer*, vol. LXXXII, no. 308, 1995, pp. 297–338.

——, 'Strategies of Migration to Upland Areas in Contemporary Vietnam', *Asia Pacific Viewpoint*, vol. 41, no. 1, April 2000, pp. 23–34.

——, 'One Hundred Years of Malaria Control in Vietnam: a Regional Retrospective. Part II, 1945–1999', *Mekong Malaria Forum*, no. 6, April 2000, pp. 98–110.

——, 'The Road to Bờ Rạ: Travel, Settlement and Contact on a Vietnamese Upland Frontier', *Journal of Southeast Asian Studies*, vol. 31, no. 2, September 2000, pp. 295–320.

——, 'Rules and Resources: Negotiating the Household Registration System in Vietnam under Reform', *Sojourn*, vol. 16, no. 2, October 2001, pp. 187–212.

——, 'State Visions, Migrant Decisions: Population Movements since the End of the Vietnam War'. In Hy Van Luong (ed.), *Postwar Vietnam: Dynamics of a Transforming Society*, Rowman and Littlefield, forthcoming.

Hardy, Andrew and Nguyễn Tiến Đông, 'Quelques intérrogations sur l'identité ethnique : le cas des Mạc de Mai Châu', *Tạp Chí Xưa & Nay*, no. 66, 1999, pp. I-III (in Vietnamese, pp. 24–25).

Henry, Yves, *Economie agricole de l'Indochine*, Hanoi: IDEO, 1932.

Hickey, Gerald C., *Some Recommendations Affecting the Role of Vietnamese Highlanders in Economic Development*, Santa Monica, California: Rand Corporation, 1974.

——, *Free in the Forest. Ethnohistory of the Vietnamese Central Highlands, 1954–1976*, New Haven and London: Yale University Press, 1982.

——, *Sons of the Mountains. Ethnohistory of the Vietnamese Central Highlands to 1954*, New Haven and London: Yale University Press, 1982.

Hitchcox, Linda, 'Relocation in Vietnam and Outmigration: The Ideological and Economic Context'. In Judith M. Brown and Rosemary Foot (eds), *Migration: The Asian Experience*, Oxford: St Martin's Press, 1994, pp. 202–220.

Ho Dac Khai, 'Contribution à l'étude de la colonisation annamite', *RIJE*, no. 7, 1938, pp. 413–425.

Honey, P. J., *Communism in North Vietnam: Its Role in the Sino-Soviet Dispute*, Cambridge, Massachusetts: MIT Press, 1963.

Huỳnh Thị Xuân, 'The Impact of Rural–Rural Migration to Resettlement Areas in Dak Lak Province'. Proceedings of the International Seminar on Internal Migration (Hanoi, 6–8 May 1998), Hanoi: Population Council Research Report no. 9, pp. 97–112.

Jamieson, N. J., Le Trong Cuc and A. T. Rambo, *The Development Crisis in Vietnam's Mountains*, Honolulu: East-West Center, 1998.

Jones, Gavin W., 'Population Trends and Policies in Vietnam', *Population and Development Review*, vol. 8, no. 4, 1982, pp. 783–810.

Jones, Gavin W. and H. V. Richter, *Population Resettlement Programs in Southeast Asia*, Canberra: ANU Press, 1982.

Jouin, B. Y., *Enquête démographique au Darlac, 1943–44*, extract from *BSEI*, vol. XXV, no. 3, 1950.

Kane, Penny, *The Second Billion, Population and Family Planning in China*, Ringwood, Victoria: Penguin, 1987.

Kemlin, Emile, *L'immigration Annamite en pays Moï, en particulier dans la province de Kontum*, Qui Nhon: Imprimerie de Qui Nhon, 1923.

Kemp, Jeremy, *Seductive Mirage: The Search for the Village Community in Southeast Asia*, Amsterdam: Foris Publications, 1988.

Kerkvliet, Benedict J. Tria, *State–Village Relations in Vietnam: Contested Cooperatives and collectivisation*, Clayton: Monash University, 1993.

——, 'Village–State Relations in Vietnam: The Effect of Everyday Politics on Decollectivisation', *JAS*, vol. 54, no. 2, 1995, pp. 396–418.

Kessel, Joseph, *Nuits des Princes*, Paris: Editions Lidis, 1953 (first published 1927).

Khérian, Grégoire, 'Le problème démographique en Indochine: Esquisse d'une politique démographique en Indochine', *RIJE*, extract from nos 1–2, 1937, Hanoi: IDEO.

——, 'Les méfaits de la surpopulation deltaïque', *RIJE*, no. 7, 1938, pp. 476–505.

——, 'La querelle de l'industrialisation de l'Indochine', *RIJE*, no. 8, 1938, pp. 629–667.

——, 'À propos de quelques ouvrages récents sur l'économie indochinoise', *RIJE*, no. 11, 1939, pp. 593–600.

——, 'Le problème du crédit en Indochine. II. Les éléments de solution', *RIJE*, no. 16, 1941, pp. 641–668.

Kleinen, John G., '"Do not pay taxes": The Anti-Tax Revolt in Central Vietnam, 1908'. In Leslie E. Bauzon (ed.), *A Comparative Study of Peasant Unrest in Southeast Asia*, Singapore: Institute of Southeast Asian Studies, 1991, pp. 74–94.

——, 'The Village as Pretext: Ethnographic Praxis and the Colonial State in Vietnam'. In Jan Breman, Peter Kloos and Ashwani Saith (eds), *The Village in Asia Revisited*, Delhi: Oxford University Press, 1997, pp. 353–393.

Lavely, William R., 'China's Rural Population Statistics at the Local Level', *Population Index,* vol. 48, no. 4, 1982, pp. 665–677.

Le Bach Duong, 'State, Economic Development and Internal Migration in Vietnam', PhD thesis, Binghamton University, New York.

Le Bo-Chanh, 'Notice sur la Province de Thai Nguyen', unpublished monograph (available at the National Library of Vietnam, Hanoi), 1933.

Lechesme, Paul, *L'Indochine Seconde, Régions Moï (Kontoum-Darlac)*, Qui Nhon: Imprimerie de Qui Nhon, 1924.

Le Duan, 'Political Report of the Central Committee of the Viet Nam Workers' Party, 5.9.1960'. In *Third National Congress of the Viet Nam Workers' Party, Documents, Volume 1*, Hanoi: Foreign Languages Publishing House, c. 1961.

Le Failler, Philippe, 'Le mouvement international anti-opium et l'Indochine (1906–1940)', Doctorat d'histoire, University of Provence, 1993.

——, 'Village Rebellions in the Tonkin Delta, 1900–1905'. In Gisèle Bousquet and Pierre Brocheux (eds), *Twentieth Century Vietnam: Essays on Vietnamese Society*, Ann Arbor: University of Michigan Press, forthcoming.

Le Fèvre, Georges, *Démolisseurs et batisseurs*, Paris: André Delpuech, 1927.

Le Roi Ladurie, Emmanuel, *Montaillou, village occitan de 1294 à 1324*, Paris: Gallimard, 1975.

Le Thi, *The Role of the Family in the Formation of the Vietnamese Personality*, Hanoi, The Gioi Publishers, 1999.

Le Trong Cuc and A. Terry Rambo (eds), 'Too Many People, Too Little Land: the Human Ecology of a Wet Rice-growing Village in the Red River Delta of Vietnam', Honolulu: East-West Center, 1993.

Li Tana, *Peasants on the Move, Rural–Urban Migration in the Hanoi Region*, Singapore: Institute of Southeast Asian Studies, 1996.

——, 'An Alternative Vietnam? The Nguyen Kingdom in the Seventeenth and Eighteenth Centuries', *JSAH*, vol. 29, no. 1, 1997, pp. 111–121.

——, *Nguyen Cochinchina: Southern Vietnam in the Seventeenth and Eighteenth Centuries*, Ithaca, New York: Cornell Southeast Asia Program, 1998.

Limerick, Patricia Nelson, 'Making the Most of Words – Verbal Activity and Western America'. In William Cronon, George Miles and Jay Gitlin (eds), *Under an Open Sky - Rethinking America's Western Past*, New York: W. W. Norton and Company, 1992.

Lombard-Salmon, Claudine, *Un exemple d'acculturation chinoise: la province de Gui Zhou au XVIII siècle*, Paris: École française d'Extrême-Orient, 1972.

Lotzer, L. E. and G. Wormser, *La surpopulation du Tonkin et du Nord-Annam: ses rapports avec la colonisation de la péninsule indochinoise,* Hanoi: IDEO, 1941.

Luong, Hy Van, 'Vietnamese Kinship: Structural Principles and the Socialist Transformation in Northern Vietnam', *JAS*, vol. 48, no. 4, 1989, pp. 741–756.

——, *Revolution in the Village: Tradition and Transformation in North Vietnam, 1935–1988*, Honolulu: East-West Centre, 1992.

Luu Dinh Nhan, 'The Migration Issue in Vietnam: A Case Study of Rural Migration from North to South', unpublished article, 1991.

Lyautey, Hubert, *Lettres du Tonkin et de Madagascar, 1894–1899*, Paris: Armand Colin, 1921.

McCauley, Martin, *Khruschev and the Development of Soviet Agriculture: The Virgin Land Programme 1953–1964*, New York: Holmes & Meier, 1976.

Madrolle, Claudius, *Indochine du Nord*, Paris: Librairie Hachette, 1932.

Maître, Henri, *Les Régions Moï du Sud Indo-Chinois. Le Plateau du Darlac*, Paris: Librairie Plon, 1909.

Mal'khanova, I. A., 'The Development of New Agricultural Lands in North Vietnam in 1961–65', *Soviet Geography*, vol. XI, no. 10, 1970, pp. 828–832.

Mallee, Hein, 'China's Household Registration System under Reform', *Development and Change*, vol. 26, no. 1, 1995, pp. 1–29.

——, 'Rural Household Dynamics and Spatial Mobility in China'. In Thomas Scharping (ed.), *Floating Population and Migration in China: The Impact of Economic Reforms*, Hamburg: Institut für Asienkunde, 1997, pp. 278–296.

Mao Tse Tung, 'Kuo-min ko-ming yü nung-min yun-tung' [The national revolution and the peasant movement]. In Takeuchi Minoru (ed.), *Mao Tse Tung chi* [Collected writings of Mao Tse Tung], Tokyo: Hokubosha, 1970–1972, vol. 1, pp. 175–179.

Marquet, Jean, *De la Rizière à la Montagne: mœurs Annamites*, Paris: Librairie Delalain, 1926.

Marr, David G., *Vietnamese Anticolonialism 1885–1925*, Berkeley, Los Angeles and London: University of California Press, 1971.

——, *Vietnamese Tradition on Trial, 1920–1945*, Berkeley, Los Angeles and London: University of California Press, 1981.

——, 'Introduction' to Tran Tu Binh, *The Red Earth: A Vietnamese Memoir of Life on a Colonial Rubber Plantation*, Athens, Ohio: Center for Southeast Asian Studies, 1985.

——, *Vietnam 1945: The Quest for Power*, Berkeley, Los Angeles and London: University of California Press, 1995.

Marseille, Jacques, *Empire colonial et capitalisme française: Historie d'un divorce*, Paris: Albin Michel, 1984.

Marty, Louis, 'Plan et modalités de l'action administrative locale pour déterminer l'installation progressive de colons indigènes dans les moyenne et haute régions des pays annamites', *BEI*, 1938, pp. 742–745.

Matthews, Mervyn, *The Passport Society: Controlling Movement in Russia and the USSR*, Boulder, Colorado: Westview Press, 1993.

M.G. [Maurice Graffeuil], 'Le paysannat en Annam', *BEI,* 1938, pp. 11–29.

Ministry of Labour, Invalids and Social Affairs, 'Report on the Result of the Survey on Rural Migration in Dak Lak province', Hanoi: Project VIE/95/004, July 1997.

Moise, Edwin E., *Land Reform in China and North Vietnam: Consolidating the Revolution at the Village Level*, Chapel Hill: University of North Carolina Press, 1983.

Monfleur, A., *Monographie de la Province du Darlac (1930)*, Hanoi: IDEO, 1931.

Morel, J., *Les concessions de terre au Tonkin*, Paris: Pedone, 1912.

Morin, Henry G.-S., *Entretiens sur le Paludisme et sa Prévention en Indochine*, Hanoi: IDEO, 1935.

Morris, Stephen J., *Why Vietnam Invaded Cambodia: Political Culture and the Causes of War*, Stanford, California: Stanford University Press, 1999.

Murray, Martin J., *The Development of Capitalism in Colonial Indochina (1870–1940)*, Berkeley: University of California Press, 1980.

Murzayev, E. M., 'The Geographical Names of Vietnam', *Soviet Geography*, vol. XI, no. 10, 1970, pp. 809–820.

Mus, Paul, 'The Role of the Village in Vietnamese Politics', *Pacific Affairs*, vol. 22, no. 3, 1949, pp. 265–272.

——, *Sociologie d'une guerre*, Paris: Seuil, 1952.

Nam Cao, 'In the Jungle'. In *Chi Pheo and Other Stories*, Hanoi: Red River, 1983, pp. 125–180.

Nash Smith, Henry, *Virgin Land: The American West as Symbol and Myth*, Cambridge, Harvard University Press, 1950.

Ng Shui Meng, *The Population of Indochina: Some Preliminary Observations*, Singapore: Institute of Southeast Asian Studies, 1974.

Ngo Vinh Long, *Before the Revolution: The Vietnamese Peasants under the French*, Cambridge, Massachusetts: MIT Press, 1973.

Nguyễn Đức Nhuận, 'Contraintes démographiques et politiques de développement au Vietnam, 1975–80', in *Population*, 30 (1984).

Nguyen Khac Vien, 'Confucianism et Marxisme au Vietnam'. In Nguyen Khac Vien, *Expériences vietnamiennes*, Paris: Editions Sociales, 1970, pp. 201–232.

Nguyễn Thế Anh, 'Le Nam Tiến dans les textes vietnamiens'. In P. B. Lafont, (ed.), *Les frontières du Vietnam: Histoire des frontières de la Péninsule Indochinoise*, Paris: L'Harmattan, 1989, pp. 121–127.

Nguyen Tu Chi, 'The Traditional Viet Village in Bac Bo: Its Organizational Structure and Problems'. In *The Traditional Village in Vietnam*, Hanoi: The Gioi Publishers, 1993, pp. 44–142.

Nguyễn Văn Huyên, *La civilisation annamite*, Hanoi: Direction de l'Instruction Publique en Indochine, 1944. Translated into English as *The Ancient Civilisation of Vietnam,* Hanoi: Thế Giới Publishers, 1995.

Obrecht, J., 'Le problème de l'identification et l'organisation des services d'identité en Indochine', *RIJE*, no. 17, 1942, pp. 1–51.

Orwell, George, *The Road to Wigan Pier*, London: Secker & Warburg, 1965 (first published 1937).

Papin, Philippe, 'Des "villages dans la ville" aux "villages urbains" – l'espace et les formes de pouvoir à Hanoi de 1805 à 1940', Doctorat d'histoire, University of Paris 7, 1997.

——, *Vietnam, Parcours d'une nation*, Paris: La Documentation française, 1999.

Pelley, Patricia, '"Barbarians" and "Younger Brothers"': The Remaking of Race in Post-Colonial Vietnam', *Journal of Southeast Asian Studies*, vol. 29, no. 2, (September 1998) p. 374–391.

Phan Dai Doan, 'Tien Hai and Kim Son Districts in the 19th Century'. In *The Traditional Village in Vietnam*. Hanoi: The Gioi Publishers, 1993, pp. 244–261.

Pietrantoni, Eric, 'La population du Laos de 1912 à 1945', *BSEI*, vol. XXVIII, no. 1, 1953, pp. 25–38.

Pike, Douglas, *Viet Cong*, Cambridge, Massachusetts and London: MIT Press, 1966.

Pinto, R., 'Chronique législative: La réforme des impôts personnels dans les pays de l'Union Indochinoise', *RIJE*, no. 10, 1939, pp. 426–446.

Pooley, C. and I. Whyte, 'Introduction: Approaches to the Study of Migration and Social Change'. In C. Pooley and I. Whyte (eds), *Migrants, Emigrants and Immigrants*, London: Routledge, 1991.

Popkin, Samuel L., *The Rational Peasant: The Political Economy of Rural Society in Vietnam*, Berkeley: University of California Press, 1979.

Porter, Gareth, *Vietnam: The Politics of Bureaucratic Socialism*, Ithaca and London: Cornell University Press, 1993.

Pressat, Roland, *Population*, translated by Robert and Danielle Atkinson, Baltimore: Penguin, 1970.

Rémery, Charles, *Notice sur le repeuplement de la moyenne et haute région du Tonkin*, Hanoi-Haiphong: IDEO, 1908.

Réteaud, L., 'Office Indochinoios de colonisation et de propriété paysanne', *BEI*, 1938, pp. 720–737.

Reynolds, Siân, *France between the Wars: Gender and Politics*, London: Routledge, 1996.

Robequain, Charles, *Le Thanh Hoa. Etude Géographique d'une Province Annamite*, Paris and Brussels: Editions G. Van Oest, 1929.

——, *The Economic Development of French Indochina,* translated by Isabel A. Ward, London: Oxford University Press, 1944.

Robinson, W. Courtland, *Terms of Refuge: The Indochinese Exodus and the International Response*, London and New York: Zed Books, 1998.

Rosaldo, Renato, 'From the Door of His Tent: The Fieldworker and the Inquisitor'. In James Clifford (ed.), *Writing Culture*, Berkeley: University of California Press, 1986, pp. 77–97.

Sakurai, Yumio, 'Lei-cho ka Vietnam Sonraku ni okeru Hyosan Nomin no Bunseki' [A Study of the abandonment of villages by peasants in vietnam during the Lê dynasty] (I), *Tonan Ajia Kenkyu* [Southeast Asian Studies], vol. 15, no. 4, 1978, pp. 552–572.

——, *Betonamu Sonraku no Keisei* [The formation of the Vietnamese village], Tokyo: Soubunsha, 1987, pp. 233–238.

——, 'Peasant Drain and Abandoned Villages in the Red River Delta between 1750 and 1850'. In Anthony Reid (ed.), *The Last Stand of Asian Autonomies: Responses to Modernity in the Diverse States of Southeast Asia and Korea, 1750–1900*, New York: St Martin's Press, 1997, pp. 133–152.

Salemink, Oscar, 'Mois and Maquis: The Invention and Appropriation of Vietnam's Montagnards from Sabatier to the CIA'. In George W. Stocky Jr. (ed.), *Colonial Situations, Essays on the Contextualization of Ethnographic Knowledge*, Madison, Wisconsin: University of Wisconsin Press, 1991, pp. 243–284.

——, 'The King of Fire and Vietnamese Ethnic Policy in the Central Highlands'. In Don McCaskill and Ken Kampe (eds), *Development or Domestication? Indigenous Peoples of Southeast Asia*. Chiang Mai: Silkworm Books, 1997, pp. 488–535.

——, *The Ethnography of Vietnam's Central Highlanders: A Historical Contextualization, 1850–1990*, London: RoutledgeCurzon, forthcoming.

Sallet, A., 'Les esprits malfaisants dans les affections epidémiques au Bình Thuận', *BAVH*, 1926, pp. 81–88. CD-ROM ed. by Võ Duy Dần, Nguyễn Hồng Trân, Philippe Papin and Philippe Le Failler, Hanoi: Pacific R.I.M., 1998.

Salmon, Lorraine, *Pig Follows Dog*, Hanoi: Foreign Languages Publishing House, 1960.

Schama, Simon, *Landscape and Memory*, London: Fontana, 1995.

Scott, James C., *The Moral Economy of the Peasant: Rebellion and Subsistence in Southeast Asia*, New Haven and London: Yale University Press, 1976.

Services du Protectorat, 'Activité colonisatrice du Tonkin–Colonisation dans la haute et moyenne région du Tonkin', *BEI*, 1938, pp. 757–779.

Seybolt, Peter J., *Throwing the Emperor from his Horse: Portrait of a Village Leader in China, 1923–1995*, Boulder, Colorado: Westview Press, 1996.

Shiraishi, Masaya, 'State, Villagers, and Vagabonds: Vietnamese Rural Society and the Phan Ba Vanh Rebellion', *Senri Ethnological Studies*, vol. 13, 1984, pp. 345–400.

Skeldon, Ronald, 'The Challenge Facing Migration Research: a Case for Greater Awareness', *Progress in Human Geography*, vol. 19, no. 1, 1995, pp. 91–96.

Smolski, T., 'Note sur le mouvement de la population en Indochine', *BEI*, 1929, pp. 86–103.

——, 'Progrès et incertitude de la statistique en Indochine', *RIJE*, no. 17, 1942, pp. 96–117.

Starobin, Joseph, *Eyewitness in Indochina*, New York: Cameron & Kahn, 1954.

Ta Thi Thuy, 'Les concessions agricoles françaises au Tonkin de 1884 à 1918', Doctorat d'histoire, École des Hautes Etudes en Sciences Sociales, Paris, 1993.

Takken, W., W. B. Snellen, J. P. Verhave, B. G. J. Knols and S. Atmosoedjono, *Environmental Measures for Malaria Control in Indonesia – an Historical Review on Species Sanitation*, Wageningen, The Netherlands: Agricultural University Wageningen, 1990.

Tan, Stan B.-H., 'Coffee Frontiers in the Central Highlands of Vietnam: Networks of Connectivity between new Productive Spaces and Global Markets', *Asia Pacific Viewpoint*, vol. 41, no. 1, 2000, pp. 51–67.

Taylor, Keith W., 'Nguyen Hoang and the Beginnings of Vietnam's Southward Expansion'. In Anthony Reid (ed.), *Southeast Asia in the Early Modern Era: Trade, Power, Belief*, Ithaca, New York: Cornell University Press, 1993.

——, 'Surface Orientations in Vietnam: Beyond Histories of Nation and Region', *Journal of Asian Studies*, vol. 57, no. 4, 1998, pp. 949–978.

Tran Tu Binh, *The Red Earth: A Vietnamese Memoir of Life on a Colonial Rubber Plantation*, Athens, Ohio: Center for Southeast Asian Studies, 1985.

Tran Van Thong, 'Mémoire sur la colonisation indigène en Indochine', *BEI*, 1938, pp. 1117–1125.

Truong Chinh and Vo Nguyen Giap, *The Peasant Question*, translated by Christine Pelzer White, Ithaca, New York: Cornell University Southeast Asia Program, 1974.

United Nations, *Handbook of Population Census Methods*, New York: UN, 1959.

UNDP, *The Dynamics of Internal Migration in Viet Nam*, Hanoi: UNDP Discussion Paper, 1998.

UNHCR, 'Insight into the Return of the "Boat People": UNHCR's monitoring experience in Vietnam, 1989–1998', Hanoi: UNHCR, 1998.

Unruh, John D., *The Plains Across: The Overland Emigrants and the Trans-Mississippi West, 1840–1860*, Urbana and Chicago: University of Illinois Press, 1993.

Vu Van Hien, 'Les institutions annamites depuis l'arrivée des Français: L'impôt personnel et les corvées de 1862 à 1936', *RIJE*, no. 13, 1940, pp. 84–107.

Wang Feng, 'The Breakdown of a Great Wall: Recent Changes in the Household Registration System of China'. In Thomas Scharping (ed.), *Floating Population and Migration in China: The Impact of Economic Reforms*, Hamburg: Institut für Asienkunde, 1997, pp. 149–165.

Woodside, Alexander B., *Community and Revolution in Modern Vietnam*, Boston: Houghton Mifflin Company, 1976.

Yan Hao, 'Population Distribution and Internal Migration in China since the Early 1950s'. In Wang Jiye and Terry H. Hull (eds), *Population and Development Planning in China*, Sydney: Allen & Unwin, 1991, pp. 212–234.

Yu, Y. C., 'The Demographic Situation in China', *Population Studies*, vol. 32, no. 3, 1978, pp. 427–447.

Biographical Index

*T*his index lists some of the people whose stories form the basis of this history, with a brief description of their migrations. A number of caveats are in order, regarding dates, names and itineraries.

Dates of birth are estimated from the ages people gave in answer to questions like 'How old are you?' Note that according to the Vietnamese system of counting age, people are usually one year 'older' than in the West. In addition, some people estimated rather than knew their age. No attempt has been made to take these factors into consideration – adjustment might simply contribute to the confusion. Dates of birth should be regarded, then, as rough guides to age.

Names of places of origin are given as I was informed of them. Except in clear cases of error, I have not attempted to make allowances for name changes in villages and communes, or administrative boundary changes of provinces and districts. In the absence of a detailed historical atlas of Vietnam, such adjustments would require considerable local research. Out of respect for their anonymity, I have not used people's real names here.

Itineraries mentioned here are limited to principal migrations, intended for basic reference purposes. Many people actually moved a great deal more. Reference to the text will furnish greater detail.

Anh was born in Luang Prabang (Laos) in 1927. He moved to Thailand in 1945 and returned to Vietnam in October 1961. I met him in Phù Yên district (Sơn La) in December 1996.

Ba was born at Bờ Rạ village (Phúc Thọ commune, Đại Từ district, Thái Nguyên) in 1920. He moved to Đất Đá village (Bình Sơn commune, Phổ Yên district, Thái Nguyên) in 1976. I met him there in October 1996.

Bắc was born at Phong Châu commune (Đông Hưng district, Thái Bình) in 1961. He moved to Tân Tiến village (Buôn Tría commune, Lak district, Dak Lak) in 1990. I met him there in November 1996.

Bình was born at Quốc Phước commune (Quảng Điền district, Thừa Thiên Huế) around 1940. He moved to Tam Giang commune (now Krông Năng district, Dak Lak) in November 1978. He returned to Quốc Phước in 1982 for two years. I met him at Tam Giang in May 1996.

Bùi was born at Bắc village (Đông Xá commune, Đông Hưng district, Thái Bình) in 1925. He moved to Tân Xá village (Tân Thịnh commune, Văn Chấn district, Nghĩa Lộ) in February 1974. He was visiting Đông Xá when I met him there in January 1997.

Cầm was born in Ninh Bình in 1940. She moved to Laos in March 1945 and to Thailand a year later. She returned to Vietnam in September 1961. I met her in Phù Yên district (Sơn La) in December 1996.

Chiến was born in Bình Son district (Quảng Ngãi) around 1917. He travelled widely after leaving home in 1944, to the Việt Bắc resistance base and Điện Biên Phủ, down the Hồ Chí Minh trail to Tây Ninh, as well as to China and Russia, before his retirement in 1976. He then moved to Hòa Bình village (Buôn Tría commune, Lak district, Dak Lak). I first met him there in May 1996.

Doanh was born at Hương Điền district (Thừa Thiên Huế) in 1951. He moved to Tam Giang commune (now Krông Năng district, Dak Lak) in March 1978. I met him there in May 1996.

Dũng was born in Xuân Trường district (Nam Định) in 1937. He moved to Mai Châu district (Hòa Bình) in 1963. I met him at Tiền Phong village (Mai Hạ commune, Mai Châu district, Hòa Bình) in July 1995.

Dương was born in Định Hóa district (Thái Nguyên) and was working at the People's Committee there when I met him in January 1997.

Đại was born at Đao Lý commune (Lý Nhân district, Hà Nam) in 1930. He moved to Tân Tiến village (Tân Quảng commune, Định Hóa district, Thái Nguyên) in 1936. I met him there in January 1997.

Đức was born in Laos in 1934. He moved to Thailand in 1946 and to Vietnam in 1961. I met him in Phù Yên district (Sơn La) in December 1996.

Giang was born at Nam Bình commune (Kiến Xương district, Thái Bình) in 1928. He fought the French in the northern uplands and in 1954 participated in the battle of Điện Biên Phủ, staying there for five years afterwards to build the roads. He moved to Hào Tráng commune (Đà Bắc district, Hòa Bình) in 1963 and to Bình Lý village (Tu Lý commune, Đà Bắc district, Hòa Bình) in 1979. I met him at Bình Lý in July 1995.

Hà was born in Thanh Hóa provincial town in 1928. She participated, as a porter, in the battle of Điện Biên Phủ. Later, while her husband Chiến was away, she stayed at Thanh Hóa town and moved to Hòa Bình village (Buôn Tría commune, Lak district, Dak Lak) when he retired in 1976. I first met her there in May 1996.

Hảo was born in Phổ Yên district (Thái Nguyên) in 1935. She moved to Cà Phê village (Minh Lập commune, Đồng Hỷ district, Thái Nguyên) in 1966. I met her there in October 1996.

Hoa was born at Xuân Thanh commune (Xuân Trường district, Nam Định) in 1922. He moved to Định Hóa district town (Thái Nguyên) in 1926. I met him there in January 1997.

Hoài was born at Nguyệt Lâm village (Vũ Binh commune, Vũ Thư district, Thái Bình) in 1913. He moved to Kim Bảng village (Phúc Thọ commune, Đại Từ district, Thái Bình) in 1945. I met him there in October 1996.

Học was born in Hưng Hà district (Thái Bình) in 1951. He moved to Bình Nguyen village (Điềm Mạc commune, Định Hóa district, Thái Nguyên) in January 1963. I met him there in July 1995.

Hợp was born in Xuân Trường district (Nam Định) around 1920. He moved to Nhà Thờ village (Tân Cường commune, Thái Nguyên city, Thái Nguyên) in 1936. I met him there in October 1996.

Hùng was born at Xuân Hòa commune (Xuân Trường district, Nam Định) in 1922. He moved to Tiền Phong village (Mai Hạ commune, Mai Châu district, Hòa Bình) in January 1963. I first met him there in October 1995.

Hùng's neighbour was born at Xuân Hòa commune (Xuân Trường district, Nam Định) around 1920. He moved to Tiền Phong village (Mai Hạ commune, Mai Châu district, Hòa Bình) in January 1963. I met him there in July 1996.

Hỷ was born at Nông Quang commune (Gia Lộc district, Hải Dương) in 1929. He moved to Cà Phê village (Minh Lập commune, Đồng Hỷ district, Thái Nguyên) in 1935. I met him there in October 1996.

Khiêm was born in Quỳnh Phụ district (Thái Bình) in 1933. He moved to Thái Nguyên city in the late 1950s, and to the Sông Cầu State Farm (Đồng Hỷ district, Thái Nguyên) in 1960. I met him in Dong Hy in October 1996.

Khoa was born at Bờ Rạ village (Phúc Thọ commune, Đại Từ district, Thái Nguyên) in 1936. He moved to Đát Đá (Bình Sơn commune, Phổ Yên district, Thái Nguyên) in 1976. I met him there in October 1996.

Kiệt was born at Tây 2 village (Đông Xá commune, Đông Hưng district, Thái Bình) in 1936. He moved to Tân Xá village (Tân Thịnh commune, Văn Chấn district, Nghĩa Lộ) in February 1974, but returned home several months later. I met him at Đông Xá in January 1997.

Kim was born at Thái Hoa village (Tân Thái commune, Đại Từ district, Thái Nguyên) in 1931. I met her there in October 1996.

Kim's husband was born at Thái Hoa village (Tân Thái commune, Đại Từ district, Thái Nguyên) in 1928. He was for many years Party Secretary at this commune. I met him there in October 1996.

La was born in Hòa An district (Cao Bằng) in 1949. He moved to Tân Tiến village (Buôn Tría commune, Lak district, Dak Lak) in 1992. I met him there in November 1996.

Lăng was born in Huế in 1912. He moved to Lak district town (Dak Lak) in 1953. I met him there in November 1996.

Liên was born at Đại Vĩ village (Liên Hà commune, Đông Anh district, Bắc Ninh) in 1916. She moved to Tân Tiến village (Tân Dương commune, Định Hóa district, Thái Nguyên) around 1936. I met her there in January 1997.

Loan was born at Trung Lương commune (Bình Lộc district, Hà Nam) in 1927. She moved to Bờ Rạ village (Phúc Thọ commune, Đại Từ district, Thái Nguyên) in 1964, and then in the mid-1970s to Đại Từ district town (Thái Nguyên), where I met her in October 1996.

Mẫu was born at Lê Lợi village (Đông Xá commune, Đông Hưng district, Thái Bình) in 1955. He moved to Đông Giang village (Buôn Tría commune, Lak district, Dak Lak) in October 1977 and returned to Đông Xá in 1991. I met him there in January 1997.

Minh was born in Tiền Hải district (Thái Bình) in 1909. He moved to Phúc Khánh village (Phúc Thọ commune, Đại Từ district, Thái Nguyên) in 1917. He moved to Phú Sơn village (Bình Sơn commune, Phổ Yên district, Thái Nguyên) in 1976. I met him there in October 1996.

Mơ was born in Vũ Thư district (Thái Bình) in 1973. She moved to Sơn La in 1994 and Ban Mê Thuột city (Dak Lak) in 1995. I first met her in Ban Mê Thuột city in May 1996.

Ngọc was born at Đông Xá commune (Đông Hưng district, Thái Bình) in 1958. He moved to Tân Xá village (Tân Thịnh commune, Văn Chấn district, Nghĩa Lộ) in February 1974, but returned home several months later. He moved then to Đông Giang village (Buôn Tría commune, Lak district, Dak Lak) in October 1977. I met him there in November 1996.

Ngô was born in Lo Giang commune (Đông Hưng district, Thái Bình) in 1931. He moved to Đông Giang village (Buôn Tría commune, Lak district, Dak Lak) in 1979. I met him there in November 1996.

Nguyên was born in Thừa Thiên Huế in 1951. He moved to Tam Giang commune (Krông Năng district, Dak Lak) in October 1978. I met him there in May 1996.

Phụng was born at Võ Lanh commune (Tiền Hải district, Thái Bình) around 1920. She moved to Tân Thái commune (Đại Từ district, Thái Nguyên) in 1965. I met her there in October 1996.

Quảng was born at Phú Lương commune (Đông Hưng district, Thái Bình) in 1947. He moved to Cam Doi village (Chia Cam commune, Krông Pa district, Gia Lai) in 1984 and then to Tân Tiến village (Buôn Tría commune, Lak district, Dak Lak) in May 1996. I met him there in November 1996.

Quốc was born at Xà commune (Đông Hưng district, Thái Bình) in 1958. He moved to Đông Giang village (Buôn Tría commune, Lak district, Dak Lak) in October 1977. I met him there in November 1997.

Tam was born at Liên Giang commune (Đông Hưng district, Thái Bình) in 1942. He moved to Liên Kết village (Buôn Tría commune, Lak district, Dak Lak) in 1978. I met him there in November 1997.

Thân was born in Quận Cống village (Xuân Thọ commune, Xuân Trường district, Nam Định) in 1926. He moved to Nhà Thờ village (Tân Cương commune, Thái Nguyên city, Thái Nguyên) in 1936. I met him there in October 1996.

Thắng was born in Xuân Trường district (Nam Định) in 1952. He moved to Dak Ro commune (Krông Nô district, Dak Lak) in 1988. I met him there in May 1996.

Thành was born in Thừa Thiên Huế in 1956. He moved to Tam Giang commune (Krông Năng district, Dak Lak) in March 1978. I met him there in May 1996.

Thức was born at Quận Cống village (Xuân Thọ commune, Xuân Trường district, Nam Định) in 1900. He left Quận Cống in 1906 and later settled at Nhà Thờ village (Tan Cuong commune, Thai Nguyen city, Thai Nguyen). I met him there in October 1996.

Tiến was born at Đông Sơn commune (Đông Hưng district, Thái Bình) around 1930. He moved to Buôn Triết commune (Lak district, Dak Lak) in 1977. I met him there in May 1996.

Tuấn was born at La Lương village (Hoàng Nông commune, Đại Từ district, Thái Nguyên) in 1919. I met him there in January 1997.

Vân was born in Nam Định in 1910. She moved to Laos in 1924, Thailand in 1946 and returned to Vietnam in 1961. I met her in Phù Yên district (Sơn La) in November 1996.

Vì was born in Chiếng Châu commune (Mai Châu district, Hòa Bình) in 1916. I met him there in October 1995.

Vượng was born at Long Hội village (Phúc Thọ commune, Đại Từ district, Thái Nguyên). He moved to Đình village (Bình Sơn commune, Phổ Yên district, Thái Nguyên) in 1976. I met him there in October 1996.

Yêm was born in Thái Bình province in 1950. He moved to Thái Nguyên city (Thái Nguyên) after graduating from university and was later posted to the People's Committee in Đồng Hỷ district (Thái Nguyên). I met him there in October 1996.

Index

GENERAL INDEX